Mimi Sheraton's
𝕿𝖍𝖊 𝕹𝖊𝖜 𝖄𝖔𝖗𝖐 𝕿𝖎𝖒𝖊𝖘
Guide to
New York
Restaurants

Mimi Sheraton's
The New York Times
Guide to
New York
Restaurants

New and Up-to-Date

Times
BOOKS

Published by TIMES BOOKS, a division of
The New York Times Book Co., Inc.
Three Park Avenue, New York, N.Y. 10016

Published simultaneously in Canada by
Fitzhenry & Whiteside, Ltd., Toronto

Library of Congress Catalog Card
Number 80-5140
ISBN 0-8129-0930-5

Book design by Tony Yee and Faye Eng

Cover design by Paul Bacon

Manufactured in the United States of America

83 84 85 86 5 4 3 2

This book is dedicated to the dozen or so friends who make up the first team of loyal and intrepid eaters who accompany me on visits to restaurants and who must remain anonymous because reservations are so often made in their names.

Most of all it is dedicated, with love and thanks, to my husband, Richard, the loyalest and most intrepid of them all, and our son Marc. It is their companionship that makes this work seem like play.

Contents

Introduction

No city in the world offers more diversity and delectable satisfaction, or more frustration and disappointment, in its restaurants than New York. It is the attempt of this book to maximize the possibilities of the former and minimize the chances of the latter.

Drawn from the six hundred or so reviews that have appeared in *The New York Times* since 1976, when I became the restaurant critic, this book includes reports on three hundred fifty establishments, ranging in quality from poor to extraordinary. All reviews have been brought up to date as necessary and the latest information on prices, hours, specialties, décor, credit cards, reservation policies and, of course, addresses and telephone numbers. The lead time on printing and distributing a book being what it is, there may have been some changes since this manuscript was completed. In addition to the complete reviews of restaurants, there is an A la Carte section that guides you to my few favorite places for country and western American foods, such as ribs and chili, hamburgers, pizzas, kosher and nonkosher pastrami and corned beef sandwiches, dairy specialties and the oldest antique restaurants in the city.

After six and a half years of restaurant going, I am now recognized in about one-third of the places I visit — a decided handicap, since I believe in the value of anonymity, but one I try to overcome in several ways. I do wear wigs, glasses and other disguises that work in a surprisingly large number of restaurants in which I am recognized when wearing my own face. I never make reservations in my own name when reviewing, so I am not expected in advance. Guests eating with me arrive first, allowing me to see what kind of table they are given and to judge the kind of greeting they are accorded. I try to eat at least some dishes that have to be made in advance. In this way, everything cannot be made especially for me, as it otherwise surely would be. In addition, in those places where I am known, I go even more times than usual, arriving at the most crowded times and ordering and reordering dishes. For the rest, I am unrecognized and the task is simpler.

My method and technique of rating restaurants, and my standards, are described under Ratings.

On the off chance that such a thing needs saying, let me assure readers that my sympathies are with them and not with the restaurant owners. As much as I love restaurants and eating out, as I have since childhood, I deplore the all-too-prevalent theory of many restaurant owners that the public exists for their convenience, rather than the other way around. Restaurant owners constantly call or write, asking me to explain their problems to the public. And while I do think a satisfying restaurant experience is something of a two-way street, I feel the burden of adjustment is on the restaurant and its staff, not on the customers.

There are customers who go into restaurants angry or in a challenging mood, daring the staff to please them. That is a fairly common occurrence in restaurants that have received three- and four-star ratings. But in general, the fault is with the restaurant owner, who either does not know how to train a staff or who himself has a poor attitude toward customers and transmits it to the staff.

I do not think the public should understand the restaurant owners' problems except in a most limited way. If you are paying top prices you have a right to expect top professonalism. That is true from the minute the restaurant doors are opened. Some owners have been angry with me for reviewing their restaurants after they have been open for only two months. I have always felt that if there are serious kinks to be ironed out and the restaurant is not yet operating at top efficiency, then prices should be lowered, in the manner of theater previews. It is outrageous to expect the public to finance a restaurateur's education.

I have sometimes been accused of having a "consumerist" approach to restaurant reviewing. No accusation could be more welcome. I do indeed have exactly that approach. I relate food, service, décor, cleanliness and so on to price and to the feeling of the overall experience.

If this book is more complete, detailed and up to date than any other New York restaurant guide, that is due to two factors — my own obsession about being thorough and making as many visits as necessary to arrive at a fair and accurate rating and the support of *The New York Times* editors and management. I have never been told that I am spending too much money (although the annual tab is staggering) or that I have gone to a restaurant too many times. I select the restaurants to be reviewed, and I go until I am satisfied, returning when necessary to make changes. No one at the *Times* attempts to alter my reviews, and the management has stood behind me during threats of lawsuits from irate restaurateurs who have received low ratings. The fact that I review usually two restaurants a week (a total of ten to twelve visits) means that I eat dinner in restaurants almost every night and usually have four or five lunches as well and an occasional Sunday brunch if that seems appropriate.

These reviews are written with two basic types of restaurant patrons in mind. The first, and by far the larger group, is made up of those who simply want to go out and have a wonderful meal and who are not interested in the whys or wherefores of a restaurant or in the psyche and concepts of the chef or owner. The second and much smaller group is made up of buffs, interested in restaurants and culinary developments, even if the results are not always perfect or perhaps not even passable. Members of the second group will often go to a mediocre restaurant if there is one dish or style of service that is interesting or innovative. It is much the same as film and theater buffs who risk bad plays and movies for the sake of seeing a single actor perform or a single technique attempted. This is quite a costly hobby these days, and I suspect that many people have been conned into thinking they should act and feel like buffs by an overzealous press. But those who have such genuine interests, as I do myself, will find special features highlighted in these reviews.

Believe it or not, I still love going to restaurants, and the promise of eating out is almost as exciting now as it was to me as a child, when my parents took me along, as they frequently did. A restaurant is exciting because it is a living theater, and at each meal a new and often bizarre or beautiful scene may unfold. There is also the possibility of eating exactly what you want, independent of others at the table — a luxury I value — and the privilege of not having to decide what sort of food you want until fairly close to mealtime.

For diversity and overall quality in restaurants, New York is hard to beat. Paris has better French food, there is better Italian food in Rome and so on, but diversity with an astonishingly high level of quality and authenticity is New York's very special advantage. I hope this book helps you enjoy eating out in New York as much as I do.

Prices

Because restaurant prices change (increase) so rapidly, it seemed more misleading than helpful to include specific prices in these reviews. I have chosen instead to describe price categories that will remain relatively the same, even if exact prices change.

Because the amount of a tip or the cost of wine or liquor can vary, I have based those price categories on a three-course dinner for one, with tax, but excluding tip and drinks. Lunches are usually less expensive than dinners, and in some cases there are fixed-price menus that are less than the average. It is important, therefore, to remember that the range given is an *average;* you can have a meal for less if you are careful, and without trying too hard you can certainly spend more. Also, in some restaurants where portions are large, few people will want three courses; so the overall price will be lowered by some sharing of appetizers or desserts. Where this is possible or customary or where economical pretheater dinners exist, this is noted in the text.

The price ranges that precede each review approximate this range for a three-course dinner for one person with tax but without tip and drinks:

Inexpensive: under $15
Moderate: $15 to $25
Moderately expensive $25 to $40
Expensive: Over $40

A special caveat: In too many restaurants, it is becoming the practice to have waiters describe daily specials not on the menu. Rarely is the price given for such dishes, and they are usually at the high end of the menu prices, if not the highest. If customers would consistently ask those prices, the waiters would soon give them automatically or would leave a printed or handwritten list with prices on the table. This is the only cure for a practice that is deplorable but for which customers have only themselves to blame.

Tipping

The tip is one of your two best weapons against bad service, the other being simply to stay away from restaurants in which you are treated rudely or served ineptly. If the staff is rude, careless or otherwise unsatisfactory, leave no tip at all, or one so small the point of it cannot be missed. Too many people seem to feel the standard 15 to 20 percent tip is mandatory no matter how badly they have been treated. If service is slow, try to figure out whether it is the fault of the waiter or the kitchen; a waiter cannot deliver food that is not prepared. In the latter case, complain to the manager or the owner about the slowness and leave a moderate tip for the waiter. If you cannot ascertain the cause, leave a small tip and let the waiter fight it out with the kitchen or the owner, as they surely will. That way, maybe something will be done about the situation in the future.

The standard 15 to 20 percent tip should be divided between captain and waiter if a restaurant has both. Usually, the captain gets between one-fourth and one-third of the total, but that may vary, depending on who did how much and how well. It is not unusual for guests to leave as much as 23 percent if waiter and captain have given exceptional service or if inexpensive menu items were ordered and the table was held for a long time. If you do not designate the captain's tip, in some restaurants he will get none, and in others he will get a share of the waiter's.

It is not necessary to tip a busboy unless he does something exceptional, such as getting you cigarettes. Waiters generally give busboys part of their tips for servicing their tables efficiently.

A handy rule for figuring tips in New York is to utilize the sales tax of 8.25 percent that appears (or should appear) as a separate entry on checks. Doubling that tax figure gives you a 16.5 percent tip, and you can adjust that up or down.

If there is a wine steward, or sommelier, a fast-disappearing group, he should get a tip of $2 for each bottle of wine you order, no matter what the price of the wine.

The maître d'hôtel or manager may be tipped if you are a regular and use the restaurant often or if he has provided some exceptional help or service. If you patronize a restaurant regularly, you can give a maître d'hôtel or manager $5 to $10 every three or four visits. It is completely unnecessary to tip him in the ordinary course of restaurant going.

Coat checkrooms these days all too often post signs announcing the tip expected. This makes it a price, not a tip, for a service the management should automatically provide. Tip between 50¢ and $1 per garment, as you see fit, and depending on the tone of the restaurant and the number of coats and other objects you leave. The management cannot make that suggested amount mandatory unless it is put on your bill and sales tax is charged for it, so don't be intimidated.

A washroom attendant should get between 25 cents and 50 cents, depending on whether the person really does anything, such as give you a clean cotton towel and brush lint off your clothes, or just sits there and watches you wash your hands. If the attendant does anything more, such as provide thread to sew a hem or a falling button (or actually does the sewing!) you may want to leave $1.

If you fail to tip anyone along the line, either by intent or error, do not be intimidated if that person follows you to the door and asks for a tip. That is inexcusable under any circumstances. If you really have forgotten — a most unlikely occurence — you may want to redress the wrong. If you have deliberately failed to tip, say so and stand firm. Also inform the owner.

Credit cards

Do not automatically assume that all restaurants take all credit cards or you often will be unpleasantly surprised. Some take all, some take only American Express, others take anything *but* American Express. If you do not have enough cash to cover a meal, call in advance and ask what cards if any, are accepted, or if a personal check will be accepted and with what kind of identification. It is unfair to get angry at a restaurant owner for not honoring credit cards, just as it is ridiculous, and inhospitable, for a restaurant owner to refuse payment by personal check if a credit card is offered as identification.

On the other hand, it is not fair for restaurant owners who do accept credit cards to do so in only a limited way. Some young restaurant owners who are short of funds ask that tips be paid in cash so they do not have to lay out the money to pay the staff before the money has been collected from the credit-card company. This may have a certain charm, but if the restaurant did not warn you about this policy when you called to make a reservation, the management will have to accept your card or forgo the tip. There are also some small restaurants that do not accept credit cards for a check below a certain figure; if they do not tell you that when you call or have that fact posted, insist on paying with a credit card anyway and report them to the credit-card company. If their policy is posted on the menu or by a sign on the premises, decide whether you want to stay and if not, make it plain why you are leaving.

Hours and closings

Although all hours and closing schedules were checked as this book went into print, they may still be subject to change, so it is a good idea to recheck. This is especially true for major holidays and summer vacations.

Dress codes

Anyone with a penchant for casual dressing should check on dress requirements in advance. Some restaurants require ties and jackets of men but have no fixed codes for women. Some require jackets but no ties, and some vary the code at different times of day.

Reservations

If you possibly can, call to make reservations before going to a restaurant. Most restaurants in New York take them. The exceptions are inexpensive to moderately priced restaurants where they cannot afford to have tables unoccupied while waiting for people with reservations to appear. If you have a preferred type of table, such as a round one with chairs instead of a banquette, request it and if you like one part of the room more than another, ask for it. Unless you are told your request cannot be filled, demand what you have been promised when you get there.

If you cannot keep a reservation, call and cancel, and call also if the number of your party changes. Some restaurants — especially those that are new and small — have a problem with no-shows because it means empty tables that could have been filled. If you find that a restaurant consistently overbooks and keeps guests waiting at the bar for more than fifteen minutes, do not go there again.

If there are empty tables in the restaurant when you arrive, insist on being seated, even if all members of your party have not arrived, unless you prefer waiting. Some restaurant owners have established the absurd and pointless policy of keeping the first guests waiting at the bar or in the reception area until all members of the party are together. Again, this is excusable only in the least expensive restaurants that do not take reservations and cannot afford empty seats. It is especially awkward if the first arrival is a woman alone, but even that does not deter some of the least sensitive and least hospitable managers.

When you make reservations, ask about credit cards, and dress codes, and, if you think it may be an issue, ask if the house has a wine or liquor license or if you may bring your own. If you drive, ask about parking, and if you have a favorite dish you expect to eat, ask if it will be on the menu. Also, if the dinner is to be followed by theater or some other scheduled performance, ask if you are allowing enough time for a complete meal. If wheelchair access is important, ask about that, too.

If a restaurant has an absurd and uncomfortable seating schedule — say at 6:30 and 9:30 — be sure you think a visit there is really worthwhile before making the too-late or too-early choice. Usually such places allow favored regulars more civilized hours.

If the person taking reservations sounds rude, pretentious, impatient, annoyed at your questions or pushy, go elsewhere. You have had what is probably a taste of service to come.

Ratings

What the stars mean (and how they are arrived at):

(none)	Poor or Fair
★	Good
★ ★	Very Good
★ ★ ★	Excellent
★ ★ ★ ★	Extraordinary

As the legend explains at the end of the restaurant reviews each Friday in *The New York Times,* "These ratings are based on the reviewer's reaction to food and price in relation to comparable establishments." Those words were carefully arrived at and mean exactly what they say. For better or for worse, the opinions expressed in the reviews — whether for the paper or this book — are strictly my own and do not represent a consensus of friends or loved ones with whom I eat. They order dishes I want to see; I taste them and form my own opinions. Nor do I take into account what the public might like. Second-guessing the mass palate would be as pointless as having a theater critic run up and down the aisles asking for opinions before he writes his reviews. My opinions are as highly personal as my tastes.

My reactions, however, are not mercurial or easily arrived at. The fewest visits made before a review appears is three, and that occurs only when there is a very small menu and when the three visits — with at least four people each time — are wholly consistent. I do not think this has occurred more than eight or ten times during six and a half years of reviewing. Usually four to six visits are required, and I have gone as many as twelve times to a particular restaurant before I felt secure about fixing a rating. Generally I go with three other people, although sometimes just my husband and I go, especially in the earliest stages of scouting. At times there have been as many as eight people, but that is usually for a Chinese or Indian restaurant where it is customary to go with a crowd and sample many dishes.

In sampling a menu, I try not only different foods (chicken, duck, fish, veal), but different preparations (fried, poached, sautéed, etc.), and I like to see house creations, classics and the sort of simple sleepers the management does not expect anyone to order. That is because I get impatient when people recommended a restaurant highly and then caution against the "wrong" dishes. Every chef is bound to have specialties at which he excels, but none should offer a dish he considers beneath his best efforts.

The ratings represent an averaging out of my experiences. It may be possible to have a two-star dinner in a one-star restaurant, but that means it is also possible to have a no-star meal there. A one-star rating, meaning good, often indicates there is some special point of interest that makes this restaurant worth a visit, even though it may have only six or eight recommendable dishes. Such a factor might be an unusual view or setting (Windows on the World and the River Café are cases in point), or the restaurant may be in a neighborhood where there are few decent alternatives, such as Lincoln Center, around Madison Square Garden or in the theater district.

Food is the primary and overwhelming factor in arriving at a rating, and if I had to assign a percentage, I would say it accounts for about 85 percent of the total rating. Cleanliness and service are also important. If a restaurant does not look clean, I check on its latest inspection made by the New York City Health Department.

Service sometimes influences the food rating, as when, for example, a captain is inept at preparing a dish or sauce at the table, or when a waiter lets food stand too long under a heat lamp or accepts something incorrectly prepared by the kitchen. But rudeness, disorganization or other flaws of service mitigate the rating even if they do not affect the food.

As much as I prefer handsome surroundings to tacky ones, I place the least emphasis on décor; all other things being equal, a beautiful room tips the balance.

Price is another important factor in determining a rating. One has a right to expect certain skills and ingredients at one price that are not expected at another. If, for example, a neighborhood restaurant like the Green Tree Hungarian American turns out a thoroughly savory and satisfying meal that includes good soup, goulash or chicken paprikash and a wonderful homemade cream puff for under $15, I will not fault it for serving canned string beans or a salad with terrible bottled dressing or for having paper napkins. I do not eat the beans and the salad, for they taste no better at that price, but the value of the complete dinner is unmistakably good — one star. Let that price go to $25 for dinner, and the beans and salad are no longer excusable. There is no excuse for really bad food at any price, not even for a dinner that costs a dime. No restaurant owner should offer what cannot be delivered with some measure of decency.

It would also be unfair to compare, let us say, Czechoslovak food to French food and make a categorical judgment that all Czech food is inferior to all French food, and therefore all Czech restaurants automatically get lower ratings. "Comparable establishments" means exactly that.

And because perfection is virtually impossible on every dish, every day, it should be remembered that even four-star (extraordinary) restaurants have some flaws, few and far between though they may be.

Poor restaurants are included only when they are well known or highly visible.

Complaints

All too often, dissatisfied restaurant customers quietly accept what happens to them, pay the check, leave and do not return. That may be what a careless restaurateur deserves, but for those interested in giving the establishment a second chance or in helping other guests, the best thing to do is express dissatisfaction immediately, firmly, politely and quietly. If a waiter is rude or inefficient, ask for the manager. If food is badly prepared but not as ordered (well-done when you wanted it rare, for example) or if ingredients are not fresh, send it back to the kitchen.

Too many Americans here and abroad assume that if the food is unpleasant, they are somehow at fault and not the kitchen. If you receive unacceptable food or treatment in a restaurant and get no satisfaction from the owner or manager, it might help to write to the owner and send a copy of the letter to me at *The New York Times*. Even though I must be wary of letters that may have been instituted by competitors or that come from customers who were themselves at fault, once the complaints begin to add up I revisit the restaurant and, if it seems appropriate, publish a caveat or a revised rating.

Index of Restaurants

RATINGS

★ ★ ★ ★

Coach House
La Grenouille
Lutèce
Vienna 79

★ ★ ★

Captain's Table (East Side)
Gargiulo's
Il Nido
Kitcho
Kurumazushi
La Côte Basque
La Tulipe
Le Cirque
Le Cygne

Madras Woodlands
Palm
Raga
Rao's
Sammy's Rumanian Jewish Restaurant
Say Eng Look
Trastevere (83rd Street)
Vienna Park

★ ★

Balkan Armenian
Beijing Duckhouse
Bistro Bordeaux
Bruno
Cabana Carioca
Chalet Suisse
Chanterelle
Christ Cella
Csarda
Da Silvano
El Coyote
Elephant & Castle
El Rincón de España
Ennio & Michael
Four Seasons
Fuji
Girafe
Gloucester House
Hatsuhana
Hoexter's Market
Home Village Restaurant Ltd.
Hubert's
Hunam
Hwa Yuan Szechuan Inn
Il Monello
Jane Street Seafood Cafe
Janice's Fish Place
Joe & Rose
Joe's Restaurant
John Clancy's Restaurant
K.O.'s
La Bonne Bouffe
La Caravelle
La Folie
La Gauloise
Le Bistro

Le Chantilly
Lello
Lou G. Siegel
Mumtaz
Nada Sushi
Nanni
No. 1 Chinese Restaurant
Omen
Oyster Bar and Restaurant in Grand Central Station
Palm Too
Pantheon
Parioli Romanissimo
Parma
Patsy's Restaurant
Peking Duck House
Pirandello
Quilted Girafe
Red Tulip
Rio de Janeiro/Boat 57 Seafood House
Russian Tea Room
Sahib
Salta in Bocca
San Marco
Seeda Thai
Shun Lee Palace
Shun Lee West
Siam Inn
SoHo Charcuterie
Takesushi
Takezushi
Tandoor
Terrace
Thailand Restaurant
Trattoria da Alfredo
Tre Scalini
Tucano

★ ★

24 Fifth Avenue
Village Green
Wings
Woods
Woods (Madison Avenue)

Woo Lae Oak of Seoul
Xenia
Ying
Yun Luck Rice Shoppe
Zapata

★

Ararat
Arnold's Turtle
Artie's Warehouse
Auberge Suise
Auctions
Baan Thai Restaurant
Bangkok Cuisine
Beirut
Berry's
Billy's
Bombay Palace
Box Tree Restaurant
Brazilian Pavilion
Bridge Cafe
Cafe des Artistes
Café Español
Cafe Geiger
Cafe Un Deux Trois
Captain's Table (Greenwich Village)
Casa Brasil
Charlie and Kelly
Chatfield's
Chef Ho's Hunan Manor
Claude's
Cottonwood Cafe
Darjeeling
Délices La Côte Basque
Demarchelier
Devon House Ltd.
Dezaley
El Charro
Elmer's
El Parador Cafe
El Tenampa
Empire Szechuan Columbus
Empire Szechuan Gourmet
Estia
Felidia
Forest and Sea International Restaurant
Foro Italico
Fortune Garden
Frankie & Johnnie's Restaurant
Gage & Tollner
Gibbon
Greene Street
Greener Pastures
Green Tree Hungarian Restaurant
Hakubai
Hunan Balcony
Il Galletto
Il Mulino
Inagiku
Jack's Nest
La Camelia
La Chaumière
Lady Astor's
La Goulue

La Louisiana
La Petite Ferme
La Petite Marmite
La Ripaille
Lavin's
Le Biarritz
Le Cherche-Midi
Le Jacques Coeur
Le Pèrigord
Le Plaisir
Le Refuge
L'Escargot Restaurant
Les Pleiades
Le Steak
L'Hostaria del Bongustaio
Little Afghanistan
Malca's
Manhattan Market
Market Dining Rooms and Bar
Marylou's
Maurice
Maxwell's Plum
Meat Brokers
Michael Phillips
Michel Fitoussi's Palace
Milestone
Mimosa
Miraku
Mitsukoshi
Monte's
Moshe Peking
Mr. Chow
Nippon
Nishi
Odeon
Oenophilia
Orsini's
Pamir
Peking Duck West
Pesca
Peter Luger Steak House
Pongsri Thailand Restaurant
Ponte's Steak House
René Pujol
Restaurant Raphaël
Ristorante Toscana
River Café
Ruc
Sea Fare of the Aegean
Sheba
Shinbashi
Shun Lee Dynasty
Sichuan Pavilion
Simon's
Sloppy Louie's
Soomthai
Souen
Sparks Steakhouse
Sweets
Table d'Hôte

★

Taj Mahal
Tamu
Tang Tang
Tastings
Tavola Calda da Alfredo
10th Street Cafe
Texarkana
Tibetan Kitchen
Toraji
Tout Va Bien
Tovarisch
Trumpets

Tse Yang
"21" Club
Uzie's
Vanessa
Variations
Vivolo
Wally's
West Bank Cafe
West Boondock
Windows on the World
Young Bin Kwan

Fair

Acute Cafe
Alfredo's
Anche Vivolo
Arirang
Assembly Steak House
Barbetta
Brasserie
Broadway Joe
Cafe St. Martin
Capsouto Frères
Century Café
Curtain Up!
David K's
Dimitri
Elaine's
Elio's
Empire Szechuan Balcony
Gallagher's
Gaylord India Restaurant
George Martin
Ginger Man
Harvey's Chelsea Restaurant
Hisae's
Hisae's Chelsea Place
Hisae's Place

Hisae's West
Horn of Plenty
Jim McMullen
Joanna
Keen's
Kippy's Pier 44
Le Veau d'Or
Mortimer's
Nuccio's
Old Homestead
O'Neals' Times Square
Pearl's Chinese Restaurant
Pietro's
Post House
Raoul's
R. J. Scotty's
Saloon
Sardi's
Shezan
Suzanne
Tavern on the Green
Ukrainian Restaurant
Victor's Cafe 52
Wise Maria
Ye Waverly Inn

Poor

Copenhagen
La Coupole
Le Relais

Le Trianon
Regine's
Szechuan Cuisine

LOCATION

(Asterisks indicate establishments reviewed in the A La Carte section but not given a full rating.)

Below Canal, East of Broadway (Chinatown, Wall Street)

Bridge Cafe
*Cam Fung
*Fraunces Tavern
*Hee Seung Fung
Home Village Restaurant, Ltd.
*Hong Gung
Hwa Yuan Szechuan Inn
*Imperial Inn

No. 1 Chinese Restaurant
Peking Duck House
Say Eng Look
Sloppy Louie's
Sweets
Szechuan Cuisine
Thailand Restaurant
Yun Luck Rice Shoppe

Below Canal, West of Broadway (TriBeCa, World Trade Center, Battery Park)

Acute Cafe
Capsouto Frères
Odeon
Ponte's Steak House

Sheba
Market Dining Rooms & Bar
*Suerken's
Windows on the World

Canal to Houston, East of Broadway (Lower East Side)

*Bernstein-on-Essex Street
*Grand Dairy Restaurant
*Katz's Delicatessen

*Ratner's Dairy Restaurant
Sammy's Rumanian Jewish Restaurant

Canal to Houston, West of Broadway (SoHo, Little Italy)

Berry's
Chanterelle
Elephant & Castle
Greene Street
Omen
Raoul's

SoHo Charcuterie
Souen
Tamu
*Tennessee Mountain
Wings
Wise Maria

Houston to 14th Street, East of Broadway (East Village & NoHo)

*B & H Dairy Restaurant
El Coyote
Hisae's Place
Lady Astor's
Luchow's

*Second Avenue Kosher Delicatessen and Restaurant
Ukrainian Restaurant

Houston to 14th Street, West of Broadway (Greenwich Village)

Arnold's Turtle
Café Español
Captain's Table (Greenwich Village)
Coach House
*Corner Bistro
Cottonwood Cafe
Da Silvano
El Charro
Elephant & Castle
El Rincón de Espana
Ennio & Michael
Horn of Plenty
Il Mulino
Jane Street Seafood Cafe
Janice's Fish Place
Joe's Restaurant
John Clancy's Restaurant
*John's Pizzeria

K.O.'s
La Chaumière
La Gauloise
La Ripaille
La Tulipe
*Lone Star Cafe
Marylou's
Monte's
Nuccio's
Pirandello
*Sweet Basil
Tavola Calda da Alfredo
10th Street Cafe
Texarkana
Trattoria da Alfredo
24 Fifth Avenue
Vanessa
Village Green
Ye Waverly Inn

14th to 33rd Streets, East of Fifth Avenue (Gramercy Park)

Empire Szechuan Balcony
*Hee Seung Fung
Hubert's
Jack's Nest
Joanna
La Coupole

La Louisiana
Mimosa (33rd Street)
Pesca
*Pete's Tavern
Salta in Bocca
Tibetan Kitchen

14th to 33rd Streets, West of Fifth Avenue (Chelsea)

Artie's Warehouse
Beirut
*Gefen's Dairy Restaurant
Harvey's Chelsea Restaurant
Hisae's Chelsea Place

Old Homestead
R. J. Scotty's
*Smokey's
Variations
West Boondock

34th to 41st Streets, East of Fifth Avenue (Murray Hill)

Ararat
Balkan Armenian Restaurant
El Parador Cafe
Hakubai

Il Galletto
La Bonne Bouffe
Young Bin Kwan

34th to 41st Streets, West of Fifth Avenue (Madison Square Garden, Garment District)

Bistro Bordeaux
Foro Italico
*Gross Dairy Restaurant
Keen's
Lavin's

Lou G. Siegel
Moshe Peking
*Paddy's Clam House
*P. J. Clarke's at Macy's
Woods (37th Street)

42nd to 46th Streets, East of Fifth Avenue (Turtle Bay)

Captain's Table (East Side)
Christ Cella
Hunam
Madras Woodlands
Mimosa (43rd Street)
Nanni
Oyster Bar and Restaurant in Grand Central Station

Palm
Palm Too
Pietro's
Sichuan Pavilion
Sparks Steakhouse
Suzanne
Takesushi
Trumpets

42nd to 46th Streets, West of Fifth Avenue (Times Square Area)

Barbetta
Broadway Joe
Cabana Carioca
Cafe Un Deux Trois
Century Café
*Charlies'
Curtain Up!
El Tenampa
Frankie & Johnnie's Restaurant

*Joe Allen
Kippy's Pier 44
Kitcho
Little Afghanistan
O'Neals' Times Square
Pantheon
Sardi's
Takezushi
West Bank Cafe
Woo Lae Oak of Seoul

47th to 51st Streets, East of Fifth Avenue

Box Tree Restaurant
Délices La Côte Basque at Olympic Tower
Gloucester House
Hatsuhana
Inagiku
Joe & Rose
Kurumazushi
La Petite Marmite
Le Bistro

Le Trianon
Lutèce
Nada Sushi
Quilted Girafe
Shinbashi
Shun Lee Dynasty
Tandoor
Tse Yang
*Wylie's
Xenia

47th to 51st Streets, West of Fifth Avenue

Assembly Steak House
Chalet Suisse
Luchow's
Pearl's Chinese Restaurant
Pongsri Thailand Restaurant
Raga
René Pujol
Seeda Thai
Tout Va Bien
Wally's

52nd to 56th Streets, East of Fifth Avenue

Auberge Suisse
Beijing Duckhouse
Brasserie
Brazilian Pavilion
Four Seasons
Il Nido
La Côte Basque
La Petite Ferme
Le Cherche-Midi
Le Cygne
Lello
Le Perigord
Manhattan Market
Michael Phillips
Nippon
*P. J. Clarke's
Ristorante Toscana
Shun Lee Palace
*Taste of the Apple
Zapata

52nd to 56th Streets, West of Fifth Avenue

Arirang
Bangkok Cuisine
Bombay Palace
*Carnegie Delicatessen and
    Restaurant
L'Escargot Restaurant
Fuji
Gallagher's
La Caravelle
Maurice
Orsini's
Patsy's Restaurant
Restaurant Rafaël
San Marco
Sea Fare of the Aegean
Siam Inn
Tastings
"21" Club
Victor's Cafe 52

57th to 72nd Streets, East of Fifth Avenue

Anche Vivolo
Billy's
Bruno
Casa Brasil
Chatfield's
Darjeeling
David K's
Demarchelier
Dezaley
Elmer's
Felidia
Fortune Garden
Gaylord India Restaurant
Girafe
Greener Pastures
Hisae's
La Camelia
La Folie
La Goulue
Le Chantilly
Le Cirque
Le Plaisir
Le Relais
Le Steak
Le Veau d'Or
Maxwell's Plum
Meat Brokers
Michel Fitoussi's Palace
Mitsukoshi
Mr. Chow
Post House
Regine's
Ruc
*Serendipity
Taj Mahal
*Tony Roma's
Tre Scalini
Tucano
Vienna Park
Woods (Madison Avenue)

57th to 72nd Streets, West of Fifth Avenue (Lincoln Center Area)

Alfredo's
Cafe des Artistes
Copenhagen
*Diane's
Dimitri
Empire Szechuan Columbus
*Famous Dairy Restaurant
*Fine & Schapiro
Ginger Man
Hisae's West
Le Biarritz
Milestone
Miraku
Peking Duck West
Rio de Janeiro/Boat 57
Seafood House
Russian Tea Room
Saloon
Shezan
Shun Lee West
Simon's
*Swiss Chalet
Tavern on the Green
Tovarisch
Ying

Above 72nd Street, East of Fifth Avenue (Upper East Side)

Auctions
*Boodles
Chef Ho's Hunan Manor
Claude's
Csarda
Devon House, Ltd.
Elaine's
Elio's
Estia
George Martin
Gibbon
Hoexter's Market
Il Monello
*J. G. Melon
Le Jacques Coeur
Le Refuge
Les Pleiades
*Madison Delicatessen and Restaurant
Malca's
Mortimer's
Mumtaz
Pamir
Parioli Romanissimo
Parma
*Patsy's Pizzeria
Rao's
Red Tulip
Regine's
Sahib
Soomthai
Table d'Hôte
Tang Tang
Toraji
Trastevere
Uzie's
Vienna 79
Vivolo

Above 72nd Street, West Side

Baan Thai Restaurant
*Balcony
Empire Szechuan Gourmet
Forest and Sea International Restaurant
Green Tree Hungarian Restaurant
Hunan Balcony
*J. G. Melon West
Nishi
Oenophilia
*Smokey's
Terrace

Brooklyn

Gage & Tollner
Gargiulo's
Peter Luger Steak House
River Café

TYPE OF FOOD

Afghan
Little Afghanistan
Pamir

African
Sheba

American
* Balcony
*Boodles
Bridge Cafe
*Charlies'
*Corner Bistro
Cottonwood Cafe
Curtain Up
*Diane's
*Elephant & Castle
*Fraunces Tavern
Four Seasons
Harvey's Chelsea Restaurant
Horn of Plenty
Hubert's
Jack's Nest
*J. G. Melon
*J. G. Melon West
Jim McMullen
*Joe Allen
Lady Astor's
La Louisiana
Lavin's
*Lone Star Cafe
Manhattan Market
Market Dining Rooms and
    Bar
Mortimer's
*P. J. Clarke's
River Café
*Serendipity
*Smokey's
*Sweet Basil
*Swiss Chalet
*Taste of the Apple
*Tennessee Mountain
Texarkana
*Tony Roma's
24 Fifth Avenue
"21" Club
Vanessa
West Boondock
Windows on the World
Woods (37th Street)
*Wylie's
Ye Waverly Inn

Armenian
See Middle Eastern

Austrian
Vienna Park
Vienna 79

Brazilian
Brazilian Pavilion
Cabana Carioca
Casa Brasil
Rio de Janeiro/Boat 57
Seafood House

Chinese
Beijing Duckhouse
*Cam Fung
Chef Ho's Hunan Manor
David K's
Empire Szechuan Balcony
Empire Szechuan Columbus
Empire Szechuan Gourmet
Fortune Garden
*Hee Seung Fung (H.S.F.)
Home Village Restaurant,
    Ltd.
*Hong Gung
Hunam
Hunan Balcony
Hwa Yuan Szechuan Inn
*Imperial Inn
Moshe Peking
Mr. Chow
No. 1 Chinese Restaurant
Pearl's Chinese Restaurant
Peking Duck House
Peking Duck West
Say Eng Look
Shun Lee Dynasty
Shun Lee Palace
Shun Lee West
Sichuan Pavilion
Szechuan Cuisine
Tse Yang
Ying
Yun Luck Rice Shoppe

Continental and New American
Artie's Warehouse
Berry's
Box Tree Restaurant
Brazilian Pavilion
Cafe des Artistes
Casa Brasil
Charlie and Kelly
Chatfield's
Century Café
Coach House
Dimitri
Elephant & Castle
Forest and Sea International
    Restaurant
*Fraunces Tavern
Four Seasons
Ginger Man
Harvey's Chelsea Restaurant
Hisae's
Hisae's Chelsea Place
Hiseae's Place
Hisae's West
Hoexter's Market
Hubert's
Janice's Fish Place
Jim McMullen
Joanna
Keen's
Lady Astor's
La Louisiana
Lavin's
Manhattan Market

Market Dining Rooms and Bar
Maxwell's Plum
Michael Phillips
Milestone
Mimosa
Mortimer's
Odeon
Oenophilia
O'Neals' Times Square
River Café
Saloon
Sardi's
SoHo Charcuterie
Tastings
Tavern on the Green
10th Street Cafe
Terrace
24 Fifth Avenue
"21" Club
Vanessa
Variations
Village Green
West Bank Cafe
Windows on the World
Wings
Woods (37th Street)
Woods (Madison Avenue)
Ye Waverly Inn

Cuban
Victor's Cafe 52

Czechoslovak
Ruc

Dairy
*B & H Dairy Restaurant
*Famous Dairy Restaurant
*Gefen's Dairy Restaurant
*Grand Dairy Restaurant
Greener Pastures
*Gross Dairy Restaurant
*Ratner's Dairy Restaurant

Danish
Copenhagen

Delicatessens
See Jewish/Kosher

English/Irish
Keen's

Ethiopian
Sheba

Fish
See Seafood

French
Acute Cafe
Bistro Bordeaux
Brasserie
Cafe Un Deux Trois
Capsouto Frères
Chanterelle
Claude's
Délices La Côte Basque at Olympic Tower

Demarchelier
Devon House Ltd.
Greene Street
La Bonne Bouffe
La Caravelle
La Chaumière
La Côte Basque
La Coupole
La Gauloise
La Goulue
La Grenouille
La Petite Ferme
La Petite Marmite
La Ripaille
La Tulipe
Le Biarritz
Le Bistro
Le Chantilly
Le Cherche-Midi
Le Cirque
Le Cygne
Le Jacques Coeur
Le Perigord
Le Plaisir
Le Refuge
Le Relais
L'Escargot Restaurant
Les Pleiades
Le Trianon
Le Veau d'Or
Lutèce
Malca's
Maurice
Michel Fitoussi's Palace
Quilted Girafe
Raoul's
Regine's
René Pujol
Restaurant Rafaël
Simon's
Table d'Hôte
Tout Va Bien
Trumpets
Tucano

German
Cafe Geiger
Luchow's
*Suerken's

Greek
Dimitri
Estia
Pantheon
Xenia

Health Foods
See Vegetarian

Hungarian
Csarda
Green Tree Hungarian Restaurant
Red Tulip
Ruc

Indian/Pakistani
Bombay Palace
Darjeeling
Gaylord India Restaurant

Indian/Pakistani
Madras Woodlands
Mumtaz
Raga
Sahib
Shezan
Taj Mahal
Tandoor

Indonesian
Tamu

Irish
See English

Italian
Alfredo's
Anche Vivolo
Barbetta
Bruno
Da Silvano
Elaine's
Elio's
Ennio & Michael
Felidia
Foro Italico
Gargiulo's
Girafe
Hostaria del Bongustaio
Il Galletto
Il Monello
Il Mulino
Il Nido
Joe's Restaurant
*John's Pizzeria
La Camelia
Lello
Monte's
Nanni
Nuccio's
Orsini's
Parioli Romanissimo
Parma
* Patsy's Pizzeria
Patsy's Restaurant
Pirandello
Rao's
R. J. Scotty's
Salta in Bocca
San Marco
Tavola Calda da Alfredo
Trastevere
Trattoria da Alfredo
Tre Scalini
Vivolo
Wise Maria

Japanese
Fuji
Gibbon
Hakubai
Hatsuhana
Inagiku
Kitcho
Mitsukoshi
Nada Sushi
Nippon
Nishi
Omen
Shinbashi
Souen
Takesushi
Takezushi

Jewish/Kosher
*Bernstein-on-Essex Street
*B & H Dairy Restaurant
*Carnegie Delicatessen and
    Restaurant
*Famous Dairy Restaurant
*Fine & Schapiro
*Gefen's Dairy Restaurant
*Grand Dairy Restaurant
*Gross Dairy Restaurant
*Katz's Delicatessen
Lou G. Siegel
*Madison Delicatessen and
    Restaurant
Moshe Peking
*Ratner's Dairy Restaurant
Sammy's Rumanian Jewish
Restaurant
*Second Avenue Kosher
    Delicatessen and Restau-
    rant

Korean
Arirang
Miraku
Toraji
Woo Lae Oak of Seoul
Young Bin Kwan

Kosher
See Jewish/Kosher

Mexican
and South American
El Charro
El Coyote
El Parador
El Tenampa
Zapata

Middle Eastern/
Armenian/North African
Ararat
Balkan Armenian Restaurant
Beirut
Little Afghanistan
Malca's
Pamir

North African
See Middle Eastern

Pakistani
See Indian

Portuguese
See Spanish

Russian
Russian Tea Room
Tovarisch
Ukrainian Restaurant

Seafood

Captain's Table (East Side)
Captain's Table (Greenwich Village)
Gage & Tollner
Gloucester House
Jane Street Seafood Cafe
Janice's Fish Place
John's Clancy's Restaurant
Kippy's Pier 44
Marylou's
Oyster Bar and Restaurant at Grand Central Station
*Paddy's Clam House
Pesca
Rio de Janeiro/Boat 57 Seafood House
Sea Fare of the Aegean
Sloppy Louie's
Sweets

South American

See Mexican and Brazilian

Spanish/Portuguese

See also the Brazilian, Cuban and Mexican listings.
Café Español
Cafe St. Martin
El Rincón de España

Steaks and Chops

Assembly Steak House
Auctions
Billy's
Broadway Joe
Christ Cella
Elmer's
Frankie & Johnnie's Restaurant
Gallagher's
George Martin

Joe & Rose
K.O.'s
Le Steak
Meat Brokers
Palm
Old Homestead
Palm Too
Post House
Peter Luger Steak House
Pietro's
Ponte's Steak House
Sparks Steakhouse
Wally's

Swiss

Auberge Suisse
Chalet Suisse
Dezaley

Thai

Baan Thai Restaurant
Bangkok Cuisine
Forest and Sea International Restaurant
Seeda Thai
Siam Inn
Soomthai
Thailand Restaurant

Tibetan

Tibetan Kitchen

Vegetarian/Health Food

See also Dairy
Arnold's Turtle
Greener Pastures
Madras Woodlands
Souen

Vietnamese

Suzanne

INEXPENSIVE

Balkan-American Restaurant
Beirut
Café Español
Cottonwood Cafe
Curtain Up!
Empire Szechuan Balcony
Empire Szechuan Columbus
Empire Szechuan Gourmet
Forest and Sea International Restaurant
Green Tree Hungarian Restaurant
Jack's Nest
Little Afghanistan
Monte's
Mumtaz
Say Eng Look
Sheba
Souen
Szechuan Cuisine
Thailand Restaurant
Tibetan Kitchen
Toraji
Ukrainian Restaurant
Ye Waverly Inn
Xenia

OPEN SUNDAY

Arirang
Ararat
Arnold's Turtle
Artie's Warehouse
Auctions
Baan Thai Restaurant
Bankok Cuisine
Beijing Duckhouse
Beirut
Berry's
Billy's
Bombay Palace
Brasserie
Bridge Cafe
Broadway Joe
Cabana Carioca
Cafe des Artistes
Cafe St. Martin
Cafe Un Deux Trois
Capsouto Frères
Captain's Table (Greenwich Village)
Charlie and Kelly
Chef Ho's Hunan Manor
Coach House
Cottonwood Cafe
Csarda
Curtain Up!
Darjeeling
Da Silvano
David K's
Devon House Ltd.
Dimitri
Elaine's
El Charro
El Coyote
Elephant & Castle
Elio's
Elmer's
El Rincón de Espäna
El Tenampa
Empire Szechuan Balcony
Empire Szechuan Columbus
Empire Szechuan Gourmet
Ennio & Michael
Estia
Forest and Sea International Restaurant
Fortune Garden
Gallagher's
Gargiulo's
Gaylord India Restaurant
George Martin
Ginger Man
Gloucester House
Greener Pastures
Greene Street
Hakubai
Harvey's Chelsea Restaurant
Hisae's
Hisae's Chelsea Place
Hisae's Place
Hisae's West
Hoexter's Market
Home Village Restaurant Ltd.
Horn of Plenty
Hunam
Hunan Balcony
Hwa Yuan Szechwan Inn
Il Mulino
Jack's Nest
Jane Street Seafood Cafe
Janice's Fish Place
Jim McMullen
Joanna's
Joe's Restaurant
John Clancy's Restaurant
Kippy's Pier 44
Kitcho
K.O.'s
La Chaumière
La Coupole
Lady Astor's
La Gauloise
La Ripaille
La Tulipe
Le Jacques Coeur
Le Relais
Le Steak
Le Trianon
Lou G. Siegel
Madras Woodlands
Malca's
Manhattan Market
Marylou's

Maurice
Maxwell's Plum
Meat Brokers
Michael Phillips
Monte's
Mortimer's
Moshe Peking
Mr. Chow
Mumtaz
Nada Sushi
Nishi
No. 1 Chinese Restaurant
Nuccio's
Odeon
Old Homestead
Omen
Oenophilia
Pamir
Parma
Patsy's Restaurant
Pearl's Chinese Restaurant
Peking Duck House
Pesca
Pongsri Thailand Restaurant
Post House
Raga
Raoul's
Red Tulip
Rio de Janeiro/Boat 57 Seafood House
River Café
R. J. Scotty's
Ruc
Russian Tea Room
Sahib
Saloon
Sammy's Rumanian Jewish Restaurant
Sardi's
Say Eng Look
Sea Fare of the Aegean
Seeda Thai

Sheba
Shinbashi
Shun Lee Dynasty
Shun Lee Palace
Shun Lee West
Siam Inn
Sichuan Pavilion
Simon's
SoHo Charcuterie
Soomthai
Souen
Szechuan Cuisine
Taj Mahal
Tamu
Tandoor
Tang Tang
Tavern on the Green
10th Street Cafe
Texarkana
Thailand Restaurant
Trastevere
Trattoria da Alfredo
Tse Yang
24 Fifth Avenue
Ukrainian Restaurant
Uzie's
Vanessa
Variations
Victor Cafe 52
Village Green
Ye Waverly Inn
West Bank Cafe
West Boondock
Windows on the World
Wings
Wise Maria
Woo Lae Oak of Seoul
Xenia
Ying
Young Bin Kwan
Yun Luck Rice Shoppe
Zapata

OPEN LATE

Acute Cafe
Arnold's Turtle
Artie's Warehouse
Auctions
Baan Thai Restaurant
*Balcony
Beirut
*Bernstein-on-Essex Street
Berry's
Billy's
Brasserie
Bridge Cafe
Broadway Joe
Bruno
Café Español
Cafe Geiger
Cafe St. Martin
Cafe Un Deux Trois
Capsouto Frères
*Carnegie Delicatessen and Restaurant
Century Café
*Charlies'

Cottonwood Cafe
Curtain Up!
David K's
*Diane's
Dimitri
Elaine's
El Charro
Elephant & Castle
Elio's
Elmer's
Empire Szechuan Balcony
Empire Szechuan Columbus
Empire Szechuan Gourmet
Estia
Felidia
Frankie & Johnnie's Restaurant
Gallagher's
Gargiulo's
George Martin
Ginger Man
Greene Street
Harvey's Chelsea Restaurant

Hisae's Place
Hisae's West
Hoexter's Market
Home Village Restaurant
Ltd.
Hunan
Hunan Balcony
*J. G. Melon
*J. G. Melon West
Jim McMullen
Joanna
*Joe Allen
*Katz's
Kippy's Pier 44
La Camelia
La Chaumière
La Coupole
*Lone Star Cafe
Marylou's
Maxwell's Plum
Meat Brokers
Mortimer's
Nuccio's
Odeon
Orsini's
Parma

*Patsy's Pizzeria
*Pete's Tavern
Raoul's
*Ratner's
Regine's
R. J. Scotty's
Russian Tea Room
Saloon
Sammy's Rumanian Jewish
Restaurant
Sardi's
*Serendipity
Shun Lee West
*Sweet Basil
*Swiss Chalet
Taj Mahal
*Taste of the Apple
Texarkana
*Tony Roma's
"21" Club
Victor's Cafe 52
West Bank Cafe
Wings
*Wylie's
Yun Luck Rice Shoppe

Reviews of Restaurants

Acute Cafe
Fair

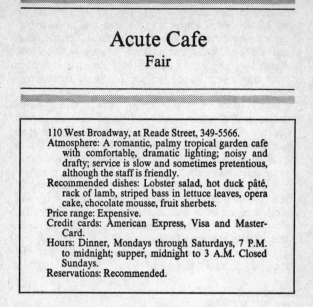

110 West Broadway, at Reade Street, 349-5566.

Atmosphere: A romantic, palmy tropical garden cafe with comfortable, dramatic lighting; noisy and drafty; service is slow and sometimes pretentious, although the staff is friendly.

Recommended dishes: Lobster salad, hot duck pâté, rack of lamb, striped bass in lettuce leaves, opera cake, chocolate mousse, fruit sherbets.

Price range: Expensive.

Credit cards: American Express, Visa and Master-Card.

Hours: Dinner, Mondays through Saturdays, 7 P.M. to midnight; supper, midnight to 3 A.M. Closed Sundays.

Reservations: Recommended.

The Acute Cafe, one of the newer and more romantically beautiful restaurants in TriBeCa, is named for the angles at which its walls meet — in keeping with the shape of the island on which it is set. After only a few months, the Acute Cafe has become a fashionable and swinging meeting place with patrons garbed in costumes from Ralph Lauren provincial to thrift shop Retro to Jean Harlow slinky. Even the young woman who serves as maître d'hôtel wears black tie and tails, giving her an antic, Chaplinesque charm.

With its gray-tile trim, glowing amethyst light reflected from neon signs, a tropical garden of potted palms and graceful mauve and white floral bouquets, the Acute Cafe is a stylish stage set. The staff is attractively dressed in chef's whites, and most of the waiters and waitresses perform with good will and efficiency. Only a few have the absent-minded half-smiles of space cadets who don't seem to quite know what they are doing or why. One gets the feeling that the slowdown between appetizer and main course is more the fault of the staff in the kitchen than in the dining room, a result, perhaps, of the elaborate nouvelle cuisine garnishes.

The food here, in fact, is nouvelled to death; considering the almost identical sauces and garnishes, it is hard to tell appetizers from main courses. As a result, it is difficult to order an interestingly varied meal. Other consistent flaws are the searingly hot plates that cook the undersides of rare lamb and duck breast, turning them tough and gray, and the overabundance of puff pastry on appetizers.

The only really poor dish was leathery, scorched soft-shell crabs but only a few other dishes are worth recommending. Among the better selections were two appetizers — the salade de printemps combining fresh lobster meat on shredded lettuce in a pungent, creamy dressing, edged with sliced peaches, and the hot duck pâté in a superdome of puff pastry rimmed by a truffle-flavored Périgourdine-style sauce. Other salad appetizers, as well

1

as the saffron-scented mussel soup, were disappoint-ingly sweet or bland.

The best main course was the rare rack of lamb, ac-cented by a verdant garlic-parsley purée. Soufflé pota-toes deflated, but other vegetables were well cooked. Three tiny nuggets of striped bass steamed in lettuce were moist and good, but the portion was absurdly small.

Sliced duck breast suffered from a honey-sweet sauce, and a cream sauce for pallid veal slices was soured with lime juice. Most of the food seems designed not to be eaten but tasted, especially such combinations as chicken and beef, or beef and veal, combinations not to be taken seriously.

Worthwhile desserts included the bittersweet choco-late mousse gilded with orange slices, the cool, crisp and mellow opera cake that combines chocolate and coffee flavors and the pastel sherbets flavored with pear, lemon, kiwi and strawberries.

Wines are undistinguished and expensive and the staff is inept at serving them.

Alfredo's
Fair

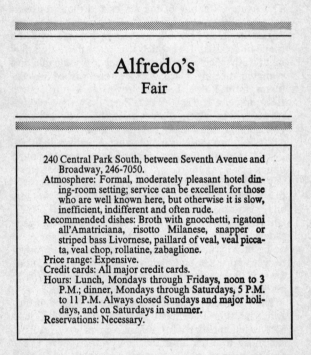

240 Central Park South, between Seventh Avenue and Broadway, 246-7050.
Atmosphere: Formal, moderately pleasant hotel din-ing-room setting; service can be excellent for those who are well known here, but otherwise it is slow, inefficient, indifferent and often rude.
Recommended dishes: Broth with gnocchetti, rigatoni all'Amatriciana, risotto Milanese, snapper or striped bass Livornese, paillard of veal, veal picca-ta, veal chop, rollatine, zabaglione.
Price range: Expensive.
Credit cards: All major credit cards.
Hours: Lunch, Mondays through Fridays, noon to 3 P.M.; dinner, Mondays through Saturdays, 5 P.M. to 11 P.M. Always closed Sundays and major holi-days, and on Saturdays in summer.
Reservations: Necessary.

Through the years, my experiences at this restaurant have been totally consistent — few places in town can match it for miserable service and icy indifference to-ward guests unknown to the management. Some of my best friends are regulars at this place, and because I re-spect their food judgment, I am willing to believe the kitchen can produce some very good dishes — a few of which I have even managed to wrest from the staff.

There often seems to be a shortage of help, especially of captains to take orders and, in addition, there are constant murmurings about unexpected crowds from

2

the nearby Coliseum. It would seem that having been in business so long, the management would be prepared to deal with all such eventualities. Were it not for the long-standing reputation for good food this place enjoys, and its proximity to the Coliseum and Lincoln Center, it would not even be worth serious consideration. The last in a long chain of harrowing experiences took place recently when five of us arrived at about 8:30 P.M. on a weekday night for dinner. As usual the place was jammed, and as usual, being unknown, we were seated in a cheerless, airless back alcove. It took thirty minutes to get appetizers (after a twenty-minute wait to order), then forty-five minutes and still no pasta. The owner, who can be gracious with friends, simmering risotto for them and making sure that things are otherwise perfect, is a master at avoiding the glance of customers trying to catch his eye. Finally we accomplished that, and said that if the pasta did not come out in five minutes, and if we could not be assured that our meat courses would follow in reasonable time, we would leave. Again he mumbled about being short of captains and overflowing with Coliseum customers, but the food did come out — dried up, tepid, tasteless. Just across the way, a man finished with dinner tried to get a check for a full thirty minutes and, in despair, got up and walked out without ever paying at all. We knew just how he felt.

One night, after broccoli with pasta, we had the house roast chicken in beer that was delicious. But because broccoli was served with it, we said we had just had some. No other vegetable was offered, even at these top prices.

Baked clams are always mushy, shrimp scampi-style can reek of iodine, indicating they are not fresh, and crostini of cornmeal polenta with Gruyère cheese, can arrive parched from having been under the heat lamp too long. California olives garnish otherwise good roast peppers and overripe tomatoes mar a mozzarella salad. There is an interesting broth flecked with tiny meat dumplings (gnocchetti de carne), and pastas that again vary with the staff's mood and pace. Rigatoni all'Amatriciana had a beautifully balanced sauce of tomato, prosciutto and onions, but the thin angel's hair pasta, capelli d'angelo, with cream, mushrooms and peas was pasty and tasted of boiled milk. Risotto Milanese, sunny with saffron, is a house special that takes thirty minutes — making it sound like fast food after our forty-five minute wait for ordinary pastas. In addition, you may be told that it is not available because of the rush. When it is, however, it can be exceptional, or may be overdosed with saffron. Potato gnocchi gratinéed in cream have also been good in the past, as were the green and white noodles, paglia e fieno, with a cream and cheese sauce. Ordering red snapper in casseruola (a thin tomato broth would be the correct thing here), we got it frankly Livornese, with tomato, olives and capers, but by any name that sauce is very well handled here on any fish. Sauces on meats have always been disappointing; paillard of veal and piccata are better alternatives, along with veal rollatine and grilled veal chop.

The bad news among the main courses came with a tough, dry beefsteak ai ferri; bland, undistinguished suprema di pollo alla bolognese (boneless chicken breast with prosciutto and cheese) and sweetbreads in a tough batter coating that tasted like an omelette and bitter liver that lacked freshness. Asparagus on two occasions were mushily overcooked, but on a third try were firm and perfect; peas, served with prosciutto, were canned.

The highly touted zabaglione was undercooked on one very rushed evening. As a result, it was thin and the marsala separated and sank to the bottom of the serving dish. On another try, it was like velvet — smooth, warm, thick but airy and altogether inspired.

Two other desserts were far less impressive — a cheesecake that tasted like nearly spoiled cottage cheese, and a really awful rum cake layered with, of all things, canned peaches.

Lunch tends to be better here than dinner — less rushed and with a little more attention from management.

Anche Vivolo
Fair

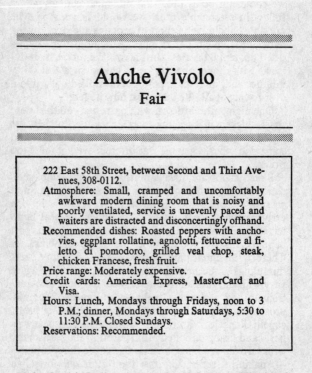

222 East 58th Street, between Second and Third Avenues, 308-0112.

Atmosphere: Small, cramped and uncomfortably awkward modern dining room that is noisy and poorly ventilated, service is unevenly paced and waiters are distracted and disconcertingly offhand.

Recommended dishes: Roasted peppers with anchovies, eggplant rollatine, agnolotti, fettuccine al filetto di pomodoro, grilled veal chop, steak, chicken Francese, fresh fruit.

Price range: Moderately expensive.

Credit cards: American Express, MasterCard and Visa.

Hours: Lunch, Mondays through Fridays, noon to 3 P.M.; dinner, Mondays through Saturdays, 5:30 to 11:30 P.M. Closed Sundays.

Reservations: Recommended.

If the food is Italian, it must be 58th Street. The block between Second and Third Avenues now has ten Italian restaurants, including the newest, Anche Vivolo. "Anche" means "also" in Italian and Vivolo is the name of the parent restaurant, which has been a successful neighborhood hangout on East 74th Street for the last several years.

Unfortunately, the new restaurant occupies a singularly uncomfortable space, noisy and cramped under a low ceiling and with so many angles and diagonals that it affords no comfortable areas for tables. Heat builds up around seats against the wall and tiny, round-bottomed vases (usually with wilted roses) tend to topple. The manners of the young waiters suggest an underlying insolence, and the kitchen can be painfully slow.

Such flaws are difficult to explain in a place run by professionals of long standing who have had enough time to smooth out the rough spots. The small but interesting menu is the same here as at the uptown Vivolo, and there are also a half dozen daily specials called out by waiters — without benefit of prices. Though most of the food is edible, the kitchen's performance does not merit the one-star rating given the uptown Vivolo.

Blandness and careless cooking are the main problems. Frying is inept, with an overpowering flavor of hot grease in such dishes as the mozzarella in carrozza appetizer or the cheese-and-ham-stuffed veal cutlet Valdostana that is a main course. Shrimp, whether topping the acceptable squid salad or in a good, spicy fra diavolo sauce, smelled of iodine, indicating that they were no longer fresh. A lack of freshness also marred the fish soup and the striped bass with mussels and clams.

Baked clams were slightly burned on two occasions and their crumbs had been mixed with what looked like paprika — a most un-Italian touch. All the cream and cheese sauces on pastas such as the undercooked tortellini and fettuccine tended to be overabundant and soupy.

A few simple dishes that were thoroughly satisfying included the appetizers of cool and meaty roasted peppers with anchovy fillets, and melenzane rollatine, eggplant slices rolled around a ricotta-cheese filling and baked with a mild tomato sauce. Sliced mozzarella with tomatoes was a near miss, flawed by a cloying oily dressing.

In addition to the regular choices of lackluster linguine with clam sauce and the much better fettuccine al filetto di pomodoro made with tomatoes and onions, there is a daily pasta specialty. You are also informed that you may have any pasta "a piacere" — "as it pleases you." That is something of an exaggeration, however, because although you can have a number of sauces, the pastas they can go on is limited. The best pastas we tried were the linguine and the agnolotti, the half-moon version of ravioli, both in an Amatriciana sauce with tomatoes, ham and onions. Pasta sauces tend to be oversalted.

Floury, innocuous sauces marred the veal piccata and the chicken scarpariello. Such specials as chicken baked with cheese in a brown sauce and slices of veal sautéed with mushrooms suggested hotel banquet cooking. Preferable choices are the grilled veal chop, the lemony sautéed chicken Francese or the broiled steak. Choosing those after one of the better appetizers or pastas and ending up with a choice of fresh fruit that usually includes a big wedge of good pineapple should result in a decent meal.

Ararat

★

4 East 36th Street, between Fifth and Madison Avenues, 686-4622.

Atmosphere: Overdone cocktail lounge décor; good service.

Recommended dishes: Ararat special hors d'oeuvres, yogurt soup, kufta plaz, harpoot kufta, choban pilaf, swordfish kebob.

Price range: Moderate.

Credit cards: All major credit cards.

Hours: Lunch, Mondays through Saturdays, noon to 4 P.M.; dinner, Mondays through Saturdays, 4 P.M. to 10 P.M., Sundays, 4 P.M. to 9 P.M. Closed on major holidays.

Reservations: Recommended.

It is hard to understand why Armenian food — with its succulent dishes, its preponderance of lamb and the intricate handwork required for many of its specialties — should be so relatively inexpensive. But that fortunate condition seems consistent among Armenian restaurants, and Ararat is no exception to that rule.

Moderately priced complete dinners include copious portions of appetizer, soup, main course with vegetables and pilaf, a salad, dessert and coffee, and many of the choices are far above average.

The best bet by far on the appetizer list is the Ararat Special, a plate filled with such soothing and savory selections as vine leaves and mussels, both stuffed with pilaf; a grainy, garlicky chick-pea purée; pleasant, if slightly bland, fish roe purée — tarama; white, bean salad, the rich eggplant and tomato stew called imam bayeldi, feta cheese and salty, thin-skinned calamata olives.

Eaten with some of the crisp, sesame-sprinkled lavash bread, that plate is almost a meal in itself. Other appetizers at Ararat are less satisfying. The artichoke hearts are frozen and the stodgy cheese pastry turnovers — beoreg — lack seasoning. A hot yogurt and cracked-wheat soup scented with mint and lemon was lovely, but an egg-lemon chicken broth, with overcooked rice, tasted of nothing but starch.

The salad is far too sharply spiked with vinegar, so skip it and save room for the better entrees — kufta piaz, six or seven grilled miniburgers of lamb showered with minced onion and parsley; harpoot kufta, balls of lamb and cracked wheat filled with currants and pine nuts and served in a peppery, though greasy, broth and choban pilaf, cubes of tenderly stewed lamb nestled under a dome of cracked-wheat pilaf garnished with braised, whole okra pods. Shish kebab was acceptable, as were the marinated lamb steak and the somewhat bland lamb stew. Swordfish remained moist after careful broiling on a skewer.

Desserts are disappointing. The usual assortment of crisp, layered pastry dripping with nuts and sugar syrup

6

tasted stale. Melon or the ekmek kadayif — the very sweet cake simmered in syrup and topped with thick, white, concentrated cream — was preferable.

Ararat is far more comfortable for lunch than dinner, precisely because it attracts more people midday and so they are dispersed throughout the three dining rooms. At night the smaller crowd is concentrated in the tightly packed and garish cocktail lounge.

Arirang
Fair

---

28 West 56th Street, between Fifth Avenue and Avenue of the Americas, 581-9698.
Atmosphere: Pleasant if unprepossessing surroundings; detached, perfunctory, unfriendly service.
Recommended dishes: Wan ja meatballs, Korean consommé, kalbui kui short ribs, sin sullo.
Price range: Moderate.
Credit cards: All major cards.
Hours: Lunch, Mondays through Fridays, noon to 2:30 P.M.; dinner, Mondays through Wednesdays, 5 P.M. to 10:30 P.M., Thursdays through Saturdays, 5 P.M. to 11 P.M., Sundays, 4 P.M. to 10 P.M.
Reservations: Recommended.

Ten years ago, Arirang seemed an interesting Korean restaurant, considering how poorly Korea's pungent cuisine was represented in New York. Now, however, the choices have expanded, and by comparison this restaurant seems to offer only bland and uninteresting versions of Korean specialties, most of them served with careless indifference.

Pul koki, a marinated sirloin beef, should be grilled at the table, but it arrived cooked, cold and stringy. Chapchae, usually a satisfying stir-fried combination of noodles, vegetables and beef, came sodden with grease; so did the sam hapcho combination of abalone, beef and vegetables.

Dinner begins with a sorry, greasy assortment of dumplings, egg rolls, batter-fried fish, chicken and shrimp fritters and salty soup. Only the tiny, spicy wan ja meatballs can be recommended.

Two very good dishes were grilled short ribs, kalbui kui, and the sin sullo, a soup-stew simmered over a brazier. But when I tried to order the sin sullo, the waitress said it would take twenty-five minutes. I chose to wait and, lo and behold, out it came in less than fifteen minutes. It was hard not to believe she had tried to discourage me from ordering it. I also had the same feeling about all à la carte selections. Clearly, the house pushes the touristy price-fixed dinners. But the broth, enriched with beef, chicken, hard-cooked eggs and vegetables, made the most satisfying main course sampled.

Kimchi, the spicy pickled Korean cabbage, had the authentic lacing of chili oil, and kim — seawood toasted

7

over charcoal — had an engaging flavor. Several fish preparations were dry, but the salad of spinach, bean sprouts and turnip was refreshing. All desserts were lackluster.

Arnold's Turtle
★

51 Bank Street, at West Fourth Street, 242-5623.
Atmosphere: Small, rustic and pleasantly Bohemian cafe-restaurant; informal, friendly service; careless housekeeping.
Recommended dishes: Miso soup, cream of parsnip soup, artichoke with mustard sauce, all salads, vegetable quiches, vegetarian lasagne, tofu with ginger tamari sauce, tabouli, huevos rancheros, total cheese sandwich, apple crumb cake, oatmeal chocolate-chip cookies, carrot cake, brown-rice pudding.
Price range: Moderate.
Credit cards: MasterCard and Visa.
Hours: Lunch, seven days, noon to 4:30 P.M.; dinner, seven days, 4:30 P.M. to midnight. Brunch, Saturdays and Sundays, noon to 4 P.M. Closed Thanksgiving Day and Christmas Day.
Reservations: Not accepted.

One of Greenwich Village's more beguiling cafes is Arnold's Turtle, in one of that area's prettiest, tree-lined sectors. This is a small, informal, rustic vegetarian restaurant, with one tiny outdoor table placed in a doorway that is no longer used, and the place is equally crowded for lunch, dinner and Sunday brunch. Unfortunately, housekeeping is careless, and a dirty carpet should be replaced or removed. Service is pleasant if at times a little too laid back.

The menu is strictly vegetarian, but eggs, cheese and other dairy products have a part in it, and a few macrobiotic ingredients, such as tamari soy sauce, are used for flavorings, but not on principle.

Anything from a glass of carrot juice to a piping-hot, baked vegetable main course can be had at any time of day; there is never a minimum. What regulars seem to prefer is a combination of small shared side orders, such as parsley and boulghor salad, tabouli (made with currants, which seems a mistake) and chomos (chicken and tahini pea purée, which is better without the cumin), bean curd, tofu with ginger tamari soy sauce and various salads decked out with alfalfa sprouts and shreds of raw carrots.

There are very good soups, including a clear and fragrant Japanese miso soybean broth, with vegetables, seaweed and tofu, and a lovely cream of parsnip, a daily soup I had recently. Artichoke in a golden, oily mustard sauce was another top choice.

Pita bread sandwiches that combine various salads are excellent, most especially the total cheese sandwich (Jarlsberg and cheddar melted with tomato and sprouts.) The tabouli and tahini sandwich tends to be dry and pasty. The only one that I did not like was a combination of Jarlsberg cheese and avocado that was baked. The heat made the avocado dark, mushy and unpalatable. Excellent huevos rancheros — fried eggs in a spicy tomato sauce — are sometimes served for weekend brunches.

Salad bowls of all sorts are so fresh they still seem to be growing, and there is usually a light, custardy quiche with whole-wheat crust, my favorite being one made with carrots.

Weaknesses come by way of the hot dishes, for though many are enclosed in very good whole-wheat or phyllo crusts, the vegetables tend to be overcooked and musty. A Russian vegetable pie sampled was overpowered by the scent of Savoy cabbage almost as strong as kale; tofu nori rolls had the same rice and carrot filling that made up the garnish around them, and a beautiful, looking brocanokopita — a phyllo layered pie of broccoli, feta and ricotta cheese — lacked creaminess, and the broccoli was overcooked.

The other flaw that earns Arnold's Turtle one star instead of two, is that in typical vegetarian-restaurant fashion, almost everything is made with everything. This means shredded carrots and alfalfa sprouts can turn up in three dishes in a single meal, and the individual characteristics of a dish are lost.

Homemade whole-wheat bread is nutty and delicious, and the oatmeal chocolate-chip cookies, the apple crumb pie and the creamy, cinnamon-scented, brown-rice pudding with nuts and raisins are all lovely. So, by the way, are the garlic-tofu and the tahini salad dressings.

Artie's Warehouse

★

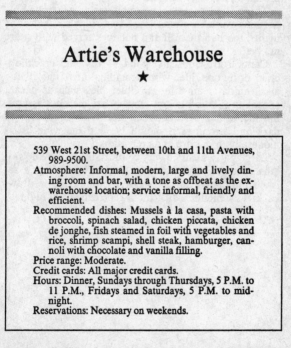

539 West 21st Street, between 10th and 11th Avenues, 989-9500.

Atmosphere: Informal, modern, large and lively dining room and bar, with a tone as offbeat as the ex-warehouse location; service informal, friendly and efficient.

Recommended dishes: Mussels à la casa, pasta with broccoli, spinach salad, chicken piccata, chicken de jonghe, fish steamed in foil with vegetables and rice, shrimp scampi, shell steak, hamburger, cannoli with chocolate and vanilla filling.

Price range: Moderate.

Credit cards: All major credit cards.

Hours: Dinner, Sundays through Thursdays, 5 P.M. to 11 P.M., Fridays and Saturdays, 5 P.M. to midnight.

Reservations: Necessary on weekends.

Lovers of offbeat locations should waste no time in getting over to Artie's Warehouse. Operating in an otherwise deserted area, it offers almost unlimited parking space, which has made it a favorite with New Jersey diners and just enough pleasantly satisfying, moderately priced food to make it popular with young people.

Except for the lights that glimmer under the loading shed, Artie's could easily be mistaken for one more warehouse on the block. But behind the totally anonymous doors is a spacious, convivial and handsome, if simply decorated, dining room. Brick walls, natural wood, rose-colored cotton-quilted wall panels and twinkling theatrical lights provide a stylish backdrop, and the young and friendly waiters and waitresses are as informal and efficient as the blue jeans most of them wear. There's almost always a lively bar scene and sometimes piano music.

Artie's flaw, cuteness, is most obvious in its appetizers, with hot specialties, such as mushrooms and fried wontons, turned mushy by a mawkish cream-cheese filling, and minced baked clams that are bland and starchy. Those who love first courses should stick to the nice, oily, marinated mussels, sparkled with minced pimento, or share the linguine with broccoli or a sprightly spinach, bacon and mushroom salad.

A daily choice of fish, steamed in a puff of aluminum foil, along with zucchini, onion, tomato and rice, was pleasant on two occasions, and shell steak, sizzlingly hot on a grill platter, has also been thoroughly satisfying. Chicken sautéed piccata style with lemon, or de jonghe (in a mustard cream sauce) has been tender and delicate, and shrimp scampi were lusty and garlic laden, if just the least bit dry. Skip the sliced beef stir-fried with vegetables, the tough and fatty spareribs and the underseasoned linguine with white clam sauce, also the house salad based on iceberg lettuce. Broiled chicken was fine one night, but stale on another.

There is an acceptable hamburger of generous proportions available after 11 P.M. on Friday and Saturday nights; too bad the roll and potatoes served with it are not better.

Cannoli are unusually good — dry and crackling-crisp; order one filled with a combination of chocolate- and vanilla-cream fillings. Other pies such as pecan, chocolate silk and lemon mousse, are merely passable, but melon has been fine and ripe. The espresso is as dark and strong as it should be, and the wine list is modest, both in price and pretention.

Large parties can be very comfortable, and Artie's — "the best little warehouse in Chelsea" — offers a relaxed alternative for Sunday-night dining. One drawback: it's sometimes difficult to get a cab late at night.

The Assembly Steak House
Fair

16 West 51st Street, between Fifth Avenue and Avenue of the Americas, 581-3580.

Atmosphere: Dark, noisy and uncomfortable dining room; staff is polite and well-meaning, but service tends to be slow.

Recommended dishes: Crabmeat cocktail, sirloin steak, lamb chops, lobster.

Price range: Expensive.

Credit cards: All major credit cards.

Hours: Lunch, Mondays through Fridays, 11:30 A.M. to 3 P.M.; dinner, Mondays through Fridays, 3 P.M. to 10 P.M., Saturdays, 4:30 P.M. to 11 P.M. (but closed on Saturdays, April 10 through November 1). Closed Sundays and holidays.

Reservations: Necessary.

Considering the many places where one can get not only high-quality steaks but also excellent trimmings to go with them, it is hard to understand the appeal of this restaurant. For while sirloin steaks and lamb chops and a beautifully broiled four-and-one-half-pound lobster were acceptable and the crabmeat cocktail was cold, fresh and altogether decent, almost everything else on this large menu proved disappointing on all visits.

The dining room here is gaudy, much in the manner of a cocktail lounge in a big chain motor inn. There is an overabundance of noise and insufficient lighting and the atmosphere is generally hectic and uncomfortable. Ventilation is poor and stale cigar smoke permeates the place. The personnel is pleasant and thoughtful, but at dinner, food can be very long in coming out of the kitchen, most especially for first courses.

Amid this discomfort one must cope with such appetizers as mushy, overly sweet chopped chicken liver, clam chowder filled with potatoes and devoid of any clam flavor whatever, and hard, dry, grilled shrimp Monagesque in a sauce that had the acrid bitterness of scorched tomato paste. Black bean soup with rice and minced onions was a good deal better but still underseasoned. Huge cherrystone clams, really meant for chowder, tasted of petroleum and had not been cut loose from their shells. Garlic steak was so heavily showered with mincings of that heady bulb that the steak's own flavor never stood a chance.

A generous slice of roast prime ribs of beef arrived medium rare as ordered but lacked the beefy richness it should have had. It appeared to have been kept warm close to steam, a practice that invariably dissipates flavor. Broiled chicken was minimally acceptable and a piece of well-grilled striped bass was ruined by overtones of petroleum, a common fault with that particular fish. Shrimp stuffed with crabmeat were overcooked and their filling was fishy and pasty. Fried shrimp were sheathed in a batter as dense as a banana peel.

A house green salad is served with main courses and a table tent advertises the presence of red-tipped lettuce in the mix. "Please notice our red-tipped lettuce," it advises, but "Try to find it" would be more appropriate. At four dinners, each salad had no more than two slim shreds of this excellent salad greeen buried among wastelands of iceberg lettuce, plus a few wisps of other decent greens tossed in. All of the salad dressings were dreadful — sweet, and overly thick and redolent of dehydrated garlic.

Greasy German fried potatoes, fair french fries and crusty, dry, cold rice were among the accompaniments offered. Only the baked potato was passable; had it been really hot it would have been excellent. Dark, overcooked spinach and watery broccoli were the only vegetables I tried. Desserts were in a class with the rest of the food.

Auberge Suisse
★

153 East 53rd Street, in the Citicorp Center, 421-1420.
Atmosphere: Shimmery, silvery handsome modern interior; fair service that can be indifferent.
Recommended dishes: Escargots, raclette, smoked trout, viande de Grison, beignet de fromage, émincé de veau, St.-Gallen veal sausage, suprême de volaille en croûte, fondue Vaudoise, lemon ice with pear brandy, chocolate fondue.
Price range: Moderately expensive.
Credit cards: All major credit cards.
Hours: Lunch, Mondays through Saturdays, noon to 2:30 P.M.; dinner, Mondays through Saturdays, 5 P.M. to 10 P.M., Sundays, 4:30 P.M. to 9 P.M. Closed Sundays during July and August. Closed on major holidays.
Reservations: Necessary.

A first cousin to Dezaley on East 58th Street, Auberge Suisse, in Citicorp, is a relatively small and compact, stunning modern restaurant, shimmering with silvery mirrors and tones of gray and beige, and with just enough sparkle to suggest a smart European modern cocktail lounge. Service, unfortunately is perfunctory, pushy and careless.

The menu of Swiss specialties includes a number of intriguing combinations, plus many more that seem overcomplicated, a fairly common flaw in Swiss cookery in general. Appetizers were, by and large, good, most especially escargots baked in a casserole with a fragrant herb butter, raclette Valaisanne, a gratin dish of melted, strong cheese, accented by boiled potatoes and pickled onions and cornichons, and beignet de fromage, hot, fried cheese puffs in a light tomato sauce. Smoked trout, though a bit small and firm, had a mild, pleasant smoke accent.

Potage balois, a thick beef soup, has always tasted like a slightly thinned-down version of Franco-American beef gravy. When we sent it back, the waiter argued, saying it was good and that it was "not nice" for us to say it wasn't.

But several main courses were thoroughly delightful, and interesting enough to make a visit worthwhile. Auberge Suisse serves a lusty fragrant fondue Vaudoise. The heavy, handsome glazed earthenware casserole is set over a burner so that its thick, wine-laced cheese stays meltingly, bubbling hot as chunks of dried bread, held on long-handled forks are swathed in the molten cheese. Although it requires a certain amount of patience for two people to finish, this is a really wonderful dish and perhaps a little easier to take if shared by four as an appetizer.

Another thoroughly satisfying main course was juicy, thick, white, St.-Gallen veal sausage grilled and served with rosti, crisp-fried Swiss potato pancakes. At Auberge Suisse that potato preparation was sometimes crisp and delicate, other times soggy and underdone.

Suprême de volaille en croûte, a chicken breast stuffed with tomatoes and cheese, then baked in a crust, was satisfying although once the pastry had been scorched. Fortunately, it is a simple matter to eat all of this creation, leaving the bottom crust intact, stuck to the bottom of the plate.

The Swiss national dish, émincé de veau, thin slivers of veal, arrived in a satiny mushroom cream sauce.

Trout with herbs smelled unpleasantly fishy, but grilled fillets of sole were acceptable. Not so the greasy calf's liver which is not nearly as good as the same dish at Dezaley. A grilled paillard of veal was pallid, watery and had a fishy smell. And tournedos Cordon Rouge, based on knotty beef, was topped with a gummy Béarnaise sauce.

Among desserts, lemon ice splashed with pear brandy was refreshing and chocolate fondue with raw fruit should appeal to chocolate freaks. White chocolate mousse tasted like sweet fat.

Auctions
★

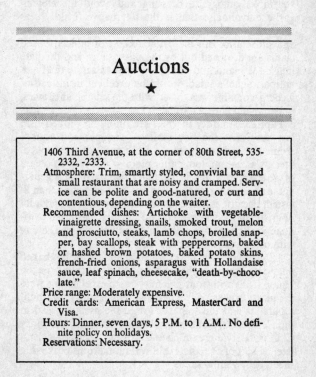

1406 Third Avenue, at the corner of 80th Street, 535-2332, -2333.

Atmosphere: Trim, smartly styled, convivial bar and small restaurant that are noisy and cramped. Service can be polite and good-natured, or curt and contentious, depending on the waiter.

Recommended dishes: Artichoke with vegetable-vinaigrette dressing, snails, smoked trout, melon and prosciutto, steaks, lamb chops, broiled snapper, bay scallops, steak with peppercorns, baked or hashed brown potatoes, baked potato skins, french-fried onions, asparagus with Hollandaise sauce, leaf spinach, cheesecake, "death-by-chocolate."

Price range: Moderately expensive.

Credit cards: American Express, MasterCard and Visa.

Hours: Dinner, seven days, 5 P.M. to 1 A.M.. No definite policy on holidays.

Reservations: Necessary.

Anyone who is bothered by noise will be especially unhappy at Auctions, an otherwise stylish and appealing little bar and steakhouse. But not everyone is disturbed by noise, and there are some people who even thrive on it, judging by the three-deep crowd at the bar most evenings and the full house that convenes in the adjacent cafe-dining room. Even after so short a trial period, expansion plans are already under way.

Both the name and décor of this restaurant derive from its location in the heart of auction country. Walls papered with the brilliantly colorful pages of auction house catalogues are in sparkling contrast to mirrored panels and a white ceiling. With just thirty-six seats so far, the small dining room is pleasantly casual, as is the service for the most part. Only occasionally is the tone marred by a waiter who is curt and contentious.

One of the three partners in this venture is Jim Downey Jr., who, with his father, was the originator and former owner of Downey's Steak House in the theater district. There is little surprise, then, in finding that broiled steaks, lamb chops and fish and some excellent potato and vegetable preparations represent the kitchen's better efforts. But there are surprises in the abundant use of iceberg lettuce, the poor preparation of sauced and sautéed dishes and the appearance of sweet cream gone sour.

What's more, unevenness marks the kitchen's performance. Smoked trout is generally moist and delicate and the horseradish cream sauce accompanying it sometimes strikes a fine balance between the hotness of the horseradish and the soothing qualities of the cream. At other times the sauce is overwhelmingly fiery. Pea soup may be velvety and gently scented with onion, or it can be slickly, unpleasantly smooth and tasteless. Among first courses, stick to artichokes. But ask for the vegetable vinaigrette dressing and avoid the cloying garlic mayonnaise that is the alternative. Mildly seasoned baked snails are satisfying, and so is the melon and prosciutto. But the briny accents of minced baked clams are drowned out by the pasty sauce and the pâté maison is bland and gummy. Chopped salad, really an antipasto-chef's salad, would be excellent if, instead of iceberg, romaine was tossed with the salami, anchovies, pimento and cheese garnishes.

Paprika is hardly the best seasoning on broiled fish, but despite it the bay scallops, snapper and scampi seemed altogether decent — fresh and not overcooked. Steak was decent, too, either plain or in a brandy cream sauce sparked with crushed black peppercorns. A generous and inviting chopped steak looked better than it tasted, because it had been too densely packed and a lot of gristle had been ground into the mix. Tasteless, overdone veal chops and chicken should be skipped, along with calf's liver sautéed to a dull gray.

Three kinds of potatoes — large and lovely hot baked potatoes, crusty hashed browns and crackling baked potato skins with sour cream — were excellent, as were the glassy slivers of french-fried onions, the firm bright asparagus and the spinach. Forgo the pseudo-bread in the form of rolls and save calories for either the fluffy California-style cream-cheesecake or "death-by-chocolate," a sort of chocolate and walnut marquise cake in a sheer, eggy vanilla sauce.

There is a minimally satisfying wine list and very silly, pretentious tulip wine glasses. Watch out for the cream that accompanies coffee or strawberries, because it can be clotted and sour. There is a small supper menu with hamburgers and salads served from 10:30 P.M. until closing — usually about 1 or 2 A.M.

Baan Thai Restaurant

★

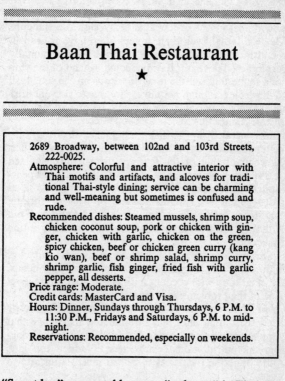

2689 Broadway, between 102nd and 103rd Streets, 222-0025.

Atmosphere: Colorful and attractive interior with Thai motifs and artifacts, and alcoves for traditional Thai-style dining; service can be charming and well-meaning but sometimes is confused and rude.

Recommended dishes: Steamed mussels, shrimp soup, chicken coconut soup, pork or chicken with ginger, chicken with garlic, chicken on the green, spicy chicken, beef or chicken green curry (kang kio wan), beef or shrimp salad, shrimp curry, shrimp garlic, fish ginger, fried fish with garlic pepper, all desserts.

Price range: Moderate.

Credit cards: MasterCard and Visa.

Hours: Dinner, Sundays through Thursdays, 6 P.M. to 11:30 P.M., Fridays and Saturdays, 6 P.M. to midnight.

Reservations: Recommended, especially on weekends.

"Sawatdee," we are told, means "welcome" in Thai. To New Yorkers, and especially those living on the Upper West Side, the huge, new Baan Thai restaurant deserves a heartfelt "sawatdee."

Although New York has its share of very good Thai restaurants, few offer anything in the way of atmosphere, and none approaches this newcomer for elaborateness and color. Baan, the management said, means a country house, and Baan Thai reflects the theme with the traditional Thai trapezoidal arch repeated in doorways, niches and frames on rustic wood-panel walls, and with Thai dance masks and artifacts displayed around the room. Sprays of tiny purple orchids, a lavish low buffet of fruit and golden custard desserts and waitresses wearing graceful fitted silk tunics add convincing touches.

This is the only restaurant I have found in New York that offers traditional Thai service in alcoves seating as many as eight people in relative privacy. Floor cushions and pyramid-shaped bolsters are authentic, although not quite authentically used; in Thailand, diners sit on the floor with legs crossed in front of them, but in Baan Thai, the cushions are grouped around a pit into which legs dangle while the diners eat from a low carved table.

Given the intriguing setting, I cannot help wishing that the food at Baan Thai were as good as it is at several other Thai restaurants in town. But that is not yet the case. Nor is the menu quite so interesting, missing as it does such favorites as princess rolls and preparations made with frog's legs, octopus and squid. There are, nevertheless, a number of well-prepared dishes served family style, which are to be eaten with fork and spoon (not chopsticks).

Right at the start, be prepared for a few problems because of language difficulties. Reservations get mixed up, so it is important to be very clear about whether you want to eat in one of the Thai alcoves or at a standard Western table. Even then, diners often have to wait in the attractive cocktail lounge, where I was accidentally served a vodka chaser for my Scotch instead of the club soda requested. But the few Americans on the staff rush to the rescue, though not always in time to prevent mix-ups. There have also been many reports of extreme rudeness since this review first appeared.

In general, fish, shellfish and chicken dishes are far better than the dry, tasteless pork and beef specialties. This means that of the few appetizers, only steamed mussels with onions are really good, the satays appearing to be precooked and reheated. The vegetable salad pales beside the sprightly salads of beef or shrimp, brightened with onions, lemon grass, mint and chili oil. Although listed as main courses, either salad is a fine first course.

Shrimp soup, heady with lemon grass and fiery hot with chili oil, is guaranteed to clear stodgy heads. Chicken soup with coconut milk is a gentler alternative. One of the problems with many beef and pork dishes at Baan Thai seems to be the incorrect use of the favorite Thai seasoning, nam pla, a fermented fish sauce that supplies protein and flavor. If added early in the cooking, the putrid aroma evaporates; if added too late, those lingering overtones impart a musty aftertaste to meat.

The chicken dishes sampled, however, have been much better, especially chicken sautéed with garlic, white pepper and soy sauce, or chicken on the green, steamed with leafy vegetables and mellowed with peanut sauce. Chicken à la Bangkok, tossed with shrimp and vegetables, was less satisfying, and so were both chicken and pork with bean curd.

Kang kio wan, made with either beef or chicken, is a rich and soupy green curry based on coconut milk and flavored with green chilies and peas, all wonderful ladled over steamed rice. Broccoli beef was only fair, but shrimp curry, sautéed with onion and chilies, and shrimp garlic, prepared much like the chicken garlic, were complex and savory. There are two enticing fish preparations at Baan Thai — slices of fried sea bass encrusted with garlic and pepper, and a whole fried fish ginger, crisp and enriched with onions, mushrooms, pork and bean sauce.

Neither fried rice nor the fried mee krob rice noodles is worth ordering. The first was tepid and mushy, while the second was too cold and too sweet.

Egg-custard desserts, cooked in sugar syrup, are better at Baan Thai, however, than in any other Thai restaurant I have tried in the city. Choose an assortment of egg threads, flower custard and beans formed of green peanuts, or fresh pineapple.

The Balkan-Armenian Restaurant

★★

129 East 27th Street, between Lexington and Park
Avenues, 689-7925.
Atmosphere: Snug, comfortable and lively.
Recommended dishes: Stuffed vine leaves or mussels,
baked eggplant, boerek, all appetizers, lentil or yo-
gurt soup, shish kebab, scara kufte, eggplant
stuffed with lamb, baked lamb with fancy pilaf or
mixed vegetables, all desserts.
Price range: Inexpensive.
Credit cards: All major credit cards.
Hours: Lunch, Mondays through Fridays, noon to
2:30 P.M.; dinner, Mondays through Thursdays,
4:30 P.M. to 9 P.M., Fridays and Saturdays, 4:30
P.M. to 10 P.M. Closed Sundays and major holidays.
Reservations: Recommended.

Inexpensive though it is, one feels no sense of deprivation when dining at the convivial Balkan-Armenian, a
70-year-old restaurant. While many of the details of the
décor prove upon close scrutiny to be somewhat corny,
the overall effect is pleasantly all-purpose Middle Eastern and Armenian combined. Tables topped with
snowy cloths at dinner are small and a bit close, and the
waiters, usually friendly, can be abrupt during peak
hours, but in general the feeling is one of relaxed good
will. Formica tabletops are unclothed at lunch, a final
bizarre touch amid the melange of oriental carpets and
lanterns, and the modern, wood wall paneling. Waiters
in printed cotton jackets suggest walking tea cozies.

Except for one token entree of chicken and a few of
fish, all the rest are based on lamb, most succulently
prepared braised, as in the tourlu guvech — golden-
brown shanks smothered under a ratatouillelike blanket
of stewed vegetables. Tender chops of shoulder lamb
are delicious on the currant-and-pignoli-studded fancy
rice pilaf, and the eggplant stuffed with ground lamb,
spices, tomato and onion is so richly seasoned it will
hardly be thought an economy dish.

While most of the entrees on the menu are under $10,
anyone willing to go a little higher should try the excellent shish kebab or scara steak, a thick broiled lamb
steak, cut from the leg and done pink inside if so ordered.

All of the appetizers come up to the superb quality of
the stuffed vine leaves and mussels, each enriched with
a cinnamon-perfumed pilaf; the fragrant eggplant and
tomato stew that is imam bayildi; the golden lentil soup,
or the rich hot madzoonabour, a pungent, minty yogurt
soup thickened with barley. Desserts include outstanding examples of the flaky nut-and-syrup-enriched
Armenian pastries, the two best being the rolled che-
ckme and tel kadayiff, a similar affair based on a shred-
ded-wheat pastry.

There is full wine and liquor service here, and the only real flaw is the lack of the authentic sesame-encrusted Armenian bread, lavash. Sesame breadsticks and Italian bread have to suffice. A full dinner at Balkan-Armenian, with soup, entree, dessert and coffee (try the syrupy Armenian brew) is inexpensive, and lunch runs even less.

Bangkok Cuisine
★

885 Eighth Avenue, between 52nd and 53rd Streets, 581-6370.
Atmosphere: Flowery, atmospheric, colorful Thai setting; cramped and slightly noisy; service is perfunctory and careless.
Recommended dishes: Minced kingfish, soups, seafood in foil envelope, salads of beef, shrimp and squid, whole crisp-fried fish with sauce.
Price range: Moderate.
Credit cards: MasterCard, Visa and Diners Club.
Hours: Lunch, Mondays through Saturdays, 11:30 A.M. to 5 P.M.; dinner, Mondays through Saturdays, 5 P.M. to 11:30 P.M., Sundays, 5 P.M. to 10 P.M. Closed on major holidays.
Reservations: Necessary on weekends.

Bangkok Cuisine East
Unrated (see note below)

1470 First Avenue, between 76th and 77th Streets, 744-9891.
Atmosphere: Attractive but uncomfortable two-level dining room with colorful artifacts and lampshades; service is polite but overly casual.
Note: Owned by the same management as Bangkok Cuisine, and with the same menu, this restaurant opened too late to be rated in this book. One visit, however, indicates it is on a par with the original.

THAI FOOD

Of all the national cuisines the traveler may sample in the Far East, the most exotic is unquestionably that of Thailand, the country formerly known as Siam. And exotic here is used in its strictest sense, meaning foreign, strange, fascinating and enticing. So truly exotic is Thai food that it may take a Westerner several days to feel comfortable with some of its more aromatic seasonings, several of which, at first taste, might not seem appropriate to food at all. But familiarity, in this case, breeds enchantment, and finally and almost invariably, the novice becomes a devotee.

Anyone fortunate enough to study Thai cooking, either by eating it frequently on home ground or by spending time in a native kitchen, has to be impressed by its subtle counterpoints of texture and flavor. Crispness is offset by silky tenderness, and its peanuts, cucumbers, aromatic coriander and rice all help cool palates flambéed by fresh ginger, pepper, raw onions and chilies that may be red, green, fresh, dried, crushed, pounded to a paste or reduced to a clear and incendiary oil. Garlic, scallions, lemon juice and sugar or honey provide a familiar flavor spectrum with surprises coming through such exclusive Thai herbs as lemon balm and grass, the limy rind and leaves of the makrut, horapa — a kind of sweet basil, soy sauce and a fermented fish sauce, nam pla, that fortunately tastes much better than it smells, uncooked.

Thai dishes resemble a cross between Indian and Chinese cooking, with curries and stir-fried dishes and a few Malaysian classics, such as meat satays broiled over charcoal, and peanut-based chili sauces are thrown in for very good measure.

No restaurant found in this search serves food nearly so attractively as it is presented in Thailand. In the most traditional setting, Thai diners eat on floor cushions, reclining against triangular bolsters, using chopsticks or forks and spoons with red or black buffalo-horn handles and a brasslike alloy for tines and bowls. Low tables hold footed dishes of brass or porcelain, enameled in the colorful mosaics that testify to the Thai love of surface ornamentation.

But though New York's Thai restaurants are short on authentic atmosphere, they provide a more than adequate range of the national cuisine.

For appetizers, there are the satays of pork, beef or chicken; ground, spicy pork balls that may be wrapped in crepes or lettuce with sauce and scallions, in the manner of Peking duck; cold salads of slivered squid or beef in a chili marinade, frilled with scallions and coriander leaves, or vegetable salads, such as bean sprouts with a peanut-curry dressing.

Soups have either a clear, astringent lemon-lime base and are adrift with shrimp, crabmeat or chicken, or they may be creamy with a base of coconut milk.

Each meal should include either a rice or noodle dish. Kow pud, Thai fried rice, is a gentler variation on the Chinese version, and may be adorned with shrimp, crab, meat or poultry. Noodles are the clear cellophane rice type or egg noodles, boiled or fried with toppings similar to the rice. Mee krob, a personal favorite, is a fried-noodle dish in which the noodles achieve the golden fragility of spun glass. This must be ordered in advance from most Thai restaurants, though Bangkok Cuisine always has it on the menu.

The romantic, colorful setting is created with dark walls, colored-glass lampshades, paintings and prints of Thai royalty and scenes, a big fish tank with a pair of fabulous-looking, black-spotted fish flown in from Bangkok (said to be used as an appetizer) and floral cloths topped with stone rubbings under glass. Minced kingfish, crisply fried and mellowed in a curry sauce, was the best appetizer. All soups, especially chicken coconut and lemon shrimps, were delicate and refreshing. Mee krob is always on the menu and is sometimes well done with sugar-glazed shrimp. A house specialty of scallops, crab, shrimp and vegetables steamed in a big foil packet was richly fragrant in its own seafood broth, and one of the best low-calorie dishes one could expect. Mixed satays of pork, beef and chicken, and fried or steamed whole fish are delicious.

Beef, pork, chicken, duck, frogs' legs and seafood are prepared in half a dozen different ways — sautéed with garlic and pepper, in fiery curry sauces, stir-fried with vegetables, such as baby corn and mushrooms or bamboo shoots. Barbecued chicken, marinated in garlic-and-herb-enriched soy sauce, is succulently broiled over charcoal, and perhaps the most ubiquitous and intriguing specialties on local menus are whole red snapper or sea bass, fried with slivers of ginger, mushrooms and bean sauce, or, drier, with a spicy chili sauce, or steamed to snowy perfection.

Throughout the meal there is much dipping into complementary sauces, many of which seem to combine honey and hot chilies, and into relish dishes of cucumber chips brightened with chilies, coriander and vinegar. The best beverage to go with all of this is Thai beer — either Singha or Amarit — much like the clean and airy Danish beer and available in most of the city's Thai restaurants. Others permit you to bring your own beer — or wine, if you prefer, although wine's more delicate flavor is overpowered by Thai seasonings.

The only disappointing course to most Western palates is dessert. Though in Thailand one finds exquisite fruit salads, with grapes and even the tiny sections of mandarins peeled, and a marvelous coconut custard — sankhaya — baked right in the coconut shell, neither of these is presented in New York. Instead, Thai restaurants offer a series of bland, sweet pudding desserts that seem to be set with a gelatinlike agar-agar or tapioca, unappetizingly presented in plastic, lidded cups.

When originally reviewed in 1977, Bangkok Cuisine was one of the best Thai restaurants, well worth a two-star rating. But though it still gives a fair representation of that cuisine in lovely, romantic surroundings, the food is not quite as special as it was. Dishes are never sufficiently spiced, no matter how insistent one may be, and both fried rice and mee krob are marred by greasiness. But there are still enough good dishes to make a visit worthwile. The newer Bangkok Cuisine East seems to be exhibiting the same flaws and strengths as the original.

Barbetta
Fair

321 West 46th Street, between 8th and 9th Avenues, 246-9171.

Atmosphere: Formal, elegant but dated dining-salon setting with a lovely Roman garden in summer; service is generally pushy, rude and overbearing.

Recommended dishes: Risotto Piemontese, seafood risotto, pasta primavera, calf's liver Veneziana, fried brains and artichokes, rum cake.

Price range: Expensive.

Credit cards: American Express, MasterCard, Visa and Diners Club.

Hours: Lunch, Mondays through Saturdays, noon to 2 P.M.; dinner, Mondays through Saturdays, 8 to 11:30 P.M. Pre-theater dinner, Mondays through Saturdays, 5 to 6:30 P.M. Closed Sundays and holidays.

Reservations: Necessary.

Consistent rudeness spoils what is an otherwise lovely setting, in this elegant and formal if dated version of what used to be called a Continental dining salon. In summer there is a graceful, leafy courtyard garden with white umbrellas and garden statuary. But at a recent lunch, a friend and I were indifferently herded toward our table, as usual here for unknown guests, and when one of us asked for the sautéed spezzatini of chicken, the captain said: "Forget it, Lady" — not exactly the soul of grace. When I was recognized at that lunch, the captain switched gears mid-meal, substituting obsequious solicitude for brusque rudeness. He also switched desserts on the wagon, bringing fresh ones to replace yesterday's leftovers, and he began to take extra pains with all dishes.

A seafood risotto I ordered took thirty minutes to arrive, a delay that should have been announced. The cold stuffed breast of veal, cima, which is a specialty of Genoa, arrived greasy and garnished with papery, unpeeled roasted peppers. The tiny whitebait-like fish, gianchetti, fried then marinated, were stale and much too vinegary. Calf's liver Veneziana style, sautéed with golden slivers of melted onion, was very good, as was the spinach and broccoli purée served with it. Fried calf's brains with artichokes can be crisply gilded with breading and delightful.

But at other times, I have been subjected to stiffly cold tortellini in a cream sauce that tasted much like boiled milk, and tough, stringy veal paillard.

In addition to being out of many interesting specials, the staff consistenly touts diners away from dishes the kitchen obviously does not want to make at given moments.

One I wish I had been warned against was the incredible crème caramel with a burned, scablike skin at the bottom. Rum cake with cloudlets of whipped cream was preferable. Obviously Barbetta can turn out good food when the staff has a mind to, but at prices such as these and so many better alternatives in town, why run the risk?

Beijing Duckhouse
See Peking Duck House

Beirut
★

> 43 West 32nd Street, between Fifth Avenue and Avenue of the Americas, 840-9154.
> Atmosphere: Noisy, convivial and informal Middle Eastern nightclub setting with brass lanterns and red walls; service polite and helpful.
> Recommended dishes: Tabboule, yogurt with cucumbers, fava-bean salad, falafel, raw kibbee, stuffed squash with hot yogurt sauce, meat pies, shish kebab, kefta kebab, rice pilaf, broiled lamb hearts, all meze appetizers except feta cheese.
> Price range: Inexpensive.
> Credit cards: American Express, MasterCard and Visa.
> Hours: Lunch, seven days, 11:30 A.M. to 4 P.M.; dinner, Mondays through Thursdays, 4 P.M. to 11:30 P.M., Fridays and Saturdays, 4 P.M. to 3 A.M., Sundays, 4 P.M. to 11 P.M. Closed on Thanksgiving Day and Christmas Day.
> Reservations: Necessary on weekends.

Among the world's great ethnic appetizer combinations, none is more sensual or diverting than Middle Eastern meze, that array of salads, spreads and dips accented with sesame, mint, scallion and yogurt, and meant to be eaten with hot and grainy pita bread. The most subtly delicate version of these hors d'oeuvres are Lebanese in origin, and so it should come as no surprise to find really wonderful meze at Beirut, the lively restaurant and nightclub.

The setting is typically informal and darkly mysterious, with muted red walls and pierced-brass lanterns casting lacy shadows. Sunday through Thursday, dinner is fairly slow paced and quiet, except for some recorded Middle Eastern music played at low pitch. But things really take off on Friday and Saturday nights, when there is a live band, a singer, a professional belly dancer, complete with seven veils, and best of all, customers who get up and sing and dance to Lebanese folk music.

Forget about all conversation at such times and give yourself up to the ear-splitting moment, and you can have an unusual and entertaining time, even if you don't find yourself humming the less-than-catchy tunes on the way out. Sunday afternoons and evenings, families sit around large tables, eating for hours — also colorful and a whole lot quieter.

Although most of the menu, with its grilled or stewed chicken and lamb dishes, averages out to rate only one star, the meze at Beirut deserve three stars. Tabboule, the salad of parsley, cracked wheat, scallions, mint and tomatoes can be scooped up on pita bread, as can the yogurt cheese, labanee, mellowed with olive oil and mint; the homus bi tahini, which is a purée of chickpeas and sesame seeds, and the baba gannouj, smoky eggplant whipped with oil, lemon and a bit of garlic. Falafel (or tomieh), those fried-bean croquettes, are delicious dipped into a creamy sesame sauce, and the fava-bean salad sparkles with a generous splash of fresh lemon juice. Cooling yogurt and cucumbers and sliced brains vinaigrette (stale on one visit, fresh on two others), along with rice-stuffed grape leaves and kibbee, raw lamb tartar, round out the elaborate meze course that is ordered à la carte. Cooked kibbee, however, was uniformly dry from reheating. Triangular meat pies with crisp pastry were lusty additions to the meze assortment.

Those not given to pressing their luck may want to end the meal here. Those who continue can rely on the oniony grilled ground lamb, kefta kebab, a decent shish kebab with vegetables, tender lamb heart grilled on skewers or broiled sweetbreads. A real sleeper among main courses was zucchini stuffed with meat and rice and served in a piquant hot sauce of lamb broth and yogurt. The chicken sampled, whether broiled on skewers or in halves, lacked freshness and was dry. All stews of vegetables and lamb were short on meat but deep in grease. Dry bits of lamb layered and stuffed with rice proved disappointing, but rice pilaf by itself had the proper succulence.

Typical pastries, based on phyllo leaves, nuts and sugar syrup, were tough and leaden. Thick, sweet Turkish coffee proved to be dessert enough. Order arrack and you will probably get Greek ouzo, which is thinner and less mellow; still, the licorice-flavor drink, which turns milky with ice and water, seems most appropriate with meze. Scotch and beer are second choices.

Berry's

★

180 Spring Street, corner of Thompson Street, 226-4394.

Atmosphere: Small, noisy and stylish Victorian pub-tavern; service generally friendly and good, but falters at peak hours.

Recommended dishes: Brunch: Fried troutlings, French toast, omelets. Dinner: Vegetable flan, cucumber and yogurt soup, gravlax, salade Chinoise, roast lamb, calf's liver, soft-shell crabs, tarragon roast chicken, fresh fruit.

Price range: Moderate.

Credit cards: American Express, Mastercard and Visa.

Hours: Lunch, Tuesdays through Fridays, noon to 3 P.M.; dinner, Tuesdays through Thursdays, 6 P.M. to 11:30 P.M., Fridays and Saturdays, 6 P.M. to midnight, Sundays, 5 P.M. to 10:30 P.M. Brunch, Saturdays, noon to 3:30 P.M., Sundays, 11 A.M. to 4 P.M. Closed Mondays and most major holidays.

Reservations: Recommended.

Berry's inspires a love-hate relationship. Step into this snug and intimate Victorian pub-tavern dining room when it is not too crowded, and you can have a satisfying, diverting, moderately priced meal. But try it at peak hours, when Berry's is full and when thumping background music compounds the high noise level, and you may well be miserable, especially if you happen to be seated at one of the city's most uncomfortable tables for two — wedged between bar, water station, the credit-card machine and a garbage pail — a table that simply should not exist. Similarly, service ranges from thoughtful and friendly when things are slow, to careless when tables are full.

Weekend brunches have always been Berry's strongpoint, and several recent visits indicate that this is still true. Bloody Marys, though decked out with wild flags of celery, are well spiced and generously spiked with vodka, and if that drink is requested without ice, there is an even chance that it will be cold enough. By far the most outstanding brunch feature is French toast made of sliced brioche, an eggy, moist bread that puffs to golden perfection. Golden-brown, fried troutlings can be had as a shared appetizer or a full main course. The omelets are generally well made, and so is tender calf's liver with bacon. Skip the fancier concoctions, such as eggs Burgundy style, poached in a somewhat indelicate and salty red-wine sauce, and a misnamed chicken hash, which is more like a soupy filling for a chicken pie.

Dinner at Berry's can be pleasantly relaxed. Appetizers are more original and entertaining than main courses, the best being warm flan custard with a sauce of fresh vegetables in cream and a salade Chinoise of fine noodles in a sesame dressing tossed with flowerets of broccoli and straw mushrooms. The cured salmon, gravlax, though properly satiny, would have been better in a dill sauce that had just a little more bite. A thick yogurt and cucumber soup proved to be another bright and refreshing starter. Not so an abominable shrimp bisque, which tasted like stale fish stock and which appeared on our check, although it had been sent back to the kitchen with a complaint that was noted by a manager.

Freshness and careful cooking result in decent main courses, such as calf's liver, sautéed pink as ordered, and on certain days, roast lamb that is also rosy and tender. Slightly limp soft-shell crabs meunière took on delicate gilding in the sauté pan, but grilled swordfish was watery and tasteless. Half a roast chicken, moist and delicate with its tarragon accent, is one of the city's better buys. An assortment of firm, bright vegetables and delicious new potatoes cut in chunks and sautéed in their jackets accompany main courses. A bright rainbow assortment of fresh fruit makes up the only really good dessert; cakes and pastries lack character.

Portions at Berry's are comfortably adequate, if not generous, and seem in keeping with the fairly moderate checks.

Billy's

★

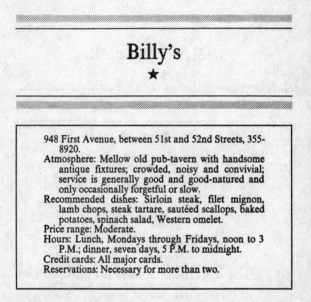

948 First Avenue, between 51st and 52nd Streets, 355-8920.
Atmosphere: Mellow old pub-tavern with handsome antique fixtures; crowded, noisy and convivial; service is generally good and good-natured and only occasionally forgetful or slow.
Recommended dishes: Sirloin steak, filet mignon, lamb chops, steak tartare, sautéed scallops, baked potatoes, spinach salad, Western omelet.
Price range: Moderate.
Hours: Lunch, Mondays through Fridays, noon to 3 P.M.; dinner, seven days, 5 P.M. to midnight.
Credit cards: All major cards.
Reservations: Necessary for more than two.

In 1966, Billy's moved from First Avenue and 56th Street to its present location. Time has mellowed the reconstructed interior, harking back to 1870, so that it has regained much of its original charm. The dark paneling, brass-trimmed fixtures and converted gaslight chandeliers were moved from the original setting and now seem as though they've always been there. Checkered tablecloths add a lively note, as does the handsome and crowded bar.

This neighborhood pub-tavern offers some very good broiled meats, but they're compromised by some very ordinary trimmings. Still, with fairly moderate prices, Billy's is worth remembering for the juicy, beefy quality of the sirloin and filet mignon steaks and the lusty lamb chops, all broiled exactly as ordered. Thick hamburger steaks are lightly formed so they remain tender, and the beef is coarsely chopped so the burgers have a meaty texture. Steak tartare is unusually good — lean, bright and pungent with capers, onion, mustard and Tabasco.

Appetizers such as the watery shrimp cocktail and the bland onion soup or Manhattan clam chowder can be passed up in favor of a shared order of sautéed bay scallops that is really a main course. Each tiny scallop is at once crisp and tender.

Among the cooked daily specials, the roast veal was decent although uninspired with its floury American-style brown gravy. Both broiled chicken and pork chops were unpleasantly dry. Thick, rare slices of roast prime ribs of beef looked inviting, but by the time I ordered, the waitress said the roast ranged from medium to well-done, so I passed. Lunchtime hamburgers were minimally acceptable, but spinach salad and a puffy Western omelet were fine.

Instead of the french fries and the onion rings that were all batter, choose the crusty baked potatoes. All desserts were disappointing. Better to wind up with the excellent Irish coffee.

Service is friendly and generally efficient, but at busy times a request for water or a check may be overlooked.

Bistro Bordeaux
★ ★

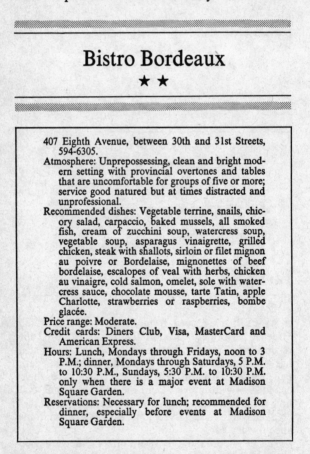

407 Eighth Avenue, between 30th and 31st Streets, 594-6305.

Atmosphere: Unprepossessing, clean and bright modern setting with provincial overtones and tables that are uncomfortable for groups of five or more; service good natured but at times distracted and unprofessional.

Recommended dishes: Vegetable terrine, snails, chicory salad, carpaccio, baked mussels, all smoked fish, cream of zucchini soup, watercress soup, vegetable soup, asparagus vinaigrette, grilled chicken, steak with shallots, sirloin or filet mignon au poivre or Bordelaise, mignonettes of beef bordelaise, escalopes of veal with herbs, chicken au vinaigre, cold salmon, omelet, sole with watercress sauce, chocolate mousse, tarte Tatin, apple Charlotte, strawberries or raspberries, bombe glacée.

Price range: Moderate.

Credit cards: Diners Club, Visa, MasterCard and American Express.

Hours: Lunch, Mondays through Fridays, noon to 3 P.M.; dinner, Mondays through Saturdays, 5 P.M. to 10:30 P.M., Sundays, 5:30 P.M. to 10:30 P.M. only when there is a major event at Madison Square Garden.

Reservations: Necessary for lunch; recommended for dinner, especially before events at Madison Square Garden.

Whether Rangers or Knicks fans are satisfied with the performances of their teams, there is now cause for cheering among those who want to have a good dinner near Madison Square Garden. The new Bistro Bordeaux turns out stylish versions of authentic bistro-grill dishes at moderate prices.

The kitchen is capable of some delicious, well-seasoned and carefully prepared food, and the menu is judiciously planned so that there are no unsold leftovers such as stews or roasts to grow stale. The partners in this new venture — Alain Jones, who runs the dining room, and Gérard Uhrik, the chef — gained experience at Demarchelier on Lexington Avenue.

Uncertain about the size of the crowds they will attract, they stick to main courses that are grilled or sautéed to order. The fish, meats and chicken are complemented by savory sauces and by generally firm, fresh vegetables, usually one combination for all main courses on a given day. The menu is, in fact, a valuable object lesson in how to impart style and interest to what is basically short-order cooking.

The dining room is generally comfortable, with good acoustics and lighting that is adequate at all but a few front tables. The décor is best described as motel provincial, and at times there's an unattractive neighborhood bar scene, a result of the television set that is turned on in the evening. Another shortcoming is the absence of large tables so that groups of five or more can be accommodated comfortably. Service is better at the crowded lunch period than at dinner, when the place is virtually empty. The staff is good natured and polite, but the waiters, perhaps lulled by the lack of evening activity, seem distracted and mete out a sort of benign neglect.

One appetizer is that a personal favorite rarely found in New York is Lyonnaise salad frisée aux lardons — crisp, spiky chicory with hot bacon and garlic croutons. Although there were a few too many croutons one night, the salad was pungent with a vinaigrette dressing and mellowed by the touch of hot bacon grease. There is just the right rustic flavor to snails baked in a green-gold sauce of garlic, shallots, parsley and butter, the same combination of seasonings that accents mussels baked on half shells. The raw beef carpaccio, though unconventional on a bistro menu, was rose red and fresh here, enlivened by a brassy mustard mayonnaise. Smoked fish such as salmon, trout and eel with horseradish whipped cream could not have been moister or more subtly edged with smoked flavor. It would be hard to match the colorful terrine of vegetables heightened by a purée of fresh tomatoes.

Soups are exceptional. Cream of zucchini soup, so often tasteless, has an unmistakable squash flavor here, and both cream of watercress and a velvety purée of mixed vegetables are bracing yet subtle.

Grilled sirloin and filet mignon steaks are equally satisfying whether done au poivre with a light touch of cream in the sauce or in a sheer, red wine sauce Bordelaise. Tender mignonettes of beef can also be ordered with the Bordelaise sauce, and there is a rich, beefy boneless strip steak topped with raw slivered shallots; light sautéeing would make those shallots a little less biting, if a little less true to the Bordeaux style. Delicate sautéed scallops of veal take on the heady perfume of tarragon, and chicken au vinaigre, a special one night, was glossed with a beautiful golden sauce sharpened mildly with red wine vinegar.

Sliced potatoes baked in butter are delicious when

crusty; only once were they uninvitingly limp. Sautéed julienne strips of zucchini and carrots, or firm string beans, are both more interesting than plain carrots, either steamed or puréed.

A thick grilled fillet of sea bass is topped with paprika, a touch that detracts from the delicate effects of a perfectly made beurre Nantais, the whipped, thickened butter sauce. Better fish choices are poached fillet of sole with a watercress sauce and cold poached salmon with cucumber salad. Paillard of beef also proved a slightly disappointing main course, once because it was marred by the aroma of overheated oil and once because it was sinewy.

At lunch there is a custardy quiche flavored with onion and a puffy omelet fines herbs. The quiche, the country pâté and an occasional sauce tend to be oversalted.

Avoid the cloying cheese and chocolate Grimble torte and the innocuous cheesecake, and try such homemade desserts as hot, caramelized apple tarte Tatin with lightly whipped cream, and cold apple charlotte with vanilla perfumed crème Anglaise. Lusciously soft and bittersweet chocolate mousse proved much better than a heavy crème caramel. Raspberries or strawberries topped with Triple Sec-flavored whipped cream are lovely, and bombe glacée, streaked with praliné, is cool and refreshing.

Such good food deserves bread with more substance and character than the dry, airy rolls, and the absurd bar snack of mixed dried cereals should be eliminated, especially when a wine is ordered as an apertiff.

There is a decent list of wines at fairly moderated prices. Three I enjoyed among the reds were Château Larose Trintaudon, a 1978 Haud-Médoc; Château Nottin, a 1979 Margaux, and a chilled 1980 Broilly.

Bombay Palace

★

30 West 52nd Street between Fifth and Sixth Avenues, 541-7777.

Atmosphere: Attractive, plush setting with Indian artifacts, comfortable seating and a bearable noise level; service is uneven.

Recommended dishes: Alu papri, mulligatawny and murgh shorba soups, naan, Palace naan, seekh kebab, gosht patiala, vegetarian bhojan, butter chicken, saag gosht with lamb, dal, eggplant bharta, peas pullao, palace and chicken biryanis, mango ice cream.

Price range: Moderate.

Credit cards: All major credit cards.

Hours: Lunch, seven days, noon to 3 P.M. (Sunday lunch is buffet); dinner, Mondays through Saturdays, 5:30 P.M. to 11:30 P.M., Sundays, 5:30 P.M. to 10 P.M. Open major holidays.

Reservations: Necessary.

In a handsome and spacious red dining room that allows for a blessedly bearable noise level, the Bombay Palace offers, for the most part, the mildly spiced specialties of northern India. The dining-room staff will arrange to have hot chili added to dishes, but only upon the most fervent request because few of the offerings are meant to be highly seasoned.

Tandoori broiled meats, chicken and seafood are the mainstays of the menu, and it is sad to have to report that this category is the least satisfactory of all because of consistent dryness. The exception was the delicate, sausage-shaped ground lamb seekh kebab, which was properly moist and gently seasoned.

Appetizers such as the vegetable fritters (pakoras) and the patties of peas and potatoes (samosas) were soggy and undstinguished, and an order of chooza chat (bits of chicken that should be marinated in a fiery sauce) were completely unsatisfactory both because the chicken did not seem fresh and the sauce was positively sweet.

Slightly better choices included the alu papri (crisply-fried chopped potato croquettes with a sweet and pungent yogurt sauce), and the chooza pakora (batter-fried bits of chicken in a ginger-and-garlic-perfumed yogurt dressing).

Soups had unusual body and finesse. The mulligatawny was heartier than most watery versions of that romatic spice broth and the murgh shorba — a chicken broth redolent of ginger, cinnamon, cardamon and garlic — seemed a bracing restorative.

Indian breads are among the world's most varied, and two basic types are represented on the Bombay Palace menu. Naan is made of a pizza-type dough that is baked on the curved stone walls of the tandoor oven. It may be had plain or as keema naan, stuffed with spiced, ground lamb that is almost a meal in itself. Palace naan, stuffed with chicken and almonds, is also delicious. But the onion kulcha, flavored with dried mango and spices, lacked authoritative flavoring. Paratha, wheat pancake bread baked on a stone griddle, is far too limp and greasy here.

There are several savory braised lamb and beef dishes available, and among these the best I tried was the gosht patiala (boneless chunks of lamb simmered with ground onion, ginger and garlic mixed with yogurt) and saag gosht, lamb with a mellow spinach and spice sauce. Vindaloo curries are most traditionally served in a blaze of chili pepper, but even two special requests brought forth comparatively mild results.

Indian vegetarian dishes were rich and so satisfying one hardly noticed they did not contain meat. The assortment of vegetables served on a tali tray (Palace vegetarian bhojan) was fragrant and satisfying with its several eggplant variations, its stewed lentil dal, the cucumber and yogurt raita, and the spiced chickpeas, among others. These same vegetable preparations may be ordered as side dishes and, with the exception of the saag paneer, homemade cheese with mushy spinach, are all worth trying.

Chicken specialties were, in general, better than other meats at Bombay Palace. The butter chicken that is broiled in the tandoor, then simmered with a gentling sauce of ginger, garlic, vinegar, yogurt, tomatoes and cream, is rich and exotic and can be had hotly spiced on demand. Murgh keema masala, minced chicken and peas in a tomato, spiced, garlic-and-onion sauce however, was disappointing on my latest visit.

It is a good idea for several diners to share dishes and to round them out with one of the rich rice combinations such as the peas pullao or a biryani. My favorites were the Palace nawabi with tiny lamb balls stuffed with almonds and raisins, or the chicken biryani with saffron, nuts and, as the menu says, "21 exotic spices." Mint-flavored yogurt sauce is served with many of the dishes, and both the dal and raita are enriching additions.

Desserts other than mango ice cream proved eminently skippable, and for reasons that must remain a mystery, the house was out of Darjeeling tea for at least half a week. Spiced tea was a fair alternative but coffee was dreadful. If Bombay Palace must be rated one star instead of two, it is because of the poor tandoori broiling and the often inferior basic ingredients. Sauces and cooking are skillfully done, but the meats should be fresher and of better quality. Service can be friendly and helpful or distracted and indifferent.

Box Tree Restaurant

★

242 East 50th Street, between Second and Third Avenues, 758-8320.
Atmosphere: Attractive but uncomfortably cramped town house setting, with tables so close it is impossible to have a private conversation; service is attentive but embarrassingly pretentious.
Recommended dishes: Cold yogurt soup, cream of sorrel soup, fillet of beef, rack of lamb, poached salmon, raspberry purée, chocolate orange layer cake.
Price range: Expensive.
Credit cards: None.
Hours: Lunch, Mondays through Fridays, noon to 2 P.M.; dinner, daily, 6:30 P.M. and 9:30 P.M. seatings. After theater, until 11 P.M.
Reservations: Necessary.

If anyone wanted fully to understand the meaning of the words "pretentious" and "precious," all that would be necessary is one dinner at the Box Tree. The uncomfortable, tiny and cramped dining room allows for no private conversation, and the waiters' overbearing manners seem much like a musical-comedy parody. Not even the genuinely handsome antique setting and beautiful table appointments can quite dispel the embarrassment of the outdated and corny service.

Food at the Box Tree seems to be based on perfectly fine and fresh ingredients, and it is obvious that no short cuts are tolerated in the kitchen. But preciousness again prevails, with overcomplicated, prettified seasonings and sudden flashes of sweetness where none are called for. The final results of the chef's efforts simply could not be taken seriously, edible though they all were. Recent visits have not given me any reason to change my opinion.

If there was one dish that epitomized the poor culinary concepts followed at Box Tree, it was a soup — crème d'oranges et tomates — a cream of orange and tomato soup that tasted as though someone had made a dreadful mistake by accidentally spilling orange juice into the tomato soup. Both the hot, verdant cream of sorrel soup and a cold Bulgarian soup of yogurt, cucumber and dill were far better.

A silky textured duck-liver pâté was bitter with an overdose of brandy. Mousse of smoked haddock had the consistency of bean curd, and an artichoke cooked with cloves was awful. Snails laced with Pernod and glazed with cheese evidenced no flavor of their own, and a croustade of tiny shrimp was inoffensive, if uninspired.

An order of calf's liver was well cooked, but the truffle and Madeira sauce had been so reduced it caramelized and became a little too sweet. The opposite flaw — blandness — marred breast of chicken in a morel cream sauce. The chicken breast was so thick that most of it remained dry because it did not come in contact with the sauce.

Three very good main courses were the filet de boeuf with sauce brûlée, rare beef in a rich brown sauce, the carré d'agneau, a perfectly acceptable rack of lamb, and poached salmon in a lemony hollandaise sauce. The fresh flavor of a steamed trout turned musty from too much thyme. Duck with green peppercorns was fair; the duck itself was moist and lean, but the sauce had none of the necessary sting.

There is a salad course on the table d'hôte dinner, — two sheaves of endive with a sweetish dressing, slices of apples and shavings of good Stilton cheese, along with a glass of weak port. The best dessert — and perhaps the best dish in the place — was crème brûlée — gentle, satiny custard under a crackling, caramelized mantle of sugar. Chocolate orange layer cake and a purée of raspberries with burnt sugar cream were almost as good. A vacherin of meringue filled with cream and raspberries was dry and stale.

Brasserie
Fair

100 East 53rd Street, between Park and Lexington Avenues, 751-4840.

Atmosphere: Trim, modern, bright and bustling setting with counter and table service; service is inept, disorganized and careless.

Recommended dishes: Onion soup, snails, oysters on the half shell, filet mignon, hamburger Provençale, omelet Lorraine, French toast, shirred or fried eggs with bacon, spinach salad with oil and vinegar, croissants, cappuccino.

Price range: Moderately expensive.

Credit cards: All major cards.

Hours: Seven days, twenty-four hours a day. Breakfast, 6 A.M. to 11 A.M.; lunch, 11 A.M. to 4:30 P. M; dinner 4:30 P.M. to 10 P. M.; supper 10 P.M. to 6 A. M.; Sunday brunch 11 A.M. to 4 P.M.

Reservations: Necessary for dinner only.

The scene is Sunday brunch at the Brasserie. Main courses have been served, but there is still no bread although I have requested it three times.

Finally, I get the attention of the man who seems to be in charge and ask him, "Are you the manager?"

Answer: "Yeah. Something the matter?"

Well, yeah, something *is* the matter. In fact, almost everything is, beginning with service and ending with food. Were this not a twenty-four-year-old restaurant operated by Restaurant Associates since the day it opened, and were it not so well known, it would not be worth reviewing at all. But given its interesting menus available twenty-four hours a day, the convenient East Side location and the pleasantly bright and casual modern setting, the Brasserie has remained in the public eye, most especially for off-hour meals, and so its inclusion seems in order.

Flaws here can be attributed to a total lack of authoritative management. Right from the start one gets the feeling that nobody's in charge. The seating procedure is vague and slow, the staff lackadaisical. Checks are mixed up, and on one occasion I was given someone else's credit card — an oversight not discovered until I started to charge a dinner at another restaurant.

At breakfast, the beautifully bright and fresh grapefruit is so badly cut that fork and knife are needed to extricate the fruit. Asking for the Alsatian yeast coffee cake, kugelhopf, one morning, I was told there would be none that day. As I finished coffee, a complete kugelhopf was deposited on the dessert stand. Returning for dinner that night, I again requested the cake and was told there was none that day. When I informed the waiter that I was looking straight at it, he put on his glasses, checked and served some. The cake proved to be dry, hollow and overloaded with raisins — hardly worth the effort of obtaining it.

The framework for the various menus here is that of an Alsatian brasserie — a casual restaurant originally owned by a brewery and serving food that went with beer. Choucroute garni, the combination of sauerkraut with various sausages, smoked ham and bacon, is the most classic brasserie dish. Here, it was consistently a disaster, with salty, greasy sauerkraut and stiff, tough and salty meats. All other cooked food, such as stews, hot sandwiches and gray, watery broiled fish (be it salmon or snapper) are reminiscent of airline cooking.

After three breakfasts, one lunch, one brunch, two dinners, one take-out meal and one after-theater supper, I can report on just a few moderately dependable offerings. Breakfast is the best meal because eggs are generally well turned out. Shirred eggs (minus their cold, stale chicken livers) were perfectly cooked and the omelet Lorraine with cheese, bacon and chives was consistently above average, and so were fried eggs and the French toast with orange slices and bacon. Other dependable choices are oysters on the half shell, filet mignon and hamburgers either Provençale or with Gruyère.

Quiche Lorraine is fair if the crust is thoroughly baked on the bottom — a chancy circumstance at best — and snails are passable if slightly salty. But pâtés were uniformly stale and bitter.

Croissants are excellent if absurdly large, the spinach salad is fresh and bright and you can keep it that way by asking for oil and vinegar instead of any house dressing.

Ask for the onion soup hot and you will have a bracing light meal; if it arrives tepid, as sometimes happens, send it back. If you order ratatouille and that Provence vegetable stew consists only of green pepper and onion, ask for eggplant and zucchini and they'll probably dig down into the pot and get you some.

Brazilian Pavilion

★

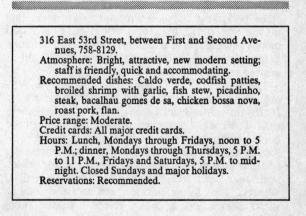

316 East 53rd Street, between First and Second Avenues, 758-8129.

Atmosphere: Bright, attractive, new modern setting; staff is friendly, quick and accommodating.

Recommended dishes: Caldo verde, codfish patties, broiled shrimp with garlic, fish stew, picadinho, steak, bacalhau gomes de sa, chicken bossa nova, roast pork, flan.

Price range: Moderate.

Credit cards: All major credit cards.

Hours: Lunch, Mondays through Fridays, noon to 5 P.M.; dinner, Mondays through Thursdays, 5 P.M. to 11 P.M., Fridays and Saturdays, 5 P.M. to midnight. Closed Sundays and major holidays.

Reservations: Recommended.

BRAZILIAN FOOD

Portugal ruled Brazil for almost three hundred years, so it is understandable that the Brazilian cuisine combines the simply prepared stewed and grilled pork, beef, seafood, black beans and rice dishes of Portugal with native South American ingredients such as coconut, corn and manioc or cassava, the root from which a dry floury farina is made to be used as both flavoring and thickening. Dende oil (extracted from palms), coconuts, hot peppers and exotic spices were added by slaves from West Africa.

As presented in New York, Brazilian food is hefty and rustic, with few accents that could be described as delicate or subtle.

Appetizers are generally disappointing, but there are a few notable exceptions. Among them are clams steamed in garlic-laden broth and fried or grilled slices of salty, pleasantly fat and meaty linguica sausages. A few places offer empadinhas, the small, crisp, meat-filled pastry turnovers, or pasteizinhos — croquettes of bacalhau, dried salt codfish.

Caldo verde, a Portuguese soup that has a potato base enriched with sausage and slivered kale or collards, can be delicious, and sopa alentejana, a garlic broth with poached eggs and bread, would be welcome on a cold autumn afternoon or evening.

Shrimp are prepared in a number of simple but interesting ways. Paulista style, they are grilled in their shells with a snowfall of minced garlic, and in the manner of Bahia (baiana), they are served in a tomato and onion sauce, which should be hotly spiced with chili oil, but rarely is in New York. Shrimp doré, dipped in batter and fried, are also good. Bacalhau gomes de sa is cooked with potatoes and onions and is garnished with black olives and hard-cooked eggs. Another specialty is mariscada, a soup-stew of shellfish, with tomatoes, onions and green pepper.

Chunks of crisp and moistly tender chicken, fried golden brown with garlic (bossa nova or bossa velha style), is excellent when not too dried out, and chicken with okra and tomatoes is cooked in a gumbolike stew. Italian names crop up on Brazilian menus, risotto foremost among them. The Brazilin style calls for flecks of chicken with red rice, which is then molded into a sort of igloo.

Churrasco-style meats, barbecued over charcoal, include pork, veal and beef chops and thin steaks that may be topped with fried eggs, minced garlic or sautéed onions and peppers or a combination of several of those garnishes. Picadinho is also on local menus, a sort of sautéed beef hash topped with a fried egg.

The national dish, feijoada (pronounced fezh-WA-da), derives its name from feijao, the Portuguese word for the tiny, shiny black beans that are its main component. The beans are simmered for hours with sauteed onions, sometimes garlic and green pepper, and are seasoned with bay leaves and spices. To the mixture are added chunks of smoked and fresh pork, pigs' knuckles, beef tongue and both fresh and dried beef, as well as sausages. Rice forms the base, and garnishes include sliced oranges, kale or collard greens, hot sauce, occasionally a topping of minced tomato, onion and green pepper, and always farofa — ground manioc flour toasted in butter and mixed with raisins, nuts and eggs, alone or in combination. Feijoada is a filling meal, best eaten in cool weather.

Desserts are mainly caramel custard flan, or a similar coconut custard pudding, and guava, either in shells or paste, is served with slices of a bland, slightly saline cheese. Native coffee, beer and Portuguese wines are good accompaniments. Cachaça, a Brazilian rum distilled from sugar cane, is mixed with lime juice, sugar and ice to make a cocktail ("batida" in Portuguese) called the caipirinha, after Brazil's mountain hillbillies.

Now in a bright new setting with white walls and green glass lampshades, the Brazilian Pavilion serves well-made caipirinhas. Caldo verde is thin with potatoes in chunks rather than in a purée, but the effect is light and satisfying. Broiled shrimp with garlic and the spicy peixe a Brasileira, a fish stew, are good. Picadinho and steaks are fair, and the bacalhau gomes de sa would have been excellent had it not been served nearly cold. Chicken bossa nova and roast leg of pork are other dependably good choices.

Feijoada is served Wednesdays and Saturdays for lunch but every night for dinner. Codfish patties are Monday lunch specials worth remembering. Skip the Continental menu choices. The flan is excellent, and is the only dessert worth ordering. Appetizers are overpriced.

Bridge Cafe

★

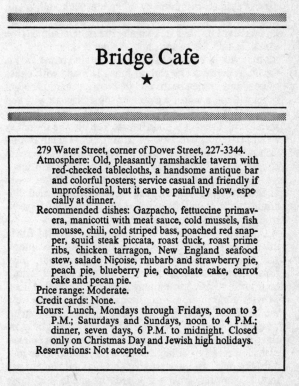

279 Water Street, corner of Dover Street, 227-3344.
Atmosphere: Old, pleasantly ramshackle tavern with red-checked tablecloths, a handsome antique bar and colorful posters; service casual and friendly if unprofessional, but it can be painfully slow, especially at dinner.
Recommended dishes: Gazpacho, fettuccine primavera, manicotti with meat sauce, cold mussels, fish mousse, chili, cold striped bass, poached red snapper, squid steak piccata, roast duck, roast prime ribs, chicken tarragon, New England seafood stew, salade Niçoise, rhubarb and strawberry pie, peach pie, blueberry pie, chocolate cake, carrot cake and pecan pie.
Price range: Moderate.
Credit cards: None.
Hours: Lunch, Mondays through Fridays, noon to 3 P.M.; Saturdays and Sundays, noon to 4 P.M.; dinner, seven days, 6 P.M. to midnight. Closed only on Christmas Day and Jewish high holidays.
Reservations: Not accepted.

What every good neighborhood deserves is at least one small, moderate-priced and delightful eating place. Such a restaurant is under the shadow of the Brooklyn

Bridge in Lower Manhattan, the Bridge Cafe. Tucked away on Water and Dover Streets, one of the more obscure corners of the city, this rejuvenated pub-tavern is pleasantly ramshackle, with an old pressed-tin ceiling, wainscotting on the walls, handsome posters and prints and red-checked tablecloths. The food is a mix-match of Continental and American dishes, with the sort of vegetarian accents that have become the trademark of the young American chefs.

The Bridge Cafe is distinguished by a clientele headed by Mayor Koch and including a loyal following from City Hall, the nearby municipal departments, the Financial District and, at night, residents of the surrounding neighborhood. The young staff exudes good will and cheery helpfulness. The only really off note is service that is slow at all times, but agonizingly so at night, especially between appetizers and main courses.

Lunch is even more casual and less expensive than dinner: paper napkins replace cloth, there are no taco chips at the bar or the stupendous, tough and chewy Italian white and whole-wheat bread from the D. & G. Bakery on Spring Street. Such refinements are left to evening, when the prices are slightly higher than at lunch. At all times, portions are generous, and there is a very decent house red wine, Cuvée Rouge from Prosper Maufoux, available by the bottle, half-bottle or the glass.

None of the food at the Bridge Cafe is in any way sensational, but much of it is original, diverting and satisfying. Only a few of the dishes that were sampled proved less than minimally adequate. Although menu items change daily, the same type of selection is maintained. Cool mussels in a vinaigrette or remoulade-type dressing are fresh and not sandy, and a light fish mousse would be as satisfying for a main course as it is for an appetizer. The chili at lunch is made with cubes of beef and kidney beans and delivers a generous belt of cayenne, and a warm escarole or spinach salad with red onions is gentle and sustaining. Green fettuccine primavera, listed as a main course, can also be shared as an appetizer; either way, its firm, fresh vegetables and rich cream sauce are above average. A lunch main course of manicotti with a thick meat and tomato sauce was also lusty and convincingly seasoned. Other pasta dishes, such as bland green noodles (misnamed linguine) with a watery white clam sauce and a pasty, stodgy cold tortellini salad, can be skipped.

Gazpacho is sharp and pungent, served with finely minced green peppers, onions, cucumbers and croutons, but a cream of celery soup was so thick it could have passed for a side dish. A ham sandwich served with it on a tasteless and grotesquely large roll made that inexpensive combination a questionable value. But a well-made salade Niçoise, heavy on tuna fish, crisp string beans and green pepper, and a delicate roast tarragon-flavored chicken were far preferable. The same chicken dish is generally available at dinner also, and so is crisp peppery duck and a New England seafood stew, much like a chowder, but with clams in shells and large chunks of fish.

Also delicious were cold striped bass, an unusual squid steak piccata, tenderized and lightly sautéed in egg batter then sparked with capers and lemon, and poached red snapper in a creamy herb sauce. Pork medaillons, much like scaloppine, were dry, although apple slices and plum sauce brightened them considerably. Soft-shell crabs were creditable, though not inspired. Chicken with bourbon and apples was acceptable, if just a bit too sweet, and both calf's liver and roast prime ribs of beef were above average but somewhat dried out from a long wait under a heat lamp. Good vegetables and rough-cut potatoes sautéed in their skins complement most main courses, and so do genuinely ripe tomatoes and the best red-tipped leaf or romaine lettuce.

Leave room for the home-crafted pies — rhubarb and strawberry, peach and blueberry being the best — along with a velvety chocolate-nut cake and a somewhat extraordinary carrot cake, aromatic with spices. Pecan pie and ripe figs with chèvre cheese were also excellent, but watermelon spiked with vodka gave little cause for celebration.

Broadway Joe
Fair

315 West 46th Street, 246-6513.
Atmosphere: Small pleasant dining rooms and convivial bar; noisy and cramped when full; service is unprofessional, overbearing and often rude.
Recommended dishes: Lamb chops, scampi, baked potato, minute steak.
Price range: Expensive.
Credit cards: All major cards.
Hours: Lunch, Mondays through Fridays, noon to 3 P.M.; dinner, Mondays through Saturdays, 4:30 P.M. to midnight, Sundays, 5 P.M. to midnight.
Reservations: Recommended.

Broadway Joe, long a well-known steakhouse in the theater district, was purchased several months ago by a group that includes the journalist Sidney Zion. At tables in the small, cheerful dining rooms or at the convivial front bar, Mr. Zion holds forth with all the writers and Broadway personalities who are his friends and who make up his clientele. Unfortunately, he confuses the role of mine host with that of mine guest.

What Broadway Joe needs is a firm, experienced hand to direct dining room and kitchen staffs. Given the snug feeling of the place and the lively caricatures of journalists by Al Hirschfeld, it would be nice if the food made it possible to enjoy a meal in this very New York atmosphere.

From the sassy manager at the door who places hands on guests' shoulders to herd them toward tables to some of the overbearing, hustling waiters who argue with guests and one another, a meal here is hardly a rewarding experience, especially at such astronomical prices.

Waiters tout the steak as prime and perhaps it is so

marked. But of five sirloins tried, none had any of the beefy zest expected. All were too dry and hard and few were cooked as ordered. Minute steaks proved far better. Filet mignon comes as two thin slices of beef, well done when ordered medium rare. The waiter removed the meat when I objected, but the manager came over to argue. "Could you please tell me just exactly what you mean by medium rare?" he asked. It was replaced with a sirloin, not a filet, and went back again; finally, a filet arrived, this time blood rare. The waiter offered drinks by way of compensation, and when they were refused he removed the cost of desserts and coffees from the check. On another occasion, a waiter adjusted a check after he replaced burned onion rings with soggy, musty substitutes that were also returned.

A few dishes were consistently good, such as a vegetable soup that seemed fresh and satisfying although not hefty enough to live up to its name, minestrone. Lamb chops were fine when broiled as ordered, and scampi in an herb-garlic butter on rice were delicious. Not so the sinewy steak sandwich, the underdone, dried-out pork chops, the burned broiled chicken or the tasteless, washed-out veal chop.

Onion soup was watery, and shrimp cocktail tasted of iodine. Cottage fries were fair one night, soggy another; hashed brown potatoes were cold and greasy, and potato shells tasted of stale fat. Baked potatoes were fine. Underripe, mushy tomato slices alternated with limp onion rings, and fried zucchini was badly burned.

The banal desserts include plain or chocolate cheesecake, chocolate layer cake and fair apple-walnut crumb pie. Despite some edible food, the thrill of seeing Norman Mailer plain and the prospect of listening to live music after ten o'clock most evenings, Broadway Joe has a long way to go to regain its former reputation for quality.

Bruno

★ ★

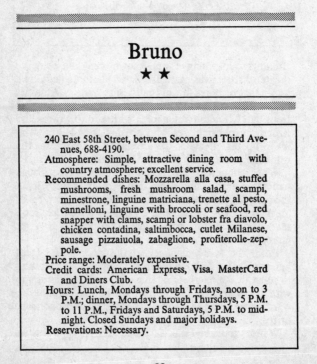

240 East 58th Street, between Second and Third Avenues, 688-4190.

Atmosphere: Simple, attractive dining room with country atmosphere; excellent service.

Recommended dishes: Mozzarella alla casa, stuffed mushrooms, fresh mushroom salad, scampi, minestrone, linguine matriciana, trenette al pesto, cannelloni, linguine with broccoli or seafood, red snapper with clams, scampi or lobster fra diavolo, chicken contadina, saltimbocca, cutlet Milanese, sausage pizzaiuola, zabaglione, profiterolle-zeppole.

Price range: Moderately expensive.

Credit cards: American Express, Visa, MasterCard and Diners Club.

Hours: Lunch, Mondays through Fridays, noon to 3 P.M.; dinner, Mondays through Thursdays, 5 P.M. to 11 P.M., Fridays and Saturdays, 5 P.M. to midnight. Closed Sundays and major holidays.

Reservations: Necessary.

The simple, almost pristine setting of this North Italian restaurant is in welcome contrast to some of the overly lavish interiors we have been subjected to lately. Dark mirrored panels and rough white plaster walls hung with large colorful and simply framed botanical prints give the dining room a country atmosphere, yet one that has a certain urban sophistication. Lighting is good at all but the center row of tables, where it is difficult to read the menu, and the noise level is fairly moderate. Tables are not crammed too closely together and the staff is polite, genuinely concerned and efficient.

In general, the food is pleasant and satisfying, the only two consistent flaws being underseasoning and poor frying. Among appetizers, broiled stuffed mushrooms in a gossamer tomato sauce, a salad of raw mushrooms with chips of red onion, and mozzarella alla casa (one of the few well-fried specialties) were all excellent. The mozzarella preparation differs from the standard mozzarella in carrozza in that the cheese is sandwiched between paper-thin slices of bread instead of being on one thick slab, and the sandwich is then dipped into an egg batter and lightly fried. An assortment of salami, prosciutto and roasted peppers was acceptable, but it seemed a shame to serve canned California olives with it. Clams oreganata were decent, if lacking the bite of the garlic and the perfume of oregano they should have, and the broiled scampi would have been perfect had there not been the out-of-character addition of paprika to their bread crumbs.

Bruno's served one of the best minestrones I've ever eaten, a veritable garden patch of vegetables with just enough pasta and beans in a delicate tomato base. Unfortunately, the broth for the cappelletti in brodo was far less distinguished, clouded with starch and much like the water in which pasta was cooked. But the meat-filled pasta "hats" — cappelletti — were fine.

Most pastas were delicious, especially the linguine matriciana with a sauce of tomato, prosciutto and onion, the thin noodles called trenette in a basil pesto sauce, the linguine with chopped broccoli in a tomato and garlic sauce, the linguine with seafood, and the lusty meal-in-itself cannelloni with a Bolognese sauce at once dense and hearty with meat yet light with a touch of tomato and cream. But linguine with white clam sauce needed a little more golden-brown garlic, and the tortellini in cream sauce were gummy.

Fish dishes, in general, were beautiful, including the red snapper with clams in a thin marechiare-type tomato sauce and the scampi fra diavolo in a thick tomato and herb sauce. Zuppa di pesce, the Italian answer to bouillabaisse, also had a lovely broth, and the shrimp, clams and squid in it were perfect. Fish fillets, however, were overcooked. A glowingly fresh, plump, two-pound lobster was ordered oreganata style and served immaculately baked — moist and tender. But the bread-crumb topping again lacked sufficient garlic and oregano and included paprika. Lobster fra diavolo seems like a much better choice.

The only fried dish that was impeccably done was the large, crisp, breaded veal cutlet Milanese. The best meat dishes were sausage and green peppers in a bracing pizzaiuola sauce, calf's liver Veneziana, unusually good saltimbocca served with leaf spinach, and chicken contadina sautéed with sausage, peppers and almost enough garlic. Kidneys were nicely prepared in a white wine sauce, and the grilled veal chop was acceptable although it was so thick it dried a bit in the broiling and absorbed no flavor of seasonings, if in fact any had been applied. Veal cutlet Valdostana, stuffed with cheese and ham, would have been good if it had not been flawed in the frying. A veal piccante and a paillard of veal were inadequately seared and were bland and watery as a result.

Golden julienne strips of fried zucchini were served with lunches but must be ordered à la carte for dinner. Again, the frying was a problem. Either the vegetable oil used is allowed to reach the boiling point or it is reused too often.

Cheesecake was sometimes wonderfully light, fluffy and creamy, other times heavy and watery. The napoleon, rum cake and fruit tart were not worth eating. But the fried crullers, zeppole, filled with crème pâtissière and topped with chocolate sauce, were wonderful, as was the zabaglione, with or without strawberries — light, frothy and heady with Marsala as it should be.

Lunch and dinner menus are the same at Bruno, with slightly lower prices during the day. The wine list is fairly standard for an upper-class Italian restaurant and overpriced by about 20 percent.

Cabana Carioca
★ ★

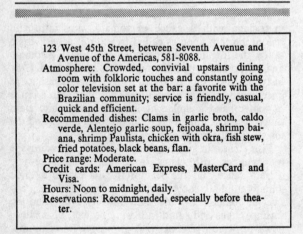

123 West 45th Street, between Seventh Avenue and Avenue of the Americas, 581-8088.
Atmosphere: Crowded, convivial upstairs dining room with folkloric touches and constantly going color television set at the bar: a favorite with the Brazilian community; service is friendly, casual, quick and efficient.
Recommended dishes: Clams in garlic broth, caldo verde, Alentejo garlic soup, feijoada, shrimp baiana, shrimp Paulista, chicken with okra, fish stew, fried potatoes, black beans, flan.
Price range: Moderate.
Credit cards: American Express, MasterCard and Visa.
Hours: Noon to midnight, daily.
Reservations: Recommended, especially before theater.

Note: For a fuller description of the sort of Brazilian dishes served here, see the review of the Brazilian Pavilion.

In a setting that is noisy, crowded and informally folkloric, the Cabana Carioca is one of the liveliest and most popular of this city's Brazilian restaurants. Convenient to the theater district, this place offers outstanding value by today's standards. The stairway leading to the second-story dining room looks a bit sleazy, but once inside, you will find a jumping bar scene with television turned on night and day and a convivial house-party atmosphere with many Brazilians who make this their headquarters. Seating is elbow to elbow, and tables are tiny.

The best appetizers to have, as you sip a caipirinha are the excellent clams in garlic broth and either the caldo verde or Alentejo garlic soup. Feijoada, served Wednesdays and Saturdays, is very good, as are the spicy shrimp baiana and the garlicky shrimp Paulista. Chicken with okra is delicious, as is the salt codfish bacalhau, either braised in sauce or with egg sauce. Steaks and pork chops are thin but acceptable, and the tomato and onion sauce for the frutos do mar fish stew is pleasant, as are most of the fish and shellfish, excepting only the tiny, tough frozen shrimp. Flan is decent.

Cafe des Artistes
★

1 West 67th Street, between Central Park West and Columbus Avenue, 877-3500.

Atmosphere: Graceful, romantic Continental cafe with lush murals; service friendly and efficient, but sometimes careless and slow.

Recommended dishes: Cauliflower salad, snails with prosciutto and onion, curried mussels in avocado, clams with Mexican relish, swordfish, soft-shell crabs, cold salmon, paillard of beef, calf's liver with avocado, orange savarin, carrot cake, strawberry ice cream.

Price range: Moderately expensive.

Credit cards: All major cards.

Hours: Lunch, Mondays through Fridays, noon to 3 P.M., dinner, Mondays through Saturdays, 5:30 to 11 P.M., Sundays, 5 P.M. to 9 P.M.; brunch, Saturdays, noon to 3 P.M., Sundays, 11 A.M. to 3 P.M.

Reservations: Necessary.

Considering the graceful charm of the Cafe des Artistes, it's a pity that the kitchen's performance level is so much less enduring. This Continental cafe, with its greenery, leaded glass windows and the sensuous, sylvan murals that Howard Chandler Christy painted when it opened in 1917, is enchanting. In the true spirit of a cafe, the dining room is cramped and noisy, a characteristic that makes service difficult, but adds conviviality.

Since this is one of the most inviting dining places on the Upper West Side, it is unfortunate to have to report that the level of cooking has gone down since the Cafe des Artistes was given a two-star rating in 1979. Only a few of the appetizers and desserts are as good as they were then, and main courses have also deteriorated. Nevertheless, this cafe can still provide enough good dishes to make a diverting meal, especially at weekend brunches.

Appetizers that have held up include cauliflower salad with an herbed vinaigrette dressing, a good choice even if the broccoli in that salad ranges from fresh bright green to slightly worn khaki brown. Clams as fresh as an ocean breeze get an added lift from a sprightly Mexican pepper relish, and the silken roast peppers, when available, make a subtly satisfying first course. For lustier appetizers, there are usually sand-free mussels tossed with curried mayonnaise and heaped into an avocado. Not nearly so savory as they used to be are the cochonailles, assorted sausages and pâtés, which are now often bland and stale. Much the same can be said for salmon appetizers, whether smoked, dill cured as gravlax, raw or in aspic.

The bland seafood gazpacho I had was served tepid instead of chilled, and its mushy fish seemed to have been dropped in by accident along with a slice of unripe avocado. Other misguided appetizers include asparagus wrapped in gravlax and in leathery slices of aircured ham, a terrine of vegetables bound by a leaden veal forcemeat and a bizarre combination of cold oysters with a hot, sausage-flecked tomato sauce. Although overcomplicated, snails sautéed with onions and strips of prosciutto are acceptable.

Simple broiled and sautéed main courses were the most satisfying. Among them, a rare and tender paillard of beef with a shallot and red-wine-butter sauce was exceptional. Sautéed soft-shell crabs with almonds could hardly be improved upon, nor could a well-grilled swordfish steak. And though the avocado lacked flavor, the slices of calf's liver sautéed with it were pink, fresh and satisfying. But walnuts and soggy zucchini slivers overpowered scallops. Apples and raspberries made chicken seem like a misplaced ingredient in a fruit salad.

Bourride, the Provence fish soup, is enriched by aioli, the heady garlic mayonnaise, but contained only a few tiny nuggets of fish and four mussels.

Desserts used to be spectacular, but now only three are above average: an airy orange savarin cake, spiced carrot cake and strawberry ice cream. Peach tart was a near miss, marred by an oversweet layer of almond cream.

The staff is polite and generally efficient. But at back tables, at crowded times, the waiters seem distracted and forgetful, and the kitchen doesn't seem able to turn out all appetizers or main courses for members of the same party at the same time.

Café Español
★

172 Bleecker Street, between Sullivan and Macdougal
    Streets, 475-9230.
Atmosphere: Small, crowded, folkloric Spanish set-
    ting; polite and generally good service that is
    sometimes slow.
Recommended dishes: Octopus, mussels vinaigrette,
    guacamole, nachos, chalupas, Mexican combina-
    tion, mariscados in green sauce or egg sauce,
    clams, shrimps or mussels in green sauce, broiled
    or boiled lobster, whitings in green sauce, paella
    Valenciana, chicken Mexican-style.
Price range: Inexpensive.
Credit cards: American Express, Visa, MasterCard
    and Diners Club.
Hours: Lunch, seven days, noon to 4 P.M.; dinner,
    Sundays through Thursdays, 4 P.M. to midnight,
    Fridays and Saturdays, 4 P.M. to 1 A.M. Open on
    major holidays.
Reservations: Recommended.

Considering the current rage for seafood and the equal
interest in finding bargains, the popularity of Café
Español is easy to understand. For, though most of the
selections on the Spanish and Mexican menus leave
much to be desired, there are several savory and satisfying appetizers and copious seafood main courses that
are exceptional buys. Add to that the snug and engaging
adobe hacienda setting and the friendly, concerned and
generally efficient staff, and you have the makings of a
pleasant dinner, especially before or after Off Broadway
theater.

Start with the tequila-based margarita, which has just
the right limy, salty pungency, and between sips nibble
on freshly warmed taco chips dipped into hot sauce or
the onion-scented guacamole, which can be ordered as
an appetizer. Then if you restrict your choices to what
the house does best, you'll go on to just about a two-star
meal. The overall rating, however, is one star because
all the meat dishes, and most chicken and Mexican specialties, are not good enough to be considered bargains,
even at such low prices.

But in these times, consider the tender and moist
pound and a quarter lobster, freshly boiled or broiled,
served with melted butter and rice or crisp-fried rounds
of Spanish potatoes a bargain at less than $10. Or have
two helpings from a generous potful of mariscados —
mussels, clams, shrimp, scallops and half a baby lobster
in a satiny-green sauce, combining parsley and garlic,
or in a smooth, custardy garlic-egg sauce. The same
shellfish in a diablo sauce proved acceptable, but for a
dish named after the devil, it lacked the proper hellfire
touch of hot pepper.

Paella Valenciana, with chicken, lobster and other
seafood, arrived slightly mushy on one try, but gently

moist and flavorful on another, and it, too, is a buy that's hard to beat. Much the same can be said of any of the shellfish or the whitings in green sauce, even if the rolls are tasteless and the salad is made with iceberg lettuce and bottled dressing. At these inexpensive prices, one can afford to skip those dreary additions and still get full value.

The veal with almond sauce was sweet and disappointing, and so was the dry chicken, prepared either in garlic sauce or Riojano style, with tomatoes, onions, peppers and wine. But Mexican chicken, with peppers, onions and tomatoes in a mildly spicy sauce, made far more interesting eating. The other good choice among Mexican main courses was the combination of a chicken taco, a beef tostado and an overcooked but soothingly rich enchilada.

Appetizers at Café Español are large enough to be shared, whether you choose cold, plump mussels vinaigrette topped with minced onion and pimento, tender octopus in a mild paprika sauce, or nachos or chalupas — fried tortilla chips glazed with cheese and jalapeño peppers or black beans.

Dishes not worth eating your way through at any price include the special shrimp with mushrooms in a characterless wine sauce, the pasty zarzuela, the sinewy, stewy steak rancheros and the Galician and black bean soups. There is good Mexican beer and a hearty, smooth Spanish red Rioja. It is reasonably priced and far preferable to sangría — as what would not be?

Anyone with an insistent sweet tooth should try the flan instead of the dully commercial cream cheese cake. Espresso is strong and restorative. Things get lively at Café Español after eight, and the kitchen runs a bit slow at peak hours.

Cafe Geiger

★

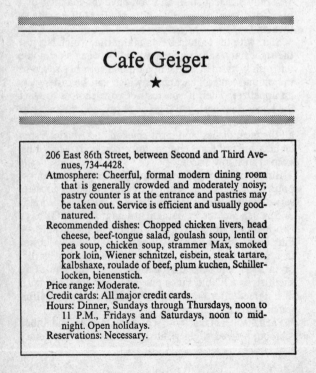

206 East 86th Street, between Second and Third Avenues, 734-4428.

Atmosphere: Cheerful, formal modern dining room that is generally crowded and moderately noisy; pastry counter is at the entrance and pastries may be taken out. Service is efficient and usually good-natured.

Recommended dishes: Chopped chicken livers, head cheese, beef-tongue salad, goulash soup, lentil or pea soup, chicken soup, strammer Max, smoked pork loin, Wiener schnitzel, eisbein, steak tartare, kalbshaxe, roulade of beef, plum kuchen, Schillerlocken, bienenstich.

Price range: Moderate.

Credit cards: All major credit cards.

Hours: Dinner, Sundays through Thursdays, noon to 11 P.M., Fridays and Saturdays, noon to midnight. Open holidays.

Reservations: Necessary.

Although the number of good German restaurants in New York City has dwindled noticeably in the last 15 years, there are still a few above-average choices left for lovers of sauerbraten and gemütlichkeit. A favorite of mine for a number of years was the Cafe Geiger in Yorkville, at first glance a pastry cafe in the true konditorei tradition. But it is really a full-fledged restaurant, and though not up to its former level, it is still a good option at moderate cost.

Considering the costs and logistics of running a restaurant in New York today, the job turned out by the management here borders on the amazing, with dependably well-prepared, generously portioned entrees at moderate prices. The look of the place is simple and modern, with dark wood-grain paneling, banal oil paintings and pleasant lighting from modern crystal ceiling fixtures. The quarters are a bit close for comfort but bearable, and the service is efficient and brisk.

The best choices here are, not too surprisingly, the German specialities. Among appetizers that includes the finely puréed chopped chicken livers with minced onion, the head cheese (sülze) or the beeftongue salad, oxenmaulsalat, both with a vinaigrette dressing. Herring fillets in a thick sour cream and onion sauce can be too soft and bland.

Soups are especially good, whether you choose the paprika-burnished beef goulash soup, the thick purée of lentil or green pea or the golden consommé with noodles.

For lunch, light dinners and between-meal lifts, there is a fine array of cold dishes, most based on raw Westphalian or cured Black Forest country hams and what is beyond doubt the freshest, rosiest beef steak tartare the city has to offer. Strammer Max, a Berlin specialty, is an open sandwich of buttered rye bread heaped with meaty slivers of Westphalian ham, topped with a sizzling hot fried egg, a snack that offers a new lease on life, especially if downed with a shot of ice-cold Steinhager, the clear and fiery German gin.

For more formal gorging, the most satisfactory main courses include the gently smoked pork loin, Kasseler Rippchen, served with piquant sauerkraut and homemade mashed potatoes, and good schnitzels of all sorts, especially the Wiener, which is encased in a fluffy, crisp breading. Wursts are passable, nothing more.

Eisbein, the Berlin favorite of steamed pigs' feet, is always on the menu, as is the glowingly fresh calf's liver, beautifully sautéed and crowned with thick, crisp slices of bacon. Duck is crisp, but a portion included two hind quarters, which is not fair; the orange sauce with it is awful. Fish is invariably overcooked

Good weekend specialties are the kalbshaxe, a tender braised veal shank so enormous it is almost embarrassing, and the pork fillet piccata in a cheese-flavored golden breading. Roulade of beef filled with onion and pickle is braised in a velvety meat gravy.

Choose such German-style vegetables as winy sweet and sour red cabbage or the sauerkraut. Alternatives such as peas and carrots are straight from the can, and creamed spinach approximates library paste. The apple pancake, heavy, tasteless and underdone within, was the most blatant disappointment suffered here.

Desserts are almost exclusively the whipped-cream extravaganzas displayed at the entrance. Get up and choose for yourself and keep an eye out for the kuchen made with fresh blue plums, the almond triangles, the beinenstich, and the Schillerlocken, cream-filled pastry coils named for the curly locks of the poet and playwright Schiller.

The wine list is, unfortunately, undistinguished, and the selections are overpriced. Instead, try a Berliner Weissebier mit Schuss, and be prepared for beer, frothy and ruby-colored with its lacing of raspberry syrup.

Cafe San Martin
Fair

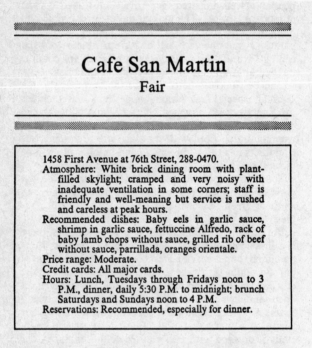

1458 First Avenue at 76th Street, 288-0470.

Atmosphere: White brick dining room with plant-filled skylight; cramped and very noisy with inadequate ventilation in some corners; staff is friendly and well-meaning but service is rushed and careless at peak hours.

Recommended dishes: Baby eels in garlic sauce, shrimp in garlic sauce, fettuccine Alfredo, rack of baby lamb chops without sauce, grilled rib of beef without sauce, parrillada, oranges orientale.

Price range: Moderate.

Credit cards: All major cards.

Hours: Lunch, Tuesdays through Fridays noon to 3 P.M., dinner, daily 5:30 P.M. to midnight; brunch Saturdays and Sundays noon to 4 P.M.

Reservations: Recommended, especially for dinner.

Moderate prices for what sounds like interesting Spanish and Continental food keep Cafe San Martin jammed and deafeningly noisy almost every night. There is a crowded bar scene, live piano music and tables are close together, making conversation virtually impossible. And even though white brick walls and green plants hanging from a skylight lend a coolly pleasant look, ventilation is inadequate in some corners of the two-level dining room, making things uncomfortable on hot summer nights,

The simple broiled specialties such as the thick rib beefsteak for two and the rack of baby lamb chops are good buys. Ask to have the red wine and marrow sauce served on the side because it compromises the flavor of the meat. Much the same can be said for the floury brown gravy served with the otherwise delicious rack of baby lamb chops. Having either of these after an appetizer such as a shared order of fettuccine Alfredo or baby eels sizzling in a garlic sauce or shrimp in a spicy garlic sauce results in a satisfying dinner, a far better one than you will have by ordering Spanish food.

Both black bean soup and the gazpacho were tasteless and Alaskan king crab meat in a sweet, sherry sauce had a threadlike texture and a fishy flavor. Dessicated slices of sausage in red wine, dramatically served in the foil pouch in which they were cooked, had no hint of wine or seasoning.

Shellfish such as shrimp, clams, scallops, mussels and lobster are dry and tasteless, and they seem to have been cooked long in advance then mixed into the preparation ordered. That flaw marred the zarzuela of mariscos, the dish called Mediterranean Delight (the shellfish in green sauce) and the paella, which also had woody, dried-out nuggets of sausages in the overcooked rice. The lobster-claw meat in the paella was not fresh, although half a lobster in the parrillada (broiled and steamed shellfish and striped bass in a pink, peppery Romesco sauce) was fresh and moist; it was, in fact, the only acceptable seafood dish.

Green sauce made with parsley and garlic is a Spanish favorite and appears in many shellfish preparations. Here it is gluey and almost devoid of garlic flavor. Fillet of hake Madrilene is a murky, overcooked combination with prosciutto and cheese.

There is a dazzling table of desserts, with huge oranges orientale, flan and coconut custard, fruit tarts and a loaf-shaped chocolate mousse. All but the oranges proved disappointing.

Service is efficient and friendly but at peak times it is somewhat slapdash. At one dinner, I overpaid the check by $80 in cash, and as I left, it was returned by the cashier, an all too rare occurrence.

Cafe Un, Deux, Trois

★

123 West 44th Street between Avenue of the Americas and Broadway, 354-4148.
Atmosphere: Large, noisy, convivial and funky cafe restaurant; service unprofessional but amiable.
Recommended dishes: Baked mussels, mussels marinère, seafood salad, fried chicken wings, chicken in the pot, fish soup, sole Meunière, brochette of chicken, entrecôte, calf's liver grand'mère, cold breast of chicken and duck, cold salmon, dame blanche, profiteroles, fruit salad.
Price range: Moderate.
Credit cards: American Express, Visa and MasterCard.
Hours: Lunch and dinner, Mondays through Fridays, noon to 1 A.M., Saturdays and Sundays, 3 P.M. to 1 A.M.
Reservations: Not accepted.

In five years, Cafe Un, Deux, Trois, has become a lively meeting place for a young and engaging crowd. Unlike several cafe meeting places that have become popular in recent years, this establishment exhibits absolutely no pretension. It provides a pleasantly diverting setting for light to heavy fare for lunch, dinner or late supper on the edge of the theater district. Set in what appears to be the funky, grandiose lobby of a shabby hotel, this cafe has a young staff that makes up in good will what it lacks in professionalism. Service may be slow and forgetful, but it is neither rude nor indifferent. Crayons and white paper tablecloths are provided for technicolor doodling or a fast game of tic-tac-toe to while away the minutes between courses. After nine, the costumed clientele, wearing what looks like thrift-shop finds, shows up and provides an entertaining floor show.

The dishes presented on the menu or blackboard are primarily French and American, and portions are generous enough to be shared, a popular practice with appetizers. The best of these are hot baked mussels with garlic and parsley; a cool, refreshing seafood salad, plump, sand-free mussels marinière in a garlic-butter-and-white-wine broth, and crisp-fried chicken wings, best eaten without the sticky-sweet dip. Pâtés are murky and greasy, and among soups, only the bouillabaisse-style fish creation is worth eating — the others are floury and bland.

There is a fair salade Niçoise, somewhat short on tuna fish. In summer, it is worth remembering the cold poached salmon with cucumber salad and green herb mayonnaise, and cold breast of chicken and duck, both moist, flavorful and satisfying. Sole meunière may lack the crisp veneer that usually distinguishes the dish, but it is creditable nonetheless. The brochette of moist chunks of chicken, lightly glossed with orange, is delicious on a bed of savory rice.

Plain entrecôte is a wiser choice than the pallid steak au poivre, and calf's liver grand'mère, with its golden, crunchy glaze, is perhaps the best of the meat selections. Poule au pot, with a Cornish hen in the pot instead of chicken, provides soothing sustenance with a light broth, leeks and carrots.

The sauce for the fish en papillote seemed made of undiluted canned tomatoes, and the Un, Deux, Trois version of pasteelya, a Moroccan pigeon pie, was musty and soggy. Fruit tarts are heavy with a sticky, gelatinous substance, but both the hot fudge sundae (dame blanche) and cream puff profiteroles with ice cream and chocolate sauce were irresistible. It would be hard to find a sliced fruit salad more sparkling than the rainbow of kiwi, peaches, strawberries, oranges and apples the cafe serves. That, following mussels mariniere, would make a fine pre-theater dinner.

Capsouto Frères
Fair

451 Washington Street, corner of Watts Street, 966-4900.

Atmosphere: Spacious and handsome brick-walled cafe-restaurant; service polite and good-natured, but inept and slow.

Recommended dishes: Ragoût of artichokes, ratatouille, artichoke with scallops, cold asparagus with garlic mayonnaise, striped bass with anchovy butter, steamed mussels in garlic broth, ham and cheese omelet.

Price range: Moderately expensive.

Credit cards: American Express.

Hours: Lunch, Tuesdays through Sundays, 11:30 A.M. to 5:30 P.M.; dinner, seven days, 5:30 P.M. to 2 A.M. Closed Christmas day only.

Reservations: Recommended.

Ask a mountain climber why he must scale the highest and most treacherous peak, and he will probably answer, "Because it's there." Much the same reason can be given for the popularity of Capsouto Frères, a bistro that has attracted the young and the costumed. In this case, "there" is a remote pocket of TriBeCa (the triangle below Canal Street) that is desolate at night, but fine for those who drive. Finding a cab can take twenty minutes and a long, lonely walk through deserted streets. But it is probable that the offbeat location is the reason for the restaurant's success. If the same food and careless, unprofessional (though good-natured) service were offered in midtown, it is doubtful that anyone would give the place a second chance. There is a sort of reverse chic in knowing of such remote eating places, especially if they are handsome in a trendy way. Set in a reclaimed warehouse, with brick walls and authoritative cast-iron columns, the dining room and bar occupy a lofty and pleasant space, albeit one that is drafty.

But though all the food is freshly made and edible, little more can be said for it. Three meals gave ample evidence that the kitchen staff just doesn't know much about the preparation of food. Roast lamb, ordered medium rare or pink, arrived in heavy cuts that ranged from raw to overdone. Pink was the only shade not represented, and much the same was true of roast duck. Steaks on two tries were as fibrous as if they had been frozen, and twice the linguine with shrimp and scallops was watery, undersalted and milky. Even a simple green salad suffered from wet lettuce that shed its dressing. A version of choucroute garni, made with red cabbage instead of sauerkraut, had the cloying sweetness of a dessert, and the roast pork and sausage in it tasted musty and stale.

The few acceptable choices included appetizers such as a brightly fresh ratatouille, a gently oily ragoût of artichoke hearts, simmered with carrots, potatoes and onions, and an artichoke bottom filled with a ceviche of scallops. Just a mild overdose of cumin marred the artichoke-scallop dish, but not enough to make it really unpleasant.

Mussels steamed in garlic broth, and a small but savory slice of grilled striped bass, veneered with anchovy butter, were the only good main courses, although a ham and cheese omelet at brunch seemed satisfying compared with most alternatives. So did clams on the half shell and cold asparagus with garlic mayonnaise. But not so the stale, greasy pâtés and faded saucisson, the murky onion soup or the butternut-squash soup, much like baby food.

Dessert pastries look gorgeous but are only passable. Strawberry and kiwi tarts outshone the surprisingly tasteless, though tantalizingly fragrant, chocolate cake, and nut tart was made with rancid nuts. Spinach salad looked wonderful, but when I ordered it at a later meal, none was available.

The menu offers an interesting variety of light and heavy choices all day and evening. There are numerous daily specials, which are described by the staff, some times with prices and sometimes without.

The Captain's Table (East Side)

★ ★ ★

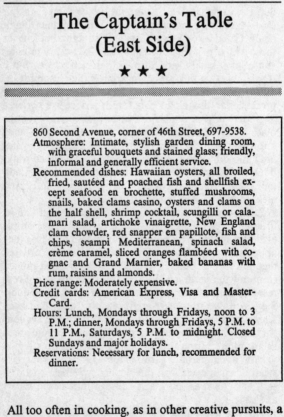

860 Second Avenue, corner of 46th Street, 697-9538.
Atmosphere: Intimate, stylish garden dining room, with graceful bouquets and stained glass; friendly, informal and generally efficient service.
Recommended dishes: Hawaiian oysters, all broiled, fried, sautéed and poached fish and shellfish except seafood en brochette, stuffed mushrooms, snails, baked clams casino, oysters and clams on the half shell, shrimp cocktail, scungilli or calamari salad, artichoke vinaigrette, New England clam chowder, red snapper en papillote, fish and chips, scampi Mediterranean, spinach salad, crème caramel, sliced oranges flambéed with cognac and Grand Marnier, baked bananas with rum, raisins and almonds.
Price range: Moderately expensive.
Credit cards: American Express, Visa and MasterCard.
Hours: Lunch, Mondays through Fridays, noon to 3 P.M.; dinner, Mondays through Fridays, 5 P.M. to 11 P.M., Saturdays, 5 P.M. to midnight. Closed Sundays and major holidays.
Reservations: Necessary for lunch, recommended for dinner.

All too often in cooking, as in other creative pursuits, a highly individualized style is celebrated for its own sake. Novelty, one might say, has become its own excuse for being. But when such individuality is successful, and is based on high quality ingredients and careful preparations, the results are hard to beat. That, in short, is the success story that can be told of the Captain's Table, the recent offspring of the forty-year-old original, which still operates in Greenwich Village.

Credit for the sure and gradual development of this beguiling, flowery little seafood restaurant, with its lavish bouquets and sparkling stained-glass panels, belongs to Gino Musso, a native of Italy's Piedmont region, and his wife, Sabine, who was born in Lyons, France. Together they have gradually collected a mixmatch of accessories that magically work so well together, and they have also evolved original recipes and a friendly relaxed style of service that almost always manages to be efficient. The result is an unusually intimate and charming dining room where the noise level is benign and the food is generally excellent.

Such a combination would be welcome in any restaurant, but it is unusual where seafood is the specialty. For reasons that so far remain a mystery, seafood restaurants in this country are generally large, sprawling and devoid of atmosphere. In recent years this has changed somewhat, but even our best seafood restaurants could not for the most part be called intimate or personalized, although they may be handsome.

The menu at the Captain's Table borrows from two worlds, combining simple, classic American seafood-house specialties (New England clam chowder, shellfish cocktails, broiled and fried fish and shellfish) with house creations that are basically Mediterranean in tone, reflecting the combined backgrounds of Mr. and Mrs. Musso.

Among the most outstanding of these creations are appetizers such as snails sizzling in an herb and butter sauce, herbaceous stuffed mushrooms, baked clams casino with mincings of crisp bacon and pimento, slivers of calamari (squid) or scungilli (conch), marinated to cool tenderness in a sparkling oil-and-lemon dressing, and cold artichoke in a sunny vinaigrette dressing that is one of the city's best.

A blend of Provençale herbs burnishes a number of superb broiled fish specialties, and diners make selections from a huge board displaying the day's catch. Whole fish, such as pompano and gray sole, are the most extraordinary choices, although all of the fish, whole or in fillets, are, in general, beautifully prepared this way. The occasional exception occurs when the cook wields a heavy hand with the herbs, leading to a mustiness that obscures the airy freshness of the fish.

Also Mediterranean in inspiration is the house specialty of long standing — red snapper en papillote, with scallops, mussels and shrimp in a bubbling, lightly garlicked tomato sauce presented in a silvery balloon of foil.

The daily array of fish is in itself enticing for variety and glowing freshness. Sharing equal billing with the luxurious salmon, striped bass, authentic red snapper, pompano and swordfish are the humble blowfish, tilefish, white snapper (really gray porgy), mako shark, flounder and butterfish, to name only a few that are intermittently available. Those preferring unadorned fish can forgo the sprinkling of herbs, but in that case it is a good idea to ask that the paprika be withheld as well. A lemony, crêpe de chine froth of hollandaise accompa-

51

nies delicately moist poached salmon, and lobster is broiled without becoming dry or tough.

Scampi Mediterranean are mellowed by a sheer sauce, combining lemon, white wine, a touch of glacé de viande and the pungency of capers, and the two wide, thick fillets of sole that are billed as fish and chips are models of expert frying with their dry, savory, absolutely greaseless breading. The chips — french fries that are said to be homemade from scratch — were slightly limp and unevenly fried on one occasion, a mild flaw in the otherwise excellent main course.

An above-average tartar sauce, boiled new potatoes in their jackets and a sprightly house salad accompany main courses, and crisp-skinned, properly floury, baked potatoes or nicely seasoned rice are alternatives. So is a knockout spinach-and-raw-mushrooms salad, gentled with an oily bacon dressing. The firmly cooked vegetables sampled, such as broccoli and zucchini, needed just a glossing of butter and a sprinkling of salt to achieve perfection.

The most refreshing and carefully turned out desserts include crème caramel, sliced fresh oranges flambéed with cognac and Grand Marnier, strawberries in a zabaglione sauce and lengthwise slices of bananas baked in a butter-rum sauce and finished with raisins and almonds.

A few consistent flaws held over from the early days of the Captain's Table still persist. Mussels marinières can be lovely in their delicate garlic broth, but they can also be gritty with sand, and the gazpacho is a cloyingly thick mass of chopped canned tomatoes, closer to chili sauce than to soup. Shellfish grilled en brochette was chokingly dry and, as already mentioned, an overkill of aromatic herbs sometimes mars broiled specialties.

Of the meat offerings on the menu, the steak, plain or au poivre, is a better choice than the scaloppine of not very good veal, which was tough and fibrous.

The Black Forest cake, because of the bland dryness of its chocolate layers, remains ordinary. Better bread would be a welcome addition, as would a more sensitive choice of sauces for the excellent clams and oysters.

The Captain's Table is every bit as pleasant for lunch as for dinner. In the evening, a hospitable touch is generally added by way of a giveaway appetizer, such as fried smelts or scungilli salad. There is a limited but adequate wine list, on which the less-expensive standard Italian choices are the best buys.

The Captain's Table
(Greenwich Village)

★

410 Avenue of the Americas, between Eighth and
Ninth Streets, 473-0670.
Atmosphere: Small, bright, flowery setting that is
somewhat cramped; generally good service.
Recommended dishes: Clams casino, clams or oysters
on the half shell, squid salad, all broiled sliced or
whole fish, broiled lobster, fish and chips, chicken
Kiev, crème caramel.
Price range: Moderate.
Credit cards: American Express, MasterCard, Visa
and Diners Club.
Hours: Lunch, Tuesdays through Saturdays, noon to
3:30 P.M.; dinner, Tuesdays through Fridays, 5
P.M. to 11 P.M., Saturdays, 5 P.M. to midnight,
Sundays, 1 P.M. to 10 P.M. Closed Mondays and
major holidays.
Reservations: Necessary.

One of Greenwich Village's most enduring landmark
restaurants, this pretty, flowery, garden-cafe seafood
house is operated by Gino Musso, who has owned it
since 1971. Although not quite so sparkling and stylish
as its newer uptown offspring, this remains a pleasant if
slightly cramped setting for generally good seafood
dishes. Service in the Cape Cod-inspired dining-room is
friendly and concerned but often slow.

Broiled fish is expertly prepared and the array is one
of the most varied in the city. Whole fish such as pompano, red snapper, striped bass and bluefish are grilled
and perfumed with the herbs of Provence or broiled in
slices that are generally not at all overcooked. Mako
shark, white snapper and tile fish are among the more
unusual offerings.

Fried fillets of fish and chips (thick french fries) also
are done as they should be — light, golden and greaseless. Stick to such simple fare, along with the clams or
oysters on the half shell, the clams casino, the squid
salad and the boiled lobster, and you will have a thoroughly satisfiying meal.

It is in the sauces and fancier preparations that the
kitchen's shortcomings become apparent. Clam chowder is fresh and made from scratch but is overly thickened with flour and lacks flavor, and the otherwise decent artichoke is served too cold and undrained so that
its water dilutes the excellent vinaigrette dressing. Snails
are dry, rubbery and afloat in a soupy sauce, mussels
marinière were full and well flavored with garlic, but
their broth was too sharply acidic. Sautéed bay scallops
tasted of overheated oil or butter that drowned out their
sweet sea flavor. The biggest disappointment here was
the red snapper en papillote baked with mussels and
scallops in a tomato sauce. This sauce used to be rich
with garlic, which helped make the dish superb. But re-

cently it has been far too sweet, a pity because all ingredients are beautifully cooked.

Bouillabaisse, awkwardly served in a wide, flat, redhot skillet that makes the ingredients difficult to handle, also was too sweet, perhaps a result of an overabundance of carrots in the sauce. The striped bass in it tasted of petroleum oil, a failing so common these days that we have about given up hope for that fish entirely. Sweetness also maimed the sauce for scampi Mediterranean style.

Steak is decent and though the chicken Kiev with its garlic butter is not authentic, it is interesting.

Desserts are weak. The Black Forest cake lacks a rich chocolate flavor and the perfume of kirsch, and the zabaglione sauce for strawberries is overly eggy and cloyingly sweet. Crème caramel is the best choice.

Casa Brasil
★

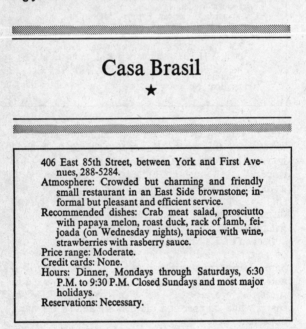

406 East 85th Street, between York and First Avenues, 288-5284.
Atmosphere: Crowded but charming and friendly small restaurant in an East Side brownstone; informal but pleasant and efficient service.
Recommended dishes: Crab meat salad, prosciutto with papaya melon, roast duck, rack of lamb, feijoada (on Wednesday nights), tapioca with wine, strawberries with rasberry sauce.
Price range: Moderate.
Credit cards: None.
Hours: Dinner, Mondays through Saturdays, 6:30 P.M. to 9:30 P.M. Closed Sundays and most major holidays.
Reservations: Necessary.

In the last year or so, we have seen the advent of a number of small restaurants with limited menus that have about them a friendly, informal and personal aspect — much as though one is dining in a private (or at least a semiprivate) home. Although this phenomenon is considered to be a recent trend, it actually began almost twenty years ago, when the Brazilian-born Doña Helma Dellorto opened Casa Brasil on the garden floor of her East Side brownstone house. Floral tablecloths and centerpieces, walls covered with photographs of celebrities who are her fans, and a mixmatch assortment of souvenirs and bric-a-brac give this place a cheerful and informal charm, and though the service is not crisply professional, it is good-natured and efficient.

This is the sort of find one loves to show off to out-of-town guests and it would not take much to make the food live up to the rest of the experience. All of the main items on the menu at Casa Brasil are of high quality and very well prepared, but they are devalued by an unnecessarily wide array of vegetables that are secondrate, if not third-rate.

There is a set menu here each evening with just a few choices among appetizers, main courses and desserts. Everyone gets the uninspired canned hearts of palm in an overly rich Parmesan-thickened cream sauce that contains flecks of ham and hard-cooked egg. The choice between the beautiful lump crab-meat salad and the equally excellent prosciutto with golden slices of papaya melon is a difficult one; either makes a delightful second course. The salad of buttery bibb lettuce in a scallion-vinaigrette dressing seems an excess after the two appetizer courses and would be more welcome after the main course.

Five nights a week those main courses include a superb half of roasted duck — crisp skin, moist and flavorful meat with no sauce to add a distracting touch. A delicate rack of lamb that usually contains about five petite chops is just as carefully roasted. Sliced roast veal with a mushroom cream sauce is less interesting but acceptable, but beef Wellington, an ill-conceived dish at best, hardly seems worth ordering.

It is a shame that the excellent duck and lamb are rounded out with such sorry trimmings as frozen green peas, packaged herb-flavored rice, cloyingly sweet orange-flavored carrots, canned artichoke bottoms and overcooked broccoli. Only a warm fruit salad accompanying the duck was at all satisfying.

On Wednesday nights, Casa Brasil's only main course is the Brazilian national dish, feijoada, and a very authentic one it is, in itself worthy of two stars.

In addition to the bowl of smoky, black beans that have been simmered with spices, pigs' knuckles, tongue, beef and sausages, there is a separate bowl of a meltingly rich beef stew, a platter of sliced London broil, orange sections, the mellow and crunchy manioc flour so traditional with this dish, and steamed white rice. This makes a really generous and wonderful dinner, to be enjoyed only at great leisure and after a day of very light eating.

On all nights, desserts are the same. There is an improbable but seductive combination of wine-scented tapioca with a vanilla and fruit sauce, strawberries in a ruby, raspberry purée, and lemon mousse that is sometimes pallid but at other times sharply astringent and refreshing. Good Brazilian coffee is served in pretty cups that match the floral tablecloth. The house has no liquor license, so guests may bring in their own beverages.

There is a small and appealing parlor upstairs where guests can wait for tables when necessary.

Century Cafe
Fair

132 West 43rd Street, between Avenue of the Americas and Broadway, 398-1988.

Atmosphere: Bright, noisy and handsome modern dining room and balcony plus a lively bar; service is friendly and accommodating if often slow and unprofessional.

Recommended dishes: saucisson vinaigrette, hot wonton wrappers, smoked salmon, julienne herb-roasted chicken, spinach salad, salade Niçoise, London broil, shell steak, grilled lamb, asparagus or lobster omelet, hot fudge sundae and cold lemon soufflé.

Price range: Moderately expensive.

Credit cards: American Express, MasterCard and Visa.

Hours: Mondays through Saturdays, 11:30 A.M. to 2 A.M.; bar service until 4 A.M. Closed Sundays. Open major holidays.

Reservations: Recommended.

A newcomer to Times Square, this cafe, beautifully designed along clean modern lines, takes on sophisticated overtones with dramatic lighting. All this is accented by a stunning neon sign from the old Loew's Delancey that shimmers in purple and gold over the bar, popular with a young, attractive crowd. Unfortunately, noise is compounded by thumping background music.

Considering the limited choice of restaurants in this area and the fact that the Century Cafe offers a wide-ranging menu from 11 A.M. to 2 A.M. and bar service until 4 A.M., it would be nice to be able to give it an unbridled welcome. So far, however, the kitchen's performance is only fair, although it offers a wide variety of dishes ranging from light choices such as sandwiches, pastas and salads to full-fledged main courses of game, meat, fish and poultry.

The kitchen fails because of overly complicated dishes that work only occasionally. One of the more successful efforts is the hot won-ton wrappers filled with chorizo sausage, Monterey jack cheese and jalapeño peppers. This dish is really spicy fried tortellini in an Italian tomato sauce. Mozzarella in carrozza arrives as rubbery squiggles of greasy fried cheese, but hot saucisson in a tangy vinaigrette sauce is lusty and interesting and smoked salmon is quite acceptable. Dishes flawed by sweetness include the appetizer of duck breast with papaya and chicken sautéed with apples and Calvados. Basically well-made pastas are often left under the heat lamp until they become crusty.

Julienne herb-roasted chicken makes a savory, satisfying salad heaped on fresh greens and garnished with celery root and black radish. But a so-called salad of warm sautéed leeks, endive and watercress is more roughage than anyone needs. Spinach salad and salade Niçoise are among the better choices. Avoid the shrimp over fruit salad with hazelnut dressing unless you like salads that are whipped up in television commercials.

Omelets such as those made with asparagus or lobster and Gruyère cheese are decent if a bit heavy-handed. London broil sliced on French bread arrived rare, juicy and properly beefy. But croquette madame is an outrageous version of the fried ham and cheese sandwich, done here with huge slabs of deep-fried French bread. Hamburgers are dry.

More ambitious main courses such as duck and very tough lobster leave much to be desired. Stick to plain steak or grilled lamb with sorrel cream sauce.

An extravagant hot fudge sundae and a cool and delicate lemon soufflé mousse almost make up for what the other desserts lack.

Prices are high, but portions are large and there is much sharing. The young and friendly staff announces daily specials, sometimes stating the price, sometimes not. There is no minimum, so small dishes can be ordered for off-hour eating.

Chalet Suisse
★ ★

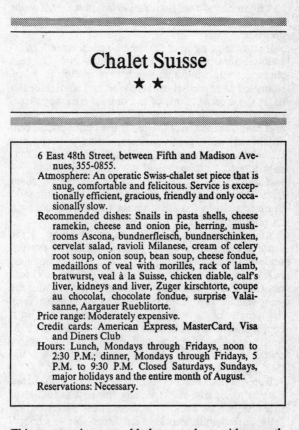

6 East 48th Street, between Fifth and Madison Avenues, 355-0855.

Atmosphere: An operatic Swiss-chalet set piece that is snug, comfortable and felicitous. Service is exceptionally efficient, gracious, friendly and only occasionally slow.

Recommended dishes: Snails in pasta shells, cheese ramekin, cheese and onion pie, herring, mushrooms Ascona, bundnerfleisch, bundnerschinken, cervelat salad, ravioli Milanese, cream of celery root soup, onion soup, bean soup, cheese fondue, medaillons of veal with morilles, rack of lamb, bratwurst, veal à la Suisse, chicken diable, calf's liver, kidneys and liver, Zuger kirschtorte, coupe au chocolat, chocolate fondue, surprise Valaisanne, Aargauer Rueblitorte.

Price range: Moderately expensive.

Credit cards: American Express, MasterCard, Visa and Diners Club

Hours: Lunch, Mondays through Fridays, noon to 2:30 P.M.; dinner, Mondays through Fridays, 5 P.M. to 9:30 P.M. Closed Saturdays, Sundays, major holidays and the entire month of August.

Reservations: Necessary.

This twenty-nine-year-old charmer glows with warmth and hospitality. The setting is operatic Swiss chalet, complete with dark wood beams, rough plaster walls, black wrought iron and waitresses in folkloric costumes, a combination that would be considered corny if newly created but is altogether felicitous as a longstanding tradition.

Considering the sort of offhand treatment most restaurant staffs accord customers these days, it is almost nourishment enough to be in a place where the owner and all the waitresses really seem to care whether guests are satisfied or would like anything else, whether silverware has been polished before it is laid out on the table and where one never feels rushed even at peak lunch and pre-theater dinner hours. Dining after 7:30 P.M. is the most leisurely experience of all here and only occasionally does service become a bit slow — usually for large parties at busy times.

The Chalet Suisse moved to its present location in 1966 and the clientele it attracts is exceptional for New York — generally quiet and radiating a Mittel-Europa love of the good life. It becomes hard to believe one is indeed in Mittel Manhattan.

The delicious, solid, countrified food presented attractively seems almost like a bonus. Appetizers and desserts are generally excellent and main courses very good; it would take only a little fine tuning in the kitchen to bring the all-important main course up to the level of the other two, thereby making this a three-star restaurant.

A lighter hand with flour would improve cream soups and sauces, and fish could be more carefully and subtly prepared.

If you are going to opt for the classic fondue Neuchâteloise, that blend of Emmenthaler and Gruyère cheeses, white wine and kirsch kept molten in a red enameled saucepan set over a flame, it is a good idea to begin the meal with one of the simpler meat appetizers — bundnerfleisch, the impeccable, paper-thin air-cured beef made in the Grison Alps, or the bundnerschinken, a delicately pink, gently saline variation of prosciutto. Cervelat salad — rosy slices of a fine pork and beef sausage topped with onions in a vinaigrette dressing — would also be appropriate before this cheese main course. Let the fondue cook down a bit before you begin to swirl in the bread crusts and it will take on a more velvety patina.

Richer appetizers are better suited to many of the other main courses. Among those appetizers are the smoothly pungent herring with sour cream and onions, puffy, hot cheese and onion tart, the soufflélike cheese ramekin that is worth the twenty-minute wait, and the spicy spinach ravioli Milanese glazed with cheese. Garlicky snails in pasta shells or mushrooms Ascona in a cool tomato and onion sauce are also excellent. A light bean soup was refreshing and a lusty cream of celery root soup was worth having, even though it was too thickened.

Rare-roasted rack of lamb encrusted with bread crumbs and garlic ranks among the best examples of that dish in New York. Thin slices of calf's liver beautifully sautéed and a knockout chicken diable — a boned, flattened breast that was grilled, peppered and topped with crisp bacon — also were among the best main courses. Satisfying, if somewhat less inspired, were the kidneys braised with liver, the roast loin of pork and a veal roast with kidneys that was just a bit tough, also a flaw in the otherwise pleasant breaded veal cutlet.

Bratwurst here could be classified as weisswurst, so tender and white was the thick, grilled sausage, succulent in its braised onion sauce, and the medaillons of veal in a pale, creamy sauce took on the earthy over tones of morilles.

Fondue Bourguignonne — chunks of bright, fresh beef held on long forks and cooked in hot oil by the diners, then seasoned in a combination of sauces — is a popular dish here, one I have enjoyed many times, if not on my most recent visits. The ingredients appeared to be impeccable.

Veal à la Suisse, known more authentically and descriptively, if less eloquently, as geschnetzeltes kalbfleisch, is a dish one must decide about for oneself. This stew of slivered veal simmered in cream is virtually the Swiss national dish, and though its charms have long escaped me, good and bad versions are still discernible. The version at this restaurant is definitely among the better renditions.

The tiny, dough dumplings, spaetzli, would be better if served right on the dinner plate with meat so that a sauce or gravy could keep them hot and moist. Rosti, the wonderfully lacy, golden-crisp Swiss potato pancake, is excellent here at night, but it is sometimes cold at lunch. Creamed carrots are less interesting than the creamed spinach, and some dishes arrive with diverting garnishes, such as the sautéed polenta slice with the veal and kidney roast.

Bread lovers should be forewarned about not overindulging on the salt and caraway topped rye rolls, and dessert buffs will have a field day, whether they give in to the temptation of the coupe au chocolat — vanilla ice cream, whipped cream and just the sort of elegant bittersweet hot-chocolate sauce one might expect from the Swiss, or the surprise Valaisanne layer of meringue, cloudlets of whipped cream and roseate strawberries. Chocolate fondue — a tiny ceramic casserole of silky chocolate kept hot over a burner — can be dipped into with bits of fruit or tiny fluted profiteroles. Aargauer Rueblitorte is a sugarless cake combining almonds, carrots, spices and whipped cream, and the Zuger kirschtorte, with its meringue layers, genoise sponge cake, kirsch and buttercream, offers subtle contrasts in both flavor and texture. Dessert disappointments included a crème caramel that was too firm, a bland chocolate mousse and completely undistinguished apple cake. Switzerland is not noted for the excellence of its wines, but one of the better choices is the red Dole de Sion.

Chanterelle
★ ★

89 Grand Street, corner of Greene Street, 966-6960.

Atmosphere: Beautifully simple, spacious and romantic dining room with antique overtones; comfortable lighting and noise level. Service is polite and friendly but occasionally slow and a bit pretentious.

Recommended dishes: Crab bisque, oyster stew, sorrel soup, seafood terrines, terrine of smoked salmon with caviar, asparagus in puff pastry, barquettes of mussels and spinach, squab, rack or noisettes of lamb, steak with cèpes, shad roe with rhubarb and leeks, sweetbreads, cassoulet, green salad, cheese, lemon tart, ice cream, reine de saba.

Price range: Expensive.

Credit cards: American Express, MasterCard and Visa.

Hours: Lunch, Tuesdays through Saturdays, 12:30 P.M. to 2:30 P.M.; dinner, Tuesdays through Saturdays, 6:30 P.M. to 10 P.M. Closed Sundays and major holidays.

Reservations: Necessary.

Since it opened in 1981, this graceful and romantic SoHo restaurant with its delicate pink walls and beautiful white embossed tin ceiling has settled in to become one of the city's more felicitous outposts for the new light and inventive cooking that is halfway between nouvelle French and new American cuisines. David Waltuck, who owns this restaurant in partnership with his wife, Karen, is also the chef. Trained at the Culinary Institute of America, he also worked at several local restaurants before opening his own.

Except for some lengthy slowdowns in the kitchen and the somewhat pretentious tone of the service that seems to be set by Mrs. Waltuck, Chanterelle is a delight for lunch and dinner. Here and there some preparations are more inventive than palatable, and a few presentations are awkward to negotiate as served, but in general the food is far above average, both in quality and in price.

Right from the start, it was evident that Mr. Waltuck is a talented chef, and though a few of his dishes seemed less good the second time around, many others showed marked improvement. Grilled seafood sausage bathed in a silken sauce has become tough and is too coarsely ground, but all seafood terrines, such as those made with pike and salmon or the other with smoked salmon and rivulets of caviar, remain excellent. So is an appetizer of oyster stew with threads of finely slivered leeks and the spring-green asparagus in puff pastry with a buttery green herb sauce.

The only unsuccessful terrine on the menu when this restaurant was first reviewed was the oxtail with carrots, looking like a beef stew that had simply been allowed to jell. Barquettes of crisp puff pastry were filled with spinach and mussels in a tomato-pink cream sauce that was briny with mussel essence. Soups have all been excellent, including the crab bisque and a sorrel and bean combination.

In the beginning, Mr. Waltuck exhibited a tendency to overseason dishes, so that the flavor of the main ingredient was lost. Lamb, for example, was overpowered by thyme on one occasion and by ginger on another. That flaw seems to have been corrected and on recent tries, both the rose-red rack and noisettes of lamb were succulent, delicately graced with garlic and in sheer, well-balanced wine sauces.

Squab, first roasted then mellowed in a red wine sauce, were as good as ever, and sweetbreads glazed with sherry wine vinegar could not be improved upon. At lunch one wintry day I had a lusty and altogether marvelous cassoulet with a variety of sausages, duck and pork, each large bean beautifully developed in a garlic-and-herb-flavored broth.

Shad roe with sorrel butter, though delicious, was so meagerly portioned it would barely satisfy as an appetizer, and lobster in Sauterne with julienne strips of vegetables hardly seemed to weigh the two pounds it was said to; it was also almost impossible to extricate the meat from the shell in the slippery sauce.

Quail, though tender and pink at the bone, lacked the golden brown richness that distinguished the squab, primarily because the smaller birds had been braised without being sufficiently browned. The quail were also awkward to negotiate, served as they were on limp cabbage leaves in a shallot cream sauce delicately balanced by a touch of vinegar.

Vegetables, such as squash blossoms, and potatoes and spaetzle so light they seemed more like egg drops were among the best accompaniments. Rolls were yeasty, chewy and superb. The cheese selection is always well varied and in top condition. Green salad in a restoratively fresh vinaigrette dressing is also well worth ordering.

Excellent desserts such as the homemade ice creams have now been joined by such equally fine selections as the pungent lemon tart and a light and airy but intensely chocolate orange flavored reine de saba torte that is accompanied by whipped cream. Petits fours, especially the big crunchy tuiles, and chocolate truffles are delectable wind-ups to the meal.

The selection of dishes is small, with four appetizers and six main courses on a weekly menu that changes every Tuesday. In additon to the à la carte arrangement, there is an enticing weekly set tasting menu of six courses that must be ordered by everyone at the table. The only flaw in its planning is that at times it contains too many similar sauces and too many seafood preparations.

The setting at Chanterelle deserves almost as much attention as the food. Aficionados of pressed-tin ceilings should look upward, for the specimen here is as lavish and frosty as wedding cake icing. Cleverly placed spotlights outside the windows reflect onto the creamy-beige-pink walls (the color, I was told, of the chanterelle, the wild mushroom for which the restaurant is named) to create a glow much like that of the sun late on a summer afternoon. The dining room is spacious, tables are large and the noise level is benign. Service is generally efficient but waivers between laid-back casualness and haute pretension.

Charlie and Kelly

★

259 West Fourth Street, corner of Perry Street, 675-5059.

Atmosphere: Romantic, candlelit Greenwich Village storefront restaurant; service is friendly, good-natured and inept.

Recommended dishes: Quiche, marinated scallops, mushroon soup, chicken pie, rack of lamb, steak, chicken breast with tomato and basil, fettuccine with clams, scallops, broccoli salad, baked peach, chocolate silk pie.

Price range: Moderate.

Credit cards: All major credit cards.

Hours: Dinner, Sundays through Thursdays, 5 P.M. to 11 P.M., Fridays and Saturdays, 6 P.M. to midnight.

Reservations: Necessary.

This is the epitome of a small, romantic Greenwich Village restaurant. Storefront windows filled with plants, dark green walls and tablecloths topped with white paper mats, candles in tall hurricane chimneys, prints and paintings and a charming little service bar add to the overall effect. Waiters and waitresses are young and friendly, if somewhat laid back and inept. The kitchen often seems to be out of selections and the staff does not always know what is unavailable until long after an order has been taken.

But the most serious failing at this well-publicized restaurant is the menu that includes a number of dishes far beyond the skills of the kitchen staff. The cooking is decent, but the style is straight American tearoom, a genre that would be perfectly acceptable if the menu did not include so many Continental dishes.

The best appetizers were the quiche Provençale, made with tomatoes, and the scallops marinated in their shells. Raw vegetables were less than fresh and inadequately cleaned although their avocado dip was mild and pleasant. I skipped the improbable-sounding melon and mint soup but found the gazpacho pleasant, if in need of a sharper accent of vinegar, and the cream of mushroom soup was delicious.

Every pasta I tried tasted as bland as though it had been created by a home economist working for a woman's magazine. Butter appeared where olive oil belonged. If any garlic had been used, it was obviously just waved over the dish briefly. The one exception was the fettuccine with clams, tomato and basil, as briny and fragrant as it should be.

Broccoli salad with anchovies, though short on dressing, was sprightly and refreshing. What was called rack of lamb came as four broiled rib lamb chops and was one of the best main courses, coming with a boiled potato and overcooked carrots. Also good was the breast of chicken in a tomato-basil sauce, but pork chops were dry and leathery.

Fresh sea scallops in a mild garlic and herb sauce would have been less disappointing had they not been dubbed Provençale, thereby raising false expectations, but an order of sole en croûte with shrimp and mushrooms was an overcooked, pasty mess.

The chicken pot pie with a very good crust was satisfying, although the vegetables in the creamy sauce were slightly scorched.

Desserts could only be called insipid, most especially the mint-flavored sabayon poured over strawberries and the unthinkable icebox cake made of packaged chocolate wafers and whipped cream. Chocolate silk pie and coffee mousse were a cut above the other two, but hardly worth the calories. Bread pudding was ice cold and soggy, and baked peach was awkwardly served, but lovely.

With all of its faults, Charlie and Kelly still offers enough good moderately priced dishes so that one can rely on a fairly pleasant dinner when casually dressed and spending an evening in the Village. This is also a felicitous setting for Sunday brunch.

Chatfield's
★

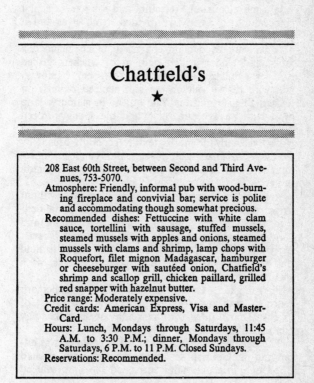

208 East 60th Street, between Second and Third Avenues, 753-5070.

Atmosphere: Friendly, informal pub with wood-burning fireplace and convivial bar; service is polite and accommodating though somewhat precious.

Recommended dishes: Fettuccine with white clam sauce, tortellini with sausage, stuffed mussels, steamed mussels with apples and onions, steamed mussels with clams and shrimp, lamp chops with Roquefort, filet mignon Madagascar, hamburger or cheeseburger with sautéed onion, Chatfield's shrimp and scallop grill, chicken paillard, grilled red snapper with hazelnut butter.

Price range: Moderately expensive.

Credit cards: American Express, Visa and Master-Card.

Hours: Lunch, Mondays through Saturdays, 11:45 A.M. to 3:30 P.M.; dinner, Mondays through Saturdays, 6 P.M. to 11 P.M. Closed Sundays.

Reservations: Recommended.

Although it is accurate to describe the casually comfortable Chatfield's as a neighborhood restaurant, when the neighborhood happens to be Bloomingdale's backyard, casualness takes on stylish overtones. This stylishness is more apparent at lunchtime than at dinner, when dress ranges from designer blue jeans to blazers.

Chatfield's suggests a tavern-restaurant in an Ivy League college town, with its brick and wainscotting-trimmed walls, the wood-burning fireplace and long convivial bar. Young preppy waiters in pink Brooks Brothers shirts are friendly and accommodating although sometimes pretentious. They also tend to forget who gets what, but their good will makes up for this shortcoming.

There are several happy surprises on the small but varied menu that is basically Continental — or nouvelle Continental — in style. On first consideration, a dinner appetizer of hot steamed mussels with apples and onions seems like a mistake, but the touch of white wine and the restrained use of the fruit mellows the combination. At lunch, equally good mussels are baked with minced walnuts. Another improbable combination that proved delicious was the thick, rare double rib lamb chops in a rich demiglace meat sauce with Roquefort cheese. Because the cheese was used sparingly, it burnished the meat without adding an acidic note.

But duck salad needed more dressing, and pâté was gray and stale, as though it had been sliced and kept in the refrigerator for several days. Skip such soups as the greasy, sourish lentil and the watery cream of cauliflower in favor of half portions of the lovely fettuccine (erroneously described as linguine) in a butter and garlic white clam sauce. Although the chef refused to divide a main course of tortellini and sausage as a first course for two diners, we divided it ourselves and it proved excellent despite the canned California olives.

Other very good main courses at lunch included a moist and tender grilled paillard of chicken, grilled snapper with hazelnut butter and thick, beefy hamburgers (with or without cheese and sautéed onions) on toasted English muffins. The quiche in a floury, limp crust with an avocado salad and the spongy, frozen Alaskan king crab aren't worth ordering, nor is the calf's liver with the mushy texture generally caused by freezing. The mixed grill of sea scallops and shrimp remained moist under the protective coating of lemon butter.

Among the specials, which are described without prices, one that generally appears at dinner is the delicate, satisfying bijou de mer — mussels, clams and shrimp steamed with garlic, white wine and parsely. Covered with the glass bowl that is later used to hold the discarded shells, this dish gives the effect of a steamy seafood terrarium.

Filet mignon Madagascar — in a green peppercorn sauce — was also well prepared, but the breast of chicken Diane, filled with ham and cheese, lacked any contrast of seasonings or textures.

The Lebanese eggplant purée, baba gannouj, was bitter, and the German air-cured ham, lachschinken, had dried out. Fried zucchini surpassed the limp sautéed version. Iceberg lettuce marred salads.

Baked desserts were either stale or virtually tasteless, carrot cake the least disappointing. Prices are fairly moderate considering the pleasant surroundings and generous portions.

Chef Ho's Hunan Manor
★

1464 Second Avenue, between 76th and 77th Streets, 570-6700.

Atmosphere: Simple, unprepossessing dining room that is crowded and noisy. Service is impatient and cursory.

Recommended dishes: Honeyed Hunan spareribs, bean curd roll, snow-white sliced fish soup, sautéed jumbo shrimp, frogs' legs, whole sea bass Hunan style, steak with scallops and vegetables, eggplant with garlic sauce, pan-fried noodles, fresh pineapple.

Price range: Moderate.

Credit cards: All major credit cards.

Hours: Lunch, Mondays through Fridays, noon to 3 P.M.; dinner, Mondays through Thursdays, 3 P.M. to 10:30 P.M., Fridays, 3 P.M. to 11:30 P.M., Saturdays, noon to 11:30 P.M., Sundays, noon to 10:30 P.M. Open on major holidays.

Reservations: Not necessary.

Chef Ho, who used to hold forth at Uncle Tai's and later at Fortune Garden, now runs the kitchen at this simple, virtually unadorned modern outpost. He produces fairly good Chinese food, devoid of the imaginative spicing one might wish for and geared more toward timid palates than to those who like authentically socko seasonings.

The restaurant is fairly crowded and the service is definitely of the slam-bam school. Seeing a group of six people reading through menus, a captain rushed over and said, "Why don't I just bring you assorted appetizers?" perhaps hoping that would speed things up. At peak hours, empty glasses are rarely removed from tables and dishes are practically thrown in front of guests.

And though all ingredients seem to be of high quality and the cooking is careful, flavors are bland and vary little from one dish to another. On all visits I did everything but beg for food that was really hotly spiced; only once did a dish even begin to approach that state. The most the captain would do was to bring a small dish of red chili oil so I could mix it in myself. But oil added without being cooked can never be evenly distributed through solid food and its sauce, and the results were far from satisfactory.

Other than this failing, much of the food is fresh and pleasant. Tenderly braised, honey-glazed spareribs had a delicate undertone of garlic, and rolled bean curd filled with vegetables and topped with coriander was an enticing appetizer. A vegetable package of diced mushrooms and bean curd rolled in lettuce leaves would have been also, but the lettuce leaves were withered and brown-edged. Hacked chicken was downright sweet, and each time I asked to have it more hotly spiced it came back redder and sweeter. Sweet was also the word

65

for the sweet and sour cabbage Hunan style, and spring roll home style oozed overheated grease.

There was a delicate, lovely snow-white sliced fish soup — a clear broth with lots of fish and airy puffs of poached egg white. All bean curd, meat and vegetables in the hot and sour soup were sprightly and well cooked, but again, all was sour without a trace of hotness.

Firm, snowy, giant sautéed shrimp more or less Cantonese style were perfectly cooked, as was the whole sea bass Hunan style with the one really pungent brown sauce I managed to get from the kitchen. The fish was crisply fried, then braised in the sharp sauce. Boneless frogs' legs were also very good if one could forget that they were supposed to be hot, and the steak with sautéed scallops and vegetables was thoroughly satisfying. So was satiny eggplant melted into a garlicky sauce and the golden, soft, pan-fried noodles tossed with bamboo shoots, pea pods, mushrooms and pork.

Dishes that were acceptable if unexciting included Mandarin double crown (lobster and chicken in separate sauces), beef with orange flavor, sliced lamb Hunan style, bean curd Szechuan style and twice-cooked sliced pork. An order of deep-fried sesame banana fritters was redolent of overheated or overused oil. Fresh pineapple proved a far more acceptable alternative.

Christ Cella
★ ★

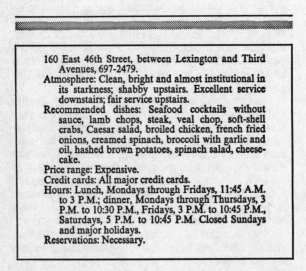

160 East 46th Street, between Lexington and Third Avenues, 697-2479.

Atmosphere: Clean, bright and almost institutional in its starkness; shabby upstairs. Excellent service downstairs; fair service upstairs.

Recommended dishes: Seafood cocktails without sauce, lamb chops, steak, veal chop, soft-shell crabs, Caesar salad, broiled chicken, french fried onions, creamed spinach, broccoli with garlic and oil, hashed brown potatoes, spinach salad, cheesecake.

Price range: Expensive.

Credit cards: All major credit cards.

Hours: Lunch, Mondays through Fridays, 11:45 A.M. to 3 P.M.; dinner, Mondays through Thursdays, 3 P.M. to 10:30 P.M., Fridays, 3 P.M. to 10:45 P.M., Saturdays, 5 P.M. to 10:45 P.M. Closed Sundays and major holidays.

Reservations: Necessary.

No type of cooking leaves less margin for error than that done in a typical steakhouse. The quality of the ingredients and the skill with which they are prepared cannot be corrected or disguised by spiced-up sauces and attention-distracting garnishes. With such stringent requirements it is not too surprising that there are very few truly first-rate restaurants for broiled steaks, chops, fish and the variety of potatoes, onions and salads that make the classic menu. Of these, certainly one of the better is Christ Cella, a steakhouse that has enjoyed a completely justifiable reputation for excellence since 1926.

Considering the high quality of both service and food and the lofty prices, it is difficult to understand the décor, so barren and sparse with its gloomy indirect lighting and bare wood floors. One might almost suspect a kind of reverse snobbism operates — a sort of "less is more" philosophy that works to the detriment of the dining experience.

This is one of several expensive New York restaurants that offer no menus. Waiters call off choices, and as for the prices, well, as J. P. Morgan is supposed to have said on the purchase of a yacht, "If you have to ask the price, you can't afford it."

Shellfish appetizers are superb, whether you order the big, firm shrimp and snowy lump crab meat or the expensive half lobster out of its shell, but ask for cocktail sauce on the side if you want it, or the seafood will be ruined. Sirloin steaks at Christ Cella have good beefy flavor, tender but with just enough texture to let you know you're eating meat instead of tenderized mash. Filet mignon is also excellent. Lamb chops are above average, although they are fatty and sometimes muttony, but broiled veal chops are impeccable. Sautéed calf's liver with greasy pan-sautéed onions was lumpy and made up of small, vein-toughened slices. Broiled half chicken and crispy sautéed, tiny soft-shell crabs are usually good.

Paprika overpowers and dries the broiled bay scallops, fresh fillet of sole, swordfish and red snapper that was far from fresh at lunch one Monday. The big disappointment was lobster, for the lobster itself was not so large as it should have been at that price, although it was well broiled.

An advantage of eating lobster at Christ Cella is that the waiter picks out all the meat, claws included, so all the diner has to do is swirl each forkful in a pool of hot golden butter and swallow it down — surely the height of luxury.

Hashed brown potatoes were properly done one night, but on another were burned black outside although remaining cold within, and cottage-fried potatoes were on all tries limp and greasy. Baked potatoes were perfection, but an order of leaf spinach was not quite so good as creamed spinach. Fresh, firm broccoli sprinkled with olive oil and flecks of lightly browned garlic was delicious. Both Caesar salad and spinach salad were sprightly and properly dressed.

Bread at Christ Cella borders on the disgraceful, considering the quality of the other food served, the prices and the availability of better choices.

The napoleon, with its layers of flaky puff pastry and its whipped cream filling, is now often soggy or too sugary sweet. The cheesecake is made by S & S, the same bakery that supplies many other steak restaurants in the city and, as always, strikes just the right combination of creaminess and grainy solidity.

Perfect strawberries and melon, and lemon sherbet

that is much too sweet and not nearly acidic enough complete the dessert choices. There is a fair wine list, some good imported beer and excellent coffee, always served steaming hot.

If Christ Cella rates only two stars, it is because cooking is uneven although prices continue to climb.

Claude's
★

205 East 81st Street, 472-0487.
Atmosphere: Gleaming and stylish mirrored Art Deco setting; chairs are uncomfortable. Service is polite and friendly but painfully slow.
Recommended dishes: Lobster, shrimp, crabmeat and mussel salad, pastry shells with snails, hearts of palm salad, fish soup, oysters with snail butter, poached fillet of Dover sole, grilled red snapper, mousse of pike with bay scallops, quail, filet of beef with madeira sauce, apple tart, fruit sherbets, fresh fruits.
Price range: Expensive.
Credit cards: All major cards.
Hours: Dinner, Mondays through Saturdays, 6 P.M. to 10:45 P.M. Closed Sundays.
Reservations: Necessary.

Claude Baills, the owner of Claude's, is undoubtedly a talented chef. But his basic skill has been compromised time and again by what appears to be an inability to organize a kitchen. When he opened this polished little Art Deco restaurant, it seemed that he had finally mastered the organization of the kitchen and had corrected the agonizingly slow service that discouraged diners at the Palace and at the earlier Claude's on Lexington Avenue. In addition, the food he turned out when he opened on 81st Street was excellent — meriting three stars.

Subsequent visits indicate, however, that one star is more appropriate. The wait between courses has become painfully long, so much so that one loses the thread of the meal, and much of the food proves unworthy of the wait or the high price.

Appetizers and some fish courses have held up much better than meat and poultry main courses. Except for some moistly tender quail and a rose-red filet of beef in a rich madeira sauce, meat dishes were disappointing. Rack of lamb arrived encased in a soggy crust, the meat's delicate flavor overpowered by a bitter concentration of herbs. Diced loin of veal with sweetbreads had the greasy overtones of bad Chinese cooking, and greaseless, flavorful duck was overpowered by stingingly salty cèpes.

Some of Claude's artistry showed through in the grilled red snapper mellowed by a marrow-laden sauce and in the poached Dover sole in a cream and butter sauce brightened with shallots, lemon and green herbs. A chardonnay-accented beurre blanc sauce was satiny and fragrant, but the meat of the Maine lobsters served with it was inexplicably hard, to the point of being hard to cut. Mousse of pike and bay scallops with both a sorrel and a lobster sauce was garnished with beautiful vegetables and wedges of potato pancake and could not be faulted, but when we asked if two could share this as an appetizer, some of the management's intransigence became obvious. The captain insisted that the dish could not be shared, although it easily could have been, and when we ordered two as appetizers, they arrived fully garnished with potatoes and vegetables. It would have been easy to leave off such garnishes, knowing that main courses would follow.

Among the better appetizers were the peppery, garlic-laden fish soup of Provence, the artfully arranged salad of hearts of palm, bibb lettuce and endive or the oysters lightly baked with shallot-flavored snail butter. Snails in a garlic cream sauce were held in a packet of flaky puff pastry and the assortment of impeccably fresh and cool lobster, shrimp, crab meat and mussel salad could have served as a satisfying main course. The only near misses among first courses were the artichoke with morels, the flavor of the wild mushrooms conflicting with that of the artichokes, and the pallid vegetable soup baked under a dome of pastry.

There is a fine array of cheeses in top condition accompanied by a well-made green salad, but the only exceptional desserts were the fruit sorbets, the exquisite cut fresh fruits and the apple tart.

The Coach House

★ ★ ★ ★

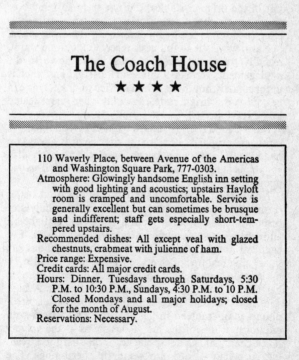

110 Waverly Place, between Avenue of the Americas and Washington Square Park, 777-0303.
Atmosphere: Glowingly handsome English inn setting with good lighting and acoustics; upstairs Hayloft room is cramped and uncomfortable. Service is generally excellent but can sometimes be brusque and indifferent; staff gets especially short-tempered upstairs.
Recommended dishes: All except veal with glazed chestnuts, crabmeat with julienne of ham.
Price range: Expensive.
Credit cards: All major credit cards.
Hours: Dinner, Tuesdays through Saturdays, 5:30 P.M. to 10:30 P.M., Sundays, 4:30 P.M. to 10 P.M. Closed Mondays and all major holidays; closed for the month of August.
Reservations: Necessary.

The most difficult and enviable creation of all is a restaurant with a style so completely its own that its dishes and menus cannot be compared to those of competitors.

The Coach House in Greenwich Village is exactly such a restaurant. An immaculate and stunning establishment, it is a day-in, day-out tribute to the tireless and skilled efforts of Leon Lianides, who has operated here for more than thirty years. The menu and cooking style can best be described as contemporary, exactly suited to its time and place. And, like the best of new creations, its techniques of cookery and combinations of dishes are drawn from the best the past has to offer.

But rather than rely on the past alone, Mr. Lianides has developed a repertory of dishes that reflects the world crossroads that New York is and the period in which we live. The best American products and dishes, such as prime beef, corn sticks and Maryland crab meat, are in perfect harmony with such European classics as veal piccate à la Française, quiche Lorraine, gazpacho or steak au poivre. What may well be the world's mellowest crunchy Mississippi pecan pie does not seem out of place alongside an equally exceptional Grand Marnier Bavaroise. Above all, it is the consistency of excellence that makes this restaurant worth four stars.

Even the setting combines traditional principles with a totally contemporary look. Built over 140 years ago as a coach house for the Wanamaker estates, the small, comfortable dining room with its brick walls and warm, red-painted trim, collection of fine nineteenth-century English oil paintings (many with food or hunting themes), the gorgeous fresh floral bouquets and the perfect level of lighting has the look of an English country inn.

One cannot help wishing that there were more room at (and between) banquette tables, or that being seated in the semibalcony called the Hayloft (actually the hayloft in the original stables) did not seem so remote or cramped, but that merely suggests that being extraordinary does not mean being perfect. By the same token, one also wishes that all guests received the same warm, friendly treatment accorded those well known to the management; from a number of observations, that is unfortunately not the case and service to unknowns can be cool or downright rude, especially when one is seated in the Hayloft.

But the food itself is, almost without exception, above reproach, primarily because the proprietor is always on hand, and because he knows exactly how each dish should be prepared and could do it himself if called upon.

Nowhere in or around the city will you find better fresh mushrooms à la grecque, whole or large halves of firm, white mushrooms soothingly bathed in light oil and lemon juice, perfumed with oregano and dill. The eggplant Provençale, another appetizer, combines the interesting textures of celery, currants and pignoli nuts, all dressed with a light tomato-olive oil combination, heightened by the flavors of onions and garlic. A high and fluffy quiche that is nothing short of inspired, plump snails sautéed in garlic butter and served with croutons, or one of the marvelous soups — the velvety black bean that is a house classic, or the sharply refreshing gazpacho — are also wonderful beginnings. The pâté maison is perhaps the most skippable of the lot. If crab cakes are offered, they are not to be missed —

high, puffy, gently crisp and lightly touched with mustard and lemon.

If duck is on the menu and if you like yours crisp, this will be the main course to select. The skin is always parchment thin and crisp, the meat moist and tender. Order it with cherry sauce if you do not mind sweetness, but green peppercorn sauce is to one palate, at least, a more sublimely sophisticated alternative. Tender, thickly cut prime ribs of beef, a delicate rack of lamb (available even in a single portion) and whole striped bass roasted and then graced with a fresh creamy dill sauce are just a few of the more irresistible choices. If soft-shell crabs sautéed in butter and lemon are available, that ends the problem for me every time.

The only fault to be found with the steak au poivre is that it is too large and too good, and the giant, triple-loin lamb chop is poetic, but only if you like lamb rare to pink; it simply becomes too dry if ordered well done.

The only main courses about which one might have reservations are the mignonettes of veal with glazed chestnuts, because the finished dish is too sweet, the lump crab meat sautéed with ham, because the ham in the cooking can become stingingly salty, and the chicken livers sautéed with mushrooms in Madeira, because the livers are sometimes served underdone.

Crisp fresh corn sticks or crusty Italian bread, well-made green salad or — upon request — a Greek salad accented with tiny black Niçoise olives and feta cheese, perfect dry and snowy baked potatoes or crisp-crusted butter-glossed potatoes Anna and fluffy white rice, each grain firmly separate from the others, are among the standard main course accompaniments.

As if all this weren't enough, there are the truly fabulous homemade desserts, many of which are set out on a table at the entrance, fair warning to pace yourself so you make it to the glorious windup.

Thin, crunchy hazlenut meringue and mocha buttercream make up the dacquoise. Dark, bittersweet chocolate with a fudgey, mousse-like texture comprises the house chocolate cake, and chunks of toasted bread set in an egg-rich custard combine for the inspired bread pudding, served with a purée of raspberries. It would be difficult to improve on any of the fruit tarts, most especially the blueberry tart and the apple tarte Tatin.

With the same careful study and concentration as he plans recipes and menus, Mr. Lianides makes up his wine list, with an encouragingly large number of fairly reasonable selections.

Copenhagen
Poor

68 West 58th Street, between Fifth Avenue and Avenue of the Americas, 688-3690.

Atmosphere: Dingy and tacky bar and dining room, noisy and cramped; service is sometimes good but often pushy and careless.

Recommended dishes: None.

Price range: Moderate.

Credit cards. All major credit cards.

Hours: Lunch, Mondays through Fridays, noon to 3 P.M., Saturdays, noon to 4 P.M.; dinner, Mondays through Fridays, 5 to 11 P.M., Saturdays, 4 to 11 P.M. Closed Sundays and major holidays.

Reservations: Recommended, especially for lunch.

Twenty-five years ago, New York had about half a dozen excellent Scandinavian restaurants offering the cuisines of Denmark, Sweden, Finland and Norway. Now only a few marginal Norwegian restaurants exist in the Bay Ridge section of Brooklyn, and Copenhagen is the sole survivor in Manhattan. Once an excellent and glowingly handsome restaurant on East 52nd Street, it moved some years ago to its present location and began a slow but steady decline. Now the food is as tacky and depressing as the seedy brown and yellow dining room that is much in need of sprucing up.

Much the same can be said for the kitchen's efforts, for food from both the smorgasbord cold table and the menu has all of the appeal of cafeteria steamtable fare. Salads on the cold table might have been ordered in from a corner deli, so overloaded were they with celery and acrid mayonnaise. Chicken in what tasted like commercially sweet barbecue sauce could hardly be considered Danish at all, and just about all ingredients on that table were second- and third-rate. Tuna fish salad was fifth-rate.

This will be especially disappointing to anyone who loves the fresh, clean, immaculately prepared country food that Denmark is justly famous for. Things were not the least bit better when four of us ordered from the menu, a feat accomplished even though the waiter tried to tout us onto the cold table because, he said, all orders from "downstairs" — the kitchen — would take at least twenty-five minutes. All were served in about fifteen, a small wonder considering that they seemed to have been cooked long ago and were barely reheated.

Gray, dry gravlax lacked the moist coral luster and fresh dill flavor that the cured salmon specialty should have, and the mustard sauce tasted like spiced cream. Unusually dark and lusty liver pâté could have been commercial liverwurst, and mustard herring lacked pungency. Chopped ham topped with a raw egg yolk proved the only mildly interesting first course.

Good Danish pumpernickel and crisp bread and cold Carlsberg beer were the only things that sustained us

72

when the poached chicken with horseradish cream sauce proved disastrous and tepid. Greasy duck seemed barely edible. Chicken was stale and its sauce had a floury pastiness and almost no hint of horseradish. The Danish pork and potato sausage, medisterpolse, a daily special, had obviously been cooked hours before and left to dry out. Only the fried meat cakes, frikadeller, could be considered decent, as was the red cabbage served with them. There was virtually no sugar glaze on the "sugar-browned" potatoes and if the string beans were not canned, they might as well have been.

Desserts such as the cold lemon soufflé pudding, citronfromage, and the apple crumb cake were a cut above other courses. Not so the chocolate mousse and the strawberry trifle.

Cottonwood Cafe

★

---

415 Bleecker Street, between Bank and 11th Streets, 924-6271.

Atmosphere: Casual and lively cafe with a young, friendly and accommodating staff.

Recommended dishes: Cheese and broccoli soup, fried chicken livers, nachos, chili, baked barbecued chicken, pork chops, burritos, cheese enchiladas, fried okra, cornbread, chili cheese omelet, buttermilk biscuits, pecan pie.

Price range: Inexpensive.

Credit cards: None.

Hours: Dinner, seven days, 5 P.M. to 11:30 P.M.; brunch, Saturdays and Sundays, 10 A.M. to 3 P.M. Closed on major holidays.

Reservations: Not accepted.

In the beginning, there was Texas music, progressive country-western sounds as represented by Willie Nelson, David Allen Coe and Waylon Jennings. Then came the television soap opera "Dallas," closely followed by the popularity of Texas clothing — studded jeans, embossed leather boots and J. R. Ewing Stetsons. Inevitably, Texas food has come north, in all of its earthy, countrified simplicity.

One of the more colorful and lively places offering the limited but entertaining range of Texas dishes is the Cottonwood Cafe in Greenwich Village. The style here is so laid back that you'll feel overdressed in anything more elaborate than a cotton shirt and jeans, but after one of the huge and marvelous frozen tequila and lime juice margaritas, you would be likely to feel at home in anything, even white tie and tails.

Barbecued beef and pork and fried chicken are the only missing elements on this typical Texas menu, along with some of the hefty spices that would make this fare more authentic. Recently added barecued ribs are disappointing and overpriced. Nevertheless, there are well-prepared Tex-Mex specialties, including appetizers such as the mild and soothing cheese and broccoli soup and nachos, the taco chips baked with a topping of mashed, refried black beans, cheese and a slice of jalapeño pepper, here a little milder than it should be. Chili with beans and plenty of beef is good if sometimes tepid, a flaw corrected upon request. Only the bland and overly slick guacamole was a disappointment among first courses, but it is hard to imagine that anyone would not love the large and tender, crisply fried chicken livers.

Several dashes of pepper improve both the livers and the cream gravy served on the side, although that floury pan sauce takes considerable getting used to at best. It appears on the mediocre chicken, fried steak and excellent mashed potatoes. To be safe, ask for it on the side. Large, thin, broiled pork chops made a delicious main course, as did the huge half of baked barbecued chicken in a sweet-sour sauce. Cheese enchiladas proved more successful than those filled with chicken, and the burritos made with wheat tortillas enfolding chili were lusty and satisfying. Pallid huevos rancheros, on the weekend brunch menu, are made here with scrambled eggs in tomato and pepper sauce instead of with the fried eggs that the dish should be based on. Better to try the chili cheese omelet or fried eggs with buttermilk biscuits and creamy, buttery grits.

The best side dishes are hot cornbread, refried beans, fried okra, pinto beans and black-eyed peas that are improved with a little seasoning. Skip the iceberg lettuce and American cheese salad, but save room for the wonderfully dark and rich warm pecan pie with a crisp and flavorful crust.

There is Tecate beer, and, after 10 P.M., there is entertainment — music or a standup comic. The Cottonwood's staff is refreshingly friendly and accommodating.

Csarda
★ ★

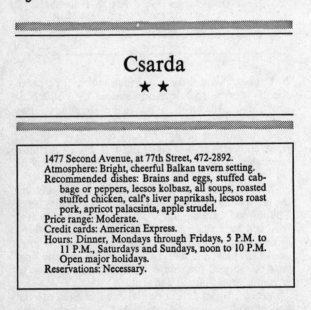

1477 Second Avenue, at 77th Street, 472-2892.
Atmosphere: Bright, cheerful Balkan tavern setting.
Recommended dishes: Brains and eggs, stuffed cabbage or peppers, lecsos kolbasz, all soups, roasted stuffed chicken, calf's liver paprikash, lecsos roast pork, apricot palacsinta, apple strudel.
Price range: Moderate.
Credit cards: American Express.
Hours: Dinner, Mondays through Fridays, 5 P.M. to 11 P.M., Saturdays and Sundays, noon to 10 P.M. Open major holidays.
Reservations: Necessary.

This trim, spotless and moderately priced Hungarian restaurant is typically Mittel-Europa. The rough, white-plaster walls are hung with colorful, geometrically patterned rugs, glazed earthenware and garlands of dried red peppers. The back bar gleams, hanging plants are at the windows, and red-and-white tablecloths and dark wood tavern chairs add to the comfortable aspect of the place. So do the friendly, helpful and concerned waitresses. This is, in fact, very much a cuisine de femme, with women doing all the cooking, among them Elizabeth Donas, the owner.

The food is hearty, warmly fragrant with sweet paprika, garlic and meltingly tender onions. Portions are large enough to be shared, and this may be done with all main courses for a small extra charge.

Appetizers are unusually good, whether you opt for the stuffed peppers filled with rice and meat in a slightly sweet-sour tomato sauce, the same meat filling in stuffed cabbage dressed with a piquant paprika sauce, the lecsos kolbasz (a sort of stew of sliced garlic sausage, green peppers and onions in a very pungent paprika sauce) or the gently sautéed brains, eggs and onions. This last is good served as a main course.

Soups make less expensive but no less satisfying starters. If the daily special is the giblet soup (chicken giblets with mushrooms and vegetables in a sort of goulash-type broth), don't bypass it.

Crisp cucumber salad, just a shade too sweet, is served to everyone, as is a basketful of dark and light bread and toasted rolls, all of which are only fair.

Main courses tend to come out of the kitchen in better shape on busy days than on slow ones. On a crowded Mother's Day, all was fresh, flavorful perfection. There was an exceptional roasted stuffed chicken with a thyme-flavored bread stuffing layered between the crisp chicken skin and the tender white and dark meat, thereby imparting its flavor to both.

Veal flecken, small steaks of veal with sautéed mushrooms and onions and topped with cheese, were good, although they would have been better had the cheese not been processed American. Duck was crisp and greaseless, with moist, tender meat, as was a roasted veal shank. Home-fried potatoes were delicious. An à la carte order of truly inspired fried onion rings was as beautiful as spun glass and much kinder to the palate.

On the next night, a deserted, rainy Monday, the duck and veal shank were so stiff and dry they might have been reheated leftovers from the previous day. But even then, the paprika-sauced calf's liver with buttery nockerl (a cross between a noodle and a dumpling) was a satisfying main course, and the appetizers were as good as they were on Sunday. On a busier Tuesday, all was near perfect.

All paprikash dishes, whether of veal, chicken or chicken livers, were fresh and delicate. The lecsos roast pork in a paprika-bright gravy and the chicken in the pot with noodles were excellent buys.

The only real disappointment was the dish I expected the most of, the erdelyi fatanyeros, a towering pyramid of a mixed grill that included grilled pork chops, knockwurst, bacon, breaded veal schnitzel and breaded livers, all inexcusably dry and tasteless.

The thin crepes, or palacsinta, filled with tart apricot preserves and topped with ground walnuts, were better than the version blanketed with what tasted like Hershey's syrup. Strudel — cheese, cherry or apple — was flaky and seemed to be homemade. The warm apple was best. All desserts are also large enough to be split between two.

There are some pleasant Hungarian red wines here, especially the Egri Bikaver and the Hajosi Cabernet.

Curtain Up!
Fair

402 West 43rd Street, at Ninth Avenue, 564-7272.
Atmosphere: Attractive cafe setting with convivial bar. Housekeeping is poor; service is careless and slow though polite.
Recommended dishes: Tomato egg-drop soup, chili, mushrooms in beer batter, omelets, hamburgers, eggs with bacon or sausages, chicken salad or tuna fish salad.
Price range: Inexpensive.
Credit cards: All major credit cards.
Hours: Brunch or lunch, seven days, noon to 5 P.M.; dinner, Sundays and Mondays, 5 P.M. to midnight, Tuesdays through Thursdays, 5 P.M. to 1 A.M., Fridays and Saturdays, 5 P.M. to 2 A.M.
Reservations: Recommended.

Curtain Up! has proved to be a disappointment at Manhattan Plaza, which is too bad because it is smartly and trimly decorated with theater posters and an attractive bar. Housekeeping is careless and service is lackadaisical. Nevertheless, it has become a sort of junior-grade Sardi's, attracting young hopefuls and newly established theater personalities.

With only a few exceptions, food is at the average coffe-shop level. The best choices included decent hamburgers served on toasted English muffins, slightly greasy but hardy and spicy chili, and acceptable omelets and egg dishes at brunch. Mushrooms fried in crisp beer batter served with a sharp mustard sauce made a good appetizer large enough to be shared by two. Chicken salad and tuna fish salad are also acceptable, although they are banally garnished with iceberg lettuce, canned California black olives and hard-cooked eggs that had gray-rimmed yolks, indicating they were overcooked. But tomato egg-drop soup with scallions was surprisingly good and seemed to include a chicken-broth base. Crab bisque, though far from the classic elegant preparation, was also soothing and satisfying.

Quiches invariably had nearly raw crusts, fish was very poorly prepared and steak was tough and stringy one night and half spoiled another time at lunch. Steak teriyaki and roast loin of pork were equally discouraging.

Lavish-looking cakes are displayed at the entrance, but the only moderately interesting one is the carrot cake, and even that would be better without its cloyingly sweet frosting. If one sticks to the recommended dishes, a light meal before or after theater can be minimally satisfying.

Darjeeling
★

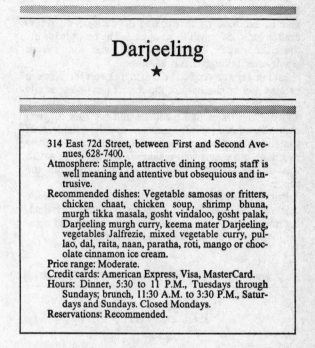

314 East 72d Street, between First and Second Avenues, 628-7400.
Atmosphere: Simple, attractive dining rooms; staff is well meaning and attentive but obsequious and intrusive.
Recommended dishes: Vegetable samosas or fritters, chicken chaat, chicken soup, shrimp bhuna, murgh tikka masala, gosht vindaloo, gosht palak, Darjeeling murgh curry, keema mater Darjeeling, vegetables Jalfrezie, mixed vegetable curry, pullao, dal, raita, naan, paratha, roti, mango or chocolate cinnamon ice cream.
Price range: Moderate.
Credit cards: American Express, Visa, MasterCard.
Hours: Dinner, 5:30 to 11 P.M., Tuesdays through Sundays; brunch, 11:30 A.M. to 3:30 P.M., Saturdays and Sundays. Closed Mondays.
Reservations: Recommended.

Billed as the home of Indian nouvelle cuisine, Darjeeling serves traditional, carefully prepared food from various parts of India with standard if above-average presentations of tandoori grilled meats and fish, spicy curries and intriguing breads. What nouvelle means here is a secret shared only by the owners.

Offering a pleasant option for dinner in this neighborhood, Darjeeling has savory appetizers such as the deep-fried vegetable fritters, the dried-pea-and-potato-filled samosas, and chicken chaat, a salad fired with seasonings of green chili peppers and mint. Giveaway appetizers include the crackling chickpea flour wafers called pappadum and fried vermicelli of chickpea flour, all to be dipped into minted yogurt. Among soups, the chicken with yogurt proved better than the milky, bland lentil soup.

The most disappointing category here is the tandoori grilled chicken, lamb and seafood. All were dry and salty even though they arrived most appetizingly on sizzling platters. Far better choices were the shrimp bhuna in a green herb spice sauce and the murgh tikka masala, nuggets of tender chicken swathed in a pink cream sauce with curry spices, garlic and chili peppers. Lovers of fiery seasonings should try the gosht vindaloo — moist chunks of lamb in a breathtaking blaze of spices, modified by the rice pullao with peas, the cool yogurt sauce, raita, and the stewed lentils, dal.

The milder but no less enticing gosht palak — lamb stewed with spinach — and the special Darjeeling murgh curry, chicken with onions and mellow herbs, were equally good. Keema mater Darjeeling was a satisfying combination of lamb with peas and herbs. Fish in curries were stale and innocuous. Whether as main courses or side dishes, mixed vegetable curry and the spicier vegetables Jalfrezie are well worth ordering.

It is the counterpoints of sauces and condiments — hot and cool, spicy and subtle, sharp and gentle — that give Indian food its charm, and the delicate, crisp layered breads add much to its appeal. The best breads are the naan, much like pizza dough, and the layered whole-wheat dough that is paratha.

Indian desserts tend to be cloyingly sweet for Western palates. Better choices are the ice creams — especially the mango and chocolate cinnamon flavors. Pistachio with saffron tastes like medicine and the rose suggests cheap soap. A generally pleasant and hospitable staff sometimes becomes obsequious to the point of embarrassment, but seems well meaning. Any hint that a dish was unsatisfactory resulted in its removal from the check.

Prices are uneven — moderate for dishes such as the chicken tikka masala, the gosht palak and the Darjeeling murgh curry, but exorbitant for the tough and meager lobster and the rubbery tandoori shrimp.

Da Silvano
★ ★

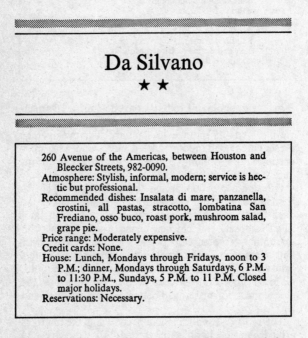

260 Avenue of the Americas, between Houston and Bleecker Streets, 982-0090.
Atmosphere: Stylish, informal, modern; service is hectic but professional.
Recommended dishes: Insalata di mare, panzanella, crostini, all pastas, stracotto, lombatina San Frediano, osso buco, roast pork, mushroom salad, grape pie.
Price range: Moderately expensive.
Credit cards: None.
House: Lunch, Mondays through Fridays, noon to 3 P.M.; dinner, Mondays through Saturdays, 6 P.M. to 11:30 P.M., Sundays, 5 P.M. to 11 P.M. Closed major holidays.
Reservations: Necessary.

Considering how much status is now being accorded to the food of northern Italy, it is surprising how narrow a range of that region's specialities is represented on local menus. Even restaurants that firmly declare themselves northern Italian seem to arrive at the same set of dishes that usually begins and ends with fettucine al pesto, Alfredo and Bolognese, perhaps a risotto, a few veal scaloppine variations, Florentine beefsteak and some sort of chicken preparation with white wine sauce.

Few such restaurants, if any, present so interesting a collection of northern Italian fare as one finds at Da Silvano, a smartly trim Greenwich Village store-front restaurant recently expanded to more than double its original size, into a handsome adjoining room. A natural rose-brick wall sets off white tablecloths, flowers, hanging white metal lampshades, green plants and a sparkling little service bar where drinks or espresso are dispensed. The young, friendly Italian waiters are as handsome as the place itself, and proud enough of their establishment to take time to explain the unusual kitchen offerings. In addition to the daily specials described by the waiters, there is a blackboard menu, unfortunately, almost illegible.

Cold artichokes with a pungent oil dressing and lightly grilled, but often soggy, breaded scampi are the more conventional appetizers. Far more interesting is the crostini, a spread of chicken livers, capers and anchovies on Italian bread, which is delicious but would be even more so if served at room temperature instead of chilled.

Panzanella, a tangy salad of roasted peppers, cut tomatoes, cucumbers and onions seasoned with garlic-and-oil-soaked bread croutons, is a refreshing hors d'oeuvre, and the insalata di mare, a cold combination of sliced squid and sea-fresh mussels in a garlic-parsley dressing, was so good one might be tempted to order seconds and forget the rest of the meal. Smoked mozzarella was delicious but not recommended with the mushy tomatoes accompanying it.

Pastas are exceptional. Try the short, quill-cut penne in a thick but delicate Bolognese sauce; petite tortellini with a spicy meat filling in a flourless sauce comprising butter, cheese and sweet cream that had been allowed to reduce in the pan, and spaghettini puttanesca, the almost threadlike pasta in a sauce of tomatoes, garlic, salty black olives, capers and anchovies. This last was an intriguing and complex combination of ingredients, considering that its name, puttanesca, means streetwalker-style and refers to a sauce simple enough for a busy working girl to make.

At times there is a wonderful combination of duck livers and tagliarini. The cannelloni were far removed from the usual presentation — filled with spinach and cheese, then baked to near-golden crispness without any sauce whatever.

It's hard to remember a better osso buco than the plat du jour presented here, the thick cut of veal knuckle gently simmered to a lean and melting tenderness with garlic, onions, white wine and carrots, all heaped on perfectly cooked rice. The missing gremolada blend of lemon, garlic and minced parsley would have added a clarifying astringent touch, but the osso buco was otherwise flawless.

So was the lombatina San Frediano, a sautéed veal chop with chicken livers, white wine, tomatoes and peas. Stracotto, the beef pot roast simmered almost imperceptibly for hours until it virtually melts at the touch of a fork, was also done well, although some rice or polenta would have been a welcome blotter for the rich gravy.

Less satisfactory main courses included a tough and fatty shell steak in a greasy pizzaiuola sauce, a bland beefsteak Fiorentina and pollo ubriaco, "drunken" chicken that was poached to moist and tender perfection in beer but lacked any distinctive seasoning. Game birds are well cooked but masked in overly complex sauces. Not so the fine pork roast with rosemary.

A salad of watercress and freshly sliced raw mushrooms was good enough to serve as an appetizer, and each main course came with chunks of roasted, rosemary-scented potatoes and bright zucchini.

Desserts were fair, including an interesting grape pie topped with whipped cream that did not seem quite real, and a chocolate mousse a bit too much like butter cream. Espresso, strong without any trace of bitterness, was several cuts above the usual variety presented in local restaurants.

David K's
Fair

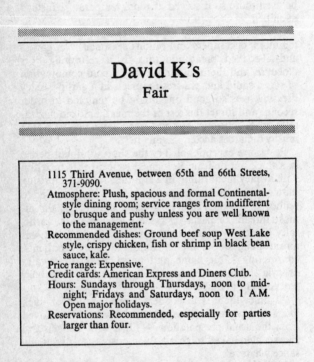

1115 Third Avenue, between 65th and 66th Streets, 371-9090.
Atmosphere: Plush, spacious and formal Continental-style dining room; service ranges from indifferent to brusque and pushy unless you are well known to the management.
Recommended dishes: Ground beef soup West Lake style, crispy chicken, fish or shrimp in black bean sauce, kale.
Price range: Expensive.
Credit cards: American Express and Diners Club.
Hours: Sundays through Thursdays, noon to midnight; Fridays and Saturdays, noon to 1 A.M. Open major holidays.
Reservations: Recommended, especially for parties larger than four.

The darling of the food establishment, this restaurant has proved nothing but a disappointment to me since it opened as Chung Kuo Yuan in 1976. I have no doubt that the kitchen can produce exceptional dishes when it is known that the customers are James Beard or Danny Kaye. But I also know that, unrecognized, I have had at least a dozen totally lackluster meals here, undistinguished except for the most exceptional prices. Now that I am recognized, food is just passable. In 1982 a seafood room opened here and was given a one-star rating, for some of the dishes were delicate and satisfying. That room has since closed.

My most memorable experience here occurred several years ago, on a jam-packed Saturday night, when Danny Kaye was hosting a large group that got all of the attention of the dining-room staff. At our table for four, white wine was poured into water glasses, right to the brim, and when we asked for wineglasses, the waiter said he would see if they had any. Finally he arrived with them, and from a second bottle again poured right to the brim, topping the drink in the manner of the most accomplished bartenders. The usually excellent little dumplings had savory fillings but pasty dough, and bean curd sheet, fried into vegetable pie, was hard and fishy and the crepe in which it was wrapped was mushy and half disintegrated.

Peking duck, always available, came as brittle, glassy skin, obviously stale, and the meat of the duck, served as a separate course, did not seem to be duck at all, but rather ropy beef. Lobster in a sauce that was supposed to be spicy was bland, and beef with broccoli was slightly spoiled. Food was automatically dished out with no question asked about our wanting it in the traditional Chinese family style in the center of the table.

Not even the gorgeous floral arrangements and the sparkling Rosenthal china and silver can make up for such food and service, but it is so popular and so intensely hyped by devotees, it seemed remiss not to report on my experiences.

More recently, when I was recognized, service was attentive but food at best was mediocre. Steamed dumplings were greasy and looked as though they had been reheated, and the tiny egg rolls oozed rancid oil. One of the better dishes was the gently soothing ground beef soup, West Lake style, and there was also a deliciously moist and crispy chicken served with a spicy salt dip.

Jade coral jumbo shrimp proved to be a silly contortion of something like watercress stems pulled through the shrimp, which were filmy with heavy oil. In the past, consistently good dishes have been the various fish preparations in black bean sauce and kale done in intersting ways. On the new menu it is prepared with oyster sauce. Yang chow fried rice was another dish acrid with stale oil.

Délices La Côte Basque
at Olympic Tower

★

1 Olympic Tower, 51st Street and Fifth Avenue, 935-2220.

Atmosphere: Lobby-level cafe is bright and pleasant and looks out on waterfall; downstairs restaurant La Cascade is stylish, modern and comfortable and focuses on waterfall beyond glass. Service is uneven — sometimes friendly, other times rude, slow and confused.

Recommended dishes: Le Cafe: Consommé, cheese omelet, eggs Benedict, quiche Lorraine, ice cream and pastry desserts. La Cascade: consommé, salade Parisienne, poached egg in aspic, snails, smoked salmon and trout, sausage in crust, stuffed baby salmon, chicken with morels, steak au poivre, rack of lamb, tenderloin of beef with marrow, chicken in puff pastry with morels, broiled striped bass with mustard sauce, pastry and ice cream.

Price range: Expensive.

Credit cards: American Express, Diners Club and Carte Blanche.

Hours: Le Cafe: Breakfast, lunch, cocktails, Mondays through Fridays, 8 A.M. to 10:30 P.M.; Saturdays, 9 A.M. to 8 P.M. Closed Sundays and major holidays. La Cascade: Lunch, Mondays through Fridays, 6 P.M. to 10:30 P.M. Closed Saturdays, Sundays and major holidays.

Reservations: Not accepted at Le Cafe; necessary at La Cascade.

One of the most original and inviting new restaurants to open in New York in quite a while is Délices La Côte Basque at Olympic Tower, the handsome black glass building on Fifth Avenue with a thoroughfare lobby running from 51st to 52nd Street. A modern version of the covered-street concept that inspired Milan's Galleria, the Olympic Tower setting is enhanced by a monumental waterfall and tall boxed trees. On the street level, Délices operates a retail pastry shop, a convivial bar and Le Cafe, a terrace area with bright tablecloths and an attractive menu offering breakfast, light lunches and snacks.

Downstairs it operates La Cascade, a full-fledged restaurant that looks out on the waterfall and that offers lunch, tea and dinner in a bright and comfortable modern setting. No longer connected with La Côte Basque, the French restaurant on 55th Street, Délices La Côte Basque is a patisserie and cafe on Lexington Avenue whose management also operates at Olympic Tower. Guy Pascal, the master pastry chef and guiding light behind the Délices ventures, and his chef, Xavier Leroux, have worked out excellent menus for both the cafe and the restaurant. What they have yet to work out is a pattern for smooth operation.

I have received many complaints about service at Olympic Tower, and though I was recognized whenever I was there, some flaws were apparent. At one lunch, a very efficient waitress seemed to have been pulled away from her station to serve me, much to the consternation of the diners who were abandoned. On another occasion, after having made a reservation for dinner, I was told upon arrival that the restaurant was closed for a private party. As gracious as the staff was about that mix-up, it should not have occurred. Neither should the captain have forgotten the salads ordered at dinner. Both at a Saturday morning breakfast in the cafe and at dinner on a quiet weeknight, service was uncomfortably slow. What the young, attractive and friendly staff needs is firm direction.

What the kitchen needs is a little more confidence. Already turning out generally pleasant and creditable dishes, the chef and his crew must develop a stronger character in seasonings. Combining classic French dishes with nouvelle cuisine creations, the kitchen does best by a deep golden, fragrant consommé, a salade Parisienne appetizer based on shrimp and mixed vegetables in a mayonnaise aspic, poached eggs in aspic and snails in garlic and parsley butter. Delicately moist smoked Norwegian salmon and trout garnished with horseradish cream could not be improved upon. Less successful appetizers included a very salty ham in parsley aspic and a heavy cotteghino sausage in crust and the scallops in puff pastry. Both onion soup and lobster bisque lacked character. So did the bisque in the form of a sauce Nantua on the otherwise well-made pike dumplings, quenelles de brochet.

Baby salmon stuffed with pike mousse gained subtle overtones from a light red wine sauce. The tender breast of chicken with cream and morels layered between squares of puff pastry was a big improvement over old-fashioned creamed chicken in a patty shell. Other nicely turned out dishes were mignonettes of beef tenderloin with marrow in a red wine sauce and broiled striped bass in mustard sauce, although the bass would have been better without paprika. There is a delicious rack of lamb coated with parsley and garlic and a satisfying steak au poivre.

Medaillons of veal were tender and mellow, but their creamy sauce with morels needed more seasoning. Breast of rare duck with a peppercorn sauce lacked pungency, and a paillard of beef that was not properly seared tasted of overheated grease.

The most successful dishes in Le Cafe proved to be perfect eggs Benedict and a light and delicate Swiss cheese omelet. Croque monsieur had overtones of burned butter, and the cheese layered in with the ham had not melted. Many dishes featured in La Cascade are also served in Le Cafe. Among these are the excellent pastries, the best of which are the mocha and meringue Délices cake, the individual St.-Honoré whipped cream pastries, very lemony lemon tarts and café Liègeois, an irresistible frozen parfait of mocha ice cream in espresso coffee with whipped cream.

Demarchelier

★

---

808 Lexington Avenue, near 62nd Street, 223-0047.
Atmosphere: Intimate, attractive and comfortable,
typical Parisian-style bistro. Service is friendly but
sometimes distracted and slow.
Recommended dishes: Hot saucisson with potato
salad, cream of celery soup, artichoke vinaigrette,
snails, grilled bass with mushroom sauce, sirloin
steak with béarnaise sauce, steak au poivre, roast
lamb, lamb chops, lemon tart, crème caramel,
crème a l'orange, tart Tatin, strawberries with
crème fraîche.
Price range: Moderate.
Credit cards: All major credit cards.
Hours: Lunch, Mondays through Saturdays, noon to 3
P.M.; dinner, Mondays through Saturdays, 6 P.M.
to 11:30 P.M. Closed Sundays.
Reservations: Recommended.

Named for its proprietors, Eric and Patrick Demarchelier, this very French bistro offers comfortable, competently made food in a variety of settings.

Those who like the street theater afforded by a sidewalk cafe can choose the glassed-in street-side tables.
Others who prefer the casual informality of a grill will
want to sit in the front room or at one of the small
tables facing the magnificent, overscale darkwood bar
with its canopies of old stained glass, an import from
some Texas extravaganza. But the back room is club-
bier and quieter, although there are two badly placed
tables with chairs in the direct path of the kitchen door.

Thumping background music in the early evening is
turned off as soon as the place begins to fill up (or as
soon as a patron asks that it be turned down), and after
8 o'clock the glass-topped tables opposite the bar are
covered with cloths for dinner.

Many of the same specialities appear on both lunch
and dinner menus. By far the best appetizers sampled
were cool, fresh-cooked artichokes in a smooth, mustardy vinaigrette dressing; lusty, hot garlic-accented
saucisson on a bed of warm French potato salad, and
sensational snails bubbling hot in a ceramic dish that
holds their heady garlic-parsley butter in convenient
wells.

Beautifully ripe honeydew melon was covered with
slices of prosciutto that were of fair quality, but much
too cold, and pâté de campagne was greasy, dense and
too finely ground. Cream of celery soup was a thick,
fragrant and bracing first course, but both the bland
watercress soup and a starchy, tasteless concoction
billed as red snapper bisque could have come out of a
hospital kitchen. There are nicely made, bright fresh
salads to nibble on between courses, my favorite being
mixed greens and raw mushrooms.

Gigot — the classic French roast leg of lamb — is a plat du jour, usually on Friday or Saturday, and because it is the best dish in the house, it is worth checking on in advance. With the properly rose-red meat are served the traditional pale-green beans, flageolets, and potatoes Maxim — sliced potatoes baked to attain a crusty outer layer and a silky inner softness.

Among the best main courses tried were excellent grilled lamb chops, good sirloin steak with a creditable béarnaise sauce and hefty steak au poivre in a cream-based sauce spiked with green and black peppercorns. At lunch a daily special of grilled striped bass with a mushroom-and-herb cream sauce proved delicious, but that was the only fish dish worth recommending. Sautéed scallops with mushrooms was fair, but grilled sole was hopelessly overcooked and crusty. Poached striped bass, though well cooked, carried the faint hint of petroleum that oftens taints this particular species. The beurre-blanc sauce served with it was so badly made that it was unrecognizable by that name — this version was overacidic and had an unpleasant starchy and slippery texture.

Moderately good main courses included a grilled paillard of veal that was just a little dry and a sautéed escalope of veal in a pleasant white-wine-and-cream mushroom sauce that derived extra body from the reduced veal stock it included.

Lightly cooked vegetables, and in some cases a grilled (unripe) half-tomato, accompany various main courses, and at lunch delicious, slim french fries replace the evening potatoes Maxim. Quiche at lunch one day had a very good onion-and-ham filling that was unfortunately set in a soggy, underbaked crust.

The classic French apple-cake, tart Tatin, had the perfect burnish of caramel, but is occasionally served so warm that the glaze melts. Both crème caramel and crème à l'orange (crème caramel with slivers of orange peel) were exceptional, as was a fluffy lemon tart. Cream cheesecake, chocolate mousse and sherbets were all banal. Fresh strawberries in what seems a homemade crème fraîche would be fine if the fruit were really ripe.

What one misses at Demarchelier are a few of those precooked, stewed and braised dishes that are in the true bistro style. Also, Perrier should be poured from the bottle at the table; it should also be cold, so no ice is needed. Here, it arrives poured over ice, with no bottle in view. But even considering lapses that occasionally include slow or careless service, there is enough delicious, authentically prepared food on the menu to enable one to enjoy lunch or dinner in an engaging setting. There are some moderately priced wines on the menu and a number of others that are overpriced.

Devon House Ltd.

★

1316 Madison Avenue, corner of 93rd Street, 860-8294.

Atmosphere: Gracefully romantic, small dining rooms with British colonial overtones; service is well meaning and polite but slightly pretentious.

Recommended dishes: Asparagus au gratin, artichoke with mushrooms, scallop and spinach pâté, cold cucumber soup, rack of lamb, scallops amandine, sole with lemon and caper sauce, sweetbreads, apple tart, chef's special chocolate dessert, fresh fruit.

Price range: Moderately expensive.

Credit cards: American Express and Diners Club.

Hours: Dinner, seven days, 6:30 P.M. to 11 P.M.

Reservations: Necessary.

Neatly and gracefully designed in a motif that the owner, Yvonne Scherrer, describes as British colonial, the restaurant gains character from an antique mahogany mantelpiece, delicate floral arrangements set off by candlelight, handsome tableware, celadon-green walls and tightly shirred, sheer white curtains — a pristine look inspired, according to the owner, by the original Devon House, a mansion in her native Jamaica.

In general, Devon House is a pleasant dining experience. But it could be more so if the tone were less pretentious and the service less self-consciously intrusive. The format is based on a simple Continental menu with about five appetizers, three main courses, a salad, a fruit and cheese course, dessert and coffee. Unfortunately, slow service makes the parade of courses string out far too long. The food was acceptable but barely at the high prices.

Some of the dishes sampled succeeded far more than others. While the cold cucumber soup needed only a dash of salt, the other soups were skippable. The cream of onion was too sweet and the mushroom soup was ruined by a cloying topping of melted Brie. Far better starters were the artichoke in a vinaigrette dressing and topped with marinated mushrooms, the asparagus au gratin given body with thin slices of prosciutto, and a scallop terrine with spinach.

Lackluster meat pâtés can be bypassed and so can the dry, tough shrimp in a lovely pink sauce and served in a puff-pastry shell.

Rack of lamb was consistently tender, rose-pink and delicately seasoned with garlic, red wine and herbs. Equally good were satiny nuggets of golden, sautéed sweetbreads. Bay scallops sautéed to exactly the right nut-sweet crispness made a thoroughly satisfying main course and so did sole in a lemon and caper sauce — a much better creation than a sole overpowered by foie gras and truffles. Chicken breasts sautéed to precisely the right moist tenderness were marred by a hot sauce of lime, lemon and orange juices, too sweet and dessert-like.

The sprightly green salad deserved a less vinegary dressing, and the cheese selection was dull, the cheeses in poor condition.

Save room for such excellent desserts as the apple tart or the chef's special, a crunchy almond cookie edged with velvety bittersweet chocolate mousse and topped with marinated strawberries and whipped cream. A passable pear tart is available, but for a lighter, more refreshing windup, try a rainbow layering of pineapple, watermelon, cantaloupe, kiwi and a strawberry.

There is a modest wine list, and a decent white and red Bordeaux is sold by the glass. Port is poured with the cheese course, and both coffee and bread are above average.

Dezaley

★

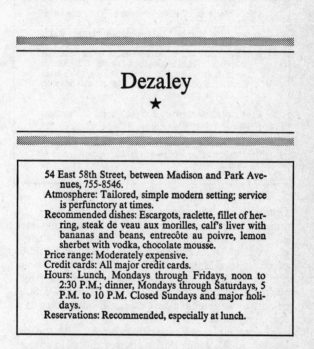

54 East 58th Street, between Madison and Park Avenues, 755-8546.
Atmosphere: Tailored, simple modern setting; service is perfunctory at times.
Recommended dishes: Escargots, raclette, fillet of herring, steak de veau aux morilles, calf's liver with bananas and beans, entrecôte au poivre, lemon sherbet with vodka, chocolate mousse.
Price range: Moderately expensive.
Credit cards: All major credit cards.
Hours: Lunch, Mondays through Fridays, noon to 2:30 P.M.; dinner, Mondays through Saturdays, 5 P.M. to 10 P.M. Closed Sundays and major holidays.
Reservations: Recommended, especially at lunch.

This is a trim, handsome, modern Swiss restaurant with a variety of enticing dishes but service is distracted and perfunctory, although it can be good. Escargots in casserole with herb butter were as pleasant as the raclette, a gratin dish of strong melted cheese, served with boiled potatoes and pickled onions.

Iced herring fillets were brightened with slivers of red peppers and onions. Tortellini maison, however, were thick and pasty in a heavy sauce that included mushrooms and cheese.

Steak de veau aux morilles was pleasant and, to my surprise, so was some very nicely sautéed calf's liver and bacon served with the improbable accent of sautéed bananas, a combination I expected to dislike but found interesting. A huge, dry, stuffed breast of chicken, however, tasted of stale grease. Steak au poivre was good, if not inspired.

Salads and vegetables were pleasant, and Dezaley offers excellent crusty Swiss mountain bread. Dark chocolate mousse and lemon sherbet with vodka were the best desserts.

I have never found a Swiss wine worth drinking anywhere, including here, but there is excellent Swiss beer.

Dimitri
Fair

152 Columbus Avenue, between 66th and 67th Streets, 787-7306.

Atmosphere: Simple, Art-Deco-inspired setting that is slightly gloomy; acceptable service.

Recommended dishes: Greek spinach pie, mussels marinière, linguini seafood Verdi, fish Skaras style, salad of cold fish and shellfish, calf's liver sauté, sirloin steak, shish kebab, all salads (with oil added), fruit tart.

Price range: Moderate.

Credit cards: American Express, Visa, MasterCard and Diners Club.

Hours: Lunch, Mondays through Fridays, noon to 2:30 P.M.; dinner, seven days, 5 P.M. to midnight.

Reservations: Not accepted at lunch; recommended at dinner.

Dimitri is the epitome of a neighborhood restaurant, with its long, convivial bar, simple but decent Greek and Continental food and atmospheric, if slightly gloomy, Art-Deco-inspired setting. Its appeal would be primarily local, convenient if one were nearby, but not quite worth a visit for its own sake. When that neighborhood happens to be Lincoln Center, though, with its paucity of acceptable eating places, Dimitri takes on a special meaning.

The menu presents interesting choices, with appetizers that double as light main courses and main courses that do just as well shared as appetizers. It is the sort of menu that allows for any appetite, and a number of the choices are stylish and intriguing. Unfortunately, cooking has become uneven and sometimes careless since this place opened, but there are still some dependable choices.

Flaky, well-filled Greek spinich pie was one of the better appetizers tried, as were mussels marinière in a green-garlic sauce. Insalata di frutti del mare, a maincourse salad of cold scallops, mussels, octopus, shrimp and squid marinated in oil and vinegar, made a pleasant first course when shared, as do any of the salads if you pour on extra oil to counteract their sharp overdose of wine vinegar.

Mixed Greek hors d'oeuvres included the spinach pie and the seafood salad, but was spoiled by a dollop of very salty tarama and another purée which was totally unidentifiable. Quiche was floury and dense. Linguine seafood Verdi, properly al dente and done with garlicky, peppery parsley sauce, was savory and satisfying and salted, so that the fragrant oil coated all the pasta. Fettucine Alfredo had a miky sauce and needed added sprinklings of freshly grated pepper and cheese.

There are several fish available each day that are broiled "Skaras style," a method the menu describes as "open grilling." Porgies and pompano were especially good done this way. Sautéed calf's liver, tender, fresh and pink, was the best main course, followed by sirloin steak and a creditable lamb shish kebab. Tough veal proved unsatisfactory in a limp, pallid piccata al limone, and an order of Long Island duckling was only halfway acceptable, one piece being crisp, fresh and meaty while the other tasted stale and of overheated grease.

With each main course is served a combination of firm, fresh vegetables, such as green beans, carrots and zucchini or cauliflower, as well as roasted or scalloped potatoes or rice. Unfortunately, the vegetables were much in need of some parsley and melted butter to perk them up.

The best dessert sampled was a paper-thin apple tart, served warm and topped with half-whipped cream. A version with apricots was cloyingly sweet. Cheesecake was gummy and lacking in flavor contrasts, baklava had a good, nutty flavor but was thick and tough, and chocolate mousse was thick, creamy and puddinglike, not at all light and airy as it should be. Espresso, cappuccino and Irish coffee, as well as herbal teas, are available. The wine list is modest and adequate, with mostly moderate prices.

Elaine's
Fair

1703 Second Avenue, between 88th and 89th Streets, 534-8103.

Atmosphere: Casual old bar-and-grill tavern with clublike overtones; service is brusque but professional.

Recommended dishes: Stuffed mushrooms, cavatelli all'Amatriciana, pastas with tomato sauces, broiled veal chop, sirloin steak, broccoli, string beans, fried zucchini.

Price range: Moderately expensive.

Credit cards: American Express.

Hours: Lunch, Mondays through Fridays, noon to 3:30 P.M.; dinner, seven days a week, 6 P.M. to 2 A.M. Closed major holidays.

Reservations: Necessary.

Since it opened about twenty years ago, Elaine's, the pleasantly old-fashioned bar-and-grill tavern, has become one of the most popular hangouts for writers and local media celebrities. As a result, it is also high on the list of curiosity seekers trying to spot the media celebrities and writers who use the restaurant as a sort of club.

If you enjoy watching writers eat steaks, chops and some basic Italian trimmings, you may find a visit to Elaine's worthwhile. Should you be lucky enough to be given a table within staring distance of these charter customers, and if you recognize them from dust-jacket photographs, you may hardly notice the brusque service and the careless and indifferently prepared food.

The small printed menu is supplemented by daily specials that are recited without benefit of price; and certain specialties are not mentioned to ordinary mortals. You have to know somehow that the appetizer list includes a seafood salad and steamed mussels, both of which are highly touted by regulars. Each time we have had them, the mussels were plump but sandy and swimming in a broth that could easily have been pure salt water. The squid and shrimp in the salad were stale and cottony on at least four visits. Baked clams arrived not more than eight minutes after they were ordered. Judging by their dryness and scorched crust of crumbs, they had been reheated, not cooked, to order. A few pastas made with meat and tomato sauce (spaghetti Bolognese and anything marinara) were delicious, and the best of these was the cavatelli all'Amatriciana. Never mind that the shell-shaped pasta had unfurled into long, thick ribbons; the result was hearty and satisfying, far more so than the soupy fettuccine Alfredo and doughy tortellini, both ruined by a dismal grade of waxy Romano-type cheese.

The overcooked, totally unsalted linguine gained nothing from its so-called sauce of chopped clams; neither oil nor garlic was present to add the necessary texture and flavor. The dish tasted merely boiled.

The thick broiled veal chop and the sirloin steak are consistently good and moderately priced. Chicken al limone, a half-chicken that might have been broiled, then steamed, proved minimally acceptable, but veal scaloppine piccata had a pasty flour coating and virtually no seasonings. It is hard to understand how chicken Parmigiana could become as poor as the version served here, inedible under a cheese topping that tasted downright soapy. Calf's liver Veneziana, soured with what tasted like distilled white vinegar, was just as bad and scampi Livornese had been so overcooked that the meat could not be pried from the shell. Moist and fresh red snapper, inexplicably topped with slices of apple, could be considered a good main course, if the apples are brushed aside.

Amid all this there are some very firm, bright and well-cooked vegetables — broccoli, string beans and crisp fried zucchini. Desserts such as floury cheesecake and an improbably orangy and grainy zabaglione made me wonder whether any regulars had ever tried them and still remained regulars. One hopes that the dilapidated women's washroom, with missing tiles and blistered plaster, is not an indication of the management's level of respect for the customers.

El Charro

★

4 Charles Street, between Greenwich and Seventh
Avenues, 242-9547.
Atmosphere: Small, lively little Greenwich Village
restaurant with typical rustic Mexican décor; serv-
ice friendly and helpful, but occasionally hectic.
Recommended dishes: Chalupas, guacamole with hot
sauce added, beef tacos or tostados, chilies relle-
nos, chicken mole poblano, fried chicken El
Charro, ropa vieja, picadillo, fried green bananas,
mariscada with green sauce, paella Valenciana
with lobster.
Price range: Moderate.
Credit cards: All major credit cards.
Hours: Mondays through Thursdays, 11:30 A.M. to
midnight, Fridays and Saturdays, 11:30 A.M. to 1
A.M., Sundays, 1 P.M. to midnight. Closed on
Thanksgiving Day.
Reservations: Necessary.

For almost thirty years, El Charro in Greenwich Village
has had a loyal coterie that has come to rely on certain
dishes. The setting is friendly, convivial and rustically
Mexican, the prices are low to moderate, and if you pick
your way carefully among menu choices, you can leave
well satisfied.

The two consistent flaws that could be corrected
easily are the commercial, textureless tortillas that lend
an inferior quality to the dishes that include them, and
the bland and slick tomato sauce basic to so many
preparations.

Those who like Mexican food to be fiery hot should
say so at the beginning of the meal and be insistent. The
ordinary dipping sauce for tostado chips is bland, but a
properly incendiary one is forthcoming on request. Stir
it into the guacamole, and it becomes delicious, and it
also does a lot for otherwise characterless huevos
rancheros — fried eggs in a mild tomato-and-pepper
sauce.

Chalupas, the appetizers of tostado chips baked with
cheese, refried beans and jalapeño peppers are better
than the pasty nachos, and for soup lovers, there is a
lusty Galician specialty, adrift with sausages, white
beans and kale. Garlic soup is heady if greasy and contains chunks of bread and egg drops.

Beef fillings, gently seasoned and meaty in texture, do
more for such Tex-Mex creations as tacos and tostados
than the overcooked chicken filling does. Enchiladas
were so soft and overcooked they had to be scraped off
the plate to be eaten, but chilies rellenos were about as
good as we have ever had them in a New York restaurant — spicy, luxurious with melting cheese and greaselessly fried before being baked.

The sautéed shredded flank steak called ropa vieja
(old clothes) had a good bite and subtle flavor, and so

did picadillo, the ground beef hash, studded with raisins. Crunchy fried green banana slices garnished both these dishes, along with fresh-made, savory yellow rice. Skip the banal iceberg lettuce salad for more interesting choices. Foremost among these is chicken à la Charro, a dish that should win the hearts of all garlic lovers. It is fried golden brown in a haze of garlic and crisp onions. Only slightly less distinguished is chicken mole poblano, in the traditional chocolate-and-spice-burnished sauce.

The only two worthwhile dishes we found among Spanish specialties proved to be freshly made paella Valenciana, with lobster, and the mariscados (mussels, clams, shrimp and scallops) in a garlic-and-parsley green sauce. Beef and veal dishes and clams in hot sauce are only minimally acceptable, and desserts do not achieve even that status.

The house is very good about allowing dishes to be shared, and the portions are generous. Divide the chilies rellenos as an appetizer, then do the same with such main courses as garlic chicken, paella or picadillo. Margaritas have the right bite of salt and tequila, the Mexican beers are properly chilled, and for those who fancy sangría, the white is more refreshing than the red.

El Coyote
★ ★

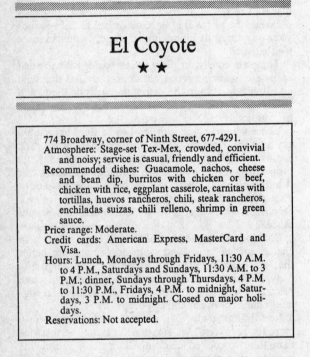

774 Broadway, corner of Ninth Street, 677-4291.
Atmosphere: Stage-set Tex-Mex, crowded, convivial and noisy; service is casual, friendly and efficient.
Recommended dishes: Guacamole, nachos, cheese and bean dip, burritos with chicken or beef, chicken with rice, eggplant casserole, carnitas with tortillas, huevos rancheros, chili, steak rancheros, enchiladas suizas, chili relleno, shrimp in green sauce.
Price range: Moderate.
Credit cards: American Express, MasterCard and Visa.
Hours: Lunch, Mondays through Fridays, 11:30 A.M. to 4 P.M., Saturdays and Sundays, 11:30 A.M. to 3 P.M.; dinner, Sundays through Thursdays, 4 P.M. to 11:30 P.M., Fridays, 4 P.M. to midnight, Saturdays, 3 P.M. to midnight. Closed on major holidays.
Reservations: Not accepted.

Think more Tex than Mex and you will not be disappointed by this rustic, adobe and knotty-pine eatery with its comfortable booths, convivial clientele and its young and obliging staff. A folkloric mural and accessories that suggest a border-town souvenir shop create a cheerful backdrop against which the hefty platters of satisfying, typical specialties can be enjoyed at relatively modest prices.

If none of the food quite fills the void in New York City for really great Mexican fare, it is all at least freshly and honestly prepared and a good deal above average. Even the taco chips on each table are crisper and sprightlier than most, and the chili-relish sauce, salsa piquante, served with them is hotly seasoned and can be even more so on request, an accommodation possible with all other food at El Coyote as well. Stir some of that sauce into the smooth guacamole, and it will improve that decent if slightly bland avocado dip. It also does a lot for the nachos, tortilla wedges topped with refried beans, melted cheese and jalapeño chilies, and for the chalupas, tortillas topped with cheese and guacamole. A porridgy dip of mashed black beans and cheese is also a delicious appetizer to be scooped up with the taco chips.

With all of these first courses, a margarita of lime juice and tequila, or a coppery Mexican beer, such as Dos Equis, is a better choice than the red wine and fruit punch sangría, because El Coyote makes an especially awful version of that basically poor drink.

At lunch, the menu includes well-made huevos rancheros, fried eggs underlined with black beans on a crisp tortilla base, and at any time there are shrimp in an exceptionally verdant and fiery green sauce of minced jalapeño peppers, tomatillos and garlic. Arroz con pollo, the standard chicken-and-yellow-rice special-ty, is subtly seasoned and succulent, with moist white meat of chicken and juicy rice. Equally satisfying is a casserole of eggplant luxuriously topped with melted cheese and accented by green peppers. Although nug-gets of pork and beef carnitas, served with soft wheat tortillas, were the least bit dry, they still had pleasantly acidic undertones of marinade and a hearty grilled flavor, and proved slightly better than the carne asada and the gloppy Mexican meat casserole. Chilies rellenos were best with cheese. The enchiladas suizas, with chicken, sour cream and green sauce, were as rich and soul warming as the chili con carne and juicy, grilled steak ranchero topped with onions and peppers.

Disappointing dishes included a characterless array of tortilla-based specialties, such as the folded taco sandwiches and tostados with beef, chicken, cheese and bean toppings. The best in the category were burritos, crisp-fried wheat tortillas, with a chicken or ground-beef filling. The only acceptable dessert is flan.

All portions are large enough to allow sharing.

Elephant & Castle
★ ★

183 Prince Street, between Thompson and Sullivan
Streets, 260-3600, and 68 Greenwich Avenue, near
Seventh Avenue, 243-1400.
Atmosphere: Simple, attractive, lively and noisy modern settings that suggest a high-style coffee-shop
cafe. Prince Street location is the more spacious
and atmospheric of the two. Service is polite and
casual, but sometimes slow at peak hours.
Recommended dishes: Soups, quiches, hamburgers,
omelets and all egg dishes, green salads, cakes and
ice cream desserts at both. Chicken Nepal,
chicken Niçoise, sautéed scallops, steak tartare, sesame chicken, New England boiled dinner and
grilled Portuguese sausage on spinach salad
recommended at Prince Street. Chicken salad with
aioli dressing, Caesar salad and chicken sautéed
with sesame seeds recommended at Greenwich
Avenue.
Price range: Moderate.
Credit cards: All major credit cards.
Hours, Prince Street: Mondays through Thursdays, 8
A.M. to midnight, Fridays, 8 A.M. to 1 A.M.,
Saturdays, 10 A.M. to 1 A.M., Sundays, 10 A.M.
to midnight. Saturday and Sunday brunch, 10
A.M. to 5 P.M. Greenwich Avenue: Mondays
through Thursdays, 9 A.M. to midnight, Fridays,
9 A.M. to 1 A.M., Saturdays, 10 A.M. to 1 A.M.,
Sundays, 11 A.M. to midnight.
Reservations: Not accepted.

Elephant & Castle originated in Greenwich Village,
where its first outpost remains a popular and jam-
packed slice of a restaurant. At first glance, it looks very
much like a coffee shop, but the attractive, rustic interi-
or, simply done with dark, varnished wood paneling,
mirrors, lots of white trim and pleasant lighting, lends a
convivial cafe atmosphere. In much the same way, the
framework of the menu is that of a short-order coffee
shop, but again style lifts it above that category, for enticing, innovative and decorative dishes have been
created to fulfill the quick-cooking requirement. The
food is American-international with health-food vegetarian overtones, coming by way of yogurt dressings
and desserts, lots of bright, lightly cooked vegetables
and carrot cake.

No liquor is served at the Elephant & Castle on
Greenwich Avenue, but there are interesting soft drinks,
some based on European fruit concentrates, and you
may bring your own beer or wine.

At the newer Elephant & Castle, in SoHo, the menu
follows the same format but offers different choices of
hot dishes and daily specials. It also has a full liquor license and interesting, moderately priced wines. The atmosphere, though similar to that in the Village, is far
more pleasant because the SoHo restaurant is more spacious and more visible and has romantic, roseate lighting and mirror-backed glass shelves holding honey and
preserves, which are for sale. But here, as on Greenwich

Avenue, there is distracting and intrusive background music.

At both branches of Elephant & Castle, you can get wonderfully rich and fluffy omelets, always cooked to the correct degree of doneness and filled with such combinations as green chili and sour cream, Portuguese sausage and cheese, asparagus and Gruyère cheese, caviar and sour cream, zucchini, tomatoes and Parmesan cheese, and when basil is in season, a verdantly pungent pesto filling is available. Such fillings as nuts and bananas are best ignored.

Creditable hollandaise sauce covers eggs Benedict, which is available for weekend brunches, and at all times there are well-prepared egg dishes with thick bacon fried to crisp but chewy perfection.

The hamburgers at Greenwich Avenue may have a slight edge over those on Prince Street, mostly because they generally are a bit more carefully grilled, but in both places they are far above average, grilled in thick rounds though no longer served on the crusty kaiser rolls. Only occasionally do they seem to be preseared and dry. Slim, savory french fries can be had as side orders. My favorite among the hamburgers is the plain one, or the combination of bacon and Gruyère cheese, but for more exotic tastes there are those with sour cream and scallions, mustard ravigote sauce, mushrooms and herbs, or even spinach and a fried egg.

Hot soups vary from day to day, and all except a watery, corn, spinach and bacon chowder at Prince Street have been delicious. Lentil with tomato and sausage, cream of broccoli, parsnip and carrot, and cold beet borscht in summer are deliciously restorative. Grilled sandwiches, all with cheese, are good at both places, although the combination of tuna fish and cheddar cheese at Prince Street seems a mistake. Quiches with vegetable fillings are always light and custardy, and their crusts are golden brown and crisp. Salads, such as the Caesar and the house salad of Boston lettuce with a creamy sesame dressing, are sprightly and refreshing. Chicken aioli — cold chunks of fresh-cooked chicken breast with a garlicky mayonnaise dressing and a salad of boiled new potatoes in rosy skins — is served at Greenwich Avenue, and is every bit as good as chicken Nepal at Prince Street — chicken salad with an avocado-based dressing that has a lemony, mint-tarragon tang. Sliced-steak salad in a mustard-vinaigrette dressing at Greenwich Avenue may have been a little too rich as a full main course, but it would be an excellent appetizer for two of three to share.

What are listed as warm entrees — main courses — are the weak spots on these menus, especially in the Village. Having tried all of them, plus a few daily specials, I can recommend only chicken sautéed with sesame seeds and spinach. On Prince Street, however, the cooking is much better in this category. All delicious were chicken Niçoise, with olives and tomatoes; sautéed scallops with dill-and-caper-flecked rice; grilled Portuguese sausage on spinach salad, and a daily special of New England boiled dinner, with corned beef, carrots, new potatoes and cabbage. Not so the dreadful steak, the drab daube of beef or the bitter oysters Rockefeller. Steak tartare was fresh and came with all the necessary condiments. Homemade-looking cakes, such as carrot, chocolate brownie, cheesecake and apple poundcake, are far above average. The crepes are better on Greenwich Avenue than on Prince Street. Try the Vienna Woods, with vanilla ice cream, chocolate sauce, walnuts and whipped cream. Coffees and teas of various sorts are also available.

Service at Elephant & Castle is casual but polite and usually efficient. It can, however, be slow, especially for hot main courses at peak hours.

Elio's
Fair

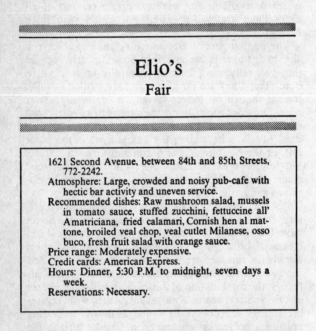

1621 Second Avenue, between 84th and 85th Streets, 772-2242.
Atmosphere: Large, crowded and noisy pub-cafe with hectic bar activity and uneven service.
Recommended dishes: Raw mushroom salad, mussels in tomato sauce, stuffed zucchini, fettuccine all' Amatriciana, fried calamari, Cornish hen al mattone, broiled veal chop, veal cutlet Milanese, osso buco, fresh fruit salad with orange sauce.
Price range: Moderately expensive.
Credit cards: American Express.
Hours: Dinner, 5:30 P.M. to midnight, seven days a week.
Reservations: Necessary.

Almost as soon as it opened, Elio's began packing in trendy Upper East Siders and celebrities such as Woody Allen, Mia Farrow, Henry Morgan and Lillian Hellman. Whether in discreet blazers complete with rep ties and polka dot pocket handkerchiefs, ranch mink greatcoats or jeans and gilded sweaters, guests elbow their way through the crowds as though they were at a wildly noisy house party. What they are willing to wait for is some of the most characterless Italian food in New York.

Blandness, in fact, may be Elio's secret of success, appealing as it does to those who want to eat Italian food but who don't really like Italian food.

Basic quality is respectable, the menu is enticing and most of the food is edible, but almost every dish I tried on four visits lacked sufficient seasoning. Service is hectic, ranging from friendly to brash, and generally too fast; four courses invariably were ordered, served and eaten within an hour. Turnover seems to be the theme in this wood-paneled pub-cafe that is a takeoff on Parma, the very good Third Avenue restaurant in which Elio Guaitolini, now of Elio's, was formerly a partner.

Crisp-crusted white and whole wheat breads are about as good as things get, so if you are hungry, don't hold back. The only recommended appetizers are the raw mushroom salad with oil and lemon juice, the mussels steamed in a light and spicy tomato sauce and warm meat-filled zucchini topped with tomato. Lackluster appetizers included the seafood salad, the thick and tough raw beef carpaccio and both the hot and cold antipasti. Really poor first courses were the heavy, stodgy vitello tonnato and squares of cornmeal polenta awash in a sort of gorgonzola cream soup.

Oddly enough in an Italian restaurant, pastas were the weakest course. Cream and cheese sauces on pastas such as fettuccine Alfredo, paglia e fieno and tortellini were milky and as abundant as soup. Only the fettuccine all'Amatriciana, with tomatoes, Italian bacon and onions, had the proper herbaceous accents. The sauce on the spaghetti primavera could be approximated with overcooked vegetable soup, and the rice in a risotto with porcini mushrooms tasted as though it had been cooked separately, then stirred in with a mushroom sauce.

One of the touted specials is grilled gamberoni, the giant red Spanish shrimp. The scent and flavor of mine were so stale and fishy that I sent them back, only to be told by the waiter: "It's just the smell. Nobody likes that dish the first time." It's hard to imagine anyone giving it a second try. Scampi sautéed with butter, lemon, white wine and garlic tasted of iodine, and the mixed fish and shellfish soup, zuppa de pesce, though decent, lacked either the briny overtones of its main ingredients or the flavor of garlic and herbs. Fried calamari was the most satisfactory seafood choice, the squid being tender and the breading crisp.

Broiled veal chop, fried veal cutlet Milanese and a good and peppery Cornish hen grilled flat under pressure (al mattone, or under a brick) were the most acceptable among meat and poultry main courses. The osso buco, an occasional special, was also good. The veal shank was well braised, tender and flavorful, although its rice had obviously been reheated. Veal scaloppine dishes were ruined by floury, saltless sauces and the liver Veneziana bristled with an overdose of vinegar. Roast suckling pig, another special, was virtually pure fat with barely a shred of meat on it, and roast veal was the sort you might find on a hospital tray.

Desserts were consistent with the rest of the meal, the only exception being fresh fruit salad with a creamy orange-flavored crème Anglaise.

Elmer's

★

1034 Second Avenue, between 54th and 55th Streets,
751-8020.
Atmosphere: Flashy, overdone, Broadway-style steakhouse, hectic and noisy; service polite and professional but unevenly paced.
Recommended dishes: Clams or oysters on the half-
shell, asparagus or string beans vinaigrette, lobster, crab meat or shrimp cocktail, minestrone,
Rumanian steak, rib eye steak, filet mignon, sirloin steak, broiled chicken, poached striped bass,
broiled lobster, veal chop, sautéed calf's liver, cottage-fried potatoes, baked potatoes, fried broccoli,
spinach.
Price range: Expensive.
Credit cards: All major credit cards.
Hours: Lunch, Mondays through Saturdays, noon to 5
P.M.; dinner, Mondays through Saturdays, 5 P.M.
to 1 A.M., Sundays, 4 P.M. to midnight. Open on
major holidays.
Reservations: Necessary for large groups.

With the arrival of Elmer's, about a year ago, Broadway
brass with all of its flashy excesses began to vie with the
gold-plated East Side singles country, and so far,
Broadway seems to be winning. The noisy and hectic
activity can perhaps best be described as Runyonesque
— short of elegance and refinement, but entertaining to
old New York hands who miss the raffish scenes that
used to be played out at the original Lindy's and uptown at the Tip-Toe Inn.

After my first dinner at Elmer's, I was certain a three-
star rating was in order. Midway through the second
meal, I wondered if it would merit even a single star.
Considering the alternatives in this price range, Elmer's
has a long way to go. This is true, even though beef, the
main business at hand, proved first-rate on all tries. It
was equally good in the form of a hefty sirloin steak,
filet mignon, rib eye steak, roast beef or as that puffy,
tender, narrow belt of beef known as Rumanian tenderloin, which at Elmer's is served with smothered onions.
Only once did filet arrive well done when it was ordered
medium rare, and the replacement was undercooked —
blue and cold at the center. Otherwise the broiling of
steaks was flawless, and so was the broiling on golden,
hot, grilled half-chicken, a thick and properly pink veal
chop and delicately moist lobster. Similarly, sautéed
calf's liver had the rosy glow it should have had, although lamb chops were much too lean and conse-
quently dry and lacking in flavor.

Broiled fish was poorly executed. Fillets of what were
said to be gray sole and cuts of striped bass had been so
overcooked that they emerged dry and tasteless. And
though tiny bay scallops were sweet and fresh, they had
been dried out by overcooking and by a heavy topping
of paprika. Poached striped bass, a special one evening,
was more carefully cooked, although its hollandaise
sauce was too heavily salted. But an order of chicken

hash exuded the stale, greasy frying taste associated with low-level Chinese cooking.

As at most New York steakhouses, potatoes are available as cottage fries, french fries, hashed browns and baked. French-fried onion rings are also served. The onions ordered on three occasions could have come out of three different kitchens — once perfect in crisp sheathings of batter, a second time with the batter completely off the onions and the third time cooked dark brown and coated with crumbs instead of batter. Cottage fries were done to a suntan-gold once, but were too darkly fried another time. Both hashed browns and french fries were acceptable, if undistinguished. Baked potatoes had the correct fluffiness and crackling-crisp skins.

Firmly cooked string beans and near-crunchy asparagus, both with an egg-and-pimento-flecked vinaigrette dressing, added refreshing notes either as side dishes or appetizers, and leaf spinach was mellow and bright. Fried broccoli had a fresher, cleaner flavor than a lackluster cauliflower prepared in the same way.

Simple seafood cocktails, such as a large shrimp cocktail, cold and briny oysters and clams on the half-shell, lump crab meat and lobster, all made fine and satisfying appetizers. Not so a thin, tough and salty smoked trout, dry prosciutto, bland pâté in a bitterly salty green sauce and Elmer's salad, based on iceberg lettuce drowned in a heavy mayonnaise-style cream dressing. Even Caesar salad left much to be desired with its unevenly mixed dabs of mashed anchovy and overpowering mustard. Of three soups tried, only minestrone is worth recommending. Cream of asparagus was terribly salty, and beef barley soup suggested a starchy breakfast porridge.

Desserts look spectacular, but their appeal is strictly visual. Even the cheesecake had been so overchilled that it had turned gummy.

El Parador Cafe
★

325 East 34th Street, between First and Second Avenues, 679-6812.
Atmosphere: Dark, lively Mexican cocktail-lounge setting; staff friendly, polite and efficient.
Recommended dishes: Chorizos, guacamole, hot sauce, cheese crisp royal, picadillo à la criolla, shrimp in garlic sauce, shrimp in green sauce, chicken mole, chicken Parador, chilies rellenos, burritos, chimichanga, huevos à la Tampiqueña, shredded spiced beef.
Price range: Moderately expensive.
Credit cards: None.
Hours: Dinner, Mondays through Saturdays, 5 P.M. to 11 P.M. Closed Sundays and holidays.
Reservations: Not accepted.

El Parador Cafe stands as evidence of how minimal a performance New Yorkers are willing to settle for in Mexican food. For over twenty years, this dark, informal and atmospheric restaurant, with its convivial bar scene and friendly, accommodating staff, has been invariably mobbed. Reservations are not accepted, but the house seems to maintain an absolutely fair first-come-first-served policy. Prices are moderate for enormous portions of food, some of which is quite good, but most of which is as characterless as the over-refined, tasteless tortillas on which so many specialties depend.

Tex-Mex, rather than classic, elegant Mexican fare, strikes the tone on the menu. Fortunately, the very well-made Margaritas, with their generous belt of tequila and their tongue-tingling salt rims, take the edge off much of the disappointment induced by the meal itself. Everything looks quite marvelous as presented at the table, whether artfully arranged on plates or heaped into cheerful red enameled cast-iron casseroles, but after that, it is mostly downhill.

Fairly greaseless and crisp taco chips can be dipped into a mildly pungent green sauce while you sip your drink, and if the sauce seems too mild, a truly incendiary replacement is available on request. Stir some of that hot sauce into the guacamole to give it the proper lift; otherwise that avocado purée is distinctly lackluster.

Appetizers beyond redemption were soggy nachos and a ceviche of stale fish. Only grilled chorizo sausage slices and the lavish, excellent cheese crisp royal were worthwhile. The cheese crisp royal appeared as a sort of Mexican pizza — a huge crisp tortilla baked under a blanket of melting cheese, sausages, onions and mashed beans — practically a meal in itself or an appetizer that would easily satisfy two or three. Neither chili bean soup nor baby-cactus salad can be recommended, but huevos à la Tampiqueña — eggs scrambled with onions, tomatoes, chorizo and cheese — would be as welcome for brunch as for dinner. Only a pasty cheese enchilada spoiled the dish. Soothing and soul-satisfying, if unexciting, was picadillo à la criolla, a chopped creole hash with leaden, fried green bananas and sliced and shredded spiced beef in a pungent mole sauce that again came to life when mixed with the hot green chili sauce.

Fairly firm and decent shrimp made fine main courses, in either a garlic sauce flecked with parsley or in a green sauce that looked like a purée of the same ingredients. Green mole sauce on a generous portion of chicken lacked any flavor whatever, but the brown mole based on chocolate, sesame and spices turned out to be delicious, and one order will certainly do for two (a practice so common at El Parador, there is a standard $4 charge for an extra plate). Chicken Parador, marinated in spices and graced with garlic, was even better than the mole.

Forget about tacos, tostados and enchiladas at El Parador because all represent wasted calories. Instead choose chilies rellenos, burritos, wheat-flour crepes rolled around the picadillo or the spicy shredded beef, or chimichanga — crisp rolls of wheat tortillas with the same fillings, topped with sour cream and guacamole. Rice and a bland bean stew accompany all main courses, and so does an acceptable house salad.

The five desserts were all poor. If you must end on a note of sweetness, have hot Mexican coffee spiked with Kahlua and an orange liqueur. The Mexican beer, Dos Equis, is the drink to have with this heavy fare.

El Rincón de España
★ ★

226 Thompson Street, between Third and Bleecker Streets, 475-9891 or 260-4950.

Atmosphere: Small, dark, noisy Bohemian rustic Spanish tavern; efficient, prompt service that is somewhat impersonal.

Recommended dishes: Mussels à la Carlos, all soups, all shellfish dishes with white, green, egg, garlic or hot sauces, octopus, codfish Gallego-style, all paellas, chicken with rice.

Price range: Moderate.

Credit cards: All major credit cards.

Hours: Dinner, Mondays through Thursdays, 5 P.M. to 11 P.M., Fridays, 5 P.M. to midnight, Saturdays, 1 P.M. to midnight, Sundays, 1 P.M. to 11 P.M.

Reservations: Necessary.

Note: El Rincón de España also has a restaurant at 82 Beaver Street between Pearl and Hanover Streets (344-5228) in the financial district. Both lunch and dinner are served and the menu and management are the same as those at the Thompson Street restaurant, but it has not been visited and so cannot be rated.

Good Spanish cooking is not easy to come by in this city, but some of the best continues to be served at this small, crowded and convivial Greenwich Village landmark. Although not strictly a seafood restaurant, El Rincón's best dishes are based primarily on an abundance of sea-fresh shellfish such as clams, mussels, shrimp, lobster and scallops.

The shellfish are served in a variety of combinations, bathed in any one of a half dozen or so fragrant and enriching sauces. Green sauce with parsley and garlic, egg sauce also accented with garlic, a mildly spiked red hot sauce and a creamy pink garlic sauce are just a few of the possible choices to play up the briny flavors of the mollusks and crustaceans.

Octopus in a pungent tomato sauce is tender and meaty, and the dried salt codfish, bacalao, is carefully soaked so it will not be stingingly salty. It is then gently simmered to tenderness along with tomato sauce, onions, green peppers and thick slices of potatoes.

There are a variety of paellas here, based on steaming hot, moist rice flecked with peas, pimentos, sausages, chicken, seafood and, if you like, chunks of lobsters. These are not the most elegant or delicately refined paellas one can think of, but they are certainly among the heartiest and most satisfying. Like many of the seafood dishes, the paella, as well as the chicken with rice, are served by the potful and portions are copious enough to be shared, a practice that does involve a modest surcharge.

Because main courses are so large, it is probably just as well that there are few appetizers to offer temptation. Only the mussels à la Carlos, again in a hot red sauce, are worth having, and these usually conflict with a seafood main course. The real winners among first courses are the soups — the gazpacho which should be a bit colder but which has the pleasant crunch of raw vegetables, the light lentil soup with greens that might be kale, Swiss chard or mustard greens, and the caldo Gallego with white beans, potatoes and greens in a pork and chicken broth only slightly lacking in body.

The biggest flaws have been the salads of iceberg lettuce and unripe tomato, the poorly made desserts and the meat dishes. If you do not like seafood, stick to chicken and rice, for meat dishes range from passable to poor.

A guitar player, who also sings, can be fairly diverting and performs at dinner every night except Saturday. Service is good-natured but hectic.

El Tenampa
★

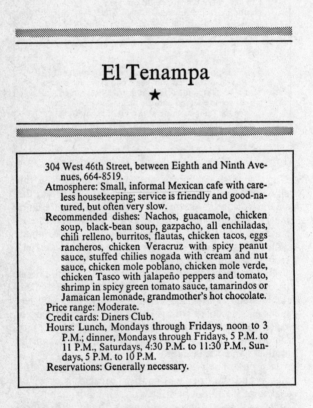

304 West 46th Street, between Eighth and Ninth Avenues, 664-8519.

Atmosphere: Small, informal Mexican cafe with careless housekeeping; service is friendly and good-natured, but often very slow.

Recommended dishes: Nachos, guacamole, chicken soup, black-bean soup, gazpacho, all enchiladas, chili relleno, burritos, flautas, chicken tacos, eggs rancheros, chicken Veracruz with spicy peanut sauce, stuffed chilies nogada with cream and nut sauce, chicken mole poblano, chicken mole verde, chicken Tasco with jalapeño peppers and tomato, shrimp in spicy green tomato sauce, tamarindos or Jamaican lemonade, grandmother's hot chocolate.

Price range: Moderate.

Credit cards: Diners Club.

Hours: Lunch, Mondays through Fridays, noon to 3 P.M.; dinner, Mondays through Fridays, 5 P.M. to 11 P.M., Saturdays, 4:30 P.M. to 11:30 P.M., Sundays, 5 P.M. to 10 P.M.

Reservations: Generally necessary.

Three things that are hard to find in New York are inexpensive restaurants, decent Mexican food and good places to eat in the theater district. All three of these needs are fairly well met by El Tenampa, a small, casual cafe on Restaurant Row. Well-spiced Mexican food at low prices is offered for lunch and dinner, and both menus include not only the standard Tex-Mex panoply of such dishes as tamales, tostados, tacos, burritos, flautas, enchiladas and taquitos, but also a full array of chicken, beef and pork specialties, complemented by subtle and heady sauces.

These sauces are, in fact, far better than most of the meats they cover, and the big flaw at El Tenampa is the poor quality of tough, stringy beef and pork, most of which seems to have been cooked long ago. Chicken can be obtained in most of the same sauces and is far preferable. Done mole poblano style, chicken was blanketed with a dark, smooth bitter-chocolate and toasted-sesame-seed sauce burnished with peppers and garlic. Chicken Veracruz style was distinguished by a chili-brightened peanut sauce, and jalapeño peppers and green tomatoes gave a brassy edge to Tasco-style chicken. Much the same green sauce did as well by firm, fresh shrimp, of which there were only six in each portion. Sour cream and peanut sauce enriched cheese-stuffed chilies nogada pueblo.

The more usual tortilla-based dishes are a bit overcooked and too soft, but nonetheless diverting and satisfying. Flautas — crisp enchiladas filled with beef and topped with sour cream and guacamole — is one of the best, and so are burritos, wheat tortillas enfolding shredded beef. Chili relleno, long green peppers dipped in batter and luxurious with melted cheese, are also good, as are green enchiladas, the enchiladas with mole sauce and cornmeal tamales steamed in corn husks. Chicken fillings were juicier and more flavorful than beef in tacos and atop tostados.

Huevos rancheros are satisfying at El Tenampa with deep fried eggs on tortillas sparked by a pepper-and-tomato sauce that can be as spicy as you want it to be. The kitchen is accommodating about spiciness, and there is a good chili sauce on the table that can fire things up even more. Guacamole that needs salt and hot sauce, and nachos — tostados chips topped with cheese and jalapeño pepper — are the best appetizers. Such soups as gazpacho, black bean with onion and cheese, and chicken and tomato soup with lime juice and coriander are exceptional. Desserts are disappointing, but there are interesting drinks. Mexican hot chocolate is flavored with cinnamon and crowned with whipped cream. Jamaican lemonade is cranberry red from sorrel blossoms steeped in it to produce a winy drink, and tamarind lemonade is pleasantly, stingingly astringent. There is no liquor license, but your own can be served.

Both housekeeping and service could be sharper; the staff is friendly and helpful, but service can be painfully slow on weekends when some of the things ordered, such as soft tortillas, are forgotten.

Empire Szechuan Balcony
Fair

381 Third Avenue, between 27th and 28th Streets,
685-6215.

Atmosphere: Attractive modern setting with balcony
and street-level dining rooms that are cramped.
Service is prompt and sometimes good-natured,
but generally inept.

Recommended dishes: Hacked chicken, fried dumplings, hot or cold noodles with sesame sauce, bean
curd with black-bean sauce, crispy scallops, crispy
shrimp in Hunan spicy sauce,

Price range: Moderate.

Credit cards: American Express, MasterCard and
Visa.

Hours: Sundays through Thursdays, 11:30 A.M. to
11:30 P.M., Fridays and Saturdays, 11:30 A.M. to
midnight. Closed only for Thanksgiving Day.

Reservations: Necessary.

Empire Szechuan Columbus
★

193 Columbus Avenue, between 68th and 69th
Streets; 496-8778.

Atmosphere: Simple, modern dining rooms that are
crowded, noisy and sometimes drafty. Housekeeping is careless. Service can be accommodating, but
is generally slow and indifferent, and occasionally
rude.

Recommended dishes: Cold duck with bean sauce,
hacked chicken, spareribs, fried or boiled dumplings, hot noodles Szechuan style, hot, spicy Szechuan cabbage, cold bean curd with sesame oil,
shredded pork with bean sauce, beef with orange
flavor, Empire special shrimp, crispy sea bass,
crispy shrimp, crispy scallops, fried rice noodles
with pork, banana stuffed with bean paste.

Price range: Inexpensive.

Credit cards: American Express, MasterCard and
Visa.

Hours: Lunch, Mondays through Fridays, 11:30 A.M.
to 3 P.M.; dinner, Mondays through Fridays, 3
P.M. to midnight, Saturdays and Sundays, 11
A.M. to 2 A.M. Open major holidays.

Reservations: Accepted.

The better of the two newcomers is Empire Szechuan
Columbus, near Lincoln Center. Too bad it is not also
the one with the better service. Besides the language
barrier, which interferes with getting orders straight,
and a slow kitchen at peak hours, the restaurant's waitresses are sometimes downright rude. Because the
street-level dining room is small and drafty, I asked to

sit in the upper level on one occasion when that room was empty. When I was told I could not, I left. At times, however, the young waitresses can be polite and well meaning.

One dish at Empire Szechuan Columbus that is fiery hot with chili peppers is the cold appetizer of spicy cabbage — a masterpiece of crisp, clean contrasts in flavor and texture. Hacked chicken sprinkled with coriander in a lovely combination of sesame and soy-chili sauce is delicious, though mild. So are the meaty, greaseless, fried or boiled dumplings and the sliced cold duck in bean sauce. Scallions brighten noodles, either hot or cold in a soy and mild chili-oil bath. Hot and sour soup is thick with bean curd, mushrooms, meat and vegetables, though thin on both hot and sour accents. But other soups, such as the pork and cabbage, the bean curd with mushrooms and the Hunan special soups seem to be based on hot water.

Meaty, sizzling hot spareribs and strips of barbecued beef on satays also are good appetizers. So is the cool, white bean curd in hot sesame oil with scallions. Among main courses, chewy slabs of beef with dried orange peel are satisfying, although they are not spicy. Eggplant with garlic sauce has a satiny, richly soothing effect.

Empire special shrimp, dry sautéed in their salt and pepper encrusted shells, are masterpieces. Scallops, either with a crisp finish in a pungent Hunan sauce or stir-fried with black-bean sauce, also can be counted among the better choices. So can the crispy shrimp, also in Hunan sauce. And the crispy sea bass in a hot, sweet and vinegary pink sauce was properly crunchy on one occasion, though not fresh enough on another. If there are any hungry corners in your stomach that still need filling, wind up with a steaming mound of soft, savory fried rice noodles tossed with pork and flecks of cabbage.

Rancid cashew nuts ruined the combination of chicken with cashews, just as rancid oil put an acidic edge on the stale-smelling sliced flounder, one of the worst dishes I have ever eaten. String beans lacked interest. So did the house special called "sliced prawns versus pork Hunan style" and the special garden vegetables that included canned mushrooms, ordinary broccoli, carrots and a few more authentic Chinese additions. Crispy-fried duck was acceptable, although it had been reheated once too often. Lamb with scallions would have been better had there been more lamb and fewer scallions. Other lackluster dishes included lamb Hunan style, shredded beef with garlic sauce and Ta-Chien chicken bulked up with red and green bell peppers. The quartered oranges offered free for dessert are refreshing, but for those who prefer a more auspicious ending there are hot, crisp and lightly sugared fried banana chunks filled with sweet red bean paste.

At the Empire Szechuan Balcony on Third Avenue, the cabbage appetizer is crunchy and refreshing, if inadequately spiced. Rancid oil marred barbecued beef strips on satays, the fried rice noodles and the beef with dried red pepper. A good deal better were the shredded pork with garlic sauce, the bean curd in black-bean sauce and both the crispy scallops and crispy shrimp, though they were not up to those at the other Empire Szechuan outposts. Hot and cold noodles in sesame sauce were delicious first courses, as were the puffy, meaty fried dumplings. But spareribs and fried duck had the texture of rubber. An overabundance of red and green pepper, carrots and cold, American-style broccoli added bulk if not flavor to many dishes, and soups here were the blandest of all. None of the standard Cantonese appetizers — egg roll, wonton, shrimp toast — are worth ordering. Beware of sweet and sour dishes at all Empire Szechuans and know that the so-called chef's specialties and daily specials tend to be tourist concoctions, rarely as good as other choices.

Both places serve good, hot jasmine tea. Only the Third Avenue restaurant has a liquor license, but drinks come with half-melted ice cubes. Both restaurants do a land-office takeout business.

Empire Szechuan Gourmet
★

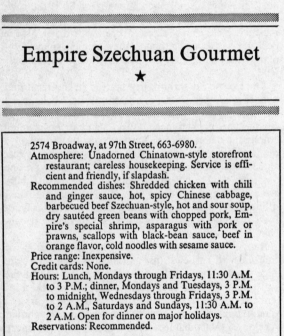

2574 Broadway, at 97th Street, 663-6980.
Atmosphere: Unadorned Chinatown-style storefront restaurant; careless housekeeping. Service is efficient and friendly, if slapdash.
Recommended dishes: Shredded chicken with chili and ginger sauce, hot, spicy Chinese cabbage, barbecued beef Szechuan-style, hot and sour soup, dry sautéed green beans with chopped pork, Empire's special shrimp, asparagus with pork or prawns, scallops with black-bean sauce, beef in orange flavor, cold noodles with sesame sauce.
Price range: Inexpensive.
Credit cards: None.
Hours: Lunch, Mondays through Fridays, 11:30 A.M. to 3 P.M.; dinner, Mondays and Tuesdays, 3 P.M. to midnight, Wednesdays through Fridays, 3 P.M. to 2 A.M., Saturdays and Sundays, 11:30 A.M. to 2 A.M. Open for dinner on major holidays.
Reservations: Recommended.

If ever there was an uptown version of a typical Chinatown restaurant, it is the Empire Szechuan Gourmet. It is an absolutely unadorned, crowded and noisy Chinese luncheonette with plastic tablecloths, typically careless housekeeping and typically low prices for food that is freshly prepared and decently serviceable. Untypically, there are young Chinese waitresses who are friendly and efficient, if somewhat slapdash about their presentation. The menu is large and varied and divides evenly between dishes that are familiar and others that are unusual.

If you like to have hot and spicy food that is really hot and spicy, make that clear at the start, otherwise you will find the dishes here far too mild. Three appetizers were sufficiently spicy — the cold shredded chicken in a chili and ginger sauce, the cold spiced Szechuan pickled cabbage, and the cold noodles with scallions in sesame oil. Hot and sour soup had a pleasant needling of chili oil and generous lacings of bean curd, meat and vegetables. Flat strips of beef satays billed as barbecued beef Szechuan-style were tender and interesting, and fried dumplings were acceptable, if not the best examples of that Cantonese specialty.

Dried sautéed green beans with garlic and minced pork were delicious. But eggplant in garlic sauce and bean curd Szechuan-style lacked the fiery sauce one expected, since they were indicated as being "hot and spicy" on the menu.

Empire special shrimp, a Taiwan dish, was among the best choices. Shrimp in the shell sautéed with garlic are served with spicy salt that adds a perfect accent to the crisp shrimp. Sliced sea scallops sautéed in a fragrant black sauce with bamboo shoots and peppers were delicious, but a whole, crisply fried fish was spoiled by an improbably red, sticky sweet sauce.

There is always a fresh vegetable in season, available stir-fried with beef, pork, prawns, or scallops. I tried the combination with the prawns and found it to be a soothing and bright, mild-flavored Cantonese main course. Beef in orange flavor was at once hotly spiced with dried chili pods and mellowed by dried tangerine peel.

Although of decent quality, beef in garlic sauce and sliced lamb Hunan-style lacked sufficient seasoning.

More expensive dishes such as fried chicken and Peking duck are mildly disappointing; stick to the less expensive stir-fried offerings here.

At dinner, fresh fruit is served gratis. Beer is available, including a rather thin, sourish Chinese brew.

Ennio & Michael
★ ★

504 La Guardia Place, between Bleecker and West Houston Streets, 677-8577.

Atmosphere: Attractive and stylishly casual cafe-restaurant; noisy when full. Service is friendly and generally good, but the kitchen is sometimes slow or unevenly paced.

Recommended dishes: Hot antipasto, baked clams oreganate, fish salad, roast peppers with mozzarella, clams Posilippo, spiedini, spaghetti alla puttanesca, linguine with clam sauce, manicotti, ravioli with meat filling, rigatoni with tomato sauce, tortelloni, fried zucchini, broccoli di rape, arugula salad, veal scaloppine with mushrooms, broiled veal chop, veal cutlet Parmigiana, filet mignon with eggplant and mozzarella, chicken all'arrabbiata, calf's liver Veneziana, shrimp fra diavolo, striped bass Livornese, cheesecake, cannoli.

Price range: Moderately expensive.

Credit cards: American Express.

Hours: Dinner, Tuesdays through Saturdays, 5:30 P.M. to 11:30 P.M., Sundays, 3 P.M. to 10 P.M. Closed Mondays.

Reservations: Necessary for parties of four or more.

At a time when many owners of Italian restaurants seem to feel that they can only succeed with overrefined versions of dishes from such northern regions as Piedmont, Lombardy and Tuscany, it is encouraging to see a frankly southern kitchen achieve a large and loyal following. Eating would be much less fun if, because of fashion's whim, we lost such southern Italian specialties as linguine with white clam sauce, clams Posilippo or oreganate, the bitter broccoli di rape affogato (literally "suffocated") with garlic and oil, shrimp fra diavolo and even veal Parmigiana, a dish whose time may have come again.

It is precisely the skillful preparation of these dishes and others like them that has led to the success of Ennio & Michael, opened in 1979 on Bleecker Street and moved in January 1981 to larger, livelier and more stylish modern quarters on La Guardia Place. Fortunately, success has not spoiled this simple, unpretentious restaurant, which not only still delivers what it promises but also has improved with time. Originally given a one-star rating, it now merits two.

To be sure, a few northern dishes appear on the menu, but it is obviously the delicate representations of specialties from the Campagna and the Abruzzi that stand out. This is just what might be expected from Nicola Di Laurenzio, the chef from the Abruzzi, the region much celebrated for its cooking, who is one of the three owners. Ennio Sammarone and Michael Savarese, the other two, oversee the dining room and coordinate the kitchen's pacing. In the new home, this pacing is not yet entirely worked out; at crowded hours, one or two diners in a party get dishes as much as five minutes before others, and there is sometimes a long wait between courses.

The menu is short and uncomplicated, though enticing, and simple specials not listed will be prepared on request. Friendly and accommodating waiters also suggest off-menu choices to frequent visitors to add variety. In addition to such listed appetizers as good garlic- and oregano-scented baked clams oreganate, the kitchen will prepare unlisted clams Posilippo, adrift in a light tomato-garlic broth. And if you prefer an enrichment to the simple well-roasted peppers, you may have them with slices of fresh mozzarella and tomato.

The hot antipasto, with its baked clams, shrimp marinara and eggplant rolled around mozzarella, was gently satisfying, although the stuffed mushrooms needed a livelier filling. A fish salad for two, made with cool, tender octopus, squid, shrimp and celery, profited from an extra splash of lemon juice and black pepper. Spiedini alla Romana, the fried mozzarella and bread appetizer, is well doused with an anchovy and caper sauce. On one night, a stuffed artichoke, warmly fragrant with Gaeta olives, anchovy, capers and garlic croutons, was a most welcome specialty. Only the mushrooms and the cold antipasto with its characterless prosciutto and salami were disappointing.

Before or after the appetizer, or sometime during the meal, try the crisp slivers of fried zucchini. They are satisfying with drinks or as a side dish to main courses, far better than the dismal overcooked and tough string beans. The broccoli di rape, often available as a vegetable when in season, is preferable plain rather than combined with the underseasoned, densely packed sausage.

Pastas are well handled, among the best being the spaghetti alla puttanesca in heady sauce spiced with basil, olive oil, garlic, black olives and a touch of anchovy, and the linguine with white clam sauce, properly accented with garlic. Baked manicotti and the meat-and-spinach-filled ravioli were lusty in flavor and texture, and a daily special of rigatoni with a light tomato sauce and cheese was exceptional. The large veal-and-prosciutto-filled tortelloni in tomato-cream sauce were better than the smaller tortellini, undercooked and dry whether gratinéed with tomato sauce or in an unpleasantly milky cream sauce. The marinara sauce on gnocchi had just the right zest, but the tiny potato dumplings should have been lighter and less pasty.

The least pleasant main course was the zuppa di pesce, a Friday night special, which was spoiled by dry and fishy-tasting squid, although the soup's other ingredients such as clams, whiting, shrimp and sole were acceptable, as was the garlic and tomato broth. Preferable choices are the pungent striped bass Livornese style with olives and capers or the shrimp in a fiery fra diavolo sauce, combining tomato, garlic and hot peppers.

Veal Parmigiana is delicious. So are the carefully broiled veal chops and the calf's liver Veneziana, usually prepared on Friday. The excellent chicken all'arrabbiata, sautéed with garlic and rosemary and enlivened with white wine and red vinegar, is a better choice than the underseasoned, ordinary chicken Margherita. Neither the pasty, bland veal piccata nor the cutlet Milanese overpowered by the flavor of the bread crumbs held as much interest as the veal scaloppine sautéed with sherry and mushrooms or the medaillons of filet mignon topped with eggplant, mozzarella and tomato.

There is an exceptionally light, almost fluffy — if unauthentic Italian — ricotta cheesecake made here, lightly flavored with vanilla. It will probably disappoint those who favor the moister, more solid version, but I prefer this more delicate variation. Cannoli are filled when they are ordered, so that the crisp tubular crusts are not made soggy by the creamed ricotta filling, which is flavored with vanilla, sugar and bits of chocolate. Rum cake is decent though undistinguished. Fresh fruit and strawberries are also available. So is very good espresso.

Estia

★

---

308 East 86th Street, between First and Second Avenues, 628-9100.

Atmosphere: Typical folkloric taverna setting, crowded and noisily convivial; service is fast, friendly and informal.

Recommended dishes: Eggplant salad, cucumber and yogurt salad, keftedakia, souvlakia gitonias, fried smelts, spinach pie, octopus salad, warm shrimp with oil and lemon, fried zucchini with skordalia sauce, egg-lemon soup, shish kebab, baked lamb with orzos, fried squid, stewed veal, estifado, grilled porgy, baked striped bass with feta cheese and tomatoes, crème caramel.

Price range: Moderate.

Credit cards: American Express, Visa, MasterCard and Diners Club.

Hours: Dinner, seven days, 4:30 P.M. to 1 A.M. Live music continuous to 3 A.M. except on Mondays.

Reservations: Necessary.

To have a good time at Estia, you must like not only Greek food but plenty of noise as well. For this small, bustling, white taverna is a lively, jam-packed meeting place for a large, lusty segment of the Greek community in New York, and that means a band playing Greek music every night starting at nine and customers getting up to dance and sing at a volume that obliterates all conversation. On Tuesdays and Wednesdays, there is an especially noisy duo, and on those nights it seems as though a closetful of pots and pans has been sent clattering about one's head.

Yet it is that noise, and the floor show provided by the clientele, that make Estia worth visiting. Were it for the food alone, Estia could easily be matched or surpassed by several other Greek restaurants in Manhattan: the level of cooking ranges from mediocre to good. But the convivial atmosphere and ethnic authenticity provide added sauce to the proceedings.

With a glass of ouzo — the milky, licorice-flavored apéritif — order an assortment of mezedakia, which are Greek appetizers and the best course by far at Estia. These include crisp chips of hot fried zucchini to be dipped in a thick, garlicky skordalia sauce; keftedakia (hot, grilled ground-lamb patties, with slivers of red onion); warm shrimp in oil and lemon, and excellent spinach pie. Crisply fried, tiny smelts and small, grilled nuggets of lamb (souvlakia gitonias) are equally good.

Among cold appetizers at Estia, eggplant salad and a salad of yogurt and cucumber are worth trying, and tender pink octopus marinated in a fragrantly seasoned oil-and-lemon dressing demands to be sopped up with bread. But the stuffed vine leaves were tough and fibrous, and the taramasalata, while smooth and creamy, lacked any of the tingling saline sprightliness associated with this fish-roe purée. Egg-lemon chicken broth with rice was decent and soothing.

As a matter of fact, the best meal at Estia would be one made up entirely of shared appetizers. Among regular main courses, however, you will fare best by sticking to the simplest choices. Cheaper braised cuts of meat were the most satisfactory sampled. Yuvetsi Parnassus — baked lamb with orzos, the soft, slippery, rice-shaped pasta in tomato sauce — was a gentle and soul-warming dish. So was a plat du jour of shoulder of veal braised to melting tenderness with tomatoes, which created a flavorful sauce for the accompanying rice. Estifado (cubes of beef stewed with tomatoes and onions and scented with cinnamon) and lamb shish kebab are also among the acceptable main courses. Kapama, chunks of stewed lamb, was less satisfactory because the meat was fatty and full of sinews. Rings of fried squid were crisp, greaseless and delicious, and both grilled porgy and striped bass with feta cheese and tomatoes were fresh, bright and well seasoned.

The Estia platter, an assortment that includes moussaka, the meat and macaroni pie called pastitsio, braised lamb shoulder and large, stuffed vine leaves, proved, by and large, dreadful. On another night, moussaka was as dry and dreary as on the first try. Veal chop in lemon sauce and a phyllo strudel filled with meat were disappointing. Vegetables were overcooked, but nevertheless pleasantly herbaceous.

Pastry desserts, such as baklava and galatoboureko, were dry and leaden. Crème caramel was a better alternative.

Felidia

★

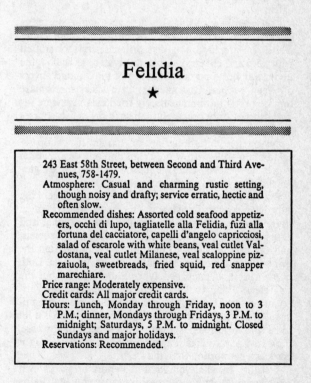

243 East 58th Street, between Second and Third Avenues, 758-1479.

Atmosphere: Casual and charming rustic setting, though noisy and drafty; service erratic, hectic and often slow.

Recommended dishes: Assorted cold seafood appetizers, occhi di lupo, tagliatelle alla Felidia, fuzi alla fortuna del cacciatore, capelli d'angelo capricciosi, salad of escarole with white beans, veal cutlet Valdostana, veal cutlet Milanese, veal scaloppine pizzaiuola, sweetbreads, fried squid, red snapper marechiare.

Price range: Moderately expensive.

Credit cards: All major credit cards.

Hours: Lunch, Monday through Friday, noon to 3 P.M.; dinner, Mondays through Fridays, 3 P.M. to midnight; Saturdays, 5 P.M. to midnight. Closed Sundays and major holidays.

Reservations: Recommended.

The more attractive a restaurant is, the greater the promise of good food it holds out, for it is logical for diners to assume that an owner who spends a great deal of money and effort to create a beautiful dining room will be able to effect equally felicitous results in the kitchen. That such optimism can be somewhat misplaced is evident at Ristorante Felidia, where the food is disappointingly inconsistent.

The dining rooms, arranged on two levels with a skylit balcony and an attractive bar, take on a rustic airiness from white walls, leafy plants and terra-cotta tile and brick. But the noise in certain areas can be deafening, especially on the balcony. Moreover, the windows and skylights still afford uninterrupted views of an open construction pit and the back of a drab brick building, and the air-conditioning is excessive, although it will be adjusted on request. Add to that the badly organized service, and the diner begins to feel that the food will have to be fairly sensational to compensate.

For the most serious eaters, a number of the kitchen's most serious efforts are consistently good enough to do just that. Among such excellent offerings are the assorted cold seafood appetizer, which includes a sprightly salad of squid and shellfish, the mussels topped with minced pimento and onion and slivers of tripe vinaigrette. The homemade pasta bow ties called fuzi alla fortuna del cacciatore — according to the luck of the hunter — were wonderful topped with braised quail and their savory sauce. Occhi di lupo, the short tubular pasta suggesting wolves' eyes, is served with a subtle, creamy ricotta-and-tomato sauce accented by bacon and grilled sausage, and a lunch special of the fine angel's hair pasta, capelli d'angelo capricciosi, was heavenly under a sauce of tomato, onion and Italian bacon.

Consistently excellent also were such main courses as sautéed sweetbreads in a lemony sauce and good, tender white veal prepared in cutlets Milanese style, or stuffed with ham and cheese Valdostana style, or as scaloppine under a delicate pizzaiuola sauce of tomato and slivers of green pepper. Red snapper in a sheer marechiare tomato broth and immaculately fried calamari were far more successfully prepared than such other fish courses as shrimp reeking of iodine, indicating staleness, or a heavy-handed interpretation of Italian fish soup. A salad of escarole with white beans and one day's special vegetable — savoy cabbage mashed with potatoes, garlic and olive oil — would be hard to match.

But very good though much of it is, Felidia's cooking is bedeviled by inconsistency. The menu, which is often stained with wine and grease, lists many original and enticing selections, but the house pushes daily specials, and the captains tend to discourage ordering from the printed menu. This is especially true of the pasta. Both homemade and packaged types are available, but the staff steers diners to the homemade, probably for a variety of reasons. Homemade pasta is, of course, more unusual and, with many sauces, superior. But there is a lot to be said for dried pasta with other sauces. In any case, the dried pasta takes longer to cook, and at Felidia it costs less per portion than the fresh.

Insisting on what you want at Felidia brings its own punishment, usually in the form of a long wait. That is true not only of pasta but also of the bland and soggy hot appetizers.

Inconsistencies are apparent even with such pastas as tagliatelle, delicate green noodles, sublime when cooked al dente and folded into a cream-and-tomato sauce dotted with prosciutto and fresh peas (alla Felidia), but a travesty when so overcooked that they melded into a single mass. Potato dumplings — gnocchi — sometimes had the airy lightness expected, while at other times they were gray and gummy, and the pesto sauce included very little basil. Linguine with clam sauce was overcooked and undersalted, and its sauce needed a more authoritative belt of garlic. Risotto with seafood would have been excellent if it had not been tossed with salty cheese, and the cornmeal polenta was hard and stodgy.

"Piatti gastronomici" is the menu's polite way of saying innards. Among them are listed tripe, kidneys, calf's liver Veneziana and the excellent sweetbreads. But the calf's liver and the kidneys were drowned in wine that did not cook off, and mushrooms outweighed kidneys by at least eight to one.

A daily special of chicken breast stuffed with vegetables and cheese was also overpowered by its wine sauce, and the pallid version of the garlic-sautéed chicken scarpariello lacked flavor.

A single pass at zabaglione resulted in a very sweet and overfoamy version of that whipped egg-yolk-and-Marsala dessert. Similarly, all the cakes sampled were toothachingly sweet and unsophisticated.

Forest and Sea
International Restaurant

★

477 Amsterdam Avenue, at the corner of 83rd Street, 580-7873.
Atmosphere: Plain, pleasant, informal dining room that requires more ventilation; service is polite and well meaning, if a little slow.
Recommended dishes: Onion soup, baked clams in garlic, stuffed mushrooms, spinach salad, Thai-style rabbit, pork chops in hoisin sauce, roasted chicken in soy sauce and black pepper, steak au poivre, chicken cutlet.
Price range: Inexpensive.
Credit cards: American Express, Visa, MasterCard and Diners Club.
Hours: Lunch, seven days, 1 P.M. to 4 P.M.; dinner, seven days, 4 P.M. to 11:30 P.M. Closed major holidays.
Reservations: Accepted.

With food prices soaring upward almost by the minute, there is some cause for celebration when a restaurant offers pleasantly prepared and interesting main courses such as Thai-style rabbit sautéed in soy sauce with ginger and mushrooms, pork chops sautéed with onion in hoisin sauce and a crisp, buttery stuffed chicken cutlet for a reasonable price, complete with rice or potatoes and well-cooked vegetables. Not all creations at the

Forest and Sea International Restaurant live up to those three dishes, but it is nevertheless possible to put together a satisfying and entertaining meal here very inexpensively. The Thai owners offer food that is basically Continental with Oriental accents and overtones, a combination that works better in some instances than in others.

The setting is simple and just a few cuts above a coffee shop, with dark wood-grain paneling and plants. Service is friendly and polite, if a bit slow, and except for radio background music and inadequate ventilation, the dining room is comfortable.

At a first dinner for four, there were so many enticing dishes I felt I was on the way to at least a two-star rating. Thick, mellow onion soup with a bubbly cheese topping and an original chicken-vegetable soup flavored with thyme and reminiscent of Manhattan clam chowder, were bracing, steaming hot and far above average.

Baked clams were exceptional with their topping of minced garlic, bread crumbs, paprika and hot chili pepper, and snails baked in a light, minty sauce were a close second. Another good choice was mushrooms baked with a melting cheese filling.

The only disappointment among first courses that night was the pasty, gray pâté maison. Nor was the salad we shared up to the earlier dishes. Called Noi's Thai salad, it consisted of bean sprouts, cucumbers, tomato and iceberg lettuce, all of which remained banal despite a fiery chili-spiked coconut dressing.

In addition to the three main courses already mentioned, Bangkok chicken marinated in soy sauce and pepper, then roasted and served with crisp, sliced cucumber in a spicy Thai dressing, was an excellent buy. Although not as tender as it might be, steak au poivre had a good beefy edge to it, and the sauce was heady with its pepper-brandy counterpoints.

At other meals, results were less encouraging. Carrot soup was overly sweet and mawkish; a daily special of beef carbonnade à la Flamande came forth as dry, tough, tasteless pot roast; something billed as white snapper was only minimally acceptable; shrimp with a fish stuffing were tough and dry. Spinach salad with mushrooms and bacon was far superior to Noi's Thai salad, and well worth ordering.

At lunch another day, spaghetti with tomato, onion and basil sauce would have been delicious had it not also contained tarragon, and sliced steak for a sandwich was almost raw and completely cold, although the meat itself was decent and fresh. Moules marinière were properly garlicky, but at least half of them were sandy.

Desserts are poor and drinks seem expensive compared to food.

Foro Italico

★

455 West 34th Street, between Ninth and Tenth Avenues, 564-6619.

Atmosphere: Modern, gaudy, bright and pleasant but sometimes cramped and noisy; service is efficient and friendly.

Recommended dishes: Hot antipasto, clams oreganate, seafood salad, tortellini in brodo, all pasta, scampi, veal piccata and parmigiana.

Price range: Moderately expensive.

Credit cards: All major credit cards.

Hours: Lunch, Mondays through Fridays, noon to 3 P.M.; dinner, Mondays through Fridays, 5 P.M. to 10 P.M., Saturdays, 5 P.M. to 11 P.M.

Reservations: Suggested for lunch and dinner; necessary before major events at Madison Square Garden.

This small, comfortable and felicitous restaurant would be welcome in any neighborhood, but when the neighborhood is that of Madison Square Garden, it is a downright blessing. Although the kitchen's performance is unexciting, there are still more than enough decent and satisfying Italian dishes to add up to a pleasant dinner before a basketball game or a hockey match.

In appearance it seems to suggest a cocktail lounge, with dark, wood-grained wall panels and a wild mismatch of colored glass chandeliers. It is dark and candlelit at night and pleasant, too, during the day despite the uninspired details of its décor. Table linens are impeccably laundered, the help is courteous and efficient, and the owner is solicitous.

One of the more refreshing and interesting appetizers is the cold mixed seafood salad, a bright tossing of squid and shrimp with celery, lemon juice and olive oil. Only the unnecessary addition of frozen Alaskan king crab meat spoils the mix slightly. Unfortunately, other second-rate garnishes include limp lettuce leaves and canned California olives, a pointless lapse with so many good barrel olives available on nearby Ninth Avenue. Paprika on broiled fish and scampi dishes is another unfortunate touch that not only dries the fish but compromises its fresh flavor.

The hot antipasto here is a savory combination of stuffed mushrooms, baked clams and eggplant simmered in tomato. Among soups, the tortellini in brodo, tender meat-filled circular pasta in a flavorful broth, is exceptional. So is this same pasta with a sauce of tomatoes and onion or of cheese, cream and butter. White clam sauce on linguine and cannelloni filled with spinach and meat were decent, but the seafood mixture on the fine angel's hair, cappelli di angelo, was stale.

Shrimp scampi-style are delicately done, well basted with a garlic and oil sauce to keep them moist as they broiled. Only the paprika slightly spoiled the effect.

And even a dish as banal as veal parmigiana was distinguished by a fluffy tomato-onion sauce under the creamy fresh melted mozzarella topping. Veal piccata, in a lemon sauce, was equally good, although the meat was mushy from having been overtenderized. Chicken dishes, however, tended to be a bit too dry.

Fortune Garden

★

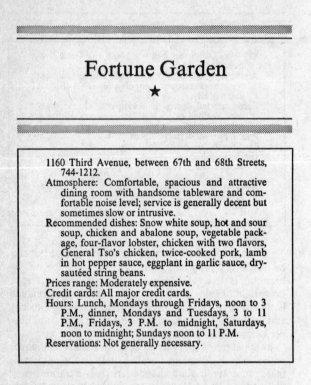

1160 Third Avenue, between 67th and 68th Streets, 744-1212.

Atmosphere: Comfortable, spacious and attractive dining room with handsome tableware and comfortable noise level; service is generally decent but sometimes slow or intrusive.

Recommended dishes: Snow white soup, hot and sour soup, chicken and abalone soup, vegetable package, four-flavor lobster, chicken with two flavors, General Tso's chicken, twice-cooked pork, lamb in hot pepper sauce, eggplant in garlic sauce, dry-sautéed string beans.

Prices range: Moderately expensive.

Credit cards: All major credit cards.

Hours: Lunch, Mondays through Fridays, noon to 3 P.M., dinner, Mondays and Tuesdays, 3 to 11 P.M., Fridays, 3 P.M. to midnight, Saturdays, noon to midnight; Sundays noon to 11 P.M.

Reservations: Not generally necessary.

Because of the pleasantly spacious setting and interesting menu, Fortune Garden tends to instill high expectations. But the promise has neven been quite fulfilled. The biggest improvement is the compliance with requests that spicy food be really spicy. In the early days that was not so, but based on recent experiences it seems that reluctance has been corrected. When you say *hot* here, be sure you mean it.

Because it is a comfortable restaurant, with large, widely spaced tables, attractive china and a bearable noise level, and as the food is fresh and decent, it's the sort of place one might go to if in the neighborhood and in search of a satisfying meal.

Service is uneven, generally good and polite but occasionally slow and perfunctory. Waiters automatically portion food out American-style, without asking guests. Many diners prefer that type of service, but those who enjoy the traditional Chinese family service, with dishes in the center of the table so food can be picked up with chopsticks, hardly stand a chance.

A few specialties were above routine interest. Among these was a vegetable package appetizer — a savory mix of minced bean curd and black mushrooms wrapped in an iceberg lettuce leaf, to be eaten out of hand. Good as this was, it would have been more comfortable to negotiate served in two delicate portions, instead of one so large it was virtually impossible to handle. Also worth trying were a sharp and pungent hot and sour soup and a chicken broth with abalone and vegetables, both served at a banquet, and snow white soup, a mild and subtle fish broth with pearly fish slices and puffy cloudlets of poached egg white. The best main courses were chicken with two flavors (white and silky, mild-flavored shreds, with bean sprouts and chunks of chicken, in a spice-burnished brown sauce), tender flecks of twice-cooked pork with a chili-spiked sauce, eggplant with garlic and lean, tender bits of lamb in hot-pepper sauce.

The most exceptional dish was four-flavor lobster — sliced, fresh-cooked lobster meat served with sauces that progressed from a mild vinegar and soy blend to an incendiary mustard mixture. Arranged around the shell of a mammoth lobster, which the waiter said weighed six pounds, the meat we were served seemed far less than that and, at the price, seemed a meager portion for each of the six people who shared it, though outstanding in quality. Exquisitely tender beef in a Malaysain barbecue sauce, another special-order dish, was almost as good as the lobster.

All other dishes left something to be desired. As tender as orange-flavored beef was, its sauce proved banal. Shrimp in Sichuan sauce was far too sweet and tasted of tomato ketchup, and several dishes were overcooked and greasy: anise-flavored braised duck, honeyed spareribs, noodles stir-fried with vegetables and a dessert of fried bananas. Lobster two ways, on the standard menu, was boring both ways, and an appetizer of aromatic beef tasted like corned beef straight from the refrigerator.

Another appetizer, crab meat to be rolled in lettuce leaves, was made with Alaskan king crab, always an inferior ingredient, and again, too much filling was spooned into each lettuce leaf. Crispy-fried sea bass had a lovely spicy sauce, but the fish itself had the musty flavor indicating a lack of freshness.

Dry sautéed string beans with crumbles of pork were delicious, as was the spicy General Tso's chicken.

Peking duck was acceptable with crisp skin and moist meat, but it would have been more entertaining if we could have filled the crepes ourselves. Again, two small filled crepes make a much more graceful presentation than one that is gross.

Black mushrooms and hearts of Chinese cabbage were leaden and greasy. Both a crisp-fried flounder and a deep-fried sea bass tasted of overheated frying oil. The bones and skin of the flounder were not nearly so shatteringly crisp as they had to be to be edible. What the captain described as "Chinese Jell-O with bananas" tasted much like Junket's Danish Dessert, a cloyingly sweet, soft, red pudding with bananas and a topping of totally rancid walnuts.

The wine list at Fortune Garden is more interesting than at most Chinese restaurants, although my preference with this food runs to beer or Scotch and soda.

Four Seasons
★ ★

99 East 52nd Street, between Park and Lexington
Avenues, 754-9494.

Atmosphere: Handsome, spacious and plush modern
setting, in bar and pool dining room. Good acoustics make it comfortable for conversations, although some tables in the grill are tightly packed;
service is good.

Recommended dishes: Marinated salmon, clams and
oysters on the half shell, wild boar pâté, game bird
pâté or galantine, calf's brains or sweetbreads in
mustard crumbs, feuilletage of oysters and vesiga,
oysters and artichokes, fettuccine with wild mushrooms, tortelloni, broiled squab, vegetable potage,
lobster bisque, sautéed Dover sole, broiled swordfish, calf's liver with avocado slices, steak tartare,
crisp shrimp with mustard fruits, breast of pheasant with glazed apples, rosemary roasted rack of
lamb, côte de boeuf, paillard of venison, poached
salmon in thin velouté, partridge with bacon and
mustard, gratin of knob celery, roesti potatoes,
sautéed snow-pea pods, chocolate soufflé, grapefruit sherbet, chocolate velvet cake.

Price range: Expensive.

Credit cards: All major credit cards.

Hours: Pool dining room, lunch, Mondays though
Fridays, noon to 2:30 P.M.; dinner, Mondays
through Saturdays, 5 P.M. to 11:30 P.M. . Grill,
lunch, Mondays through Fridays, noon to 1:45
P.M.; dinner, Mondays through Fridays, 8 P.M. to
11:30 P.M. Closed Sundays.

Reservations: Necessary.

Opened almost twenty-five years ago, The Four Seasons has weathered so well that it is still the handsomest
and grandest mordern restaurant in the country if not in
the world.

It took an extraordinary collection of talent to plan
and execute the creation of this landmark in the Sea-
gram Building. The high-flown palatial interior, with its
swagged, rippling, coppery-chain curtains, the marbled
splendor of its reflecting pool, the garden of greenery
and the gleaming, dark, French-rosewood-paneled
walls and black upholstery of the barroom, brightened
by Richard Lippold's hanging brass-rod sculptures all
came from the drawing board of Philip Johnson, and
table appointments were also innovations in restaurant
tableware at that time, and much of the silver hollo-
ware, china, crystal and serving equipment are now in
the Museum of Modern Art's good-design collection.

This was conceived as a restaurant that would feature
the foods of each season, with menu, plants and accessories changing accordingly, and this was an entirely
new idea twenty years ago. Rather than simply repeat-
ing classic cuisine, the originators drew from the whole
history and geography of cookery, recombining elements into new dishes appropriate to New York as a
crossroad of the world.

The late Albert Stockli, then the executive chef, tested

and retested many of the dishes, which are still prepared under the expert hand of the chef, Seppi Renggli.

In a way, the Four Seasons really could be considered as two restaurants — the trim, tailored and handsomely masculine, two-level barroom, where a simple but stylish grill menu prevails at lunch and late dinner on weekdays, and the glamorous sparkling pool dining room where larger and more elaborate menus are served Mondays through Saturdays.

But though the menus differ in style, all of the food comes out of the same kitchen, and the same strengths and weaknesses prevail in both rooms. Broadly speaking, the Four Seasons does best by simple dishes based on ingredients of impeccable quality that are usually just as impeccably grilled or sautéed. Weaknesses come in some of the frying, the darker sauces for meat dishes and in the desserts. Menu changes are frequent, so dishes recommended are not always available.

It would be difficult to find fresher oysters and clams than those offered here, served with a variety of dipping sauces, most of which tend to be a bit heavy. Our choice is the freshly grated horseradish and lemon. Crab meat is always represented by the largest, snowiest lumps available but is probably from Florida rather than the Chesapeake Bay, and thus is a bit mild in flavor. Scottish smoked salmon is above average, but a far more interesting choice is the Swedish marinated salmon, gravlax, served with an airy dill sauce. That salmon is also delicious grilled as a main course.

The best pâté is the galantine of game birds, but the wild boar is also very good, although not identifiable as boar. A fish pâté with insets of scallops and salmon was, on three occasions, too densely compact and rubbery. One excellent hot appetizer was feuilletage of oysters with vesiga, a rectangle of puffed pastry sandwiching a layer of plump, poached oysters in a silky sheen of vesiga — the marrow from the backbone of a sturgeon that is the classic liaison in a traditional couilibiac and another was a gratiné of oysters and artichokes. Calf's brains encrusted with mustard-flavored crumbs and sautéed in brown butter were also delicious. A nest of tiny shrimp in shoyu, one of the holdovers from the original menu, came as limp tasteless shrimp in a deep-fried potato basket with a knockout sauce based on fiery aromatic Japanese green horseradish. The preserved goose confit d'oie, served hot in a ramekin, was pasty and unplesantly mushy.

Mixed vegetable potages are always well done, but the duck consommé, though pleasant, had no identifiable flavor and could have been just about any strong clear brown stock.

Fish is beautifully cooked at the Four Seasons, rarely to an overdone state. A grilled, thick swordfish steak was perfectly moist and tender and is especially good with olive butter. Sautéed Dover sole would have profited by a slightly lighter lemon-butter sauce. Poached salmon in a sheer velouté, flavored with leeks, was a lovely replacement for a truite au bleu sent back because it had the muddy taste of a bottom fish. Sautéed shrimp and scallops said to be in lobster butter came in a sauce that seemed like a thinner version of the bisque to make a fair dish. Crisply fried, battered, gilded shrimp with Italian preserved mustard fruits were as good as they have been since the restaurant opened twenty years ago.

There were two extraordinary meat main courses — a grilled côte de boeuf, with a rich but gossamer sauce, and a rosemary-roasted rack of lamb. Both were served with bones and roasted trimmings for nibblers. Sautéed calf's liver was also excellent, garnished with avocado. I also enjoyed the breast of pheasant topped with glazed apple slices in a delicate sauce not much heavier than au jus.

Duck and a few other game dishes (wild boar and venison) at times are overpowered by sweet and sticky sauces much like Chinese barbecue glaze in texture. Game in this country has little enough flavor, and heavy sauces kill any chance of having the meat distinguishable. Grilled game in the barroom was far superior — both partridge with bacon and mustard paillard of venison.

An exceptional side dish with the wild boar or other game is Gorgonzola polenta, a soufflélike puff of cornmeal flavored with cheese and so good it should be available as an à la carte side order. Steak tartare has always been of high quality and delicious at the Four Seasons, and it still is.

Veal scaloppine, sautéed to a perfect golden brown finish and dressed with lemon butter, were necessarily needled for added tenderness, a touch that imparted the texture of ground meat, and a thick veal chop was dry and overpowered by rosemary. Cassoulet served in the grill at lunch as a plat du jour was baked in individual gratin dishes to give it a crusty topping but,unfortunately, this also made it dry and pasty, and its meats lacked distinction. There is also a spectacular puff-pastry-topped chicken pie in the grill at lunch, and a very stylish late dinner menu that includes good pasta and broiled squab.

Many dishes are garnished with an Oriental-style, stir-fried vegetable combination, a touch that is not always successful. Better to order single vegetables, such as firm bright broccoli in good lemony hollandaise or sautéed, faintly crisp snow-pea pods or, best of all, sliced knob celery, gratinéed under a light cheese-and-cream topping. Roesti potatoes, grated and fried, have been wonderful; baked and steamed potatoes are also excellent, no small triumph in this city.

To anyone who remembers the original Four Seasons desserts, this final course will come as a huge disappointment. Nothing on the impressive wagon is nearly so good as it looks, with the sole exception of a thick, mousselike, chocolate velvet cake. This thick and rich combination would be a little easier to take with a spoonful or two of half-whipped cream. The mousses are too soft and blend with the whipped-cream garnish, and the poached fruits are too sweet. Chocolate soufflé is better than vanilla here, as the half-and-half harlequin specialty proved, and the homemade fruit sorbets are generally lovely, especially the grapefruit.

If the cakes and pastries are below par, the croissants certainly are not. They are tiny, flaky and excellent, although to my taste, to achieve real perfection, they still need a pinch less sugar and a pinch more salt.

Prices at the Four Seasons are astronomical, especially in the pool dining room (unless you have the under $30 pre-theater dinner or late supper). One should, therefore, be very choosy about the table one accepts. To be seated in the upper back level behind the pool dining room is not to be at the Four Seasons at all, unless you have one of the few rail tables. At lunch there is also an upper and outer Siberia behind the barroom, so insist on the room you want when making reservations.

The best wine buys are among California selections. French wines are considerably overpriced.

Frankie & Johnnie's Restaurant

★

269 West 45th Street, corner of Eighth Avenue, 245-9717.
Atmosphere: Simple, noisy and crowded upstairs dining room with many uncomfortably placed tables; service ranges from efficient and helpful to slapdash.
Recommended dishes: Broiled sirloin and filet mignon steaks, veal chops, lamb chops, chicken, calf's liver, baked or hashed brown potatoes.
Price range: Expensive.
Credit cards: All major credit cards.
Hours: Dinner, Mondays through Saturdays, 4:30 P.M. to midnight. Closed Sundays and most major holidays.
Reservations: Necessary.

For over fifty-five years, Frankie & Johnnie's has been a popular steakhouse in the middle of the theater district, especially favored by a Broadway crowd. Operated by the same family since it first opened, this upstairs dining room still attracts devotees, especially in the hours before curtain time. How it manages to do so is a mystery I have never been able to fathom.

The simple dining room has a cramped and hectic bar and few comfortably placed tables. All are too close together, and many are in awkward spots; one, smack up against the coatrack and directly in the path of the entrance, should not exist at all. After peak hours, the staff becomes pleasant and efficient, but during rush hours, service is brusque and slapdash. Even the manager can be rude to customers encountering long waits for tables reserved well in advance. Add to this the noise that seems to plague all New York steakhouses, and you have an altogether unfelicitous evening.

Oddly enough, the only real points in this restaurant's favor (besides its proximity to theaters) are the delicious broiled meats and chops it serves. As good as they are, however, they are not quite enough to earn it more than a one-star rating, simply because everything else on the menu is second or third rate. And because it is possible to get excellent broiled meats with equally good appetizers, potatoes, vegetables, salads and desserts at several other steakhouses in town, the visitor will hardly find Frankie & Johnnie's worth a visit for either food or a pleasant dining experience.

From bread and appetizers right through to desserts and coffee, and with the exception only to broiled meats and chicken, the food is dreary and totally unremarkable. Clams and oysters often are shrunken in the shells, indicating they had probably been opened long in advance of serving, and at two dinners they arrived afloat on half-melted ice. Grainy chopped liver, drowned in pools of melted fat, was inedible, and chicken broth had the musty flavor and aroma of stale grease.

But, lo and behold, steaks, whether filet mignon or sirloin, lamb chops or thick loin veal chops and even hefty cuts of calf's liver arrive carefully broiled and full of rich, heady flavor. Steaks and lamb chops are so carelessly trimmed that much of the enormous-looking portions is waste fat; nevertheless, the meats are exceptional, and so is the broiled chicken. These meats are also nicely served, with steaks carved at the tables, unless customers request otherwise.

The broiled fillets of sole sampled were far less satisfactory — watery, overcooked and loaded with paprika. Baked potatoes were acceptable, although they had been cooked in foil, and hashed brown potatoes were interesting, although greasy and in larger chunks than usual. Cottage fries were limp and greasy, and potato pancakes lacked onion, salt, pepper or anything else to distinguish them; crispness is not enough to make acceptable pancakes. Potatoes au gratin had fairly good flavor but were too milky. French-fried onions, on two tries, had the bitter sting that results from overcooking.

Creamed spinach, though only average, seemed far superior to the broccoli, which must have been held in an aluminum pot too long and took on the acrid aroma of boardinghouse cabbage. The house salad is based on iceberg lettuce, and while the lettuces in the tossed green salad looked fresh and sprightly, the dressing included too much vinegar.

Cheesecakes and pies were soggy and banal, strawberries unripe.

Fuji
★ ★

238 West 56th Street, between Eighth Avenue and
   Broadway, 245-8594.
Atmosphere: Trim, modern Japanese dining room
   with cooking done at table; service is exceptionally
   efficient and gracious.
Recommended dishes: Asparagus with crab sauce,
   fried oysters, chawan-mushi, suzuko, yakitori,
   yakinori, soups, tonkatsu, teriyaki broiled meats
   and fish, seafood sukiyaki.
Price range: Moderate.
Credit cards: All major credit cards.
Hours: Lunch, Mondays through Fridays, noon to
   2:45 P.M.; dinner, Mondays through Saturdays,
   5:30 P.M. to 10 P.M. Closed Sundays and major
   holidays.
Reservations: Recommended.

New York still has a few small, simple, almost self-ef-
facing restaurants that go on doing dependable jobs,
satisfying a loyal clientele year after year, almost being
taken for granted and getting little publicity. Typical of
these is Fuji, a consistently dependable and satisfying
Japanese restaurant fairly convenient to both the theater district and the Coliseum.

In existence for almost thirty years, Fuji boasts no
high-style, with-it interior but is a neat and restful dining room with the typical shoji screens, scroll-like wall
panels, some cheerful Japanese music in the background and immaculately polished wood tables. The
waitresses are sublimely courteous and efficient, and the
dishes, on the somewhat standard menu, are very well
prepared and presented.

For some reason, the one dish that has always been
poorly prepared here is the tempura, and for years it has
been soggy with an unpleasant flavor of overheated
cooking oil. Other frying, such as the quite wonderful,
crusty-fried oysters and the breaded pork cutlet, tonkatsu, is flawless, and both of these dishes are worth trying.

Appetizers are well prepared, including the custard
chawan-mushi steamed in a cup with flecks of fish and
vegetables, and suzuko, a salmon caviar with grated
vegetables. In spring there is usually firm, bright-green,
cold asparagus to be dipped into a crab sauce that has
eggs and bean curd as its base, and there are refreshing
versions of such Japanese standards as the wilted spinach, oshitashi, and pickled vegetables.

Sukiyaki is not among my favorite dishes, but there is
a variation here made with fish, lobster, clams, salmon
and a white fish such as halibut that is lovely. All of the
fish with bean curd, bean thread noodles and vegetables
are simmered in fish stock in a casserole at the table,
and the final broth is as briny as a sea breeze.

Mellow nuggets of chicken grilled on skewers (yakitori) is made with bits of green pepper, mushrooms and

123

onions and is as satisfying as a main course as it is an appetizer. All teriyaki broiled meats and fish are delicious with the sweet-salty marinade forming a flavorful glaze. Dipping sauces are all properly piquant.

Fresh fruit is the best dessert, and throughout there is fragrant tea arriving in a hot and steady supply. As alternatives you could have beer, sake, or anything else you might want from the bar.

Gage & Tollner
★

372 Fulton Street, near Jay Street, Brooklyn. 875-5181.

Atmosphere: One of the city's handsomest antique pieces, dating from 1879; generally good service.

Recommended dishes: Crab meat Virginia, oysters casino, clams or oysters on the half shell, broiled soft clam bellies, crab meat à la Dewey, fried seafood combination, broiled striped bass, broiled lobster, mutton chop, lobster Thermidor, brandy Alexander pie, applesauce spice cake.

Price range: Moderately expensive.

Credit cards: American Express, Diners Club, MasterCharge and Visa.

Hours: Lunch and dinner, Mondays through Fridays, 11:30 A.M. to 9 P.M.; dinner, Saturdays, 4 P.M. to 11 P.M.; Sundays, 3 to 9 P.M. Closed Sundays, during July and August.

Reservations: Recommended.

Specializing primarily in seafood, Gage & Tollner, near Borough Hall in downtown Brooklyn, is by far the city's most beautifully intact landmark restaurant, reflecting the Gay Nineties style. In 1879, when Charles M. Gage opened this restaurant, Brooklyn was still a separate city. (In 1884, Eugene Tollner became a partner, and the restaurant was renamed.) Original features in the long, formal dining room include rows of mahogany-framed arched mirrors, garnet velour walls topped by embossed, gold-painted, Lincrusta-Walton wall covering (a composite of linseed oil and powdered sawdust), and gas-lighted chandeliers with etched crystal shades. If you have an early dinner there as daylight wanes, you will see a lamplighter igniting gas jets with an old-fashioned key and alcohol taper on a slender rod.

The menu, although wisely reduced in size in recent years, offers old-fashioned fish and meat dishes, very much in keeping with the style of the restaurant's original period. When they are available, soft bellies of steamer clams are delicious broiled as an appetizer, in cream soup or bisque, or in what is known as a celery broil — a gratinéed combination of clams (or oysters or scallops), heavy cream and diced celery. Oysters are better than the larger clams, whether on the half shell or baked casino-style.

Preparations to ignore entirely are those made with any kind of sauce, especially the bland, pasty cream sauces, and all of the soups. The cream soups and bisques are just thicker and thickest versions of the cream sauces, and fish chowder was fresh and lively one night but tasted stale, fishy and floury on another. Stick to such plain and impeccable appetizers as clams and oysters on the half shell and baked Virginia crab meat appetizer.

Although clams casino was dried out, the larger, softer oysters casino, with dottings of pimento and bacon, was delicious. Crab meat à la Dewey, prepared with the only decent cream sauce I tried and bits of pimento and green pepper, was very good, as was the cheese-topped lobster Thermidor baked in a large scallop shell. Although it dried out a bit more in that wide, flat shell than it would have stuffed back into the lobster's own tail, it was one of the kitchen's better efforts.

Mixed seafood fry (and all other fried specialties) was crisp and greaseless although I tasted no difference between those marked as plain fries and others designated as "seasoned" fry.

Oyster stew lacked seasonings and was short on the oyster's own liquor for brininess, but was otherwise fresh and decent. Broiled lobster was tender and moist and the broiled fish was acceptable; only the striped bass had real flavor. Sole, halibut and shad with roe were disappointing.

In addition to seafood, there are a few meat offerings that sound tempting. When steak, lamb chops or mutton chops are ordered, the raw cuts are presented for approval, then are promptly ruined in the broiling. A steak ordered rare came drily well done, and the lamb chops that replaced it were raw. At another dinner, the lamb chops were well broiled, but served cold. Thick mutton chop with sausage, bacon and a nugget of kidney was the only really good meat selection. Fried chicken would have been excellent with some seasoning, but the corn fritters served with it were starchy, dense and leaden.

Though potatoes and salads are dreadful, there is a peculiarly appealing version of cole slaw — shredded raw cabbage topped with seafood cocktail sauce.

Among desserts, the most acceptable were brandy Alexander pie and applesauce spice cake. Rice pudding had a nice crusty nutmeg topping, but was very short on rice, and other cakes and pies were commercially banal.

Gallagher's
Fair

228 West 52d Street, between Broadway and Eighth
Avenue, 245-5336.
Atmosphere: Convivial and informal dining rooms
with a bustling and noisy bar scene; inefficient
and indifferent service.
Recommended dishes: Shellfish appetizers, oxtail
soup, roast beef, lamb chops, broiled scrod,
creamed spinach.
Price range: Expensive.
Credit cards: All major credit cards.
Hours: Seven days, noon to midnight.
Reservations: Recommended.

This convivial, lusty eating place, with its paneled walls,
checkered tablecloths and photographs of sports, theater and political personalities, is one of the few real
landmarks remaining in the Broadway area. Almost all
of the food that makes up Gallagher's standard steakhouse menu is of superb quality, but unfortunately the
ingredients are reduced to minimum acceptability by
careless cooking and even more careless handling. What
does it profit a restaurateur if he buys prime beef and
then overcooks it or serves it barely tepid? If the shrimp
are fresh and firm but not deveined? And sparkling
fresh clams and oysters are insufficiently chilled?

The food is further compromised by chaotic and
often sullen service. At 7:30 one Sunday night, a waiter
explained that the house was out of four desserts, but
that strawberry shortcake and apple pie were available,
although not cheesecake. The other waiter came to say
that there was no apple pie — only cheesecake. The
lunch menu one Monday offered roast beef hash and
Mulligan stew, but the waiter explained that there was
never hash on Mondays and no stew ever at lunch any
day, no matter what the printed menu said. After the
theater on a Saturday night, the waiter literally threw
four menus across the table, then gazed absent-mind-
edly around the room as he asked, "Wadda ya wanna
drink?" At all times, food was shoved onto the table instead of being truly served.

With luck, the seafood cocktails can be in perfect
shape, and even the coarsely chopped chicken liver can
be good, although not with the beet horseradish and
wilted iceberg lettuce served with it. But that liver can
also be fatty and bitter. Herring is overmarinated in
vinegar and so becomes sour and mushy. An otherwise
delicious beefy oxtail and vegetable soup tends to cook
down during the day and to become bitingly salty at
night.

Except for a really tough, grizzled sirloin steak, all
meats were of excellent quality. But they were consistently tepid to cool and often not cooked as ordered.
This was true of calf's liver, roast beef, tasteless broiled
chicken and sliced steak with the good, brassy, house

barbecue sauce. Only lamb chops and a snowy, pearly cut of scrod were broiled exactly as requested. Fillet of sole with almonds had been broiled to crumbles at lunch, and at the same meal, scallops were unevenly cooked so that some were charred and others remained nearly raw. Shrimp fried in beer batter and fried onion rings were heavy with grease, and if the french fries were not purchased frozen, they might as well have been.

Baked potatoes were better, but potato skins were as dry as wood, and the slivers of Gallagher potatoes invariably seemed to have been standing around growing cold. Creamed spinach was excellent, but it is not possible to report on the house salad, as those we ordered never arrived. This may be the only restaurant in town that considers heated canned tomatoes a suitable vegetable. That is what was served along with hard, dry nuggets of beef tenderloin Schmeling at lunch.

Desserts also used to be much better than they are now, and that includes the gummy cheesecake and the soupy rice pudding with a raspberry sauce that is overly sweet. Apple pie is good if it is not ice cold, and the biscuit strawberry shortcake can have a lovely homespun quality when it is not portioned out so far in advance that it turns soggy. Prices are at standard steakhouse highs. At peak hours, there is a raucous and deafening bar scene straight out of Schaefer City.

Gargiulo's
★ ★ ★

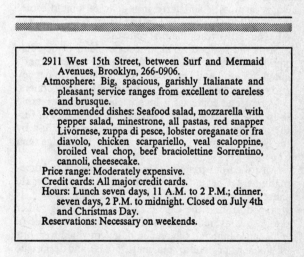

2911 West 15th Street, between Surf and Mermaid Avenues, Brooklyn, 266-0906.

Atmosphere: Big, spacious, garishly Italianate and pleasant; service ranges from excellent to careless and brusque.

Recommended dishes: Seafood salad, mozzarella with pepper salad, minestrone, all pastas, red snapper Livornese, zuppa di pesce, lobster oreganate or fra diavolo, chicken scarpariello, veal scaloppine, broiled veal chop, beef braciolettine Sorrentino, cannoli, cheesecake.

Price range: Moderately expensive.

Credit cards: All major credit cards.

Hours: Lunch seven days, 11 A.M. to 2 P.M.; dinner, seven days, 2 P.M. to midnight. Closed on July 4th and Christmas Day.

Reservations: Necessary on weekends.

Just a few doors away from Surf Avenue, with its seedy, blaring and raunchy attractions, is what certainly must be one of the city's best Italian restaurants — a high, wide, bright and spacious setting for Neapolitan cooking so lightly and subtly turned out that it gives lie to the canard that the food of that southern region is necessarily heavy and indelicate.

Gargiulo's is a huge, gaudily Italianate restaurant in the Coney Island section of Brooklyn. It seats 500 diners when all of the private party rooms are full. Its main dining room — with a soaring, dark-beamed ceiling, imitation brickwork, adobe-color walls, lavish gold-brocade draperies and high fanlights that let the sun pour in — suggests the dining rooms of countless hotels that one comes across along the Mediterranean or Adriatic. Diners here may wear anything from T-shirts to navy-blue suits, but the courtly, impeccably professional waiters are always in black tie. And because of the high ceiling, the noise level is bearable here, even when the room is jam-packed, as it often is on weekends. Families, local pols and neighborhood kibitzers congregate here for lunch or dinner, creating the atmosphere of a club.

In the true Italian tradition, most regulars order their meals a course or two at a time. First an antipasto or two, then some pasta, then they wait and see. They might feel like some fish, then wait and see, and then decide on meat, vegetables and salads then wait and see and have fruit, and finally wait and see and have some pastry and cheesecake, on and on through courses whose numbers become lost in a delectable shuffle.

Mozzarella is made on the premises and accounts for two of the best appetizers. Freshly sliced, sweetly moist mozzarella, sprinkled with grated black pepper and a few drops of olive oil, can be ordered with tissue-thin slivers of pink prosciutto and a salad of roasted green and red peppers bathed in fragrant olive oil.

Mozzarella in carozza is a personal favorite, the cheese sandwiched between slices of bread, then dipped in a light egg batter and deep-fried to golden crispness. Only a piece of lemon is missing in the Gargiulo format to make that appetizer complete. Baked clams nestled under a light garlic-scented topping of bread crumbs, clams or mussels simmered in a delicate tomato broth, and a fritto misto that is a mixed fry of vegetables, are other equally irresistible first courses.

So is the seafood salad, a roseate blend of octopus, squid, mussels, scallops and shrimp, all tenderly marinated in an oil and lemon dressing flecked with parsley and ever so slightly stung with flakes of hot red peppers.

Minestrone comes as a lovely, clear, fresh vegetable soup, not so heavy that it obviates the possibility of further eating; but the escarole and bean soup, if had by the bowlful, almost does, being more of a porridge than a soup.

All rolled-out pasta in the noodle category is homemade here. Cheese-filled ravioli in a chiffonlike tomato sauce, an unusual lasagna for which the dough is wrapped around the cheese and sausage filling rather than being layered in with it, fettuccine alla Gargiulo (a pink-sauced mound of green noodles entwined with bits of chicken, prosciutto and mushrooms) and fettuccine carbonara with a sunny sauce of cheese, cream, eggs, butter and prosciutto are all extraordinary.

White sauces such as oil and garlic with clams or anchovies are as pungent as they should be, and the twisted pasta lengths, fusilli al filetto, are lightly glossed with a sheer tomato sauce enriched with onions and prosciutto.

Fish is particularly well prepared, with first prize going to the red snapper Livornese, the thick white fillet gently simmered with tomatoes, black olives and capers. Ocean fresh lobsters baked oreganate with garlic and parsley bread crumbs, or cooked fra diavolo in a hot tomato sauce, perhaps just a shade too greasy, and firm, meaty shrimp marinara are all cooked to a perfection most seafood houses might envy.

Among meat main courses, try the tender beef braciolettine Sorrentina (broiled beef rollups filled with mozzarella and parsley and blanketed with sautéed mushrooms), the well-broiled, thick veal chop, or the tender, golden chunks of chicken sautéed scarpariello style, with lemon, and just a hint of garlic.

Veal for scaloppine may not be the tenderest or palest but it is more than merely decent, especially when one considers that most veal main courses, with vegetable or salad and a crisp, meltingly creamy potato croquette are inexpensive.

Broiled sausages were the only main course tried recently that left much to be desired, primarily because the sausages themselves lacked character.

There are wonderfully coarse, fragrant bread and beautiful vegetable dishes at Gargiulo's, among them crisp, fried slivers of zucchini, escarole with oil, olives, currants and capers, string beans braised with tomatoes, sautéed chunks of artichokes and bitter broccoli di rape or standard broccoli in a garlic and oil sauce — all good news to vegetarians tired of the sterile approach to cooking most vegetarian restaurants display.

The house salad does this restaurant discredit, made as it is with iceberg lettuce, an ingredient that should never be allowed to darken the kitchen's doorway. Sprightly, emerald green arugula, though charged for à la carte, is a more fitting salad course.

Fruit platters brilliant with cuts of cantaloupe, watermelon, strawberries, grapes and whatever else is in season, is a favorite dessert. But even if I have that, I cannot quite forego the city's best cannoli, made in the restaurant's bakery. The small, crisp and greaseless pastry tubes are filled with whipped, snow-white ricotta hauntingly perfumed with the slightest hint of oil of cinnamon, a filling with a velvety texture unspoiled by bits of chocolate or nuts. Cheesecake is unusual here too, light, soufflélike and seasoned only with lemon, vanilla and sugar.

Although Gargiulo's has been a landmark in Coney Island for seventy years, its real success is due to the Russo family who took it over seventeen years ago. It is a completely family-run operation, with Nino and Mike Russo as the main overseers aided by their sister Louisa, and brothers Victor and Ralph. All kitchen help are relatives imported from the area around their native Sorrento, and the pride of family is apparent in what the kitchen turns out.

The menu is not the limit here, large as it is. The kitchen turns out innumerable other dishes on request, as long as the ingredients are on hand.

If Gargiulo's get three stars instead of four, it is because of an intermittent unevenness of its food. There are seemingly inexplicable lapses from time to time, when the products of the kitchen are merely good instead of extraordinary. There is also a tendency toward heavy-handedness with such northern specialties as veal piccante, which can come out of the sauté too gummy with flour. Original creations leave much to be desired, so stick to Southern classics.

Wine prices are fairly moderate. If you're lucky, you pay nothing at all. Pick a number from one to ninety-nine, and if the number you pick is the one the waiter shakes out of his cardboard box, the meal is on the house.

Gaylord India Restaurant
Fair

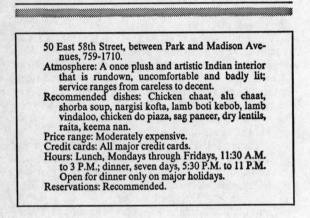

50 East 58th Street, between Park and Madison Avenues, 759-1710.
Atmosphere: A once plush and artistic Indian interior that is rundown, uncomfortable and badly lit; service ranges from careless to decent.
Recommended dishes: Chicken chaat, alu chaat, shorba soup, nargisi kofta, lamb boti kebob, lamb vindaloo, chicken do piaza, sag paneer, dry lentils, raita, keema nan.
Price range: Moderately expensive.
Credit cards: All major credit cards.
Hours: Lunch, Mondays through Fridays, 11:30 A.M. to 3 P.M.; dinner, seven days, 5:30 P.M. to 11 P.M. Open for dinner only on major holidays.
Reservations: Recommended.

The care and delicacy that once rendered Gaylord's food the best of its kind in town unfortunately seems to have disappeared. Based on visits in 1979 and 1982, the kitchen is as much in need of toning up as the run-down and almost seedy interior. Housekeeping is poor, service for the most part is lackadaisical and careless, lighting is so dim the menu can hardly be read and the divans in the large dining room are obviously in need of springs. As they are now, one sinks so low that the table top is almost at shoulder level.

The food here is on a par with the setting and service. Deep-fried fritter appetizers such as the vegetable samosas and pakora were stale and greasy. The ground meat seekh kebob, however, could be considered decent, as were the crisp papadum wafers. All tandoori-grilled food — chicken, stale shrimp that tasted of iodine and lamb — was dried out and had a flavor that suggested charcoal lighter fluid.

An order of chicken makhanwala in a fairly good sauce of tomatoes, spices and butter consisted only of backbones, a piece of neck, a third wing joint and a tip of breast meat. Rice for the vegetable biryani was hopelessly overcooked, and a dish of shrimp (called prawns) in a green pepper and chili masala sauce was far from fresh. The properly fiery lamb vindaloo curry seemed the only dish of any merit at all during the first two meals, and even then the meat did not seem to have been simmered with the sauce. Even breads were far less interesting than at most Indian restaurants.

Dishes that can be recommended include fried pieces of chicken chaat that were crisp and gently spiced and the pungent potato salad, alu chaat. The tart vegetable soup, shorba, had an authentic and intriguing sting; not so the watery mulligatawny nor the insipid tomato soup.

The lamb-filled bread keema nan had much more flavor than the onion kulcha, the plain nan, cauliflower-filled sobi paratha.

Nargisi kofta, ground meat packed around hard-cooked eggs, then braised in a rich, brown curry sauce, lamb boti kebob masala with onions, tomatoes and spices and chicken do piaza braised with onions and spices, were far more acceptable than any other dishes I tried.

Spinach cooked with cheese (sag paneer) was a much better vegetable preparation than the scorched okra. Dry lentils, or the soupier dal and the cucumber and yogurt sauce, raita, were refreshing accompaniments to the rest of the meal.

The usual syrupy sweet Indian desserts are available here, prepared with no particular distinction. Mango ice cream was a preferable alternative.

George Martin
Fair

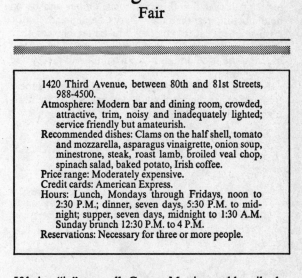

1420 Third Avenue, between 80th and 81st Streets, 988-4500.

Atmosphere: Modern bar and dining room, crowded, attractive, trim, noisy and inadequately lighted; service friendly but amateurish.

Recommended dishes: Clams on the half shell, tomato and mozzarella, asparagus vinaigrette, onion soup, minestrone, steak, roast lamb, broiled veal chop, spinach salad, baked potato, Irish coffee.

Price range: Moderately expensive.

Credit cards: American Express.

Hours: Lunch, Mondays through Fridays, noon to 2:30 P.M.; dinner, seven days, 5:30 P.M. to midnight; supper, seven days, midnight to 1:30 A.M. Sunday brunch 12:30 P.M. to 4 P.M.

Reservations: Necessary for three or more people.

If being "in" were all, George Martin would easily deserve a top rating. Seldom has a restaurant gained such popularity so rapidly. Owned by George Martin and the former New York Knicks basketball star Dave DeBusschere, the place is popular with sports-world figures, and on weekends the singles action at the bar becomes so intense that it is sometimes necessary to lock the doors.

As a result, the noise level is generally head-splitting, a condition greatly exacerbated by the constant thump of background music. That, plus inadequate lighting at table level and a good-natured but confused and inept dining room staff, combine for an experience that could hardly be called felicitous.

Inept is also as good a word as any to describe the kitchen's average performance. Overcooking and underseasoning are consistent failings, and in some instances the food sampled was stale or had been reheated once too often. An order of grilled salmon, with a dry crust of paprika, reeked of a fishiness that implies staleness, and an order of spareribs had apparently been steamed and resteamed until tasteless. Breast of chicken is prepared in a different way each night; mine had been sautéed in a floury and sweet Marsala sauce more suitable to a dessert than a main course.

Stringy duck, which was almost burned in an attempt to render it crisp, was not helped by a sticky, mustardy, orange sauce, and calf's liver had the mushy texture that meat acquires when frozen.

The simplest choices can result in an acceptable meal for those interested in taking in the scene. A sirloin steak on one try arrived properly seared and done as ordered, but another time, requested rare, it arrived unseared with a cold blue center. A thick veal chop, grilled medium, was delicious, and remarkably pink and rosy roast lamb was one of the more satisfactory alternatives.

For first courses, stick to clams on the half shell or asparagus vinaigrette. Sliced tomatoes with mozzerella, though pleasant, will undoubtedly be improved when ripe tomatoes and fresh basil are available to enhance the combination. Minestrone or onion soup were both hot and decent. Despite a slightly oversweetened dressing, spinach salad with mushrooms, onions and bacon held more interest than the watery Caesar salad. Fluffy, crisp-skinned baked potatoes are better choices than any of the special potatoes. Skip the overcooked vegetables and the fried onions and zucchini, both greasy and nearly burned.

Fresh strawberries, a hot-fudge sundae and superb Irish coffee are the worthwhile desserts. Prices are fairly high considering the quality.

The Gibbon

★

24 East 80th Street, between Fifth and Madison Avenues, 861-4001.

Atmosphere: Comfortable, attractive and quiet surroundings that suggest a private club; service is generally good, occasionally slow.

Recommended dishes: Cucumber stuffed with lobster, mussels in garlic and bean paste, Japanese pâté, usuzukuri, tataki, prawns à la Kyoto, sushi, sashimi, lobster, kamo-hasamiyaki, rack of lamb, sirloin steak Chester, negima, banana ice cream, fresh pineapple.

Price range: Moderately expensive.

Credit cards: All major credit cards.

Hours: Lunch, Mondays through Fridays, noon to 2:30 P.M.; dinner, Mondays through Saturdays, 5:45 P.M. to 10:30 P.M. Closed Sundays and major holidays.

Reservations: Necessary.

The sudden and enduring popularity of The Gibbon is not due solely to the food, which combines French and Japanese influences. What makes most devotees want to keep the place a secret is its spacious, comfortable and blessedly quiet dining room. The Gibbon (named for the small, slender ape that is the subject of a Japanese scroll hanging over the downstairs fireplace) feels very much like a private club. And glancing around the dining room most nights of the week, one might easily assume the members of that club are all media executives and art dealers, for those groups seem to have claimed this as their own.

Both lunch and dinner menus offer light and savory enticements, and the intertwining of Japanese and French influences is done with considerable sensitivity, both in décor and food.

Appetizers are so appealing and satisfying one could have an entertaining meal with an assortment of several. Cucumbers crisped in ice water are filled with fresh, briny lobster at night — a better choice than the decent but less interesting Alaskan king crab meat used in a similar way at lunch. Other excellent appetizers are hot steamed mussels in a garlic-burnished bean broth, a soothingly bland Japanese duck-liver pâté in plum sauce and usuzukuri — pearly slices of translucent white fish accented by a fiery radish dressing. Whether served as a main course at lunch, or an hors d'oeuvre at dinner, tataki (scallion-flecked charred slices of filet mignon that are rose-red at the center) are delicious.

Raw fish sashimi and some well-crafted fish, seaweed and vinegar-rice sushi are attractively served, although these are often far less sprightly than those in restaurants that specialize in such intricate delicacies. King crab meat rolled in cucumbers, a limp tempura that tasted of cooking fat, and shrimp and lotus roots in a strawberry purée were all disappointing. Cream of

133

cauliflower soup, though good, seemed at odds with the rest of the menu.

Main courses at dinner were better designed than those at lunch. The most exceptional choice was the kamo-hasamiyaki, roasted slices of duck breast layered with Oriental vegetables. The duck meat was firmer and more flavorful than that meat usually is in this country, and the concept of the dish itself is right in line with French nouvelle cuisine.

Negima, paper-thin rolls of beef wrapped around scallions, can be delicious but sometimes are steamy and soggy, and the same is true of the prawns à la Kyoto that were really large shrimp topped with a dark, rich, shallot, lemon and soy sauce. Both the rare, lean rack of lamb and the sirloin steak Chester were mellowed by a subtle blend of Japanese sweet wine, tomato, soy sauce, garlic and ginger. A glowingly fresh steamed lobster with a sesame oil, shallot, saki and tomato sauce were also worth trying, although not quite up to the earlier dishes. Although some dishes on the menu change, the general level of cooking averages out to be the same.

A few dishes at The Gibbon failed slightly although all were above minimal levels of decency. Somewhat pedestrian were the chicken breasts filled with watercress, red snapper wrapped around tofu and a rather fishy crab meat filling, and slices of salmon rolled around soba buckwheat noodles. The salmon was not quite suited to this preparation and crumbled as it was steamed.

Dressing for the green salad should have been slightly less acidic, but firm, near-crisp string beans were pleasant with main courses. Rice stuffing in a tomato, however, dried out in the heating.

A velvety homemade banana ice cream, astringent lemon sherbet and fresh pineapple ingeniously cut and sprinkled with Cointreau seemed the most appropriate ending for the meal. Chocolate mousse was smooth and rich, but the carrot cake needed more spicing. There is a fair, moderately priced wine list, and a variety of Oriental teas in addition to regular coffees.

The Ginger Man
Fair

51 West 64th Street, just east of Broadway, 399-2358.
Atmosphere: Large, sprawling and attractive pub-tavern, noisy and lively; seating is uncomfortably cramped, and service is uneven.
Recommended dishes: Onion soup, tomato and shrimp soup, spinach salad, chicken salad, lamb kebab, sautéed vegetables with melted cheese, sirloin steak, calf's liver, rack of lamb without sauce, chocolate nut roll, chocolate ice cream, cassis sherbet, fruit salad.
Price range: Moderately expensive.
Credit cards: All major credit cards.
Hours: 11:30 A.M. to midnight daily.
Reservations: Necessary before Lincoln Center performances and recommended at peak lunch and dinner hours.

Opened in 1964, The Ginger Man is one of the oldest restaurants in the Lincoln Center area. One of the first pub-tavern restaurants with tile floors and fancy glass, the Ginger Man had excellent food in its early days, when omelets were made in an open kitchen by the late food writer and cooking-school teacher Dione Lucas. Under the present owners, Michael and Patrick O'Neal, who also operate several other old-timy O'Neal pubs on the West Side, the kitchen's skills seemed to be in a steady decline. A recent series of meals at the Ginger Man indicated that the food now averages out as fair. Nevertheless, the Ginger Man is larger and apparently more successful than ever, especially before performances.

Success does not necessarily mean excellence, unfortunately, especially where Lincoln Center restaurants are concerned. Proximity is the key. Because the Ginger Man is so conveniently situated, it is worth devising a strategy that makes eating there a relatively satisfactory possibility.

The several dining rooms, though jammed and noisy at peak hours, are convivial and suited to quick preperformance dining. The help can be careless and brusque, but most waiters and managers are friendly and accommodating, trying to seat people where they wish to be seated, and working hard to get diners out on time.

Omelets are huge and leaden and lack the light flavor of freshly broken eggs. Hamburgers used to be excellent at The Ginger Man, but four tried recently were made of spoiled meat. When one was sent back, the replacement also smelled and tasted high. The kitchen is also careless about cooking to the correct degree of doneness.

For appetizers, stick to the onion soup and, if available, tomato and shrimp soup, both far better than the overcooked, unsalted artichoke, the greasy pâté, the floury shrimp in garlic sauce and the chokingly dry fettuccine.

For a light main course, rely on spinach, mushroom and bacon salad or the very decent chicken salad garnished with diced tomato and onion. At lunch, there is a fresh and interesting main course of stir-fried vegetables topped with melted cheese. The most reliable of the meat main courses are sirloin steak, though expensive, calf's liver with onions, leeks and chives, and rack of lamb (if it arrives hot with sauce on the side). Duck was a near miss — well roasted but almost ice cold and with a cloyingly sweet tangerine sauce. And broiled fillet of sole was acceptable when not overcooked.

Chocolate ice cream, cassis sherbet and a chocolate mocha and praliné nut roll are fine for dessert. Bloody Marys are watery, but other drinks are poured with a generous hand. Prices are very high, all things considered.

Girafe

★ ★

---

208 East 58th Street, between Second and Third Avenues, 752-3054.

Atmosphere: Dark, intimate, supper-club setting with wild-animal theme; crowded and slightly noisy downstairs but quieter upstairs; excellent service.

Recommended dishes: Spiedino di mozzarella, antipasto caldo, vongole oreganate, cozze marechiare, peperoni e acciughe, minestrone, cannelloni, paglia e fieno, gnocchi, fettuccine filetto di pomodoro, spaghetti carbonara, zuppa di pesce, pollo funghi e aglio, scaloppine al limone, scaloppine Martini, grilled veal chop, bistecca peperonata, zuppa inglese, zabaglione.

Price range: Expensive.

Credit cards: American Express, Diners Club, Visa and MasterCard.

Hours: Lunch, Mondays through Fridays, noon to 3 P.M.; dinner, Mondays through Thursdays, 5:30 P.M. to 10:30 P.M., Fridays and Saturdays, 5:30 P.M. to 11 P.M. Closed Sundays and all major holidays.

Reservations: Necessary.

Girafe is one of those only-in-New York phenomena — a highly successful, uncommonly good restaurant which, in spite of its loyal following, has never been considered fashionable and which is rarely talked about. Why that is so must remain a mystery, I suppose, but I am always struck with how solidly delicious the food is here, where service is clickingly efficient. Little misses the eyes of owners and captains, who seem to have some extrasensory perception of customers' wishes.

At first glance, one might make the mistake of not taking this place seriously. First of all, there is the slightly silly Disneyland giraffe sculptured in metal, almost two stories high, outside. Only the discreet bronze plaque saying "Ristorante" tips one off as to the real business at hand. Inside, the animal theme persists in paintings of wildlife of the African plains. The rooms are darkened to supper-club intimacy, there are flowers and candles at most tables and a busy, lively bar at the entrance, all suggesting what used to be known as a "hideaway." A winding staircase leads to the Treetops, a white-brick room with attractive basket lampshades, somewhat lighter, quieter and more restful than the downstairs room. Although generally open to the public, the Treetops room is also the setting for private parties.

The only uncomfortable section of the whole place is the back of the downstairs dining room, which is excessively cramped and airless, a condition made worse by the proximity of the kitchen from which cooking odors occasionally come forth, and where aisle chairs are often bumped by waiters rushing past.

Although the cooking at Girafe is billed as North Italian, there are a number of delectable Neapolitan specialties, and the overall style of the cooking suggests a fine southern Italian hand at work somewhere in the kitchen.

Before planning your meal it is a good idea to keep in mind that the captain turns out one of the most extraordinary zabaglione custards in town, well beaten over heat until frothy and hot, laced with exactly the right amount of Marsala and topped with crumbled amaretti, the bitter almond macaroons that give this dessert a crunchy textural contrast.

Remember that windup as you try to avoid overeating on the other fine courses, and because portions are generally huge, consider dividing orders. Among appetizers I especially liked the spiedino di mozzarella (fried cheese and bread cubes blanketed with a thick anchovy and butter sauce), cozze marechiare (mussels in a light, spicy tomato broth) and the very fresh and dewy clams oreganate topped with nice dry garlic-herb bread crumbs.

The antipasto caldo was a hot assortment of baked clams, scampi, stuffed mushroom caps and a nugget of deep-fried mozzarella, all well prepared, and the firm but silky roasted peppers, almost certainly homemade, complemented by plump, mildly salty anchovies (peperoni e acciughe), was one of the lighter but appealing first courses. Unfortunately, prosciutto served with melon was third-rate and tasted much like plain boiled ham. Mozzarella in carozza, fried cheese deep-fried in a crust, seemed to be done with bread crumbs rather than in an egg batter and was slightly soggy.

The heavy soup, pasta e fagioli, had a delicate, smoky flavor, but would have been better made with the traditional pasta, ditali, instead of tiny acini di pepe, which did not provide the right textural accent to the beans. Minestrone was not the ordinary heavy tomato-masked soup, but was a green, clear mélange of zucchini, carrots, potato, celery, parsley and tiny ditalini pasta cylinders. Grated cheese thickened it just enough, and the combined result was an exceptionally fresh and bracing soup.

Pastas were for the most part beautifully prepared — a bit heavy on oil in their sauces, as is much of the cooking at Girafe, but savory nonetheless. Fettuccine filetto di pomodoro was exceptional, with perfectly al dente noodles bathed in a tomato and onion sauce enriched with flecks of ham. Carbonara was not the usual white creamy concoction but had an almost brown glaze and a wonderfully velvety flavor of the bacon, pancetta and onions in a rich oil-and-butter sauce. If there was egg, it had created just the right transparent but satiny finish. Cannelloni filled with a spicy meat, much like sausage filling in a good Bolognese meat and tomato sauce, was delicious, if a bit heavy for an intermediate pasta course.

All equally irresistible were the tiny, delicate potato dumplings, gnocchi, in the same meat sauce, the green and straw-colored noodles, paglia e fieno, with peas and a cheese-laden cream sauce, fettuccine Alfredo and the finest of spaghetti strands, capelli di angelo (angel's hair), in a sheer tomato-clam sauce.

Although one night's specialty of striped bass Livornese was burdened with an overpowering sauce of onions and olives, and a dish of veal Sorrentino (scaloppine baked with eggplant and mozzarella cheese) did not do justice to the very fine white and tender veal, most other main courses were more than minimally satisfying.

Zuppa di pesce, a picturesque still life of shiny black mussels, sea-fresh clams, shrimp, squid and firm white fish not a bit overcooked, was in a briny, highly seasoned tomato-shellfish stock. Pollo funghi e aglio, bits of moist, tender chicken redolent of garlic, white wine and herbs, was just a shade better than the cacciatore, a similar chicken dish slighty sweetened by the tomatoes added to its sauce. Chicken scarpariello, sautéed in garlic after the chicken skin was removed, had dried out slightly but was above average.

All veal here was unquestionably prime quality. The lombata alla griglia — a thick chop grilled to just the right faintly pink stage of being done without being dried out — showed that superb meat off to great advantage, and veal scaloppine Martini, with a slight touch of Parmesan sautéed in butter and finished with lemon, was beyond reproach, as was the fried breaded veal cutlet Milanese. Only a misguided "taster" special of veal and chicken Sorrentino (parmisiana) indicated a slight tendency to pander.

At lunch one day, a combination of sautéed chicken and mild, meaty Italian sausage in garlic butter was meant for those who are serious about their garlic, and an enormous plateful of calf's liver Veneziana was satisfactory, if a shade too brown and bland, and much too overwhelmingly apportioned. Very good beefsteak with a mild tomato herb sauce and slivers of roasted green peppers (bistecca peperonata) was gentle and carefully sautéed.

A salad of dark green arugula was as sprightly and fresh as possible, although the somewhat overgrown leaves were a bit tough, and a side order of fried zucchini, like the mozzarella in carozza, had been cooked a little too long in fat just a bit too hot.

There is very good, solid whole-wheat bread at Girafe and there are several gloppy, sensuously rich desserts — a rum, custard and meringue extravaganza known as zuppa inglese, a stickily rich napoleon with custard as thick as cold honey, and that altogether inspired zabaglione.

Gloucester House

★ ★

East 50th Street, between Park and Madison Avenues,
755-7394.
Atmosphere: Simple, bright and attractive Cape Cod
décor, fair service.
Recommended dishes: Clams and oysters on half
shell, all plain seafood cocktails, Manhattan clam
chowder, all plain broiled or fried fish, all vegetables, apple pie, fresh berries.
Price range: Expensive.
Credit cards: All major credit cards.
Hours: Lunch, Mondays through Fridays, noon to
2:30 P.M.; dinner, Mondays through Fridays, 5:30
P.M. to 10 P.M., Saturdays and Sundays, noon to
10 P.M. Closed Thanksgiving and Christmas.
Reservations: Recommended.

There is no restaurant in New York where one can find
consistently fresher or higher quality fish and seafood
than at Gloucester House, a restaurant with a pleasantly
simple, airy and clean Cape Code décor. There are
panels with interesting displays of eel spears and sailor's
knots, beautiful luster tiles over the bar, and pleasant
deep-sea-blue walls contrasting with white trim and
scrubbed, oak-top tables.

Not only is the quality of the ingredients high, but the
basic broiling, frying, sautéeing and poaching are also
expertly done. Rarely does one get a piece of overcooked fish here. Swordfish, scrod, snapper and sea
bass are expertly done and only one piece of salmon recently seemed less than glowingly fresh.

There are wonderfully cold, clear and plump assorted
oysters, including Canadians, Cape Cods and Long Islands, and the lump crabmeat and large, firm shrimp
are near perfection. This is also one of the few places
that serves true lemon sole, and a thick fillet, ordered
fried, was a masterpiece of golden crispness outside,
while the fish inside remained moist and full of flavor.

There are also some excellent vegetables — the slices
of broiled eggplant, the crisp chips of fried zucchini and
the parchmentlike french-fried onion rings.

All of this might sound as though we were well on the
way to a three-star if not a four-star rating, but there is a
serious flaw at Gloucester House that obviates either of
those two ratings. Whenever the kitchen attempts a dish
that is Continental, that has a sauce or any sort of
vaguely complex preparation, the results are disappointingly tasteless.

An appetizer or main course of beautiful lump crabmeat, wrapped in bacon and broiled, is a sheer waste of
the crabmeat, totally overpowered by the smoky accent
of the bacon. Then there were mussels in a watery curry
sauce and roast shrimp in garlic butter that barely
hinted at having any garlic at all. Among soups, only
the Manhattan clam chowder was consistently excellent.

The New England, light and creamy one night, was thick and pasty the next. Lobster bisque could easily have been canned, and billi-bi tasted one night as briny as creamed salt water, while on another occasion it didn't taste of the sea at all, only of a sharp, acidic sherry.

Deviled crabs, again made with glorious snowy lump crabmeat, had none of the peppery character required for a dish truly "deviled," and a fair broiled lobster, somewhat dry, was ridiculously small. Snapper Creole was merely broiled snapper topped with a fair Creole sauce, and, similarly, snapper amandine, instead of being sautéed, was broiled with dry almonds sprinkled on top. Potatoes au gratin were dry and sticky, and french fries limp and underfried at one dinner but crisply perfect at another. These are home-cut fries with tips of peel at each end, a pleasant and crunchy touch. At times, dreadful potatoes au gratin are served instead of french fries.

Very good crusty biscuits are passed several times with the meal, and when they ran out, thinly crisp and delicious corn sticks replace them, but the green salad was drowned in an overabundance of the garlic-mayonnaise dressing that is one of the standards in seafood houses in town.

Among desserts, there were a decent hot apple pie and beautiful fresh berries. Pecan pie had too high a proportion of gelatin to nuts, and the floating island was served so ice-cold one could not discern any flavoring in its smooth egg-custard sauce. The Gloucester House special, a sort of orange Bavarian cream topped with what seemed to be orange marmalade, might appeal to those who lean toward childhood desserts; we found it a bit cloying after the first three bites. Rice pudding, which used to be wonderful, was an overcooked starchy mass when I last had it.

Service here can be downright curt and abrupt (especially upstairs at lunchtime) or pleasantly relaxed and friendly, the reasons for the differences being impossible to fathom. One waiter didn't remove a soup cup before trying to get down the main course, but another carefully observed that more of the big cheesecloth-covered lemon halves were required and brought them unasked.

Greener Pastures

★

117 East 60th Street, between Park and Lexington
Avenues, 355-3214.

Atmosphere: Attractive modern dining room with
garden view; pleasant service.

Recommended dishes: Egg, tuna and vegetable
chopped-liver salads, all salad plates and sandwiches, lentil, pea and mushroom and barley
soups, Sichuan fish, eggplant steaks parmigiana,
broiled bluefish and scrod, snow peas, broiled
mushrooms, quiches.

Price range: Moderate.

Credit cards: None.

Hours: Lunch, seven days, noon to 4 P.M.; dinner,
Mondays through Thursdays, and Saturdays, 4
P.M. to 9:30 P.M., Fridays and Sundays, 4 P.M. to
8:30 P.M. Open major holidays.

Reservations: Not accepted.

Vegetarian restaurants, for the most part, seem to im-
pose a penalty on their clientele because their settings
are so drably dull and often unkempt. But that is hardly
so at Greener Pastures, where food is served in a handsomely designed room that is pleasant and exhilarating.

Rose-brick walls, natural-pine wainscotting, a terra-
cotta floor, blond-wood chairs and a skylight greenhouse cafe make this restaurant as bright and sunny for
lunch as it is romantically atmospheric at night. The
help is young, cheerful, efficient and professional. The
only fault is a tendency to get rid of the worst tables
first.

The menu is as imaginative and satisfying as the
room, combining vegetarian, health food and kosher
principles in the vegetable, egg and fish dishes it offers.
The kitchen does best with straightforward salads, each
a veritable garden of sparkling crisp and fresh ingredients, and its well-broiled fish selections, all served on
beds of grainy brown rice flecked with bits of vegetables. Breads are nutty and whole-grained, and there is
the usual array of health-food natural fruit and vegetable drinks.

Vegetarian chopped liver, egg and tuna salad, plain
or heaped in avocado halves, are excellent. So were
three soups tried — a smoky, thick lentil, a vegetable-
sparkled split pea soup and a creamy fresh mushroom
and barley soup. There was a quiche of the day that we
divided as an appetizer; ours was made with spinach
and mushrooms, and though the greens turned the crust
soggy, the flavor was delicious.

Guacamole is mildly spiced with cumin, a spice
somewhat out of keeping with the fresh taste of avocado.

There is a fresh and colorful salade Niçoise made
with an excellent grade of white tuna fish that seems to
be water-packed and string beans, potatoes, and greens.

All fish is carefully broiled, most especially the bluefish and the scrod. The main problem is with some of
the ethnic concoctions, none of which are authentic and
many of which are disappointing. Among the best

choices are fried eggplant steak parmigiana in a slightly bland tomato sauce, topped with properly runny cheese (rennetless to observe kosher restrictions) and garnished with russets of carrots and slivers of onions, and a Sichuan-style fish, tossed with walnuts and seasoned with garlic, scallions and soy sauce. A dish billed as bouillabaisse is more like a thick, slick, sweet creole tomato creation, and sole Mexican style has a layering of the unsatisfactory guacamole inside that spoils it.

Vegetables, said to be teriyaki style, are really fried tempura style and are good — crisp, fresh and greaseless. Crunchy vegetables, almost raw and topped with melted cheese, make a strange but not totally unpleasant dish, very popular with those who seem to be regulars.

Side orders of such vegetables as crisp, green sesame-strewn snow peas and whole broiled mushrooms are done simply and well. There are beautiful sandwiches at Greener Pastures on excellent wholegrain breads, all prettily garnished with frills of salad greens and sunny bursts of freshly grated raw carrots. Cheese blintzes are of decent quality, but badly fried, so they taste of grease. Low-fat sour cream is served with them.

For dessert, there is a nicely baked apple, a fair rice pudding and crunchy molasses-bound walnut or pecan pie. Crammed is the word for the too-small overloaded plates; it is impossible to finish most portions or to handle them neatly.

There are pleasant herb teas, wine and beer. Prices are moderate because the generous portions make it possible to share dishes. Hot entrees seem more reasonably priced than salads.

Greene Street

★

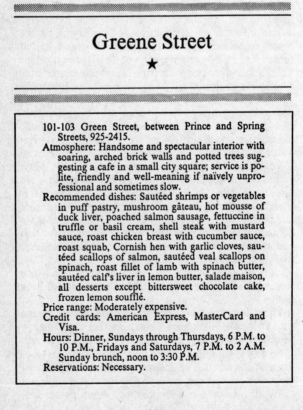

101-103 Green Street, between Prince and Spring Streets, 925-2415.

Atmosphere: Handsome and spectacular interior with soaring, arched brick walls and potted trees suggesting a cafe in a small city square; service is polite, friendly and well-meaning if naïvely unprofessional and sometimes slow.

Recommended dishes: Sautéed shrimps or vegetables in puff pastry, mushroom gâteau, hot mousse of duck liver, poached salmon sausage, fettuccine in truffle or basil cream, shell steak with mustard sauce, roast chicken breast with cucumber sauce, roast squab, Cornish hen with garlic cloves, sautéed scallops of salmon, sautéed veal scallops on spinach, roast fillet of lamb with spinach butter, sautéed calf's liver in lemon butter, salade maison, all desserts except bittersweet chocolate cake, frozen lemon soufflé.

Price range: Moderately expensive.

Credit cards: American Express, MasterCard and Visa.

Hours: Dinner, Sundays through Thursdays, 6 P.M. to 10 P.M., Fridays and Saturdays, 7 P.M. to 2 A.M. Sunday brunch, noon to 3:30 P.M.

Reservations: Necessary.

Greene Street in SoHo is a Chinese puzzle of surprises, offering a series of unexpected delights that slowly reveal themselves. First there is the pleasant shock of beauty — soaring arched brick walls, a profusion of potted trees, a big airy mural across one wall and a catwalk balcony where drinks are served.

Wicker chairs on tiered platforms create an atmosphere reminiscent of an outdoor cafe in a town square, all centered around a stage on which jazz and classical musicians perform. The menu brings another surprise, for in such a setting, one hardly expects to find sophisticated attempts at nouvelle cuisine. But they abound here and many are turned out with considerable success.

Further surprises come in the views of the restaurant from its varied angles. And if you walk around the balcony, there is the added diversion of an adjoining art gallery. Make the full tour of the balcony and your interest will almost certainly be piqued by two tentlike cozy corners — dark, fabric-draped alcoves with pillows on the floor where drinks are served.

The kitchen excels at poultry dishes such as roast squab with sautéed apples and pears, the rock Cornish hen roasted with whole nut-brown cloves of garlic and sliced breast of chicken in a delicately bright cucumber sauce cozily bedded down on fine green tagliatelle. Cooks also generally do well by breast of duck that is lean and moist and is accompanied by figs. Only once, when the sauce was burnished with cassis, did the duck meat seem dry and tough. Ordering it medium rare, a diner was told by a waiter that duck had to be well done to be tender. And sure enough, that's how it arrived — well done to the waiter's taste.

There were a few other gaffes by members of the staff, all of whom were polite and well-intentioned though lacking in professionalism. After reeling off a dizzying list of daily specials (without bothering to mention prices), a waiter advised us to order those rather than dishes from the regular menu because, he said, the specials were prepared by the head chef whereas other dishes were done by the sous chef. Order wine and you may be told, as we were, "They say that one is pretty good," and don't be surprised if the cork is broken off as the bottle is being opened.

Despite such amateur performances, there is a genuine feeling of welcome from this staff and enough very good food to add up to a pleasant evening. Main courses that come close to the excellence of the poultry included roast fillet of lamb with a spinach and butter sauce and a shell steak sparked with a sauce of grainy, brassy Meaux mustard. A creamy and crisp-topped gratin of potatoes and gently sautéed julienne filaments of vegetables round out many of the main courses. Veal scaloppines, though slightly tough from insufficient pounding, were saved by a beautifully balanced, pale golden sauce and a cushioning of firm, fresh leaf spinach. But the chef's way with meat and poultry is not equaled by his understanding of fish, whether in appetizers, soups or main courses.

Exceptional appetizers included a velvety hot mousse of duck liver, in a mellow golden-brown wine sauce with grapes, and the mousse of mushrooms (called a gâteau) enriched with marrow. Fettuccine in cream accented by truffles or basil was equally engaging as an appetizer or a main course.

Brunch, though pleasantly accompanied by chamber music, left much to be desired. Bloody Marys needed more generous belts of vodka, omelets were tough and leathery and a salad of sliced chicken, pignoli nuts and broccoli actually was composed mostly of lettuce with barely any dressing for textural and flavor contrast. A croque monsieur (the French toasted ham and cheese sandwich) was made on bread that was much too thick and dry and had been cooked too rapidly. Scrambled eggs with salmon cavier in puff pastry, calf's liver in lemon butter and a bagel with cream cheese and silky, saline smoked salmon would be preferable choices.

' Desserts at dinner and brunch are the same, and generally worthwhile. A creamy mousse of white chocolate gains substance from a cool bittersweet chocolate sauce, and fragilely crisp squares of puff pastry were layered with whipped cream and kiwi slices. An upside-down orange layer cake in a satiny vanilla sauce was unexpectedly exceptional — "unexpectedly" because layer cakes generally are banal and cloyingly sweet. Also improbable but delicious was the pear "poached in white peppercorn," whatever that means, but perfect in its frothy, creamy honey-vanilla sauce. Cubes of fresh pineapple macerated in brandy provided a cold, clear contrast with the otherwise rich food.

Three flaws that detract somewhat from the overall pleasure of a meal at Greene Street are the upstairs check room that is a bottleneck, the wicker chairs, some of which are too low and others that are rough and snag stockings and loose-woven fabrics, and the many levels and steps throughout the premises; "eyes down" is the rule to follow as you wander through.

There is a music charge after 10:30, and a two-drink minimum if no food is ordered.

Green Tree Hungarian Restaurant

★

1034 Amsterdam Avenue, at West 111th Street, 864-9106.

Atmosphere: Lively, informal, no frills, old cafe-restaurant popular with students; friendly, helpful and sometimes slow service.

Recommended dishes: Chicken soup, borscht, cherry soup, potato pirogen, stuffed cabbage, chicken paprikash, stuffed roast chicken, beef or veal goulash, scrambled eggs with brains, breaded veal cutlet, napoleon, cream puffs, apple strudel, palacsinta.

Price range: Inexpensive.

Credit cards: None.

Hours: Lunch, Mondays through Saturdays, noon to 3 P.M.; dinner, Mondays through Saturdays, 3 P.M. to 9 P.M. Closed Sundays.

Reservations: Not accepted.

Prices being what they are, it is no small challenge to find a friendly and convivial restaurant offering hot, lusty and well-seasoned three-course dinners with coffee for under $10. Considering that such prices are still in effect at the Green Tree Hungarian Restaurant, it may seem downright ungrateful to report a decline in overall quality. There are still enough good choices to provide a satisfying dinner, but the choice used to be even wider. Therefore, a one-star rating is more in order now than the two-star rating given several years ago.

Reminiscent of the homey, Bohemian cafe-restaurants of Europe, the Green Tree is a favorite with students from Columbia and Barnard and the staffs of St. John the Divine and St. Luke's church and hospital. Diners seated at oilcloth tablecloths are supplied with paper napkins and get familial concern from waiters and from the owners, Ali Kende and his wife, Clara. Mrs. Kende still turns out her wonderful cream puffs and napoleons filled with custard and whipped cream and the warm flaky apple strudel after 7:30. Service may slow down at busy times and the kitchen runs out of popular choices early, but at these prices it is understandable.

Less understandable are the staleness of such reheated main courses as the duck, goose and pork and the frequent scorching of sauces. Dishes that remain good are the golden, aromatic chicken soup with the best matzoh balls in the city, and the cold beet borscht. The potato- or meat-filled dumplings, pirogen, are at their best fried and topped with cool sour cream and they may be shared as an appetizer or eaten as a stick-to-the-ribs main course.

Stuffed roast chicken is now far superior to the dried-out veal shank and duck, and rising costs have apparently taken their toll of such cuts as veal cutlet and rib steak. Order sauce dishes like the meltingly rich and tender chicken paprikash and the beef or veal goulash brightened with paprika and you probably will not be disappointed. Vegetables are canned and potato pancakes are leaden, but the mashed potatoes enriched with sautéed onions and paprika and the tiny dough dumplings, nockerl, were soul-warming.

Cakes other than those mentioned are overly sweet and characterless. Beers and wines are moderately priced.

Hakubai

★

Hotel Kitano, 66 Park Avenue, at the corner of 38th Street, 686-3770.

Atmosphere: Pleasant, trim Japanese setting with some quiet corners and attractive tatami rooms, though main dining room can be noisy at peak hours; service sometimes good, but generally off-hand and careless.

Recommended dishes: Chawan-mushi, miso bean soup, grilled lobster, kara-age fried fish, seafood nabemono and yosenabe, shabu-shabu, seaweed with herring roe, eggplant with soy sauce, nuta.

Price range: Moderately expensive.

Credit cards: All major credit cards.

Hours: Lunch, daily, noon to 2 P.M.; dinner, daily, 6 P.M. to 10 P.M.

Reservations: Necessary, especially at lunch.

Hakubai, tucked away on the first and second floors of the Hotel Kitano, can still provide a very good meal, as it did in 1979, when it received two stars, but it does so with much less consistency. A one-star rating seems more in order now. The main fault is the decline in service, with an often brusque and careless staff. At busy times, dishes arrive slowly, hot tea is not replenished and often some diners get their main courses long before others at the same table. Greetings at the door can be equally offhand, and a parting thank you is rarely forthcoming.

The kitchen also performs inconsistently. Shrimp and vegetable tempura, which was formerly light and greaseless, now generally arrives reeking of overused or overheated frying oil, and so do the tatsuta-age, fried chicken nuggets. Sashimi and sushi, once fresh and pearly, now often seems to have been cut long in advance of serving.

Dishes that have held up include chawan-mushi, a sheer custard steamed in porcelain cups with flecks of vegetables and shrimp. It is now on the English dinner menu, and so are a number of the more esoteric and interesting dishes formerly restricted to the Japanese menu. Among such small dishes worth trying are raw sea urchin, seaweed with herring roe, baked eggplant with soy sauce and nuta, raw tuna or chicken and scallions in a silky soybean paste.

Kara-age, a whole deep-fried fluke, escapes tainting with the oil that mars the tempura, and the fish remains moist within. Teriyaki steak is tough and bland, and negimayaki, rolls of marinated beef wrapped around scallions, are generally soggy. Seafood casseroles, however, steamed at the table, are still excellent, especially yosenabe, a sort of bouillabaisse with vegetables, shrimp, clams and fish. Two halves of a lobster are done in different ways — one grilled with bean paste, the other as a sort of French-style salad with mayonnaise and vegetables. The combination is delicious and diverting. Butter-grilled salmon, once among the better dishes, is now often chokingly dry. There is a lot of limp iceberg lettuce in evidence, both as salad and garnish.

I had not previously tried Hakubai's shabu-shabu, which proved to be a beautifully fresh and colorful combination of beef and vegetables boiled over a brazier at the table, then dipped into aromatic sesame and soy sauces. It is well worth ordering and should offer savory diversion to dieters.

Fruit remains the best dessert.

Harvey's Chelsea Restaurant
Fair

108 West 18th Street, between Avenue of the Americas and Seventh Avenue, 243-5644.
Atmosphere: Handsome, restored turn-of-the-century bar and restaurant that is noisy and lively; service is friendly but unprofessional.
Recommended dishes: Pea soup, broiled mushrooms, roast duck with cherry sauce, broiled salmon, steak, Alsatian sausage with potatoes, omelets, bagel with cream cheese and smoked salmon.
Price range: Moderate.
Credit cards: None.
Hours: Lunch, Mondays through Saturdays, noon to 5 P.M.; dinner, Sundays through Thursdays, 5 P.M to midnight, Fridays and Saturdays, 5 P.M to 1 A.M. Sunday brunch, noon to 4:30 P.M. Closed major holidays.
Reservations: Recommended.

With its enormous polished mahogany bar, the gleaming brass wall clock and cut-glass panels, Harvey's Chelsea is another turn-of-the-century set piece. At brunch, lunch and dinner it is a favorite of local residents, and there are just enough nicely prepared dishes at moderate prices to justify the popularity. A thick pea soup with ham and firm broiled mushrooms proved thoroughly satisfying first courses, and freshly roasted duck with a cherry sauce lacked the cloying sweetness such sauces usually have. Broiled salmon, though a bit overdone, was acceptable, as was steak. One of the best main courses can be Alsatian sausage with hot potato salad — "can be" because it is occasionally slightly high with spoilage. Shepherd's pie is comfortable and homey, a combination of vegetables, beef and lamb stew, although its potato topping suggests a dehydrated mix.

Sunday brunch is pleasant and a very good buy with soda bread and a drink (mine a Bloody Mary short on vodka) included in the fixed price. Above-average omelets offer a variety of fillings. A generous bagel, cream cheese and smoked salmon sandwich garnished with scallions and capers is an alternate main course as is the good beefy steak of an unrecognized cut of meat topped by three fried eggs. Competently prepared eggs Benedict could be improved with better Canadian bacon.

Wines are overpriced and there is a marked tendency of the management to fill the worst tables first. Refuse a table you do not like and you will be rewarded with a better one.

Hatsuhana
★ ★

17 East 48th Street, between Fifth and Madison Avenues, 355-3345.
Atmosphere: Handsome Japanese sushi bar with tables; crowded and noisy; service difficult if you do not speak Japanese.
Recommended dishes: All sushi and sashimi, nuta, natto, chawan-mushi, broiled scallops, broiled squid feet, broiled giant clams, seafood kushiyaki, soups and pickled vegetables.
Price range: Moderately expensive
Credit cards: All major credit cards.
Hours: Lunch, Mondays through Fridays, 11:45 A.M. to 2:30 P.M.; dinner, Mondays through Fridays, 5:30 P.M. to 9:30 P.M., Saturdays, 5 P.M. to 9:30 P.M. Closed Sundays. Open on major holidays.
Reservations: Necessary for dinner.

Among the more rarified and intricate of Japanese culinary specialties, sushi is perhaps the most artfully enticing and antique, dating back some 2,000 years. Created in Southeast Asia, then traveling to China and finally to Japan, these exquisitely molded combinations of sweet vinegar rice, bits of raw fish and vegetables and wrappings of spinach-green seaweed, come in endlessly diverting and satisfying forms.

That brief bit of sushi history comes to us from the menu at Hatsuhana, a small, stylishly modern Japanese restaurant with an upstairs dining room recently redecorated. The real action is at the street-level sushi bar, where one can watch the prestidigitators who are the sushi makers as their hands fly to mold rice under raw shrimp, squid or tuna (nigri sushi) or the variety of offerings neatly wrapped in seaweed (nori sushi).

A natural adjunct to sushi (those with large or small red caviar, and sea urchin roe were the most subtly spectacular) is sashimi, raw fish such as tuna (the half fatty toro being the most highly prized), squid, shrimp, mackerel with silvery strips of skin, or pearl-pink fluke. I watched as a party of four received a complete selection of all sushi and sashimi which was served to them at a table in a huge round lacquer tray. The colorful mosaic of food patterns made me wish I had a camera with color film on hand. Fiery green mustard, pickled ginger, soy sauce and stoneware mugs of hot, mild tea are the natural accompaniments to these delicate morsels.

But sushi and sashimi are not quite all there is to Hatsuhana's menu for it is a sort of snack restaurant with "small dishes" to be ordered in succession. This, unfortunately, is a custom not made plain to Westerners there. It is too bad the help or management does not take time to explain the more unusual specialties, many of which are not on the English menu at all.

Advised by a Japanese friend, I ordered natto, a pungent mix of fermented beans, tuna fish and scallions: nuta, a sensual blend of raw fluke and scallions in a satiny yellow sauce made of soybean paste, lemon and sake, and a soft, hot, steamed custard, chawan-mushi, set with bits of greens, mushrooms, fish, shrimp, gingko nuts and lemon rind.

Tempura here varies from fair to very good. The salmon teriyaki was a bit too dry but the seafood kushi-yaki, bits of fish, pepper and mushrooms broiled on skewers, was perfect. Soups and salads were pleasant and the squid "feet" or tentacles broiled in butter, the sliced giant clams grilled with pepper, and the sliced sea scallops boiled in butter, were all as satisfying as they were interesting. No meat is served. Sake, beer, wine, and whiskey are available, but tea and sake seemed the most appropriate beverages. Pineapple and cantaloupe are often unripe.

The sushi and sashimi at Hatsuhana are certainly worth three stars, as are the more obscure dishes. However, the more ordinary dishes are not as well prepared, and the most interesting choices are not offered to non-Japanese. Therefore, an averaging of the menu results in a two-star rating.

Hatsuhana is wildly busy at peak meal hours and takes no reservations. Prices are low per dish, but portions are small and it is easy for two people to consume quite a costly variety.

Hisae's
Fair

45 East 58th Street, between Madison and Park Avenues, 753-6555.

Atmosphere: Three garish but amusing nightclub-style dining rooms where service can be abrupt.

Recommended dishes: Broccoli with garlic and oil, squid or scungilli salad, eggplant with miso, red snapper in garlic butter, sea bass with black-bean sauce, salmon with mushrooms, tortellini, spinach salad, apple pie, pecan pie, chocolate torte.

Price range: Moderately expensive.

Credit cards: American Express, Visa, MasterCard and Diners Club.

Hours: Lunch, Mondays through Fridays, noon to 4 P.M.; dinner, daily, 4 P.M. to midnight.

Reservations: Recommended.

Hisae's Place
Fair

35 Cooper Square, near Fifth Street, 228-6886.
Atmosphere: Convivial tavern with sloppy house-keeping; service is slow and can be polite or surly.
Recommended dishes: Broccoli with oil and garlic, eggplant with miso, scungilli salad, tortellini, eggplant stuffed with lamb, red snapper with garlic, sea bass with black beans, cheesecake.
Price range: Moderate.
Credit cards: None.
Hours: Dinner, Mondays through Thursdays, 5 P.M. to midnight; Fridays and Saturdays, 5 P.M. to 1 A.M., and Sundays, 5 to 11 P.M.
Reservations: Recommended.

Flushed with an early and well-deserved success, Hisae Vilca, who originated one of New York's most original cuisines by combining elements of Oriental, Italian and vegetarian cooking, overexpanded, and the quality of her restaurants has slowly declined. Judging by recent visits, a demotion from a two-star rating to fair is in order for both Hisae's Place on the Bowery, and Hisae's on East 58th Street.

The uptown restaurant, with its upholstered supper-club dining rooms, is still lively, if garish, but the more Bohemian tavern on the Bowery has become sloppy and unappetizing. In both places, service can be friendly and helpful or rude and pushy. When an order of musty, stale mussels was returned at the Bowery restaurant, the waiter seemed concerned, and without argument he scratched the item off the check, but on another night another waiter refused to replace rotted bean sprouts. During a busy lunch at 58th Street, a waiter threw menus across the table and brought a check before it was requested.

Worst of all, the quality of ingredients and cooking in both restaurants has declined. The once-sprightly creamy dip for raw vegetables tastes like a commercial mayonnaise-style dressing. Cold asparagus and artichokes are held too long in the refrierator, and one night the sauce for artichokes seemed to be undiluted mustard. Meager quantities of shrimp or scallops are bulked up with a veritable mountain of limp, wet vegetables.

Dishes that have held up consistently are such appetizers as conch (scungilli) or squid in vinaigrette dressing, hot broccoli bathed in garlic and oil and satiny eggplant slices glossed with miso bean paste. The creamy scallop chowder with onions and potatoes should be brinier and hotter, but is still acceptable. Two dependable classics are sea bass braised with black beans and ginger and red snapper with garlic butter. Above average are spinach salad, tortellini with peas and poached salmon with mushrooms.

The chicken and meat dishes have always been second-rate and remain so, the one exception being the savory eggplant stuffed with ground lamb served downtown.

Such fish as flounder, swordfish and trout, which are sautéed with vegetables, are usually drowned in heavy sauces, the worst being sweet and sour.

Desserts are much better uptown than downtown. Thick, fresh apple crumb cake, a lean, fragrant chocolate nut torte and excellent crunchy pecan pie are ususally on hand. The same desserts downtown are entirely different and often stale. For example, the apple pie is thinner and tasteless, the spice cake and chocolate rum cake are underbaked and the pecan pie is dry.

Hisae's Chelsea Place
Fair

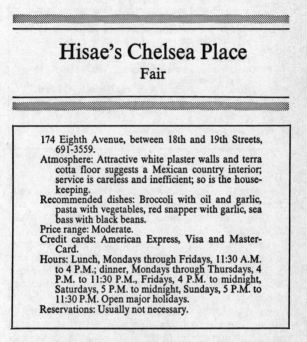

174 Eighth Avenue, between 18th and 19th Streets, 691-3559.

Atmosphere: Attractive white plaster walls and terra cotta floor suggests a Mexican country interior; service is careless and inefficient; so is the housekeeping.

Recommended dishes: Broccoli with oil and garlic, pasta with vegetables, red snapper with garlic, sea bass with black beans.

Price range: Moderate.

Credit cards: American Express, Visa and MasterCard.

Hours: Lunch, Mondays through Fridays, 11:30 A.M. to 4 P.M.; dinner, Mondays through Thursdays, 4 P.M. to 11:30 P.M., Fridays, 4 P.M. to midnight, Saturdays, 5 P.M. to midnight, Sundays, 5 P.M. to 11:30 P.M. Open major holidays.

Reservations: Usually not necessary.

Never one of Hisae Vilca's better efforts, the tiled and rough-plastered Chelsea outpost of her chain has deteriorated noticeably. Originally rated one star, it now deserves no more than fair, which is really an average of its poor-to-good range. Housekeeping has become careless and the staff inefficient. On a good night, the Continental-Oriental vegetarian specialties do Hisae credit, with firm bright broccoli properly perfumed with garlic, the pasta al dente with a vegetable sauce and her well-known fish dishes fresh and cooked to pearly, moist perfection. But good nights are few and far between, and we have often had wilted raw vegetables in salads, a red snapper fillet that was not fresh and not really red snapper, stale mussels and shrimp and brown rice studded with rancid nuts. Mrs. Vilca apparently is spreading her supervisory talents too thin, and Chelsea is the loser.

Hisae's West

Fair

12 West 72nd Street, off Central Park West, 787-5656.

Atmosphere: Huge, funky, fallen-grandeur Tudor dining rooms with large, widely spaced tables; service uneven and distracted.

Recommended dishes: Mussels in tomato broth, broccoli with oil and garlic, scallop chowder, spinach pasta with peas and mushrooms, eggplant in miso sauce, sautéed mako shark with zucchini, steak, pecan pie, apple crumb pie, chocolate cake, fruit salad.

Price range: Moderate.

Credit Cards: American Express, Visa, MasterCard and Diners Club.

Hours: Dinner, Mondays through Thursdays, 5 P.M. to midnight, Fridays and Saturdays, 5 P.M. to 1 A.M., Sundays, 4 P.M. to 11 P.M. Open major holidays.

Reservations: Recommended.

If any student of the restaurant business needs an object lesson in the consequences of one owner's operating too many restaurants, the perfect illustrations are this and the foregoing restaurants begun and now only partly operated by Hisae Vilca.

Even small details such as the bread and raw-vegetable giveaway appetizer testified to carelessness and lack of interest on the part of the management. The bread was stale and insubstantial, and the bean sprouts among the faded raw vegetables had aged to a soggy, brown limpness. Shrimp sautéed in black-bean sauce tasted so strongly of iodine (indicating staleness) that not even the garlic and ginger in the sauce could mask the medicinal tang. A sea bass also had a suspiciously fishy smell and taste, tuna fish was dry and soft-shell crabs arrived mushy and watery. When a complaint was registered about the crabs, a waitress nodded matter-of-factly, saying that the sautéed soft-shell crabs were supposed to be mushy and watery, and that if we wanted them crisp, we should have ordered them deep fried. Don't order bouillabaisse at Hisae's West unless you're in love with canned tomatoes, for that is the bulk of this tasteless dish. And the broiled Maine lobster seemed to have been precooked and reheated. Equally poor were a breast of chicken stuffed with vegetables and both the calamari and the conch salads. These were once Hisae triumphs, but on recent visits they were sour with vinegar.

Just a few dishes reflected their former quality, among them such appetizers as juicy sandless mussels steamed in a tomato-garlic broth; firm broccoli bathed in garlic-scented oil, and smooth, gently oiled eggplant in miso sauce. There were also a decent creamy spinach pasta tossed with peas and mushrooms and, surprisingly delicious among so much depressing food, a lovely creamed-scallop-and-potato chowder. The only halfway decent main course was a sautéed mako shark steak with julienne strips of zucchini and a good beefy sirloin steak. Some desserts also seemed to be holding up well, with a crisp pecan pie, a cinnamon-perfumed apple-crunch tart, a dark chocolate cake and a respectable fresh fruit salad.

The setting here is somewhat funky and bizarre — huge dining rooms done up in a sort of stony, apartment-house Tudor, complete with stained-glass windows. There is a big gloomy bar with piano music several evenings, and a newly added sushi counter.

Hoexter's Market
★ ★

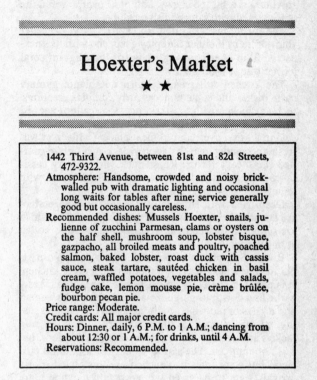

1442 Third Avenue, between 81st and 82d Streets, 472-9322.

Atmosphere: Handsome, crowded and noisy brick-walled pub with dramatic lighting and occasional long waits for tables after nine; service generally good but occasionally careless.

Recommended dishes: Mussels Hoexter, snails, julienne of zucchini Parmesan, clams or oysters on the half shell, mushroom soup, lobster bisque, gazpacho, all broiled meats and poultry, poached salmon, baked lobster, roast duck with cassis sauce, steak tartare, sautéed chicken in basil cream, waffled potatoes, vegetables and salads, fudge cake, lemon mousse pie, crème brûlée, bourbon pecan pie.

Price range: Moderate.

Credit cards: All major credit cards.

Hours: Dinner, daily, 6 P.M. to 1 A.M.; dancing from about 12:30 or 1 A.M.; for drinks, until 4 A.M.

Reservations: Recommended.

Since Hoexter's Market opened in 1977, the kitchen has had a few ups and downs, beginning with a two-star rating and dropping to fair two years ago. Now, fortunately, things have obviously taken a turn for the better, and the earlier expertise is again evident in the preparation of the remarkable grilled meats and poultry, baked lobster, luxurious soups, firm, fresh vegetables, crackling crisp waffled potatoes and such irresistible desserts as tangy lemon mousse pie, mellow chocolate fudge cake, bourbon pecan pie and a rich and well-caramelized crème brûlée. The impeccability of such specialties far overshadows the shortcomings of others.

Moreover, the brick walls and tin ceiling that looked handsome but which heightened noise have been modified with a carpetlike wall hanging and panels of a patterned mauve padding, making the noise level more bearable.

Associated with Hoexter's, the food market on Lexington Avenue known for its fine meats, this restaurant has always excelled in the quality of its beef, lamb, veal, chicken and duck. They are best simply prepared —

153

with peppercorns, mustard sauces or herb butters. The raw-beef appetizer carpaccio, brightened by a dressing of capers, peppers, olive oil and Parmesan cheese, and the freshly ground steak tartare are excellent, too. Only the prosciutto has been disappointing because of its lack of ripeness, and the smoked chicken is sometimes dry.

Consistently good appetizers include snails (especially if served in puff pastry with a garlic cream sauce accented by tomatoes and mushrooms), steamed mussels Hoexter, in a tomato-and-cream broth, clams and oysters on the half-shell and julienne of zucchini gratinéed with Parmesan cheese. Among fish appetizers, the gravlax was a bit too chewy, and basil overpowered the sauce served with sautéed fish escalope.

The menu changes often, so choices vary. Consider yourself lucky if either the spicy gazpacho with its unexpected fillip of red salmon caviar or the fragrant coral lobster bisque is offered.

The kitchen still seems to turn out bland, gummy pasta dishes and some unnecessarily complex creations, such as chicken with lobster sauce, sea scallops zapped by an overdose of curry and slightly tough scallops of veal in a salty, overreduced meat glaze. Calf's liver was fresh and tender, but the syrupy dark meat glaze muffled the meat's flavor. Roast duck with a winy cassis sauce was delicious, and so was chicken breast with tomato in a basil cream sauce.

Deep-fried waffled potatoes, salads and vegetables are beautifully prepared, even though pistachios, which are supposed to accompany cauliflower, were forgotten at one dinner.

Robert Schapiro, who owns Hoexter's, is also a partner in Uzie's next door, and there is a common kitchen. It is possible, therefore, to get Uzie's fragrant and zesty garlic bread with its gorgonzola sauce; that, with a salad and a glass of red wine, would make an elegant and sustaining late supper. A dress code requiring ties and jackets and prohibiting denim is posted on the door, but it is not enforced. The staff is usually pleasant and efficient, but sometimes it is rushed and distracted. Early arrivals seem to be given the worst tables, while more comfortable ones are being kept vacant for regulars. After 9 P.M., there can be a long wait at the jam-packed bar, even if you have reservations.

This becomes a disco after 12:30 or 1 A.M. when dinner is over.

Home Village Restaurant Ltd.
★ ★

20 Mott Street, between Mulberry Street and the Bowery, 964-0381.

Atmosphere: Neat and orderly upstairs and downstairs dining rooms with tablecloths and typically atmospheric decorative touches; service is generally good but can be perfunctory at busy times.

Recommended dishes: House egg roll, braised shark's fin and crabmeat soup, sliced-pork soup with assorted vegetables and bean curd, baked chicken with salt, roast chicken, roast duck, steamed sole, sautéed sea bass with soy sauce, braised seafood in bird's nest, lobster or clams with black bean sauce, lobster with cheese, baked prawns with chili and spiced salt, sautéed squid, baked crabs with curry, fried oysters, deep-fried fresh rolled liver, beef ball with brown sauce, baked giblets with salt, Chinese-style pork chop, chef's special fried steak, steamed stuffed bean curd, sautéed spinach with preserved beancake sauce, fried vermicelli rice noodles Singapore style.

Price range: Moderate.

Credit cards: None.

Hours: Lunch, Mondays through Fridays, 11 A.M. to 3 P.M.; dinner, Mondays through Thursdays, 3 P.M. to 1 A.M., Fridays and Saturdays, 3 P.M. to 2 A.M., Sundays, 11 A.M. to 1 A.M. Open major holidays.

Reservations: Recommended for dinner, especially on weekends.

Although I paid six visits to the Home Village Restaurant in Chinatown and tried some forty dishes, including several that were not on the menu, this review probably should be marked "To be continued." That's because the forty dishes represent only 20 percent of a menu listing 185 dishes as well as fifteen or more available for special house dinners.

Moreover, as far as I know, this is the only restaurant in the city that presents a menu with the food of the Hakka — the mountain people of Canton — listed clearly for the most part, in English. According to E. N. Anderson Jr. and Marja L. Anderson, writing on the modern cuisines of south China in the book "Food in Chinese Culture," the Hakka have been regarded as simple mountain folk who do little cooking. The authors say that this is a mistaken belief and that on any given night a Hakka restaurant can provide patrons with more than 100 dishes prepared from local products.

Since its opening in 1980, the Home Village Restaurant, with its two floors of trim, bright and cheerful modern dining rooms, has lived up to this reputation for instant variety. The Chinese patrons outnumbered the non-Chinese by about thirty to one on my visits, and there seemed to be no difference in the way food was prepared for the two groups.

Service is best when the restaurant is least crowded — week nights and afternoons — when waiters and managers offer patient explanations and show a desire to please. Friday and Saturday night and all day Sunday can be hectic and customers may be treated perfunctorily.

Hakka or non-Hakka, most of the food here is unusual and much of it is positively delicious. Only a few preparations were lackluster; the most serious failures were bland beef and veal dishes in brown sauces that were heavy with cornstarch and in overdone and soggy vegetables, most especially mushrooms with dried scallops.

Appetizers are not listed on the menu as such, so it is not easy to decide where to start. Several of the Hakka dishes make good beginnings, however, including the crisp, tender poultry giblets baked in salt and the tiny beef balls of finely ground, tightly packed meat braised in brown sauce and decorated with broccoli. The house egg roll, which has a thick, puffy, crisp skin, is far above average. So is a variation — fried rolled beef liver in the same skin. Shrimp (called prawns) baked in the shells with salt and spiced with green chilles could be eaten shell and all. Curried crab also makes an excellent appetizer and chunks of lobster in the shell baked with a fine crust of cheddarlike cheese were succulent and pungent. Either lobster or clams in black bean sauce also is a satisfying appetizer or main course.

Two soups worth considering are the blend of assorted vegetables, diced bean curd and sliced pork, and the shark's fin with crabmeat, which at first was overly thick but which was lightened with some rice wine vinegar and hot mustard. Both condiments were offered and their uses explained on a slow night, but they had to be requested on a busy one.

Steamed and braised fish dishes were superior to those that were fried. Sole steamed with scallions and ginger achieved a pearly, custardy consistency, as did a sea bass (listed as C B on the menu) in a soy and wine sauce. Sea bass in sweet sauce can be skipped and so can the fried or panned sole, which were too dry and greasy. Sautéed shrimp mixed with frozen peas or rancid cashew nuts also should be passed up in favor of sautéed squid, crackling with tender, briny freshness. For a dish that tastes as delightful as it looks, order the stir-fried assorted seafood and vegetables in a deep-fried basket of noodle-fine grated taro root, described on the menu as a bird's nest.

It would be a mistake to pass up the tender, moist golden-skinned chicken baked in salt and left rose-pink at the bone so the meat remains snowy and silky, or the roast chicken that is equally good. Both were excellent when dipped into a sauce that seemed to combine sesame, soy, ginger and star anise. Chunks of chicken in black bean sauce had mustily stale overtones, but half-crisp roasted duck could not have been better.

Among the more esoteric Hakka main courses are the combinations based on what the menu lists as "biche de mer," apparently taken from the French bêche-de-mer. The Chinese refers to a sort of giant sea slug that attains a gelatinous consistency not unlike a chewy steamed cucumber. Combined with black mushrooms, beef balls or roasted duck feet, this may be something that the more adventurous will want to try. Another Hakka dish that was served at a special dinner seemed to be smoked and sugar-glazed sole, a fishy and pungent delicacy inexplicably served with bottled orange-colored French dressing. Our Chinese neighbors dipped into this happily, but for our taste it spoiled the fish.

An extraordinary meat dish, chef's special steak, could be a variation on chicken-fried steak. The meat must have been pounded to tenderness, then breaded and fried to crispness and finished off with a soy and wine sauce. Pot-roasted veal and kale was decent, but it was no match for the marvelous Chinese-style pork chops — thin, chewy and mellow in a honeyed hoisin glaze.

Only two vegetable dishes proved interesting — spinach melted in a sharp sauce of preserved bean curd, and pillows of fresh bean curd stuffed with finely minced pork and shrimp.

There is a ghastly fried rice specialty here that is topped with a syrupy-sweet tomato ketchup and onion sauce, but the white version with strands of egg, shrimp and pork can be recommended. So can the savory, curry-gilded Singapore fried rice vermicelli sparked with cayenne and green chilies.

When a large group appears at Home Village, the management tries to sell a special house dinner — its version of the French menu de dégustation. Resist the temptation to take this easy way out and choose the dishes you prefer no matter how long the deliberation takes. When a house dinner was ordered, the captain agreed to some substitutions, but they were not made. It is better and cheaper to plan your own menu. Order just a few dishes at a time so that all do not arrive at once and grow cold.

Soft drinks are available, but you must provide your own liquor or beer. Oranges are the only satisfactory dessert. Avoid the dreadful white agar gelatin pudding topped with canned fruit salad that comes as a banquet dessert. Plastic chopsticks are heavy, slippery and hard to handle.

Horn of Plenty
Fair

91 Charles Street, corner of Bleecker Street, 242-0636.

Atmosphere: Intimate and Bohemian indoor dining room plus a large and attractive covered garden with a greenhouse effect; service is concerned, efficient and accommodating.

Recommended dishes: Deviled crabmeat, Cajun crab and eggplant, chopped chicken livers, pan-fried chicken, barbecued spareribs in hot sauce, stuffed pork chop, broiled pork chop without sauce, pecan pie, chocolate walnut pie, apple cobbler, fresh fruit.

Price range: Moderate.

Credit cards: All major cards.

Hours: Dinner, Mondays through Thursdays, 6 P.M. to 11:45 P.M., Fridays and Saturdays, 6 P.M. to 1 A.M., Sundays, 5 P.M. to 11:45 P.M. Open major holidays.

Reservations: Recommended.

Each year there are fewer bona fide outdoor eating places in New York because owners put roofs over their gardens so they can realize profits from the space regardless of the weather. Usually when gardens are covered they lose their outdoor feeling. But a successful conversion was completed recently at Horn of Plenty in Greenwich Village. One of the larger and more popular garden restaurants in the city, its open space was covered with clear plastic supported by natural wood, and hanging plants were placed throughout.

Unless you are there on a busy night, and in a group of three or fewer, you will be completely comfortable in this pleasant space, especially with the friendly, concerned and efficient dining room staff. Smaller parties generally are seated in cramped corners on the bar side of the garden, where the heat and noise are unfelicitous.

Most of the dishes turned out by the kitchen also could be described as unfelicitous — overcooked, oversweetened, oversalted or drowned in pasty, characterless sauces. Marmalade sweet curries are the poorest, followed by Italian and Creole main courses. But fortunately, there are about a half-dozen good soul food specialties that enable the visitor to have a satisfying dinner in this garden setting.

Peppery deviled crabmeat is perhaps the best appetizer, followed closely by Cajun crab and eggplant, and fresh and meaty chopped chicken livers. Giant clams casino were tough and musty, and shrimp bisque was so thick it could almost be cut with a knife.

Choose one of the three very good main courses and you should be satisfied. Meaty spareribs in a hot pepper and vinegar barbecue sauce were delicious. So was the bacon-crisp chicken, only lightly floured and fried so that it remained moist and tender within. A gigantic pork chop stuffed with cornbread would have been better without its floury sauce, nevertheless, it was well above average. Not so the fatty ham hocks, the pasty smothered chicken or the dried-out duck in a sauce that seemed to be nothing but hot honey. A number of larger-than-life layer cakes are on display, all as characterless as if they had been made from mixes. The best desserts were the pecan pie, the chocolate walnut pie, the apple cobbler and fresh fruit.

Hubert's
★ ★

102 East 22nd Street, between Park Avenue South and Lexington Avenue, 673-3711.

Atmosphere: Subtle lighting lends a romantic touch to this simple yet sophisticated dining room, that is cramped and noisy when full. Service is gracious and concerned, but slow; cigar and pipe smoking are not permitted.

Recommended dishes: Chicken soup with fall vegetables, homemade white cheese, wild mushrooms with puff pastry, pâté of smoked salmon, sautéed duck livers, eggplant caviar, smelt fritters, sausage with sweet potato gratin, potato and zucchini pancakes, broiled swordfish, chicken soufflé, fish with fish mousse, loin of pork braised in bourbon, filet of beef with mushrooms, rack of lamb in rosemary crust, breast of Muscovy duck, vanilla roulade, chocolate cake, quince tart, cheesecake, lemon tart with lemon cream, dacquoise or dacquoise tarts, persimmon sherbet, vanilla ice cream with brandied figs and grapes.

Price range: Moderately expensive.

Credit cards: American Express.

Hours: Lunch, Mondays through Saturdays, noon to 3 P.M.; dinner, Mondays through Saturdays, 6 P.M. to 10:30 P.M. Closed Sundays except Sunday holidays, Mother's Day, Father's Day and Easter. Open on major holidays.

Reservations: Necessary.

Brooklyn's loss was Manhattan's gain when Hubert's, the charming and very good restaurant that was in Boerum Hill, moved to Manhattan, in the premises formerly occupied by E. F. Barrett. The new restaurant, still operated by Karen Hubert and Len Allison, the partners who share kitchen and dining room chores, is already up to the two-star performance of the original. Despite the kitchen's consistency in Brooklyn, the location was too remote to attract a steady following.

If the new Hubert's lacks some of the romantic appeal of the mellow old Victorian corner bar in Brooklyn, it is nonetheless dramatic and handsome, with outdoor street lamps casting a theatrical glow through uncurtained windows. The young staff is as gracious and hospitable as the owners — all refreshingly unpretentious. But service is slow and, judging by complaints from readers, often indifferent. A problem of noise also needs correcting.

Right from the roasted corn "nuts" offered at the bar to the delicate lemon tarts and vanilla roulade, each culinary detail is given the most careful thought and execution. Everything looks, tastes and is homemade, including piquant cherry-tomato and lime relish, basil and tomato jelly and warm, fragrant bacon-flecked muffins at lunch, and the gentle vegetable purées and gratins that round out main courses at dinner.

The culinary style is New American in the best sense of the term, borrowing freely from European cooking traditions and combining them with native influences.

159

Perfect cases in point are the lunchtime appetizers of warm herb-scented country sausage alongside a creamy gratin of sweet potatoes and the crisply fried smelt fritters in beer batter. Also at lunch, tart applesauce and sour cream are soothing contrasts to crisply fried pancakes of grated zucchini and potatoes.

The dill-scented chicken soup that was so extraordinary in Brooklyn apparently travels well, for it is just as good in New York even though there are a few too many slices of root vegetables adrift in it. An interesting first course is the creamy fromage blanc, the whipped cream cheese sparked by gentle overtones of garlic. An equally good appetizer is the satiny warm eggplant caviar nested on roasted sweet pepper and underlined with the oily, edible skin of the eggplant. Also recommended are a pâté of smoked salmon flavored with dill and aquavit that is as rich as ice cream, and wild mushrooms or duck livers that gain crunchy contrast from the puff pastry served with them. A few appetizers seemed uninteresting, but only so when compared with more exciting alternatives. Two dishes lacking interest were the shrimp and oysters in coriander cream and the overly contrived tomato that held a small fillet of fish filled with salmon mousse. A combination of chanterelles on a tiny mound of pasta sounded tempting but was short on flavor.

Meat main courses are especially well prepared. Tender pork loin braised in bourbon and garnished with prunes and delicate fruit and vegetable purées has a lusty goodness even though it is slightly sweet if you're planning to drink wine. Both the rare-roasted rack of lamb encrusted with rosemary and the filet of beef sautéed with mushrooms, scallions and crème fraîche approach perfection. So do the slices of rare Muscovy duck breast. At lunch, choices include a delicate, flavorful chicken soufflé topped with morels, and a delicious and carefully broiled fish with garlicky spinach and a sliver of stuffed eggplant. There are also daily specials.

Not all main courses were as good as those described above. The quail, for instance, was too tough to be pierced with a knife and was virtually inedible as served. At lunch, the tortellini needed more of the creamy sauce and the turkey pot pie was soupy and bland. The ham had too much of a sweet pineapple topping, although the molasses-glazed baked beans with it were properly dark and mellow. The most consistent culinary flaws are tendencies to sweetness where it doesn't belong and blandness.

At dinner, the least interesting main courses included steamed trout and chicken marinated with citrus fruits served over tasteless couscous. Lobster on pasta with a sauce of brandy, cream and shallots was lovely, but at the high prices, there should have been more lobster meat. Portions here tend to be small, this was most noticeable on the lobster-pasta combination. Fish filled with fish mousses are frequent specials and are pleasant, and green salads are fresh and pungent.

There are some superb desserts, including a spongy lemon tart with lemon whipped cream, a nut-encrusted roulade of Génoise sponge cake filled with whipped cream, and a crisp and luscious hazelnut dacquoise.

Dacquoise also appears in small tarts at times and there is a rich cheesecake brightened with orange and lemon. Snow mousse is an irresistible cross between a cassata and tortoni and there is usually a homemade ice cream. The vanilla is topped with brandied figs and grapes, and the tart persimmon sherbet is accented with raspberry purée. Chocolate brownie cake, a thin quince tart and bourbon sponge cakes were only slightly less tempting than other desserts. Pear Bavaroise was the only one really short on flavor.

There are some interesting modestly priced wines among the more lavish offerings.

Hunam
★ ★

845 Second Avenue, between 45th and 46th Streets, 687-7471

Atmosphere: Standard Chinese modern setting, dimly lit; generally excellent service that only occasionally falters.

Recommended dishes: Hacked chicken, corned pork, pearl balls, turnip cakes, shrimp puff, hot and sour soup, hot and sour fish broth, lamb Human style, crispy whole sea bass, bamboo steamers, spareribs, crisp fried boneless duck, Hunam beef, orange-flavored beef, sautéed smoked chicken, tangy and spicy green beans, eggplant family style and, for the most adventurous, preserved duck.

Price range: Moderately expensive.

Credit cards: American Express, Diners Club and Carte Blanche.

Hours: Lunch, seven days, noon to 3 P.M.; dinner, Sundays through Thursdays, 3 P.M. to midnight, Fridays and Saturdays, 3 P.M. to 1 A.M. Closed Thanksgiving Day.

Reservations: Necessary for lunch.

One of the more dependable sources of the hot, spicy and gingery dishes of the Hunan province of China is this simple modern restaurant, with its sophisticated brown and mirrored cocktail lounge décor. Although that décor is somewhat in need of sprucing up, it remains one of the more attractive settings in which generally very good Chinese food is served. Owned by T. T. Wang, the chef who is also the proprietor of the Shun Lee restaurants, Hunam has its off moments but still manages to maintain a fairly high level of cooking. Service ranges from excellent to pushy and distracted. It can take several requests to get tea and water, and at lunch a captain tried to dissuade me from ordering fried bananas for dessert. It seemed that he might be rushing me when he said the bananas were terrible, but tasting proved he was only being honest; terrible they surely were.

Others dishes were far better and much up to the level when I first reviewed this restaurant in 1977. Only some occasional greasiness in dishes such as the pan-fried noodles, the shrimp toast and those bananas seems a recurrent flaw.

Appetizers at Hunam make up the consistently best course, whether one tries such thoroughly delicious cold selections as the piquant paper-thin slices of corned pork or the tender morsels of hacked white meat of chicken in a fiery chili sauce soothed with a lacing of sesame oil. The dough for the steamed dumplings was a bit sticky and pasty, although their pork filling was subtly seasoned with ginger, and the spring rolls were slim, delicate and glassily, crisply green-free.

Hot and sour fish broth with egg drops and chunks of white, firm fish was exquisite with its counter-points of spicy and astringent flavors. So was the more common hot and sour soup, heavier on the hot than on the sour and enriched wth an abundance of vegetable and meat slivers. Winter melon soup was poor, tasting much like hot water and including hard undercooked squares of melon. The broth for the wonton soup was also tasteless, but the wonton were excellent and the extra garnish of shrimp added a nice touch.

Among the specialties the scaloppine-like slices of leg of lamb, Hunam style, has remained as excellent as it ever was, the tender meat well complemented by slivered scallions and a translucent, incendiary red chili oil sauce. Also marked with the red triangle that indicates a dish is hot and spicy is the crispy whole fried sea bass, golden brown in its thick sauce of minced vegetables and nuggets of ginger.

Exceptional were bamboo steamers, spareribs, thickly coated in a velvety anise-scented sauce after being steamed in a rice flour batter, and Hunam beef, also in a hot sauce and brightened with watercress. So were the mild-flavored boned, pressed crisp fried duck with a vegetable sauce, the julienne bits of sautéed smoked chicken with pungent fresh coriander and the orange-flavored beef in which the sweetness of the fruit juice offset the spiciness of chili oil. Both the crisp, dry sautéed tangy and spicy green beans and the oily, garlic and hot-sauce flavored eggplant family style, a dish that suggested Provence as much as it did Hunam, were as satisfying as they were interesting.

Unfortunately a number of other dishes, formerly made as well as those above seem to have fallen out of favor with the chef, so cursory was the attention he gave them. The fried noodles and Lake Tung Ting shrimp being cases in point.

Fillet of sea bass with shrimp roe sauce, once a truly poetic specialty at Hunam, was served totally lacking in the hotness and tang it formerly had. Unlike too many restaurants where dishes billed as hot arrive bland, Hunam takes you at your word when you request fiery seasonings.

Moo shu pork, that combination of crepes rolled around a shredded vegetable and pork filling, was decent, as were both the lobster Hunam style and the mixed seafood combination in Neptune's platter, but none of those were in any way distinguished.

The bar and two dining rooms here are done more or less in a flashy modern Chinese idiom-dark, fairly banal and much in need of refurbishing, as are the washrooms, which were inexcusably messy.

Hunan Balcony

★

2596 Broadway, at 98th Street, 865-0400.
Atmosphere: Pleasant, modern, informal downstairs, somewhat seedy upstairs; service ranges from good to indifferent.
Recommended dishes: Moo shu pork, bean-curd Sichuan style, sliced lamb Hunan style, spicy, crisp sea bass, golden crispy chicken, Hunan roast duck, stuffed honey banana.
Price range: Moderate.
Credit cards: All major credit cards.
Hours: Lunch, Mondays through Fridays, noon to 3:30 P.M.; dinner, Mondays and Tuesdays, 3:30 P.M. to midnight, Wednesdays through Fridays, 3:30 P.M. to 2 A.M., Saturdays, noon to 2 A.M., Sundays, noon to midnight. Open holidays except Thanksgiving.
Reservations: Necessary for five or more people.

The newer downstairs of this Chinese restaurant is the more pleasant level, done up as it is with spanking white, rough plaster walls and greenery at the window. The upstairs is still somewhat depressing and dismal and, unfortunately, is the only facility for large private parties. Better to insist on sitting in the light, bright downstairs dining room.

Considering the high prices at most of the new and fashionable Chinese restaurants, especially those featuring Hunanese food, this place is a find. If dishes are not breathtakingly poetic, they are at least decent, and many are interesting. At off hours, however, such as Saturday lunch, food can be stale and greasy.

Save money and your appetite by skipping appetizers and soups; all of my attempts in those categories were washouts, although I tried three different appetizers (fried dumplings, hacked chicken and an assortment of three cold meats), and all of the soups except the ham and winter melon and the abalone and chicken.

Instead, start with something like the moo shu pork, the savory meat, egg and vegetable filling to be wrapped in thin crepes that should be hotter than mine were. The main courses that proved best included spicy, crisp sea bass — whole, golden and crunchy under its mild sweet-sour sauce — and boned tender, golden crispy chicken, a dish children will adore.

A square of firm but creamy bean curd in a spicy Sichuan pepper sauce, garnished with peas, was one of the better things sampled. The sliced lamb Hunan style — lean and tender and sautéed with bamboo shoots, mushrooms and slivered leeks — was another. Fork-tender beef with slivers of broccoli and a lean, roasted half duck to be dipped in spiced salt and eaten with steamed buns were as good as they were unusual. A dish that was a half-and-half combination of shrimp in chile sauce and pork in black-bean sauce was merely acceptable.

163

No so the iodine-tinged crispy shrimp, nor the soggy General Ching's chicken, nor the greasy, hard, ten-ingredients fried rice.

Desserts are, for the most part, ice cream and canned fruits, but one offering — banana fritters stuffed with a sweet bean paste — was delicious.

This place already has a loyal following among students and faculty members of nearby Columbia University and is a pleasant find in this neighborhood. Service is erratic.

Hwa Yuan Szechwan Inn
★ ★

40 East Broadway, near Catherine Street, 966-5534.
Atmosphere: Simple, typical and trim modern Chinatown setting; hectic when crowded; efficient service.
Recommended dishes: Shredded chicken with pepper sauce, aromatic sliced beef, preserved duck, hot spicy Chinese cabbage, noodles with sesame sauce, large shrimp with black bean sauce, all kidney dishes, fishhead or pork meatball casseroles, beef or pork with hot green chili peppers, chunk chicken with hot sauce, bean curd with hot sauce, eggplant, moo shu pork, carp with hot sauce.
Price range: Moderate.
Credit cards: All major credit cards.
Hours: Sundays through Thursdays, noon to 10 P.M., Fridays and Saturdays, noon to 11 P.M. Open major holidays.
Reservations: Necessary for groups of six or more.

It is not often that one comes across a Chinese restaurant with a menu that reflects a fairly strict commitment to the food of one particular region of China. Whether the featured cuisine is Hunanese, Fukienese or Sichuanese, the management generally feels compelled to add such trademark Cantonese appetizers as egg roll, roast pork, spareribs and egg-drop and wanton soup in order to appeal to the mass audience that would not consider a Chinese meal complete without those touches.

And because in most such cases the chef or proprietor considers these dishes lower ground, they give them short shrift, often purchasing them ready-made from mass producers in Chinatown.

Fortunately, no such compromises are in evidence at the Hwa Yuan Szechwan Inn in Chinatown. Here, in a clean, pleasant modern dining room, the management offers a fascinating array of unusual dishes, very well prepared, without attempting to be all things to all eaters. And the few Cantonese-style dishes that do appear on the menu — shrimp (large, not baby size) with black bean or lobster sauce, sizzling rice with chicken, meat or shrimp and vegetables — are given the same careful attention as the true Sichuan specialties.

Forget all about egg rolls and wonton when dining here and instead try the lean, moist slivers of shredded chicken in chili pepper sauce (better than the blander though decent "wonderful taste" chicken), the paper-thin, spicily cured, aromatic sliced beef, the slivered jellyfish or fragrant, succulently melting preserved duck and, for crisp contrast, hot spicy Chinese cabbage. Cold noodles perfumed with sesame sauce and fired with chili oil can also be had as a first course. Kidneys are well done, whether as a cold appetizer with chili and ginger sauce or as a hot main course, sautéed with the cocoa-brown, hot and spicy "home-style" sauce.

That same home-style sauce does wonders for thick custardy triangles of sautéed bean curd, tender stir-fried chunks of chicken or slices of beef or pork.

Among the soups, I sampled only a thick, rich and properly balanced hot and sour because I was beguiled by the category of "casserole" dishes — really main-course soups served in handsomely rustic ceramic pots and consisting of rich broths laden with either braised fish heads or giant, subtly seasoned pork meatballs, combined with vegetables that include Chinese cabbage.

Cold dishes and casseroles are unquestionably the highlights of the menu, but a number of other choices, though somewhat less exotic, were thoroughly satisfying. Among these were the Cantonese dishes already mentioned, excellent moo shu pork with a generous amount of meat in its filling, shredded beef or pork with hot green chili peppers and whole carp in a velvety but stinging hot sauce.

The only unsatisfactory dishes I had here were fried chicken chunks and smoked duck with camphor and tea flavor, both of which were parched dry, and though the beef, stir-fried with broccoli, was about as tender as I have ever had it, the dish in general was unexciting.

Dry sautéed string beans were a bit tough and salty, although generously sprinkled with meat. Eggplant with bean sauce was lusciously soft and silken, a perfect foil for spicier fare. Desserts consist mostly of canned fruit. Beer, domestic and imported, is available.

As usual in Chinatown, prices are moderate and portions huge. Other Hua Yuan outposts have opened in various parts of the city, but the comments and rating here refer only to this Chinatown original.

Il Galletto

★

120 East 34th Street, between Lexington and Park Avenues, 889-1990.

Atmosphere: Pleasant, modern, somewhat noisy dining room with inadequate ventilation; service polite and professional but sometimes pretentious.

Recommended dishes: Cappelletti in brodo, taglierini al filetto, linguine with clam sauce, spaghetti carbonara, scampi Adriatico, brodetto al Adriatico, cernia Livornese, chicken with rosemary, chicken Bolognese, chicken piccata, veal scaloppine al limone, veal cutlet Valdostana, veal cutlet Milanese, grilled veal chop, arugula and endive salad.

Price range: Expensive.

Credit cards: American Express, MasterCard and Visa.

Hours: Lunch, Mondays through Fridays, noon to 3 P.M.; dinner, Mondays through Fridays, 5 P.M. to 10:30 P.M., Saturdays 5 P.M. to 11 P.M.. Closed Sundays and major holidays.

Reservations: Recommended.

Il Galletto is a convenient and convivial North Italian restaurant worth remembering when visiting in the neighborhood. Just four blocks from Madison Square Garden, it is jammed at lunch but only moderately crowded at dinner.

The setting is simple and slightly formal, and more adequate lighting would lend a needed cheerful glow. A slight improvement in the ventilation would also be advisable, doing away with the sudden whiffs of canned fuel that emanate from the cooking done in the dining room. But the most consistent flaw at Il Galletto is an unsure hand in the kitchen, resulting in seasonings that lack authority and character. There is also a tendency to put too much flour in the sauces and to overuse what tastes like corn oil.

Nevertheless, several pastas, most fish dishes and a number of the chicken and veal specialties that were tried proved reliable and satisfying. Antipasto choices, though acceptable, did not seem worthwhile alternatives to some far better choices, such as cappelletti in brodo — lusty meat-filled dumplings in a rich, golden broth — or pastas, such as taglierini al filetto (fine noodles in tomato, prosciutto and onion sauce), linguine with a garlicky red clam sauce or velvety spaghetti carbonara, silky in a coating of onion, bacon, and egg yolk. Pasta primavera, made with either linguine or cappelli d'angelo, fine angel's hair, is a popular favorite at Il Galletto, but at various times it was too soupy or too dry, with vegetables too raw or too overcooked. A floury white sauce made pasty masses of both cannelloni and manicotti, and green peas that had obviously been frozen were served with paglia e fieno, the green and white noodles, and were ice cold in the center. A basil-based pesto sauce lacked the necessary freshness and appeared on gummy gnocchi, as well as on chicken breasts and veal scaloppine.

All of the fish dishes sampled were fresh and well seasoned. Scampi Adriatico maintained a firm texture and was complemented by a lemony onion and mushroom sauce, and brodetto al Adriatico, made with striped bass and clams in an herb-gentled sauce, were excellent on several tries. Only slightly less so was cernia Livornese, snowy and moist snapper in a sauce pungent with olives and capers.

Although a thick veal chop is difficult to broil properly, the kitchen met the test well, turning out correctly seared meat that remained moist and rosy at the center. A paillard of veal, however, dried out in the grilling. Ham, cheese and a mushroom sauce lent an elegant richness to veal cutlet Valdostana, although here, too, less flour would have led to a more refined sauce, just as it would have for the otherwise fine veal scaloppine al limone and chicken breast, both piccata and Bolognese. Boneless and tender breast of chicken with rosemary benefited from the same skillful cooking that distinguished a breast of chicken in white wine sauce, which, however, had an inexplicable topping that seemed to be made up of frozen mixed vegetables (the corn kernels were the giveaway).

Arugula and endive in a sprightly combination made the best salad. Desserts can all be marked near misses, including ice-cold cheesecake, bland chocolate-mousse cake and zabaglione overdosed with Marsala wine.

Il Monello
★ ★

1460 Second Avenue, between 76th and 77th Streets, 535-9310.

Atmosphere: Intimate, plushy if overdone setting; generally efficient, pleasant service that can be distracted at times.

Recommended dishes: Carpaccio with green sauce, antipasto caldo, vongole alla Capri, spiedini, artichoke oreganata, risotto, brains dorata, pasta e fagioli, all pastas except spaghetti carbonara and linguine with clam sauce, crostacei marinara, red snapper with clams, pollo scarpariello, pollo Bolognese, grilled veal chop, cotoletta Milanese, bocconcini di vitello, torta San Onorato, zuppa inglese, zucotto.

Price range: Expensive.

Credit cards: All major credit cards.

Hours: Lunch, Mondays through Saturdays, noon to 3 P.M.; dinner, Mondays through Saturdays, 5 P.M. to midnight. Closed Sundays and major holidays.

Reservations: Necessary for dinner.

This plush and convivial restaurant is one of the city's more solid and dependable sources of very good north Italian food. Under the watchful eye of Adi Giovannetti, who also owns Il Nido, it has developed interesting dishes that complement the north Italian standards. Although the cooking here is a bit less inspired than its counterpart on 53rd Street, there is an obvious effort to obtain the freshest seasonal fruits and vegetables, such as the red radicchio lettuce, white truffles and wild mushrooms that are wonderful with pasta, in salads or in a creamy risotto.

Service is thoughtful and professional, if sometimes distracted and rushed. As for the setting, it is restfully, dimly lit yet with enough light on tables themselves to enable one to read both the menu and the check with ease, and also to appreciate the visual appeal of the food. But the whole adds up to more than the sum of the parts, for close inspection proves all details to be corny and overdone. It is amazing that such details create so urbane and felicitous a backdrop, an accomplishment that owes much to the lighting and the snowy tablecloths, albeit on tables that are much too close together.

Rosily bright and fresh carpaccio, a raw beef appetizer, is served here with a choice of green herb sauce or an Italian oil-and-cheese dressing. Having chosen the dressing, I regretted bypassing the herb sauce, the cheese being too overpowering for the paper-thin, satiny beef slices. Antipasto caldo — a hot assortment of shellfish with moist, tender broiled shrimp, plump, fresh mussels in a light tomato sauce and baked clams — was altogether satisfying, even though the clams were ever so slightly tough and their bread-crumb flavor drowned out the herbs mingled with them.

Vongole alla Capri, clams in a light tomato sauce, were excellent. Spiedino alla Romana, the brochette arrangement of bread squares and mozzarella cheese fried and dressed with an anchovy sauce, had ham in the combination at Il Monello but was flawed in the cooking, for most of the cheese disintegrated to the point of near disappearance. Artichoke oreganata, baked with garlic and bread crumbs, was delicious.

Two soups — pasta e fagioli, the bean and pasta combination in tomato broth, and the vegetable minestrone — were acceptable, the pasta e fagioli being the better. The management explained that since minestrone is not ordered frequently, it tends to sit around all day and become overcooked, and to avoid that, when the soup is ordered, fresh but separately cooked vegetables are added to the tomato base. The result lacked the subtle blending of flavors this soup has at its best, and because so many other restaurants manage to cope with this problem successfully, there must be a better solution than the one found here.

Pastas ranged from spectacularly good to merely delicious. Green lasagna with a filling of cheese, meat sauce and crumbled sausage was certainly one of the best, as were the delicate rounds of tortellini alla panna, in a chiffon-light cream and cheese sauce. The thin pasta strands known as capelli d'angelo (angel's hair) in a Bolognese meat sauce, the paglia e fieno (hay and straw symbolized by green and white noodles) and the very similar green and white fettuccine Il Monello, both in creamy sauces, were excellent. So was linguine matriciana, a lusty sauce of tomatoes, chunks of onions and bits of ham. Linguine with white clam sauce, though good, included tough bits of clams, and the spaghetti carbonara swam in what seemed to be an undercooked sauce of eggs, butter, cheese, onions and prosciutto, although its flavor was fine. Ravioli malfatti, really spinach dumplings without a pasta covering, could have been firmer but were nonetheless satisfying.

Fish preparations were exceptionally well done. The extravagazana known as crostacei marinara, a veritable still life of lobster, langoustine, shrimp, mussels and clams in a pungent tomato sauce, proved to be one of the best seafood dishes in the city. Red snapper with clams, in a lighter sauce, was equally well prepared, if less glamorous. But broiled striped bass tasted of petroleum.

I tried the very good chicken dishes here, the pollo scarpariello (shoemaker's style), for which tender nuggets of chicken were braised with garlic, and pollo Bolognese, a sort of chicken breast cutlet with prosciutto and cheese mantled by a light, tangy lemon sauce. Pollo Toscana, however, was a pastiche of dried-out hard bits of chicken, chicken livers and overcooked eggplant, all gratinéed with cheese, so that the whole melded into a solid, almost inseparable mass.

Veal at Il Monello is a beautiful, pale, mauve-pink color, indicating it is young and milk fed. A thick chop, well grilled, was excellent, as was the cotoletta Milanese, a breaded, flattened cutlet that still has a piece of its bone attached in classic style. Although the cutlet could have had a little more salt (and again the bread crumb flavor was too strong), it was a gorgeously crisp and a greaseless triumph.

When I ordered the sausage with pizzaiuola sauce, the owner winced, saying that he was not happy with the sausage itself. I tried it anyway and found he was right, although the sauce of tomato, carefully peeled green pepper, mushrooms and garlic was lovely. But since he knew the sausage was not right, and far better examples are available in town, it is a wonder why he has not found a replacement or removed the choice from the menu.

Bocconcini de vitello Il Monello, thin scaloppine of veal sautéed at the table with a sauce of tangerine liqueur and white wine and a pinch each of sage and rosemary, was good, if a touch too sweet. The calf's liver Veneziana was spoiled only by being too heavily sautéed, so that the sauce was browner and stronger flavored than it should have been. Brains dorata, gilded in a light breading, were fresh, moist and beautifully cooked.

Beautifully golden articoke hearts, crisply fried zucchini and a fresh, sprightly arugula, radicchio, and endive salad were the best accompaniments among those we tried. In fall, white truffles make an appearance along with porcini mushrooms.

Zuppa inglese, that Italian version of trifle, mounded with baked meringue over layered, rum-soaked cake and custard, was luxuriously rich as was the torta San Onorato, better known perhaps by its French name, gâteau St.-Honoré. The star among desserts is the cloudlike chocolate combination of cake and cream, zucotto.

Wines are, as might be expected, overpriced, and the list, like the menu, holds few surprises but many dependable standards.

Il Mulino

★

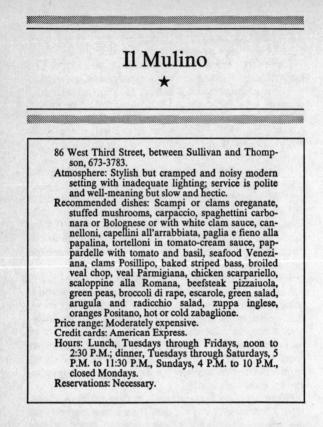

86 West Third Street, between Sullivan and Thompson, 673-3783.

Atmosphere: Stylish but cramped and noisy modern setting with inadequate lighting; service is polite and well-meaning but slow and hectic.

Recommended dishes: Scampi or clams oreganate, stuffed mushrooms, carpaccio, spaghettini carbonara or Bolognese or with white clam sauce, cannelloni, capellini all'arrabbiata, paglia e fieno alla papalina, tortelloni in tomato-cream sauce, pappardelle with tomato and basil, seafood Veneziana, clams Posillipo, baked striped bass, broiled veal chop, veal Parmigiana, chicken scarpariello, scaloppine alla Romana, beefsteak pizzaiuola, green peas, broccoli di rape, escarole, green salad, arugula and radicchio salad, zuppa inglese, oranges Positano, hot or cold zabaglione.

Price range: Moderately expensive.

Credit cards: American Express.

Hours: Lunch, Tuesdays through Fridays, noon to 2:30 P.M.; dinner, Tuesdays through Saturdays, 5 P.M. to 11:30 P.M., Sundays, 4 P.M. to 10 P.M., closed Mondays.

Reservations: Necessary.

Jimmy Durante said it best: "Did you ever have that feeling that you wanted to go, still you have the feeling that you wanted to stay?" His measured chant came to mind on each of my visits to the fashionably popular Il Mulino (The Water Mill) in Greenwich Village.

What made me want to go were the crowded tables and uncomfortable chairs, the deafening noise and the soporific lighting. Unable to see or hear, and often unable to move, I grew impatient at the service, which would first be slow and then become hectic. Throughout, however, the staff was friendly and accommodating.

What made me want to stay were some dishes that were about as good as they can be. The menu blends southern and northern Italian dishes with overly complicated house creations.

There seems to be the feeling in many Italian restaurants that fanciness is a matter of complexity, of combining as many "gourmet" ingredients as possible in one dish. At Il Mulino, for example, a veal specialty may combine mushrooms, Gorgonzola cheese, cream and Calvados, masking the gentle flavor of the meat. But when Il Mulino is good, it is very, very good, beginning with the giveaway appetizer, its version of the bread salad panzanella. Here toasted slices of Italian bread are rubbed with garlic, then topped with oil, tomato and shallots, and are served with thinly sliced salami and silken roasted peppers.

Anyone who still wants an appetizer after that should consider the spicy stuffed mushrooms, the scampi or clams oreganate or the carpaccio with a verdant green herb and mustard sauce that almost makes one forget that the meat is too thickly sliced. Artichoke hearts baked with salty Canadian bacon and the pallid prosciutto can't match the other appetizers. Skip the murky zuppa all'ortolana, a salty broth with an overabundance of vegetables.

Similarly, a huge mass of overcooked vegetables strangles the fine pasta strands, capelli d'angelo primavera, and in another dish that angel's hair pasta is smothered with the house sauce combining tomato, chopped pâté, mushrooms, cognac, prosciutto and cream.

But there are a few marvelous pasta dishes: the large squares, pappardelle, that hold up better under the thick house sauce, and the big meat-stuffed tortelloni in a lively tomato sauce scented with fresh basil. Spaghettini carbonara gets a savory brown haze of sauce based on pancetta, onions, egg and butter, and nutmeg, veal and beef enhance the cream and tomato Bolognese sauce. Spaghettini with white clam sauce is every bit as good as the capellini in a fiery tomato arrabbiata sauce. And the green and white noodles, paglia e fieno, are delicious in a cream sauce flecked with prosciutto and fresh green peas. Tortellini were meagerly filled and their sauce was milky.

There are a few very well prepared seafood dishes, among them little-neck clams Posillipo in a sheer tomato broth with garlic toast, and the mixed seafood stew pescatora alla Veneziana in a similar though brinier broth combining shellfish, tender squid and fish. A whole striped bass for two baked in foil was moist and delicious although carelessly boned and scaled. Peppery scampi fra diavolo would have been perfect if the shrimp did not taste of iodine.

Meats were the weakest course. The most rewarding exceptions were the veal Parmigiana made with Muenster cheese in a bright tomato sauce, immaculately broiled veal chops and veal scaloppine alla Romana, sautéed with artichoke hearts and mushrooms. Beef steak pizzaiuola, a blend of tomato, herbs, garlic and mushrooms, was also delicious, and so was the lightly floured and sautéed garlicky chicken scarpariello. Osso buco was undercooked and tough as a result. Veal piccata proved totally lackluster and so did the rolled veal birds and a complex chicken breast dish with wine, ham and cheese. Similarly disappointing were roast veal, a tasteless paillard and beef alla Romana in a tomato and caper sauce. A dense mushroom sauce flawed the otherwise excellent veal chop Valdostana, stuffed with cheese and ham.

Salads and vegetables were fresh and delicate, especially the peas with ham and onion, the sautéed escarole and the radicchio and arugula salad.

It's been a long time since I have had such excellent hot zabaglione — thick as velvet and heady with Marsala wine. The cold zabaglione, bound with crushed macaroons, was almost as good, plain or spooned over raspberries. The Italian rum cake zuppa inglese was delicate, and the sliced oranges Positano had just the right bittersweet accents of rind, Grand Marnier and framboise. Not quite so good were the poached pears and the chocolate ganache cake from Délices la Côte Basque.

Il Nido

★ ★ ★

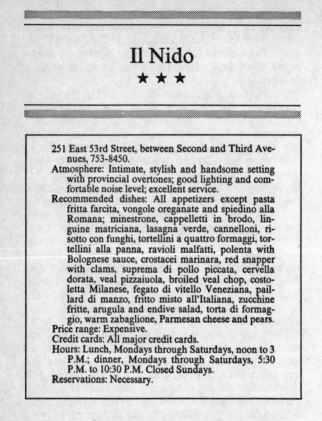

251 East 53rd Street, between Second and Third Avenues, 753-8450.

Atmosphere: Intimate, stylish and handsome setting with provincial overtones; good lighting and comfortable noise level; excellent service.

Recommended dishes: All appetizers except pasta fritta farcita, vongole oreganate and spiedino alla Romana; minestrone, cappelletti in brodo, linguine matriciana, lasagna verde, cannelloni, risotto con funghi, tortellini a quattro formaggi, tortellini alla panna, ravioli malfatti, polenta with Bolognese sauce, crostacei marinara, red snapper with clams, suprema di pollo piccata, cervella dorata, veal pizzaiuola, broiled veal chop, costoletta Milanese, fegato di vitello Veneziana, paillard di manzo, fritto misto all'Italiana, zucchine fritte, arugula and endive salad, torta di formaggio, warm zabaglione, Parmesan cheese and pears.

Price range: Expensive.

Credit cards: All major credit cards.

Hours: Lunch, Mondays through Saturdays, noon to 3 P.M.; dinner, Mondays through Saturdays, 5:30 P.M. to 10:30 P.M. Closed Sundays.

Reservations: Necessary.

If there is a single combination that should guarantee success, it is excellent North Italian food beautifully served in a handsome, restful and completely felicitous dining room. On that basis, few Italian restaurants deserve success as much as Il Nido. Adi Giovannetti, who also operates the very good Il Monello, has already made this latest addition even better than his earlier effort.

Graceful, old, rose-etched glass, beveled mirrors, half-timbered walls and a display of antique bric-a-bric create a snug and stylish backdrop against which is served some unusual and unusually delicious food. Tables are tightly cramped in the back room, although well spaced up front.

The enticing menu includes many offerings rarely seen around town. Most welcome is an impeccable risotto con funghi — Po River rice simmered in stock and enriched with porcini, earthy wild mushrooms. Equally good is polenta. As an appetizer (crostini di polenta), the cooked, sliced cornmeal is fried and topped with sautéed chicken livers and a combination of fresh and dried mushrooms. Instead of pasta, one can have a softer, velvety polenta with any sauce, my favorites being the chicken-liver mushroom combination and the rich, meaty Bolognese classic.

Il Nido also offers a delicate but interesting choice of appetizers, from simple but perfect roast peppers and anchovies to the more elaborate crostini di polenta. In between there is the superb raw sliced beef, carpaccio, with a tingling sauce of oil and vinegar flecked with finely minced celery; roasted peppers, capers and anchovies, and either mussels or clams in gossamer tomato sauces. The hot antipasto consists of sautéed shrimp and clams with a square of spiedino alla Romana, and the cold antipasto includes fresh and sprightly squid and seafood salad, silken eggplant simmered with tomatoes, excellent salami and prosciutto. Broiled scampi are moist and tender, and if your taste runs to something as elemental as celery and olives, you can expect to have spicy yet mellow, small brown-black Gaeta olives served correctly on crushed ice.

Dried beef bresaola is of the finest quality — deep rose in color and moist enough to have flavor. Although no appetizer sampled was really poor, a few simply did not stand up to the others. Among the less successful were spiedino alla Romana (a bit too soggy and too heavily sauced), vongole oreganate (the breadcrumb topping on the clams was too wet and too bland) and pasta fritta farcita (an interesting but heavy first course). In season, white truffles and fresh porcini mushrooms are prepared in interesting ways.

One of the more amusing and delectable pasta selections is ravioli malfatti, which means "badly made ravioli." This Tuscan Lenten specialty, which dates back to the seventeenth century, was considered malfatti because it lacked the traditional pasta covering. It is really dumplings of spinach, eggs and cheese — a classic ravioli filling. At Il Nido, the verdant puffs are complemented by a light tomato sauce. Linguine matriciana in a hearty tomato, prosciutto and onion sauce and the green-and-white fettuccine Il Monello, much like Alfredo, were done to perfection. So were lasagne verde, with its creamy melted cheese and sheer tomato topping; tortellini alla panna, meat-filled and done with cheese and butter, and tortellini a quattro formaggi — a sauce of four cheeses, taleggio, fontina, Gorgonzola and bel paese, to which a fifth, grated Parmesan, is added at the table.

The pastas I liked far less were capelli d'angelo (fine angel's hair) with a sauce based on Alaskan king crab, always a disappointing ingredient; tagliarini, with a tomato sauce made with tough bits of shrimps; spaghetti carbonara, which was greasy and would have been better with Italian bacon, pancetta, than with dry chips of prosciutto, and linguine, with a white clam sauce that was much in need of garlic. Trenette al pesto was passable, but again greasy and not in the same league with the more glorious alternatives.

If you prefer soup to pasta, choose between soothing, buff-colored, tomatoless minestrone — with its beans, vegetables, spinach and the subtle hint of garlic — and the fine, slightly saline chicken broth in which tender, meat-filled cappelletti are set adrift.

If there is a consistent flaw in the main courses, it is in the sautéeing. All too often the oil became overheated, and its odor and taste were mildly unpleasant. This flawed a number of the menu's fancier creations, such as the veal and chicken dishes sautéed with mushrooms, artichokes and white wine. Skip those and opt for the grilled meats or the immaculately greaseless fried specialties or the finer seafood dishes.

Moist and pearly red snapper, simmered with tomatoes and clams, and a bright, fragrant mélange of lobster, shrimp, clams and mussels in a lusty tomato sauce (crostacei marinara) were far better than the sautéed striped bass.

Seldom have I seen more savory frying than is done at Il Nido, whether for costoletta Milanese or the gorgeous fritto misto all'Italiana — a Tuscan combination of thinly breaded veal scaloppine, brains, sweetbreads, calf's liver and a slim, delicate lamb chop that will be replaced with baby goat in the spring. A side order of crisply fried zucchini adds green crunch to this array of gilded meats. Much the same preparation is done for the brains alone — cervella dorata. Fegato di vitello (calf's liver) done Veneziana style with onions and white wine, and suprema di pollo piccata — lemony piccata of chicken breast — were the two expertly sautéed dishes. A thick, grilled veal chop had more flavor than the thinner dry paillard of veal, but the robust beef version — paillard di manzo — had more richness brushed with garlic.

The only really excellent desserts were a creamy, lemony cheesecake and the froth of hot zabaglione heady with Marsala. Crushed, crisp macaroons (amaretti) are sprinkled over it, but I prefer that step eliminated because the crumbs become soggy midway through the dessert. Cold zabaglione is pleasant enough over strawberries, although a little too sweet.

The management has tried to bring some unusual wines along with the fine menu. I especially enjoyed the inexpensive, clean, crisp white Sardinian alghero (known as vermentino in Italy), and the costly but distinctive 1974 drago from Piemonte. Vino santo, a Tuscan after-dinner wine that seems halfway between sherry and brandy, and which is served with hazelnut biscotti to be dipped into it, is sold by the glass.

Inagiku

★

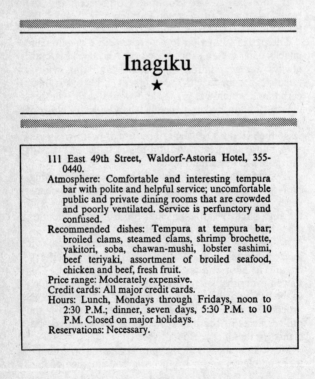

111 East 49th Street, Waldorf-Astoria Hotel, 355-0440.

Atmosphere: Comfortable and interesting tempura bar with polite and helpful service; uncomfortable public and private dining rooms that are crowded and poorly ventilated. Service is perfunctory and confused.

Recommended dishes: Tempura at tempura bar; broiled clams, steamed clams, shrimp brochette, yakitori, soba, chawan-mushi, lobster sashimi, beef teriyaki, assortment of broiled seafood, chicken and beef, fresh fruit.

Price range: Moderately expensive.

Credit cards: All major credit cards.

Hours: Lunch, Mondays through Fridays, noon to 2:30 P.M.; dinner, seven days, 5:30 P.M. to 10 P.M. Closed on major holidays.

Reservations: Necessary.

Inagiku, the Japanese restaurant in the Waldorf-Astoria Hotel, is a Chinese puzzle of dining rooms — public and private, some serving food Western style at tables and chairs, others serving in the Japanese fashion with guests seated at low tables on tatami-matted floors. Of all the settings on these large and sprawling premises, the one providing the most exceptional food is the tempura bar, a traditional counter seating area where cooks deep-fry the crisp coated seafood, fish and vegetables to order and in full view.

Service at the tempura bar is polite and gracious, far more so than it is in other dining rooms. Waitresses at the bar guide those not well grounded in the art of tempura dining, explaining various combinations and suggesting single items that can be ordered as well. Among those choices is a personal favorite, kakiage, the final offering in the traditional tempura ritual. It is a fritter of leftover bits of shrimp, fish and vegetables swirled in batter then deep fried in what is here described as a blend of sesame, camellia and olive oils. Dipped into radish-flavored soy sauce, or simply into lemon and salt, the tempura variations at Inagiku sparkle with flavor. Although there are several other good dishes at this restaurant, if it were not for the tempura bar, Inagiku would hardly be worth recommending. Both private and public dining rooms are gloomy, poorly ventilated and unevenly heated. Service in the noisy public rooms is perfunctory and confusing. The language gap is not too serious if one orders from the standard menu, but it results in considerable frustration for those who want to try more esoteric specialties offered only on the Japanese menu.

The management seems reluctant to present Japanese menus to Westerners and has only a few waiters who can interpret them. Diners willing to persist can find such interesting and well-prepared specialties as soba (the cold buckwheat noodles enlivened with soy sauce and scallions), or chawan-mushi, the soft, winy custard steamed in porcelain cups with shrimp and vegetables. Even more exotic are small dishes such as nimono, a combination of simmered vegetables and bean curd or torono, a taro-root porridge mixed with raw egg yolk, seaweed and a dab of the fiery green horseradish, wasabi. Lobster sashimi is another specialty not on English menus, and the pearly, snowy raw meat is served sliced on the back of the lobster shell to be followed by the baked claw and upper body meat served with melted butter.

Other sashimi such as raw tuna fish and sea bass are listed on the English menu and were as fresh and attractively served as the lobster, but sushi were lackluster. Clams, either grilled or steamed in a sake-and-scallion-scented broth, are also delicately satisfying, as is the yakitori, tender moist nuggets of marinated chicken, onion and green pepper grilled on small bamboo skewers. In fact, broiling is generally well done here as the beef teriyaki and shrimp brochette illustrate. Only the teriyaki fish and the negima-yaki — thin slices of beef rolled around scallions — were limp and tasteless and seemed to have been cooked in advance then reheated.

Shabu-shabu, the boiled beef, noodle and vegetable main course, lacked a properly rich stock and so was bland and uninteresting. The sukiyaki proved a more savory alternative but it could hardly be considered inspired.

There is much confusion here as to what is available when. At one dinner I asked a waiter for natto, a cool side dish of fermented soybeans in a spicy, eggy sauce, and he said it was never served at the restaurant. On the way out I asked the hostess about natto and she said it was always available. But on my next visit the waitress said she had never heard of it.

Forgo the pseudo-Polynesian extravaganzas such as a melon daiquiri. Instead, stay with sake, beer or that time-honored Japanese favorite, Scotch whisky.

Jack's Nest

★

> 310 Third Avenue, between 23d and 24th Streets, 260-7110.
> Atmosphere: Pleasant and trim modern dining room with comfortable booths; service is exceptionally friendly, cooperative and efficient.
> Recommended dishes: Fried chicken livers, fried chicken, barbecued chicken, fried pork chops, barbecued spareribs, ham hocks, fried whitings or porgies, collards, black-eyed peas, sweet potato pie.
> Price range: Inexpensive.
> Credit cards: American Express, MasterCard and Visa.
> Hours: Lunch, Mondays through Fridays, 11 A.M. to 3 P.M.; dinner, Sundays through Thursdays, 3 to 11 P.M., Fridays and Saturdays, 3 P.M. to 1 A.M.
> Reservations: Necessary only for large groups.

The simple, hearty and savory dishes originating with poor blacks in the South is the most characteristic soul food served at Jack's Nest, where the menu includes fried chicken, smoked barbecued ribs, ham hocks, fried fish, chitterlings, corn bread, collard greens, black-eyed peas and yams, to name only a few of the classics.

Brightly decorated with colorful caricatures of the entertainment and sports celebrities who frequent the place, and with comfortable orange plastic booths and crisply fresh paper placemats, Jack's Nest is something like a super-luncheonette.

Best of all is the staff. Rarely will you find more congenial, hospitable and accommodating waitresses. And wonder of wonders, the diner can have almost anything on the menu in any size portion or combination. If you want a half order of the crackling, crisp-fried chicken with a half order of the lean and meaty barbecued spareribs, just ask for it that way and it's yours. If you want only one of the meaty, crisp-crusted fried pork chops and one tender smoked ham hock, the management sees no reason to refuse you.

Delicious fried chicken livers can be ordered as an appetizer to share, or in combination with fried chicken wings, or in-the-basket with french fries, which should be better than they are. That holds true for all side dishes, unfortunately, and it is the commercial, lackluster quality of the potato salad, cole slaw, mashed yams, string beans and all vegetables except collard greens and black-eyed peas (easily doctored with salt and pepper) that makes the difference between a one-star rating and a two.

Corn bread, though hot and served with plenty of butter, is a bit too soft and sweet, and the so-called Carolina beef stew could come right out of a can. Chopped pork barbecued, served for lunch on weekdays, is one of the better specialties, especially if a generous shot of Tabasco sauce is added.

Barbecued chicken is far better than the chicken smothered in a gravy that looks like chocolate pudding, and fried shrimp must surely be purchased pre-breaded. The fried whitings and porgies were better than all other fish and seafood. And order the pork spareribs rather than the dry and relatively tasteless beef ribs.

With all barbecues, ask for an extra serving of very hot sauce. Sweet potato pie, when served warm, is smooth and fragrant. Other desserts, most especially the awful cobbler made with canned peaches, were as commercially bland as the vegetables.

Despite its flaws, and because of the typical dishes done well here, Jack's Nest offers good value, and it is a perfect place for children, who will have plenty of choice. Adults, meanwhile, can relax with one of the good-sized drinks mixed at the service bar.

Jane Street Seafood Cafe
★★

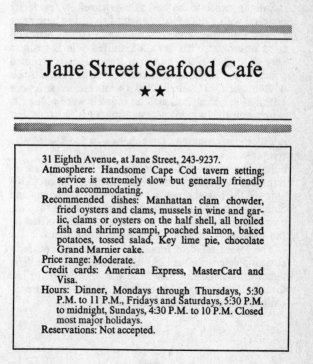

31 Eighth Avenue, at Jane Street, 243-9237.
Atmosphere: Handsome Cape Cod tavern setting; service is extremely slow but generally friendly and accommodating.
Recommended dishes: Manhattan clam chowder, fried oysters and clams, mussels in wine and garlic, clams or oysters on the half shell, all broiled fish and shrimp scampi, poached salmon, baked potatoes, tossed salad, Key lime pie, chocolate Grand Marnier cake.
Price range: Moderate.
Credit cards: American Express, MasterCard and Visa.
Hours: Dinner, Mondays through Thursdays, 5:30 P.M. to 11 P.M., Fridays and Saturdays, 5:30 P.M. to midnight, Sundays, 4:30 P.M. to 10 P.M. Closed most major holidays.
Reservations: Not accepted.

This handsome Greenwich Village restaurant has a refreshingly spare and simple New England charm. Natural rose-colored brick, darkly stained wood wainscotting, parchment-colored walls, a few old photographs, just a few well-placed plants, pleasant lighting and big ceiling fans create an intimate and restful backdrop particularly well suited to seafood, given its Cape Cod overtones. A young and pleasantly accommodating staff adds to the felicitous experience of dining here, although service is often painfully slow.

Along with a decent whole-wheat bread, a giveaway at each table is an improbably irresistible cole slaw — improbably, because I do not usually like cole slaw with mayonnaise and this one is really adrift in the dressing. But somehow the freshness of the cabbage and the seasonings combine to make the cole slaw at the Jane Street cafe an exception.

There is solidly delicious, sprightly Manhattan clam chowder with plenty of fresh vegetables and abundant clams that can occasionally be a bit tough. Golden-brown fried oysters or clams with a verdant tartar sauce, which can be ordered as an appetizer or main course, were crisp, hot and properly briny. Large, shiny mussels steamed in white wine with garlic were plump and fresh, and both clams and oysters on the half shell were icy cold and crystal clear. The only appetizers that were unpleasant were the ill-conceived steamed top neck clams in garlic butter (unpleasant because the large chowder clams were too tough for steaming) and the minced, mushy baked clams.

Broiled seafood of all kinds was moist, not overcooked and generously portioned. Among the best are the firm, snowy gray sole, the plain sole, the whole flounder, the shrimp scampi, the thick, meaty bluefish or the dewy, pink salmon with its spring-green dill sauce.

Salmon can also be had that is carefully, perfectly poached with a dill sauce. Fancier fish dishes here are a bit less satisfying, however, than the plain broiled and fried offerings. What is called stuffed sole is really a very good fillet of sole on top of a meaningless creamed combination of mushrooms and onions, and the mussels with linguine, in what is called a white cream sauce, is a mishmashed combination. The mussels were piquantly saline, and the linguine pleasant in its gentle sauce, but the two elements lacked a unifying thread of flavor. In addition, mussels are in their shells — an awkward presentation.

Baked potatoes and brown rice are perfect and are alternates to vegetables. In this last category, I thoroughly enjoyed the baked acorn squash glazed with honey and cinnamon. But I thought the fresh greenness of the delicious combined broccoli and zucchini was muffled by the addition of sautéed mushrooms and onions.

The tossed salad of romaine lettuce, tomatoes, radishes and celery with a light dill dressing was excellent. Among desserts, the Key lime pie and the chocolate Grand Marnier cake, both with clouds of authentic whipped cream, were the best choices.

Janice's Fish Place
★ ★

570 Hudson Street, corner of 11th Street, 243-4212.
Atmosphere: Pleasant, informal cafe-restaurant, crowded and moderately noisy when full; erratic service.
Recommended dishes: Broccoli with garlic and oil, eggplant with miso vinaigrette, steamed mussels, scallop chowder, shrimp with Oriental vegetables, steamed lobster, sea bass with black beans and ginger, red snapper with garlic and scallions, stuffed shrimp, carrot cake, lemon cheesecake, "disaster" cake, pecan pie.
Price range: Moderately expensive.
Credit cards: American Express, MasterCard and Visa.
Hours: Dinner, Sundays 5 P.M. to 11 P.M., Mondays, 6 P.M. to 11 P.M., Tuesdays through Fridays, 6 P.M. to midnight, Saturdays, 5 P.M. to midnight. Sunday brunch, noon to 4 P.M.
Reservations: Necessary.

More than two years have passed since Hisae's Fish Place on Hudson Street in Greenwich Village became Janice's Fish Place, and it is encouraging to see not only how well the original formula has been maintained, but even improved upon. When the restaurant opened three years ago, Hisae Vilca and Janice Rubin were partners, but Miss Rubin took over when the partnership was dissolved. However, the same Oriental-Continental-vegetarianesque menu is offered in this casual cafe-restaurant with its large bar and rustic wood-paneled walls. Service, unfortunately, is too often distracted and thoughtless.

Vegetables and fish dishes are still the winners, while the few poultry and meat dishes offered leave much to be desired. Portions are large, and it is most entertaining to go with four or six in a party so that many dishes can be shared and sampled. Good, grainy whole-wheat Italian bread and a platter of nearly raw vegetables with a yogurt dip are placed in the center of each table.

Hot emerald-green broccoli, only lightly blanched, is served in a fragrant bath of olive oil and nut-brown cracklings of garlic, and a portion will easily satisfy four diners as a first course. So will the fat, glistening mussels steamed in a scallion-flecked tomato broth, which needs only a little more substance to achieve perfection. Satiny eggplant in a miso vinaigrette and a salad of slivers of scungilli (conch), marinated to melting tenderness, are both superb, as are the asparagus in a pungent blue-cheese dressing and the creamy chowder of sea scallops.

Among the daily specials, two excellent choices that seem to be constants are a modestly priced hot, steamed, pound-and-a-quarter lobster with drawn butter, and a whole, coral red snapper steamed with bits of golden garlic and slivers of scallions. Shrimps stuffed

179

with scallops and lobster and only the merest hint of
bread crumbs were moist and delicious, and swordfish
teriyaki, with Oriental vegetables, had a subtle appeal
that unfolded as I ate my way through it. Far less successful was the pasty, dense and pedestrian curry sauce
on otherwise fine seafood and vegetables.

The regular menu at Janice's always offers excellent
steamed sea bass with black beans and ginger, shrimp
stir-fried with vegetables, plain stir-fried vegetables and
steamed, snowy codfish in a mustard sauce.

Although tender and of good quality, chunks of filet
mignon simply do not profit from being stir-fried with
shrimp and black mushrooms, and the added sprinkling
of sesame seeds and a soupy soy sauce dressing does not
help. Chicken Hawaiian, cooked with pineapple, has always been a disaster in the Hisae-Janice format. Better,
but not by much, are sautéed bits of chicken in a sourish
chive-vinegar sauce.

Carrot cake, a crunchy pecan pie, lemon cheesecake,
strawberries and fruit salad are satisfying desserts.
Three chocolate cakes are also displayed. The one
called a "disaster" — moist, velvety and bun shaped —
is good, but obscured by an overkill of chocolate sauce,
whipped cream and strawberries. Chocolate cake with
apricot jam between layers will appeal to lovers of
Sacher torte, but sour-cream chocolate cake is only fair.

Sunday brunch is far below the dinner-time standards.

Jim McMullen
Fair

1341 Third Avenue, between 76th and 77th Streets,
861-4700.
Atmosphere: Attractive, modern pub-restaurant with
Art Nouveau accents; noisy and cramped. Bar
scene is a madhouse, staff is young, unprofessional, good-natured and inept.
Recommended dishes: Mussels vinaigrette, cream of
spinach soup, broiled chicken, broiled fish, calf's
liver, chicken paillard, steak sandwich, spinach
salad.
Price range: Moderate.
Credit cards: None.
Hours: Lunch, daily, 11:30 A.M. to 4:30 P.M.; dinner,
daily, 4:30 P.M. to 1:45 A.M. Open major holidays.
Reservations: Not accepted.

Since its 1976 opening, Jim McMullen has managed to
become one of the swingingest and most popular pub-
restaurants on the East Side. No reservations are taken,
and standbys are four deep at the bar at almost any time
of day, from Sunday brunch to Saturday night supper.
It is handsomely, if simply, gotten up, with natural-
brick walls and a décor that is basically modern, but

gets a few Art Nouveau accents via etched patterns on mirrors and a few carved wood panels in the dining room.

Although the quality of cooking has declined since this place first opened, that fact does not seem to discourage the trendy crowd that backs up to form a single's scene at the bar. Late at night, high-fashion-model types appear, and at earlier hours, the crowd might best be described as aging preppy. The food is aging preppy too — bland, pallid, soft and characterless. Plain broiled dishes, such as chicken, fish, a thin but juicy paillard of chicken and a steak sandwich were all thoroughly decent. Mussels vinaigrette, served hot in a fragrant broth, were one of the best things sampled. Calf's liver is also done with a light hand.

At lunch one day, shepherd's pie, the ground meat baked under a mashed potato topping, was soupy and salty and reminiscent of school cafeteria lunch offerings, and a salade Niçoise seemed to have come straight from the refrigerator where it had remained all set up in its bowl.

Cream of spinach soup and spinach salad are a cut above other dishes. Chicken pot pie arrived with a crust that had been scorched black, tortellini in a salad were pasty, and a combination of mozzarella cheese and tomatoes, although pleasantly flavored with basil, swam in a sea of oil. Roast-beef hash seemed fine for the first few bites when it was hot, but became salty and uninteresting as it cooled. Having tried desserts such as the chocolate brownie pie, the chocolate mousse, the cheesecake and the deep-dish apple pie, I can assure you that none is worth the calories.

Service often is chaotic. Orders are confused, the kitchen slows down, it is hard to get utensils, water or a check, and as though that were not bad enough, you may be subjected to the kindergarten "we," as in, "Are we ready for our coffee?"

Joanna
Fair

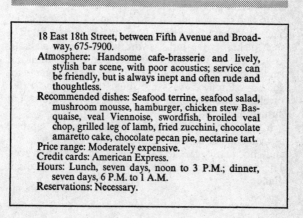

18 East 18th Street, between Fifth Avenue and Broadway, 675-7900.

Atmosphere: Handsome cafe-brasserie and lively, stylish bar scene, with poor acoustics; service can be friendly, but is always inept and often rude and thoughtless.

Recommended dishes: Seafood terrine, seafood salad, mushroom mousse, hamburger, chicken stew Basquaise, veal Viennoise, swordfish, broiled veal chop, grilled leg of lamb, fried zucchini, chocolate amaretto cake, chocolate pecan pie, nectarine tart.

Price range: Moderately expensive.

Credit cards: American Express.

Hours: Lunch, seven days, noon to 3 P.M.; dinner, seven days, 6 P.M. to 1 A.M.

Reservations: Necessary.

Chaotic service and poorly conceived, ineptly executed food do not seem to discourage the attractive crowd of fashion models and photographers who favor the big front bar and the banquette-lined dining room at Joanna's. At this handsome cafe-brasserie, the Art Nouveau backdrop alone seems enough to keep them coming back, and perhaps in this context and with this following, food is regarded as merely a necessary prop.

Sometimes, you can get a good dish at Joanna's and have it served with reasonable dispatch and good will, but such an experience is indeed a sometimes thing. As in too many restaurants, the management follows the unfortunate practice of giving away the worst tables first (at least to unknown guests). When I found myself seated next to heavy smokers in a dining room that was only half full, I requested a change and was put smack up against a busboy station, where dishes were being scraped and slammed down. Requesting another change, I incurred the wrath of waiters and busboys who showed their displeasure with grimaces, grunts and a punishing lack of attention.

The menu at all times offers an array of heavy, light and in-between choices, so it is especially disappointing to see how badly many of them turn out. There is also a tendency toward cutesy language such as "Everyday a Stew or Ample Pot Full of Enriching Soup," so that even if that stew is the delicious chicken Basquaise, one feels slightly full at the start. Some dishes are good one time, bad another. A case in point is an appetizer of green vegetables vinaigrette. The zucchini, broccoli and peas in it may be firm and bright or mushily overcooked, and the dressing can be caustic with vinegar, or it may be properly mellow.

The dill-cured salmon gravlax is fine, but it is served in an absurdly small portion, and its mustard sauce is candy sweet. About a half teaspoon of fishy California caviar, served in the skins of new potatoes with sour cream, is in no way worth the price ($14 at the time of this writing), and various pastas have been overcooked and tossed with sauces that were either pasty or soupy.

The best appetizers were a sprightly seafood salad, an airy seafood terrine and a mushroom mousse brightened by a lemony sauce.

But minestrone tasted like a greasy, thin creole sauce. Omelets are heavy, and a sandwich of so-called Black Forest ham and Brie was disappointing because the ham seemed like the ordinary boiled variety and the Brie was far past its prime.

Broiled meats and fish and a crisply fried veal cutlet Viennoise were the most reliable main courses. Stick to such dishes as the moist swordfish, the thick slabs of grilled leg of lamb with Provence herbs, the small but tender veal chop and the creditable hamburger with good ratatouille. Steaks are tough and sinewy. Fried zucchini was fine and crisp on three occasions but burned on a fourth.

Much is made of chocolate desserts, and a sampler assortment can be obtained. Only chocolate pecan pie and chocolate amaretto cake are exceptional, however. There was also a nice fresh nectarine tart at a recent dinner.

Joe & Rose
★ ★

747 Third Avenue, between 46th and 47th Streets, 355-8874.

Atmosphere: Intimate, typical New York steakhouse décor, with several small, comfortable dining rooms; excellent service.

Recommended dishes: Prosciutto, clams, manicotti, spaghetti with clam sauce or meat sauce, sirloin steak, sirloin for two, roast prime ribs of beef, veal cutlet picatta, Milanese or parmigiana, broiled fish, broiled or sautéed scallops, cottage-fried, baked or hashed-brown potatoes.

Price range: Expensive.

Credit cards: American Express, Diners Club.

Hours: Lunch, Mondays through Fridays, noon to 3 P.M.; dinner, Mondays through Saturdays, 5:30 P.M. to 10 P.M. Closed Sundays. Open most major holidays.

Reservations: Necessary.

Originally opened on 45th Street in 1913 by Joe and Rose Resteghini and called then Mamma Rosa's, this restaurant changed to its present name and location in 1941. Now run by Alfred (Freddie) Resteghini, the son of the original owners, and his wife, Rene, Joe & Rose provides one of the most felicitous, comfortable and almost neighborly settings for excellent steak and roast beef, rounded out with some competently prepared Italian specialties.

The usual masculine steakhouse décor is softened somewhat by mellow lighting, an ornately handsome, pressed-tin ceiling, a convivial bar and, here and there, some aging, brown and moss-green murals of Italian hill towns. Divided into several small dining rooms, one with booths, another with roomy tables and two inner-sanctum back rooms for the most devout regulars, the restaurant is snug and pleasant in its proportions, and the service follows suit. For though the waiters handle the constant rush of business crisply and efficiently, they also manage a smile and never seem to show a trace of impatience over an indecisive diner.

Appetizers and soups are not the strong points at Joe & Rose. Both prosciutto and minestrone were decent, though unexciting, and clams were cold and fresh.

Pastas were delicious, and splitting orders on a first course is a wise decision made by many devotees of this place. The manicotti, with its creamy ricotta filling and its meaty tomato sauce topped with a cheese sauce and then gratinéed, is elegant and lusciously irresistible. The same spicy meat sauce can be had on spaghetti, as can a briny, garlic-scented, white clam sauce. The only flaw was slightly overcooked, undersalted pasta. So savory a clam sauce deserved a better base.

Steaks and roast prime ribs of beef, whether cut thickly with a rib bone or thinly sliced, as I prefer, were

183

pungently beefy and would be hard to top anywhere, and the sirloin for two is extraordinary. Lamb chops, though of excellent quality, were carelessly trimmed and just a bit overcooked, and calf's liver had the mushy texture that meat acquires when it has been frozen.

Veal, however, was impeccably snowy and tender, whether piccata style with a lemony sauce or crisply fried for cutlet Milanese or parmigiana.

Tiny, nut-sweet bay scallops were lightly broiled or sautéed, and a snowy, moist fillet of sole would have attained the same perfection had its sprinkling of paprika been eliminated. Crisp rounds of cottage-fried potatoes are generally good as are crusty baked potatoes and hashed browns. French-fried onion rings range from crisp to limp. Osso buco was generously portioned and well seasoned but somewhat overcooked. So were most of the vegetables, which are purchased fresh daily. The tired mixed green salad was bulked up with iceberg lettuce.

There is very good, chewy bread at Joe & Rose, passable cheesecake, a standard collection of Italian wines, and the drinks are generously portioned.

Joe's Restaurant
★ ★

79 Macdougal Street, between Bleecker and West Houston Streets, 473-8834.

Atmosphere: Simple, unpretentious modern dining rooms that are noisy when full. Excellent service.

Recommended dishes: Clams oreganate, spiedino alla Romana, mozzarella in carrozza, hot antipasto, pasta e fagioli, stracciatella Romana, linguine with white clam sauce, ziti alla Joe, spaghetti with garlic, oil and anchovies, baked lobster oregante, striped bass marechiare, fried squid, veal piccata, grilled veal chop, broiled veal rollatine with dry sautéed mushrooms, steak pizzaiuola, chicken scarpariello, fried zucchini, sautéed escarole, arugula salad, zabaglione.

Price range: Moderately expensive.

Credit cards: American Express, MasterCard and Visa.

Hours: Wednesdays through Mondays, noon to 11:30 P.M. Closed Tuesdays. Closed on Thanksgiving Day and Christmas Day.

Reservations: Necessary for four or more.

One southern Italian restaurant that has managed to survive the trend toward North Italian cooking is Joe's. Lunch at this 41-year-old landmark is relaxed and easygoing and, though noisy at dinner, the spirit is always convivial. Some of the food served in the trim, unpretentious modern dining rooms could certainly be classified as excellent. Overall, however, the kitchen strikes a very good, solid average, and the dining room staff is friendly, thoroughly professional and helpful.

Surprise is not the specialty here, not among appetizers, not in main courses, not in desserts. But if you start with the deep-fried bread, anchovy and mozzarella creation, spiedino alla Romano, you will have as fine a rendition of the dish as can be found in the city. Glistening fresh baked clams, moist and tender under their veneer of breadcrumbs, garlic and oregano, illustrate just how good that dish can be. And the hot antipasto, including shrimp, a baked clam and a silken sliver of eggplant in tomato sauce, is a fine choice when the shrimp are fresh — on one occasion they had the stale flavor of iodine. Two soups were excellent — the steaming hot pasta e fagioli, with tender beans well seasoned by garlic and bacon, and the lighter Italian egg drop, stracciatella Romana.

Some of the pastas here are far better than others. Forget the heavy, doughy potato gnocchi in a salty, pasty tomato sauce, the bland spaghetti carbonara and the slightly sweet and sticky stuffed shells. Instead, try the lusty spaghetti with olive oil, nut-brown cloves of garlic, anchovies and tiny black Gaeta olives, or the linguine with white clam sauce. The house specialty is ziti alla Joe — a soul-soothing dish of the short tubular pasta under a downy blanket of ricotta and mozzarella cheeses, baked in a mild tomato sauce.

Shrimp fra diavolo was disappointing because the shrimp were not fresh and because the sauce lacked the proper fire. The Italian variation on bouillabaisse, zuppa di pesce — a Friday special — lacked the sparkle it can have when it is cooked to order. As a matter of fact, all daily specials had this failing, so it is safer to avoid them.

But it is doubtful that the fried squid could appear in better form than they do here — golden and greaseless. The baked lobster oreganate also deserves an excellent rating. However, the lobsters run small (about one and one-half pounds) and the price is inordinately high. The menu at Joe's is only the beginning, for there are innumerable simple Italian dishes available on request. Among those I asked for were the fried cheese sandwich, mozzarella in carrozza, and striped bass marechiare, distinguished by unusually fresh-tasting fish and a richly garlicked light tomato sauce.

The quality of the veal is high — tender and full of flavor. Try it in the pungent, lemony piccata or grilled in one thick chop or two thin ones or wrapped around a tangy cheese filling and broiled as rollatine. Dry-sautéed mushrooms, savory fried zucchini and subtly garlicked escarole are fine accompaniments. Arugula salad is sprightly and refreshing and is far preferable to the house salad based on iceberg lettuce. Again, very good beef goes into the steak pizzaiuola, lavishly garnished with green peppers, mushrooms, onions and a thin tomato sauce. Chicken scarpariello, in properly sautéed chunks, has a perfect golden haze of garlic.

The Italian cheesecake was mediocre and the rum cake wet and heavy, but the hot zabaglione had an almost magical, velvety thickness and exactly the right accents of Marsala and sugar. I cannot remember ever having tasted a better version.

Wines are banal and overpriced.

John Clancy's Restaurant
★ ★

181 West 10th Street, at Seventh Avenue South, 242-7350.

Atmosphere: Delicate and airy gray-and-white modern dining room that is informal and convivial; upstairs room for private parties. Service is polite and well meaning but often affected, confused and slow.

Recommended dishes: Pickled mussels, gravlax, shrimp cocktail, mushrooms stuffed with crab meat, broiled clams with herbed butter, lobster bisque, mussel soup, oyster stew, watercress soup, cream of caviar soup, fisherman's stew, lobster à l'américaine, mesquite-broiled swordfish or scallops, mousse of sole with lobster sauce, poached coho salmon, soft-shell crabs amandine, Portuguese clams and sausage, chocolate-mousse cake, lemon meringue tarts, strawberry shortcake, lemon mousse, strawberries cardinale. At brunch, chicken hash, omelets and creamed finnan haddie.

Price range: Expensive.

Credit cards: All major credit cards.

Hours: Dinner, Tuesdays through Saturdays, 6 to 11:30 P.M., Sundays, 5:30 P.M. to 11:30 P.M. Sunday brunch, noon to 3:30 P.M. Closed Mondays. Open major holidays.

Reservations: Necessary.

It is one thing to teach the art of perfect cooking in a school or to develop and explain perfect recipes in a cookbook, but quite another to lay it on the line by opening a restaurant. A teacher-author-chef who was willing to take this risk is John Clancy, whose "eclectic seafood restaurant" John Clancy's Restaurant is just off Sheridan Square in Greenwich Village.

Moving into the premises formerly occupied by Julius Lombardi's and doing little more than giving the suave setting brightening coats of pearl gray and white paint, hanging some pastel posters, adding graceful china and adjusting the lighting to a felicitous level, Mr. Clancy set about developing a small but diverse menu with an international range of fish and shellfish specialties.

Because his own credentials as a cook were obviously being relied on to draw a clientele, it was surprising to learn that at first Mr. Clancy was not doing the cooking himself. Now, however, he generally cooks, and when he does, the food is even better than it was earlier.

Russell Carr, who assists at Mr. Clancy's baking school, is on hand, too, and he has created the most extraordinary course at this restaurant — an array of breathtakingly beautiful cakes, most of which taste every bit as fantastic as they look. Keep your eye on such possibilities as the dome of whipped-cream bittersweet chocolate-mousse cake, the inspired individual lemon meringue tartlets and, if available, the rose-pink strawberry shortcake, for which berries are blended through the cream.

Although cakes such as the Grand Marnier torte and the walnut layer cake are a little too sweet, and blueberries are not quite ripe enough to do justice to tarts and shortcakes, they are all far above the usual run. A combination of chocolate and raspberry purée in a cake was the least effective among these offerings, but nonbaked desserts such as a pungent lemon mousse and strawberries mellowed by a raspberry cardinale sauce gave the best cakes stiff competition.

I have listed the desserts first deliberately, because anyone who eats to full satisfaction on other courses will regret doing so when these beauties are paraded for selection.

Meanwhile, back at the appetizers, there are some lovely choices. Cool pickled mussels with just enough pungency to set off their freshness are among the best cold appetizers, along with silky gravlax, the dill-cured salmon that is sparked by a mustardy sauce, and a perfectly simple shrimp cocktail based on slightly warm, tender shrimp rather than the tasteless ones usually presented.

The only near miss among cold first courses were the clam bellies, little satiny cushions that blended too closely in texture to the bland rémoulade sauce. Spice in the sauce and a bit of crunch somewhere would help. The same lack of textural contrast was apparent in the stuffed mussels, minced under a topping of béchamel sauce. Better to choose mushroom caps stuffed with crab meat or the bright cherrystone clams broiled with herbed butter. Those who do not mind cheese with oysters may select the creamy baked oysters, but the combination of tastes is not one I can accept with ease.

Despite so many fine choices, it seems a failing that plain cold clams or oysters on the half shell are not really available when both mollusks are on hand. On request, a waiter said he would ask the chef and, probably because I was recognized, bluepoint oysters were served — fresh, bright and unchilled. There is a question as to just what a restaurant should be responsible for beyond the limits of its menu, but a request such as this seems simple enough to fill.

Soups are exceptional, if less than steaming hot. Lobster bisque could not have had a richer, brassier edge to it, and the cream of mussel soup and the watercress soup both had exactly the right counterpoints of flavor. Cold cream of caviar soup sounded dreadful but tasted wonderful, with its underpinning of chives modifying the gentle fishiness of the red caviar.

Broiling is done over briquettes of brushwood mesquite shipped in from Texas. The result is a mild smoky flavor that permits the character of the fish to come through. The technique, excellent on Dover sole and halibut, worked even better on swordfish and scallops.

Fisherman's stew, a near-bouillabaisse full of mussels, clams, shrimp and a variety of fish, could easily be zapped by the powerful garlic rouille, but added with caution, the sauce does much for the aromatic broth. Portuguese clams, a frequent special, was another exceptional dish, a combination of clams steamed with the garlic and pepper-flavored linguica sausage and Serrano ham in a tomato, wine broth perfumed with coriander.

It would be hard to beat the lobster à l'américaine done here, with a whole lobster cut through the shell and simmered in a brilliant blend of tomato, wine, cognac, thyme and tarragon.

Mousse of sole in lobster sauce, another intermittent special, was beautifully done, but paupiettes of sole in combined lobster and hollandaise sauces were stiffly overcooked.

Sautéeing was accomplished successfully only on soft-shell crabs amandine, which were as tender, juicy and crunchy as they should be. But shrimp with jalapeño chilies had been overly sweetened with sherry and were pasty with flour. Bay scallops in garlic butter needed more seasoning.

Two casseroles missed entirely: the pallid mixed seafood pie, uninteresting and not a pie at all, and the crab au gratin, in which the crab meat had been puréed to resemble mashed potatoes. Served along with broccoli purée, it was a plateful of mush.

Texture, in fact, is the element that needs work here, and so does the combination of vegetables and main course. There is probably no single vegetable that works with every main course on a menu such as this, and the purées with dishes such as the stew, the lobster and Portuguese clams are blatant errors, conflicting as they do with both the spirit and flavors of those lusty specialities.

A green salad was bright and fresh, although it needed more dressing. Our waiter forgot orders of salad on two occasions, and at a nearby table, bread did not appear until requested. It also took fifteen minutes to get a glass of water. All of which is to say that service is not yet smooth. Neither is the kitchen's timing, which lags, especially between appetizer and main course.

In general, John Clancy's is comfortable, but chairs could be more capacious, and in the back room, noise and the sound of rushing air in a duct were disconcerting. So was the room's uneven temperature.

California white wines make up the bulk of the wine list. Not being very fond of such wines made my choice difficult. Nevertheless, three were pleasing — the 1979 Sauvignon Blanc of Joseph Phelps, the 1979 Chardonnay from Lambert Ridge and my favorite among whites, the 1979 Pinot Blanc-Chalone. Over all, my preference was for one of the only two reds on the list — the 1978 Pinot Noir from Joseph Phelps, which was decidedly better than the whites with the robust Portuguese clams, lobster and fisherman's stew.

Excellent Sunday brunches follow the restaurant's seafood theme. Fish and shellfish specialties are featured, along with chicken hash, omelets and country ham and chicken shortbread made with toasted cornbread. There is a luxurious version of creamed finnan haddie that is gratinéed, and Monterey Jack cheese and fiery jalapeño peppers add zest to to a delicate omelet. A creamy and elegant oyster stew and a rich lobster bisque are soothing and sustaining first courses and the brie baked in a brioche is an interesting main course or appetizer. Homemade Danish pastry is flaky and fragrant and the margaritas and Bloody Marys are expertly made.

Keen's
Fair

72 West 36th Street, between Fifth and Sixth Avenues, 947-3636.

Atmosphere: Large, noisy and handsome English pub, with cramped seating; service is well meaning but inept.

Recommended dishes: Shrimp and scallops vinaigrette, smoked salmon, snails with cèpes and walnuts, ballotine of duck, rack of lamb, mutton chop, grouper with mustard sauce, Cambridge burnt cream.

Price range: Moderately expensive.

Credit cards: All major credit cards.

Hours: Lunch, Mondays through Saturdays, 11:45 A.M. to 3 P.M.; dinner, Mondays through Saturdays, 5 P.M. to midnight. Clam bar, Mondays through Saturdays, 3 P.M. to midnight. Closed Sundays.

Reservations: Necessary for lunch.

When it was first announced that the English chophouse Keen's was being restored, lovers of New York landmarks found cause to celebrate. Long a cherished spot for mutton chops, steak and kidney pie and other English chophouse specialties, the old tavern had been missed since it closed in 1976. Reopened late in 1981 by Dr. George Schwarz, a radiologist whose earlier entries into the restaurant business included One Fifth and the two Elephant & Castle cafes, Keen's so far gives little cause for joy where food and service are concerned. Even a change of chefs has not helped at all.

The setting is much like the original, with clay pipes on the low ceiling and dark paneled walls, though the renewed interior is a far less mellow interpretation. Seating is extremely uncomfortable because of badly placed tables and booths that are pinched and cramped. The staff is good-natured enough but the service is detached, thoughtless and unprofessional.

Most disappointing of all is the menu. Instead of offering the savory grilled and roasted meats and fish and the meat pies that would be appropriate to the setting, and which would be relatively simple to prepare, the menu is primarily nouvelle cuisine. It's as though the owner, having had the courage to invest in the restoration of this old place, then hedged his bet with flossy and trendy food.

A few chophouse classics appear on the menu, but these are meagerly and indifferently turned out. On one occasion, a mutton chop was thin and bland, but on another, it came properly thick and juicy, topped with a kidney and good bacon. On two visits the mixed grill consisted of little dried out twists of innocuous meats and the mutton en brochette did not taste like mutton, but like lamb that had been frozen. Rack of lamb scented with thyme proved far better, but a Chateaubriand steak for two was barely enough for one. Filet mignon with three peppers in a winy sauce was fair, but its totally inappropriate accompaniment was a cold, stale baked potato with sour cream already in place. Grilled calf's liver took on musty, greasy overtones from the sautéed onions that blanketed it, and medaillons of veal with morels were just about passable. Sweetbreads in a Calvados-spiked sauce were good, though overly rich as a main course, and the puff pastry casing had gone soggy.

Fish dishes proved no more felicitous than meats, the one exception being the grouper baked en papillote in a mustard sauce. Poached salmon was overcooked and hard. And there is an incredibly poor lunch main course of sole baked with salty, pasteurized black caviar. If you think this form of caviar is bad cold, just try it hot.

Oysters and little neck clams, though fresh and bright, were not chilled. But prosciutto and the Scotch salmon were delicious. So was the ballotine of duck, a coarse pistachio-studded pâté. Avoid the red and fibrous house pâté, but try the interesting snails with cèpes and walnuts in a light cream sauce, or the avocado baked with a poached egg and topped with béarnaise sauce. Oysters baked under a froth of leek mousse should have been hotter, but the dish was one of the better appetizer choices. Also skip such soups as the Bermuda fish chowder, the improbably green vichyssoise and the bland cold cucumber concoction.

Having tried all of the desserts, I can recommend only two — the banana Britannica, which is an old-fashioned American banana split, and the Cambridge burnt cream, otherwise known as crème brûlée.

Kippy's Pier 44
Fair

261 West 44th Street, at the corner of Eighth Avenue, 221-1065.

Atmosphere: Heavy-handed and commercial rendition of a pub that is more or less Cape Cod Colonial in style. Ventilation is poor and service is amateurish, ranging from good-natured to contentious.

Recommended dishes: Clams or oysters on the half shell, melon, grapefruit, shrimp or clams fra diavolo or marinara, mixed seafood on fettuccine, broiled Dover sole, stone crabs, cold fisherman's platter, broiled chicken, broiled lobster.

Price range: Expensive.

Credit cards: All major cards.

Hours: Mondays through Saturdays, 11:30 A.M. to 1 A.M., Sundays, noon to 1 A.M.

Reservations: Generally recommended, especially before matinee and evening theater performances.

As welcome as a good fish restaurant would be in the theater district, there is little cause for celebration in the arrival of Kippy's Pier 44 in the Milford Plaza Hotel, operated by Joe (Kippy) Kipness, known for Pier 52 on 52d Street. The menu at Pier 44 is a carbon copy of the 52d Street Pier, and there has been no noticeable improvement in the food or service in the course of nine meals.

The dizzying number of dishes on the huge menu may be part of the problem. Having eaten my way through all appetizers and desserts, as well as a representative group of fish, shellfish, meat and poultry dishes that are broiled, fried, poached and served plain or in fancy sauces, it appears that in almost every area the restaurant falls short.

Only a few choices are acceptable and these are worth noting for anyone who yearns for a fish dinner before the theater, the only reason to consider this restaurant. Among appetizers, clams and oysters on the half shell are invariably fresh, cold and sparkling. Melon and grapefruit are alternatives. Moderately acceptable first courses include the lobster cocktail and the shrimp cocktail, said to be made with "the world's largest shrimp," which they certainly are not. All soups were floury and pasty, though the Boston fish chowder proved less offensive than the others. But shrimp or clams, with marinara or fra diavolo sauce, were surprisingly lusty and spicy. A similar preparation made with king crab meat, shrimp, clams and scallops on fettuccine was just about the best main course. Broiled chicken was fresh and sizzling and the prime ribs of beef were creditable but would have been even better had the meat not dried out under a heat lamp.

One night I ordered lobster but was told that all six portions had been sold. It was available at lunch the next day and was just about perfectly broiled. This unevenness was also true of the the Dover sole. It was soggy and soupy when sautéed one night but above average when grilled the next day.

Cold seafood specialties proved preferable to hot ones. A platter of lobster, shrimp, clams, oysters and stone crabs, a house specialty, was satisfying, but a chef's seafood salad made with cheese was barely edible. Poor choices were the sweet-sour curries, the creole-sauce dishes in which the tomato sauce had been scorched, and the unpleasantly fatty poached fish dishes served with a stiff lobster sauce.

Thick, sweet dressings spoil decent mixed greens in salad, and cole slaw is often gray and wilted. Canned clam juice and broth were inexplicably stale, and baked potatoes, done in foil, were invariably cold and lumpy. Smoked trout was a dead ringer for smoked whitefish, prosciutto was stiff and salty, and crab meat cakes, as well as the crab meat stuffings, were shredded into something like fishy-tasting threads. Sirloin steak could be equaled in any nightclub.

The setting is as undistinguished as the food; both dining rooms and bar are done up in the Cape Cod Colonial style often found in the tonier dining rooms of chain motels. The restaurant is noisy and drafty and the service ranges from friendly and amateurish to downright contentious. I discovered frequent errors in the check — sometimes in the house's favor, other times in mine. In any case, reach for one of the apples or bananas offered in a big seashell as you leave. Either makes a better dessert than the cloying commercial cakes, pies and puddings on the menu, although ice creams are fine.

Kitcho
★ ★ ★

22 West 46th Street, between Fifth Avenue and Avenue of the Americas, 575-8880.

Atmosphere: Attractive modern dining room downstairs with tatami rooms on second and third floors; excellent service.

Recommended dishes: All except sushi.

Price range: Moderately expensive.

Credit cards: American Express and Diners Club.

Hours: Lunch, Mondays through Fridays, noon to 2:30 P.M.; dinner, Mondays through Fridays, 6 P.M. to 10:30 P.M., Sundays, 5 P.M. to 10:30 P.M. Closed Saturdays and major holidays.

Reservations: Necessary.

Although dozens of Japanese restaurants have opened in New York since Kitcho first came into being almost twenty-five years ago, few, if any, have managed to maintain the degree of excellence and authenticity the management here has achieved. Its trim, handsome, modern downstairs dining room, plus its two floors of traditional tatami compartments where guests remove their shoes and sit on the floor, are marked improvements upon this restaurant's former home.

The clientele is overwhelmingly Japanese, usually in the ratio of fifteen to one. It was interesting to note that almost all of the Occidentals drank sake and almost all of the Japanese drank Scotch, usually with a whole bottle buried in a bucket of ice. Most of the waitresses are gracious, charming and painstakingly polite, even with Westerners asking endless questions at the busiest times. Oddly enough, the television set playing continuously at the bar is never heard in the dining room, and the wonder is that the busy bar staff find time to watch it at all, considering their hectic pace. Flowers on shiny black tables, a stunning array of stoneware service pieces and amenities such as hot towels at the beginning of the meal add to the felicitous experience.

Best of all, of course, is the food, which is based on glisteningly fresh ingredients, meticulously prepared and subtly seasoned. Some of the most common dishes are done here with a finesse that takes them out of the ordinary. Among these are the clear soup suimono and a smoky rich bean paste variation, misoshiru, and the tenderly marinated teriyaki grills of pork, chicken, beef or fish, all perfumed with hints of ginger, soy sauce and sweet sake. Kushikatsu, boneless nuggets of pork deep-fried to golden crunchiness, and to-banyak, meat or fish marinated and grilled and served with glazed zucchini slices, mushrooms, vegetables and rice, were exceptional.

Tempura of shrimp with fried slivers of sweet potatoes, zucchini, green pepper and eggplant could perhaps have been more glassily crackling for my taste, but it was far above run-of-the-mill in quality. With all of these dishes, of course, come the subtle accents of salty soy sauce or stinging mustard or horseradish.

More unusual appetizers include shitashi (braised fresh spinach enriched with sesame oil), sunomono (a salad of crab meat and vegetables), suzuko (fresh red salmon caviar with grated white radish), yakinori (crisp, antique-tasting dried leaves of seaweed with the green horseradish, wasabi) and yaki-hama, broiled clams topped with lemon slices and served with a mildly hot dip.

Sushi are not up to other dishes, but cold boiled soba noodles pungent with soy sauce and chopped scallions was among my other favorites. Kamameshi, rice steamed with seafood or chicken, and bits of meat or shrimp grilled on hot stones, are diverting and delicious. Exotic ice creams, flavored with green tea or sweet soy bean paste, and sparkling fresh watermelon or honeydew made up the dessert choice.

Noticing at the bottom of the menu the mysterious and intriguing offering of "chef's choice" dinners at much higher prices, our curiosity was piqued and we ordered one dinner for one price and a second for another (the highest) to compare the range and number of dishes.

The owner carefully explained that these dinners were built around dishes which the Japanese recognize as special and luxurious, among them a number of raw freshwater fish specialties, and he wanted to be sure we did not expect more lavish specialties along the lines of foie gras and truffles or complicated cooking. What unfolded before us during the two-and-a-half-hour meal was a parade of dishes of such rarified and astonishing visual beauty that seeing them was almost nourishment enough. Most were based on fish: red, white, yellow; some thick, others so thinly sliced one could read through them. Most were raw, some were pickled, others marinated, still others grilled or smoked.

A few courses consisted of dishes grouped on a bed of shaved ice mounded on lacquered, boat-shape trays and many were adorned with sprays of tiny, Japanese silver maple leaves. A rare red caviar, funa — taken from a freshwater fish and imported from Japan — was unusually rich and briny. One small round bowl held marinated mushrooms, each no larger than a raisin.

As interesting as these banquets were, I would recommend them only for advanced aficionados of Japanese food, and especially of raw fish; for the rest, the standard menu will prove more familiarly satisfying.

Sake, warm or chilled, and Japanese beer (my preference is for Sapporo) are the most suitable beverages unless, of course, you are really Japanese, in which case you may want Scotch. Kitcho in New York, by the way, has no connection with the several Kitchos in Japan.

K.O.'s
★ ★

99 Bank Street, corner of Greenwich Street, 243-0561.
Atmosphere: Handsome and theatrical modern setting, widely spaced tables, good lighting and service.
Recommended dishes: Smoked salmon, rock shrimp, asparagus vinaigrette, mozzarella in carrozza, zucchini frittata, all steaks, lamb chops, veal chop, broiled shrimp, sautéed sand dabs, soft-shell crabs, home-fried potatoes, sautéed mushrooms, stuffed baked potato, braised endive, creamed spinach, crème brûlée, chocolate cake, banana cream pie, cheesecake, apple tart, strawberries.
Price range: Moderately expensive.
Credit Cards: American Express, MasterCard and Visa.
Hours: Dinner, Sundays and Tuesdays through Thursdays, 6 P.M. to 10:30 P.M., Fridays and Saturdays, 6 P.M. to 11:30 P.M. Closed Mondays.
Reservations: Recommended.

Soon after it opened last year, K.O.'s, the attractive, dramatically lighted modern steakhouse, rated one star, and two seemed not far behind. That early promise has now been fulfilled because the kitchen staff has developed a more authoritative hand with seasonings and corrected some earlier flaws. The characteristic steakhouse sizzle may still be lacking as meats come from kitchen to table, but that shortcoming is compensated for by the superb quality of the carefully broiled meats and fish and the diverting side dishes and appetizers that are more stylish than those in the standard steakhouse format.

The owners are Karen Ortenzio, whose initials inspired the restaurant's name, and her husband, James, who is a wholesale meat dealer. His experience accounts for the exquisite prime quality of cuts such as rib steak and the porterhouse as well as the sirloin and the filet mignon. As good as the standard steaks are, they are far outdistanced by the juicy rib steak and the well-marbled and, therefore, richly flavored porterhouse for two.

These steaks, as well as the lean and the tender lamb chops, are better seared now than in the past, so their juices are sealed in. The thick rose-pink loin veal chops are still inadequately seared, so some flavor is lost, although they are well above average. Rack of lamb, also served for two, is delicious, but it is so heavily coated with fat that it is hard to get at the meat and pointless to gnaw on bones. It was the only dish that did not seem worth ordering. Our rack, ordered medium rare, arrived almost raw.

It is hard to get crisply roasted duck that is neither dry nor stale, but it is found at K.O.'s, though it is much better without the cold, honey-sweet sauce that is served on the side. Wild rice with the duck was fresh, hot and fluffy without being mushy. White rice was the base for lightly broiled, moist shrimp that were fragrant with herbs and for sand dabs, the popular West Coast fish that are first cousins to flounder. They are sautéed with as much skill as the tiny, crisp-coated soft-shell crabs.

Hashed-brown potatoes are scented with onion and are fine when they are not burned, and the scallion-flavored stuffed baked potato is satisfying. Spinach is better creamed than plain, and endive is carefully braised and tender. Herbs add flavor and fragrance to sautéed mushrooms, but the salad greens have been wet and so shed their dressing.

Mozzarella in carrozza, although still not the classic version, has improved somewhat with the cheese slices much thicker between the bread and a lively anchovy sauce that brightens the fried sandwich. Stuffed artichokes, which were mushy on earlier visits, have not been available of late, but asparagus in vinaigrette dressing could not be improved upon. Scotch salmon is firm, pale pink and only gently smoky in flavor. Steamed Florida rock shrimp served hot with melted butter remains an excellent appetizer and the zucchini frittata, a sort of crustless quiche, seems lighter and more custardlike than in the past.

Rough textured breads, both the white and whole wheat, are especially good topped with the herb and garlic cottage cheese spread, but go easy on this combination so that you can manage dessert. Desserts vary from day to day, but consistent winners have been the satiny banana cream pie, the apple tart and the light cheesecake. The moist and intensely chocolaty chocolate cake is less cloying than it used to be, and the crème brûlée retains a custardy base and a glassy caramelized topping.

Service is excellent but plates are sometimes searingly hot.

Kurumazushi
★ ★ ★

423 Madison Avenue, between 48th and 49th Streets, 751-5258.
Atmosphere: Small, simple upstairs sushi bar with a few tatami alcoves and one private room; service gracious and helpful.
Recommended dishes: Everything except honeydew melon, cold omelet and warm eel.
Price range: Expensive.
Credit cards: American Express and Diners Club.
Hours: Lunch, Mondays through Fridays, noon to 2:30 P.M.; dinner, Mondays through Fridays, 5:30 P.M. to 10 P.M. Closed Saturdays, Sundays and major holidays.
Reservations: Necessary.

Kurumazushi, perhaps the least prepossessing of all the sushi restaurants in New York, is also the best that I have found so far. Set above a Larmen Dosanko fast-food noodle restaurant, Kurumazushi has a simple sign that could easily be missed. To enter the restaurant, you must first walk into the Dosanko, climb the stairs and slide open a more or less Japanese wood-and-glass door, all of which might cause you to suspect you are in the wrong place. The interior is equally uninspiring, with its big bar, small sushi counter and a few tatami alcoves lined up against the front window. But the crush of Japanese customers eating sushi and sashimi is testimony to the superiority of this establishment, especially when one realizes they are paying a very high price for the privilege, especially at dinner. Nowhere in New York have I found sushi so well made and so delicately balanced in texture, temperature and flavor. The only recurrent flaw is a tendency to serve fish that is too cold.

Sit at the counter so you can appreciate the hands of the sushi masters as they work magically, pressing out oshi-zushi, warm, lightly seasoned rice finished with such dew-fresh toppings as raw tuna, pearly, pink-edged flounder and sea bass and vinegar-marinated mackerel. Among other exceptional choices are cooked shrimp, satiny squid meat either from the body or the lacy tentacles, and cooked rose-pink octopus and abalone. And for the real prize, ask for the pale-pink fatty tuna. All these are available in the deluxe sushi assortment or can be ordered a piece at a time.

Maki-zushi is the category of rice and fish rolled in nori, a dried, spinach-color seaweed, that should be eaten first in an assortment so that the seaweed wrapping does not become soggy. Some of the best choices among these are roe of sea urchins with the intense flavor of lobster roe, large, pale-golden salmon caviar and slices from long rolls containing tuna and rice, and cucumber with a sort of minty parsley. A satisfying windup favored by most Japanese is what they call an ice cream cone, a handheld cone of seaweed filled with rice and tuna.

All the fish and seafood made into sushi can also be obtained sliced without rice as sashimi, usually eaten first. In either case, small dishes of soy sauce mixed with the searingly hot green horseradish, wasabi, are near at hand. On some assortments, crunchy fernlike seaweed cools palates. Both clear soup with vegetables and smoky-flavored miso bean soup are delicious. So is the nutta, an appetizer salad of tuna and scallions in a wine-and-mustard sauce, sometimes available at dinner.

The complete sushi and sashimi dinner also includes a mound of slivered tuna and scallions to be dipped into soy sauce. But fruit and additional sushi and sashimi are billed as à la carte, so order with care. Ripe pineapple makes for a refreshingly astringent finish, but the unripe honeydew melon served to us had no color at all and was hard and bitter — inexcusable at this price level. Although at this price, one might expect a more attractive setting and platters that are more elaborately garnished, apparently all the creative energies here are expended on the food. Lunch specials are fairly reasonable, such as chirashi, a lacquer box layered with rice and an assortment of raw fish and pickles, soup and tea.

Sake, whiskey and beer are served, but bear in mind that the most serious sushi connoisseurs may drink sake or whiskey before starting to eat, but only tea once the rice is served. Those who have trouble handling chopsticks can take comfort from the information in a new cookbook, "The Book of Sushi" by Kinjiro Omae and Yuzuru Tachibana, published by Kodansha International. The authors explain that it is best to hold sushi with the fingers and to invert the sushi so that the fish is dipped into the soy sauce instead of the rice. They also say it is desirable to feel and taste the fish on the tongue before the rice. This book, primarily intended for home sushi makers, contributes greatly to the appreciation of sushi.

La Bonne Bouffe
★ ★

127 East 34th Street, between Lexington and Park Avenues, 679-9309.

Atmosphere: Small, charming, provincial bistro; noisy when full; friendly and efficient service.

Recommended dishes: Marinated vegetables, quiche, snails, coquilles St.-Jacques, salade Niçoise, mignonettes de boeuf, escalope de veau, sole Grenobloise, scallops Provençale, brochette of lamb, duck with orange sauce, strawberries with Grand Marnier sauce, crème caramel, fruit tarts, cheesecake.

Price range: Moderately expensive.

Credit cards: American Express.

Hours: Lunch, Mondays through Fridays, 11:30 A.M. to 2:30 P.M.; dinner, Mondays through Saturdays, 6 P.M. to 10 P.M. Closed Sundays. Open major holidays.

Reservations: Not accepted for lunch, but necessary for dinner.

The charming and solidly good La Bonne Bouffe is just the sort of engaging bistro one comes across constantly in Paris but rarely sees in New York. It is indeed a jewel — unpretentious, with a small but well-planned menu and carefully prepared French food in the comfortable tradition of la cuisine bourgeoise. The long, narrow dining room is inviting, with rough, off-white plaster walls and dark beams, copper pots and wall lamps casting a restful but adequate light. Tables are small and close together, banquettes are uncomfortable, and when the restaurant is full the noise level is distracting. Nevertheless, La Bonne Bouffe has a friendly, personal atmosphere that is maintained by several efficient and thoroughly delightful waitresses as well as by the owners, Marcel Moine, who is the chef, and his wife, Janine, who runs the dining room.

There are three very good appetizers at La Bonne Bouffe, beginning with small, tender snails sizzled under a golden mantle of butter and parsley, not so zapped with garlic that they numb the palate for courses to come. Large, gently simmered sea scallops in a satiny cream sauce (coquilles St.-Jacques) were carefully gratinéed so that they had a savory crust but were not dried out. Marinated vegetables are somewhere between ratatouille and mixed vegetables à la grecque — a rainbow combination of eggplant, peppers, tomato, carrots, cauliflower and more. It deserves better than the accompaniment of a canned California black olive.

Pâté de campagne was good one night but only fair on another try, when it was in need of more authoritative seasonings. Soups have been lackluster, whether one tries the watery onion soup or a clam chowder that tasted as though it had come straight from a can with only the slightest and most inadequate doctoring.

In addition to five or six regular main courses there are two to four daily specials. Greaseless golden-brown duck in a delicate sauce that contains chunks of orange is on the standard menu, as are lusty, sharply-spiced mignonettes of beef in a green-peppercorn sauce made with red wine and shallots. Escalopes de veau Bonne Bouffe was another winner — two pale and slender slices of veal fillet gratinéed under a blanket of mushroom duxelles, Gruyère and a light glace de viande. Tiny, sweet bay scallops sautéed with tomato and garlic (à la Provençale), were delicious, too. Fillet of sole Grenobloise was sparked with capers and lemon. Grilled salmon or bass, just a bit dry, were helped by a pungent sorrel sauce.

A daily special of grilled lamb brochette with a good brassy mustard sauce was lovely. The only main course, in fact, that was below standard was a Rock Cornish hen — and that's mainly because that bird is not worth eating in the first place. Main courses were graced with a platter of such bright, firm, freshly cooked vegetables as sautéed, sliced potatoes with a herbaceous edge to their flavor, steamed carrots in parsley butter, whole string beans or, at times, a creamy zucchini soufflé.

Mr. Moine's cooking deserves better French bread. The type served at Bonne Bouffe is dry and tasteless.

Fruit tarts are homemade and far above average, as is the cheesecake, although sometimes garnished with canned fruit — an unnecessary touch. Strawberries in a silky Grand Marnier sauce topped with whipped cream were totally irresistible. So was crème caramel. But chocolate mousse tasted a bit like package chocolate pudding, and the strawberry tart's puff pastry was leaden.

A three-course dinner is moderately expensive, but portions are large, and most diners will find two courses enough. The lunch menu offers lighter selections and prices that are about half those in the evening. Quiche, salade Niçoise and chicken with mushrooms and tomatoes were all delicious, as was a simple veal scaloppine sautéed with mushrooms.

La Camelia

★

---

225 East 58th Street, between Second and Third Avenues, 751-5488.

Atmosphere: Formal and pleasant if unimaginative setting with inviting view of the kitchen. Noise level is high and ventilation poor; service ranges from professional and efficient to hectic.

Recommened dishes: Assorted shell fish appetizers, clams and mussels in saffron broth, carpaccio, coteghino sausage with lentil purée, crab meat crepe, baby octopus, gnocchi Bolognese, spaghettini with fresh tomato sauce, tortelloni, tortellini in crust, vermicelli with fresh greens, broiled Spanish shrimp, cacciucco, sautéed veal chop, paillard of veal, lamb chops with mint, calf's liver with sausage, fruit tarts.

Price range: Moderately expensive.

Credit cards: American Express, MasterCard and Visa.

Hours: Lunch, Mondays through Fridays, noon to 3 P.M.; dinner, Mondays through Saturdays, 5 P.M. to 11 P.M.; supper, Mondays through Saturdays, 11 P.M. to 1 A.M. Closed Sundays and holidays.

Reservations: Necessary for dinner.

Fifty-eighth street between Second and Third Avenues is fast becoming Italian Restaurant Row. The line of black and silver-gray stretch limousines has lengthened considerably there since La Camelia opened late in 1981. Lunch, dinner and supper menus in this pleasantly plush if undistinguished new setting offer North Italian cooking with strong overtones of novella cucina, the Italian version of the French nouvelle cuisine. Kiwis are featured with prosciutto as well as in dessert tarts, and there are combinations such as oranges with shrimp cocktail in Russian dressing, strawberries doused with balsamic vinegar, smoked salmon folded into creamy fettuccine and chicken with a sauce of pistachio nuts. Some creations prove more successful than others.

Owned by Tony May, who is also a partner in the Rainbow Room, his brother Luciano Magliulo, who is the manager, and the chef, Carlo De Gaudenzi, La Camelia plays to a full house most nights, although the lunch traffic is light. After ten at night, guests sit around a big white piano bar where a trio plays, and at one in the morning the chef stirs up pasta at the bar and serves it without charge.

There are a lot of entertaining ideas here that need working out. So do the service, the acoustics and the ventilation. Reservations are not always honored on time, a condition that the manager handled with ill grace one evening. When I was recognized at two lunches, cut pastries, probably from the night before, were replaced with fresh tarts.

Based on five visits, I found the kitchen's performance uneven, with main courses the most critical weakness. Pastas that are excellent when hot too often arrived tepid. Appetizers are the most successful course. Clams and mussels in a tomato and saffron broth and assorted baked shellfish are among the best hot choices. Close seconds are the sliced coteghino pork sausage with a smooth lentil purée and a gratinéed crab meat crepe. At lunch, the tender, tiny baby octopus in a subtle tomato and olive oil sauce, and sparked with anchovies, is lusty enough to be a main course instead of an appetizer.

Equally good cold appetizers include superb smoked salmon layered over slivers of fennel, fine, firm airdried beef, bresaola, the raw-beef carpaccio in a pungent green herb sauce, and a smooth chicken liver pâté with truffles. The combination of Russian dressing and oranges in the shrimp cocktail made for an unpleasant contrast and prosciutto lacked age and, therefore, character.

The only soup I tried — the meat-filled pasta squares, agnolotti, in capon broth — tasted like hot salt water, and my one pass at risotto was equally disappointing, probably because the broth simmered with the rice was itself pallid. Better to opt for pastas such as the steaming hot tortellini in meat sauce baked under a pastry crust or the large, gentle tortelloni, filled with spinach and cheese and glossed with a light tomato and cream sauce. When hot, vermicelli or capellini in a green herb and garlic sauce is bracing. So is the spaghettini with an airy, fresh tomato and onion sauce.

Green and white noodles (paglia e fieno) in a cream sauce with peas, and fettuccine with smoked salmon seemed bland and stodgy. Wilted, hot arugula turned stringy in the cooking, spoiling the marinara sauce that topped the short tubular quills called penne. Linguine del Golfo, more than any other dish, summed up the creative confusion in the kitchen. Done in a fragrant garlic, parsley and oil white sauce, the linguine had been tossed with bits of shrimp and lobster; over that went clams and mussels in their shells, making this awkwardly messy.

Frying is not well executed, judging by the fritto misto of fish, the veal cutlet Milanese and the fried zucchini. Sautéeing of dishes such as fillet of sole with zucchini and veal with white truffles is inept, although it is more successful with the veal chop flavored with sage and porcini mushrooms.

The best fish dishes were the red Spanish shrimp broiled with garlic and butter and the Livornese fish stew cacciucco, made with lobster, scallops, shrimp, clams and mussels in a sheer tomato broth.

Capon breast blanketed with a thick pistachio sauce and stuffed roasted chicken proved cloying. But excellent calf's liver, sautéed pink as ordered, was fleshed out with neat pork sausages and gently sautéed onions. Both the grilled paillard of veal and lamb chops with mint were expertly rendered.

Zabaglione, though a bit too airy, had just the right balance of sugar and Marsala. Wholly successful desserts were the light banana cream pie and the tart combining kiwis, figs and strawberries. My favorite dessert is the aged, properly gritty grana cheese with a ripe pear.

La Camelia has a well-chosen and fairly priced wine list, with more than 100 selections representing Italy's most important regions. There are five excellent versions of Burnello do Montalcino, perhaps Italy's finest red wine.

La Caravelle
★ ★

> **33 West 55th Street, between Fifth Avenue and Avenue of the Americas, 586-4252.**
> Atmosphere: Beautiful, romantic, plushly elegant Parisian setting; service can be excellent but is often rude and impatient.
> Recommended dishes: Oysters, clams, cold striped bass or terrine of seafood, smoked salmon, pain de brochet, poached sole with pike mousse, mussel soup with curry, roast veal or beef, chicken au vinaigre, poached chicken gros sel, braised squab, chicken Normande, salade Lyonnaise, grilled red snapper, roast duck with peppercorns, Grand Marnier or raspberry soufflés.
> Price range: Expensive.
> Credit cards: American Express, MasterCard, Visa and Diners Club.
> Hours: Lunch, Mondays through Saturdays, 12:15 P.M. to 2:30 P.M.; dinner, Mondays through Saturdays, 6 P.M. to 10:15 P.M. Closed Sundays and major holidays.
> Reservations: Necessary.

Almost from the day it opened in 1960, La Caravelle has been counted among the top three or four haute-cuisine restaurants in the city, and for most of that time it has, quite justifiably, been awarded four-star ratings.

Given the enduring beauty of this gastronomic landmark, it was with much sadness that I felt compelled to report a marked decline in the quality of food preparation in 1978, and recent visits indicate no improvement. For although all of the products used are still of impeccable quality, there is overwhelming if depressing evidence that the kitchen's performance has become markedly uneven.

The romantic beauty and gracious charm of this dining place have not faded, although its décor was so much in vogue when it was created that it bordered on a fad. The leafy, sun-dappled murals of Parisian park scenes, the lipstick-red velvet banquettes and the pale, soothing colors of walls and draperies that reflect a comfortable golden glow of light are all impeccably maintained, a prodigious and costly feat considering the wear and tear this crowded restaurant gets.

What has deteriorated is the service, and there is no restaurant about which I get more complaints than this one. Unknown customers are given tables that should not even exist in an expensive restaurant, and the reports of blatant rudeness, more from management than from waiters, are numerous and consistent. Robert Meyzen, one of the original partners, now owns La Caravelle with its former chef, Roger Fessaguet, who is graceless and unwelcoming in the dining room.

Because La Caravelle could be such a lovely place in which to spend an evening, it is worth noting the gastronomic highlights. Among appetizers, the best choices are the excellent, high-quality purchased items — the silky, mild smoked Scotch and Nova Scotia salmon, the perfect, clear, cold briny oysters and clams, the succulent imported French pâtés of duck with green peppercorns or of goose with truffles, as well as all fish mousses and meat or fish pâtés that are homemade.

Three well-prepared choices on the hors d'oeuvres wagon were cold striped bass, plain or in a mixed salad, and lemony calf's brains vinaigrette. But charcuterie — the assortment of homemade pâtés, purchased cured hams and salamis — was blandly undistinguished on two early visits, though much improved on two later samplings.

Except for one order of onion soup that was almost inedibly salty, other soups sampled — a creamy, curried mussel soup and a heady consommé — were above average, as was the onion soup on a previous try.

Among other good dishes worth a visit are tiny whitebait crisply fried and available only occasionally, in season, and perfectly poached striped bass with a delicate cream and tomato sauce Dugleré. Not so the rubbery, leaden main course quenelles in a cream sauce so starchy it formed a cracked film before it could be eaten, nor fillets of sole amandine so overcooked and drowned in a lake of burned butter that it was difficult to pick morsels up on a fork. Frogs' legs were more acceptable though far from the best I've had.

The roast meat plats du jour are among the more reliable choices. I had a creditable, if less than poetic, roast leg of pure white veal that rated a more distinctive sauce, and some sliced roast of beef sirloin — a little tough but richly and satisfyingly beefy. Duck, tried twice, might have been done in two different kitchens. The breast of duck, magret de canard, was tough and fibrous, having been too thickly sliced. But duck in a piquant cream and green-peppercorn sauce was glowingly plump, moist, crisp and altogether delicious.

One more winner, and perhaps the best dish I had in the entire six encounters, was a luncheon specialty of poached chicken gros sel, about as moist and tenderly poached as chicken could be, served with firm bright vegetables simmered in the chicken stock and with coarse salt. Chicken in a heady vinegar sauce is also far above average. And at dinner one night I was served a carefully braised squab mellowed by steamed salsify, not the least bit dry and very rich in flavor.

But also at lunch was a jarret of veal in a starchy, tasteless cream sauce and a paillard of beef that was acceptable, though insufficiently seared. A saddle of lamb, listed as a house specialty served for two, included in each portion one chop rosily rare as ordered, and one chop that was dry, tough and completely well done. The escalopes of salmon are dry and tasteless; thicker cuts are more successful.

Pastries are all second-rate, but soufflés flavored with raspberries or Grand Marnier are unbeatable. I had a Jekyll and Hyde experience with a house specialty, les crêpes "ma pomme," crepes filled with sautéed apple slices and flambéed with brandy and liqueurs. One Saturday night it took the kitchen two tries to come up with usable crepes, but even those burned to the chafing dish, and later stuck to the palate, their filling reduced almost to applesauce. But, lo and behold, on another visit this dessert came out as sheer perfection — light, durable crepes, firm yet tender apples, a caramelized sauce the color of honey. Pretty petits fours accompanied dessert; only the glazed fruits had any real flavor, although the baked miniatures were crisp and habit-forming despite their blandness.

La Chaumière

★

310 West Fourth Street, between Bank and Twelfth Streets, 741-3374.

Atmosphere: Intimate, pleasant and relaxed French country setting with good acoustics. Tables are uncomfortable for parties of more than four; service is good, if somewhat strained.

Recommended dishes: Snails, beignets of salmon, string bean and mushroom salad, entrecôte, grilled leg of lamb, veal chop, duck, vanilla ice cream with strawberries, iced cake with hot chocolate sauce, lemon meringue cake.

Price range: Moderately expensive

Credit cards: American Express, Visa, MasterCard and Diners Club.

Hours: Dinner, Sundays through Thursdays, 5 P.M. to midnight, Fridays and Saturdays, 5 P.M. to 1 A.M.

Reservations: Necessary.

La Chaumière has a snug, friendly, provincial charm, a limited but interesting French menu with English translations, a casually dressed young staff that is just a little tense and prices that are fairly moderate by today's standards. It has existed quietly and successfully as a Village bistro since its opening in 1972. Recently remodeled, the bar section is a sort of cafe, with a limited menu made up of appetizers.

The food is neither startlingly original nor breathtakingly delicious. But almost everything is carefully cooked, well seasoned and satisfying. Sauces are especially subtle and balanced and are the strong point in the kitchen. A mustardy vinaigrette dressing lends cool pungency to such appetizers as the string bean and mushroom salad and the artichoke, served just a little too cold. That same flaw dissipated the flavor of the slightly dry country pâté, generously served in an individual terrine. Snails in parsley-flecked garlic butter were excellent and so was the puffy onion quiche in a crisp and buttery crust. A creditable French onion soup arrived tepid and was almost completely absorbed by the heavy slice of toasted bread under the glazed cheese crown.

The only fish I tried was the beignets of salmon, crisply fried and served with a sorrel sauce, an altogether satisfying dish.

An ice-cream scoop of parsley butter did wonders for the entrecôte, a tender and rose-red prime shell steak, and a thick slice of leg of lamb, grilled rare with Provençale herbs, was even better than the steak. Duck was crisp, moist and tender, and the burnished orange sauce with it was one of the few that was not sticky-sweet.

Medaillons of veal were overly sweetened by an apple and Calvados sauce. A sautéed veal chop chausseur in a delicate sauce that included shallots, tarragon, tomato and cognac turned out to be far better.

The only worthwhile desserts were the chocolate ice cream cake with hot, dark and bitter chocolate sauce, the vanilla ice cream with strawberries and the lemon meringue cake. The apple tart was limp and sticky-sweet, the chocolate mousse lacked texture and richness, and the strawberries were virtually drowned in a caustic dose of Cointreau.

La Côte Basque
★ ★ ★

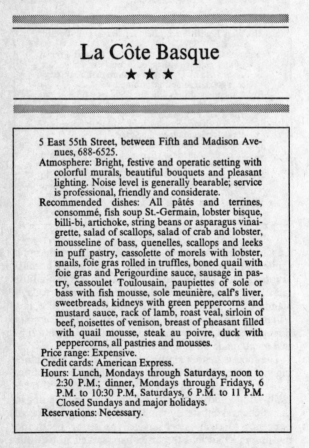

5 East 55th Street, between Fifth and Madison Avenues, 688-6525.

Atmosphere: Bright, festive and operatic setting with colorful murals, beautiful bouquets and pleasant lighting. Noise level is generally bearable; service is professional, friendly and considerate.

Recommended dishes: All pâtés and terrines, consommé, fish soup St.-Germain, lobster bisque, billi-bi, artichoke, string beans or asparagus vinaigrette, salad of scallops, salad of crab and lobster, mousseline of bass, quenelles, scallops and leeks in puff pastry, cassolette of morels with lobster, snails, foie gras rolled in truffles, boned quail with foie gras and Perigourdine sauce, sausage in pastry, cassoulet Toulousain, paupiettes of sole or bass with fish mousse, sole meunière, calf's liver, sweetbreads, kidneys with green peppercorns and mustard sauce, rack of lamb, roast veal, sirloin of beef, noisettes of venison, breast of pheasant filled with quail mousse, steak au poivre, duck with peppercorns, all pastries and mousses.

Price range: Expensive.

Credit cards: American Express.

Hours: Lunch, Mondays through Saturdays, noon to 2:30 P.M.; dinner, Mondays through Fridays, 6 P.M. to 10:30 P.M, Saturdays, 6 P.M. to 11 P.M. Closed Sundays and major holidays.

Reservations: Necessary.

As though it were not difficult enough to keep his first restaurant, Le Lavandou, operating at a consistent two-star level through the years, Jean Jacques Rachou, the chef-owner, bought La Côte Basque in the spring of 1980. Almost immediately he brought that much-neglected culinary landmark up to the same rating and soon managed to correct so many of the early shortcomings that La Côte Basque merits three stars.

Excellent it surely is, and festive, too, with fanciful murals of Basque scenes glimpsed through stage-set windows. The décor, which is a refurbished rendition of the dining rooms created for Henri Soulé when he opened this restaurant in 1958, would be considered corny by many designers. But with red banquettes, gorgeous floral arrangements and pleasant lighting, the overall effect is as exhilarating as Christmas. Because tables in the back dining room are a bit too close together the noise level at peak hours can be distracting, but less so than at comparable places in town. The dining room staff is friendly, gracious and professional. Only occasionally is an unknown customer treated indifferently.

The most marked improvement has been with the desserts and pastries, now made by Jean Pierre Le Masson, but that is not the only category for which congratulations are in order. Even the pâtés and terrines of fish, game, meat and poultry that were so good right from the start now have added subtleties. The terrine of salmon with sole is flecked with fresh herbs or the slimmest string beans. Pistachio- or pepper-studded pâtés of duck or game and the fresh foie gras rolled in minced black truffles and served in a basket of puff pastry are not only delicate but also stunning. The same description applies to the airy pike quenelles as main course or appetizer, the dainty, fez-shaped mounds of bass mousseline verdant with herbs and the appetizer salad of sliced sea scallops in crème fraîche with a touch of Ricard liqueur and sections of pink grapefruit.

Mr. Rachou has long been known for his lavish garnishes, but they now seem to be more delicate, which is another improvement. A combination of three sauces is worked into sprays of flowers for appetizers such as the puff pastry casing filled with poached scallops and leeks or the ragout of lobster with morels, or for main courses such as paupiettes of sole or bass filled with lobster or fish mousse.

A satiny vinaigrette dressing for salads brings life to such first courses as string beans, asparagus or the artichoke, which is served with its petals fanned out in circles around the sliced base. Norwegian salmon is sometimes excellent but twice had a medicinal flavor caused by heavy smoking.

Escargots Méridionale had just the right overtones of herbs and garlic. A novel and successful appetizer at lunch is the small, rough-textured garlic saucisson baked in puff pastry and served whole with oily, parsley-flecked French potato salad. Prosciutto is as impeccable as other ingredients here, and not even the quiches and céleri rémoulade are taken for granted. They get the special attention that makes the diner appreciate them anew.

Game appetizers and main courses are braised to tender perfection. The kitchen is equally skillful with such birds as the boned quail filled with foie gras and sweetbreads adrift in sauce Perigourdine, the pheasant breast filled with quail mousse and with the noisettes of venison grand veneur.

There are excellent soups at La Côte Basque, including a bracing golden consommé, the creamed pea soup St.-Germain, hot billi-bi full of mussels and two soups that crackle with bright shellfish flavor: a lobster bisque and a Marseilles-style fish soup.

As for the appetizers, all rolled paupiettes of fish with seafood mousse fillings are worth trying, but lobster can be tough. Perhaps the only real failure among dishes we tried was the sole meunière, overcooked in butter that had gone black and smothered in slightly bitter mushrooms. Another time, however, it was impeccably sautéed and, fortunately, mushrooms were withheld.

Pepper sauces all have just the right sting, whether they accompany veal kidneys, lean and tender duck or the steak au poivre. Had the generous, beefy steak not been served medium when ordered rare, it would have been perfect. But nothing less than perfect is the way to describe the thyme-and-garlic-scented rack of lamb that magically stays rose-red right to the edges of each slice. Roast veal and beef are close seconds to the lamb.

Although the noisettes of veal were delicately tender, they needed a more flavorful garnish than steamed cucumbers. Calf's liver with shallots, and sweetbreads with wild mushrooms are excellent choices at lunch. Vegetable garnishes taste as good as they look. Sauce Perigourdine is relied on too often, when lighter, herbaceous alternatives would be more suitable.

Soufflés, oddly enough, make up the only dessert category that seems to have declined. They are acceptable, if bland, and the elusive flavor of pear soufflé demands a more subtle sauce than chocolate. Nevertheless, there are still about a dozen beautiful temptations, none more successful than the velvety chocolate and chestnut ganache. Apple slices in the tarte Normande are topped with baked custard and caramelized sugar. All fruit tarts, such as the kiwi with banana and the plum, are superb. So are the oeufs à la neige, the gâteau de riz, the chocolate and mocha dacquoise, the charlottes with raspberry or vanilla and bitter-almond cream, and the Grand Marnier and chocolate mousses.

Amid such culinary splendors, a rather dull cheese platter, teabag tea and instant decaffinated coffee are inexcusable lapses. Captains should state prices for the daily specials not on the menu.

Selections on the wine list are carefully orchestrated to include typical and classic choices from each region, and in almost every case a range of vintages allows for a range of prices.

La Coupole
Poor

2 Park Avenue, entrance on 32nd Street, between Park and Madison Avenues, 696-0100.

Atmosphere: Stunning Art Deco reproduction of Paris brasserie; noisy and drafty; staff is confused and inefficient.

Recommended dishes: Cream of mushroom soup, quiche Lorraine, grilled chicken, mussels in poulette sauce, almond torte, bombe pralinée, kiwi tart.

Price range: Moderately expensive.

Credit cards: All major credit cards.

Hours: Lunch, 11:30 A.M. to 6 P.M.; dinner, 6 P.M. to 2 A.M. Open seven days.

Reservations: Recommended.

By now, anyone who cares must know that La Coupole is a line-for-line copy of the handsome Parisian brasserie of the same name. Jean Denoyer (owner of La Golue) and Jean Manuel Rozan operate the New York look-alike, and they borrowed interior Art Deco design elements, the china and the menu with the permission and cooperation of the management of the renowned meeting place on the Boulevard Montparnasse. What they should have borrowed, however, were the kitchen and dining room staffs. After a steady stream of publicity that has drawn a huge, amusingly costumed crowd, La Coupole is turning out badly prepared food that is a perfect match for the inept service.

The poor management becomes obvious right at the threshhold, where a variety of problems can occur. Your reservation may not be on the book at all. Or if it is there, you might be made to wait for fifteen to forty-five minutes. A third and recurrent possibility is that the man or woman at the desk may be on the phone, not only finishing a call but making and receiving others without even a nod to waiting customers. A line of guests often backs up at the door, crowding those already seated at uncomfortable tables near the checkroom, where low clothespoles keep coats resting on the floor.

Red velvet banquettes are too low for comfort and tables skid on the slippery tile floor; many are in the paths of chilling drafts. Each table seems to have three waiters who rarely communicate, so diners are asked the same questions several times, and no one knows who gets what when food is delivered. Meanwhile, busboys pour water into glasses of Perrier, remove clean silver, leaving the soiled, and take away condiments before the food is finished.

The menu itself is in the best brasserie tradition, listing light, heavy and in-between choices well suited to all hours. It is especially disappointing then to realize just how bad most of the food is. Twice I had oysters that had been opened hours before they were served, so that some were spoiled while others had dried to the shell. Crab meat in a salad at lunch was so far past its prime that it smelled like tuna fish. At one dinner the leaves of an undercooked artichoke could hardly be wrenched from their base, and the dressing was made with a musty, no-name oil flecked with acidic pimentos. At lunch, another and slightly better artichoke was served with bland vinaigrette dressing.

Pâté may be acceptable or cold and greasy, smoked trout had a strong medicinal aftertaste, and snails were so crusty and dried out that I was happy that six arrived instead of the twelve ordered. Presliced, darkly dry prosciutto was as poor as a tasteless jambon persillé. Though of good quality, smoked salmon was meagerly portioned.

Onion soup was stale one night and bitterly salty on another. An otherwise good cream of pea soup was served tepid. Of four soups tried, cream of mushroom alone can be recommended.

The only really decent main courses included a quiche Lorraine, mussels in an egg-enriched poulette sauce, and grilled chicken. Pot au feu was fair, with good beef in an oversalted broth.

All other dishes failed, from a leaden omelet to choucroute garni and a cassoulet that seemed made of canned beans stirred through with washed-out meats and sauce. Brown sauces on coq au vin and sweetbreads were dead ringers for institutional brown gravy spiked at the last moment with overdoses of wine. The expensive steaks, gigot and rack of lamb were tough, gray and much like steam-table meats. Calf's liver had the mushy interior that results from freezing, and all fish was stale, overcooked and tasteless. A salade Niçoise seemed to have been made up hours in advance and held in the refrigerator, and so did cold roast chicken.

Desserts at La Coupole offered some bright spots, especially a fine ice-cream bombe with layerings of nut praline and a spongy almond torte. Crème caramel was very good at lunch, very bad at dinner. A pear in red wine with cream was impossible to extricate from the narrow, topple-prone wine goblet into which it had been wedged, and assorted cheeses were lifeless and served ice cold.

Lady Astor's

★

430 Lafayette Street, between Astor Place and Fourth
Street, 228-7888.

Atmosphere: Romantic, amusing gaslight-era reproduction that is pleasantly threadbare; service is
polite and well meaning but often slow.

Recommended dishes: Caesar salad, snails, sautéed
mushrooms, artichoke, onion soup, avocado with
chicken salad, prime ribs of beef (if rare), breast of
chicken Provençal, fillet of chicken sautéed in
white wine, calf's liver, rococo chocolate cake.

Price range: Moderate.

Credit cards: Not accepted, but personal checks are
taken when accompanied by a major credit card.

Hours: Dinner, Sundays through Thursdays, 5 P.M. to
11 P.M., Fridays and Saturdays, 5 P.M. to midnight.

Reservations: Recommended.

Directly across from the Public Theater, Lady Astor's
comes as something of a surprise with a seamy, drab ex-
terior hiding an amusing and lavish reproduction of a
gaslight-era sporting house. Heavy velvet hangings,
crystal chandeliers and huge gilt mirrors make this a
restful and engaging setting that somehow suggests a little girl dressed up in grandiose old clothes that she
found in the family attic. Service is friendly, but at
times the young and good-natured help is careless about
bringing utensils. The kitchen can be slow, but an effort
is made to speed things up when guests say they are
going to the theater. Allow about an hour and a half if
you plan to have a full three-course meal.

The food at Lady Astor's is far from brilliant, but it is
pleasantly serviceable, and the menu includes light
choices such as sandwiches and salads as well as more
substantial steaks. It also includes hamburgers, but they
are so small and dry that it is best not to consider them.
High points are three chicken dishes — a boneless
breast of chicken smothered under a Provençal mélange
of tomatoes and zucchini, a moist, white-wine-and-but-
ter-flavored fillet of chicken and a half avocado filled
with a generous portion of luscious, dill-scented chicken
salad.

Good, if slightly less so, were sautéed calf's liver
topped with golden-brown garlic cracklings, and roast
prime ribs of beef, fine if they are served rare but dull if
overcooked or held too long under a heat lamp. New
potatoes in their jackets were roasted to crunchy perfection, just right with the roast beef. Chateaubriand au
poivre was delicious, but the tiny portion was much
overpriced. Sirloin steak, though a little tough, had a
good beefy flavor and was accompanied by corn on the
cob and snow peas. The worst main course was fillet of
sole so smelly that it could not have been fresh and so
badly cooked that it turned watery. Eggs Benedict were

cold, and their hollandaise sauce lacked a fresh lemon flavor; so did the green salad.

Like main courses, appetizers are decent. The most engaging proved to be a steamed artichoke in an emerald-green parsley and garlic-butter sauce. That sauce also did well by snails in mushroom caps, as well as by plain meaty sautéed mushrooms. Onion soup had a good rich flavor, but croutons, instead of a larger piece of toast, disintegrated rapidly and made the soup mushy. Caesar salad needed fresh lemon juice and sharper cheese, but it was refreshing nonetheless.

Mousselike rococo chocolate cake was far better than an overwet carrot cake and an insipidly sweet and soggy orange, chocolate Grimble torte. Plum pudding with a butter-rum sauce improved with whipped cream, which is available on request.

Lady Astor's might not be worth a trip for its own sake, but it is a handy option when visiting the area.

La Folie
★ ★

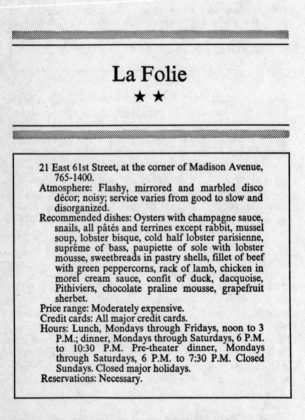

21 East 61st Street, at the corner of Madison Avenue, 765-1400.
Atmosphere: Flashy, mirrored and marbled disco décor; noisy; service varies from good to slow and disorganized.
Recommended dishes: Oysters with champagne sauce, snails, all pâtés and terrines except rabbit, mussel soup, lobster bisque, cold half lobster parisienne, suprême of bass, paupiette of sole with lobster mousse, sweetbreads in pastry shells, fillet of beef with green peppercorns, rack of lamb, chicken in morel cream sauce, confit of duck, dacquoise, Pithiviers, chocolate praline mousse, grapefruit sherbet.
Price range: Moderately expensive.
Credit cards: All major credit cards.
Hours: Lunch, Mondays through Fridays, noon to 3 P.M.; dinner, Mondays through Saturdays, 6 P.M. to 10:30 P.M. Pre-theater dinner, Mondays through Saturdays, 6 P.M. to 7:30 P.M. Closed Sundays. Closed major holidays.
Reservations: Necessary.

If ever there was a restaurant that had a décor and tone that belied its food, it is La Folie in the Carlton House. Formerly a discothèque, its décor is far more suitable to that function than to a restaurant that rates the impressive talents of Bernard Norget, who previously served as a chef at the Connaught in London. All is a glitter of mirrors, and there are so many types of inlaid marble that it makes the place look like the sample showroom of the Marble Institute.

Seats in the pink marble ladies' room are clear Plexiglas, and a long-lash eye is painted at the bottom of each bowl. The big curvy bar outside has as its base dozens of pairs of mannequin feet, each wearing a different pair of shoes. Completing the garish interior are swirls of stained glass and paintings so bad they wouldn't even be accepted in the Washington Square outdoor art show. Service, although courteous and considerate, is often slow and disorganized.

The bar area is a fairly comfortable cocktail lounge and dining room where caviar and blini are served during cocktail time at moderate prices. The disco action has been replaced by "touch dancing" after 10:30 P.M., Wednesdays through Saturdays. Even so, hard surfaces make for maximum noisiness almost everywhere in the place, even when the rooms are only half full.

Nevertheless, La Folie still has many dishes worth the attention of serious eaters. Among the appetizers that have remained excellent since the restaurant's opening are tender snails seasoned with parsley, garlic and shallots, then baked in individual timbales, each with a puff-pastry cap; oysters gratinéed in a champagne cream sauce and topped with caviar, and two fragrant and subtle pâtés — one a country pâté of pork, pork liver, cream, garlic, brandy and vermouth, and the other a terrine of duck perfumed with Armagnac. A rabbit terrine was too cold to evaluate. A light puff pastry blanketed with creamed scallops was also an interesting, if overwhelming, first course. Also offered is a satiny cream of mussel soup mellowed with saffron and thickened with julienne strips of vegetables, but the portion is so large and the soup so rich that it would be barely possible to eat another course if you finished it all. The same is true of the equally good, rose-pink lobster bisque (which should be served hotter than it was when I tried it).

Less successful hors d'oeuvres included a combination of slightly dry and tough shrimp in a cream sauce overpowered by Pernod and a tasteless gratin of mussels listed as "la mouclade du Maine." Cold half lobster had a dawn-pink sauce and a filling of bright, cool vegetables.

It would be hard to fault the suprême of bass in a Chablis velouté sauce with fresh tomato, or the tender, snowy chicken or veal, both graced with a perfect sauce of butter, cream and morels. The heart of a beef fillet, rare as ordered and heightened by a top and bottom crust of black and green peppercorns, was served with potatoes amandine — crisply fried puffs of mashed potatoes and sliced almonds, an unusual and somewhat sensational combination.

Confit de canard, duck melted and perserved in its own drippings, is expertly roasted at La Folie, although it is a main course best left to the fall and winter months.

Provençale herbs lent their airy perfumes to a rack of lamb served perfectly pink.

Paupiettes of sole enveloped an airy lobster mousse, and sweatbreads, though mellow and delicious in their winy sauce, arrived in two super-domes of puff pastry; flaky and butter-gilded though the pastry was, it proved too much to eat.

Desserts have declined since the earliest days here, and even the homemade sherbets and ice creams are less interesting, although the grapefruit sherbet remains exceptional. The flaky pastry Pithiviers filled with almond paste, and a crunchy dacquoise layered with mocha butter cream are also good. Chocolate praline mousse almost makes up for the absence of the ethereal chocolate ice cream that used to be offered.

An exceptionally good buy at La Folie is the moderately priced pre-theater dinner available from 6 P.M. to 7:30 P.M. Mondays through Saturdays. The menu is large and the choice excellent, and you certainly don't have to go to the theater to qualify for it.

La Gauloise
★ ★

502 Avenue of the Americas, between 12th and 13th Streets, 691-1363.
Atmosphere: Handsome, pleasant brasserie-cafe setting; excellent service.
Recommended dishes: All appetizers, onion soup, cream of mussel soup, mousse of scallops, capelli d'angelo with caviar, cassoulet, choucroute garni, scallops sautéed with herbs, venison with wild mushrooms, medaillons of veal forestière, entrecôte au poivre, calf's liver with shallots, eggs Benedict, omelet fines herbes, all desserts except apple tart and Brie.
Price range: Moderately expensive.
Credit cards: All major credit cards.
Hours: Lunch, Mondays through Fridays, noon to 3 P.M.; dinner, seven days, 5:45 P.M. to 11:30 P.M. Brunch, Saturdays, noon to 3 P.M., Sundays, noon to 4 P.M. Open on Thanksgiving Day.
Reservations: Necessary.

Good to better is the direction devoutly to be wished for, and it is clearly the direction of things at La Gauloise, an altogether handsome and engaging cafe-brasserie that has been operating for just a little over two years. With its mirrored panels, dark-wood trim, Art Deco lighting fixtures and capacious banquettes and chairs, this charming restaurant from the first offered pleasant and decent food, although service was somewhat brash.

But a change for the better was clearly evident on later visits. The owners, Camille Dulac and Jacques Alliman, the latter from Alsace, must be credited with more polished, professional and efficient service and even better food.

As is so often the case these days, appetizers make up the best course, and those at La Gauloise are distinguished by their bright freshness and tantalizing flavor counterpoints. Vegetables, such as leeks, slim asparagus and string beans, sparkle in a pungent vinaigrette dressing. Snails are meltingly tender in their verdant herb-butter sauce, and tiny troutlings, crisply fried and served with a mustardy hollandaise sauce, are as remarkable as the pâtés and the coarse and rich saucisson chaud, with its warm, parsley-and-onion-flavored potato salad. Mushrooms à la grecque, in a cool, spicy tomato sauce, plump coral mussels ravigotte and a cloudlike mousse of scallops, served hot in a rose-pink Nantua-style sauce satisfy enough to be main courses, while a creamy mussel soup arrived hot, gently briny and soul-soothing. There is also a delicate pasta, capelli d'angelo with a pale blond caviar-butter sauce.

Grilled, sautéed and poached fish are acceptable, but not up to the excellence of the snowy and tender sautéed sea scallops, aromatic with herbs.

Entrecôte au poivre profits from a generous crunch of black pepper, all enriched with a velvety brown sauce. Noisettes of venison with wild mushrooms and spätzle, a seasonal special, could hardly have been improved on. Brochette of lamb was among the few disappointments, along with magret de canard — the first because the chunks of lamb varied in quality from tender to tough, the second because it was overdone on two tries, although otherwise delicious. Unless it is served rare, the duck breast meat becomes tough. Similarly, thin slices of salmon were dried out and relatively tasteless, although their accompaniment of sautéed spinach and tomato sparkled with flavor. Cassoulet, a Sunday specialty, proved to be one of the better versions around, firm but tender beans under a crusty topping, studded with garlicky sausage and chunks of duck and lamb. The Wednesday feature is choucroute garni, and the brightly blond sauerkraut with an almost crunchy crinkle was perfection; the pink and delicate smoked pork, bacon and sausages did the choucroute justice.

Only a limp and lardy apple tart and an unripe Brie marred the dessert selection. A lush, creamy chocolate marquise, an ice cream bombe, mellow with praline, and an inspired parfait, sunny with mandarin orange juice and topped with caramelized orange rind, proved excellent. So did the profiteroles with a bittersweet hot fudge sauce and oeufs à la neige, also accented by caramelized orange rind.

There are some interesting hors d'oeuvres passed at the bar in the evening — tiny quiches, periwinkles and sometimes the fried troutlings. Lunch is a somewhat quieter experience than dinner at La Gauloise, but at either meal, one has a sense of being very well cared for. At both lunch and brunch, peppery onion soup, the impeccable eggs Benedict and omelet fines herbes are excellent choices.

La Goulue

★

---

28 East 70th Street, between Madison and Park Avenues, 988-8169.

Atmosphere: Handsome, turn-of-the-century Parisian brasserie setting; service is efficient and polite but distracted.

Recommended dishes: Mushrooms à la grecque, céleri rémoulade, potage St.-Germain, smoked trout, moules marinières, chicken Portugaise, roast baby chicken, kidneys Dijonnaise, bass Goulue, duck with apples, bombe pralinée, crème caramel.

Price range: Moderately expensive.

Credit cards: American Express, MasterCard, Visa and Diners Club.

Hours: Lunch, Mondays through Saturdays, noon to 3 P.M.; dinner, Mondays through Saturdays, 6 P.M. to 11 P.M. Closed Sundays and major holidays.

Reservations: Necessary.

With its handsome antique interior, its dark wood paneling and art nouveau trimmings, La Goulue is a pleasant reminder of the Brasserie Lipp in Paris, but ever since it opened about ten years ago, it has been plagued by unevenness. Though it was formerly rated two stars, the kitchen's performance has again declined.

The restaurant is as popular as ever, both at lunch and dinner, with art dealers and residents of the surrounding area in spite of the erratic quality. The unevenness is evident right from the start — in the appetizers. Crunchy céleri rémoulade and silky mushrooms à la grecque can be excellent, but the terrine de canard turns out to be a grainy, mealy pâté almost devoid of flavor, especially because it is served ice cold. The artichoke vinaigrette also suffers from a long stay in the refrigerator, and the aspic around the oeufs en gelée is heavy and rubbery. Smoked trout at one dinner was acceptable, but the snails needed more garlic. At lunch one of the best first courses is the moules marinières — briny, fresh mussels perfectly steamed in a garlic and white wine broth.

Main courses can be discouraging at first glance, because the plates are overloaded. To be served half a duck, wild rice, a huge sheaf of broccoli and a grilled half tomato on the same plate is to be given the impossible task of tackling the duck without scattering food all over the tablecloth. The same can be said of the chicken Portugaise and a whole baby chicken, although it was delicious in a lightly browned butter and herb sauce. The chicken Portugaise had not sufficiently absorbed its savory, light tomato sauce, and the duck, though good, was dried out on top because the apple slices over it were too heavily caramelized. Bass Goulue, in a light, white wine sauce, has been consistently dependable. The saddle of lamb and the entrecôte with mushrooms could have been dished out of any hotel kitchen, and the unsalted broccoli appeared to have done time in a steam table.

Only the ice cream bombe with its accents of praline and the gentle crème caramel are worthwhile desserts. Wines are greatly overpriced. Service in this noisy setting is prompt, professional and polite, but distracted.

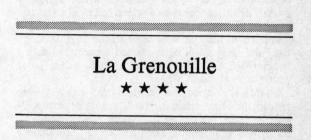

La Grenouille
★ ★ ★ ★

3 East 52nd Street, between Fifth and Madison Avenues, 752-1495.
Atmosphere: Lavishly beautiful and opulent dining rooms with glorious floral arrangements and excellent lighting; tables are jammed together and noise level is high. Service can be excellent but is sometimes indifferent.
Recommended dishes: All cold appetizers, hot saucisson with French potato salad, clams Corsini, all soups, frogs' legs Provençale, grilled Dover sole, poached salmon, quenelles, lobster Nantua, bay scallops à la nage, roast veal, roast pork, braised chicken with tarragon, poached chicken, roasted duck, calf's liver Bercy, Alan King's veal chop, all desserts and soufflés.
Price range: Expensive.
Credit cards: American Express and Diners Club.
Hours: Lunch, Mondays through Saturdays, noon to 2 P.M.; dinner, Mondays through Saturdays, 6 P.M. to 10 P.M. Closed Sundays and generally in August.
Reservations: Necessary.

With its sparkling mirrors reflecting spring-green walls, lipstick-red banquettes and the glorious, impressionistic floral bouquets, La Grenouille is clearly the most stylish and graceful of the city's four-star restaurants. Small wonder that it has become the favorite and most flattering setting for members of the high-fashion world. Charles Masson, once maître d'hôtel at Henri Soulé's Pavillon, opened La Grenouille eighteen years ago, and since his death in 1975 it has been coolly, charmingly and efficiently run by his widow, Gisèle, and their son, Charles, who, among other tasks, has taken over the arrangement of the flowers that cost about $75,000 a year. André Joanlanne, the chef for the last fifteen years, is functioning at peak performance, judging by recent visits.

Neither the lunch nor the dinner menu is large — each offers no more than a dozen main courses; yet each always seems to present an embarrassment of choice, so well-balanced and enticing are the possibilities.

At both meals there is a sparkling and totally irresistible assortment of cold appetizers, available singly or in a grand assortment. Among regular offerings are the crunchy cucumbers in a gentling, light cream dressing, shoestring-slim haricots verts or asparagus tips only occasionally less crisp than they should be, chunks of firm, satiny, cold striped bass, impeccable shrimp in a pink dressing and a terrine de campagne and pâté du chef that manage to be lusty and delicate all at once.

Hot saucisson with a soothing, warm French potato salad was perfect, and so were oeufs en gelée, the poached eggs with runny yolks caught in pale amber aspic. The littleneck clams Corsini, baked in a parsley-garlic-butter and white-wine sauce, made one long for a small nest of silky pasta to catch all the fragrant sauce. Only the saucisson d'Arles seemed more pallid than I remembered and the prosciutto, though decent, paled beside other choices.

Soups are wondrous concoctions, whether one chooses the briny, creamy hot billi-bi with its plump, roseate mussels, the potage St.-Germain, which must be the world's best rendition of that puréed pea soup, the lobster bisque mellowed with tarragon and cognac, or the gazpacho with minced raw vegetables served on the side.

Les grenouilles Provençales are always on the menu, as might be expected. Rarely in this country will you find frogs' legs that are tinier or more immaculately sautéed and seasoned. Dover sole is grilled to golden succulence and though its mustard sauce would profit from more bite, the combination as served is hard to beat. Other excellent fish specialties include, at lunch, moist poached salmon, sharpened by a verdant tarragon, basil, and mild-vinegar sauce, airy quenelles and a lobster Nantua that is a marvel of subtle spicing.

In season, bay scallops à la nage are served at lunch, poached in a court bouillon that is glossed with heavy cream, all set off by wisps of carrots and celery to make a dish I have difficulty resisting whenever it is available. And poached chicken fricasee, also at midday, is a miracle of pearly moistness.

A leg of veal as a plat du jour had to be the snowiest, most tender example of that meat extant, and the purée of carrots and pork and sage-stuffed zucchini served with it were worthy complements. Le poulet de grain poêlé à l'estragon proved to be succulently moist braised chicken perfumed with tarragon, and steak au poivre, though somewhat less inspired, was far above average. Thin, sautéed calf's liver Bercy with shallot butter, and nut-brown roasted duck garnished with fruits, remain among the house masterpieces.

Disappointments were veal kidneys that were too thinly sliced and virtually drowned in a soupy mustard-cream sauce. The veal Orloff, despite a good creamed duxelles of mushrooms, was a failure because of the dried-out toughness of the meat. There is also a slight tendency here to oversalt sauces.

All desserts can be recommended. The oeufs à la neige is consistently the best in the city, and so is the dark, rich chocolate mousse. Raspberries with cloudlets of Grand Marnier sauce, a velvety chocolate cake touched with orange flavor and dusted with cocoa, and newer creations such as peach charlotte and strawberry whipped-cream cake with a froth of banana purée are all superb. So are the lofty soufflés, here miraculously available in half-and-half combinations of flavors.

Amid all this elegance, only the service is occasionally flawed, either by an overbearing maître d'hôtel who takes unknowns by the elbow and literally pushes them to the bar when he wants them to wait there, or an instrusively obsequious captain who interrupts conversations with his unnecessary "Bon appetit" and "Is everything all right?" A waiter brings sherbet long after other desserts have been served from the wagon because, he says, sherbet, like coffee, comes from the kitchen and why should he make two trips? Although high-fashion regulars sit in the front room, the back room always seemed more comfortable to me. Parties larger than six cannot be comfortably accommodated here, and even that number crowds the largest tables.

La Louisiana
★

132 Lexington Avenue, between 28th and 29th Streets, 686-3959.
Atmosphere: Small, attractive, but cramped and noisy dining room; service is friendly and efficient.
Recommended dishes: Scallops Rockefeller, gumbo, pickled Gulf shrimp, boudin, catfish, fried chicken, Southern-fried steak, roast duck, lamb chops, pecan pie, chocolate almond torte, blackberry pie, strawberries.
Price range: Moderately expensive.
Credit cards: None, but checks written on New York banks are accepted.
Hours: Dinner, Mondays through Thursdays, 6 P.M. to 11 P.M., Fridays and Saturdays, 6 P.M. to 11:45 P.M. Closed Sundays and most major holidays.
Reservations: Necessary.

Among the cuisines virtually missing from the New York menu, none would be more welcome than Louisiana's, for surely the rich and heady specialties of Cajun and Creole kitchens make up this country's most original and best regional food. Several years ago, Abe de la Houssaye, a native of Breaux Bridge in Cajun country, began to fill the culinary gap somewhat at his small and polished restaurant, La Louisiana. He combined highly stylized versions of Louisiana dishes and more-or-less nouvelle cuisine interpretations of Continental food with results that were rated fair but promising when first reviewed. Later visits indicate that early optimism was well placed, for La Louisiana has improved to a one-star rating.

Almost from the start, a young and stylish crowd began to back up at the small bar or sit on the window ledge and suffer (or perhaps enjoy) head-splitting noise compounded by background music, waiting their turn in the cramped but softly glowing dining room where walls are the deep creamy coral color of crayfish bisque.

The best dishes here are the Louisiana specialties that are not prepared well anywhere else in the city even though the chef-owner still exhibits a penchant for misplaced sweetness. Who, for example, really wants raisin-studded pumpernickel rolls with a mellow, chicken-okra gumbo or with a sophsticated appetizer such as the scallops Rockefeller, baked with spinach and delicately scented with Pernod? Nor do those rolls help the gentle, warm and meaty pork and calf's liver sausage called boudin, or the spicy pickled Gulf shrimp tossed with mushrooms.

Not all the first courses are as successful as those already mentioned. A crayfish bisque lacked the crackling bite this pungent crustacean should add, and the smoked chicken was dry and bland.

Frying is beautifully, greaselessly accomplished, whether for the thick fillets of fresh catfish with a verdant tartar sauce or for the boned half chicken with its crisply ruffled breading accented by honey butter and Creole mustard and cayenne sauce. A crunchy veneer of golden-brown flour sealed in the beefy juices of the Southern-fried steak.

Overgarnishing obscured the delicacy of tender, carefully sautéed calf's liver. Much the same could be said for the pork fillets, which were smothered in fruity sauce. Additional cloying sweetness came by way of apple butter on musty, greasy croutons served as a garnish. The half-moon, ravioli-style pasta, agnolotti, in basil tomato sauce was delicate and savory on earlier visits; on a later visit it was tepid and pasty.

Rum pecan pie and a velvety chocolate almond torte were delicious and would have been even better with sweet whipped cream instead of acidic crème fraîche, but that cream seemed just right for a beautiful purple-red blackberry tart and for the ripe, red strawberries burnished with brown sugar. A characterless, fresh peach tart and a cherry-filled brownie tart were mediocre. So was the chicory coffee blend, bitter enough but not thick enough to be in the Louisiana tradition.

La Petite Ferme

★

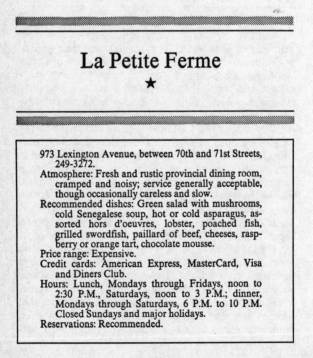

973 Lexington Avenue, between 70th and 71st Streets, 249-3272.

Atmosphere: Fresh and rustic provincial dining room, cramped and noisy; service generally acceptable, though occasionally careless and slow.

Recommended dishes: Green salad with mushrooms, cold Senegalese soup, hot or cold asparagus, assorted hors d'oeuvres, lobster, poached fish, grilled swordfish, paillard of beef, cheeses, raspberry or orange tart, chocolate mousse.

Price range: Expensive.

Credit cards: American Express, MasterCard, Visa and Diners Club.

Hours: Lunch, Mondays through Fridays, noon to 2:30 P.M., Saturdays, noon to 3 P.M.; dinner, Mondays through Saturdays, 6 P.M. to 10 P.M. Closed Sundays and major holidays.

Reservations: Recommended.

It has often been suggested that one should see a play early in its run because with repeated performances the cast loses its freshness and enthusiasm. Apparently that can also be true of a restaurant, judging by recent visits to La Petite Ferme. The bloom certainly seems to be off the performances of kitchen and dining-room staffs, and perhaps even of the management. Started as a pocket-size provincial restaurant in Greenwich Village about a dozen or so years ago, La Petite Ferme moved to this larger location in 1977, still under the close scrutiny of its owner, Charles Chevillot. The same array of brightly fresh and simple dishes was presented on a blackboard menu, and if the enlargement was accomplished at the expense of the original excellence, the food at this newer restaurant was worth two stars when originally reviewed. Simple floral bouquets, checked linen dish towels for napkins and a fresh country setting added to the charm and originality.

But as the owner divided his interests, first with Les Tournebroches at the Citicorp Center, then with an outpost on St. Martin in the Caribbean, his East Side restaurant suffered. Now, he seems to be trying to restore the original quality by staying on these premises. But though almost all the food is pleasantly acceptable and some of it is very good, La Petite Ferme is now worth going to only if one happens to be nearby.

Prices have soared, which also alters the perception of value. Promised acoustical improvements were never made, so the closely packed room is noisy. Anyone unfortunate enough to be seated under the stairway may have to fight off feathers drifting down from the cage of the mourning doves above and at the same time cope with the thundering herd of waiters running to and from the kitchen. Members of the dining room staff, which is sometimes pleasant and efficient, can be thoughtless, chatting among themselves while customers wait unacknowledged. A few occasionally wear dirty aprons, and others are unshaven.

Still, the brief blackboard menu offers some pleasantly simple food, beginning with an hors d'oeuvres assortment that included first-rate smoked trout, smoked salmon, vegetable salads and salami. The assortment was stale on only one occasion. A cold Senegalese soup, golden with curry, had been puréed with banana, a touch that added only the slightest counterpoint of sweetness plus a creamy texture. Nevertheless, a full portion was overrich as a first course. The mussels, which on earlier occasions were sparkling and sharp, arrived completely lackluster one evening, and a cold cucumber soup at lunch tasted of nothing at all. A sprightly, crisp green salad with raw mushrooms and a pungent vinaigrette dressing was refreshing as a first course, and the asparagus was suitably firm and green.

Poached fish such as halibut and coho salmon had the proper moistness and silky butter sauces, and a rose-pink Choron sauce did justice to pearly grilled swordfish. Grilled fillet of sole at lunch arrived dry and suspiciously fishy in smell and taste, but a young lobster could not have been more carefully steamed. Paillard of beef was well grilled, but veal sautéed with lemon was watery and bland. Vegetables are firm and bright, and cheeses in a large assortment are carefully chosen, with chèvres being the most distinguished.

At one lunch raspberry tart was apparently a leftover, judging by its mushy crust, but at dinner another sample had exactly the right butter-cookie crispness. Fresh orange slices in a satiny pastry cream, all on a buttery crust, made a lovely tart, and chocolate mousse was delicious if a little heavy on whipped cream,

House wines, bottled by the Chevillot family in Beaune, seemed to have less bouquet and depth than in the past.

La Petite Marmite
★

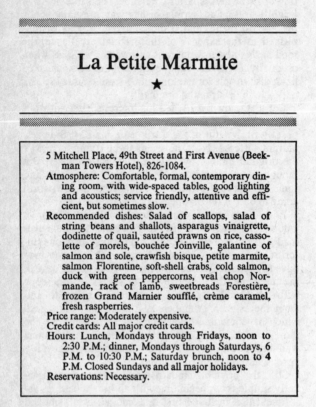

5 Mitchell Place, 49th Street and First Avenue (Beekman Towers Hotel), 826-1084.
Atmosphere: Comfortable, formal, contemporary dining room, with wide-spaced tables, good lighting and acoustics; service friendly, attentive and efficient, but sometimes slow.
Recommended dishes: Salad of scallops, salad of string beans and shallots, asparagus vinaigrette, dodinette of quail, sautéed prawns on rice, cassolette of morels, bouchée Joinville, galantine of salmon and sole, crawfish bisque, petite marmite, salmon Florentine, soft-shell crabs, cold salmon, duck with green peppercorns, veal chop Normande, rack of lamb, sweetbreads Forestière, frozen Grand Marnier soufflé, crème caramel, fresh raspberries.
Price range: Moderately expensive.
Credit cards: All major credit cards.
Hours: Lunch, Mondays through Fridays, noon to 2:30 P.M.; dinner, Mondays through Saturdays, 6 P.M. to 10:30 P.M.; Saturday brunch, noon to 4 P.M. Closed Sundays and all major holidays.
Reservations: Necessary.

Recently, Pascal Dirringer, formerly at La Gauloise in Greenwich Village, took over in the kitchen here to cook his way into partnership with Jacky Ruette, who has owned La Petite Marmite since 1968. With a more ambitious and expensive menu than the one at La Gauloise, but with some of the same specialties, Mr. Dirringer's performance is uneven, ranging from fair to very good, although at La Gauloise his cooking was well worth two stars.

The most important difference seems to be one of style and perhaps the lack of a strong rein on Mr. Dirringer's creativity. Sticking to simple preparations, such as slim French string beans or asparagus with a vinaigrette dressing, a cool salad of pearly bay scallops, cold poached salmon, delicately sautéed soft-shell crabs or rare-roasted rack of lamb, he displays his former skill. Marked capability is also exhibited in such soups as the heady, golden-brown beef-and-chicken broth flecked with meat, marrow and vegetables that inspired the restaurant's name — la petite marmite — and in a creamy coral bisque of crawfish.

Mr. Dirringer achieves very good results with near classics, such as an appetizer of crawfish in a Nantua sauce held in puff pastry (la bouchée Joinville), with cold boned and stuffed quail masked with topaz aspic (la dodinette de caille) and with a hot mousse or galantine of salmon and sole also offered in a velvety bisque-style sauce.

But by associating too freely, he is also capable of placing a blob of absolutely raw duck liver on a plate of otherwise decent charcuterie or of serving an absurdly small copper cassolette of snails and chanterelles much too heavily spiked with cognac. The same miniature cassolette was adequate in size, however, for fresh morels glossed with butter, shallots and parsley. And among the better appetizers there were also immaculately cold and sparkling littleneck and cherrystone clams, offered with a mignonette sauce of wine vinegar and red onions. But when served in an assortment of shellfish, the clams were in poor company with pallid mussels rémoulade and spongy crab meat.

Main courses display a similar lack of restraint. Such snowy, subtly flavored fish as French rouget and brill were overpowered — the first with heavy-handed doses of anchovies, garlicky tomatoes and salty olives, the second with not only a sauce Nantua, but also a thick purée of mushrooms. Many dishes were oversalted, and beautifully sautéed sweetbreads Forestière, although delicious, were too generously portioned, considering the complexity of flavors they presented. Far better choices include simple sautéed salmon Florentine on a bed of bright leaf spinach or prawns lightly sauced with butter and basil and served on rice. Sliced, rare breast of duck in a green peppercorn sauce was also a very good main course, if somewhat less impressive than the same dish at La Gauloise, and a veal chop Normande, soothed with a fragrant Calvados and a touch of cream, was rich and heady.

Medaillons of veal were overcooked and so stringy they might have been boiled, and both roast chicken with herbs and poached chicken with truffles were minimally acceptable.

Cakes and pastries are mediocre. Choose instead from the fairly good assortment of cheeses, or try the raspberries, crème caramel or frozen Grand Marnier soufflé. Hot soufflés were undistinguished and virtually unrisen.

Considering the courteous and accommodating staff, the widely-spaced tables and the felicitous lighting and acoustics, it is easy to understand why at both lunch and dinner this restaurant has a loyal following among neighboring United Nations delegates and residents of the Beekman Place area. Choose correctly, and you can have a thoroughly satisfying and delightful dinner.

La Ripaille

★

605 Hudson Street, between West 12th and Bethune Streets, 255-4406.

Atmosphere: Rustic, attractive French setting; service is friendly and efficient.

Recommended dishes: All cold vegetables vinaigrette, all salads (especially seafood), broccoli mousse, snails, mignonettes of beef au poivre, kidneys, sweetbreads, roast duck, roast veal, fruit tarts, berries with Grand Marnier cream, bombe pralinée.

Price range: Moderately expensive.

Credit cards: American Express, MasterCard and Visa.

Hours: Dinner, Mondays through Sundays, 6 P.M. to 11:30 P.M. Closed Sundays from May to November.

Reservations: Recommended, especially on weekends.

Ripaille, a sixteenth-century French word designating a feast amid an atmosphere of revelry and carousal, inspired both the name and the décor of La Ripaille, a charming, rustic and handsome little wood-beamed restaurant facing Abingdon Square in Greenwich Village. All chores are divided among the four young French owners — Patrick and Alain Laurent, who are brothers, and their wives, Theresa and Nelly. The women do the cooking, while their husbands manage the dining room that seats between thirty and thirty-five guests. The informal and felicitous setting makes for congenial, relaxed dining although the high noise level when the room is full can make conversation difficult.

Cooking has improved slightly since La Ripaille opened in 1980, but a few persistent flaws cause it to fall a little short of a two-star rating. Dishes are all carefully, honestly prepared from generally excellent ingredients, and the menu represents a well-balanced combination of nouvelle and traditional French specialties. The kitchen still tends to be a bit tentative with seasonings so that dishes lack a certain convincing authority, but most are satisfying and diverting.

Menus here change daily, and favorites are rotated. Some favorites sampled when this place first opened still appear on menus, among them the airy hot broccoli mousse with a lemon-butter sauce, snails in cream accented by a walnut purée and baked in ramekins, and a seafood salad in a sunny vinaigrette dressing. More recently I tried a terrine of scallops studded with bits of crisp vegetables and gentled with a green herb sauce, a house pâté that was lusty if a little too salty and fettuccine al pesto, the basil sauce achieving heady perfection although the pasta was too firmly al dente. Cold vegetables in vinaigrette sauce are also good first courses.

Main courses that were best when La Ripaille opened, and which have become standards on the menu, are the mignonettes of filet mignon with four peppers in a sheer cream sauce, the properly roseate kidneys with the brassy accents of Dijon mustard, and golden sautéed sweet breads in champagne sauce. Roast veal flavored with thyme and rosemary was itself tender, moist and delicious, although its cream and white-wine sauce was pallid. Beautifully cooked, pearly fresh paupiettes of sole needed a slightly thicker beurre blanc sauce, but it was hard to tell whether the sauce had simply been made too thin or had been diluted by juices from the fish. Lean, moist and savory duck that seemed to have been braised rather than roasted would have been better with fresh peas instead of canned. Odd that the French persist in thinking that canned petits pois are still acceptable ingredients when so much emphasis has been placed on freshness. Potatoes in their jackets sautéed with shallots and nicely firm julienne strips of vegetables accompany main courses, and the green salad is refreshing.

White chocolate mousse includes disturbing chunks of solid white chocolate, making a mawkish, cloyingly sweet desert. Far better were mixed berries with whipped cream, a smooth ice cream bombe burnished with praline and the fruit tarts.

La Tulipe
★ ★ ★

104 West 13th Street, between Avenue of the Americas and Seventh Avenue, 691-8860.

Atmosphere: Intimate, stylish and romantic bistro; friendly and considerate service that is sometimes pretentious.

Recommended dishes: Everything except cream of mussel soup, marinated salmon in dill sauce and ballotine of duck.

Price range: Expensive.

Credit cards: American Express, Diners Club, MasterCard and Visa.

Hours: Dinner, Tuesdays through Sundays, 6:30 P.M. to 10 P.M. Closed Mondays and major holidays, and usually mid-August through Labor Day.

Reservations: Necessary.

Laid out in the garden-floor apartment of a renovated brownstone, La Tulipe has a small and intimate dining room that takes on a felicitous glow from the mellow plum-colored walls, the graceful floral bouquets, the simply framed mirrors that add a sparkling illusion of space, and the comfortable light cast by white glass lampshades. The noise level is generally tolerable and the front room, with its antique zinc-topped service bar, its oyster bar and Parisian cafe chairs, is a hospitable area in which to wait for friends or a table.

Although there often are some exaggerated time lapses between appetizers and main courses, service is generally efficient and friendly, if sometimes pretentious. Tables along the wall are a bit too small to accommodate four diners comfortably and create a slight service problem, but the overall charm of La Tulipe and the really lovely food made such flaws seem minor.

Kitchen and dining room chores are divided between John and Sally Darr, the husband and wife who own and operate La Tulipe. Mr. Darr, who manages the dining room, was the head of the lower school at the Brooklyn School of Friends until his retirement, and there is still something of the schoolmaster in his manner. Sally Darr, who plans the menus, cooks, bakes and oversees the kitchen, is a former textile designer who always loved to cook and who is basically self-taught. Deciding that cooking was what she liked to do, Mrs. Darr assisted in the test kitchens of Time-Life, preparing a series of cookbooks on the world's cuisines, and later worked for "Gourmet" magazine, where she supervised the test kitchens and also wrote and edited articles. La Tulipe is the culmination of her food career, and one can sense that it is in every way a labor of love.

The menu is small but enticing and well-balanced. Seasonal foods are featured as Mrs. Darr alters the selections to take advantage of the produce she finds at the market.

Such offerings might be the minuscule soft-shell crabs sautéed meunière-style and topped with a froth of nut-brown butter poured from a copper casserole, or the hot and cold soup that combines the pungent, sour sorrel with cream and potatoes. Served hot, the soup has flecks of potato and the intriguing crunch of croutons. The cold version is puréed then thickened with an extra splash of cream and finally given a verdant sprinkling of green herbs. Only a cream of mussel soup flavored with saffron was thin and watery.

Long, crisp zucchini fritters arrive in small baskets, a pretty if slightly awkward arrangement since one is not quite sure whether to pick up the zucchini and eat it out of hand or to move the basket off the plate so the very hot vegetable can be handled with knife and fork. But either way, it is sheer perfection. A buttered and toasted croustade holds wild morilles and champignons in a cream sauce for another delectable first course, and pâté lovers will surely appreciate the langue Valenciennoise, that combines smoked beef tongue with chicken-liver mousse and foie gras de canard, seasoned with green peppercorns. Scallop and watercress mousse and ravioli filled with sweetbreads and spinach were delicious.

The only appetizer that needed improvement was the raw salmon marinated in dill sauce. Slices were too thick and had been left too long in a lime marinade, so the final result was less mild and silky than it should have been.

In addition to the soft-shell crabs, excellent main courses were the nuggets of golden brown sweetbreads tossed with peas on a bed of fine and tender noodles, the pearly fillet of red snapper baked with vegetables and cream en papillote, and properly rare noisettes of lamb with green herb butter that were adorned by slices of tomatoes baked on thin crusts of eggplant. All other vegetables and potato garnishes were equally decorative and delicious.

A rack of lamb was just a bit too overdone to achieve total perfection, and grilled breast of duckling, whether with glassy red sour cherries or green peppercorn butter, was acceptable if far less exciting than other choices.

Slices of squab breast, grilled rare, are cushioned on a bed of couscous flecked with pine nuts and raisins, and a delicate sweet-sour sauce brightens calf's liver. Chicken is roasted as moistly golden brown as the garlic cloves that flavor it.

Almost all diners order the refreshing green salad and the excellent cheeses.

Mrs. Darr's baking is every bit as good as her cooking, judging by the cocoa-powdered, flourless chocolate and whipped cream roll and the immaculate, astringent lemon tart with its buttery pâté brisée crust holding a lemon-custard-soufflé filling.

Floating island reaches new heights with egg whites enfolding toasted hazelnuts, all poached in a fez-shaped charlotte mold and set adrift in a vanilla-scented sea of crème anglaise. Peach Melba, made with a fresh peach and fresh raspberry purée, was served in a "tulipe" of frilled pastry, and the same form also held the lemon sherbet doused with Russian vodka — a nearly perfect combination slightly marred by sherbet that was too frozen and icy. Freshly baked thin apple tart, an apricot soufflé and a layered chocolate cake with crème anglaise are all exceptional. Raspberry Bavarian cream is skippable. Coffee was excellent, but tea should be brewed from leaves, not bags.

As Mrs. Darr characterizes her own cooking, it is "a fresh approach to classic cuisine," and definitely not "nouvelle." Like many other cooks, Mrs. Darr avoided flour long before the nouvelle cuisine creators gained attention, and all of her sauces are gossamer reductions of stocks and juices, glistened with last-minute additions of butter.

Mrs. Darr still needs a slightly more authoritative hand at seasoning so her fresh and beautiful food takes on the character and personality that would make it worth four stars instead of three.

Wine prices are almost insultingly high here, as though any amount will be paid by a captive audience, a feature that limits enjoyment.

Lavin's

★

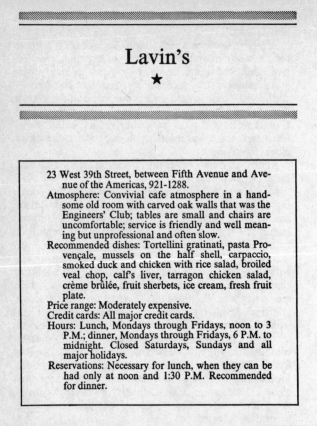

23 West 39th Street, between Fifth Avenue and Avenue of the Americas, 921-1288.

Atmosphere: Convivial cafe atmosphere in a handsome old room with carved oak walls that was the Engineers' Club; tables are small and chairs are uncomfortable; service is friendly and well meaning but unprofessional and often slow.

Recommended dishes: Tortellini gratinati, pasta Provençale, mussels on the half shell, carpaccio, smoked duck and chicken with rice salad, broiled veal chop, calf's liver, tarragon chicken salad, crème brûlée, fruit sherbets, ice cream, fresh fruit plate.

Price range: Moderately expensive.

Credit cards: All major credit cards.

Hours: Lunch, Mondays through Fridays, noon to 3 P.M.; dinner, Mondays through Fridays, 6 P.M. to midnight. Closed Saturdays, Sundays and all major holidays.

Reservations: Necessary for lunch, when they can be had only at noon and 1:30 P.M. Recommended for dinner.

A welcome addition in an area notably short of good restaurants, Lavin's has become a trendy, popular favorite since it opened in 1980. A high, wide and handsome dining room, in what was the Engineers' Club, it is distinguished by carved golden oak-paneled walls, heavy, sunny lace curtains and a lively lunch clientele, drawn mostly from the nearby fashion and garment districts, with wine buffs frequenting it in the evenings. Food and drinks are served at the big rectangular bar, where there is also a Cruvinet wine dispenser that makes it possible to hold many open bottles in good condition, thereby providing a variety of wines by the glass. That most are California wines is a disappointment to those who think that state's vintages are much overrated, as I do. But the idea is a good one, nonetheless.

The staff here is young, bright and good-natured and distinctly preppy in style. What is annoying is the habit some waitresses have of using the kindergarten "we" and of smiling in that vacuous, cheerful way associated with hospital nurses. "Are we ready for our dessert?" and a certain "now, now" tone bring to mind nurses who come into the hospital room at dawn asking if "we are ready to have our temperature taken." Service can be agonizingly slow, probably because the kitchen staff is so involved in intricate garnishing.

The food is nouvelle American, with all of the flaws and advantages that this still developing cuisine exhibits. On the plus side are the fresh vegetables lightly

cooked, the attractive cold dishes intriguingly garnished
and the range of light to heavy dishes always on the
menu. Drawbacks include sweetness via such ingredients as honey, currants, orange and overly reduced wine
sauces that caramelize and become syrupy. There are
also some embarrassingly pretentious touches. A case in
point is the appetizer known as the Oriental box, not a
torture device but rather a lacquer box filled with thick
slices of cucumber containing the merest wisps of
smoked salmon and overly vinegared raw bay scallops.
Chopsticks accompany this dish, which takes about
twenty-five minutes to get out of the kitchen, all a silly,
pointless contrivance in an otherwise Western-style restaurant. In the same vein, vegetables are served in a
Chinese bamboo steamer but are almost totally devoid
of salt and flavor.

Strengths at Lavin's are pastas, broiled meats and
cold plates. Weaknesses include almost anything served
with sauce, especially such choices as the lamb ribs
sticky with an orange-ginger glaze, duck that tastes as
though it were candied with orange marmalade and a
game hen with honeyed mustard.

Tortellini, filled with veal and chicken and glossed
with cream, butter and cheese, is the best pasta. A close
second is the pasta Provençale, linguine with an herbaceous dressing of olive oil, tomato, capers and garlic.
Pasta primavera, overloaded with carrots, red pepper,
broccoli and string beans, lacked finesse. As a main
course, or shared as an appetizer, pasta is satisfying.
Appetizers, such as a very dry and salty smoked beef,
were not helped by being wrapped around unripe cante-
loupe, and the added flavors of dill and lime juice only
made things worse. Better choices were the cold mussels
on the half shell simmered with white wine, shallots and
a hint of saffron and served on shredded red cabbage
(too much, but a nice idea) and a green herbed rice
salad. That rice salad also rounded out the bright raw
beef, carpaccio, served over raw mushrooms, and a platter of smoked chicken and duck with snow peas vinaigrette — each a pleasant lunch or pre-theater main
course. The tarragon-flavored chicken salad was another good choice.

Breasts of chicken, mawkish under a jammy glaze of
black currants, and a veal demiglace combined dessert
and main course in the same dish. Better to opt for the
good, broiled veal chop, the shell steak or the calf's liver
with a winy shallot butter sauce. Poached scallops were
much too bland and characterless. Straw potatoes are
delicious — glassily crisp and greaseless and obviously
made from scratch.

On one night I sampled some ice creams and sherbets
that the house was beginning to play with, and even at
that early stage they seemed excellent, though too soft.
Blueberry sherbet promised to be bright, fresh and
properly fruity, and both vanilla and chocolate ice
creams had a satiny, creamy richness. Crème brûlée had
just the right caramelized glaze over gentle custard, but
apple tart was wet, steamy and unpleasant.

In addition to the service, other unwelcome touches
are the practice of taking lunch reservations only for

noon and 1:30 P.M. and keeping early arrivals waiting until a party is complete, making for a jammed, confused backup at the door at lunchtime. In addition, chairs are stiffly uncomfortable, and tables are small.

Le Biarritz
★

325 West 57th Street, between Eighth and Ninth Avenues, 757-2390.

Atmosphere: A pleasant and inviting well-kept bistro with erratic service.

Recommended dishes: Quiche, salade Niçoise, gigot with flageolets, calf's liver, roast chicken with chanterelles, lamb chops, rice pudding, crème caramel, chocolate mousse, fresh fruits with red wine.

Price range: Moderate.

Credit cards: American Express, Diners Club and Visa.

Hours: Lunch, Mondays through Fridays, noon to 3 P.M.; dinner, Mondays through Fridays, 5 P.M. to 11 P.M., Saturdays, 5 P.M. to midnight. Closed Sundays and major holidays.

Reservations: Necessary, especially for lunch.

A few years ago, Le Biarritz offered such good, hearty and authentic bistro-level cooking at moderate prices that it was awarded three stars. Following that review, complaints poured in regarding the carelessness of the service and the rudeness of the staff, and when research indicated such complaints were warranted, I wrote appropriate caveats. But throughout that time, the quality of the cooking remained constant.

Now, however, it is apparent that the kitchen's standards have deteriorated markedly, a pity because the dining room is still snug and glows with rows of polished copper pots, and the prices are low by today's standards. But even at those prices there are now so many flaws in the food that Le Biarritz is worth just a single star, making it a good place to keep in mind for the few things it still does very well. For the most part, the food is better, fresher and livelier at lunch; at night, things get to looking faded and warmed over.

Among the best appetizers are a high, puffy quiche Lorraine and a bright, fresh salade Niçoise. Artichoke vinaigrette is delicious when it has not passed too much time in the refrigerator, and crêpe Biarritz, with a slightly pasty seafood filling, is otherwise acceptable for those who like lavishly rich first courses.

Escargots, all soups, pâté and assorted hors d'oeuvres are to be avoided. Pass up also the sweetbreads with scorched onions, the tasteless, tepid contre-filet of beef, the bland blanquette de veau and the overcooked salmon in a Dijonnaise sauce that lacks punch.

But gigot with flageolets is consistently well prepared, with flavorful roast lamb cooked rare to pink and thinly sliced, then served with the classic gentle jade-green beans. Calf's liver sautéed "à l'Anglaise" and roast chicken with chanterelles are dependable choices. Roast duck is one of those dishes that can be good or poor, depending upon its freshness and degree of preparation.

The green salad is pleasant, and the creamy rice pudding, scented with orange rind, remains poetic — still one of the best in the city. Crème caramel, chocolate mousse and very refreshing fresh fruit salad doused with lemony red wine are the best desserts.

Coffee, even when made in the Melior pot, is weak and watery. The wine list does not include vintage years, and the quality of the year you get depends on how well known you are to the management.

Service is still nervously erratic and at its best when things are slow.

Le Bistro
★ ★

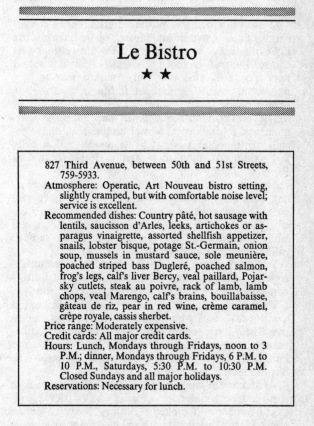

827 Third Avenue, between 50th and 51st Streets, 759-5933.

Atmosphere: Operatic, Art Nouveau bistro setting, slightly cramped, but with comfortable noise level; service is excellent.

Recommended dishes: Country pâté, hot sausage with lentils, saucisson d'Arles, leeks, artichokes or asparagus vinaigrette, assorted shellfish appetizer, snails, lobster bisque, potage St.-Germain, onion soup, mussels in mustard sauce, sole meunière, poached striped bass Dugleré, poached salmon, frog's legs, calf's liver Bercy, veal paillard, Pojarsky cutlets, steak au poivre, rack of lamb, lamb chops, veal Marengo, calf's brains, bouillabaisse, gâteau de riz, pear in red wine, crème caramel, crêpe royale, cassis sherbet.

Price range: Moderately expensive.

Credit cards: All major credit cards.

Hours: Lunch, Mondays through Fridays, noon to 3 P.M.; dinner, Mondays through Fridays, 6 P.M. to 10 P.M., Saturdays, 5:30 P.M. to 10:30 P.M. Closed Sundays and all major holidays.

Reservations: Necessary for lunch.

Le Bistro has been quietly, steadily and successfully serving up delicious examples of the cuisine bourgeoise for twenty-three years at its present address, and for twenty years before that on its original site across Third

Avenue. Purchased almost five years ago by Georges Hayon, Le Bistro plays to a packed house at lunch every weekday. Less crowded at dinner, the redecorated and colorfully festive dining room offers a leisurely option for very good food at moderate prices. Service is bustling, professional and polite, and the noise level is benign.

Those who like to sit on banquettes will be thoroughly comfortable, but those who prefer round tables might find that they are in the center aisle in traffic patterns where chairs are frequently bumped.

Most of the food, though lacking in innovative brilliance, has that convincing, old-time bistro flavor, a quality not easily found these days. If the cooking is sometimes uneven, the kitchen's performance maintains a steady two-star average.

At the bar and at most tables for dinner, there is a lusty pâté offered by the management, a gently garlicked, softly spreadable blend that goes well with the hard-toasted croutons. Pâté in the form of terrine de campagne has much the same rustic patina, and so does hot, coarse garlic sausage with lentils, snails in a froth of garlic butter and the oily, garlic-scented salami, saucisson d'Arles. A creamy, mustard-edged vinaigrette dressing lends sparkle to cold leeks, asparagus and large meaty artichokes, as well as to the house green salad, which would be improved with slight chilling.

Mussels in a pungent mustard dressing and a combination of clams, oysters and mussels on ice have just the right piquancy as appetizers. Less interesting first courses sampled included a somewhat banal assorted hors d'oeuvres, stiff and salty smoked salmon and quiche that varied from light fluffiness to a slightly soggy heaviness.

The smoky, onion-accented pea soup, potage St.-Germain, and a bright coral lobster bisque, both daily specials, abounded in hearty richness, and the volcanically hot, gratinéed onion soup had a deeply burnished flavor.

Most main courses differ from lunch to dinner. Midday, such daily specials as veal stew Marengo and veal cutlet Pojarsky, with slivers of tongue and ham in a cognac-truffle sauce, were exceptional. Both grilled veal paillard with lemon and parsley butter and sautéed calf's liver with bacon were also delicious.

To judge by typical examples, fish sautéed meunière-style is a difficult accomplishment, but it is beautifully done at Le Bistro, whether with fish fillets or, better yet, a whole baby flounder, sometimes available. Scampi in a garlic and parsley butter are tender and firm, but an overdose of tarragon muffled other seasonings. Bouillabaisse, however, was distinguished by a harmonious balance of flavors — a dish worth looking for on Fridays and sometimes Saturdays as well.

At dinner, the most exceptional main course is rack of lamb for two, gilded by a garlic and parsley breadcrumb veneer and cooked rose pink. Steak au poivre packs exactly the right punch, made elegant by a lacing of Armagnac. Duck emerged from the oven lean and succulent, but syrupy-sweet canned figs proved an unfortunate topping. So did the same sort of sweet sauce, this time with grapes, on otherwise well-braised quail.

Grilled chicken with tarragon butter was satisfying, if undistinguished, but frog's legs had exactly the right garlic overtones to set off the moist tenderness of the meat. Both poached salmon with hollandaise sauce and poached striped bass nestled under a cream and tomato sauce Dugleré were above average. Vegetables are at times brightly al dente, but at other times mushily overdone. Boiled and fried potatoes, however, were invariably just right.

The best deserts were ruby-red pear poached in red wine, a gossamer crème caramel with a brassy edge of caramelized sugar and frozen crêpe royale, with ice cream and a crunch of toasted almonds. The most outstanding dessert is gâteau de riz — not really a cake, but rather a baked rice pudding with a sugar-glazed top all in a sheer crème anglaise sauce. Cassis sherbet is coolly restorative, and so are strawberries, for those who prefer lighter endings.

A better cheese assortment would be more in character, and so would a more imaginative selection of moderate-priced wines.

Le Chantilly
★ ★

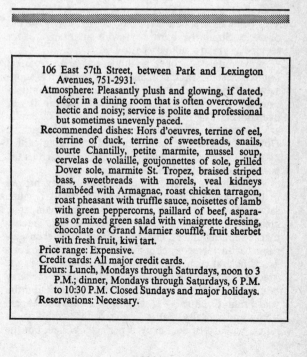

106 East 57th Street, between Park and Lexington Avenues, 751-2931.
Atmosphere: Pleasantly plush and glowing, if dated, décor in a dining room that is often overcrowded, hectic and noisy; service is polite and professional but sometimes unevenly paced.
Recommended dishes: Hors d'oeuvres, terrine of eel, terrine of duck, terrine of sweetbreads, snails, tourte Chantilly, petite marmite, mussel soup, cervelas de volaille, goujonnettes of sole, grilled Dover sole, marmite St. Tropez, braised striped bass, sweetbreads with morels, veal kidneys flambéed with Armagnac, roast chicken tarragon, roast pheasant with truffle sauce, noisettes of lamb with green peppercorns, paillard of beef, asparagus or mixed green salad with vinaigrette dressing, chocolate or Grand Marnier soufflé, fruit sherbet with fresh fruit, kiwi tart.
Price range: Expensive.
Credit cards: All major credit cards.
Hours: Lunch, Mondays through Saturdays, noon to 3 P.M.; dinner, Mondays through Saturdays, 6 P.M. to 10:30 P.M. Closed Sundays and major holidays.
Reservations: Necessary.

If Le Chantilly is now slightly below its original level of excellence, it still maintains an average far above many haute-cuisine French restaurants in the city.

The original partners still hold forth here, with Paul Dessibourg in the dining room and Roland Chenus in the kitchen.

Le Chantilly's kitchen is just a little too uneven to deserve its former three-star rating. At both lunch and dinner, the assortment of cold hors d'oeuvres salads are light, sparkling and altogether lovely, and only the pâté de campagne is somewhat characterless. Worthwhile pâtés include the terrine of eel with its sauce Cressonière, the pale and delicate terrine of sweetbreads sparked with lacy strands of blanched orange rind and the spicy terrine of truffled duck.

Tourte Chantilly, a quiche with fillings that vary daily, is puffy and well baked and the escargots in individual cups invite the dipping of bread crusts to soak up every drop of herbaceous butter. At lunch, the exceptional hot appetizer is the cervelas de volaille, a cloud-like poached sausage of chicken in a sauce combining cream, truffles and a mellowing hint of port.

Two hot appetizers exhibited the flaws that also detract from other courses. Both the plump oysters baked under a froth of champagne cream sauce and the twin mousses of fish arrived tepid, and on two visits the mousses were too densely firm and bland. Keeping food hot seems to be a real problem here, judging by several cream soups and main courses.

Only the petite marmite was served properly steaming, a rich simmering of beef, chicken and vegetables in a heady broth garnished with cheese and croutons, and a saffron-scented mussel soup attained briny perfection. A brassy lobster bisque was barely warm and totally devoid of a crackling lobster flavor.

Roast veal served as a plat du jour was tough and sinewy. One evening the specialty was beef Wellington, a misbegotten creation that I thought had long gone out of style. Similarly, roast veal with an orange sauce seemed as grave a culinary gaffe.

A marmite St. Tropez at lunch was a near-perfect bouillabaisse by another name. But a similar fish soup-stew — the bourride Pyramidiale — was pasty, indelicate and on two occasions most of the fish in it was overcooked. The fish dishes to rely on at Le Chantilly are the crisp fried goujonnettes of sole and the grilled Dover sole, both impeccably cooked and accompanied by a gentle mustard sauce, and braised fish such as the bass with cucumbers in an airy butter sauce.

Veal kidneys, properly rose-red at the center, proved to be as good as ever in their cream and Armagnac sauce. The sweetbreads with morels in champagne cream — tender and moistly flavorful — represented a marked improvement. Nut-brown roasted chicken perfumed with tarragon, equally beautiful pheasant Périgourdine and cushiony noisettes of lamb cooked to the precise medium-rare stage requested, could be the envy of many a chef. Not so the unexceptional duck and the veal Franc-Comtois — sautéed with a ham and cheese filling and so salty that it bordered on inedibility. At lunch, paillard of beef arrived perfectly grilled, but the sautéed calf's liver carried the faintest traces of bitterness, indicating it was not as fresh as it should have been.

Asparagus and salads are verdant harbingers of spring, as is the assortment of pastel fruit sherbets glistening with cut fresh fruits. Fruit sherbets and soufflés flavored with chocolate or Grand Marnier are lovely. Offerings from the pastry wagon show improvement and most are creditable. The most unaccountable dessert was the fresh strawberries, all with white tips and many roughly green — in short, underripe. It would seem wiser for the restaurant to wait until ripe berries are available.

Prices are high enough for diners to expect quieter surroundings, more evenly paced service and more space between tables.

Le Cherche-Midi
★

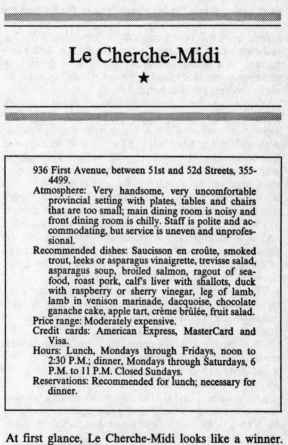

936 First Avenue, between 51st and 52d Streets, 355-4499.

Atmosphere: Very handsome, very uncomfortable provincial setting with plates, tables and chairs that are too small; main dining room is noisy and front dining room is chilly. Staff is polite and accommodating, but service is uneven and unprofessional.

Recommended dishes: Saucisson en croûte, smoked trout, leeks or asparagus vinaigrette, trevisse salad, asparagus soup, broiled salmon, ragout of seafood, roast pork, calf's liver with shallots, duck with raspberry or sherry vinegar, leg of lamb, lamb in venison marinade, dacquoise, chocolate ganache cake, apple tart, crème brûlée, fruit salad.

Price range: Moderately expensive.

Credit cards: American Express, MasterCard and Visa.

Hours: Lunch, Mondays through Fridays, noon to 2:30 P.M.; dinner, Mondays through Saturdays, 6 P.M. to 11 P.M. Closed Sundays.

Reservations: Recommended for lunch; necessary for dinner.

At first glance, Le Cherche-Midi looks like a winner. And judging by the almost full house on my visits, it is already attracting a loyal coterie. Simply but handsomely designed to suggest a countrified Provençale setting, Le Cherche-Midi's rough white walls, terra cotta tile floors, baskets, antique accessories and delicate floral arrangements create a clean, gentle and unpretentious background. In summer, meals are also served in the small back garden. The menu has equal charm and appeal.

But though dinner here turns out to be an above-average experience, the basic plan is seriously flawed. Tables are jammed together, chairs are skimpy and uncomfortable, the room is noisy when full, and main courses are heaped on plates so small that it is almost impossible to cut through a chicken breast or a half duck without scattering rice or vegetables across the table. In addition, these plates are served so hot that it is impossible to give them a steadying touch while cutting meat. And whoever designed Le Cherche-Midi's interior should also have realized that at busy times the kitchen doors swing out to hit customers backed up at the checkroom, and that some of the spotlights glare into the faces of diners.

The small well-planned menu of Provençale dishes is enticing and the food is pleasantly delicate. What is missing, however, is an authoritative hand with seasonings. The result is dishes that lack character. Ingredients could not be fresher or of better quality and the cooking is careful and precise; because efforts in the kitchen are so sincere and painstaking, it is a pity that the final step is not realized. It is as though Sally Scoville, the American owner-chef, who lived in France and who had a restaurant in Cambridge, Mass., has mastered cooking techniques but lacks the final artistic flair necessary to make food really memorable.

Among the most successful efforts are appetizers such as the mild and gently smoked trout, the cold leeks or asparagus mellowed by a vinaigrette dressing made with an excellent olive oil, and the salad of the ruby-red lettuce, trevisse, given crunch with walnuts and scented with walnut oil. The artichoke appetizer, was a near miss, however, because it was ice cold and lacked salt, a common failing here. Hot, meaty saucisson en croûte was heady with garlic. A chiffon-sheer cream of asparagus soup, though delicious, should have been hotter, and a mild and inappropriate sweetness marred the duck pâté. Mustard seems to be a problem as well, a salad of mussels having too little of it in the sauce and the céleri rémoulade having a biting overdose.

The country-style French bread with its crackling crust is irresistible, especially when service lags between the appetizer and main course. The bread is especially good dipped in the heady broth that is the basis of a seafood ragout, a sort of crystal-light bouillabaisse with mussels, shrimp and scallops. Grilled salmon steak with a generous dab of green herb butter and capers made another fine main course.

Leg of lamb, roasted after several hours in a juniper-scented marinade, suggested venison and was delicious. So was a roast lamb lightly touched with rosemary, savory, thyme and garlic. Thyme and garlic also flavored braised chicken, but so mildly that the chicken was undistinguished. Similarly, a hindquarter of chicken with morels in cream and a breast of chicken stuffed with a purée of mushrooms lacked salt and flavor. Chicken au vinaigre, in a sauce made with black currant vinegar, was also too sweet.

Rose-pink calf's liver topped with a silky purée of sautéed shallots, roast pork and half a roast duck

234

sparked with sherry or raspberry vinegar were much better than the cassoulet, in which the beans were undercooked. Nuggets of sweetbreads in a light wild mushroom and cream sauce were tough because their membranes had not been removed.

The cheese assortment was fair, but the condition of several chèvres was less than perfect. The waiter, having an awkward time balancing the tray between two tables, cut thin and crumbly slices, another example of poor functional design. But the three "in" desserts of the season are well represented here: a chocolate ganache cake that is rich, cool and very chocolatey, hazelnut dacquoise with the right contrast of crisp meringue to satiny cream, and the slightly heavy but delicious crème brûlée. Puff pastry for the strawberry tart had all the charm of wet cardboard. But a fresh fruit salad was bright and refreshing. Bracing café filtre and espresso deserve better cups than the combination of china and clumsy metal.

The wine list has some excellent choices, including fine white and red Hermitages, but prices are about 15 percent higher than they should be.

Le Cirque
★ ★ ★

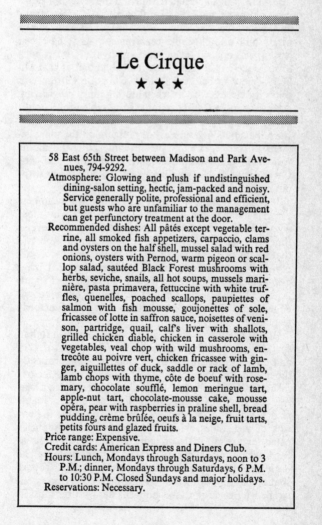

58 East 65th Street between Madison and Park Avenues, 794-9292.

Atmosphere: Glowing and plush if undistinguished dining-salon setting, hectic, jam-packed and noisy. Service generally polite, professional and efficient, but guests who are unfamiliar to the management can get perfunctory treatment at the door.

Recommended dishes: All pâtés except vegetable terrine, all smoked fish appetizers, carpaccio, clams and oysters on the half shell, mussel salad with red onions, oysters with Pernod, warm pigeon or scallop salad, sautéed Black Forest mushrooms with herbs, seviche, snails, all hot soups, mussels marinière, pasta primavera, fettuccine with white truffles, quenelles, poached scallops, paupiettes of salmon with fish mousse, goujonettes of sole, fricassee of lotte in saffron sauce, noisettes of venison, partridge, quail, calf's liver with shallots, grilled chicken diable, chicken in casserole with vegetables, veal chop with wild mushrooms, entrecôte au poivre vert, chicken fricassee with ginger, aiguillettes of duck, saddle or rack of lamb, lamb chops with thyme, côte de boeuf with rosemary, chocolate soufflé, lemon meringue tart, apple-nut tart, chocolate-mousse cake, mousse opéra, pear with raspberries in praline shell, bread pudding, crème brûlée, oeufs à la neige, fruit tarts, petits fours and glazed fruits.

Price range: Expensive.

Credit cards: American Express and Diners Club.

Hours: Lunch, Mondays through Saturdays, noon to 3 P.M.; dinner, Mondays through Saturdays, 6 P.M. to 10:30 P.M. Closed Sundays and major holidays.

Reservations: Necessary.

In the past, Alain Sailhac has shown himself to be one of the most talented French chefs working in New York. Now he seems once again to be close to the top form he exhibited several years ago when he was at Le Cygne. As chef of Le Cirque, he is proving himself as dedicated to perfection with such simple, classic preparations as grilled paillard of beef and grilled chicken diable encrusted with crushed mustard seeds and breadcrumbs as he is with more innovative creations. These include a warm salad of scallops and roe on ruffled red-tip lettuce leaves; the firm, white-fleshed fish, lotte, in a rose-gold saffron sauce, and a lusty fricasee of chicken in an herb-scented tomato and white wine sauce, brightened with fresh ginger.

Add to such beguiling cookery the sublime pastries and desserts of Dieter Schorner, and it is easy to see why Le Cirque merits an extra star, raising its rating from two to three stars. The food is so good, in fact, that it deserves a far more felicitous setting, one that would afford ample space between tables and a more benign noise level and accord equally good service to all.

Mellow lighting and a rose-beige color scheme give the room a flattering glow, although the elements of the décor are garish and dated, much in the style of a European dining salon. But graceful baskets of flowers, fruits and vegetables, arranged by Suzette Cimino, make pretty and original table centerpieces. As it has been since it was opened seven years ago by the Tuscan-born Sirio Maccioni, formerly the maître d'hôtel at that old high-society mecca, the Colony Club, Le Cirque is a celebrity circus, with much table hopping and waving across the room. Most desirable front tables go to politicians, fashion personalities and show-business superstars. This puts a great deal of pressure on the management, of course, and that pressure intensifies during the sort of emergency that occurs when Governor and Mrs. Carey arrive at 8:30 on a jam-packed Friday night without reservations.

It is understandable, then, why unknown customers are relegated to the back of the room and why those who spend a great deal of money at Le Cirque several times a week get the best tables. But it is still too bad that some of the most crammed-in tables exist at all, especially those in heavy traffic patterns. And it is regrettable also that unknown guests are often left standing several minutes at the door before they are acknowledged and that they are sometimes shown perfunctorily to the bar.

Basically French, the menu offers a few stylish Italian specialties, reflecting the combined influence of chef and owner. There are so many wonderful appetizers on the menu that one could make a wholly satisfactory meal just by combining them. Simple choices, such as smoked sturgeon, trout and salmon, are as impeccable as the oysters, clams and crab meat. Except for the terrine of vegetables, which is marred by an unsophisticated texture, all pâtés of game, meat, poultry and seafood are delicious, my own favorite being pâté de tête — a veal head cheese accented with parsley, chives, shallots and garlic. Rose-red raw-beef carpaccio is enlivened by a verdant and pungent herb sauce, mussels are enveloped in a silky vinaigrette dressing, with slivers of red onion, and the marinated raw fish, seviche of red snapper, is sparked with fresh chilies, sweet peppers and onion.

Only an overcooked and fishy seafood crepe was flawed among hot appetizers. Herbed snails and oysters gratinéed with cream and a touch of Pernod could not have been better. Nor could the meaty Black Forest mushrooms, tossed quickly in hot butter and sprinkled with herbs. Spaghetti primavera is an inspired house invention, and the blend of cream and butter enfolding broccoli, tiny peas, mushrooms, tomato and toasted pignoli nuts has not been equaled elsewhere. A close second is fettuccine with white truffles. Neither of these pastas is on the menu, but both are favorites of regulars.

Rich soups present almost irresistible alternatives to the pastas, whether one chooses bright cream of lobster, golden cream of carrot or strong onion soup kept hot over a clay brazier.

Fish and seafood are gently cooked to remain moist, an accomplishment that is realized with poached scallops in a satiny beurre-blanc sauce, as well as with the greaselessly fried strips of sole known as goujonettes, accented by a light mustard sauce, with paupiettes of salmon, filled with fish mousse, and with quenelles de brochet, those luxurious pike dumplings.

Such game birds as partridge and quail are rendered flavorful and tender by careful braising, and their intricate garnishes of wild mushroom and chestnut purées do them justice. Rarely will you find noisettes of venison that have a richer flavor. Among game dishes, only some very dry rabbit proved disappointing, though its wine-dark sauce was almost good enough to compensate.

Although veal paillard was watery and lackluster one night, a thick veal chop blanketed with sautéed wild mushrooms and lamb chops scented with thyme were perfection, and so was a huge, thick côte de boeuf for two, which was perfumed with rosemary and highlighted by an intense bordelaise sauce and a tarragon-accented sauce béarnaise. Kidneys needed slightly more crunchy searing, but two dishes, chicken braised to golden tenderness with vegetables and sautéed calf's liver with shallots, proved just how good simple cooking can be.

Roast duck with apples and Calvados are too sweet, but rare, sliced aiguillettes of duck, with their faint hint of pink peppercorns, could not be faulted. Between chef and owner, there is a constant search for the newest, youngest and best ingredients, such as truffles, New Zealand gooseberries and cherries, the Italian red lettuce, radicchio, and fish flown in from Europe.

Expensive soufflés are pushed a little too strongly by captains eager to increase their tips by creating higher checks. Few soufflés can stand up to the lemon meringue or apple and nut tarts or to the cloudlike chocolate-mousse cake. Beautiful nonpastry desserts include a luscious crème brûlée with a caramelized sugar glaze, a mousse opéra, with layers of dark and white chocolate mousse in a tapered glass, and what has to be the world's best bread pudding. Dome-shape oeufs à la neige are jeweled with candy fruits for Christmas. A creamy sauce Armagnac covers whole poached pears filled with raspberries and held in shells of hazelnut praliné — a dessert as spectacular in taste as it is in appearance. That is also true for a treasury of petits fours and such sparkling glazed fruits as grapes, kumquats and cherries.

Le Cygne
★★★

53 East 54th Street, between Madison and Park Avenues, 759-5941.

Atmosphere: New graceful, comfortable and romantic dining rooms, with Impressionistic color schemes, excellent lighting and bearable noise level; service is generally excellent but occasionally slow.

Recommended dishes: Clams or oysters on the half shell or des gourmets, all meat, duck and seafood pâtés and terrines, artichoke bottoms with sweetbreads, scallops in wine and saffron sauce, all hot fish mousses, paupiettes of sole, céleri rémoulade, snails in puff pastry, snails, crème Maximoise, billi-bi, grilled or sautéed Dover sole, quenelles, three fish in cream sauce, soft-shell crabs Provencal, chicken with morels, chicken Cévenole, breast of duck in honey-vinegar sauce, calf's liver with shallots, duck smitane, braised squab with olives, sweetbreads with chanterelles, escallop of veal with wild mushrooms, steak au poivre, rack of lamb with sage, roast veal or beef plat du jour, apple tart, Paris-Brest, all soufflés, Grand Marnier or chocolate mousse.

Price range: Expensive.

Credit cards: American Express and Diners Club.

Hours: Lunch, Mondays through Fridays, noon to 2 P.M.; dinner, Mondays through Saturdays, 6 P.M. to 11 P.M. Closed Sundays.

Reservations: Necessary.

Since it opened in 1969, Le Cygne has been one of the city's outstanding haute-cuisine restaurants. Almost always distinguished by food that was long on flavor and short on chichi, this restaurant for a long time maintained a four-star rating. But a while back, the kitchen fell far below par, making a two-star rating more appropriate. To judge by my latest visits, however, the chef, Jean-Yves Piquet, seems to be newly inspired, and the food he is turning out is excellent and well worth three stars.

What is inspiring him may well be Le Cygne's gracefully beautiful and romantic new surroundings, next door to the restaurant's original home on 54th Street. Gérard Gillian and Michel Crouzillat, the owners, worked for more than a year to create this large and stunning restaurant, which occupies an entire converted town house. Rooms glow with an Impressionistic color scheme of soft blues, pinks and ivory, and floral paintings are accented by graceful bouquets on tables. Lighting is superb, suffusing the rooms in a soft late-afternoon glow, and though the sound is a bit harsh at the most crowded times, the noise level is generally bearable. It is a surprise to learn that the proportions of these rooms are not any larger than in the original dining room, because the décor lends such a sense of spaciousness. But some chairs placed in traffic paths are kicked by waiters passing by in a hurry, which detracts from an otherwise gracious experience.

There are fine private dining facilities, too. Le Cygne can serve private parties either in the basement wine cellar or in the upstairs dining room, which can be divided for small groups.

Many of the earlier menu favorites have been combined with newer creations of the chef. Among the excellent additions are such hot appetizers as artichoke bottoms with sweetbreads in a mushroom-and-truffle sauce Périgourdine and pale golden scallops in a gossamer wine-and-saffron sauce. Hot fish mousses that fill paupiettes of sole, or which are baked in a crust, are classics of Le Cygne, and they are well represented, both as appetizers and main courses. Quenelles of scallops or pike, also served as appetizers or main courses, are light in texture but lusty in flavor and, like the mousses, are done justice by the accompaniment of a coral-pink sauce Nantua or a satiny beurre blanc.

Pâtés and terrines of meat, duck, seafood or lotte with dill are all expertly made, and all oysters and clams on the half shell arrive chilled and sparkling. Clams and oysters des gourmets are baked under a savory mantle of white wine, cream and a purée of mushrooms. Snails, either in toasted bread casing or in the classic Burgundy shallot-and-garlic butter, are heady with herbs and spices. The only appetizer not up to the rest was smoked salmon, exquisitely presented but much too thickly sliced and just a little too salty.

Soups have always been a strong point of the kitchen, and those in the new facility are up to the old standards, whether you have hot, briny, billi-bi with mussels enveloped in cream, chilled sorrel soup, crème Maximoise or pungent watercress.

In addition to the quenelles, excellent fish main courses include immaculately broiled or sautéed Dover sole with mustard sauce and three fish — firm meaty lotte, sole and striped bass, all steamed to pearly translucence — in a buttery, pink, cream sauce. Soft-shell crabs, though a little large for the season, were carefully sautéed and seasoned with garlic and aromatic herbs.

Two welcome additions to the menu are rare-roasted duck breast glossed with honey vinegar and rose-pink squab with olives. Duck smitane, in a cayenne-accented sour-cream sauce, was popular on the former menu and deserves to be so on the new one as well. Other house favorites that are beautifully prepared are chicken Cévenole, braised in a crock with cèpes, and braised chicken with morels in a champagne cream sauce. The same sauce does very well also for the sautéed escallop of veal with morels. Strips of beef filet with sauce Périgourdine, rack of lamb with sage and saddle or breast of veal are all moist and cooked to exactly the right doneness. Veal, whether as a roast or a sautéed escallop, is always pale, mild and moist, and so are veal sweetbreads. Veal kidneys, though rare and savory under their mustard-cream sauce, are stronger and brassier than they should be.

Two persistent and almost inexplicable flaws relate to vegetables and cheeses. With so much attention being paid these days to the proper presentation of both, it is hard to understand how the management can condone such overcooked vegetables. And considering that all parties are French, it is equally hard to fathom why cheeses are presented fully wrapped or in boxes, thereby missing the point that they are being shown so their inner condition can be ascertained.

Le Cygne's baking, too, still needs work, but the art of soufflé making is back to its former glory. Flavored with lemon, chocolate or Grand Marnier, these high-crowned, gently sweet masterpieces have just the right, runny interiors and are complemented by light, delicate sauces. Apple tart and Paris-Brest, filled with whipped cream and praline, were the only really exceptional baked desserts, although clafouti, the cherry tart, showed some improvement. Kiwi and strawberry tart and the Alexandra, a layered affair of meringue and mocha cream, are fair, and so is a garishly decorated napoleon. Some petits fours are fine, while others are dry and tasteless.

Details of service at the new Le Cygne still need smoothing out, but in general, the staff is professional, friendly and accommodating although rushed at peak hours. The kitchen tends to slow down a bit between appetizers and main courses. Wines are overpriced.

Le Jacques Coeur

★

448 East 79th Street, between First and York Avenues, 249-4920.

Atmosphere: Simple, small downstairs bistro that is moderately noisy when full; seating is somewhat cramped; service is friendly and generally good, if unprofessional.

Recommended dishes: Terrine maison, snails, smoked ham, onion soup, vegetable soups, quenelles, salmon stuffed with sole mousse, steak au poivre, stuffed squab, grilled red snapper, duck with orange sauce, floating island, apple tarte Tatin.

Price range: Moderately expensive.

Credit cards: All major credit cards.

Hours: Dinner, Tuesdays through Thursdays and Sundays, 6 P.M. to 10:30 P.M., Fridays and Saturdays, 6 P.M. to 11 P.M. Closed Mondays. Open holidays except for Christmas and New Year's Day.

Reservations: Generally necessary.

This simply decorated, low-ceilinged, narrow tunnel of a French eatery in a brownstone-type house is operated by Robert Renaud, the owner-chef, and his wife, Paulette, who manages the dining room. The Renauds come from the town of Bourges in the French region of Berry, and the name of their restaurant was inspired by the restaurant in which Mr. Renaud cooked for fifteen years before coming to this country. Both restaurant names are taken from the Palais du Jacques Coeur, a gothic landmark in Bourges.

The limited but well-balanced menu has a few classic touches and a few more unusual selections. The outstanding choices among appetizers are the terrine maison, a properly garlicky and peppery coarse pâté, far better than a too-firm and bland pâté en croûte. Escargots, out of their shells in an earthenware baking dish, are large and tender and have just the right accent of garlic, butter and a generous sprinkling of parsley.

The selection of hors d'oeuvres is drab and uninspired, and the smoked trout is too stiff and dry. Melon served with a ruggedly delicious smoked ham, much like the Black Forest variety, is ripe, sweet and conveniently cut.

The onion soup here is one of the best in the city, based as it is on very brown and rich stock that imparts the depth of flavor this soup never has if the onions are undercooked and light in color. Vegetable soups are also velvety and satisfying.

Quenelles de brochet, when available, are never too finely ground but have a rather interesting, velvety texture — the genuine flavor of fresh fish — and their coral lobster and mushroom sauce Nantua was subtle and fragrant. A sauce beurre blanc on well-grilled red snapper had perhaps a bit too much of a vinegar sting but was still more than merely acceptable. Very fresh poached salmon filled with a mousse of sole had a winy fish velouté sauce that was excellent.

A tender steak broiled exactly as ordered was blanketed by an authoritative sauce au poivre, the bite of the black peppercorns modified by a touch of cream, and canard à l'orange came as crisp duck in a blissfully bitter orange sauce.

Roast squab with a savory mushroom, liver and rice stuffing was cut in half so that it was easy to negotiate, and the meat was done to just the right, rosy degree of doneness.

In the past, flaws included the overroasting of a rack of lamb and an awkward presentation of stuffed paupiettes of chicken. Vegetables have improved a great deal; they now arrive bright and fairly firm, although originally they were much overcooked.

The best dessert is still the floating island, a moist, orangey cross between bread pudding and fruit cake, adrift in a frothy, sea of vanilla custard sauce. Apple tarte Tatin, though a bit too sweet, had a pleasant caramelized edge to its flavor. Oversweetness marred the slightly chewy crème caramel and the raspberry mousse that tasted like lipstick.

An acoustical ceiling has helped the noise problem a good deal, but tables are very close and a few are uncomfortably wedged in, especially the back table that conflicts with the refrigerator door. Anyone with claustrophobia will mind the deep downstairs sensation here. Others will find the boîte-like atmosphere snug and inviting. Service is friendly and informal, but waiters should remember who gets which dish.

Lello

★ ★

65 East 54th Street, between Madison and Park Avenues, 751-1555.
Atmosphere: Polished and sophisticated supper-club
setting downstairs and large and attractive upstairs dining room; service is generally professional, but slow upstairs, and treatment of unknown
guests is somewhat perfunctory at the entrance.
Recommended dishes: Smoked salmon, hot antipasto,
carpaccio, seafood salad, baked clams, snails in
mushroom caps, scampi Belvedere, broth with
spinach and eggs, linguine with seafood, tortellini
Bolognese, manicotti, paglia e fieno al filetto, spaghettini with clam sauce, risotto Certosina, grilled
scampi, fried squid, striped bass, red snapper and
clams, Mediterranean fish soup, chicken Valdostana, chicken Fiorentina, grilled baby chicken,
veal piccata, saltimbocca, calf's liver Veneziana,
grilled calf's liver, beefsteak or veal Vesuviana,
veal Milanese, veal paillard, broiled veal chop,
vegetables and salads, fedora cake, napoleon,
cheesecake.
Price range: Expensive.
Credit cards: All major cards.
Hours: Lunch, Mondays through Fridays, noon to 3
P.M.; dinner, Mondays through Thursdays, 5:30
P.M. to 10 P.M., Fridays and Saturdays, 5:30 P.M.
to 11 P.M. Closed Sundays.
Reservations: Necessary.

A fine balance of northern and southern Italian specialties appears on the enticing menu at Lello, a polished
and sophisticated restaurant opened just a few years
ago. Angelo De Cicco, the chef who was formerly at
Salta in Bocca on lower Madison Avenue, has been in
charge of Lello's kitchen for the last year. Based on five
recent visits, we found he has not lost his touch. There is
some unusually good and elegant food here, compromised only by a few ill-conceived creations that the chef
and management apparently consider fashionable, such
as chicken with oranges and melon balls in a champagne cream sauce.

The traditional Italian dishes are done with delicacy
and finesse. Several savory seafood specials make up
the hot antipasto or can be ordered separately. These include the scampi Belvedere sautéed in white wine with
shallots, clams baked with Mediterranean herbs, and
mussels steamed with tomato. Gently smoked salmon
and a sprightly seafood salad with tender rings of squid
and shellfish in a vinaigrette dressing were excellent. So
was the carpaccio, paper-thin slices of raw beef, although it was slightly overpowered by a thick, pungent
green sauce made with capers, cornichons and basil.
Snails with shallots, garlic and parsley and baked in
mushrooms caps were beautifully turned out. The cold
antipasto and the insufficiently aged prosciutto were
undistinguished.

It would be hard to find a better, sunnier version of
stracciatella Romana than at Lello's. The golden

consommé is laden with beaten egg, spinach and grated Parmesan cheese.

Oddly enough, most pastas did not come up to the fish, poultry and meat main courses. Those made with a cream, butter and cheese sauce (fettuccine Alfredo, spaghettini carbonara and paglia e fieno mimosa) tasted of boiled milk, and though a good deal better, even cream-and-tomato sauce on the spaghettini primavera was too sticky.

The kitchen excels in its tomato sauces. The green and white noodles, paglia e fieno al filetto, made with tomato and onion, had just the right accents of garlic and pepper, and the meat, cream and tomato Bolognese sauce on meaty tortellini made for a wonderful combination. Linguine with a mixed seafood sauce was better than the dry pesto. Linguine with white clam sauce could not be faulted. Butter, broth and cheese created a satiny richness in the risotto Certosina, rice studded with shrimp and asparagus or green peas.

Well-prepared fish courses include the red snapper with clams in a gossamer tomato broth and the striped bass with mussels and clams steamed in white wine with herbs. Forget the scampi baked with gluey Gruyère, and choose instead the grilled scampi. Zuppa di pesce, the mixed seafood soup-stew, is made with rock lobster, squid, scallops, mussels and clams and is delicious, though slightly salty, and squid were immaculately fried.

The whole baby chicken, veal paillard, thick veal rib chop and moist and pink calf's liver are expertly broiled. And the liver is even more irresistible sautéed with onions and white wine, Veneziana style. Chicken alternatives include buttery chicken Fiorentina with leaf spinach, and chicken Valdostana, stuffed with ham and cheese. Capon with truffles was overly complicated and the roast duck with apples and oranges was syrupy sweet. The duck also had the musty overtones induced by reheating.

Veal piccata was fine, and fried cutlet Milanese was properly crisp and buttery. The veal and ham combination, saltimbocca, gently seasoned with sage, was exceptionally delicate. Vesuviana is the spicy tomato sauce with garlic and mushrooms that is applied to beefsteak or veal.

There are three wonderful homemade desserts — the chocolate-topped napoleon, the moist, lemony Italian cheesecake and the fedora, chocolate-covered sponge cake and puff pastry layered with custard and chocolate cream.

Service downstairs is professional and accommodating, if brusque as guests enter. The upstairs dining room is spacious and quiet but service is slow and food arrives tepid. And unknown guests can be relegated to it, even if they have asked in advance for tables downstairs.

Le Périgord

★

405 East 52nd Street, east of First Avenue, 757-6244.

Atmosphere: Pleasant though undistinguished setting, suggesting a noisy, crowded hotel dining room; service ranges from good to careless and brusque.

Recommended dishes: Terrine of lamb, feuilleté of frog's legs, truffle tart, mixed hors d'oeuvres, grilled Dover sole, roast duck, confit of duck, grilled chateaubriand, shell steak, raspberry or apple tart, raspberry or Grand Marnier soufflé, crêpe soufflé, chocolate mousse cake, bread pudding.

Price range: Moderately expensive.

Credit cards: All major credit cards.

Hours: Lunch, Mondays through Fridays, noon to 3 P.M.; dinner, Mondays through Saturdays, 5:30 P.M. to 10:30 P.M. Closed Sundays and major holidays.

Reservations: Recommended.

As much as we might want a restaurant owner and staff to treat all customers equally, it is easy to understand why the best tables and warmest greetings go to the regular patrons. Nonetheless, all other treatment should be equal for regulars and newcomers. Just how uncomfortable a meal can be when that is not the policy was made obvious during two dinners at Le Périgord.

It was with high hopes that I returned to this small, plush dining salon after an absence of five years. One of the owners had written to say that a new chef, Antoine Bouterin, had taken over the kitchen. My usual fear of being recognized faded one busy Saturday night. The captain took the drink orders, dropped the menus on the table and disappeared with no explanation of specials. He soon returned to take the orders, describing the plat du jour only when asked. No wine list was offered.

Several minutes later he turned to a neighboring table, where he seemed to know all the customers, and reeled off about four appetizers and as many main courses that had not been offered to us. Much the same routine was reenacted at dinner a few weeks later. Both times, the dessert cart was rolled over perfunctorily, and if we could not see what was on the bottom shelves, too bad. Only the very good hazelnut tuiles were served with our coffee; all tables around us got miniature fruit tarts as well.

Service in the noisy, smoky, jam-packed dining room was distracted and slapdash at both dinners. One waiter, gazing across the room as he served a fine, tarragon-accented béarnaise sauce for a rare and beefy grilled shell steak, ladled the sauce over the rim of the plate and onto the cloth. And when clearing the table, he dropped a fork with pastry crumbs onto a guest's sleeve and apologized only when he caught the irate glance of the recipient.

At a third dinner, however, when I seemed on the way to becoming a regular, we were treated quite differently, with all the specials offered in advance, including what turned out to be excellent Grand Marnier and raspberry soufflés, and crêpes soufflés with Calvados cream. We were even given some of the sparkling little fruit tarts. But then the captain was called away from the table to greet important customers at the door in the middle of taking our orders. Unless you are considered important, there can be a pretty long and lonely wait at that door. If it seems that poor service is overshadowing the commendable efforts of the new chef, that's just the way it is.

The style of cooking is halfway between nouvelle and classic French, and there is an uneven hand at seasonings. Otherwise good dishes, such as a lusty fish soup and the truffle tart, were bitingly salty, while red snapper court bouillon, salmon steamed with fresh thyme and fresh noodles with truffles were as bland as hospital food.

Beef is especially well prepared at Le Périgord, whether as an entrecôte or in the grilled chateaubriand for two, both with the satiny béarnaise sauce. Overcooked noisettes of lamb and characterless medaillons of veal in lobster sauce left much to be desired, but roast duck and preserved confit of duck both had just the right tender, greaseless finish and hefty, meaty flavor. Fine flavor also distinguished lobster grilled with herb butter, but the meat unfortunately turned tough and chewy. Dover sole could not have been more carefully grilled. Firm, bright vegetables and sprigs of fresh herbs brightened all main courses.

Several appetizers were excellent, among them the mixed hors d'oeuvres, the garlic-accented terrine of lamb with ratatouille, caviar soufflé and flaky feuilleté holding boned nuggets of frog's legs in a buttery sauce. Pâté of smoked salmon was dry, and marinated salmon was so tasteless that it seemed to have been soaked merely in water, although the sauce was pungent.

In addition to the soufflés, there are some delicious desserts, such as the intensely chocolaty chocolate mousse cake, apple and raspberry tarts, and a marvelously crusty, custard-layered bread pudding. The chef may not be a finished talent, but he is obviously on the right track. Le Périgord could be a pleasant option for lunch or dinner, but not until the service is as improved as the food.

Le Plaisir

★

969 Lexington Avenue, between 70th and 71st Streets,
734-9430.
Atmosphere: Glowing and warmly pleasant supper-
club setting with uncomfortable chairs and tables;
service is friendly and well-meaning but too slow.
Cigar smoking is discouraged but permitted.
Recommended dishes: All appetizers, cream of garlic
or cream of mussel soup, noisettes of lamb, fillet
of beef, veal with noodles and foie gras, pigeon
breast with green peppercorn sauce, calf's liver,
chocolate meringue cake, chocolate marquise,
strawberry charlotte, apple tarte Tatin, pear or
Sauterne sherbet.
Price range: Expensive.
Credit cards: All major cards.
Hours: Dinner, Mondays through Saturdays, 6 P.M.
to 10:30 P.M. Closed Sundays.
Reservations: Generally necessary, especially on Fridays and Saturdays.

There are two basic ways to go into the restaurant business — either start from scratch with a brand-new name
and setting, establishing a style and character that reflect the background of the owner or chef, or buy a restaurant that already has a large following and take up
where the previous owner left off. Judging by the general lack of success that follows such takeovers, the latter seems to be the more difficult. The new owner must
tailor his style and instincts to those of his predecessor,
and he may wind up alienating the very customers he
hoped to inherit.

A case in point may well be Le Plaisir, under new
management since the spring of 1982. Formerly owned
by Stephen Spector and Peter Josten, this highly successful and trendy establishment featured the intricate
dishes of Masataka Kaboyashi, the chef who specialized
in the most avant-garde and esoteric expressions of the
nouvelle cuisine modified by Japanese garnishes. Although I was not enthusiastic about his efforts because
they seemed contrived and precious, it was obvious that
the man had style and achieved what pleased himself.
That it also pleased a loyal audience was to the restaurant's advantage, and it must be assumed that the new
proprietor, Pierre Jourdan, hoped that this following
would continue.

It is my feeling after four visits, however, that the
friendly, casual, almost rustic charm of the owner
would probably be more suitable in a snug and casual
bistro featuring the cuisine bourgeoise. Furthermore,
the new chef, Guy Reuge, formerly with La Tulipe,
turns out some delicious food and subtly balanced
sauces, but here, reconciling his own views of food with
those of the new owner, he is turning out nouvelle cuisine presentations that look clumsy and unconvincing.

Only the most serious food buffs who are willing to risk mediocre main courses in order to experience the generally excellent appetizers and desserts will want to spring for the prix fixe tab. They also can sample one of New York's best assortments of cheeses, usually in top condition. Still, those who want a wonderful dinner at that price — as compared with an interesting experience — will probably be disappointed.

Dinner starts with well-prepared appetizers that may include a cool and sprightly basil-and-dill-accented lobster salad, puff pastry sandwiching lightly blanched asparagus tips in a chive-scented butter-and-lemon sauce or a galantine of trout enfolding salmon mousse brightened by a minted mayonnaise. Slices of rare squab breast and fresh duck foie gras made a gently warm and soothing appetizer salad. So did the sautéed duck liver with raisins nested on wilted spinach and mellowed by a subtle sherry vinegar. Foie gras on slim haricots verts and a creamy salad of scallops and sheaves of endive were also lovely first courses. The best soups were the cream of mussels with asparagus and the cream of garlic with the tiny snails, petits gris. Consommé, whether garnished with red snapper or sweetbreads, was weak and salty and lacked the beefy body expected.

Fish and seafood main courses were poor. Chopped up lobster and julienne strips of vegetable proved a mishmash of flavors and textures, and the grilled pompano in a beurre blanc reeked of oily fishiness. Billed as pot au feu de la mer, a graceless seafood stew seemed like odd bits of fish and shellfish afloat in dill-flavored milk, and I have seldom had a fish course worse than the greasy salmon overpowered by marrow and a heavy red wine sauce.

Meat courses were better, particularly the delicately pink noisettes of lamb perfumed with mint and the rare, tender fillet of beef with marrow in a dark-red wine sauce. Properly pale and delicate slices of veal fillet garnished with homemade noodles and warm foie gras could not be improved upon. Delicately rare pigeon breast in a green peppercorn sauce and fresh, moist calf's liver burnished by a pungent orange sauce were above average. Sweetbreads in puff pastry with truffles and tiny green olives and chicken in a morel cream sauce were acceptable, nothing more.

Four goat cheeses of varying degrees of sharpness distinguish the cheese tray that usually includes a properly runny petit Brie, the ripe triple crème St.-André and a stinging blue-streaked pipo-crème. After that, there is a choice of enticing desserts. A savory bitter-chocolate-and-meringue cake is as irresistible as the hot apple tarte Tatin or the chocolate marquise with its velvety mousselike interior and its brassy coffee sauce. A charlotte of strawberry bavaroise is also delicious, and so are the flat, puffy oeufs à la neige, the poached egg whites adrift in a satiny crème anglaise. Poached pears and orange salad lacked distinctive flavor, but the pear and Sauterne sherbets were refreshingly astringent. The prix fixe dinner, which carries no surcharges, also includes some fair pastry appetizers and some enticing, well-made petits fours with coffee.

The setting at Le Plaisir has been somewhat refurbished, and the floral wall fabric has been replaced by bright rough silk the exact deep-coral color of a well-made sauce Nantua. There will be a rotating exhibition of art on the walls and, with luck, the future collections will be an improvement over the shoes, handbags and costume jewelry first displayed.

Service is cordial, sincere and accommodating, though painfully slow between appetizer and main course. The noise level is bearable, but chairs are too high and tables are uncomfortably shaky. The new wine list includes some excellent choices that are moderately priced.

Le Refuge
★

166 East 82nd Street, between Lexington and Third Avenues, 861-4505.

Atmosphere: Charming rustic and fresh French Provincial setting; service is friendly, accommodating and moderately efficient.

Recommended dishes: Tomato and arugula salad, mousse of smoked salmon, asparagus or artichoke vinaigrette, entrecôte maître d'hôtel, sole meunière, fish pâté with green sauce, duck without canned peas, calf's brains with capers, chocolate mousse, raspberry tart.

Price range: Moderately expensive.

Credit cards: None.

Hours: Lunch, Mondays through Saturdays, noon to 3 P.M.; dinner, Mondays through Saturdays, 6 P.M. to 11 P.M. Closed Sundays. Open some major holidays.

Reservations: Recommended.

Dark wood, bright blue-and-white country checkered cotton curtains and big, dish-towel napkins give this restaurant a relaxed and airy French Provincial charm. The front room with a handsome bar suggests a cafe-bistro, while the back room feels much like an enclosed sunporch. Service is friendly and accommodating and, if anything, dishes arrive too quickly, especially on crowded nights when one suspects turnover is on the management's mind. Generally though, a meal here is easygoing and comfortable, if noisy.

Cooking is easygoing, too, with a certain softness and sweetness pervading many dishes. What is lacking is an authoritative hand that would give dishes strength and character. Nevertheless, there are some satisfying choices for anyone who finds this neighborhood convenient for lunch or dinner, the former being especially felicitous.

Pierre Saint-Denis, the owner-chef, was formerly at the original La Petite Ferme, and much of the format is evident here. Where he got the idea for chicken livers served with blueberries had perhaps best be left a mystery; that he continues to serve it must mean that this inky mess has devotees — a most discouraging thought.

Other appetizers are a good deal better, fortunately. Among the best were a tomato salad with a creamy, mustard-brightened vinaigrette dressing, a cloud-light mousse of smoked salmon dotted with red caviar, bright, firm asparagus or artichokes in the same refreshing vinaigrette dressing and a delicate fish pâté with an herbaceous green sauce. A timbale of snails braised with butter and garlic managed to overcome the unnecessary sprinkling of raisins. A leek quiche needed a less floury pastry.

A totally characterless bouillabaisse tasted of nothing but canned tomatoes, and even the usually heady rouille sauce lacked sufficient garlic and cayenne.

Duck with flavorful skin and moist meat was compromised by canned peas, a gaffe even if they did come from France. Better the local variety or a different garnish entirely. The best main course was the calf's brains gilded in butter and piquant with capers. Sole meunière at lunch one day had just the right haze of golden butter over and around it, and entrecôte with maître d'hôtel parsley butter was several cuts above average. That is more than can be said for the pallid chicken with Calvados and cream, the stale-tasting poached salmon with a beurre blanc sauce and the stewy, stringy veal zapped with an overdose of tarragon.

Salads are bright and fresh, and bread is decent. Undersalting is a persistent flaw here, so be prepared to season to taste, as the recipe books like to say. Vegetables such as julienne strips of carrots, zucchini and yellow squash are well cooked and offer firm contrast to main courses.

Sherbets, albeit homemade, are devoid of flavor and splintered with ice. Better to opt for the excellent bittersweet chocolate mousse or the crisp-crusted raspberry tart. There is an almond mousse here that tastes as though it were made with Jergens hand lotion.

Le Relais
Poor

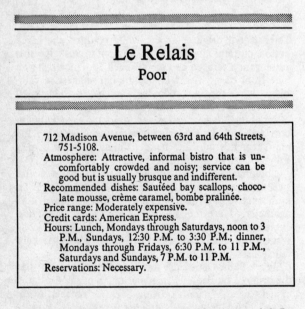

712 Madison Avenue, between 63rd and 64th Streets, 751-5108.
Atmosphere: Attractive, informal bistro that is uncomfortably crowded and noisy; service can be good but is usually brusque and indifferent.
Recommended dishes: Sautéed bay scallops, chocolate mousse, crème caramel, bombe pralinée.
Price range: Moderately expensive.
Credit cards: American Express.
Hours: Lunch, Mondays through Saturdays, noon to 3 P.M., Sundays, 12:30 P.M. to 3:30 P.M.; dinner, Mondays through Fridays, 6:30 P.M. to 11 P.M., Saturdays and Sundays, 7 P.M. to 11 P.M.
Reservations: Necessary.

If there was ever a restaurant spoiled by success, it is Le Relais, a four-year-old bistro. Although the restaurant was always head-splittingly noisy, the very good food and service once made up for this distraction, and Le Relais deserved its earlier two-star rating. Now, noise is compounded by indifferent service and by food that at its very best can only be considered passable. Much of it is underseasoned or is prepared too long in advance.

Not that these flaws have cut down on the popularity of Le Relais. At all hours there is a languidly trendy bar crowd blocking the entrance to the dining room, and tables are filled as quickly as they are emptied, which is none too quickly, for service is painfully slow and chaotic. "Don't worry. We haven't killed anyone yet," our waiter said as I ducked to avoid a bowl of soup. Even so, it was hard to relax.

It's been a long time since I have had such badly cooked vegetables, especially a bronzed and mushy spinach that might have been bottled baby food, much overcooked asparagus and broccoli with flowers falling off. An otherwise acceptable lentil salad was served ice cold, and so was the chicken liver pâté that became greasy. An overly acidic edge marred a tomato-vegetable soup. Chicken salad in mustard mayonnaise was among the original glories of this establishment, but at a recent lunch, the ample amount of meat topped soaking-wet lettuce. The water ran to the bottom of the bowl, washing the mayonnaise down with it. Roast chicken bore no traces of the tarragon it was supposed to have, sliced noisettes of lamb were tough and chewy and pasty calf's liver with a floury brown gravy could have come from a cafeteria steam table. Overcooked veal curled and dried out, and a candy-sweet orange butter marred soft-shell crabs. Only sautéed scallops can be recommended among main courses. There were, however, three good desserts — the chocolate mousse, the bombe pralinée and the lusty crème caramel. Prices would seem moderate if the food were good. No years are included on the wine list, a strange lapse in a place much frequented by wine dealers.

L'Escargot Restaurant

★

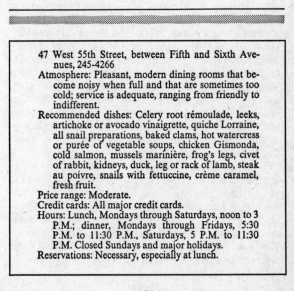

47 West 55th Street, between Fifth and Sixth Avenues, 245-4266

Atmosphere: Pleasant, modern dining rooms that become noisy when full and that are sometimes too cold; service is adequate, ranging from friendly to indifferent.

Recommended dishes: Celery root rémoulade, leeks, artichoke or avocado vinaigrette, quiche Lorraine, all snail preparations, baked clams, hot watercress or purée of vegetable soups, chicken Gismonda, cold salmon, mussels marinière, frog's legs, civet of rabbit, kidneys, duck, leg or rack of lamb, steak au poivre, snails with fettuccine, crème caramel, fresh fruit.

Price range: Moderate.

Credit cards: All major credit cards.

Hours: Lunch, Mondays through Saturdays, noon to 3 P.M.; dinner, Mondays through Fridays, 5:30 P.M. to 11:30 P.M., Saturdays, 5 P.M. to 11:30 P.M. Closed Sundays and major holidays.

Reservations: Necessary, especially at lunch.

Reasonably priced, decently prepared French food at the bistro level is hard to come by these days, here as well as in France, and for the very same reason: Rising costs dictate higher prices that can be commanded only by food that is fashionably new.

An exception to this rule in New York is L'Escargot. If the two simple but comfortable contemporary dining rooms are not the settings for rare gastronomic experiences, they do offer some solidly satisfying food at very modest prices. Service, like the food, varies from very good to minimally acceptable. And in certain corners the air-conditioner operates with a vengeance; if it is annoying, ask to be moved to another table or to have the temperature turned up a bit. The management will comply, though often less than graciously.

But with prices what they are today, consider a dinner under $15 that might begin with very good, crisp mustardy celery root rémoulade, or a refreshing artichoke, an avocado half or leeks marinated in a pungent vinaigrette dressing, to be followed by a lively, well-seasoned green salad, and a main course of mussels marinière in a white wine fumé redolent of garlic or an impeccably fried, boneless breast of chicken Gismonda on a bed of leaf spinach. A dozen plump snails in the Burgundian sauce of butter, garlic and parsley is an alternative main course at this price, and for dessert there is a light and sunny crème caramel, ripe melon or a salad of fresh fruit.

Other complete dinners are equally good values and can be built around a main course of rosy, garlic-scented rack of lamb served with fresh string beans and a potato croquette. At such moderate prices as these, a few imperfections have to be overlooked, though the items involved don't have to be eaten. Among such at L'Escargot are the terrible bread, the occasional leaves of iceberg lettuce that are added to the otherwise respectable mix of greens and the generally poor baked desserts.

Nor are all the appetizers and main courses equally well prepared. Skip banalities such as the mixed hors d'oeuvres, the pâtés, the sandy mussels ravigotte and the spinach quiche in favor of the Lorraine. All snails, whether done with the classic Burgundy sauce or with the anise-flavored Ricard liqueur or with Provençale aromatic herbs, are as delicious as the snails served as a main course, tossed into butter, garlic and parsley-sauced fettuccine. Snails and a few other appetizers carry a surcharge. Both the hot cream of watercress soup and the purée of vegetable soup were far above average. So were the frog's legs with garlic butter, the rose-red, slightly crunchy kidneys with shallots, finished with a Bordelaise sauce, and the hefty civet de lapin, a rabbit stew enriched with smoky overtones of meaty bacon in a dark, red-wine sauce.

Duck with skin as crisp as bacon had meat that remained moist and supple, and the fresh orange sauce struck the right bittersweet note, although one might wish that its accompaniment had been plain, well-seasoned white rice instead of the pretentious combination of wild and white. It would be hard to beat the rack or leg of lamb at any price but easy to outclass the soggy, oversized, sautéed soft-shell crabs, the steamy and corny beef Wellington and the salty, sourish chicken grand-mère, another special one day. The only acceptable beef dish was the steak au poivre vert, properly bloody, if a bit sinewy, in a pungent green peppercorn sauce. A lighter application of flour would help the otherwise acceptable sweetbreads as well as the calf's liver with avocado slices. But all the shrimp were stale, whether as appetizers or main courses.

There are about eight dull, commercial cakes on display — one or two good ones would be preferable. For dessert choose the crème caramel or the fresh fruit. American coffee is consistently weak and boiled; espresso is a better choice. There are some good moderately priced wines.

Lunch prices are even lower than those at dinner, and at that time of day, the cold poached salmon with green herb mayonnaise and cucumber salad is a light and lovely main course.

Les Pleiades

★

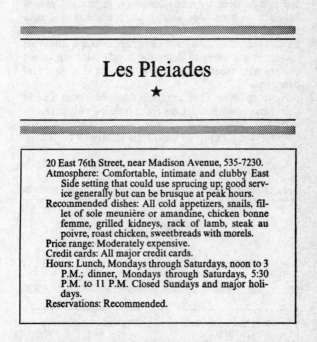

20 East 76th Street, near Madison Avenue, 535-7230.
Atmosphere: Comfortable, intimate and clubby East Side setting that could use sprucing up; good service generally but can be brusque at peak hours.
Recommended dishes: All cold appetizers, snails, fillet of sole meunière or amandine, chicken bonne femme, grilled kidneys, rack of lamb, steak au poivre, roast chicken, sweetbreads with morels.
Price range: Moderately expensive.
Credit cards: All major credit cards.
Hours: Lunch, Mondays through Saturdays, noon to 3 P.M.; dinner, Mondays through Saturdays, 5:30 P.M. to 11 P.M. Closed Sundays and major holidays.
Reservations: Recommended.

With so much going for it, it's too bad Les Pleiades has not kept up the quality of its kitchen, which used to turn out food that was savory and satisfying, if never brilliant. A recent dinner for six indicated such serious lapses (even though I was recognized) that one can only recommend the restaurant with caution. Saucisson en croûte arrived stale and gray, as though it had been sliced hours ago and held without refrigeration. Canned peaches garnished greasy, stringy reheated duck, and soggy soft-shell crabs smelled suspiciously fishy. Lunch, however, is a good deal better than dinner, as it always has been, and accounts for the one-star rating.

What have stood up well are the cold appetizers, which can be had separately or in an assortment. They usually include two excellent poached fish — salmon and striped bass — with green herb mayonnaise, well-prepared leeks or artichokes in mustardy vinaigrette dressing, a crunchy salade Niçoise or gentle mushrooms

253

à la grecque, nice, pink and mild prosciutto and rugged saucisson sec or en croûte. Céleri rémoulade and cucumber salad also are well prepared. Escargot are decent.

Pâté de campagne, formerly coarse and garlicky, is now soft and fatty. Soups have always been disappointing. Among main courses, the rack of lamb remains an excellent choice, always cooked as ordered and lightly burnished with herb and garlic flavors. Bright, firm vegetables accompany this as well as the nut-brown, moist roast chicken. But do not make the mistake of ruining that chicken with a dousing of the heavy brown sauce served with it; burned onions add the identifying flavor. Sweetbreads with morels are pleasant, served in a light and winy sauce.

Steak au povire is delicious, as are the grilled kidneys with mustard sauce, the chicken bonne femme with tiny potatoes and nuggets of bacon and the grilled or sautéed sole favored by many luncheon regulars. Desserts have always been poor, and tasting crème caramel, pale chocolate mousse and pastries indicated no improvement. Most of all, the food here seems dated, although that does not seem to deter the loyal following of art dealers who frequent the place. Neither do the awful paintings.

Another caveat I feel compelled to add. From time to time I have had complaints from readers who have visited this restaurant at very crowded times and have been treated abruptly or downright rudely.

Le Steak

★

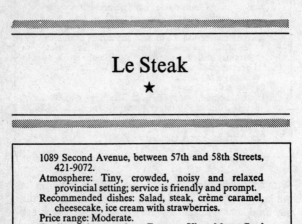

1089 Second Avenue, between 57th and 58th Streets, 421-9072.
Atmosphere: Tiny, crowded, noisy and relaxed provincial setting; service is friendly and prompt.
Recommended dishes: Salad, steak, crème caramel, cheesecake, ice cream with strawberries.
Price range: Moderate.
Credit cards: American Express, Visa, MasterCard and Diners Club.
Hours: Dinner, Mondays through Saturdays 5:30 P.M. to 10:45 P.M., Sundays, 5:30 P.M. to 9:45 P.M. Closed on major holidays.
Reservations: Recommended.

It would be difficult to match the menu at Le Steak for utter simplicity. The only offerings are a very good salad of mixed greens in a pungent mustard-and-garlic vinaigrette dressing served as a first course, a strip steak that weighs about a half-pound, a mound of decent if not inspired french fries and a large dessert menu. That, plus American coffee, makes up the one and only table d'hôte dinner, a satisfying buy, especially if one is planning to go to a movie on 57th Street or Third Avenue. The format is so simple that it has been successfully repeated in Georgetown and Houston.

The setting at Le Steak suggests a small provincial inn. It is candlelit, cramped and convivial with a jampacked bar after eight. Some background music adds unnecessarily to the confusion, but the young staff is friendly, fast and accommodating. When I sent back coffee ice cream parfait because it was caustic with rum, it was cheerfully replaced with a light and lovely crème caramel.

Tender steaks were cooked exactly as ordered — with an observable difference between one ordered rare and another ordered medium rare. Both were topped with the house sauce — a Provençale herb combination that was a bit strong on thyme and therefore overpowered the beef. Unless you are inordinately fond of thyme, ask to have the sauce on the side or eliminated. Bread, though hot, had an unpleasantly musty flavor.

Cheesecake and crème caramel are by far the best desserts. Ice cream with strawberries is preferable to the bland chocolate mousse and the parfaits frozen into their metal cups.

Le Trianon
Poor

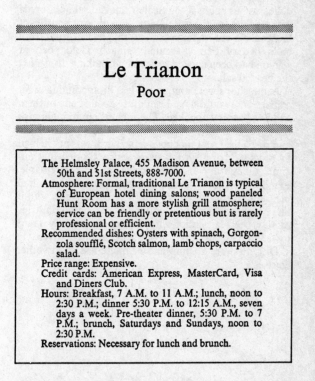

The Helmsley Palace, 455 Madison Avenue, between 50th and 51st Streets, 888-7000.

Atmosphere: Formal, traditional Le Trianon is typical of European hotel dining salons; wood paneled Hunt Room has a more stylish grill atmosphere; service can be friendly or pretentious but is rarely professional or efficient.

Recommended dishes: Oysters with spinach, Gorgonzola soufflé, Scotch salmon, lamb chops, carpaccio salad.

Price range: Expensive.

Credit cards: American Express, MasterCard, Visa and Diners Club.

Hours: Breakfast, 7 A.M. to 11 A.M.; lunch, noon to 2:30 P.M.; dinner 5:30 P.M. to 12:15 A.M., seven days a week. Pre-theater dinner, 5:30 P.M. to 7 P.M.; brunch, Saturdays and Sundays, noon to 2:30 P.M.

Reservations: Necessary for lunch and brunch.

Food and service here, so far, are precisely the kind that have given hotel restaurants a bad name. Whether in the wood-paneled, comfortably upholstered Hunt Room or in the more formal and somewhat lugubrious traditional Le Trianon, the diner is offered the same menu choices and gets the sinking feeling that nobody is really in charge.

At best the service is friendly and polite but careless. A salad for two, instead of being divided, is served on a single plate. Water and coffee refills must be requested several times. And even the most polished captain rests his hand on a diner's chair as he takes the order. At worst, the service follows the New York delicatessen style, although at times it can be embarrassingly pretentious. A captain will argue over the saltiness of the raw salmon tartare appetizer he has made — "Salty? How can it be salty? I didn't put salt in it. Did you see me put salt in it?"

Most discouraging of all is the food — consistently mediocre, sometimes totally inedible because of spoilage. The flavor of garlic and herbs in one appetizer, shrimps Riviera, was overpowered by the iodine in the shrimp, indicating staleness. A veal loin chop — called a veal T-bone steak on the menu — smelled high, as did the meat stuffing for some soggy quail. Duck pâté arrived musty and dark gray, and oysters, apparently opened at least an hour before they were served, were shrunken, yellowed and dried out.

Thick, dark-brown onion soup suggested canned beef gravy, and it was barely warm under a greasy, waxy topping of grated Jarlsberg. Cream of pea soup was a far preferable alternative, bland and characterless though it was.

Among the only really decent appetizers were the delicious but badly sliced Scotch smoked salmon served without lemon, the small, hot and savory soufflé of Gorgonzola cheese, and hot oysters gratinéed in cream on a bed of Pernod-scented spinach. Cold poached salmon had been cooked to the same choking dryness as the broiled salmon.

Lamb chops were among the less disappointing main courses and would have been quite good if one of them had not been overcooked. The rack of lamb might also have passed muster were it not for an overkill of thyme and rosemary. An innocuous mixed grill was not helped by a dousing of a syrupy sweet sauce. Grilled filet mignon, though dry and lifeless, was at least acceptable. Lemon chicken — a sautéed breaded breast — had pleasant accents of lemon, but the green noodles with it had grown cold and hard. A lunch salad based on strips of raw beef carpaccio, with a pungent, creamy sauce tossed into greens, was one of the better alternatives.

Desserts were as limp and characterless as the other courses.

Le Veau d'Or
Fair

129 East 60th Street, between Park and Lexington
Avenues, 838-8133.

Atmosphere: Crowded, noisy, quintessential small
Parisian bistro; service can be good and efficient
or indifferent and careless.

Recommended dishes: Snails, oeuf en gelée, hot sausage, vegetable soup, rack of lamb, poussin grand-
mère or bonne femme, crème caramel, chocolate
mousse.

Price range: Moderate.

Credit cards: American Express.

Hours: Lunch, Mondays through Fridays, noon to
2:30 P.M.; dinner, Mondays through Saturdays, 6
P.M. to 10:15 P.M. Closed Sundays and holidays;
closed Saturdays and Sundays in summer.

Reservations: Recommended, especially for lunch and
always for parties larger than four.

Once New York's most authentic and satisfying Parisian-style bistro, this jammed, funky and charming little
place has become increasingly careless through the
years, both in the treatment of customers and in the
preparation of food. There is still a strong sentimental
appeal about the small room with its homey posters,
Paris street signs and especially the trademark painting
of the gold calf asleep in a bed with lacy pillows under
his head. But those who have no fond memories of this
place to mitigate its present performance will feel dinner there is time ill spent.

When crowded, as it usually is at lunch, Le Veau
d'Or is a harrowing experience, as the management is
cool-to-rude to those waiting for tables, especially if
they are women unaccompanied by men, and once you
are seated it is unnerving to feel trays gliding by so close
to your head and to be elbow-to-elbow with guests at
nearby tables. Worst of all, there seems to be a formula
about which guests get which giveaway appetizers. At
lunch, it may be ratatouille or salade Niçoise, usually
meted out to all. But the famed mussels ravigote seem
to be held for particular guests, or for a particular time.
Arrive at 9 P.M. and you may be told they are gone. Arrive at 7:30 P.M. and you may get a slab of a dreadful
quiche, cakey and reeking of stale eggs, while at other
times you get slices of salami or, finally, the prized mussels. Why you were not so blessed is a mystery waiters
mumble about when a direct question is put to them.

Since this is one of the few authentic menus of bistro-
style bourgeois dishes left around, it's a pity they are not
better prepared. Among the appetizers that stand up
well are the snails sizzling in individual crocks under
mantles of green herbs and garlic, the hot garlic sausage
in a crust that is sometimes limp but generally good although the potato salad lacks flavor, and the oeuf en
gelée, a perfect egg mollet — poached with a runny yolk
— set in a flavorful aspic underlined with ham. Vegetables vinaigrette can be good or stale and overcooked.

Potage santé — health soup — is a vegetable purée with a potato base sparked by sorrel and is thoroughly satisfying. Onion soup was bitingly salty.

Lunchtime chicken in sauce dishes and stews such as veal Niçoise have recently tasted as though they were reheated several times, and the sauce had not permeated the chicken. Fish was badly overcooked. Duck at dinner had the musty flavor of reheated grease, and the green peppercorn sauce had no sting or distinction of any kind, while the wild rice with it was overcooked and undersalted. Though heavily rimmed with fat, rack of lamb had an excellent flavor and was done rare as ordered. Poussin grand-mère or bonne femme has always been above average here and still is. If bonne femme (with mushrooms and peas) is on the menu, I generally ask for the grand-mère version (mushrooms, onions and bacon), preferring that lustier sauce, and the kitchen complies.

Pastry in the form of fruit tarts is poor, but chocolate mousse and crème caramel are good.

The one policy most distressing at Le Veau d'Or is the habit of overbooking reservations, necessitating the agonizing wait on line and at the bar. I had a 12:30 reservation for lunch one day and after arriving seven minutes late was kept waiting until 1:15, at which point I left, there being several parties at the bar still ahead of me.

By now, the owner should know how many people can be seated in how long a period and book tables more realistically. Service can be polite and pleasant, if rushed, but the management's response to impatient patrons on the waiting line is a laugh and a shrug, which is not quite good enough.

L'Hostaria del Bongustaio
★

75 East 55th Street, between Madison and Park Avenues, 751-3530.
Atmosphere: Delicately pretty dining room, with tables too small and close together; service uneven and unprofessional but polite.
Recommended dishes: Carpaccio, seafood risotto, green risotto, risotto alla Milanese, linguine with seafood, fettuccine with smoked salmon, ravioli malfatti, trenette al pesto, green and white pasta with porcini mushrooms, bucatini all'Amatriciana, cannelloni, chicken in vinegar, chicken in walnut sauce, grilled chicken country-style, paillard of veal or beef, calf's liver Veneziana, red snapper Livornese, snapper in brodetto, strawberries with lemon juice and sugar.
Price range: Expensive.
Credit cards: American Express, MasterCard, and Visa.
Hours: Lunch, Mondays through Fridays noon to 3 P.M.; dinner, Mondays through Fridays, 5:30 P.M. to 10:30 P.M., Saturdays, 5:30 to 11 P.M. Closed Sundays and major holidays.
Reservations: Necessary.

Inconsistency is perhaps the most difficult condition to deal with in rating a restaurant, especially if the kitchen's talents range widely from exceptional to mundane, if the setting is gracefully pretty but uncomfortably cramped and if the staff is polite but unprofessional. Add to that high prices at which no shortcomings can be excused, and a management apparently at a loss about what managers should do, and you have the concise story of L'Hostaria del Bongustaio, a northern Italian restaurant with an original and enticing menu.

Serious eaters might want to try L'Hostaria del Bongustaio for such risotto triumphs as the saffron-gilded Milanese classic or green risotto with spinach and leeks, or the same short and wide-grained Po River rice simmered with squid, shrimp and mussels for seafood risotto.

Other hard-to-beat pasta creations include fettuccine in a satiny cream sauce mellowed with smoked salmon; trenette, or slim noodles, al pesto, in a basil sauce, velvety with puréed potatoes, or paglia e fieno — green and white noodles with butter, cheese and smoky, wild porcini mushrooms. The thicker bucatini all'Amatriciana pasta was another masterpiece, with its tomato sauce enriched by pancetta bacon and onions, the same sauce that enlivens the malfatti ("badly made") ravioli, which are dumplings of spinach and cheese, but without the pasta covering that ravioli usually have. A frothy cannelloni filled with spinach and blanketed in a creamy tomato sauce showed talent in the kitchen, and so did linguine with seafood.

But not all the pastas met the same standards. One with tuna fish was dry and barely tepid, another with zucchini and mozzarella cheese arrived too cool for the cheese to melt properly, lasagne had been mushily overcooked, and it was hard to believe that five cheeses were present in the sauce of the maccheroncini al cinque formaggi.

But even with the best food, can a restaurant be recommended in which dried edges are trimmed from stale cheesecake and fresh bread is brought to replace stale bread when a well-known customer appears? And what can be said of a place, no matter how beautiful, in which waiters wear dirty white coats and the flower vases need washing?

Then again, L'Hostaria del Bongustaio serves a rosy, raw-beef carpaccio in pungent anchovy and caper sauce and expertly grilled veal and beef paillard. Also hard to beat are calf's liver sautéed with onions, Venezianastyle, and a snapper or fish stew with a caper-and-olive-accented Livornese tomato sauce.

There are some fine chicken specialties, too, among them boneless breast of chicken in a silky sauce of crushed walnuts and cream. Pollo all'aceto, a version of sautéed boneless chicken scarpariello, has garlic overtones sparked with a mildly pungent touch of wine vinegar, and pollo novello al mattone, though not really grilled between bricks, as the name implies, had nonetheless been properly flattened and had a crunchy grilled skin and a moist and succulent interior.

But again, failures counter triumphs. A tomato salad said to include mozzarella had none until it was requested; the cheese proved to be the best available, even if the tomatoes were not. On one occasion, seafood salad had grown soggy and musty, and another time it was almost frozen. Crostini turned out to be stale chicken-liver pâté with limp slices of white-bread toast on the side, and steamed mussels in white wine, though delicious, were gritty with sand. Squid smothered in white wine had virtually no taste, and the so-called mixed fish fry proved to be all squid, with only two shrimp on the side. Medaillons of veal arrived as scaloppine, and several times incorrect orders appeared.

The chef has a heavy hand with salt at times, and still heavier hand with the indelicate pastries. Inconsistencies even extended to iced coffee. Two glasses at the same lunch table tasted entirely different — one strongly burnished with an espresso flavor, the other weak and watery.

Little Afghanistan
★

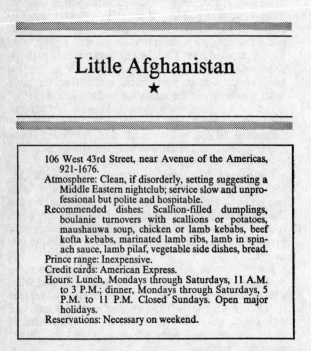

106 West 43rd Street, near Avenue of the Americas, 921-1676.

Atmosphere: Clean, if disorderly, setting suggesting a Middle Eastern nightclub; service slow and unprofessional but polite and hospitable.

Recommended dishes: Scallion-filled dumplings, boulanie turnovers with scallions or potatoes, maushauwa soup, chicken or lamb kebabs, beef kofta kebabs, marinated lamb ribs, lamb in spinach sauce, lamb pilaf, vegetable side dishes, bread.

Prince range: Inexpensive.

Credit cards: American Express.

Hours: Lunch, Mondays through Saturdays, 11 A.M. to 3 P.M.; dinner, Mondays through Saturdays, 5 P.M. to 11 P.M. Closed Sundays. Open major holidays.

Reservations: Necessary on weekend.

Resembling somewhat the cuisines of the Middle East and India, the cooking of Afghanistan has until recently been absent from the New York scene. It is now served in a pleasant and interesting way at this unusual little restaurant that offers modestly priced fare in the midst of the theater district.

In a setting that suggests an Arabian Nights cocktail lounge crossed with a disorderly luncheonette, a handsome, willing and thoroughly ingratiating staff explains the dishes on the exotic-sounding menu. Afghan music vibrates in the background, and in one corner a khima, or tent, is set up, with divans around a table that can be reserved for laid-back dining, native style. Photographs of the rugged, mountainous Afghan landscape on walls and menu covers make it obvious what a heroically handsome country it is.

The basis of the menu consists of eggplant, yogurt, ground meat in a pungent paprika sauce, kebabs, curries and a superb, crisp-crusted channeled bread flecked with black onion seeds. Many dishes appear and reappear as appetizers, main courses and side dishes, varying only in portion size and garnish. For that reason it is important to pay close attention to menu descriptions, lest you wind up with three courses of the identical ingredients. It is also important to make choices known clearly and distinctly, for orders are often confused. By far, the best appetizers sampled were thin wontonlike dumplings filled with chopped raw scallions and topped with meat sauce and yogurt. Boulanie, flat griddle-fried turnovers with a variety of fillings, such as scallions, potatoes, carrots or pumpkin, were also delicious, better choices than either the soggy, meat-filled fried sambosas or the pasty vegetarian sambosas.

The more satisfying of two soups is maushauwa, made with tiny meatballs, yogurt, rice, beans, meat sauce and aromatic herbs and spices. Unfortunately, no matter how firmly one asks, it is never served really hot in temperature, though it may be sufficiently fiery in taste. Most of the food, in fact, would be better if truly hot.

Kebabs of marinated lamb and chicken, and ground-beef kofta kebabs are all delicious, served with either white rice or the fragrant brown pilaf. Marinated lamb ribs and chunks of lamb in a spinach sauce mellowed with onion and garlic are soothing and delicate, if not breathtaking. A dish of mildly curried lamb and rice pilaf with carrots and raisins is also worth trying.

Vegetable side dishes, such as pumpkin or eggplant topped with meat sauce and yogurt, are good accompaniments to the otherwise unsauced kebabs and can be had in large portions, without meat sauce, for vegetarians. What is billed as Afghan salad is a banal combination of iceberg lettuce, unripe tomatoes, cucumbers and onion in a watery sourish dressing.

Neither the firni, a tasteless cream and cornstarch pudding, nor the baklava, which twice included rancid nuts, is worth ordering.

Cardamon-perfumed tea is a refreshing finish to a meal at Little Afghanistan. There is no liquor license, so you may take your own beer or wine.

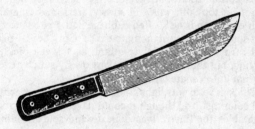

Lou G. Siegel
★ ★

209 West 38th Street, 921-4433.
Atmosphere: Comfortable, formal modern dining
    rooms that are pleasant if undistinguished; service
    is typically casual and chatty but efficient.
Recommended dishes: Gefulte fish, cold boiled fish,
    stuffed cabbage, all soups, pot roast, meatballs,
    stuffed breast of veal, duck, chicken or boiled beef
    in the pot, beef goulash, salami or tongue with
    eggs, cold plates, apple strudel, mohn cake.
Price range: Moderate.
Credit cards: American Express, MasterCard, Visa
    and Diners Club.
Hours: Lunch, Mondays through Fridays, noon to
    3:30 P.M.; dinner, Sundays, noon to 9 P.M., Mon-
    days through Thursdays, 3:30 to 9 P.M. Closed
    Friday nights always and Saturday nights in sum-
    mer; closed all Jewish holidays.
Reservations: Recommended.

Rarely have any diners been given shorter shrift in service, atmosphere and food than those who frequent kosher restaurants. In rating such restaurants, then, it is
necessary to consider them in relation to comparable establishments. By that standard, Lou G. Siegel, the 65-
year-old kosher restaurant in the garment district,
clearly deserves two stars.

This is one of the few kosher restaurants truly eligible
for the white-tablecloth category, and although the
décor is far from distinguished, it is at least solid, formal
and clean. There is full bar service and a hearty menu
of traditional Jewish meat dishes with no dairy foods on
hand. Pickled green tomatoes and fresh cole slaw are
automatically placed on each table and there is always a
range of bright, firm pickles from new to completely
sour.

Although the chopped liver is on the greasy side, and
definitely not made of chicken livers, other appetizers
were at a high level compared to their counterparts in
other kosher restaurants. Gefulte fish, lacking in pepper
and a bit too soft, was still snowy, fresh and fragrant
with onion, and the stuffed cabbage had a good sweet-
and-sour balance to its tomato sauce. Cold boiled pike
and carp were deliciously piquant, as was the pickled
herring, but the stuffed derma was overly starchy even
for that unfortunate creation.

Chicken soup was light golden in color, free of artificial colorings, and though it could have used more root
vegetables for flavor, was delicate and soul-warming.
Kreplach and the pastry soup nuts, mandel, were well
cooked and seasoned, but matzoh balls fell apart. Pea
soup was even better with its garlicky croutons.

A half duck came out of the oven crisp, greaseless
and tender, but the applesauce with it was far too sweet
and watery, and its sweet potato and string beans were
typically overcooked.

A snow-white, moistly fresh breast of chicken in the pot, a fairly lean, boiled beef flanken and very good paprika-bright pot roast were fine choices, as were the potted meat balls and stuffed breast of veal. Beef goulash with noodles was another presentable main course, but other dishes with sauces are best ignored. One unusual dish consistently done well here is braised lamb tongues in a sweet-sour Polonaise sauce, sometimes with raisins. Fish is invariably overcooked, and potato pancakes are stiff with what seems to be baking powder. But kasha varnishkes, that classic combination of crushed buckwheat groats and bowtie pasta, is rarely soggy or fatty and is a perfect foil for rich dishes such as the duck or pot roast.

Tongue or salami fried in a pancake-style omelet and beautifully fresh and copious salad platters (spoiled only by the omnipresence of iceberg lettuce) are understandably favorite luncheon choices.

The flaky, cinnamon-enriched apple strudel here would be 100 percent better if it were served warm, and the poppyseed mixture in the rolled mohn cake could use a dash of lemon juice, but both these desserts are fairly good as presented. Not so the ersatz cream concoctions based on nondairy whiteners that substitute for the verboten cream. Better to skip them and choose what can be done authentically.

Portions are generous and prices moderate. While there is rabbinical supervision of the kitchen here, Lou G. Siegel is not glatt kosher, though it closes all day Saturday and opens Sunday. It is also a choice worth considering for its proximity to the theater district.

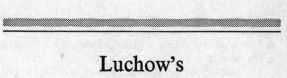

Luchow's
Unrated (see note below)

1633 Broadway, at corner of 51st Street, 247-5880.

Note: As this book goes to press, Luchow's, one of New York's most famous antique restaurants, is in limbo. Located at 110 East 14th Street since August Lüchow opened this handsome, wood-paneled German restaurant in 1882, it has fallen upon hard times in recent years because of bad service and housekeeping and a kitchen that produced almost totally inedible food.

Now it is being recreated on 51st Street and Broadway, although the original interior — or what's left of it after the owners sold the magnificent artifacts and accessories at auction — will not be brought uptown. Neither will the umlaut over the "u" in the restaurant's name.

There is also a plan to open a disco called The Palace at Luchow's original location.

Lutèce
★ ★ ★ ★

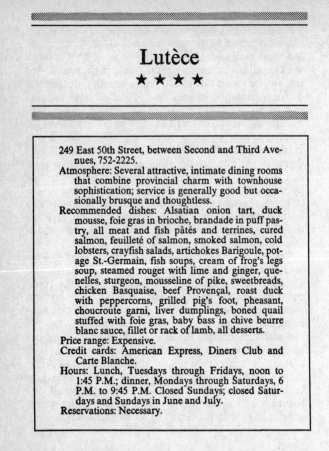

249 East 50th Street, between Second and Third Avenues, 752-2225.

Atmosphere: Several attractive, intimate dining rooms that combine provincial charm with townhouse sophistication; service is generally good but occasionally brusque and thoughtless.

Recommended dishes: Alsatian onion tart, duck mousse, foie gras in brioche, brandade in puff pastry, all meat and fish pâtés and terrines, cured salmon, feuilleté of salmon, smoked salmon, cold lobsters, crayfish salads, artichokes Barigoule, potage St.-Germain, fish soups, cream of frog's legs soup, steamed rouget with lime and ginger, quenelles, sturgeon, mousseline of pike, sweetbreads, chicken Basquaise, beef Provençal, roast duck with peppercorns, grilled pig's foot, pheasant, choucroute garni, liver dumplings, boned quail stuffed with foie gras, baby bass in chive beurre blanc sauce, fillet or rack of lamb, all desserts.

Price range: Expensive.

Credit cards: American Express, Diners Club and Carte Blanche.

Hours: Lunch, Tuesdays through Fridays, noon to 1:45 P.M.; dinner, Mondays through Saturdays, 6 P.M. to 9:45 P.M. Closed Sundays; closed Saturdays and Sundays in June and July.

Reservations: Necessary.

The French restaurant with the greatest range and most ambitious kitchen is Lutèce where André Soltner, who is both chef and owner, offers many special and lavish preparations.

Mr. Soltner, the chef-partner almost since this restaurant was opened in 1961 by André Surmain, bought the restaurant in 1972. His team now includes his wife, Simone, who keeps the dining room efficient and felicitious, and Christian Bertrand, the chef de cuisine, who understudies Mr. Soltner.

Certainly, Lutèce is the most comfortable if not the most elaborate of the town's four-star dining places, and the various rooms in this townhouse offer a variety of atmospheres, all more or less in keeping with the casual, personal charm of French country restaurants. The most stylish area is the small downstairs room in the front, although many prefer the upholstered intimacy of the upstairs dining rooms. Still other regulars opt for the enclosed garden, which has a special charm at lunch when the light filtering through the skylight puts a glow on the trellised petal-pink walls. Complaints about slow and indifferent service tend to come from diners seated upstairs, and there have been recent reports of careless service to unknown guests.

Mr. Soltner takes enormous pleasure in helping diners plan meals they will enjoy, often sending small extras out to customers he knows will like his choices. Among the lagniappes offered in such instances were tiny tartlets filled with garlic cream and sheer slices of pheasant liver, a hard act for any appetizer to follow. Nevertheless, possibilities are extraordinary, whether you choose the puffy, crisp-crusted Alsatian onion tart, the fine juniper-perfumed duck mousse or foie gras baked in eggy brioche dough, the feuilleté puff pastry, filled with the whipped, creamed salt codfish, brandade, then finished with a pink beurre blanc. Fish pâtés and terrines of country pâté are always on hand, all equally inspired, as is the fine-grained, woodsy smoked salmon and the slightly chewy, peppery herb-cured raw salmon. Alternates are cold half lobsters, composed salads with crayfish and avocado and an occasional daily attraction, such as fresh, warm langoustine in a basil-touched butter sauce or a dishful of shelled crayfish in a Nantua-flavored sauce. Tiny artichokes à la Barigoule, not much larger than rosebuds, are sometimes available, and the dish of jade-green leafy buds, adrift in a saffron-gold sauce tinged with pink peppercorns and bronzed coriander seeds, invites photographing as much as it does tasting.

The potage St.-Germain is a homier version than La Grenouille's, with a more yellow tinge to it and the slight, soul-warming hint of onion and leeks. Fish soup with crab meat, afloat with croutons topped by the red-pepper-and-garlic sauce rouille, is a satisfying lunch in itself.

Although salmon baked en croûte with tarragon was strangely lacking in flavor and its sauce was too heavily stung with vinegar, and scallops Méridionale tasted of burned butter, other fish, such as the steamed rouget touched with lime and ginger and the mousseline of pike, achieved ethereal perfection. Delicate round slices of sweetbreads gilded in the sauté pan and sparkled with capers, and roast chicken dripping butter and green herbs were each four-star dishes.

Two fine lunch plats du jour were a tender braised beef Provençale and a creamed chicken fricassee brightened by filaments of zucchini and noodles. Kidneys at one of these lunches were totally obscured by an overabundance of a very decent red wine sauce, but at dinner a roast duck with pink and green peppercorns in Provence-inspired sautéed tomatoes had fine strands of eggy homemade noodles as a subtle underpinning. Choucroute garni, when available at lunch, sets an enviable standard for this Alsatian sauerkraut specialty.

Like so may of France's haute cuisine restaurants, Lutèce now offers a nightly menu de degustation, a tasting menu of six or seven courses that must be ordered by everyone at the table. We tried such a menu and found it diverting and delectable. It began somewhat blandly with a breast of chicken stuffed with mousse of chicken and truffles and then went on to a mustard-gilded pied de porc — pig's foot. The slightly sweet-sour brown sauce vinaigre had just the right burnish to offset the richness of the meal. Half a boned baby quail stuffed with its own liver and foie gras baked in a shatteringly crisp crust was enriched with a truffle sauce, and after that came baby bass in a vegetable-and-chive-strewn beurre blanc sauce as delicate as air.

The pièce de résistance was a roast fillet of lamb in a sauce based on sautéed pimento, fresh thyme, veal glaze and a touch of tomato for overall rosiness. Unfortunately, the pimento sweetened the sauce too strongly for my palate and for the red wine I was drinking. At a later dinner a roast rack of lamb was served in a honey-mustard-vinegar sauce that was also palate-shocking in its sweetness. New and exceptional dishes include a napoleon-like feuilleté of salmon, roast pheasant, braised wild boar and sautéed liver dumplings.

André Soltner is one of the few chefs who can bake as well as he cooks, a tribute to his Alsation background. Puff pastry holding raspberries, his lemon Bavaroise in tart pastry, the extraordinary tarte Bressane with its eggy, almond-sweetened custard-cream filling, and his astringent lemony succès maison live up to the promises of other courses. So do his chocolate soufflé, with its liquid-ivory vanilla sauce, and some of the fruit sorbets, excepting only melon and kiwi, which are inelegant. The tarte Tatin lacked the glassy caramel glaze and buttery apple essence it needs to be at its best. Petits fours are miracles of crisp fragility.

Getting reservations here requires persistence. The telephone is always busy, and you must generally call four weeks ahead.

Madras Woodlands
★ ★ ★

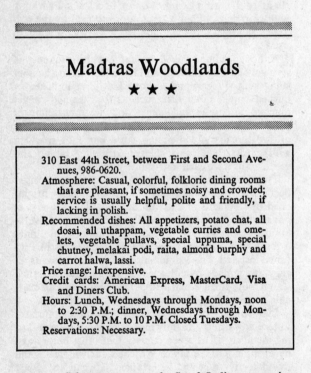

310 East 44th Street, between First and Second Avenues, 986-0620.

Atmosphere: Casual, colorful, folkloric dining rooms that are pleasant, if sometimes noisy and crowded; service is usually helpful, polite and friendly, if lacking in polish.

Recommended dishes: All appetizers, potato chat, all dosai, all uthappam, vegetable curries and omelets, vegetable pullavs, special uppuma, special chutney, melakai podi, raita, almond burphy and carrot halwa, lassi.

Price range: Inexpensive.

Credit cards: American Express, MasterCard, Visa and Diners Club.

Hours: Lunch, Wednesdays through Mondays, noon to 2:30 P.M.; dinner, Wednesdays through Mondays, 5:30 P.M. to 10 P.M. Closed Tuesdays.

Reservations: Necessary.

Using no fish, meat or eggs, the South Indian vegetarian kitchen produces an array of dishes so intricately seductive in their sparkling contrasts of seasonings and textures that they appeal esthetically even if one eschews vegetarianism as such. Outstanding examples of the wonders of the South Indian kitchen have been prepared consistently at Madras Woodlands at a location especially convenient for the United Nations delegates who favor the restaurant at lunchtime. At other times, and most especially on weekends, the two colorful and informal dining rooms with their folkloric decorations are filled with Indian families, a lively and tacit testimony to the authenticity of the preparations.

The entrance dining room where the bar is situated suggests a cocktail lounge and is a lively setting for people watchers. The newer and larger dining room is a bit more formal and restful and would be even more felicitous without the banal, elevator-style background music.

The staff is sincere, polite and willing to be helpful in explaining the dishes and the correct way to order, although there have been a few reports of rudeness. An occasional language barrier makes for a bit of confusion, but what might be considered errors in combinations of dishes or methods of ordering to Indians will probably pass unnoticed to European and American eaters. One thing to keep in mind right from the start is that seasonings are fiery when so indicated. There are appetizers, side dishes and main courses, but they mix and match with the sort of freewheeling ease we have become used to in clothing fashions, and with much the same entertaining results.

Frying, grilling, stewing and steaming are the basic types of cooking employed, and all sorts of vegetables and legumes are magically turned into fritters, dumplings, crepes and pancakes. If ordered in curry-style stews, the vegetables are best accompanied by one of the miraculous breads, such as the deep-fried, puffy wholewheat poori, or batura, balloon bread that looks like a gigantic pale golden walnut. Puffed though fried on a griddle, pulka is also based on whole-wheat flour and has a toasty wheat flavor. Paratha plain or stuffed with vegetables is a soft grilled bread,wonderful when dipped into the cool cucumber and yogurt sauce known as raita, or the soothing lentil sauce, dal, or into the special chutney based on coriander, lemony tamarind and green chilies.

These same sauces, plus a superb relish of grated fresh coconut and green chilies, and an incendiary condiment called melakai podi that seems to be pure cayenne pepper moistened with ghee, all combine and recombine to light up all the other dishes on the menu and to send electrifying charges across the palate.

To enjoy Madras Woodlands to its fullest, go with four to six eaters and share dishes. Begin with an assortment of appetizers that might include the snowy, cloudlike iddly, steamed white lentil patties that absorb the various spicy sauces. On Sunday, special iddly are made of steamed semolina and are larger and studded with bits of vegetables. Medhu vadai, deep-fried lentil-flour fritters, and special vadai, deep fried with onion, are lusty and aromatic. Puffy rounds of fried mashed lentils are called bonda, and the delicate half-moon bajjis may be filled with vegetables or a slice of sour-sweet apple. The crisp lentil fritters pakoda and the spiced cashews are other excellent appetizers, among which we also include the extraordinary potato chat, which may be the world's best potato salad. It is made of diced boiled potatoes marinated in a deceptively cool-looking green sauce; but that color is a result of coriander, tamarinds and pounded green chilies, and it signals a hotness that can be increased with onions and pepper added on request. Only a touch of lime juice ameliorates the effects of that heat.

Dosai is the family name for a series of huge, thin, crisp and golden-brown crepes made of lentil flour. Variations include sadha dosai, gently soft, paper dosai that are the largest of all and are not filled, and the masala dosai, rolled around a luxuriously soft mixture of potatoes, onions, nuts, peas and sometimes perhaps tomatoes, all spiced with turmeric and coriander. Mysore masala dosai with the same vegetables get palate-tingling doses of fresh coriander and green chilies. The clarified butter — ghee — gilds the butter dosai crepes. Special rava dosai with semolina added to the lentil flour come off the griddle lacy and bubbly and are enriched with onions, peas and coriander.

Uthappam are large puffy pancakes combining lentil and rice flours with various vegetable mixtures, and what is called a vegetarian omelet is also the same type of pancake and includes no eggs. A rich vegetable koorma makes a combined sauce-topping for the omelet. Only the fried vegetable cutlets, much like croquettes, are disappointing in this category; they are pasty and are accompanied by ordinary ketchup. The cutlets and a rather watery, acidic tomato soup are the only two dishes not worth recommending.

Five rich and satisfying vegetable curries and two pullavs are offered, to be ordered individually or combined as you please or available all together on the vegetable thali, served with wafer-thin pappadums — the way most Indians order them. Cauliflower curry, gobhi masala, in a velvety pink sauce and chickpeas, chenna masala and special vegetable curry with fresh coconut are personal favorites, as is the drier, softer koorma. Rice cooked with flecks of vegetables make up the vegetable pullav; a more unusual and interesting variation is special uppuma — a sort of vegetable pullav based on semolina instead of rice.

Flavors that enchant throughout include turmeric, mustard seeds, cayenne, black pepper, ginger, cinnamon, chilies, coriander, lime juice, onions, garlic and tamarind, all tempered by the yogurt and dal sauces.

Because Indian desserts are intensely sweet and syrupy, they are not among my favorites. Those at Madras Woodlands are a little less sweet and have a little more background flavor than others found elsewhere. Those interested in experimenting should try the crunchy almond burphy scented with saffron and the warm carrot halwa.

There is full bar service, and beer is perhaps the best drink with the food. But the most authentic is lassi, a water-thinned yogurt that may be had sweet, salty or spiced, the spiced being especially aromatic. Flavored with saffron and almond, badam kheer is interesting, if a bit overwhelming, with food. Spiced tea, with or without milk, has the most appeal to those who like sweetly fragrant beverages, but Mysore coffee, much like cappucino, is a less overwhelming alternative.

Special dinners combining elements of the menu provide easy alternatives for newcomers to this cuisine.

Malca's
★

175 East 83d Street, between Lexington and Third
  Avenues, 879-8865.
Atmosphere: Tiny, trim bistro; front dining room is
  more comfortable than badly ventilated, inade-
  quately lighted inside dining room; staff is good-
  natured but often inept.
Recommended dishes: Lebneh, baba gannouj, tab-
  bouleh, eggplant Niçoise, spinach or pigeon pie,
  lamb tajine, couscous, chicken Malca or Jerusa-
  lem, fish à la Mistral.
Price range: Moderately expensive.
Credit cards: All major credit cards.
Hours: Dinner seven nights a week, 5 P.M. to 11 P.M.
Reservations: Recommended.

If there is one thing New York does not need, it is a restaurant that serves tenth-rate French food. If there is
one thing New York could use, it is a restaurant that
serves creditable couscous along with some excellent
Middle Eastern dishes. All of those culinary features are
combined at the recently opened Malca's, a tiny two-
room bistro with decorative old movie posters that offers French, Moroccan and Middle Eastern food. The
sooner the owner concentrates on the Moroccan and
Middle Eastern cuisine, the better off eaters will be.

Malca Lothane, an Israeli by birth, who was formerly
the owner of the Garden of Delights food shop and restaurant on Lexington Avenue, prepares fresh and delicate versions of such Lebanese appetizers as lebneh, the
yogurt cheese, which she sprinkles with mint and olive
oil, baba gannouj, the smoked eggplant purée that is
sparkled with lemon and garlic, and spinach pie in
phyllo crust. Eggplant Niçoise, a gentle stew with peppers, onions and tomatoes, gets a sunny splash of lemon
juice.

Every night, Moroccan couscous is available, the
hefty stew combining chicken and lamb, yellow and
acorn squash as well as zucchini, turnip, raisins and
chickpeas — all heady with scents of coriander, cinnamon and cumin, and the thick fiery hot sauce, harissa.
The flakey pastilla, a pie that usually contains minced
pigeon but which here is made with chicken or Cornish
hen, is generally on the menu. So is chicken Malca, also
called chicken Jerusalem. By either name it is a satisfying spiced, broiled chicken marinated in lemon juice.

On Sundays Malca does all of the cooking and only
Middle Eastern food is served. On that day, a soothing
and rich lamb tajine made with apples and spices is
added to the selection of main courses.

Smoked salmon served with frozen or jarred artichoke hearts was so spoiled it smelled much like Parmesan cheese, and canned asparagus filled puff pastry.
Vegetable terrine could have been made of baby-food

269

purées, and a quiche was muddy with overcooked spinach and mushrooms.

What is billed as noisettes of lamb looked more like dried, leathery scaloppine, and stale duck was musty from having been reheated too often. Braised chicken Beausejour was somewhat more decent, but only minimally so. The only good main course on the French menu was the fish à la Mistral — "fish" because the menu promised red snapper, but what was delivered had the texture of cod.

Desserts included a leaden diplomat pudding, gummy crème caramel, gelatin-slick Grand Marnier cake, burned zabaglione on a pasty crepe and a so-called apricot pudding with enough rosewater to suggest hair tonic.

The help is good-natured and gracious about dividing shared dishes. They are, however, somewhat inept at opening wine, and the kitchen is slow.

Manhattan Market

★

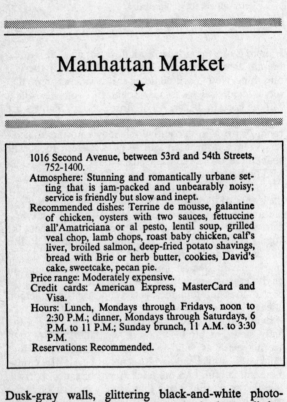

1016 Second Avenue, between 53rd and 54th Streets, 752-1400.

Atmosphere: Stunning and romantically urbane setting that is jam-packed and unbearably noisy; service is friendly but slow and inept.

Recommended dishes: Terrine de mousse, galantine of chicken, oysters with two sauces, fettuccine all'Amatriciana or al pesto, lentil soup, grilled veal chop, lamb chops, roast baby chicken, calf's liver, broiled salmon, deep-fried potato shavings, bread with Brie or herb butter, cookies, David's cake, sweetcake, pecan pie.

Price range: Moderately expensive.

Credit cards: American Express, MasterCard and Visa.

Hours: Lunch, Mondays through Fridays, noon to 2:30 P.M.; dinner, Mondays through Saturdays, 6 P.M. to 11 P.M.; Sunday brunch, 11 A.M. to 3:30 P.M.

Reservations: Recommended.

Dusk-gray walls, glittering black-and-white photographs of New York scenes and a back glass wall that opens onto a garden and skyscraper setting that echoes the feeling of the photographs lend an urbane atmosphere to this convivial restaurant. There also is a massive and handsome bar that, we were told, came from an old restaurant in the South Bronx, and beautiful chandeliers from a Philadelphia railroad station. David Liederman, a professional young American chef who trained in the kitchen of the Troisgros brothers in Roanne, France, among other places, operates this place along with David's Cookie Kitchen next door.

Mr. Liederman's menu might be described as American nouvelle cuisine, depending on the flourless sauces and unusual fruit, vegetable and herb garnishes that distinguish France's new cooking. Results remain sometimes delightful, other times merely bizarre. Creative ingenuity is too often valued for its own sake by practitioners of this new cuisine, and some of the food at Manhattan Market suffers from that predeliction and has not delivered on its earlier promise.

But before the food, there is the noise, not only caused by overcrowding, but also by the hard surfaces and the inexplicable disco music that throbs in from the bar. Acoustical remodeling has helped only a little.

Beware of the bread that appears on your table. The hard-crusted, yeasty slim baguettes baked in David Liederman's commissary are so excruciatingly delicious you might eat your fill before the main meal arrives. Served with fresh butter, or available at an extra charge with herb, garlic or Brie butter, this bread with a glass of red wine would have to be considered a four-star meal. Fortunately, the bread is also sold at the bakery next door, as are the equally extraordinary chocolate-chip cookies, which have become famous.

Between bread and cookies, there are some interesting things to eat. Fish mousses have been frothy and delicate. A terrine of pork and veal was lusty, and a smooth galantine of chicken had a meaty richness. Oysters on the half shell were decent, if lacking slightly in brininess, and two delicious sauces were served with them, horseradish cream and an Oriental soy-and-rice-wine vinegar dip. Pastas are generally enjoyable — one a fettuccine with a tomato, pancetta and onion all'Amatriciana sauce, and the other a version of the basil-based pesto, also with nuggets of unsmoked pancetta bacon. Only fish spoiled the freshness of fettuccine primavera.

A smooth, thick puréed lentil soup was smoky and subtle, but other soups in the past were failures.

The most successful main courses remain the meats, especially thick, grilled veal chop with herb butter, rosy lamb chops with perhaps just a slight rosemary overkill, and wonderfully rare and beefy shell steak in a green peppercorn sauce. Somewhat more exotic was fresh, carefully sautéed calf's liver with a sauce that combined counterpoints of shallots, currants and sherry-wine vinegar. The roast baby chicken was pleasant, but chicken breasts, breaded with pecans, were mushy.

With the exception of gray sole in lemon butter and grilled salmon, all fish dishes were disappointing. As in most nouvelle cuisine kitchens, there is the question of the new meaning of broiling. Even when ordered that way, all fish looked steamed. Grilled should mean grilled, with a light golden searing to add and protect savor.

The most dismal failure among main courses at a recent lunch was the stir-fried vegetables in sesame oil; a soggier, murkier and oilier creation would be hard to come by.

Desserts have improved enormously. Not only the cookies are wonderful now, but the same can be said for the marquise-like bittersweet chocolate sweetness cake, the fluffy chocolate torte known as David's cake, the warm pecan pie and the inspired lemon-brightened crème brûlée.

271

There are interesting Sunday brunches here, featuring assorted smoked fish, bagels, cream cheese, herring and pastries from the house bakery. Another nice touch is the inclusion of a list of bottles and half-bottles of dessert wines on the dessert menu.

Market Dining Rooms and Bar
★

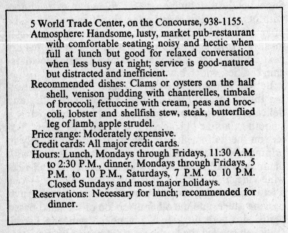

5 World Trade Center, on the Concourse, 938-1155.

Atmosphere: Handsome, lusty, market pub-restaurant with comfortable seating; noisy and hectic when full at lunch but good for relaxed conversation when less busy at night; service is good-natured but distracted and inefficient.

Recommended dishes: Clams or oysters on the half shell, venison pudding with chanterelles, timbale of broccoli, fettuccine with cream, peas and broccoli, lobster and shellfish stew, steak, butterflied leg of lamb, apple strudel.

Price range: Moderately expensive.

Credit cards: All major credit cards.

Hours: Lunch, Mondays through Fridays, 11:30 A.M. to 2:30 P.M., dinner, Mondays through Fridays, 5 P.M. to 10 P.M., Saturdays, 7 P.M. to 10 P.M. Closed Sundays and most major holidays.

Reservations: Necessary for lunch; recommended for dinner.

When the Market Dining Rooms and Bar at the World Trade Center became fully operative in 1977, it was an original and exciting pub-tavern-restaurant stressing the fresh produce, seafood and simple grilled meats befitting a place situated on the site of the old Washington Market. It was well worth a three-star rating and a visit downtown for its own sake.

But a few years later, as a result of complaints from readers, I revisited the place and found it was then worth only a single star. Two years and three visits later, that still seems appropriate because there are just a few decent dishes served in handsome surroundings, in a section where good restaurants are scarce.

Areas for quick stand-up eating and counter eating, as well as drinking, are at the entrance to the restaurant, overlooking the concourse-enclosed street scene.

The most serious eating takes place within the pub-club-steakhouse confines of the Market Dining Rooms and Bar, done up to look not quite modern, not quite antique, but blending overtones of both styles. Polished brown and golden oak, mellow terra cotta walls, clear, frosted and green gaslight-era lampshades, engraved-glass dividers with heads of steers, rooster finials on marble lampposts, black-and-white-checkered upholstery on curved banquettes that are the most comfortable in town, antique golden oak sideboards and mismatched chairs, baskets of fruits and vegetables — all these combine to create a tailored, masculine and fashionable setting that invites hearty eating, market style.

The lack of a firm management hand is obvious here, especially at dinner. Service borders on the inane. On many evenings there is no attendant in the check room, so there is confusion about putting away and retrieving coats and umbrellas. Seated at a table, one finds that utensils, bread, condiments and wine frequently have to be requested, often more than once. Staff members are good-natured enough and never rude. But almost all seem to be sleepwalkers badly in need of the wake-up tug of a supervisor.

There also seems to be a blatantly stupid regulation imposed by management in regard to the still very good giveaway appetizer at dinner. This may be sliced cotteghino sausage with lentil salad, or Italian salami with roasted peppers, but no bread is offered with that course. When we asked for bread, the waiter started to take away the still unfinished sausage and peppers. We said we wanted bread *with* that course and he said he was not allowed to serve that way. When bread came, the free appetizer was supposed to go. Since that happened on two separate evenings, with two different waiters, I assume it is a house policy, for reasons too obscure to fathom.

Freshness, once ever present in the ingredients served here, seems to have disappeared, as has the impeccably careful cooking necessary for success with simple dishes. Clams and oysters on the half shell still arrive sprightly and well chilled, but roasted clams on rock salt were rubbery, although there seemed to be a slight and delicious hint of garlic about them. A salad of crab meat in avocado was Alaskan king crab meat and, therfore, stringy and tasteless. On another visit, deviled oysters were so heavily zapped with mustard the briny flavor of the bivalves disappeared. Iced oysters, said to be served on seaweed, arrived on lettuce but were fine.

Venison pudding, a sort of hot pâté, had delicate, gently spiced overtones, and chanterelles lent earthy richness. A timbale of broccoli was also delicious, served with roasted peppers. Both swordfish and red snapper were so overbroiled, however, that they took on the texture of absorbent cotton, and noisettes of venison tasted gamy past the point of normal gaminess, indicating they were at least half spoiled. Calf's liver was neither pink as ordered nor fresh as expected.

Dishes that have held up best include fettuccine in cream tossed with fresh peas and firm flowerets of broccoli, and the still spectacular tureen of lobster and shellfish stew, served for two. Sea scallops may overpower other shellfish such as clams, mussels and lobster, but they were satisfying in a heady tomato and onion broth. Grilled steak and butterflied leg of lamb are also above average.

Desserts will disappoint anyone who experienced the originals. Cheesecake of basic high quality had soured from overage. Apple strudel, though gross in appearance, did have a crackling crisp crust and a gently savory apple filling, a far better choice than the now characterless frozen chocolate soufflé with burnt almond sauce.

Parking is free in the downstairs garage, and each diner is given two double-yolk eggs upon leaving, for the next morning's breakfast.

Marylou's

★

21 West Ninth Street, between Fifth Avenue and Avenue of the Americas, 533-0012.

Atmosphere: Graceful and handsome dining rooms on garden floor of a Village brownstone. Acoustics and ventilation need adjustment; service is polite and good natured but sometimes confused.

Recommended dishes: Onion soup, New England clam chowder, clams or oysters on the half shell, stuffed mushrooms, pasta primavera, broiled fillet of sole, broiled whole fish, sole amandine, broiled or sautéed bay scallops, fillet of the day en papillote, seafood brochette, broiled lobster, broiled chicken, shell steak, steak Madagascar, calf's liver, all desserts.

Price range: Moderately expensive.

Credit cards: All major credit cards.

Hours: Lunch, Mondays through Fridays, 11:30 A.M. to 3 P.M.; dinner, Mondays through Thursdays, 5:30 P.M. to 1 A.M., Fridays and Saturdays, 5:30 P.M. to 2 A.M., Sundays, 5:30 P.M. to 10 P.M. Sunday brunch, noon to 4 P.M. Closed only Christmas Day and New Year's Day.

Reservations: Recommended.

Marylou's is on the garden floor of a wide brownstone formerly occupied by the Penguin. The premises have been turned into three graceful, romantically handsome dining rooms hung with kitsch paintings. Only the intense noise when tables are full, complicated by piped-in music and insufficient ventilation, mar the effect.

Marylou Baratta, who owns this restaurant with her brother Thomas, has long been the owner of a successful fish market, and the preponderance of seafood dishes on the menu reflects this background. She is of Italian descent and her chef is Thai, but they have decided not to lean heavily on ethnic traditions in the kitchen. As a result, the food is fresh and decently prepared, but decidedly short on character. The shrimp gumbo is acceptable, but it lacks the Louisiana flavorings needed to give it zest. Linguine with clam sauce arrived as a creamy tomato dish light on garlic and congealed into a pasty mass, probably the result of waiting under a heat lamp before being picked up. Even shrimp Bangkok, an invention of the chef, came off as a warm and stodgy appetizer unrelieved by the timid amounts of curry spices.

But during my six visits a number of simple dishes have been very good consistently. Clams and oysters on the half shell have been superbly fresh, and stuffed mushrooms decked with cheese made a savory appetizer. Cold mussel salad was a sprightly first course, although on one occasion the mussels were gritty. They were also gritty in a main course, steamed in white wine with mustard, and as garnish on the seafood brochette. The waiter said he had many complaints on this score, but he continued to offer mussels at other tables. The same sort of lapse occurred when we ordered a grilled whole fish but were served fillets because there were no more whole fish left. Two minutes later the same waiter offered whole fish to a neighboring table.

Other appetizers among the near misses were artichokes in a sauce that seemed based on a sweet relish, stiff and salty smoked trout and pasty baked clams. Better to rely on the lusty onion soup or the New England clam chowder with potatoes and vegetables, or to share the corkscrew pasta prepared with vegetables, primavera-style.

Fish lovers should find satisfaction in any of the broiled fish or lobster, in the sole amandine with its nut-crunch breading, the moist, marvelous seafood brochette with tiny bay scallops, and the fish of the day (with luck, red snapper) simmered in a light tomato sauce, en papillote. But the trout amandine was limp, the mixed seafood was heavily fried and the stone crabs (served ice cold with hot melted butter) were pallid.

One of the better choices is the beefy, tender steak, plain or encrusted with green peppercorns, Madagascar-style. Broiled chicken glazed with a soy and ginger marinade outclassed the dry chicken pie, but calf's liver sautéed with apples proved properly pink if a bit sweet.

Well before dessert you will probably be aware that the waiters, though polite and well-meaning, are short on polish. And if there is a private party, the chaos may be exhausting. But try to muster up strength for the desserts, because they are worth it — whether you choose the airy lemon mousse or the chocolate mousse, the froth of a pecan roll with whipped cream, the angel-cloud rice pudding or the double chocolate cake.

Maurice

★

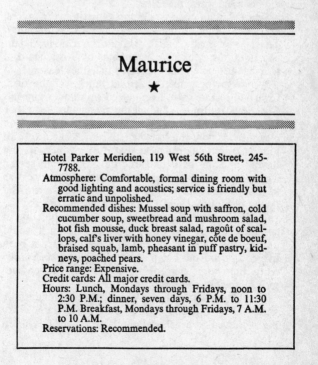

Hotel Parker Meridien, 119 West 56th Street, 245-7788.

Atmosphere: Comfortable, formal dining room with good lighting and acoustics; service is friendly but erratic and unpolished.

Recommended dishes: Mussel soup with saffron, cold cucumber soup, sweetbread and mushroom salad, hot fish mousse, duck breast salad, ragoût of scallops, calf's liver with honey vinegar, côte de boeuf, braised squab, lamb, pheasant in puff pastry, kidneys, poached pears.

Price range: Expensive.

Credit cards: All major credit cards.

Hours: Lunch, Mondays through Fridays, noon to 2:30 P.M.; dinner, seven days, 6 P.M. to 11:30 P.M. Breakfast, Mondays through Fridays, 7 A.M. to 10 A.M.

Reservations: Recommended.

Operated by Air France, the Parker Meridien hotel hired Alain Senderens, chef-owner of L'Archestrate, one of Paris's most highly touted and overrated restaurants, to set up the hotel's kitchen for the Maurice restaurant. Having tried the food while Mr. Senderens was in residence, then several times since his departure, I can report a marked improvement since he left. Now, if he just stays away long enough. . . .

Some of the dishes served in this pleasant, if undistinguished, formal dining room represent the nouvelle cuisine at its most bizarre. For instance, vanilla is used to flavor a butter sauce that underlines poached lobster. The combination is not nearly so bad as it sounds when the lobster is not tough and the sauce is not too sweet.

Food was consistently tepid, even though the plates were so hot that some of the sliced meats and poultry overcooked as they were being carried from kitchen to dining room.

Still, the Maurice already turns out some good food, including such appetizers as curried oysters on spinach, a beautifully smooth and fragrant saffron-gilded mussel cream soup, and a sparkling cold cucumber soup. Some giveaway hors d'oeuvres appear each night, with two dreadful losers always among them: limp toast triangles covered with a fishy butter and a tiny pastry roll-up with a filling that remains a mystery.

Two typical nouvelle cuisine appetizer salads — well prepared — are the rare duck breast on sprightly greens, and warm, golden-brown nuggets of sweetbreads and raw mushrooms, also on greens. Each has a pungent light-cream dressing, and each would be better with fewer greens. Tender, sweet sea scallops in a pink butter sauce were delicious, but snails in a small casserole lacked character. Salmon rolled around a sole mousse had been reduced to dry solidity. A slice of Périgord foie gras, though fine, fatty and richly flavored, did not seem worth the price.

Seafood main courses, despite expertly made sauces, did not come up to the level of the meat and poultry. The poorest seafood dish was the knuckle-hard langoustines, overcooked in wrappings of Swiss chard, a fate that also befell turbot braised in lettuce leaves.

By far the best main course at lunch was the firm, fresh and roseate calf's liver glazed with honey vinegar. Côte de boeuf for two had all the tender succulence one expects from the best beef. Sliced lamb in tarragon cream held more interest than the thick slices of dull though decent sautéed veal that did not pick up any flavor from the basil or garlic-flavored cream served with them. The bland chicken with caviar sauce was tasteless. Neatly cut, nut-brown breast of squab retained far more moisture and flavor than usual, and roasted veal kidneys were distinguished by the combination of sprightly crackle and inner rosiness. The duck would have equaled the squab and kidneys had it not been overcooked on the hot plate. Vegetables were consistently limp with overcooking, and the braised endives took on the bitterness of burned onions.

The Charolais fillet was excellent and wonderfully garnished with a tiny duck-liver tart. The same flaky pastry served as a colossal shell for a delicious sliced breast of pheasant, a robust dish for dedicated trenchermen.

Raspberries were moldy on five visits, but the poached pear filled with a praline mousse was delicious. Not so the limp, paper-thin apple tart with its caramelized glaze. Petits fours are dry as plaster, and the puff pastry filled with raspberries was tough and soggy.

Widely-spaced tables and comfortable chairs make dining at the Maurice a generally satisfying experience, though it was marred at night by downdrafts of icy air and at all times by waiters who reach across one diner to serve another. They also go through an absurd dumb show, lining up at a table to remove big domed silver plate covers simultaneously at some invisible signal.

Maxwell's Plum
★

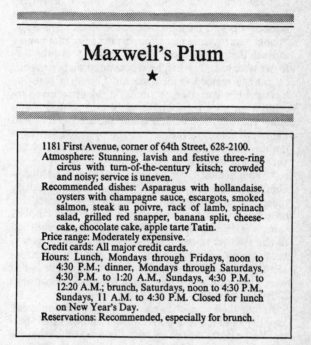

1181 First Avenue, corner of 64th Street, 628-2100.
Atmosphere: Stunning, lavish and festive three-ring circus with turn-of-the-century kitsch; crowded and noisy; service is uneven.
Recommended dishes: Asparagus with hollandaise, oysters with champagne sauce, escargots, smoked salmon, steak au poivre, rack of lamb, spinach salad, grilled red snapper, banana split, cheesecake, chocolate cake, apple tarte Tatin.
Price range: Moderately expensive.
Credit cards: All major credit cards.
Hours: Lunch, Mondays through Fridays, noon to 4:30 P.M.; dinner, Mondays through Saturdays, 4:30 P.M. to 1:20 A.M., Sundays, 4:30 P.M. to 12:20 A.M.; brunch, Saturdays, noon to 4:30 P.M., Sundays, 11 A.M. to 4:30 P.M. Closed for lunch on New Year's Day.
Reservations: Recommended, especially for brunch.

Since Maxwell's Plum opened in 1965, that monument to turn-of-the-century Art Nouveau kitsch has inspired countless imitators across the country, all pallid shadows of the exuberant original. Warner LeRoy, founder of Maxwell's Plum and son of the film producer Mervin LeRoy, is every inch a child of Hollywood who understands the true nature of the extravaganza and ascribes to the esthetic precept that more is more. For this cafe-restaurant, he amassed kaleidoscopic swirls of antique and reproduction stained glass, blazes of brass, forests of carved wood and waterfalls of crystal, combining them into the city's most fabulously festive interior. The concept of good taste has about as much validity at Maxwell's Plum as it does at a three-ring circus; in both instances, it seems very much beside the point. Those who seek peace, quiet and restrained elegance had best look elsewhere, but if razzle-dazzle suits your mood, there is no better place in which to encounter it.

The cast of customers Mr. LeRoy manages to attract is as amazing for its variety as the setting is for its opulence. The clientele ranges from the singles who gather six deep at the bar almost every evening to family celebrations, complete with cake-bearing waiters singing "Happy Birthday" and distributing balloons to all the children. There is a brunch scene on weekends, as well as lunch, dinner and supper in the enlarged enclosed sidewalk cafe and the more gussied-up back room, and the menus are wide ranging in style and ethnic origins.

But if the setting and following at Maxwell's Plum have held up, the food and service have not. Several years ago, both were surprisingly good for a place that was so enormous and theatrical. Today both are reminiscent of nightclub food service. Waiters can be efficent and helpful, or slapdash, forgetful and downright argumentative, as one was when an order of pasta with sausage was sent back because it contained no sausage. "Look, here's a little piece," the waiter said, rummaging through the paglia e fieno with a fork to prove the customer wrong. Only when he was assured that one speck of sausage seemed inadequate did he return it to the kitchen to be corrected. A similar incident occurred recently over a meager portion of ice cream. And if you allow yourself to be crammed into the table just behind the back-room reservation desk, be prepared for freezing downdrafts and waiters' arms reaching in front of your face all evening long.

Although most of the food sampled proved disappointing, there are just enough good dishes to satisfy those who enjoy the setting. Escargots baked under a crisp crust were delicately herbed and buttered. Smoked salmon is decent, and both oysters and clams gratinéed in their shells under a mantle of champagne cream sauce were plump and subtle. Avoid watery underseasoned pâtés and the bland, watery duck salad. Soups were uniformly wishy-washy, and steamed rock shrimp did not seem fresh.

Among the better main courses count the sirloin steak au poivre and the rose-pink rack of lamb with herb butter. Veal piccata was pasty with flour, and duck has always been stringy and overcooked. Mushy calf's liver appeared to have been frozen, but grilled red snapper with a mustard sauce and Dover sole were above average.

Forget about the murky curries here and the heavy-handed omelets served at brunch and lunch. Pastas have been soupy and undersalted. Salads hold up well, most especially the spinach, and vegetable cooking has improved. Hamburgers can be very good but also can be made of half-spoiled meat.

Desserts are not as good as they used to be. The once famous chocolate cake is now dry and tasteless, and the banana split is all whipped cream and very little ice cream or banana. Pecan pie and ice creams are better choices. Fresh strawberries were unripe, banana fritters tasted of overheated frying fat, and the chocolate mousse was much like chocolate Redi-Whip. Ice-cold Brie and a chalky St. André were the offerings from the cheese tray.

On two occasions we ordered wines of specific vintages but were presented with wines of other years, al-

·though no mention was made of the switch. Both breads served contained raisins, a mistake with wine, liquor and the Continental main courses.

Meat Brokers

★

1153 York Avenue, at 62nd Street, 752-0108.
Atmosphere: Dark, noisy and overcrowded pub setting; service is friendly but slow and perfunctory.
Recommended dishes: Mussels, sirloin steak, filet mignon, roast prime ribs of beef, calf's liver, baked potato, spinach salad, ice cream.
Price range: Moderate.
Credit cards: All major credit cards.
Hours: Dinner, Mondays through Thursdays, 5 P.M. to midnight, Fridays and Saturdays, 5 P.M. to 1 A.M., Sundays, 4 P.M. to 11 P.M. Open all major holidays except Thanksgiving Day.
Reservations: Not necessary.

A dark, noisy and frantic steakhouse-pub, this relatively new addition to the local scene specializes in low prices for steaks and chops said to be of aged, prime quality served in adequate, if less than lusty, portions. But to offer those low prices some corners had to be cut and, in this case, the corners are service and comfort. The cost-and-labor-saving device invoked here, as at so many out-of-town chop houses, is the salad bar, something I regard as an abomination, but which many Americans seem to adore. Because customers take their own salads, serving time is cut and greater turnover is possible. In addition, the kaleidoscopic array of gloppy toppings, dressings, chopped egg, artificial bits of bacon and the like tempt customers to load the deep (and here, often hot) bowls and fill up on roughage before the moderately sized portions of meat arrive. Rising costs have brought higher prices since this place opened, and cooking has become careless.

Very good herring fillets in cream sauce on the salad bar comprise the only real appetizer, other than a shared order of the main course spareribs that are fatty and in a dreadful sweet-sour sauce that tastes bottled. Both the sirloin and filet mignon steaks and the roast prime ribs of beef and calf's liver were very good when properly cooked, but on busy nights all arrived overdone. A veal chop and two lamb chops were small and dry. Chunks of filet mignon en brochette were fatty and steamy. Broiled red snapper was a bit moister and more acceptable than a slice of dry Pacific salmon, but mussels in tomato sauce were delicious.

Among the potatoes (à la carte extras), the baked were far better than the limp and greasy cottage fries. Onion rings in glassy, greasy batter were atrocious, as were orders of totally tasteless broccoli and string beans.

Better to select carefully from the salad bar (the spinach and mushroom salad was the wisest choice, but combine oil and vinegar with a little of the oregano dressing for the best result) and let the cooked vegetables go.

Desserts often seem stale and overchilled.

The help is friendly but slow and unprofessional, and the booths are miserably cramped.

Blackboard menus are supplemented by an electronic tickertape with green lights flashing menu choices and prices. Waiters are "brokers" and the "preferred stocks" (menu items) are described as the "investments." Any interest?

Michael Phillips
★

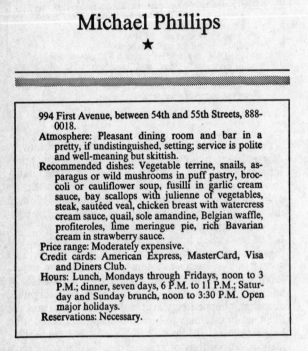

994 First Avenue, between 54th and 55th Streets, 888-0018.

Atmosphere: Pleasant dining room and bar in a pretty, if undistinguished, setting; service is polite and well-meaning but skittish.

Recommended dishes: Vegetable terrine, snails, asparagus or wild mushrooms in puff pastry, broccoli or cauliflower soup, fusilli in garlic cream sauce, bay scallops with julienne of vegetables, steak, sautéed veal, chicken breast with watercress cream sauce, quail, sole amandine, Belgian waffle, profiteroles, lime meringue pie, rich Bavarian cream in strawberry sauce.

Price range: Moderately expensive.

Credit cards: American Express, MasterCard, Visa and Diners Club.

Hours: Lunch, Mondays through Fridays, noon to 3 P.M.; dinner, seven days, 6 P.M. to 11 P.M.; Saturday and Sunday brunch, noon to 3:30 P.M. Open major holidays.

Reservations: Necessary.

There are two groups of potential customers who should be interested in Michael Phillips, the recently opened restaurant on First Avenue. The first group is made up of those who are in the neighborhood for one reason or another and would like a decent, pleasant lunch, dinner or weekend brunch. By picking their way carefully through the menu, diners should be able to come up with a diverting meal that reflects nouvelle cuisine influences. Although neither the food nor the setting is distinguished in any way, at least both are several cuts above average. The effort made by the young staff is touching in its sincerity, if somewhat short on professionalism.

But Michael Phillips should hold even more interest to a second group — professionals or amateur buffs in the restaurant field. For such serious eaters, this bright and shiny new restaurant contains valuable object lessons.

It has always seemed that any really good restaurant

expresses the ideas and style of a particular owner, a family or a chef. What we often see these days, however, are restaurants reflecting no particular, single background. In creating such a dining place, the owner has his ear to the ground, trying to come up with a sure-fire package that will "sell." The usual result is an unsure hand and palate, a restaurant in which nothing quite hangs together.

This situation is obvious at Michael Phillips as soon as one looks around the room — spacious, freshly decorated but in a style that just does not come off. Half elegant, half casual, its various elements do not blend. What probably had been conceived as a place for swingers, suggests instead a prettified tearoom in a suburban department store.

The food reflects the same lack of authority. Some of the dishes the chef turns out are very good, but most are only minimally acceptable — not a very high batting average at such prices. Hot oysters in a Chablis butter sauce emerge succulently plump and tender one time but dry and tough another. A terrine of vegetables with verdant herb sauce is among the best versions of this dish in the city, but a country pâté is gray, mushy and bland. Snails in a delicately balanced sauce of tomatoes, mushrooms, shallots and cream may be lovely, but frog's legs, overpowered by a sweet citrus sauce, prove disastrous. Cream of broccoli or cauliflower soup may be richly flavored and engaging, but pasta specialties are touch and go. Fusilli with garlic cream sauce far surpassses the pasta primavera that needs a more binding sauce, and the version with ham, vegetables and cream sticks to the overheated plate, becoming dry and pasty. And so it goes, through beautifully roasted duck turned to candy by a caramelized grapefruit sauce, and a rack of lamb with its own delicate flavor that was masked by the heavy edging of mustard on its surface.

Tiny bay scallops got just the right gloss of butter in the sautéing, and the slivers of vegetables that topped them were bright and firm. Fish steamed in lettuce was overcooked, but sautéed sole amandine held firmly and brightly to make a most satisfying main course. Other successes were the appetizers of puff pastry casing, holding either wild mushrooms or slender asparagus tips, and sautéed chicken breast in a watercress cream sauce and properly snowy veal medaillons in two sauces — a reduced brown glaze that was a triumph and a pink peppercorn sauce that had too much of this crusty aromatic spice. Quail, a specialty one night, had been braised to moist and tender perfection, although a tasteless array of complex vegetable garnishes accompanied it. Steaks on two visits were excellent, but an omelet and a chef's salad were graceless and uninspired. There are a few knockout desserts: Belgian waffles with strawberry sauce and whipped cream, a glassy green lime pie topped with meringue rosettes and rich Bavarian cream — a creamy tower in a lake of strawberry sauce. The profiteroles were marvelous, but the portion of these rich chocolate-sauced, ice-cream-filled pastry puffs could easily have served four.

The staff is sometimes forgetful and service often drags between appetizers and main courses. Though many details about daily specials are provided, prices are not among them.

Michel Fitoussi's Palace
★

420 East 59th Street, between First and York Avenues, 355-5152.
Atmosphere: Plush and spacious dining room that is somewhat banal; comfortable noise level; service is excellent.
Recommended dishes: All lobster salad appetizers, délice de crabe, raw beef, consommé, mussel soup with saffron, ravioli, bass en croûte, venison, pheasant, rack of lamb, beef with Madeira sauce, coffee ice cream with caramel sauce.
Price range: Expensive.
Credit cards: All major credit cards.
Hours: Mondays through Saturdays, 6 P.M. to 10 P.M. Closed Sundays.
Reservations: Recommended.

Ever since it opened in 1975, the Palace has been known as the city's most expensive restaurant. Recently renamed Michel Fitoussi's Palace when the chef also became the proprietor, the restaurant now has several rivals in its reduced price range. But four meals eaten there since Mr. Fitoussi took over the management indicate that it is still a one-star value.

Inevitably, when discussing the Palace, price comes before food, a situation that has existed since it opened. Previously, there were dinners for $150, $95 and $70, a confusing arrangement because each dinner had a different number of courses and unless everyone at the table chose the same format, service was awkward. That plan has been sensibly simplified. Now there is a single dinner at $70 that includes a choice of appetizers, soup or a minuscule serving of pasta, then a fish or meat main course, a salad, dessert and coffee. There are also many dishes that carry surcharges. Although no other restaurant in New York has so expensive a fixed-price meal, it is certainly possible to spend $70 for food alone at several first-class French restaurants. But in most of those restaurants, the diner receives far more value, in both variety and skillful preparation.

As adept as Mr. Fitoussi is at a number of preparations, he falls short on many more. His dishes have almost identical garnishes, meal after meal, week after week. Whether one has the lovely striped bass en croûte with a sorrel sauce, a moist and flavorful pheasant or the lackluster veal with an overly sweet mushroom cream sauce, the same vegetables are bound with slivers of leeks into tiny packets. Never mind that a steamed potato or rice would complement the fish or that crisp gaufrettes or wild rice would do much for the game or veal.

Some of the misplaced sense of value that marred the Palace before is still evident. On the fixed-price dinner, American caviar, generally too soft and musty, is often announced as one of the appetizers, and a beautifully roasted chicken covered in gold leaf is among the main courses. The vulgar and pointless golden garnish adds no flavor or special quality to the chicken. The money would be better spent on the best Russian caviar, with parsley on the chicken.

First courses include some light and lovely lobster salads and a very good raw beef in a shallot, caper and parsley mayonnaise. But you can wind up with an overly contrived rolled slice of smoked salmon filled with crème fraîche and dipped into the same inferior caviar, or a delicate fish pâté topped with foie gras, a misguided combination both from the standpoint of flavor and of texture.

Mussel soup with saffron and a heady consommé are better than the lobster bisque, and among pastas, the ravioli with sweetbreads brighten the meal far more than the angel's hair pasta, turned pasty in its overly reduced tomato and basil sauce.

Fitoussi's lusty wine sauces do well by heavier meat dishes, whether on game such as venison or pheasant, on beef or on a rack of lamb. But salad greens are weighed down with oily dressings.

All dishes are exquisitely and lavishly presented with structures such as a huge tiered bird cage of uncooked pasta, or by a schooner made of fried bread or a fisherman sculpted in tallow. The best desserts are the rich coffee ice cream bathed in a warm caramel sauce and a white chocolate mousse with bits of chocolate in it that has more character than this dessert generally has. Disappointments included a banal chocolate-mousse cake and an apple tart so hot that its pastry-cream filling tasted eggy.

The décor is slightly brighter now, but with all the damask and commercial oil paintings, it still lacks distinction. What the Palace also lacks now is a host. With Mr. Fitoussi busy in the kitchen and the very capable maître d'hôtel bustling around in the dining room, there is no one at the ready with a warm and friendly greeting.

The regular wine list is overpriced. As always, a 20 percent service charge is automatically added to the check, but upon request the amount can be reduced.

Milestone

★

75 West 68th Street, between Columbus Avenue and
Central Park West, 874-3679.

Atmosphere: Simple, pleasant and rustic setting,
crowded and somewhat hectic; service is polite
and patient.

Recommended dishes: Quiches, mushrooms à la
grecque, scrod, trout amandine, beer-batter
shrimp, whitings in black-bean sauce, bluefish,
chicken parmesan, pork chops, spinach salad, fettuccine Alfredo.

Price range: Moderate.

Credit cards: None.

Hours: Dinner, Tusedays through Fridays, 5 P.M. to
10:45 P.M., Saturdays, 4:30 P.M. to 10:45 P.M.
Closed Sundays and Mondays.

Reservations: Not accepted.

Since it opened several years ago, the Milestone, a
pleasantly informal and countrified restaurant, has been
a welcome oasis of good, reasonably priced food within
walking distance of Lincoln Center. Recently moved to
larger quarters, just across the street from its original
home, this kitchen now turns out food that does not
seem to be quite so good as it was a few years back, but
the Milestone remains more than a cut above average
and a boon in this area. Prices, though still comparatively moderate, are higher than they were, and service
remains friendly and helpful, but the house runs out of
many dishes early in the evening, limiting the choice
considerably.

No reservations are accepted, however, which means
a line forms at almost all hours. This is especially discouraging just before Lincoln Center performances.
The wait is shorter after 8 P.M., but there is almost always at least a small line, and quarters are cramped.

Home-style cooking that might be classified as tea-
room-Continental prevails. Vegetable combinations,
such as carrots and broccoli, are banal, and vegetables
are frequently undercooked and undersalted. Italian
dishes, of which there are a considerable number, are
usually too light on garlic and identifying seasonings,
but most of the food is fresh, decent, honest and often
engaging.

Forget the overthickened soups, and choose instead
such first courses as the fluffy, crusty quiches or the
pungent mushrooms à la grecque. Both the spicy fra
diavolo sauce and the garlic and parsley "bianco" sauce
can be lovely, but the mussels in them were so full of
sand that they would have been more aptly named
"True Grit."

Fish is very well handled, whether as snowy whitings
in a vaguely Oriental black-bean sauce, as bluefish fillets or as scrod nestled under butter, red onions and
lemon. Scampi parmigiana, with a glazing of cheese,
was only slightly less interesting than shrimp fried in a
puffy, golden beer batter.

Broiled pork chops, properly lean and meaty, and

chicken parmigiana, with an oozy mozzarella and tomato topping, proved far better among meat choices than a fibrous veal piccata in a floury, soupy sauce. Roulades of eggplant filled with cheese had been so overcooked that the cheese disappeared in the process. The house salad is in the coffee-shop genre. It would be better to order spinach salad with raw mushrooms, bacon and onions, a crisp and fresh alternative, which, though an à la carte extra, is large enough for four people to share.

Both cannelloni and fettuccine Alfredo had been overcooked to pasty masses. Cakes and pies were nothing but sweet, totally without sophistication. Those with an insistent sweet tooth will be better off with ice-cream sundaes — somewhat exaggerated after a full meal, but fine for sharing. There is a modestly priced and minimally acceptable wine list.

Mimosa

★

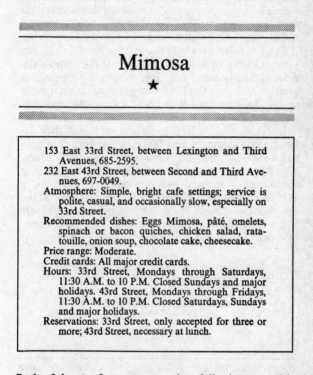

153 East 33rd Street, between Lexington and Third Avenues, 685-2595.
232 East 43rd Street, between Second and Third Avenues, 697-0049.
Atmosphere: Simple, bright cafe settings; service is polite, casual, and occasionally slow, especially on 33rd Street.
Recommended dishes: Eggs Mimosa, pâté, omelets, spinach or bacon quiches, chicken salad, ratatouille, onion soup, chocolate cake, cheesecake.
Price range: Moderate.
Credit cards: All major credit cards.
Hours: 33rd Street, Mondays through Saturdays, 11:30 A.M. to 10 P.M. Closed Sundays and major holidays. 43rd Street, Mondays through Fridays, 11:30 A.M. to 10 P.M. Closed Saturdays, Sundays and major holidays.
Reservations: 33rd Street, only accepted for three or more; 43rd Street, necessary at lunch.

Both of these cafe-restaurants, cheerfully done up with rough, white plaster walls and mimosa-yellow accents, provide moderately priced but stylish meals that are light, relatively quick and satisfying, and they are available from 11:30 in the morning until 10 at night. Except for two ill-conceived and badly executed cannelloni variations, the menu is French, with several interesting appetizers, three crepes, six or eight quiches, omelets, a few salads, several seafood and meat dishes and desserts. The menus are identical in the two restaurants, and since most of the food for both is prepared at the 43rd Street kitchen, both offer identical fare, as recent back-and-forth visits indicated.

The best of the appetizers I tried were a coarse, fragrant meatloaf-style pâté, and eggs Mimosa, three halves of hard-cooked eggs filled with their own yolks that had been fluffed with mustard-tinged mayonnaise and green herbs. The only flaw with both of these choices was that they were served too cold so that their flavors could not be fully appreciated.

Fresh, bright ratatouille can be an appetizer or side dish. Céleri rémoulade was too limp and its dressing too pungently hot and sour.

Vichysoisse tasted of nothing but starch and was decked out with chives that seemed to be fresh but were completely dried out — not quite as bad as the commercially dehydrated variety, but papery nonetheless. Onion soup with a cheese glaze had a beefy broth and rich flavor.

Individual quiches were the real triumphs here — piping hot, with gentle custard fillings and flaky, crisp crusts. Those I liked best were the spinach, the bacon and the seafood. Only the smoked salmon quiche was disappointing, because it was reminiscent of lox and eggs, a somewhat indelicate associaton for a quiche. Crepes were pleasant, although the crepes themselves were a bit too soft to provide the desirable textural contrast to sauce and filling. Sautéed scallops were tough, but the vegetables with them were fresh and firm.

Chicken salad here is as beautiful to behold as it is to eat, consisting of a lavish amount of white and dark meat of freshly cooked chicken on sprightly greens and dressed with an excellent sunny mustard vinaigrette sauce. The same dressing is used for the green salad that accompanies all nonsalad main courses.

Both cannelloni offered are awful because of their intense, salty, gummy sauces that tasted of burned tomato paste. Better to stick to quiches, salads and omelets, and skip fruit tarts. A dry chocolate cake is pleasant, as is cheesecake. Wine and beer are served at the smaller 33rd Street Mimosa, while there is full bar service at the newer outpost. Some dishes, such as quiches, appetizers and salads, can be taken out from the 43rd Street Mimosa.

Miraku

★

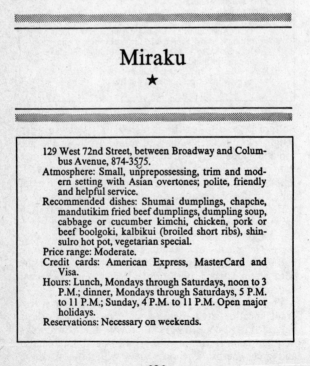

129 West 72nd Street, between Broadway and Columbus Avenue, 874-3575.

Atmosphere: Small, unprepossessing, trim and modern setting with Asian overtones; polite, friendly and helpful service.

Recommended dishes: Shumai dumplings, chapche, mandutikim fried beef dumplings, dumpling soup, cabbage or cucumber kimchi, chicken, pork or beef boolgoki, kalbikui (broiled short ribs), shinsulro hot pot, vegetarian special.

Price range: Moderate.

Credit cards: American Express, MasterCard and Visa.

Hours: Lunch, Mondays through Saturdays, noon to 3 P.M.; dinner, Mondays through Saturdays, 5 P.M. to 11 P.M.; Sunday, 4 P.M. to 11 P.M. Open major holidays.

Reservations: Necessary on weekends.

Miraku, a small and trim restaurant with a Korean and Japanese menu, provides one of the more pleasant and least expensive choices for an easygoing dinner on the Upper West Side. A few Oriental accessories enliven the otherwise simple and immaculate setting. The waitresses in their beautiful, folkloric dress, are gracious and accommodating, and even children are treated kindly and patiently.

The Korean dishes are the most successful. Among these are such interesting appetizers as the delicate shumai — steamed, fluted dumplings filled with pork, shrimp and bamboo shoots — and the mandutikim — spicy, crisp-fried beef dumplings to be dipped into a soy and scallion sauce. Chapche, sautéed mixed vegetables, was a gentle and satisfying first course. Among soups, the beef broth with spicy beef dumplings proved to be best.

Decent, but less interesting appetizers include the namul vegetable salad and the bland, but fresh, grilled shrimp. Avoid the steamed minced clams that have the stale flavor and mealy texture of canned products.

The main courses that I enjoyed most were kalbikui, the tender and savory, marinated and broiled short ribs of beef, and the shinsulro, consisting of garlicky beef, pork meatballs, hard-boiled eggs, fish fillets and vegetables served for two in a black-iron hot pot and kept steaming over a brazier, a genuine bargain.

Boolgoki, a traditional Korean dish based on strips of beef, pork or chicken grilled and simmered with vegetables, was also gentle and satisfying, and so was the vegetarian special, with its simmered bean curd, mushrooms, bean sprouts, onions and other vegetables served in a sweet and salty sauce.

But the standard Japanese appetizers, soups and teriyaki dishes left much to be desired, and although a shrimp and vegetable tempura looked beautiful, it reeked of overheated grease.

Chicken or beef teriyaki, sizzling on an iron grill platter as it arrives at the table, seems to be a favorite with children, probably because it is sweet. Kalbichim, boiled short ribs with vegetables, was acceptable but less flavorful than the kalbikui.

The fiery Korean pickled vegetables, kimchi, was best made with cabbage, although the cucumber version, made with what seemed to be kosher garlic pickles, had a refreshing sharpness. Both were preferable to the house salad, consisting of iceberg lettuce and unripe tomato. Fresh fruit or ice cream are the most dependable desserts. À la carte dishes are better than those on fixed-price dinners.

Brighter lighting and better ventilation would be welcome improvements. There is full bar service, offering Japanese beer and a number of house concoctions reminiscent of Trader Vic's early days.

Mitsukoshi

★

461 Park Avenue, corner of 57th Street, 935-6444.
Atmosphere: Handsome, restful, modern Japanese cocktail lounge and sushi bar with a cheerless, drab dining room; service is polite and willing but erratic.
Recommended dishes: Shushi, sashimi, yakitori, grilled eggplant, chawan-mushi, bean soup, chicken teriyaki, toban-yaki, fillet kuwa-yaki, pineapple, melon.
Price range: Expensive.
Credit cards: All major credit cards.
Hours: Lunch, Mondays through Saturdays, noon to 2 P.M.; dinner, Mondays through Saturdays, 6 P.M. to 10 P.M. Closed Sundays and major holidays.
Reservations: Necessary.

Recent visits to this restaurant indicate it is operating at the same level as it did when it opened in 1979. Given the sophistication and authenticity represented in New York's Japanese restaurants today, this ambitious and somewhat handsome installation, while decent, leaves much to be desired in gastronomic excitement. It would be interesting to know what sort of evaluation of the local food scene was made by the owners before they decided on the culinary level they consider adequate. Situated just below a shop (also called Mitsukoshi) selling fine Japanese porcelain and art objects, the entrance stairway, cocktail lounge and sushi bar of the restaurant are beautifully laid out with blond wood, mirrors and plants. The setting is spacious, quiet and conducive to conversation as one has a before-dinner drink or some of the vinegar-rice, seaweed and fish sushi or the raw fish sashimi that are Mitsukoshi's best offerings. There is also a single tatami room behind sliding shoji panels, and judging by a few quick peeks, this, too, is a handsome room.

The dining room, unfortunately, is less inviting than the outside room, mostly because of drab lighting and an institutional arrangement of furniture. Kimono-clad waitresses are gracious and polite, if unprofessional. There were trying waits between courses and even then diners did not receive their main dishes at the same time. Table appointments were as beautiful as they were unusual and included canopied baskets in which the fried shrimp and vegetable tempura are served, and glazed stoneware dishes holding the still-life arrangements of refreshing pickled vegetables.

Sushi and sashimi are excellent at the sushi bar, and the luxurious combination of both on a platter, to be ordered twenty-four hours in advance, is spectacular and costly.

Yakitori, the tiny satays of grilled marinated chicken, were moist and pungent, and the grilled half eggplant filled with ground chicken provided a savory beginning to the meal. So did the chawan-mushi, a custard flecked with fish and vegetables, steamed in painted porcelain cups, a specialty that would be even better if the vegetables were cut in smaller pieces. A smoky bean soup held more interest than the pallid clear soup.

The rest of the food at Mitsukoshi proved to be of the bland, characterless hotel dining-room variety and perhaps is best suited to fainthearted eaters who prefer Japanese food somewhat modified. Shabu-shabu, cooked on a burner in the center of the table, was a fresh, if underseasoned, combination of broth and seaweed in which slices of beef and a wide variety of vegetables were poached, then to be dipped into either a vinegar or a sesame sauce, both of which were excellent.

Toban-yaki, a combination of diced grilled chicken, shrimp and vegetables served over tiny, red-hot stones, was a cut above such main courses as the limp tempura, the red snapper cooked in a watery broth with bean curd and vegetables, and the dry and disappointing imported grilled eel, kabayaki. Tender, boneless sliced chicken teriyaki with its sweet and piquant soy-sauce glaze was another good choice.

Also grilled at the table was the fillet kuwa-yaki, thin cuts of top quality beef and mixed vegetables that made one of the better main courses. Beefsteak Nihonbashi, a more conventional form of sliced steak broiled in the kitchen and seasoned with soy sauce, was acceptable, though the green salad served with it was mostly a tasteless array of iceberg lettuce.

Lobster onigarayaki, in spite of its exotic name, turned out to be tepid broiled lobster with a side dish of soy sauce.

Melon and pineapple were adequate desserts, but the green tea ice cream had a pasty, musty flavor. There is Japanese beer to be had, as well as hot, nicely served sake.

Monte's
★

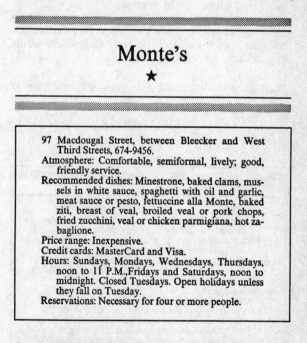

97 Macdougal Street, between Bleecker and West Third Streets, 674-9456.
Atmosphere: Comfortable, semiformal, lively; good, friendly service.
Recommended dishes: Minestrone, baked clams, mussels in white sauce, spaghetti with oil and garlic, meat sauce or pesto, fettuccine alla Monte, baked ziti, breast of veal, broiled veal or pork chops, fried zucchini, veal or chicken parmigiana, hot zabaglione.
Price range: Inexpensive.
Credit cards: MasterCard and Visa.
Hours: Sundays, Mondays, Wednesdays, Thursdays, noon to 11 P.M.,Fridays and Saturdays, noon to midnight. Closed Tuesdays. Open holidays unless they fall on Tuesday.
Reservations: Necessary for four or more people.

Good, solid Italian food at comfortingly low prices has been the big feature at Monte's for almost thirty years. The dining room, though somewhat crowded, has fairly effective acoustics and so is not ear-shatteringly loud. There are freshly laundered tablecloths, uniformed waiters, a warm golden glow of lamplight and a small bar where a television set is the focal point.

Monte's is especially inviting on Saturday and Sunday afternoons when a few regulars and Italian families gather around the tables, and service is more leisurely than during the peak rush hours.

The wide choice on the menu and the generous portions make it possible to share courses and so have a varied meal at a low price. A crisp, fresh antipasto salad, garlic-laden baked clams, steaming shiny black mussels in their garlic-and-parsley broth or pasta are all amply portioned to provide generous serving for two as appetizers. So is the excellent, thickly cut, crisp-fried zucchini. The thick, satisfying minestrone is virtually a meal when heavily layered with cheese.

Pasta here tends to be overcooked, but it is cooked to order, al dente, for fifty cents extra, a reasonable surcharge that assures near perfection. The best sauces are the white clam, the basil-and-parsley-scented pesto, the heady garlic and olive oil combination (aglio-olio) and fettuccine alla Monte's baked with tomato sauce under a mantle of mozzarella cheese.

If one skips the pasta course, spaghetti can be had with all of the meat, fish and poultry entrees, a wise move for those on the slimmest of budgets. Some vegetables served with main courses are better than others; if Swiss chard is available, order it. Potatoes in a tomato and onion sauce are delicious.

The best entree choices are veal or chicken parmigiana, chunks of veal broiled on a skewer, a thickly cut, peppery breast of veal with a spinach, egg and cheese stuffing, and charcoal-broiled veal chops or pork chops. Some sauces here tend to be greasy.

Desserts are undistinguished except for a made-to-order hot zabaglione that's a little heavy on the Marsala but otherwise frothy and soothing. Cheesecake would be good were it not served icy cold.

Mortimer's
Fair

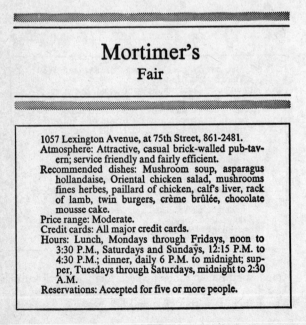

1057 Lexington Avenue, at 75th Street, 861-2481.
Atmosphere: Attractive, casual brick-walled pub-tavern; service friendly and fairly efficient.
Recommended dishes: Mushroom soup, asparagus hollandaise, Oriental chicken salad, mushrooms fines herbes, paillard of chicken, calf's liver, rack of lamb, twin burgers, crème brûlée, chocolate mousse cake.
Price range: Moderate.
Credit cards: All major credit cards.
Hours: Lunch, Mondays through Fridays, noon to 3:30 P.M., Saturdays and Sundays, 12:15 P.M. to 4:30 P.M.; dinner, daily 6 P.M. to midnight; supper, Tuesdays through Saturdays, midnight to 2:30 A.M.
Reservations: Accepted for five or more people.

Middle-aged preppies with tired stomachs can count on bland, soft, minimally decent food to see them through lunch and dinner at Mortimer's, an attractive, convivial pub-tavern. Everything about this brick-walled tavern is friendly and low key and it has become a popular neighborhood meeting place. When the neighborhood is the Upper East Side, the scene can become trendy and fashionable whether the fashion is rolled-up seersucker trousers and white bucks, safari jackets or three-piece gray suits, all of which may be on the premises simultaneously.

The menu is promising in its array of light and heavy fare, but it is disappointing in the delivery. Appetizers such as chicken liver pâté and three-custard cheese are so intensely rich that it is hard to imagine anyone eating more than a dab or two of either, spread on a cracker or a slice of toast. Tough leeks in vinaigrette dressing could not be cut but had to be torn, and ice-cold bacon turned fatty in the dressing. Mortimer slaw, based on red cabbage, ranged from cloyingly sweet to unpleasantly bitter. Both the slaw and the meager chef's salad were sodden with oily dressing.

Better appetizers were hot asparagus with hollandaise sauce, Oriental chicken salad with soy sauce and Sichuan peppercorns, and an earthy mushroom soup. Gravlax was a bit chewy but well flavored; its mustard sauce, however, lacked pungency.

Barely buttered pasta with peas and ham is the sort you'd expect on a hospital tray, and what is billed as chicken salad is merely dry, tasteless julienne strips of chicken breast on lettuce; ask for chicken-salad dressing and you get a saucer of sweet Russian dressing. The bay scallops meunière we tried, though tiny and sweet, were floury instead of slightly crisp. Roast duck had a fine flavor once it was cut, a difficult task because the skin was rubbery.

The best main courses were twin burgers of beefy, seared lean sirloin, sautéed calf's liver (although the zucchini with it was bitter), a moist, soothing, grilled chicken paillard and rack of lamb, done pink as ordered. By contrast, chicken hash was a mess — stale chicken in a pasty yellow sauce on burned toast. But it is the previously mentioned main courses, plus such good desserts as crème brûlée custard and chocolate-mousse cake, that earn Mortimer's a fair instead of a poor rating.

Moshe Peking

★

40 West 37th Street, between Fifth Avenue and Avenue of the Americas, 594-6500.

Atmosphere: Trim, pleasant, contemporary dining room; good service.

Recommended dishes: Special dumplings, fried wontons, barbecued chicken wings, egg drop soup, steamed sea bass, moo goo gai pan, pepper steak, chicken with cashews, steak kow, Peking veal with noodles, beef with broccoli or snow peas.

Price range: Moderately expensive.

Credit cards: American Express, MasterCard, Visa and Diners Club.

Hours: Lunch, Sundays through Thursdays, noon to 3 P.M,; dinner, Sundays through Thursdays, 3 P.M. to 9:30 P.M., Saturday night, one hour after sundown to 1:30 A.M. Open major holidays, but closed on Jewish holidays.

Reservations: Recommended.

One of the better-known facts of restaurant life is that Chinese restaurants are most likely to do well where they are in easy reach of a Jewish clientele, most especially if the food they serve is Cantonese. Although explanations for this phenomenon are necessarily speculative, a few reasons might explain it, at least in part. Most obviously, certain Chinese dishes seem overwhelmingly familiar to Jewish customers — plenty of hot tea and chicken broth with rice, noodles or wontons, first cousins to kreplach.

Then too, both cuisines are mildly seasoned with flavorings coming from garlic, sautéed onions, corn or peanut oils and ginger. The lure of the exotic eased by the touch of the familiar is further illustrated in a kind of cookery that features stew-type dishes of braised, cut-up ingredients. And by odd coincidence, Cantonese cooking as represented here uses no dairy products. Even Jews who do not observe kosher laws, generally by custom and habit are not used to the taste of milk products in meat dishes, and perhaps without even realizing it, they feel at home with such a cuisine.

It is little wonder then, that with this natural affinity, Moshe Peking, the glatt kosher Chinese restaurant, should be as crowded and popular as it is. Among kosher restaurants, it has to be considered special for its décor alone — a really stunning, modern cocktail lounge and dining room done in brown and beige, with soft, pleasant lighting, a huge indoor tree strung with candlelight bulbs, and starchy, well-laundered table linens. It is really the only handsome restaurant available to those who observe kosher dietary laws and must be a boon to young people who are dating.

It would be nice to be able to say that the food here is so good one should go, kosher or not, but that is hardly the case.

As a general rule, avoid all dishes based on substitutes. This includes the dry and fishy "pho-nee" shrimp

292

in mock lobster sauce (fish fillets in slippery sauce), veal sitting in for pork, tough and greasy veal or beef short ribs posing as spareribs, and so on.

Among appetizers the best choices were crisp fried wontons, a steamed Peking dumpling filled with meat and scallions, and barbecued chicken wings. Meat balls tasted as though they had come out of a fricassee, skewered beef was leathery and egg rolls oozed grease.

Thin and delicate wontons, a little light on filling, and strips of veal, chicken and green vegetables floated in a bland but not unpleasant chicken broth, which seemed to have been colored yellow with a bit of turmeric or annatto, a subterfuge not confined to this restaurant alone. Egg drop soup had more body, and the best of the three was the hot and sour soup, which need vinegar and chili oil to be convincing.

The most satisfying main courses were the moo goo gai pan with fresh, moist pieces of white chicken meat and crisp vegetables, the steamed sea bass with slivers of scallions and ginger and the pepper steak — tender, juicy bits of beef, flawlessly stir-fried with green pepper and onion. Crispy aromatic duck lacked the fresh taste it should have and was completely unaromatic, and the fried rice tasted of stale grease. Chicken with cashew nuts, steak kow, Peking veal with noodles, beef with snow peas or broccoli and a fair moo soo veal — shredded meat and vegetables rolled in crepes — were other acceptable selections.

These are a number of Polynesian-type drinks, all fruity and multicolored and topped with tiny paper parasols, and as cloying as a jar of baby-food fruit pudding. Desserts such as canned pineapple, lichee nuts, sherbet and almond cookies were on a par with those in utility neighborhood Chinese restaurants. The less said about the French pastries made with nondairy whitener "cream" fillings, the better.

Mr. Chow

★

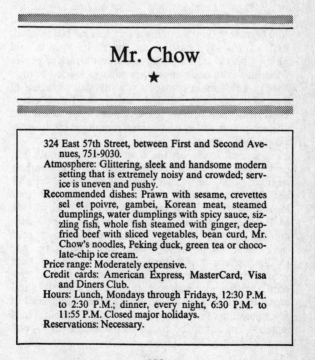

324 East 57th Street, between First and Second Avenues, 751-9030.

Atmosphere: Glittering, sleek and handsome modern setting that is extremely noisy and crowded; service is uneven and pushy.

Recommended dishes: Prawn with sesame, crevettes sel et poivre, gambei, Korean meat, steamed dumplings, water dumplings with spicy sauce, sizzling fish, whole fish steamed with ginger, deep-fried beef with sliced vegetables, bean curd, Mr. Chow's noodles, Peking duck, green tea or chocolate-chip ice cream.

Price range: Moderately expensive.

Credit cards: American Express, MasterCard, Visa and Diners Club.

Hours: Lunch, Mondays through Fridays, 12:30 P.M. to 2:30 P.M.; dinner, every night, 6:30 P.M. to 11:55 P.M. Closed major holidays.

Reservations: Necessary.

Fortunately, the absurd custom of serving Chinese food only in dining rooms that resemble the pagoda telephone booths in Chinatown is falling out of favor. New York now has several highly successful Chinese restaurants decorated in modern or Continental styles, totally devoid of bric-a-brac that looks as though it came from a souvenir shop in the Hong Kong airport. But nothing begins to compare with the dazzlement of the gleaming modern interior designed for Mr. Chow, the local branch of the restaurant that has captured chic clienteles in London, where it originated, and in Beverly Hills.

The stunning sleekness of the two-level dining room is achieved with sparkling, lacquer-white walls, white marble floors and expanses of black glass and smoke-gray mirrors. Almost every detail is handsome and impeccable from the Lalique doors to the romantic ceiling mobile that suggests the green cloth sails of a Chinese junk. Lighting is comfortable and felicitous, and the service is efficient, polite and thoughtful.

Considering the attractiveness of this restaurant, it is disappointing to have to report that the dining room is extremely uncomfortable, a result of the head-splitting noise, the cramped tables and almost painfully pinched chairs, and a couple of free-standing screens that tend to tip as they are bumped into, which is often. There also seems to be a problem with air circulation; some sections of the room are stifling. Add to that the coyly pretentious tone of the menu, and the idea that Michael Chow apparently feels he cannot operate a classy restaurant with Chinese waiters, and this restaurant can become as uncomfortable philosophically as it is physically.

The food here is as continentalized as the service and the setting, but with less success. For though I had a few very good dishes, and only two or three that were really poor, the general level of cooking is decent but ordinary. On my first visit, Mr. Chow offered to plan the meal as he was doing for many other tables. I allowed him to, asking only that prawn with sesame be included, as it caught my fancy on the menu. He agreed, and along with that dish he served crevettes sel et poivre (delicious salty and peppery shrimp quick-fried in their shells), a fair main course of prawns with cloudlets of egg white and peas, and dreadfully cold and greasy fried rice tossed with shrimp and peas. That meant four shrimp-prawn dishes on the menu arranged by the master planner himself.

Appetizers made up the best course, and both the pork-filled steamed dumplings, served in their bamboo steamers, and the water dumplings in sesame oil and hot chili were excellent, as was gambei, a dish that looked like shredded seaweed but which is really made of fried, slivered collard greens or kale topped with crushed, salty dried fish. Korean meat, slices of cold pork in a spicy garlic sauce, was interesting, but Dragon's eye, a quail's egg fried in shrimp toast, did not seem quite worth the trouble it obviously took to prepare it, although it was acceptable. Both the spring roll and aubergine en croûte represented the worst kind of frying, tasting of overheated, overused oil. Diced, spiced squab — meant to be rolled in lettuce leaves — was delicious, but the small snippets of lettuce leaves were inadequate to permit proper rolling.

Not one of the three soups I tried had any distinction whatever. The hot and sour was neither hot nor sour, the shark's fin tasted exactly like the hot and sour, and the corn with crab meat tasted of canned corn kernels.

My favorites among main courses were sizzling fish (flounder in a dark, mellow sauce with scallions and ginger), ginger-flavored whole steamed sea bass, crisp julienne strips of deep-fried beef tossed with shredded vegetables and finely diced, satiny bean curd in a pink hot-and-sweet sauce enriched with minced pork.

The kitchen exhibited marked unevenness with main courses. One night the whole baby chicken that was marinated, steamed and deep fried proved enticingly spicy — crisp, yet moistly tender. On another night it seemed as though it had stood around for hours before being reheated. On one try Mr. Chow's noodles, tossed with mild hot sauce, were rich with flecks of pork and shreds of cucumber, but on another contained almost no meat and were a bit dry.

The menu suggested that notice was needed to produce Peking duck, but when I asked for it I was told it would take only thirty minutes. The menu described the classic presentation: cold crepes, a platter of crisp duck skin, scallions, plum sauce and finally the duck meat. What I got was a magnificently golden duck, but it was sliced with skin and meat together and contained much of the fat that should have been rendered out. Despite the unconventional preparation, and perhaps because of the fat, the flavor was rich and interesting, even though lovers of the crisp standard would be disappointed.

Gambler's duck, badly overcooked, had a musty flavor, and among the completely banal dishes were Peking chili chicken, roast pork, pork with chili, imitation crab (egg white with ginger) and lamb with spring onions. Fresh live lobster was decent, if not quite worth the trouble of picking it out of the shell, and special lobster was distractingly sweet. ("The only thing that's special about this dish is that it's not lobster. We use large Pacific prawns . . ." the menu read.)

Mixed Chinese vegetables were overcooked and as ordinary looking as Birds Eye oriental mixture.

Oranges Curaçao, really sliced oranges Orientale, would have been refreshingly welcome had they been a little less sweet, and caramelized toffee bananas and apples were very good one night, only fair on another. There are two excellent ice creams — one of green tea, the other a rich chocolate chip — and soggy, tasteless apple, strawberry and apricot tarts.

Anyone who wants to visit Mr. Chow to catch the entertaining and theatrical scene can put together a good and interesting meal, but one must choose with care. Chopsticks are available on request but seem out of place, and both dinner plates and food are often cold, so ask for both properly heated. There is a tendency here to send unordered dishes over to tables, "at the captain's suggestion for you to try." Before you accept, consider that you will be charged for those pseudo-gifts. The staff can be ungracious when such largesse is refused.

Mumtaz
★ ★

1493 Third Avenue, between 84th and 85th Streets,
879-4797.
Atmosphere: Decorative, informal and festive setting;
pleasant service.
Recommended dishes: Assorted hors d'oeuvres, all
breads, chicken tandoori, chicken tikka masala,
lamb dupiaza, chicken livers with spices, shag
gosht, vegetable masala, nargisi kofta, vegetable
biryani, raita.
Price range: Inexpensive.
Credit cards: American Express, MasterCard and
Visa.
Hours: Lunch, seven days, noon to 3 P.M.; dinner,
seven days, 3 P.M. to midnight. Open on major
holidays.
Reservations: Recommended.

Unlike the more ambitious midtown Indian restaurants
that have opened in recent years, this one has no slickly
designed interior. Rather, it uses a festive, folkloric
draping of fabrics to create a tentlike effect in a room
with a black, red and white color scheme. The cuisine is
primarily North Indian with just a few of the more
hotly spiced southern dishes included.

The selection of assorted hors d'oeuvres offers a delightful array of contrasts, with the ground lamb perfectly broiled on skewers (sheek kebab), the spicier
grilled lamb patties (shami kebab), crisp fried pastry
filled with vegetables (samosas) and light, puffy cheese
and vegetable fritters (pakora). Slivered onion and
lemon complement the grilled meats, and the whole collection has a sort of rooflike pappadum, the paper-thin,
nut-flavored lacy fried bread wafer. Fried shrimp Ben-
gali style, simmered in a heady tomato sauce, was another very good appetizer.

Soups, however, were disappointing. The tomato
might have been Campbell's straight from the can, and
the mulligatawny had none of the subtle spice accents it
requires. Only the vegetable soup, with its base of the
lentil purée, dhal, was at all interesting.

Indian breads are extraordinary in their savory richness and diversity, and several are well represented
here. My favorites were the buttery, layered paratha,
served plain or as mughlai paratha, with a filling of
ground meat, chopped eggs, onions and green peppers,
itself almost a main course especially if topped with
some of the cucumber and yogurt sauce, raita. Golden
puffy poori was also delicious.

Chicken tandoori was moist, tender and fragrant with
mild spices, and boneless bits of the same chicken were
simmered in a gentle tomato, green pepper and onion
sauce (chicken tikka masala). Lamb dupiaza braised
with chunks of onion, nargisi kofta (ground lamb
packed around hard-boiled eggs, then braised in tomato

sauce) and shag gosht, fork-tender chunks of lamb cooked with spinach, were excellent.

There were also wholly satisfying vegetarian dishes here — the mixed vegetable masala in a curry sauce, the bhindi masala (okra with tomatoes and onions) and the mixed vegetable and rice dish, vegetable biryani, that had the added crunch of nuts contrasting with tender rice.

Unfortunately, those who like their Indian food hotly spiced will have a hard time convincing the management here that they really mean business. But dhal was light and delicious and the rice was always well cooked — saffron-gilded grains mingling with plain white ones.

Indian desserts have always seemed to me too stickily sweet to be edible, and those at Mumtaz proved no exception, but perhaps they are an acquired taste. I would have been happier with some cold fresh fruit to offset the highly aromatic food. Service is pleasant, friendly and efficient. Complete dinners include three courses and a beverage; breads have to be ordered à la carte.

Nada Sushi
★ ★

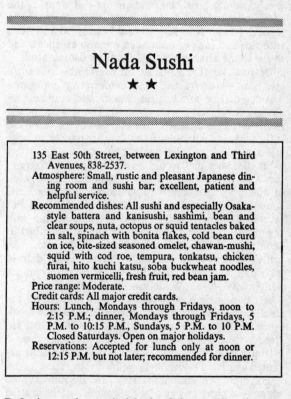

135 East 50th Street, between Lexington and Third Avenues, 838-2537.
Atmosphere: Small, rustic and pleasant Japanese dining room and sushi bar; excellent, patient and helpful service.
Recommended dishes: All sushi and especially Osaka-style battera and kanisushi, sashimi, bean and clear soups, nuta, octopus or squid tentacles baked in salt, spinach with bonita flakes, cold bean curd on ice, bite-sized seasoned omelet, chawan-mushi, squid with cod roe, tempura, tonkatsu, chicken furai, hito kuchi katsu, soba buckwheat noodles, suomen vermicelli, fresh fruit, red bean jam.
Price range: Moderate.
Credit cards: All major credit cards.
Hours: Lunch, Mondays through Fridays, noon to 2:15 P.M.; dinner, Mondays through Fridays, 5 P.M. to 10:15 P.M., Sundays, 5 P.M. to 10 P.M. Closed Saturdays. Open on major holidays.
Reservations: Accepted for lunch only at noon or 12:15 P.M. but not later; recommended for dinner.

Referring to the tropical look of the traditional Japanese bamboo and paper house, Fosco Maraini in his book, "Meeting With Japan" observed: "The Japanese often live in northern snows with the provisional attitude of southerners forced northward by events." Bernard Rudofsky, in his book "The Kimono Mind," quotes the fourteenth-century philosopher Yoshida Kenko: "A house should be built with the summer in view. In the winter, one can live anywhere."

Much the same observations can be made about Japanese food, I decided as I sampled the cooling sushi, sashimi, chilled noodles and savory cold to tepid appetizers at the small and rustic Nada Sushi restaurant during a summer heat wave.

Limp with the summer heat, I welcomed the restorative powers of soft, white bean curd chilled on ice and then dipped in a blend of dried bonita flakes, seaweed, ginger and soy sauce, the cold buckwheat noodles, soba, and the wheat vermicelli, suomen, which was doused with soy sauce sparked by green wasabi horseradish and minced scallions.

Although there are a few lusty, hot casseroles (nabe) and some steamy soups in the Japanese cuisine, for the most part food is served cool, cold or tepid. Mr. Rudofsky suggests that this is a result of kitchen and dining room logistics. Whatever the reasons, it would be hard to imagine more suitable hot-weather fare than the delicate and brightly fresh sushi prepared at Nada Sushi and available at the bar or tables. Cooked shrimp, vinegared mackerel, sea bass, cold omelet, lean tuna or the tastier fatty tuna, the sea-urchin roe called uni, the best grade of pale-gold salmon caviar, tender octopus and chewy, saline, giant clam muscle are just some of the possibilities to be packed on to the mildly sweet, gently tepid rice base. Nori sushi, rolled in seaweed and filled with rice and tuna or cucumber, are also excellent, and so are all the arrangements of plain raw fish, sashimi.

Unusual for New York are the two Osaka-style sushi selections — battera made with mackerel and vinegared seaweed on rice, and kanisushi, marinated crabmeat on vinegar rice layered with seaweed. The Osaka kitchen favors milder seasonings than that of Tokyo, and these sushi are made without wasabi; they are pressed in large cakes, then cut into rectangular portions.

Small dishes that would be considered appetizers in the Western meal format can be ordered in succession to add up to a complete and satisfying dinner here. Among my favorites were the nuta, a gently sweet and mustardy, scallion-flecked salad that can be had with raw tuna, squid or fluke, the dish that is described as squid legs baked with salt but that looks more like grilled octopus tentacles, and satiny raw squid dabbed with pink cod roe. Oshitashi — lightly wilted spinach with bonita — was also delicious and refreshing.

A banal shrimp salad was the only mistake on the small-dish menu. But it was overshadowed by the excellence of the hot steamed custard, chawan-mushi, enriched with shrimp and vegetables, and the dashi maki — puffy little pillows of a warm, wine-sweet omelet accented by grated radish mellowed with soy sauce.

For more conventional tastes, there are full-flavored soups — a clear and smoky consommé with bean curd and mushrooms and a heartier soybean soup with squares of bean curd and greens. All frying is well done — crisp, golden and greaseless — whether for the batter-dipped tempura shrimp and vegetables or for the crunchy, breaded food, such as chicken furai, the pork cutlet tonkatsu and the assorted nuggets of pork, chicken and squid that make up hito kuchi katsu.

Broiling is not nearly so satisfactory, however, and although the grilled chicken, yakitori, and the beef and pork teriyaki were acceptable, little more can be said for them. Nothing good can be said about the American salad of raw cabbage and iceberg lettuce doused with an awful French dressing that rounds out main courses.

One unusual feature at Nada Sushi is the moderately priced complete dinner served on a compartmented china platter that fits into a lacquer tray. After the diner selects the main course — tempura, for instance — the selection is rounded out with pickles, rice in various forms, vegetables, baked fish, sashimi and whatever other dishes complement the main course.

In addition to oranges and honeydew melon for dessert, Nada Sushi has a fudgy bean jam confection that is less cloyingly sweet than most Asian candies.

Prices for complete meals are moderate, but the bill mounts up considerably for the small dishes or sushi. There is full bar service and the staff is more than willing to explain dishes and the way to handle them. Tablecloths appear for dinner and so do hot towels, but a stained carpet strikes an off-note at any time of day.

Nanni
★ ★

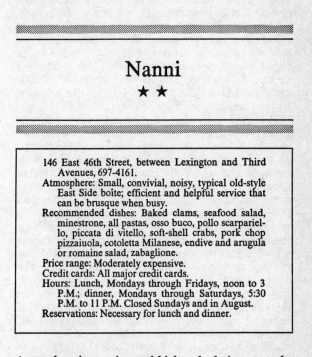

146 East 46th Street, between Lexington and Third Avenues, 697-4161.
Atmosphere: Small, convivial, noisy, typical old-style East Side boîte; efficient and helpful service that can be brusque when busy.
Recommended dishes: Baked clams, seafood salad, minestrone, all pastas, osso buco, pollo scarpariello, piccata di vitello, soft-shell crabs, pork chop pizzaiuola, cotoletta Milanese, endive and arugula or romaine salad, zabaglione.
Price range: Moderately expensive.
Credit cards: All major credit cards.
Hours: Lunch, Mondays through Fridays, noon to 3 P.M.; dinner, Mondays through Saturdays, 5:30 P.M. to 11 P.M. Closed Sundays and in August.
Reservations: Necessary for lunch and dinner.

As much as innovation and high-style design are to be applauded in the creation of both restaurant interiors and their menus, we have had such an abundance of newness recently that it can be downright relaxing to revisit an old-fashioned undesigned restaurant such as those that once abounded in neighborhoods all over the city.

The original Nanni on East 46th Street (not to be confused with its newer and fancier uptown younger brother, Nanni al Valletto) is just such a restaurant — small, clubby, convivial, noisy and with a menu offering familiar, well-prepared classics of both northern and southern Italy. Travel posters are the sole attempt at adornment, hanging on off-white and dark varnished wood walls.

Appetizers here are few and the selection is confined to piping-hot, properly garlicky baked clams, a lightly colorful minestrone soup, bland, waxy prosciutto and clam or shrimp cocktails. There is also a wonderfully refreshing, lemony seafood and celery salad, not on the menu but always on hand. But considering the treasury of excellent pastas, skipping appetizers is no hardship. Better to divide a pasta (or order a separate half portion) as a first course. You won't go wrong, whether you decide on the noodle-like trenette in their pesto sauce of basil, garlic and cheese, the baked ziti with tomato sauce and melted mozzarella cheese, the eggy fettuccine carbonara with nuggets of the cured bacon pancetta, the fine "angel's hair" spaghetti, cappelli di angel, or the meat-filled "hats," cappelletti, served with the mild tomato sauce Nanni enriched with nuggets of meat and just the right balance of herbs.

Fish and seafood dishes may be mildly disappointing. Glowingly fresh sea bass marechiaro was cooked to the correct degree of doneness and was served in a pink tomato sauce that seemed to have been thickened with flour — a culinary error in a sauce that should be delicately transparent and not bound at all. Shrimp in the scampi Sorrento were inexplicably tough and hard and they were served in a pasty sauce that included mushrooms, inappropriate with the flavor of the scampi and the sauce. Two better choices were the soft-shell crabs meunière and a Friday night special of the delightful Italian bouillabaisse, zuppa de pesce.

There are a number of very good meat dishes at Nanni, including one of the best versions of pollo scarpariello in the city. The chicken, cut in chunks that included the bone, became nicely browned while remaining moist and tender while sautéed in oil, garlic, white wine and lemon. A paillard of veal (not on the menu but available) was expertly grilled. Two tender pork chops in the spicy tomato sauce pizzaiuola, a crisp, thin veal cutlet Milanese style and the veal piccata in a light lemony sauce were excellent. Osso buco, a daily special, was tender and in a perfect herb-scented sauce. Breast of chicken valdostana, the chicken stuffed with prosciutto and topped with melted cheese and sauce, would have been better if the cheese had been inside the chicken instead of forming a gummy liaison between breading and an over-abundance of slick sauce. Calf's liver alla Veneta was dry and too heavily sauced.

All dishes came with well-cooked vegetables — firmly al dente zucchini in butter one night, nicely sautéed escarole on another. The house salad was based on cracklingly fresh greens tossed with an excellent oily lemon-edged dressing. Unfortunately, it was bulked up with iceberg lettuce.

Except for a wonderfully warm zabaglione (also not on the menu but made on request, with or without strawberries), desserts, such as rum cake and chocolate mousse cake, were banally commercial.

If Nanni no longer shines with the three-star luster of excellence it formerly displayed, it is because of the heaviness of some of its sauces, the disappointing fish dishes, the use of canned peas that are unworthy and unnecessary additions to otherwise excellent sauces, the iceberg lettuce and the sameness of the base sauces used for several pastas and meat dishes. Still, it remains one of our better choices for solidly lusty Italian food. The waiters are especially kind and friendly toward children.

Wines are overpriced by about one third.

Nippon
★

---

145 East 52nd Street, between Third and Lexington Avenues, 758-0226.

Atmosphere: Typical Japanese setting much in need of refurbishing; tatami rooms or Western tables; pleasant and good service.

Recommended dishes: Yakitori, torikawa-yaki, tempura, chawan-mushi, hama-nabe, tonkatsu, tatsuta-age, negima-yaki.

Price range: Moderately expensive.

Credit cards: All major credit cards.

Hours: Lunch, Mondays through Fridays, noon to 2:30 P.M.; dinner, Mondays through Thursdays, 5:30 P.M. to 10 P.M., Fridays and Saturdays, 5:30 P.M. to 10:30 P.M. Closed Sundays. Open on major holidays.

Reservations: Necessary.

When Nippon opened almost twenty years ago, it was by far the best and most graceful Japanese restaurant in the city, but things apparently have changed. Not only has the setting become shabby with chipped paint and peeled wallpaper, but the cooking also seems to have lost its lively glow.

Sushi, those intricately rolled and packed variations of vinegar, rice, seaweed and assorted bits of raw fish and shellfish, were only barely acceptable, but a long way from the sea-fresh, colorful arrangements formerly turned out at this sushi bar. Soup seemed little more than tepid water, and most of the dishes cooked at the table, such as sukiyaki and shabu shabu, proved pallid and boring. The meat and vegetables in them turned tough and ragged from overcooking, and sauces lacked the punch needed to bring the cooked ingredients back to life.

Most of the vegetable side dishes, such as bean curd and eggplant, were overcooked, and in some cases specialties that were excellent one night were only fair on another.

A few dishes seemed to be still above average at Nippon. Frying was done well, whether in the tempura assortment of shrimp, fish, seaweed and vegetables or in such specialties as breaded pork cutlet (tonkatsu) or nuggets of crisp, greaseless, fried chicken (tatsuta-age). Kakiage, a tempura fritter combining seafood and vegetables, was a bit pasty in the middle, but that was the only flaw among the fried foods. Negima-yaki, tender beef roll-ups wrapped around scallions and broiled in a soy marinade, were lovely and firm one night, but at another time were much too soft and drowned in sauce. A variation with striped bass was altogether unsatisfactory because the fish was dry and falling apart and had an unpleasantly fishy odor.

A few of the appetizers and side dishes that are also available as first courses were interestingly prepared. Marinated broiled chunks of chicken on tiny skewers (yakitori), and another version done with barbecued-chicken-skin cracklings on skewers (torikawa-yaki), were delicious. Nuta, slivers of red tuna fish mixed with soybean purée and mussels, was good, if not quite up to other examples in town, and masago-ae, raw squid with cod roe, was tough and bland. Chawan-mushi, a steamed custard made with sake, bits of seafood, chicken and gingko nuts, could have been a little firmer, but it was soothing and aromatic nonetheless.

One casserole dish that was rich and soul warming, and which would make an excellent soup course if shared by two or three people, was hama-nabe, a rich, brown, soybean soup in which clams, vegetables and fragrant, dry Japanese mushrooms were simmered.

Soba, cold buckwheat noodles dipped in a mustardy, scallion-flecked soy sauce, were refreshing, and though not on the menu, were forthcoming when ordered. It's just possible that a number of other dishes are also not on the menu, a situation markedly unfair to non-Japanese customers.

Ice cream, a sticky, sweet bean paste and honeydew melon were the only desserts. The melon was a nice idea after the dinner we had but was completely unripe when served.

There is a small, attractive bar at Nippon, serving Japanese beers as well as gently warmed aromatic sake, along with more usual bar drinks. Waitresses are congenial and helpful, and the hot towels presented at the beginning of each meal add a hospitable and authentic touch.

Nishi

★

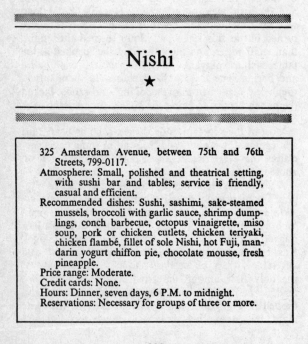

325 Amsterdam Avenue, between 75th and 76th Streets, 799-0117.
Atmosphere: Small, polished and theatrical setting, with sushi bar and tables; service is friendly, casual and efficient.
Recommended dishes: Sushi, sashimi, sake-steamed mussels, broccoli with garlic sauce, shrimp dumplings, conch barbecue, octopus vinaigrette, miso soup, pork or chicken cutlets, chicken teriyaki, chicken flambé, fillet of sole Nishi, hot Fuji, mandarin yogurt chiffon pie, chocolate mousse, fresh pineapple.
Price range: Moderate.
Credit cards: None.
Hours: Dinner, seven days, 6 P.M. to midnight.
Reservations: Necessary for groups of three or more.

Nishi is a small, dark and polished little stage set of a restaurant featuring stylized versions of Japanese dishes in a modern dining room, where spotlights reflect on glassy black walls. A white brocade bridal kimono mounted on the wall and a tiny, decorative sushi bar add dramatic Japanese accents to the setting, and the staff is friendly and accommodating. Although the food lacks consistent excellence at Nishi, a number of delicious and satisfying options are available at fairly moderate prices.

Fresh fish, fine quality nori seaweed and gently flavored rice are adeptly combined in very good sushi, and the freshness of raw fish is equally apparent in the sashimi, artfully arranged on simple black or white plates. Unfortunately, those plates, and glassware, are often chipped. Both sushi and sashimi can be obtained at the bar or at the tables, where you can order more substantial main courses.

Unlike the very traditional sushi, sashimi and smoky miso bean soup, main courses at Nishi show European influences, either in preparation or presentation. Results are far more successful with appetizers than with main courses. The most consistent flaw is the cooking oil, which is stale or overheated, giving acrid overtones to dishes such as the sautéed eggplant with miso sauce, an appetizer that otherwise would have been lovely, and the huge swirl of kakiage tempura done in great big lacy fritters combining seafood and vegetables. The unpleasant oil was less apparent in the crusty, breaded pork and chicken cutlets, masked by the thick, sweet and salty dipping sauce.

Excellent appetizers included a big bowl of large sand-free steamed mussels served with hot butter for dipping, lightly cooked garlic-scented broccoli, a beautifully arranged seashell holding slices of barbecued conch, and delicate steamed dumplings filled with shrimp or pork. Tender slices of cooked octopus marinated in vinegar with slivers of cucumber were exceptional.

Fillet of sole Nishi, braised with soy sauce and sake, was properly moist. Mildly sweet and fruity sauces complemented the tender breast of chicken flambé. The same flavor accented the seafood curry, although the sauce was too heavy.

Because the beef teriyaki lacked proper searing, the paper-thin slices were unappetizingly gray and stringy. And a large, thick salmon steak, grilled teriyaki style, was overcooked and therefore dry.

All main courses were served as Western blue-plate specials, with rice and bright, stir-fried mixed vegetables in crisp julienne slivers. A dressing of sesame seeds, soy bean oil and rice vinegar added a Japanese flavor to a very Continental green salad topped with slices of raw mushrooms.

Desserts are all Western, the most spectacular being hot Fuji, otherwise known as a hot fudge sundae. Served in a huge stemmed wine glass, it is enough for four. The thick, fudgelike chocolate mousse also comes in a generous portion. Delicious though these desserts were, they seemed overwhelming after Japanese food. More subtle and refreshing choices were the fresh pineapple and the frothy mandarin yogurt chiffon pie. Only the chocolate Grand Marnier pie seemed commercial and banal.

Nishi has liquor service and flowery, scalding hot tea. There is a minimum at tables, but none at the sushi bar.

No. 1 Chinese Restaurant
★ ★

---

202 Canal Street, near Mulberry Street, 227-1080.

Atmosphere: Downstairs dining room is typical of unadorned sloppy Chinatown settings relieved only by tablecloths and crystal chandeliers; upstairs dining room is brassy, lavish and overdone. Service is good, efficient, good-natured and accommodating although little English is spoken.

Recommended dishes: Hot and sour soup, periwinkles, clams in black-bean sauce, roast pork, cold roast duck, roast suckling pig, steamed sea bass, steamed crabs, crabs in black-bean sauce, steamed lobster, lobster with ginger and scallions, abalone with assorted vegetables, oily fried squid, squid with mixed vegetables, crystal jumbo shrimp, grilled jumbo shrimp in shell, baked salted pork ribs with hot pepper, pan-fried noodles.

Price range: Moderate.

Credit cards: MasterCard and Visa (only after 6 P.M.).

Hours: Lunch, seven days, 11 A.M. to 4 P.M.; dinner, seven days, 4 P.M. to 11 P.M. Dim sum, seven days, 8 A.M. to 4 P.M. Open on major holidays.

Reservations: Recommended.

From the street this hardly looks like a restaurant at all. The lacquer-brown roasted ducks, chickens and strips of pork and ribs, and the huge, gold-crusted sides of roast suckling pigs hanging in the window suggest a takeout food shop of the sort so common in Chinatown. No. 1 does provide that service in the front section of the shop, but in back and upstairs are dining rooms where complete meals are offered. Although there are a few dishes from Sichuan and Shantou, most of the food is Cantonese and the real specialties are the grilled, roasted and barbecued meats so tantalizingly displayed.

The simple, straightforward dining room downstairs is interesting and convivial and less gaudily gussied up than the huge upstairs rooms, and in all dining rooms, tablecloths are comfortable touches at dinner. At times, however, things get a lot messier than they should.

Very little English is understood here and ordering can be a bit confusing. Nevertheless, the good-natured staff and management do their best to get things straight and are accommodating about bringing a few dishes at a time, rather than all at once. They are also patient with the very few Caucasians who eat there and who constantly point to dishes being served to Chinese customers and inquiring what they are.

Combining that method with the more usual reading of the menu, one manages to get some very good and inexpensive food on these premises. Soups are served in huge bowls only, and easily serve six, which makes it an impossible course for two or three diners. That is not much of a loss; of the three soups tried, only the hot and sour was interesting and even that needed a heavy dosing of hot oil. Chinese parsley and fish-slice soup, and a combination of winter melon and meat were rather bland.

Among the many types of shellfish prepared in the rich, fermented black-bean sauce, I found the periwinkles (called snails), the cherrystone clams and the crabs to be the best. But crabs were also miraculously delicate and pungent steamed with lemon slices, a preparation equally sublime with lobsters. Ginger-and-scallion-accented lobsters were also delicious, and the same combination enhanced a satiny steamed sea bass.

Salty, oily grilled shrimp, crisply nestled in their shells, really needed no peeling. The crystal white jumbo shrimp, though moist and pearly, were acceptable but hardly distinctive.

Squid is done up in a number of fascinating ways. Oily fried squid combined tenderness with a light, snappy crunch. Equally delicious were corkscrew-cut squid tossed with assorted vegetables that included lotus root and sprouted mung beans. It is difficult to remember ever having abalone as meltingly tender as it was here, braised and layered over vegetables and ruffled sheets of sautéed bean curd.

Roasted and barbecued meats such as the suckling pig and the gently warm sliced roast pork were served over tiny yellow beans, almost nutlike in texture, and the suckling pig was further complemented by a light sprinkling of salted black beans. Roast duck cut in strips through greaseless, parchmentlike skin and moist meat could be dipped into the hoisin-based sauce usually served with Peking duck. Poached, salted pork ribs (really chops) had a peppery patina that made them unforgettable.

Boneless fried squab with lemon flavor, a bit too sweet, will appeal to those who like lemon chicken, while crispy-fried chicken, though not quite up to other examples in Chinatown, at least was tender and not the least bit dry.

Stir-fried dishes with brown sauces tended to be disappointing, glutinous with overdoses of cornstarch. Among these were the steak with broccoli in oyster sauce and the fillet steak with onions, although the beef itself was tender and flavorful.

Vegetable dishes such as Buddha's delight and assorted vegetables with bean curd were decent but are far surpassed in many other restaurants in the neighborhood. Similarly, the special fried rice tasted of overheated grease and included soggy, frozen shrimp. Choose instead the slim, pan-fried noodles as crisp and golden as spun glass.

Cut oranges are placed on each table along with wet washcloths at the end of each meal, but if you prefer, there are some heavy and cloyingly sweet steamed cakes and buns filled with bean paste for dessert.

The only really poor meal I had here was the Chinese dim sum tea lunch, served all day every day in the upstairs dining room. Not only were the dumplings and other dishes almost all cold, but they were far less varied and interesting than elsewhere.

Budweiser beer is sold, but you may bring in your own brand, or follow in the steps of many of the Chinese customers who set down big bottles of whiskey on their tables. Jasmine tea is served at times, on a schedule that must remain mysterious.

Nuccio's
Fair

251 Avenue of the Americas, corner of West Houston Street, 620-0545.
Atmosphere: Small, informal and stylish cafe-trattoria, cramped and noisy, but convivial; service is alert, informal, but sometimes slow.
Recommended dishes: Tortellini alla Bolognese, penne all'arrabbiata, risotto alla Certosina, chicken scarpariello.
Price range: Moderately expensive.
Credit cards: American Express.
Hours: Lunch, Mondays through Saturdays, noon to 3 P.M.; dinner, seven nights, 6 P.M. to midnight.
Reservations: Recommended.

Nuccio's, a fashionable and popular cafe-trattoria with colorful food posters and plant-filled window boxes, has everything going for it except its food. It is attractively bright — sunlit by day and theatrically romantic at night, when the street light casts rosy shadows through the plate-glass windows. It is also noisy and crowded in a convivial way, and the young, efficient waiters manage to control what occasionally comes through as a touch of insolence. Although the management grudgingly agrees to requests for the sharing of large portions by two, it is a common practice with stylish regulars.

Decent, meat-filled tortellini thickly blanketed with a lusty Bolognese meat sauce tasted as delicious as the short, quill-shaped penne prepared all'arrabbiata in a peppery, creamy tomato sauce. The most unusual and best "pasta" is risotto alla Certosina, a richly simmered blend of rice, tomatoes, frog's legs and seafood. It was served awkwardly in a huge sort of paella pan that was hard to handle and discouragingly large to contemplate. Savory though it was, it did not appear to be a true risotto, with rice first glossed in butter, then simmered in tomatoes and broth. This version seemed to be a combination of cooked rice and seafood reheated together. Pesto sauce, heady with basil, had the proper verdant belt, but the gnocchi lacked the lightness and delicacy required of these small potato dumplings.

The only main course worth having was chicken scarpariello, sautéed chunks of chicken on the bone in a garlicky white-wine sauce. Dishes tried but not recommended include a tasteless mozzarella-and-tomato salad, a pasty hot antipasto of seafood and stuffed zucchini and a couple of dishes that might have been in the refrigerator for two days, vitello tonnato and a seafood salad. Stale squid in sauce, plus a few clams, made up a watery frutti di mare sauce for linguine, and fettuccine alla primavera seemed to be doused with leftover vegetable soup.

A fra diavolo sauce had the proper sting and velvety texture, but the shrimp in it were dried out. The Italian fish soup consisted mainly of mussels and overcooked chunks of fish. Worst of all was calf's liver Veneziana, much like pickled herring with almost-raw liver boiled in an acid bath of vinegar and zapped by three huge bay leaves. Veal piccata also was much too sour.

Banally commercial desserts did nothing to redeem the earlier failures. Not even the wonderfully coarse and crusty bread could do that.

The Odeon
★

145 West Broadway, corner of Thomas Street, 233-0507.

Atmosphere: A suavely polished Art Deco cafeteria converted into a convivial, noisy dining room that is popular with a young, stylishly casual crowd; service is friendly and well-meaning but painfully slow.

Recommended dishes: Oysters with champagne sauce, leek and artichoke soup, country salad, sliced breast of duck, sliced fillet of beef, sautéed sweetbreads with lobster, pasta with zucchini, lobster à la nage, rack of lamb, crème brûlée, chocolate cake.

Price range: Moderately expensive.

Credit cards: American Express, MasterCard and Visa.

Hours: Lunch, Mondays through Fridays, noon to 3 P.M.; dinner, Mondays through Saturdays, 7 P.M. to 12:30 A.M., Sundays, 7:30 P.M. to 12:30 A.M.; supper, seven days, until 2:30 A.M.; Sunday brunch, noon to 3:30 P.M. Open most major holidays.

Reservations: Necessary.

From dinnertime to 2:30 in the morning the cast of patrons arrives at this funky Art Deco ex-cafeteria in everything from punk to black tie, from urban cowgirl and thrift-shop ragbag to plainclothed uptowners. At the Odeon, the bar scene makes guests feel as though they're at a party, and the 1930's and 40's background music is not too objectionable as a result.

A charming and accommodating staff enhances the generally felicitous atmosphere, and one suspects that the reason for the agonizing slowdowns between appetizers and main courses is a failing in the kitchen, not in the dining room.

The dinner menu focuses on nouvelle cuisine prepared by Patrick Clark, an American chef who is said to have served an apprenticeship with Michel Guérard, one of France's best-known practitioners of the nouvelle cuisine.

Leek and artichoke soup had exactly the right satiny texture and oniony overtones. Equally good were the oysters in a light champagne sauce and nested on leaves of fresh spinach. The cream sauce covering snails was heady with garlic, although the snails had a musty flavor. While terrines of chicken livers and rabbit needed more interesting textures and spicing, the silky Norwegian salmon could be faulted only for its high price tag. At one dinner, a salad of leeks, mushrooms and truffles was properly mellow, but at another the leeks were barely chewable. A huge country salad of crisp chicory, Roquefort, bacon and croutons was enough for four as an appetizer.

Rack of lamb, though overpowered by thyme, arrived rare as ordered. So did sliced breast of duck in a sauce of foie gras and pan juices. Lobster à la nage, poached in a sauce fragrant with leeks and white wine, was flawless. But at the price, portions should have been larger. The sauce on both the properly cooked calf's liver and the civet of duck was too sweet. Breast of roast chicken stuffed with an overly intense duxelles of mushrooms was bitter and barely edible. The accompanying spinach, puréed to the consistency of baby food, didn't help. Steak frites seemed made of frozen beef.

At these prices, one would expect fresh lump crab meat in a salad rather than frozen Alaskan crab meat. Pasta varies daily and the angel hair with butter, zucchini, a touch of tomato and red onion needed only a bit of pepper and a dash of salt to bring it to life.

An irresistible sourdough bread is sometimes served. Odeon's white chocolate mousse is slightly better than in most places and the crème brûlée is a marvel of creamy custard topped with a crackling sugar glaze.

Oenophilia
★

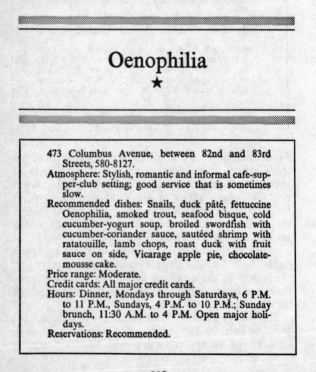

473 Columbus Avenue, between 82nd and 83rd Streets, 580-8127.

Atmosphere: Stylish, romantic and informal cafe-supper-club setting; good service that is sometimes slow.

Recommended dishes: Snails, duck pâté, fettuccine Oenophilia, smoked trout, seafood bisque, cold cucumber-yogurt soup, broiled swordfish with cucumber-coriander sauce, sautéed shrimp with ratatouille, lamb chops, roast duck with fruit sauce on side, Vicarage apple pie, chocolate-mousse cake.

Price range: Moderate.

Credit cards: All major credit cards.

Hours: Dinner, Mondays through Saturdays, 6 P.M. to 11 P.M., Sundays, 4 P.M. to 10 P.M.; Sunday brunch, 11:30 A.M. to 4 P.M. Open major holidays.

Reservations: Recommended.

The dark, atmospheric informal front room at this Upper West Side restaurant suggests a stylish cafe, while the back room with plants and candlelight has the intimate air of a supper club. The tone is young and trendy, with honest food nicely garnished, reflecting a combination of Continental and American kitchens. Sweetness remains as persistent a flaw now as when this restaurant opened in 1977, but there are enough dishes for those who have more sophisticated palates.

Snails with garlic, shallots and just the slightest gilding of cheese are sizzling hot and savory, and the duck pâté, though a little too delicate, is satisfying with its mix of pork, veal and pistachios, mildly scented with Grand Marnier. An overdose of Cognac spoiled the veal pâté and a scallop mousse was just a bit too airily soft to hold its flavor.

Fettuccine Oenophilia, a non-Italian pasta dish much in the current fashion trend, is a mellow tossing of cream, julienne strips of ham and Parmesan cheese set off by a dash of nutmeg, for which I would prefer a peppery replacement. Smoked trout is thick, moist and gently smoky but oysters baked with too much saffron and a stringy mass of Jarlsberg are best skipped. Soups have always been good here, and both the seafood bisque and the cold cucumber and yogurt soup continue the tradition. Apple seems a misplaced ingredient in shrimp salad, another example of nouvelle tearoom cuisine at its most blatant.

Swordfish was broiled to moist, pearly perfection and got a bright lift from the sauce of cucumber and fresh coriander and sautéed shrimp were well complemented by a refreshing, colorful ratatouille. Double-thick lamb chops glazed with garlic and enlivened by a red wine and pepper sauce were delicious as was the crisp duck; ask to have its peach brandy sauce served on the side so you can add it (or ignore it) at will. Too much Pernod brought an overly licorice accent to quail, and escalopes of veal, twice, were tough.

A round, Vicarage apple pie flavored with almonds, brown sugar and cinnamon and dark chocolate-mousse cake made up layerings of devil's food cake and mousse with a fudge frosting are the best desserts. Silk pie and a whipped-cream mousse sweetened with orange liqueur seemed insipid by comparison.

Service is friendly, polite and accommodating but can slow down between appetizers and main courses on busy nights.

Old Homestead
Fair

56 Ninth Avenue, between 14th and 15th Streets, 242-9040.

Atmosphere: Gaudy steakhouse décor with closely set tables; service is uneven.

Recommended dishes: Clams on the half shell, broiled lobster, sirloin steak, calf's liver.

Price range: Expensive.

Credit cards: All major credit cards.

Hours: Lunch, Mondays through Fridays, 11:30 A.M. to 3:30 P.M.; dinner, Mondays through Fridays, 4 P.M. to 10:45 P.M., Saturdays noon to midnight, Sundays, 1 P.M. to 10 P.M. Open major holidays.

Reservations: Recommended.

The Old Homestead, operating since 1868, is said to be New York's oldest steakhouse. For a long period its distinction lay in the fact that it was in the middle of the city's wholesale meat market and was especially popular for lunch with the market men, a tribute to the quality and quantity of the food served there. In recent years, however, much of the meat market has moved to the Hunt's Point area of the Bronx and, whether or not as a direct result, the quality (though not the quantity) of food at the Old Homestead has deteriorated badly.

Although it is a crowded and popular spot for both luncheon and dinner, the Old Homestead is a victim of carelessness. The dining rooms are noisy and gaudily decorated and tables are cramped and close. The noise level is deafening, and the service is sloppy. Drinks are prepared with half-melted ice, and cheap, commercial cocktail crackers are at the bar. A relish tray consisted of spiced apples, sour pickles, sweet pickles, hot Italian peppers and tasteless, overcooked chick-peas, all thrown together in the same dish so that their flavors combined hopelessly. Breads and bread sticks were either limp and soggy or stale, and salad dressings were thick and pasty, although the romaine lettuce in the salad was sprightly and crisp.

Just a few dishes sampled rated praise — the sparkling fresh, ice-cold clams on the half shell; the five-and-a-half-pound lobster for two that was beautifully broiled; the very good, beefy sirloin steaks, both in the regular and heavy-cut versions, and the excellent sautéed calf's liver with meaty strips of bacon.

All else was near disaster. Shrimp balls were pasty with bread-crumb filler, baked stuffed clams were thick and dry, and marinated herring was covered with a sour cream dressing that had coagulated, probably from having been kept portioned-out in the refrigerator for too many hours. Shrimp were water-logged and tasteless.

Foil-wrapped baked potatoes were leaden, and hashed brown potatoes were greasy and loaded with paprika, but the cottage fries were a bit better. A grossly thick cut of roast beef was steamy and flavorless, and lamb chops were dry and overdone. Overcooked, bitter creamed spinach, tasteless broiled mushrooms and french-fried onion rings that were all batter added to the sorry array of poor preparations.

Desserts such as nesselrode pie, incredibly sweet and sticky rice pudding and gummy cheesecake are beneath serious criticism. Prices are full-fledged steakhouse highs.

If the Old Homestead is rated fair instead of poor, it is only because its main business is steak, and its steaks, as well as lobsters, are commendable.

Omen
★ ★

113 Thompson Street, between Prince and Spring Streets, 925-8923.

Atmosphere: Handsome, informal Japanese dining room; service is friendly, gracious and accommodating but slow for large groups.

Recommended dishes: All small appetizer dishes and miso soup, marinated chicken (sansho), marinated chicken with radish (mizore), steamed custard (chawan-mushi), broth with vegetables and noodles (omen), tofu with vegetables (yudofu), Japanese pickles (tsukemono), rice with Japanese leaves (chiso gohan), pickled radish (takuwan-no irini), fresh fruit.

Price range: Moderate.

Credit cards: American Express.

Hours: Lunch, Thursdays through Sundays, noon to 2:30 P.M.; dinner, Tuesdays through Sundays, 5:30 P.M. to 11 P.M. Closed Mondays.

Reservations: Suggested for dinner, especially for four or more.

Omen is a dish of broth, noodles and vegetables that dates back three hundred years in Japan's culinary history. It is also the inspiration for the recently opened Omen restaurant in SoHo. In a long, narrow dining room where brick walls are accented by Japanese accessories, Mikio Shinagawa, the owner, oversees the serving of the fragrant and bracing broth dish as well as the light, bright and entertaining smaller dishes that are also on the menu of his family's two restaurants in Kyoto.

There are richly satisfying esthetic rewards in the artfully arranged, subtly flavored vegetable, fish, noodle and chicken dishes served here. The delicate specialties, while somewhat esoteric, will disappoint only those with meat-and-potato appetites.

The omen dish is the most interesting selection on the menu, a restorative main course based on a golden broth achieved by steeping kelp and the dried flakes of the bonito fish in water. Served steaming hot in a big brown-glazed ceramic bowl, the broth is accompanied by a dish of bright, lightly cooked cold vegetables, such as burdock root, spinach, scallions and ginger with toasted sesame seeds, and a tray of the hot, thick white wheat flour noodles, udon. The vegetables are added to the broth all at once while the noodles are stirred in gradually. The diner extricates solids with chopsticks. "Slurp the noodles," the charming Japanese waitress explained on our first attempt, adding that we should drink the soup directly from the bowl.

The menu also lists about sixteen delicious small dishes, each of which can be an appetizer. By ordering several, you can build a main course. Among the delightful choices were oshitashi, cold, crisp lightly blanched spinach topped with sesame seeds; goma-ae, a spinach-and-mushroom salad with sesame seeds, and shira-ae, a creamy salad of tofu with carrots and spinach. The wormlike appearance of the delicious fern dish, zenmai-no umani, may discourage the fainthearted, which would be their loss.

The most adventurous eaters will want to try the nuta, a salad of shrimp and scallions in a sauce of bean paste and egg yolks; the yamakake, raw tuna with grated Japanese yam in a satiny sauce, and sudako, cooked cold octopus marinated in rice vinegar. There are several excellent versions of the raw fish specialty sashimi. Both the steamed chicken with cucumber (tosa-zu-ae) and the sautéed burdock and carrot with sesame seeds (kinpira) are engaging, and the sansho, sautéed chicken that has been marinated in Mirin wine, sake and soy sauce, is moist and flavorful. So is the mizore, marinated sautéed chicken topped with grated radish.

Tempuras, whether based on vegetables, shrimp, octopus or tofu, were disappointing, however, because the batter lacked essential crispness, and the flavor of grease was unmistakable. Preferable choices are the yudofo, bean curd and vegetables in a mild broth, all served in an iron pot with fiery and aromatic Japanese pepper, and the chawan-mushi, a steamed custard with bits of chicken, shrimp and vegetables. The kayaku gohan, a blend of soft rice steamed with tiny morsels of chicken and vegetables, is satisfying, if somewhat bland. Chiso gohan is a soothing combination of rice with aromatic leaves that suggest dill, fennel and pine. Several types of pickled vegetables add pungency to rice dishes. Miso bean soup with tiny mushrooms and bean curd is outstanding. Fresh pineapple, oranges and grapes are the refreshing desserts.

The tableware is beautiful, and hot facecloths are offered when food is ordered. Beer and wine are not sold here, but they may be carried in.

O'Neals' Times Square
Fair

147 West 43rd Street, 869-4200.

Atmosphere: Big, convivial pub-tavern; service friendly and accommodating but often inept.

Recommended dishes: Smoked trout, fettuccine with broccoli, hamburgers, chicken salad and watercress sandwich, shirred eggs Florentine, steak, broiled chicken, chicken Maltaise, nut cake.

Price range: Moderately expensive.

Credit cards: All major credit cards.

Hours: Lunch, Mondays through Saturdays, 11:30 A.M. to 5 P.M.; dinner, Mondays through Saturdays, 5 P.M. to 10 P.M.; supper, Mondays through Saturdays, 10 P.M. to midnight; Sunday brunch, 11:30 A.M. to 5 P.M. Closed Sunday nights.

Reservations: Accepted for lunch upstairs, but not for brunch and lunch downstairs; recommended for dinner.

O'Neals' Times Square holds no surprises for those familiar with other restaurants owned by Michael and Patrick O'Neal, such as the Ginger Man and O'Neals' Baloon at Lincoln Center. The same sort of corny, if pleasant, pub-tavern look prevails, the young staff is friendly and good-natured, if unprofessionally inept, and the food to rely on if you want to eat in this area is the plainest on the menu. The pity of it all is that the kitchen goes through all the motions at the new O'Neal's, seeming to buy fresh ingredients and cooking and baking from scratch, which only proves that homemade is not enough.

Among appetizers, the only choices to be recommended are a thick, gently smoked trout fillet with an apple sour-cream sauce and creamy fettuccine with broccoli and spinach. Clams are zapped by sharp ginger and scallions, gravlax is gummy and the duckling terrine sampled was stodgy and gray. Soups are poor, with the asparagus and mushroom as thick as starchy porridge and the onion metallic-tasting and watery.

Salads are of the coffee-shop genre and seem to have been arranged on plates and held in the refrigerator hours before they were served. The trio of shellfish (three clams, three shrimp and a small mound of crab meat) was much overpriced.

Hamburgers are thick and well broiled though somewhat overpowered by their heavy whole-wheat buns, and a sandwich of chicken salad and watercress on pumpernickel was thoroughly satisfying. Not so a chewy, awkward gravlax-and-shrimp triple-decker sandwich.

Pass up the leaden omelets in favor of shirred eggs Florentine, bordered with creamed spinach. Eggs Benedict were cold, and their hollandaise sauce was salty and grainy. That same graininess marred the cold zabaglione on strawberries.

313

With the exception of sautéed chicken breast in an orangy Maltaise sauce, all the creations were unsatisfactory, including calf's liver with avocado, shrimp with sausage, duck with cherries, goulash with waxen spätzle and sole with fruit and almonds. Spongy soft-shell crabs were half spoiled.

Broiled chicken, sirloin steak and steak au poivre were acceptable. Lamb chops were fine when I was recognized, but withered and overcooked when I was not. Such home-baked breads as cornsticks tasted of stale cooking oil. A chewy nut tart was the only dessert worth its calories.

Orsini's
★

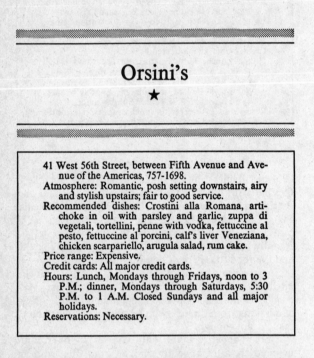

41 West 56th Street, between Fifth Avenue and Avenue of the Americas, 757-1698.
Atmosphere: Romantic, posh setting downstairs, airy and stylish upstairs; fair to good service.
Recommended dishes: Crostini alla Romana, artichoke in oil with parsley and garlic, zuppa di vegetali, tortellini, penne with vodka, fettuccine al pesto, fettuccine al porcini, calf's liver Veneziana, chicken scarpariello, arugula salad, rum cake.
Price range: Expensive.
Credit cards: All major credit cards.
Hours: Lunch, Mondays through Fridays, noon to 3 P.M.; dinner, Mondays through Saturdays, 5:30 P.M. to 1 A.M. Closed Sundays and all major holidays.
Reservations: Necessary.

Almost since the day it opened in 1953, Orsini's has been a favorite meeting place for members of the high-fashion world. The original restaurant consisted only of the present downstairs bar and small dining room with Pompeian-red walls, touches of wrought iron and a painting of a pubescent odalisque lending a somewhat sensual and romantic note to the setting, which was in every way typically Roman. Now that original room has been redone in a more cheerful and flattering pink and mauve scheme, and both lunch and dinner are also served in the loftier and more stylish upstairs dining room, which combines provincial and classic Italian overtones.

If you want to know the best place to sit, just watch where the denizens of high fashion settle down; clearly, the front part of the dining room is it. Nonentities are relegated to the aisle of seats that leads to the never-never-land of celebrities, and the passing parade of the haute-coutured can be dizzying indeed. Upstairs, service is more leisurely and more polished, but no matter where one sits, the food is much the same, a comforting, if not encouraging, thought.

For at Orsini's stupendous prices, it is reasonable to expect equally stupendous food, and though there are a few very good dishes available, not one even begins to approach greatness.

The best of the appetizers sampled were crostini alla Romana (spiedini alla Romana elsewhere), bread and mozzarella baked to runny, golden succulence, accented by a buttery sauce with capers and anchovies, and the artichoke braised in olive oil verdant with parsley and heady with garlic. Second place goes to the light and fresh zuppa di vegetali, which had little if any tomato and plenty of celery, zucchini, broccoli stems, carrots, white beans and chick peas.

All other appetizers were banally turned out, including dry, rubbery mozzarella with unripe tomato slices, bready, ungarlicked clams oreganate, passable scampi and a dreadful, pallid version of the fried bread and cheese combination of mozzarella in carrozza, which was a bit limp and tasted of overheated oil.

Pasta is usually the course that can save a fair-to-middling Italian restaurant, but only a few pastas at Orsini's are in any way inspired. If you want to go to this restaurant to bask in the glow of some of New York's best dressed, than rely on rigatoni or penne with vodka (short, tubular pasta with a lusty sauce of tomato, pepper and vodka), the decent chicken-filled tortellini, in a creamy sauce doused with cheese, or fettuccine with porcini, the rich, earthy, dried, wild mushroom. Crespelle alla Fiorentina (crepes with spinach and prosciutto in a béchamel sauce) was fair.

Linguine with white clam sauce sometimes lacks salt and sufficient garlic. Pesto sauce was acceptable if dry. At one dinner, four orders of pasta were undercooked and hard. Risotto ammiraglia, with meager dottings of shellfish, was a dreary example of this rice dish — soupy, spiked with cognac and altogether unpleasant.

Veal paillard is one of the most popular dishes with the luncheon cognoscenti, but it is impossible to understand why. On many tries, the veal was tough, the underside barely seared, and the juices that filled the plate left the meat dry and fibrous. Far preferable was calf's liver Veneziana sautéed with onions, a tender filet mignon peperonata in a spicy tomato sauce, mellowed with roasted peppers, and la pescatora, a combination of clams, lobster tails and shrimp in a savory tomato sauce.

Chicken scarpariello and chicken Margarita both tend toward dryness. Cuscinetti di vitello ("cushions" of veal, filled with slightly spoiled prosciutto and baked with cheese) and veal Sorrentina (cheese, eggplant, veal and wine sauce) were much like nightclub food. But veal piccata and beef rolls with mushrooms and prosciutto were above average.

Salads were fresh and crisp, but the limp fried zucchini lacked any flavor whatever. Zabaglione at Orsini's has been too frothy, thin and sweet, and rum cake is the best of the pastries.

Oyster Bar and Restaurant
In Grand Central Station

★ ★

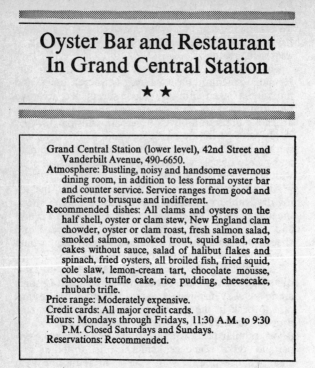

Grand Central Station (lower level), 42nd Street and Vanderbilt Avenue, 490-6650.

Atmosphere: Bustling, noisy and handsome cavernous dining room, in addition to less formal oyster bar and counter service. Service ranges from good and efficient to brusque and indifferent.

Recommended dishes: All clams and oysters on the half shell, oyster or clam stew, New England clam chowder, oyster or clam roast, fresh salmon salad, smoked salmon, smoked trout, squid salad, crab cakes without sauce, salad of halibut flakes and spinach, fried oysters, all broiled fish, fried squid, cole slaw, lemon-cream tart, chocolate mousse, chocolate truffle cake, rice pudding, cheesecake, rhubarb trifle.

Price range: Moderately expensive.

Credit cards: All major credit cards.

Hours: Mondays through Fridays, 11:30 A.M. to 9:30 P.M. Closed Saturdays and Sundays.

Reservations: Recommended.

The Grand Central Restaurant and Oyster Bar on the lower level of Grand Central Station, now nearly sixty-five years old, remains the classic landmark setting for clams and oysters on the half shell and the justly famous oyster stew and oyster pan roast.

The menu is as distinctive as the handsome, cavernous tiled and wood-paneled setting. Not only does it include all of the standard fish and shellfish varieties one would expect to find, but there also is an obvious and successful effort to offer more unusual varieties of fish such as catfish, finnan haddie, Lake Winnipeg goldeye, ling, lotte, sand dabs, mako shark, tautog, Virginia spots, whitebait and wolffish. Broiling here is immaculately well done, with the fish cooked to the point of moist and snowy perfection. Frying and poaching are also done carefully, but the broiled specialties are far and away the most laudable.

In addition to the wide variety of fish, there is usually a selection of six to eight types of oysters that may include bluepoints, Maine belons, box, Chincoteagues, Cotuits, Kent Island, Wellfleet and Apalachicola. My own favorite among these are the Wellfleets, the Cotuits, the belons and the Malpeques — all with a briny, deep-sea bite and just a slightly dry, coppery accent. Those who like milder oysters should try the Chincoteagues and the Apalachicolas. There are usually a few types of clams available as well, and, like the oysters, they are priced individually, enabling one to order an assortment for the sake of comparison. Lemon is really all these glistening, freshly opened specimens require, but there is good sharp cocktail sauce available, and for the oysters a sparkling shallot, tarragon and red-wine vinegar mignonette sauce.

The best place to have these specialties, as well as the lusty oyster or clam stew and the spicier pan roasts is at the oyster bar where you can watch them being prepared. The creamy potato and clam-flecked New England clam chowder is better than the starchy, bland tomato-based, Manhattan clam chowder.

Everything seems better, if more hectic, at lunch. At dinner, the staff is grumpier, many of the specialties are sold out after seven in the evening and even the food seems tired.

Besides clams, oysters and chowders, excellent first courses are salmon or trout smoked over fruitwood right on the premises. Shrimp cocktail is only fair, but crisp, fried oysters with a light and pungent tartar sauce can be shared as another fine starter. Fried clams, though good, are less flavorful, and, on the night I tried them, they were somewhat limp. Steamed mussels can be unbearded and gritty, or firm, plump and delicious, and mussels Dijon are too cold and their sauce is tasteless.

Beautifully fresh salads can be had as a light main course or can be shared as appetizers. Try the marinated squid salad with slivers of red onion or the halibut flakes on raw spinach with a lemon-mustard dressing or the fresh salmon on endive. Clams casino with bacon and minced peppers would have been more tender had they been made with littlenecks instead of cherrystones, and the baked stuffed clams were stifled by a mound of pasty breading.

Sauces and fancy dishes were weak spots throughout. The Belgian fish soup-stew, waterzool, combined excellent fish with a watery broth and a sauce that seemed heavily floured. Bouillabaise was not only awkwardly served, but it was completely overpowered by an overdose of saffron.

Well-fried fresh salmon cakes could have used some chives, onion or dill for flavoring and the so-called soubise sauce served with them lacked any hint of the onion it should have had. Fried shrimp in several variations were all disappointing and so was the portion size. Lobsters taken from the tank in the dining room ranged from excellent to overly dry, especially when broiled. Crab cakes are delicious, but skip the acrid tomato sauce.

But for impeccably buttery, broiled smoked finnan haddie (also available with eggs Benedict), grouper, halibut, scrod, lemon sole, or any fish with Hollandaise, this place is hard to beat.

Boiled potatoes, in and out of jackets, are served when appropriate, and such side dishes as cole slaw and green salad are cracklingly fresh and bright. Homemade biscuits are too often stone cold and hard and although they are abundant, they generally taste too strongly of baking soda.

There are some lovely homemade desserts. Among the best are the rhubarb trifle, layered chocolate truffle cake, the tart lemon-cream pie and rice pudding that seems to be based on clouds of whipped cream. Chocolate mousse is as rich as a fudge and the cheesecake is lemony and delicious. But apple pie can be cold and soggy and blueberries on a shortcake are encased in a film of gelatin.

One serious failing here is the wine list. Although it contains a very good representation of California white wines, only a few reds are included. Fair broiled chicken and steak are the only nonseafood alternatives.

Palm
★ ★ ★

837 Second Avenue, between 44th and 45th Streets,
687-2953.

Palm Too
★ ★

840 Second Avenue, between 44th and 45th Streets,
697-5198.

Atmosphere: Jammed, convivial, noisy old tavern-
steakhouse with cartoon caricatures on the walls,
sawdust on the floor and some booths; Palm Too
has reproduced the atmosphere of the original
across the street with success. Service in both is
generally good-natured, quick and professional
but at times can be pushy or brusque.

Recommended dishes: Clams or shrimp Posilipo,
clams oreganate or casino or on the half shell,
shrimp cocktail without cocktail sauce, minestrone, spaghetti with white or red clam sauce or oil
and garlic, all potatoes but especially cottage fries,
onion rings, spinach, chopped tomato and onion
salad, corned beef and cabbage, roast beef or
corned beef hash, broiled chicken, roast beef,
steak tartare, sirloin and filet mignon steaks, lamb
chops, broiled lobster, scampi, cheesecake.

Price range: Expensive.

Credit cards: All major credit cards.

Hours: Lunch and dinner, Mondays through Fridays,
noon to 10:45 P.M., Saturdays, 5 P.M. to 11 P.M.
Closed Sundays and major holidays.

Reservations: Palm, accepted for lunch but not for
dinner; Palm Too, recommended for both lunch
and dinner for parties of four or more.

Beyond question, the Palm is my favorite steak restaurant in New York and the following review, most of
which was written in 1976, still reflects my feelings. This
is true despite a slight falling off in quality and sharpness in cooking. Part of the problem, I suspect, is the
new method of grading beef, which has allowed some
top choice grades to be labeled prime. Steaks at the
Palm are generally excellent, but even so, they sometimes lack that extra edge of beefiness that used to be
standard. Among some specialties that have declined,
steak à la Stone (sliced and served with pimento and
onions) now often is lackluster, and beef Deutsch, once
made with cubes of sautéed beef tossed with peppers
and onions, now comes as a big thick steak with which
those vegetables are less effective. A recent order of
crab meat was warm and cottony, and once in a while
cottage fries are limp. Chicken Bruno, once crisply fried

nuggets of chicken sprinkled with garlic, now is somewhat bland and tastes of commercial bread crumbs.

Because the custom at the Palm is to call dishes off without presenting a menu, a list of dishes available with their 1982 prices is included.

Almost no one who has ever eaten at Palm feels lukewarm about it. This fifty-six-year-old landmark with its plain pipe rack décor, sawdust-covered floors and celebrity cartoons painted on the walls seems to inspire either rapt devotion or a total turn-off.

The difference of opinion rarely concerns the food. Even Palm's detractors usually agree that its steaks and chops are properly, gently charred without, yet cooked to a rosy tenderness within, exactly to the degree of doneness ordered and that the crisp rounds of cottage fried potatoes are close to poetic, while the cream-and-butter-basted broiled lobsters are gigantic enough to make one understand why the ancients believed in sea monsters.

What bothers anti-Palmists is the combination of noise and crowds, the brusqueness of the waiters and, most of all, the absence of a written menu that would tell them what they can order and how much it will cost.

Yet to Palm's coterie of admirers, the noise and crowds take on the conviviality of a big house party, the brusqueness passes for no-nonsense efficiency and after a few visits, they know all too well how much it costs, with a steak dinner and a drink averaging $50, and a typical lunch coming to $25.

But even though they openly defend the lack of a menu as being part of the native charm, few in their heart of hearts have not longed to know the full repertory the kitchen is capable of producing. Waiters reel off the choices of filet, sirloin and lobsters; if pressed they admit to roast prime ribs and lamb chops and may eventually get to broiled fish. Only devotees know of the many Italian dishes, now, unfortunately, less brilliantly prepared than formerly.

But there are always surprises, even to those who have frequented this establishment for ten or twenty years. Looking around, one may see someone eating the garlic-scented white clam sauce on a mound of al dente spaghetti, or shrimp and clams in an herbaceous marinara sauce Posilipo style and the town's freshest, most robust steak tartare, ground to order filet mignon.

Finally, even the most loyal supporters are driven to ask, "What else do they serve at the Palm?"

Calling it the Palm, by the way, although popular, is not correct, for the name is strictly Palm and it is a clue to the Italinate style of the menu. In 1926, when Pio Bozzi and John Ganzi decided to open an Italian restaurant, they wanted to call it Parma, in honor of the capital of their native Italian province, Emilia. But when it came to licensing, the city clerk wrote it as Palm, and thus it has remained, belying its Italian origins and cuisine.

Immediately and for a long time after, this was a favorite hangout for newspaper people whose headquarters were in the area, and now, under the aegis of Bruce Bozzi, grandson of the founding partner, it is generally jam-packed with a mixed crowd who have in common only their passion for food. Wally Ganzi,

319

grandson of the other founder, operates the Palm in Los Angeles, while Washington, Chicago, Houston and Miami also have Palms to call their own. Palm Too, an annex to the New York establishment and just across the street, has managed to recreate the look, if not quite the same hectic, ebullient pace. Some prefer it precisely for that reason.

While some might criticize the gargantuan portions, most of Palm's aficionados like them that way, and besides, the house is always willing to allow and often suggests the sharing of portions at small extra charges and the carrying out of doggie bags. Drinks are poured with equal generosity and anyone ordering Scotch and soda will have a hard time finding room for the latter.

Seafood cocktails are generally excellent here, but ask to have the banal cocktail sauce served on the side. Beside the clams in their various preparations, good first courses are the chopped tomato and onion salad, the lusty minestrone, when available, or half orders of such hearty, garlic-scented pastas as the aglio-olio, with white or red clam sauce. The sea-monster-size lobsters are miraculously tender and remain unparalleled around town, as are the lamb chops — in my experience, unequaled anywhere. Steaks and roast beef are usually first rate as are all of the other recommended dishes. No other place equals the Palm for the texture of its cottage fries when they are at their best, and the fried onions are parchment crisp and greaseless.

Salads are disappointing here, and spinach is cooked to mush. Specialties such as roast beef and corned beef hash and corned beef and cabbage are featured at lunch and are wonderful, but the veal parmigiana and veal piccata have seen better days.

THE MENU

Appetizers, soups, salads, vegetables, potaoes, pasta and desserts remain the same for lunch and dinner at both Palm and Palm Too.

Appetizers

Shrimp cocktail	$7.50
Crabmeat cocktail	$8.50
Clams on the half shell	$4.50
Baked clams, oreganate or casino	$6.50
Anchovies and pimentos	$4.00
Clams Posilipo, for an entree portion that serves two to three as an appetizer	$11.00
Shrimps and clams Posilipo, for an entree portion that serves two to three as an appetizer	$14.50

Soups
(One each day)

Lentil, onion, minestrone, split pea and clam chowder	$2.00

Salads

Mixed greens or hearts of lettuce with Russian, Roquefort or oil and vinegar dressing	$3.00
Sliced or chopped tomatoes and onions	$3.50
String beans and onion	$4.50

Pasta

Spaghetti with red or white clam
   sauce, meat sauce, marinara sauce
   or aglio-olio (garlic and oil) $8.50
   Half portion $4.50

Potatoes
(All portions serve two)

Cottage fried, hashed brown, french fried,
   mashed or shoestring $3.00
Lyonnaise $3.50
Au gratin $3.50
Baked $1.00
French fried onions $4.00

Vegetables

Leaf spinach $3.00
Creamed spinach $3.50
Peas, or peas and onions $3.00
String beans $3.00
Asparagus, in season, butter
   or hollandaise sauce $3.50

Lunch Entrees

Two or three of these entrees are available for lunch
every day, in addition to the steaks, chops, lobster and
other broiled offerings on the dinner menu. (*Indicates
dishes made only at Palm Too.)

Veal parmigiano $12.00
*Veal Sorrentino $12.00
*Veal rollatini $12.00
Veal corden bleu $12.00
Veal and peppers $11.00
Breaded veal cutlet $11.00
Ham and spinach $8.00
Corned beef and cabbage $8.50
Roast beef hash $9.00
Corned beef hash $8.00
Meat loaf $7.50
Roast duck $8.00
Roast pork $8.50
*Beef rollatini $10.50
Pot roast $8.50
Beef or lamb stew $8.50
Steak à la Stone $9.50
Beef Marsala $9.50
Beef cordon bleu $9.50
Beef piccata $9.50
Boneless chicken parmigiano $8.50
*Chicken rollatini $8.50
Scallops $11.50
Lobster Newburgh (Friday special) $12.50
Shrimp, fried, marinara or scampi $11.50
Chicken champagne $9.00
*Lasagne, cappelletti, manicotti or cannelloni $8.50

Dinner Entrees

Broiled lobster, 4 to 4½ pounds $34.00
Sirloin steak $19.00
Filet mignon $19.00
Steak tartare $11.00
Steak à la Stone $20.00

Beef Deutsch	$20.00
Prime ribs of beef	$16.00
Lamb chops, baby ribs	$16.00
Broiled pork chops	$11.00
Breaded pork chops	$11.00
Breaded veal cutlet	$13.00
Veal parmigiano	$13.00
Veal Marsala	$13.00
Veal piccata	$13.00
Veal Francese	$13.00
Broiled chicken	$8.50
Chicken Bruno	$9.50
Chicken sauté	$13.00
Shrimps and clams Posilipo	$14.50
Clams Posilipo	$11.50
Broiled filet of sole	$11.50
Fried filet of sole	$11.50
Sautéed fillet of sole	$12.50
Broiled striped bass	$14.00
Broiled shrimp, scampi style	$13.50
Fried shrimp	$12.50
Fritata of onions, mushrooms, green pepper and ham	$8.50

Desserts

Tortoni, spumoni or tartufo	$1.50
Melon	$3.00
Strawberries	$3.50
Cheesecake	$3.00

Pamir

★

1423 Second Avenue, between 74th and 75th Streets, 734-3791.
Atmosphere: Intimate, exotic, rustic dining room with folk artifacts; polite, shy and helpful service that is sometimes slow.
Recommended dishes: All appetizers, quabilli palaw, sabsi-chalaw, badenjan chalaw, aushak, kebab-e-murgh, all vegetable side dishes, Afghan tea.
Price range: Moderate.
Credit cards: MasterCard and Visa.
Hours: Dinner, seven days, 5:30 P.M. to 11 P.M.
Reservations: Necessary on weekends.

"Do you realize we are eating in the only Afghan restaurant in New York?" a man asked his friend at Pamir recently. "I doubt that," the other man said." I can't believe there is only one of anything in this city."

Such chauvinism is well-founded, because Pamir is indeed the second Afghan restaurant in town, the first being the one-star Little Afghanistan, which opened a year earlier.

Two restaurants may not indicate a trend, but there must be enough evidence of a sympathetic clientele to inspire a second investment in the presentation of the exotic, entertaining and satisfying cuisine of Afghanistan.

Pamir's dining room is informal and restful, small, snug and intimate, with rustic wood-paneled walls, colored lanterns and such folk artifacts as musical instruments and carpet saddlebags on the walls. It is operated by a sincere and friendly staff of two, and if there are occasionally extended time lapses between courses, the good will more than makes up for the wait.

A visitor gets the distinct impression that the somewhat shy, darkly handsome waiters really want guests to like their native food, and they offer helpful advice in ordering so newcomers to the cuisine will enjoy the proper contrasts of spices and textures. "Order a dish with a sauce, such as sabsi-chalaw, lamb with an onion and a garlic-flavor spinach sauce," a waiter suggests, "and the other can have plain lamb kebabs, or the spiced chicken on skewers — kebab-e-murgh."

If there are three or four people dining together, another suggestion might be quabilli palaw, a golden rice pilaf enriched with raisins, almonds and julienne strips of pimento and carrots, nuggets of lamb nestled underneath, and for the fourth dish, a vegetable will be recommended — perhaps spiced, sautéed pumpkin with yogurt (buranee kadu) or cinnamon-scented eggplant topped with yogurt and meat sauce (buranee badenjan). Combining aspects of Indian, Middle Eastern and Soviet Georgian kitchens, the rugged food of Afghanistan offers exotic and complementary flavor counterpoints — cool yogurt fired by hot chili peppers, sharp scallions soothed by fresh mint, pepper offset by cinnamon.

Lamb, eggplant, onions, tomatoes and rice appear and reappear in a variety of forms. Gently stewed as badenjan chalaw, the lamb chunks achieve a melting tenderness that the plain, slightly dry grilled kebabs of lamb or chicken do not.

The most interesting appetizers are variations on the turnover theme — bulanee gandana, crisp pancakes stuffed with scallions and topped with yogurt; bulanee kachalou, filled with potatoes, ground beef and spices, and sambosa goushti, crisp-fried pastry half-moons, plumped with ground beef and mashed chickpeas to be served with a cool-hot mint sauce. Aushak, delicate, pancake-shaped dumplings filled with scallions, are gentled with a yogurt-meat-and-mint sauce.

Were they served truly hot, the two soups would be wonderful. As it is, both aush (vegetables, noodles, spiced ground beef and yogurt) and mashawa (a clearer, meatier blend of the same elements without noodles) are at least interesting.

More tender meats for the kebabs would improve the picture also, but even so, a comfortable and diverting meal can be had at Pamir for moderate prices. There are vegetarian dishes as well, which are really smaller portions of the vegetable side dishes, and a channeled, yeasty flat bread, encrusted with toasted onion seeds, is delicious, though a little tougher than it should be.

Both desserts are skippable. Baghlawa proved dense and leathery, and firnee, a rosewater custard, was watery and cloyingly perfumed.

Cardamom gives a pleasantly heady quality to the Afghan tea, and there is full bar service, beer being a better choice than wine with this lusty fare. If you ask for extra-spicy food at Pamir, as the menu suggests, the house complies.

Pantheon
★ ★

689 Eighth Avenue, between 43rd and 44th Streets, 664-8294.
Atmosphere: Bright, clean, semiformal setting; good service.
Recommended dishes: All appetizers, egg-lemon soup, all lamb dishes, stuffed grape leaves, spinach-cheese pie, shrimp or lobster salad, broiled whole fish, galaktomboureko.
Price range: Moderate.
Credit cards: American Express, MasterCard, Visa and Diners Club.
Hours: Mondays through Saturdays, 11:30 A.M. to 11 P.M. Closed Sundays. Open major holidays.
Reservations: Not accepted.

Considering how difficult it is to find restaurants that not only offer good food in pleasant surroundings but in addition do so at moderate prices and in the theater district, the Pantheon has to be regarded as something of a minor miracle.

For in this bright, simple and comfortable Greek dining place, it is possible to have a satisfying three-course dinner at modest prices and do so in a full-fledged restaurant with clean tablecloths, comfortable lighting and complete wine and liquor service.

The creamy mullet roe purée, taramasalata, is brightened with lemon and is only mildly saline, and the fresh artichoke hearts in their cool olive oil and lemon dressing are so generously portioned, and so rich, that they make a light and satisfying lunch. Salads of cucumber, anchovies, black olives and pungent feta cheese, and the piquant egg-lemon soup are all good choices among first courses.

Lamb is the meat that appears in most of the main course dishes, as might be expected. It is tender and pink as shish kebob, light and sprightly with mint as meat balls in egg-lemon sauce, hearty and earthy braised as lamb kapama or stewed with tomatoes and okra or string beans.

Lamb innards — brains, livers, sweetbreads and kidneys — are a bit overcooked, if pleasantly seasoned, and much the same can be said for all of the vegetables.

For lighter pretheater entrees, good choices are the spinach and cheese pie between flaky layers of phyllo pastry, grape leaves stuffed with lamb and rice and swimming in egg-lemon sauce or the even more interesting yogurt, shrimp salad or a cold half lobster in lemon sauce. Broiled whole fish decked out with parsley and lemon are especially good. Fillets are too dry and do not stand up to broiler heat so well as the whole fish.

Roasts such as veal, pork and chicken are comparatively tasteless, but the moussaka has a rich, custardlike cheese topping and is delicious.

Galaktomboureko, a golden semolina pudding-cake with phyllo pastry top and bottom, has enough sugar syrup over it to quiet the most demanding sweet tooth, as will the acceptable, if not inspired, baklava. Rice pudding is interesting here — rich and eggy and fragrant with cinnamon. Greek coffee can be ordered mildly, medium or very sweet, and remember not to stir it and disturb the grounds before drinking.

The light, white wine, hymettus, or the sharply astringent resin-tinged retsina, are proper foils for the oily and herbaceous Greek food. Both are available by glass or bottle at the Pantheon, which is open late enough to accommodate post-theater diners.

Parioli Romanissimo
★ ★

1466 First Avenue, between 76th and 77th Streets, 288-2391.
Atmosphere: Small, crowded, gaudily Italianate setting; uneven and impersonal service.
Recommended dishes: Stuffed mushrooms, hot antipasto, stracciatella soup, all pastas except fettuccine carbonara, asparagus parmigiana, uccelletti alla finanzieri, costoletta parmigiana, beefsteak Parioli, pescatore Veneziana, chicken alla Romana, scallopine pizzaiuola, chocolate-mousse cake, zuppa inglese, ricotta cheesecake, strawberries with zabaglione.
Price range: Expensive.
Credit cards: American Express, Diners Club and Carte Blanche.
Hours: Dinner, Tuesdays through Saturdays, 6 P.M. to 11 P.M. Closed Sundays, Mondays and major holidays. Closed for July and August.
Reservations: Necessary.

It is doubtful that there is another restaurant in New York that enjoys a popularity more overwhelming than that of the small and stylish Parioli Romanissimo. From the standpoint of getting reservations, this is the most difficult restaurant I have had to review. Whenever I called, I was told reservations were taken only for 6, 8 or 10 o'clock, and to get them at 8, I found it necessary to call two and a half weeks in advance.

It was always surprising, therefore, to arrive at 6 and find only two or three tables occupied, then to watch people file in at 7 and 7:30. Although the management denies it, those choice hours are obviously saved for regulars, with newcomers worked in to fit the schedule. To be sure, this is a small restaurant with only 45 or 50 seats, and careful timing is necessary to accommodate the crowds, but even so it was uncomfortable to have to adjust plans to so inflexible a schedule.

Waiting for tables at a tiny front bar is uncomfortable. The service, once you are seated, is brisk, a little high pressured concerning daily specials, sometimes efficient, other times lax. Always, it is coldly impersonal. At times grated cheese and pepper mills are offered when they should be. But when we were served a bowl of stracciatella soup — broth with egg drops and spinach — no grated cheese was forthcoming until asked for, and we had to request the peppermill each time we wanted it. Often it arrived when the dish was half-finished.

There are many dishes that are very good, a few that are excellent and a surprisingly large number that are mediocre. To begin with, the bread — in this case, bland, hollow, ordinary restaurant white rolls — was inexcusable in a quality Italian restaurant. Appetizers were uniformly disappointing, the only really good choices being those dishes that were served with a tomato sauce.

It was a sauce so light and well spiced it would have made Kleenex palatable. It graced the decent stuffed mushrooms and, in a slightly different version, hot antipasto that included mushrooms, mixed shellfish and sautéed artichoke hearts. Baked clams or clams casino were no better than those in any neighborhood restaurant, and shrimp oreganate had the stale flavor of iodine and were soggy under their thick breadcrumb coating.

Pastas, however, are triumphs for the most part. Meat-filled rounds of tortellini in a creamy, meaty Bolognese sauce were as lovely as those done alla panna, in heavy cream. Fettuccine Alfredo had the right blend of cream, cheese and butter, and the delicate cannelloni filled with spinach and what tasted like sausage meat were superb under a gratinéed cheese cream sauce. Clam sauce was also above average.

Capelli di angelo — fine-stranded "angel's hair" — was irresistible, whether done all'arrabbiata, "as if stirred by a madman" (a tomato sauce spiced with green olives, capers, bits of pickled gherkins, mushrooms, and parsley), or with pescatore Veneziana, a sort of tomato-sauced shellfish array of tender mussels, squid, clams and, unfortunately, stale shrimp.

The only pasta I found unpleasant was the fettuccine carbonara. On the first try I was served fine linguine, which, the management insisted, was fettuccine. The second time the pasta was right, but both times the unconventional carbonara sauce, brownish with flecks of meat and none of the creamy egginess I expected (although it had some egg in it), was tainted with an unpleasant oil flavor such as occurs when one uses olive or corn oil that is rancid or that has been allowed to boil.

That same oil flavor spoiled some otherwise gorgeous leaf spinach sautéed with garlic, and almost ruined a beautifully sautéed chicken alla Romana, although here the accents of wine and lemon with the tender chicken pieces just about masked the unpleasant flavor.

The best main courses were the uccelletti alla finanzieri (rolled veal birds filled with ham and sauced with cream, chicken liver, morels and dried Italian mushrooms) and a superbly well done costoletta parmigiana, the beautiful white veal chop flattened, its bone still in, breaded and topped with fresh and creamy mozzarella cheese and a marinara sauce. Beefsteak Parioli, with a tomato, green-pepper sauce, much like a pizzaiuola sauce, was rich and hearty, as was a fine veal scallopine pizzaiuola.

Pescatore Veneziana, similar to the version served over pasta, was similarly delicious, although the small piece of white fish that accompanied it was slightly overcooked.

Branzino al forno, a whole striped bass cooked in the oven, was really poached rather than baked, and was done in a combination of white wine and stock. It was impeccably cooked — moist, pearly, just set, like a custard — but it and its velouté sauce were completely devoid of flavor. Breaded and fried veal cutlet Milanese was soggy.

Desserts are excellent here, whether you spring for the thick, dark, chocolate-mousse cake, the liqueur-soaked zuppa inglese, the creamy ricotta cheesecake as frothy as whipped cream, or the light, airy zabaglione on strawberries.

Also unusual but welcome in an Italian restaurant is the choice of Italian cheese with either fresh fruit or a refreshing macedoine of mixed cut frits.

Prices at Parioli Romanissimo are staggering. As a rule nothing accompanies the meat or fish ordered unless a vegetable is an integral part of the dish — such as sautéed artichokes tossed in with meat or chicken, or spinach with saltimbocca. In addition, the wine list is extremely expensive.

Parma
★ ★

1404 Third Avenue, between 79th and 80th Streets, 535-3520.
Atmosphere: Simple, clubby tavern setting; excellent service.
Recommended dishes: Insalata di calamari, antipasto, all pastas, soft-shell crabs, osso buco when available, chicken scarpara, chicken Abruzzese, broiled veal chop, arugula salad, fried zucchini, cheesecake.
Price range: Moderately expensive.
Credit cards: American Express.
Hours: Dinner, seven days, 5 P.M. to 12:30 A.M. Closed holidays.
Reservations: Necessary.

This casual tavern-cafe is brightened by posters and assorted graphics, and its properly informal mood has made it a popular haunt with a young, lively and fashionable East Side coterie. The buildup at the bar is three deep by 8:30, and unfortunately, there is a comparable buildup of decibles as the place fills up. The food reflects the solid, comfortable simplicity of the setting, and the menu is limited but attractive and adequately varied.

There are two interesting appetizers at Parma, both compromised by being served icily cold — insalata di calamari, a salad of squid, mussels, shrimp and celery in an oil, lemon and vinegar dressing, and the pleasantly diverting antipasto that includes good, fatty salami, bland prosciutto, cima alla Genovese (a herbaceous stuffed breast of veal) and a wedge of spinach frittata, along with the usual but refreshing antipasto salad.

Pastas are beautifully prepared, whether you try the linguine with its good, garlickly, white clam sauce, spaghetti all'Amatriciana in a rich tomato-onion prosciutto topping or the green and white fettuccine (paglia e fieno), with peas and bits of ham in a creamy cheese sauce. Penne militari is also delicious with its tomato and basil sauce. Meat-filled tortellini alla panna and fettuccine Alfredo were a bit blander than the other choices but satisfying nonetheless.

Among the best main courses sampled at Parma was the Thursday night special, osso buco, braised veal knuckle, exquisitely tender and succulent in a satiny lemon sauce, well suited to the just slightly overcooked potato gnocchi that accompanied the dish. Also solidly satisfying and expertly prepared were chicken scarpara, chunks of chicken sautéed to golden-brown perfection and livened with lemon and garlic, a perfectly broiled veal chop and four tiny soft-shell crabs meunière. Chicken Abruzzese in a sheer tomato sauce was also delicious.

Shrimp scampi were a bit overbroiled and dry, and veal scaloppine piccata was disappointing because the veal itself, while thinly cut, did not seem to have been pounded and so tensed up and became thick and tough when cooked. Another disappointment was mixed green salad, a limp and vinegary combination with iceberg lettuce as its main ingredient. The crackling, green arugula was far preferable.

Fresh string beans were tough and overcooked but these or escarole accompany all dishes. Slivers of fried zucchini and cold broccoli salad, both à la carte side orders, were exeptional.

The bread at Parma is properly crusty, coarse and chewy, but the cheesecake was the only worthwhile dessert. Cold zabaglione was grainy and tasteless.

Since it serves dinner until 12:30 A.M. seven days a week, Parma is a good place to remember after theater.

Patsy's Restaurant
★ ★

236 West 56th Street, between Broadway and Eighth Avenue, 247-3491.

Atmosphere: Simple, bright and pleasant dining rooms with bearable noise level; service generally good, although at times slightly impatient.

Recommended dishes: Mozzarella in carrozza, spiedino alla Romana, hot antipasto, prosciutto and melon, spaghetti marinara, linguine with white clam sauce, spaghetti puttanesca, spaghetti à la Genovese, manicotti, lasagne with broccoli di rape, clams à la Posilipo, lobster oreganata, shrimp oreganate, mixed fried fish, beef bracciole, veal and peppers, sausages pizzaiuola, veal rollatine, calf's brains oreganate, veal piccata, veal parmigiana, fried zucchini, cheesecake, fruit platter.

Price range: Moderately expensive.

Credit cards: American Express, MasterCard, Visa and Diners Club.

Hours: Dinner, Tuesdays through Thursdays and Sundays, noon to 10:30 P.M.; Fridays and Saturdays, noon to 11:30 P.M. Closed Mondays and major holidays.

Reservations: Accepted for parties of five or more.

For over thirty-five years, this Neapolitan restaurant has been holding forth fine under the guidance of the Scognamillo brothers — Salvatore, who runs the dining rooms, and Joseph, who is the head chef. Together, this team turns out delicately fresh and savory versions of lusty southern Italian classics. They do so in both the upstairs and downstairs dining rooms, each with its own complete kitchen. And though I have a preference for the Mediterranean-blue walls, the bright simplicity and the liveliness of the downstairs room, both are comfortable and only slightly noisy when full. To judge from recent visits, the lower kitchen's performance on a few dishes is a shade superior.

So many of the dishes at Patsy's are excellent that at first it looked as though the restaurant would easily rate three stars. There were, however, a few important and consistent failures that kept it short of that mark. Those flaws include a tendency to under-salt pasta in the cooking (a lack that cannot be properly compensated for by salting the finished product) and a few tomato sauces that were much too heavy and indelicate. Because those sauces covered important dishes, their shortcomings have to be considered serious.

With that unpleasantness out of the way, it is gratifying to report on some wonderful Italian food of the sort that is not quite fashionable but nonetheless soul-satisfying. Rarely have I had deep-fried mozzarella in carrozza prepared so greaselessly, with the cheese center properly hot and runny and the outside coating so crackling crisp.

Spiedino alla Romano, a Roman cousin to the carrozza dish, may be had as an appetizer or a light main course, and the combination of fried bread and mozzarella with an anchovy, lemon and caper sauce as done at Patsy's is unquestionably the best I have had in the city in the last fifteen years. Although the cold antipasto is only minimally interesting, the hot version, with its stuffed vegetables and baked clams, is beautifully prepared, and the pink prosciutto draped across ripe, golden cranshaw melon was impeccable.

Other delicious first courses are baked clams oreganate, or sandless and sea-breeze-fresh clams à la Posilipo in a tomato broth scented with garlic and oregano. Downstairs, they say no half-portions of pasta are served. Upstairs, they suggest it. See what policy reading you get, and then decide which of the many enticing choices you will have, either as a first, an in-between or a main course. The best ones sampled were linguine with white clam sauce, which might have had a few more clams but was otherwise perfect; manicotti, with a combination of ricotta, mozzarella and Parmesan cheese in one of the brighter tomato sauces; spaghetti or linguine marinara, and baked lasagne. Spaghetti Genovese is an unusual and interesting creation, with its burnished orange sauce, which is a purée of beef, carrots, celery, onion, garlic, butter and olive oil.

Noticing that pastas not on the menu were being served, I thought up a few I wanted to try and we ordered them. Fettuccine Alfredo was a soupy, milky and bland disappointment, but spaghetti puttanesca, with its small black olives, capers, anchovies, cracklings of golden garlic and a liberal dousing of light olive oil, was superb. Pasta with the bitter broccoli di rape was good but required a shorter, more workable pasta than the perciatelli served with it. That broccoli alone, suffocated in a garlic and oil bath, was poetic, as were crisp slivers of fried zucchini. Only once when I ate upstairs did that dish (as well as some of the other frying) taste of oil that had been overheated or overused. The same flaw did not exist in the downstairs frying, neither for the beautiful mixed fry of fish, with its rings of tender squid and chunks of whiting, nor in the fluffy potato croquettes that accompanied many main courses.

The best main courses at Patsy's were the most authentically Neapolitan: well-seasoned but exorbitantly expensive lobster oreganata style; sweet and hot pork sausages in a tomato and spicy pizzaiuola sauce, with slivers of red peppers; rollatine of veal filled with creamy cheese and lightly braised in a gentle wine sauce; veal and peppers; dewy, fresh calf's brains oreganate, baked with a verdant parsley and garlic overlay, and beef roll-ups, bracciole filled with raisins, pignoli nuts, cheese and prosciutto. Lemony veal piccata, though above average, had an unnecessarily sticky sauce, and veal scaloppine Francese was overpowered by a sweetish wine flavor. Chicken cacciatore, though decent, should have been more subtle and interesting.

Beefsteaks and veal chop pizzaiuola were also excellent, and the veal parmigiana obviously got more careful attention in the kitchen than that clichéd dish usually does, with rewarding results. The only really poor dish sampled was striped bass marechiare, for although the fish was snowy and delicate and not in the least overcooked, its dark brown-red acidic sauce was the

330

polar opposite of the transparently light, fresh tomato essence the term marechiare implies.

The bread at Patsy's is chewy and properly yeasty, but the standard house salad is based on iceberg lettuce. Better to choose a combination of dandelion greens and chicory, or arugula when in season. In addition to the well-made potato croquettes, Patsy's offers softly seductive stewed potatoes, baked with tomato, oil, thyme and onion.

Other than the Italian cheesecake, baked desserts are unremarkable. The cheesecake, when fresh and not cold, has the right fluffiness of texture and gentle airy sweetness. My favorite dessert, however, was a gorgeous fruit platter, mounded with shaved ice to cool wedges of cranshaw melon, quarters of persimmon, plump, blue Ribier grapes and the Christmas-red fruit of a cactus pear.

Service is brisk, efficient and generally helpful. Only at the most crowded times does one detect an impatience among waiters and, occasionally, a desire to finesse the clientele into quick and limited choices. The wine list is made up of standard basics priced about ten or fifteen percent higher than they should be.

Pearl's Chinese Restaurant
Fair

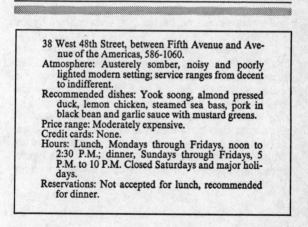

38 West 48th Street, between Fifth Avenue and Avenue of the Americas, 586-1060.
Atmosphere: Austerely somber, noisy and poorly lighted modern setting; service ranges from decent to indifferent.
Recommended dishes: Yook soong, almond pressed duck, lemon chicken, steamed sea bass, pork in black bean and garlic sauce with mustard greens.
Price range: Moderately expensive.
Credit cards: None.
Hours: Lunch, Mondays through Fridays, noon to 2:30 P.M.; dinner, Sundays through Fridays, 5 P.M. to 10 P.M. Closed Saturdays and major holidays.
Reservations: Not accepted for lunch, recommended for dinner.

Although it retains a steady following among members of the fashion and publishing worlds, Pearl's specializes in a style of Cantonese cooking that has fallen out of fashion with the more dedicated fans of Chinese food. All of the food served at this consistently crowded and noisy establishment is of high quality and is freshly prepared, but the style is a much-Americanized, tamed version of the authentic cuisine of that southern Chinese province. The result is a collection of dishes that are for the most part blandly undistinguished and even less interesting than they used to be.

The "in" high-fashion scene on Sunday nights as well as the constant crowds at weekday lunches and dinners give evidence that there is a loyal audience for this sort of unadventurous Chinese fare.

The most innovative aspect of Pearl's is its décor, a super-modern, long, dark tunnel of a setting that still represents a sharp departure from the obviously Oriental décor Chinese restaurants usually adopt. Unfortunately, the rounded shape of the ceiling causes noise to bounce around the room in a most distracting way, and the lighting is uneven by day and inadequate at night, especially since the full enjoyment of Chinese food depends on being able to appreciate the color contrast of various dishes.

One that has become a justifiable classic at this restaurant is lemon chicken — tender, crisply fried strips of chicken in a mellow sauce that has just the right lemony edge and no cloying sweetness. Other well-prepared specialties are the meaty, moist chunks of almond pressed duck and the appetizer yook soong — diced pork and water chestnuts served with a pungent, dark, scallion-flecked sauce. The ingredients are rolled into a lettuce leaf and eaten out of hand. Fried nuggets of pork in black bean and garlic sauce with mustard greens was also above average.

Steamed sea bass (not to be confused with poached sea bass with cucumber and scallion) is another simple and pleasant dish and the fish itself was well cooked.

The more banal if acceptable dishes at Pearl's were the lobster and chicken with mushrooms and vegetables, beef with lotus root and Chinese steak. Moo shu pork was greasy and seemed to be all vegetable. All of these dishes, in fact, contained vegetables that in every instance were badly overcooked, a most uncommon failing in a Chinese kitchen. At a recent lunch a soup and a sauce based on beaten eggs were marred by the staleness of the eggs used.

Dim sum and fried appetizers were pedestrian and the broth for the wonton soup was stingingly salty. The same fault also occurred with the sauce for the poached sea bass. And an order of yang chew fried rice, while generously studded with shrimp, pork and scraps of vegetables, tasted unpleasantly of overheated grease.

Because dessert selection is confined to the usual neighborhood Chinese restaurant repertory, it does not appear to be an especially popular one with the figure-conscious representatives of the fashion world who are Pearl's regulars.

Peking Duck House
★ ★

22 Mott Street, between Pell and Worth Streets, 962-8208.

Atmosphere: Informal and orderly but unadorned dining rooms; uneven service that can be surly.

Recommended dishes: Peking duck, fried spring chicken, spiced cold beef, meat and vegetables with Tientsin mung bean noodles, steamed or fried dumplings, smoked fish with bone, hot and sour soup, fried or steamed flounder, carp with fresh bean curd, lobster or shrimp in hot spicy sauce, beef with watercress, diced chicken with walnuts, broccoli, string beans, eggplant with garlic sauce, bean curd with minced pork, homemade noodles with bean sauce.

Price range: Moderate.

Credit cards: American Express.

Hours: Lunch, Mondays through Fridays, 11:30 A.M. to 3 P.M.; dinner, Mondays through Fridays, 3 P.M. to 11:30 P.M.; Saturdays and Sundays, 11:30 A.M. to 11:30 P.M. Closed on major holidays.

Reservations: Necessary for groups larger than five.

Beijing Duckhouse
★ ★

144 East 52nd Street, between Lexington and Third Avenues, 759-8260.

Atmosphere: Disorderly modern dining room; service ranges from excellent to perfunctory.

Recommended dishes: All listed above, plus fried, dried scallops, and seaweed, duck song, barbecued beef on a stick, fried spareribs with honey, sliced beef with broccoli, diced chicken with peanuts in hot sauce, pork with garlic sauce.

Price range: Moderate.

Credit cards: American Express, MasterCard and Visa.

Hours: Sundays through Thursdays, noon to 11 P.M.; Fridays and Saturdays, noon to midnight. Open major holidays.

Reservations: Necessary.

Beijing, Peking — what does it matter as long as you're healthy and as long as you can get an outstanding example of one of the world's most spectacular duck preparations. By either name, the Chinese capital is credited with the creation of Peking duck, a miraculous combination of golden, lacquer-bright skin, moistly tender meat, icy scallions and cucumbers — all mellowed with a velvety hoisin sauce and folded into a hot, paper-thin crepe to be eaten out of the hand.

Based on a fresh-killed duck that is pumped with air to loosen skin from meat, the preparation for this creation includes dousings of boiling water and hanging the duck for twenty-four hours to allow fat to drain off and the skin to achieve a parchment glaze. The skin is then rubbed with maltose (sometimes honey) and the bird is roasted in a hot oven.

Because of the lengthy and complicated preparation, most restaurants require twenty-four hours' notice for Peking duck. The few that offer it without advance notice generally turn out a cold, stale and lifeless variation.

Not so the Peking Duck House in Chinatown or the Beijing Duckhouse on East 52nd Street. Whether in the unadorned but orderly Chinatown dining room or in the somewhat more formal but often messy uptown outpost, the one dish not to be missed is the marvelous duck — available on no more than twenty minutes' notice and carved at the table by a chef who wields a scalpel-sharp cleaver with a dexterity that Dr. Christiaan Barnard might envy.

The carving is somewhat unconventional, in that skin and meat are sliced off together in long chevron strips, to be rolled in crepes with all the classic trimmings. Meaty carcasses are carried back to the kitchen to be used for soup unless they are requested by diners, in which case they are chopped in chunks so they can be picked up and gnawed on. In addition to being readily available and expertly prepared, Peking duck at both restaurants is relatively inexpensive — slightly more at Beijing — for a large duck that is ample for six, assuming other dishes are ordered.

Even without that remarkable duck, both restaurants would be well worth visiting for a number of excellent specialties. But the two consistent flaws that keep the restaurants from meriting three stars is the stubborn refusal to put the proper amount of spicy seasoning in dishes traditionally requiring them and the equally stubborn refusal to bring only a few dishes at a time. Dishes that were supposed to be hot and spicy are listed on the menu in red, and that is the only indication of hotness you will get. No amount of cajoling seems to sway the kitchen, and though much of the food was delicious, the blandness was often disappointing.

With those flaws cited, there still is much to be appreciated. Among the more outstanding first courses are the meaty, scallion-flecked dumplings — equally good steamed or fried — and a meat-and-vegetable appetizer salad, served half hot, half cold and consisting of silky Tientsin mung bean noodles, shrimp, shreds of pork, grated carrots and cucumbers and slivered scallions, in a sesame, soy and chili-oil sauce.

Also exceptional were spiced cold beef not unlike pastrami, darkly fragrant smoked fish and, at the uptown dining room, the delicate shreds of deep-fried seaweed topped with a crunchy sprinkling of fried, dried scallops. Honey-glazed spareribs were better uptown than down, and only uptown can you find duck song — sautéed chopped duck in a savory sauce, to be rolled in lettuce leaves — and the marinated barbecued beef satays on skewers. Spring rolls tasted of stale grease, and duck-feet skin will appeal only to those who like

334

cartilaginous textures. Soups at both places were uninteresting, the one exception being the hot and sour.

Crisply deep-fried Peking-style chicken in a winy soy sauce with scallions proved as satisfying a main course as the moist and tender nuggets of sautéed chicken that are served with walnuts in brown sauce or with peanuts in a chili-oil sauce, or the garlic-scented slivers of beef stir-fried with sprigs of watercress or melted in a brown sauce with broccoli. Whether steamed or fried, fish at both restaurants was cooked to the just-set, custard-like state that does most for the fresh flavor of the fish itself. Braised whole carp with sheets of fresh bean curd was perhaps the most extraordinary of the fish preparations, followed closely by the fried or steamed flounder. Both sparkled with ginger and scallions.

Shrimp with garlic sauce (a variation on the standard Cantonese sauce) and fried prawns with chili sauce were uninteresting. Both shrimp and lobster in a well-contrasted hot and spicy sauce were far better. Mutton was as strong, tough and dry uptown as down.

Cooks in both kitchens have a way with vegetables, such as the crackling slender string beans stir-fried with minced pork, the gentle slivers of eggplant simmered with garlic, the broccoli sautéed with garlic and the cubes of creamy bean curd enriched with minced pork and red chili oil. Fried rice and homemade noodles tasted unpleasantly of stale cooking oil, but the noodles with bean sauce and cucumbers had enough richness and substance to make a satisfying and most economical main course. Plain white rice is desirable here to offset the slight saltiness of some dishes.

Fried apples and bananas with walnuts were abominable at both places, suffering from the same horrendous grease that marred the rice and noodles.

Peking Duck West
★

199 Amsterdam Avenue, at 69th Street, 799-5457.
Atmosphere: Pleasant and spacious dining room; service ranges from attentive to pushy and abrupt.
Recommended dishes: Bok choy with hot sauce, meat and vegetable with mung-bean sheets, dried scallops with seaweed, barbecued beef, smoked fish, steamed sea bass, beef with watercress, orange flavor beef, Peking duck, fried duck, homemade noodles with bean sauce, crisp string beans.
Price range: Moderate.
Credit cards: American Express, MasterCard and Visa.
Hours: Sundays through Thursdays, noon to 11 P.M., Fridays and Saturdays, noon to midnight.
Reservations: Recommended, especially for dinner.

Apparently not afraid of spreading their managerial and culinary talents too thin, the owners of the Peking

Duck House in Chinatown and the Beijing Duckhouse on East 52nd Street have opened a third outpost near Lincoln Center. So far, the new kitchen's performance is not up to those of the older restaurants.

Nevertheless, this handsome restaurant, with its carpeted, well-decorated dining room, widely spaced tables and formally dressed captains and waiters, is already a welcome addition to the neighborhood. There are more than enough competently prepared dishes to make up a satisfying meal, foremost among them being an exceptional Peking duck, which, as is the case at the other two restaurants, need not be ordered in advance. The glistening roasted duck is brought to the table, where the chef carves it with lightning dexterity. The meaty duck slices, with their glassily crisp skin, wrapped in crepes, are accented by strips of cucumber, wisps of scallions and a fruity, hoisin-based sauce.

Traditionally, Peking duck is sliced after the skin and meat have been separated; at Peking Duck restaurants, the two are left intact, with just the slightest underlining of translucent fat to add richness of flavor and a satiny texture. At about $25, the Peking duck provides six people with two generous portions each, or it will make a wonderful meal for two if nothing else is added. Those who like to gnaw on bones should ask to have the carcass left; otherwise, it will be whisked away to go into duck soup with cabbage, a bland but soothing concoction.

Some of the dishes that have made the two older restaurants popular are well represented at Peking Duck West. Among them are such appetizers as the cold Chinese cabbage, bok choy, sparked by a sweet and fiery marinade, slivered cold meats and vegetables tossed with strips of sheer mung-bean sheets, crisp seaweed flecked with dried scallops, and smoked fish in a nut-flavored sauce. Also good are flat, tender strips of hot beef barbecued on skewers. But greasiness marred such appetizers as fried dumplings, stuffed eggplant, spring rolls and vegetarian duck, which is formed of bean-curd sheets. Steamed dumplings were overcooked and mushy.

Hot and sour soup was neither hot nor sour, and its slickly thick texture indicated an overabundance of cornstarch. The lack of spicy seasoning, even when requested, is another serious failing, even with dishes listed on the menu in red ink to indicate red hot. The only properly spiced dish was a delicious beef with orange flavor. In addition, what is billed as a hot spicy sauce for deep-fried fish, lobster and shrimp arrives stickily sweet and sour, and the hot pepper sauce for diced chicken with peanuts was merely a clear brown glaze. The acrid flavor of overused frying oil overpowered both chicken and peanuts as well as mutton garnished with scallions and beef with broccoli. Far better creations are the crisp fried duck, delicate steamed sea bass with threads of fresh ginger and scallions, and crisp string beans stir-fried with minced pork and garlic.

A garlic sauce for eggplant tasted more of grease than of garlic, but homemade noodles with bean sauce have the same savory overtones that made it a favorite at the Peking Duck House in Chinatown.

Besides canned Chinese fruits and Häagen-Dazs ice

cream, the only desserts are fried bananas and apples, both of which bore traces of stale oil.

One night at dinner there was a culinary floor show with the chef performing the Chinese noodle trick, showing how the dough for noodles is pulled and folded until it suddenly splays out into strips. The performance was only moderately successful, but engaging nonetheless. Service at Peking Duck West can be friendly and helpful, but the captains tend to be pushy and overbearing and definitely want customers to adhere to their timetable. This can mean, for example, that soup will be served in the middle of the appetizer course and that too many dishes arrive at once.

Pesca
★

23 East 22nd Street, between Broadway and Park Avenue, 533-2293.
Atmosphere: Elegant and romantic setting with very high noise level; service is friendly but unprofessional and erratic.
Recommended dishes: Clams cataplana, mousse of sea scallops, fresh bluepoint oysters, gravlax, smoked fish, Bermuda fish chowder, seafood lasagne, bourride cioppino, sautéed sand dabs, broiled salmon, walnut-cream layer cake, apple flan, walnut, bourbon and molasses pie.
Price range: Moderately expensive.
Credit cards: American Express.
Hours: Lunch, Mondays through Fridays, noon to 3 P.M.; dinner, Mondays through Saturdays, 6 P.M. to 11 P.M., Sundays, 6 P.M. to 10 P.M. Closed major holidays.
Reservations: Necessary.

Pesca is a perfectly exquisite restaurant with a menu devoted entirely to seafood. In this long, wide room, walls enameled in lingerie pink go from mauve to shrimp color in tone, depending on the filters in the spotlights around the room. There are long picture windows opening onto a white-brick courtyard, handsome glass lampshades over the bar, sprays of white flowers and attractive photographs, prints and paintings of shells, fishing scenes and waterfronts. But although tables are spaced widely apart, the combination of metal ceiling and uncarpeted floor contributes to a distractingly high noise level, compounded by piano music that is intrusive.

There are unusual and attractive offerings on the fish and shellfish menu. Clams cataplana, a Portuguese specialty consisting of clams and slices of spicy pork sausage braised together with tomatoes, garlic and onions (in a round cooker known as a cataplana), was absolutely delicious and hearty enough to make a satisfactory main course, although it is an appetizer. Other fine first courses included a cloud-light, warm mousse of sea scallops with a sheer tomato and dill sauce, and impeccable, well-chilled bluepoint oysters with a pale-pink tomato sauce flecked with chips of horseradish, a bit too overpowering for the delicacy of the oysters but interesting as a sort of side relish. Moist, bright coral gravlax, made of salmon cured with dill and what is described on this menu as "coarse" salt, was excellent, and so was smoked fish with a sauce of dill, capers and crème fraîche. Oysters baked with Stilton cheese and bacon, however, made an overcomplicated dish, and a pâté of sole inset with bits of asparagus was served so cold that its flavor was lost.

Bermuda fish chowder, as a first course, was a most unusual and interesting combination of chunks of fish, tomato, vegetables and just enough dried red chili peppers to give a considerable belt. Seafood lasagne, regularly on the menu, has alternating layers of green pasta with shrimp and sea scallops, with a tomato, cream and basil sauce, all baked under a light cheese glaze. It made a delicious first course when shared.

The single best main course sampled was sautéed whole baby flounder, billed as sand dabs. Fair french fries and firm, well-cooked string beans accompanied the fish, as did a remarkable tartar sauce. The only fault was the overcrowding of the plate, which made it difficult to bone the fish without scattering vegetables over the table. Also delicious but awkwardly served was that San Francisco-Italian soup-stew, cioppino. Here a high, round glass bowl arrives filled with half a lobster, mussels, clams, shrimp and nuggets of fish in a lusty soup of tomato, red wine, saffron and herbs. Unfortunately, what is needed is a wider, flatter soup bowl and lobster cut in more manageable sections.

A different assortment of fish for broiling is offered each night, but when the choices are announced no prices are given, so ask in advance. Of the daily specials, grouper, bass and trout were acceptable and king salmon was excellent. Water-broiling seems to be the method used, and as a result, flavor tends to wash out. Other daily features have included shad roe sautéed in butter with a touch of orange juice, a combination that would have been excellent had the shad roe been a bit moister. Broiled lobster, though tender and not at all dry, seemed to have been touched with an incompatible herb or liqueur that took the edge off the lobster's fresh flavor.

Bourride, always on the menu, is generally made with red snapper and is served without any of the soup traditional for that Provençale dish. It comes as poached fish topped with aioli garlic-mayonnaise, all on a crouton moistened with fish stock. It is good but disappointing if the creamy white soup is expected. Fish fillets baked in parchment were mildly pleasant. Vegetables such as kale and string beans were bright and al dente, but fried potatoes, onion chips and zucchini were too pale and greasy. Boiled potatoes were properly cooked, but the house salad had a watery, tasteless dressing.

Most of the desserts look better than they taste. The only ones worth recommending are walnut and bourbon pie, a buttery apple flan and a huge but light walnut and whipped-cream layer cake. The wine list is restricted to California products, many of them over-priced.

The staff at Pesca is friendly and well-meaning but often forgetful about orders, a failing that is especially true at peak hours.

Peter Luger Steakhouse
★

178 Broadway, at Driggs Avenue, Brooklyn, 387-7400.
Atmosphere: Antique German tavern dining room dating from 1887; service is efficient and brusque at busy times, otherwise it is friendly.
Recommended dishes: Steak, lamb chops, braised chicken, french fries, baked potato.
Price range: Expensive.
Credit cards: None.
Hours: Lunch, Mondays through Fridays, 11:45 A.M. to 3 P.M.; dinner, Mondays through Thursdays, 3 P.M. to 10:45 P.M.; Saturdays, noon to 11:15 P.M., Sundays, 1 P.M. to 9:45 P.M.
Reservations: Recommended.

Attracting a huge crowd to this otherwise desolate section of Williamsburg, the restaurant began life as Charles Luger's Cafe Billiards and Bowling Alley in 1876, and some of the original architecture exists in the Driggs Avenue entrance. Dark painted wood paneling, topped by half-timbered walls, heavy brass plates on wall shelves and scrubbed oak tables set the tone, which is reminiscent of a German tavern.

My experiences at Peter Luger's through the years have been disappointing, a view corroborated by the most recent visits. Both cooking and service can be unnecessarily sloppy and careless, even for a rugged steakhouse, but the pace and brusqueness are considerably toned down at lunch, when crowds are not backed up the full length of the bar.

The menu is so small that the preparation of each dish should be perfect. Appetizers consist only of shrimp cocktail and sliced tomatoes, with or without onions, that can be delicious when tomatoes are ripe. The shrimp (hardly the "jumbo" size they are billed as) varied from firm, cold and clean to warm, soft and haphazardly deveined.

The steak at Luger's is all top quality, hefty cuts of porterhouse, whether for one, two or three eaters. It can be delicious but often is broiled over too high a heat, so that the outside is charred dry, while the inside is almost always underdone. The biggest flaw is that all steaks are brought to the table sliced so that their juices run out and the meat turns cold before it can be eaten. On request, they can be had unsliced.

339

Double loin chops are thick and well flavored, if very badly trimmed of fat. Big, thick slabs of roast prime ribs of beef, available only occasionally, are served as ordered, but lack a distinctively beefy flavor. At lunch each day there is a specialty or two in addition, and on a Tuesday, I found braised chicken in broth with carrots, celery and boiled potato to be one of the best dishes I have had at this restaurant.

Homemade french fries and baked potatoes, done without foil wrappings, are excellent, but hash browns tend to be burned black around the edges and on the bottom. Creamed spinach may have been fresh when cooked, but it was as darkly bitter and overcooked as the version packed by Gerber's. A special house steak sauce is a typical sweet-sour, red barbeque sauce and wholly dreadful, though popular enough to be sold bottled.

The best dessert is warm apple pie, with firm apples, lots of cinnamon and a thin crust that was good, even if not crisp. Other desserts include a rummy cheesecake, cloying chocolate mousse cake, pecan pie, with a tasteless commercial crust and only the thinnest veneer of nuts, and an apple strudel that is decent only when hot.

The beer on tap is Beck's, light and dark, and served in big glass steins; both are delicious.

Pietro's
Fair

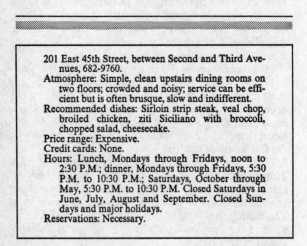

201 East 45th Street, between Second and Third Avenues, 682-9760.

Atmosphere: Simple, clean upstairs dining rooms on two floors; crowded and noisy; service can be efficient but is often brusque, slow and indifferent.

Recommended dishes: Sirloin strip steak, veal chop, broiled chicken, ziti Siciliano with broccoli, chopped salad, cheesecake.

Price range: Expensive.

Credit cards: None.

Hours: Lunch, Mondays through Fridays, noon to 2:30 P.M.; dinner, Mondays through Fridays, 5:30 P.M. to 10:30 P.M.; Saturdays, October through May, 5:30 P.M. to 10:30 P.M. Closed Saturdays in June, July, August and September. Closed Sundays and major holidays.

Reservations: Necessary.

For close to fifty years, Pietro's has been one of the city's most popular Italian-style steakhouses, with a coterie that swears by every dish. Walk up the narrow flight of stairs that lead to the first-floor dining room almost any afternoon or evening, and you will find the tiny bar that opens into the equally tiny kitchen jammed with guests waiting for tables, most of them hoping to be seated on the first level rather than the even less distinctive upstairs floor. Noise, crowds and waiters shouting orders all add up to a hectic and almost chaotic atmosphere.

Diners not known to the management may be given a table smack up against the door to the ladies' room even if the place is three-quarters empty. One night I ordered zabaglione, remembering how good the zabaglione could be, and was told there might be a short wait for it. After about twenty-five minutes I asked when it would be ready, only to be told by a waiter: "Forget it. The kitchen is much too busy and they are just not going to make it." Like that.

It is hard to understand why anyone puts up with this place, because in over a dozen visits during the past thirty years I have never had a meal that was exceptional or even memorably good.

The only dishes I have ever enjoyed have been the tomato and onion salad, whether cut up or sliced, the chopped lettuce, tomato and anchovy salad and the ziti Siciliano, which is normally baked macaroni with eggplant slices and mozzarella cheese but at Pietro's is cooked with a sauce of broccoli, garlic and olive oil. The sauce is made with chopped and puréed broccoli stems, with a few flowers, and is thoroughly delicious. Steak has been dry but acceptable, if not brilliant, and so has boiled chicken.

As for appetizers, many of which are listed among seafood main courses, there were dry, overcooked shrimp scampi in a sweet onion sauce and clam sauté, heavily breaded clams with none of the briny freshness they should have, in a sauce that desperately needed garlic. The antipasto included half a can of tuna fish, unbroken and set down in a block, prosciutto with all the flavor of waxed paper, very ordinary Italian salami, roast pepper and an anchovy or two. Minestrone was acceptable, though a bit thin.

Broiled meats other than steak, veal chop and chicken were disappointing. Good-quality, badly trimmed lamb chops were heavily edged in fat that had not charred and came almost well done when ordered medium rare. Calf's liver was done as ordered but had the pasty softness that meat usually gets when it has been frozen.

Chicken à la Pietro (a chokingly dry sauté of chunks of chicken with burned onions, mushrooms and green peppers) was awful, and what was billed as veal parmigiana was a sauceless slab of dry veal fried, topped with grated Parmesan cheese and then browned for a chokingly dry end result.

Outside of the ziti, every pasta dish I have had here has been overcooked, including a recent order of cannelloni, and the spaghetti with clam sauce did not taste of fresh clams and was awash in a watery clam liquid.

Hashed brown and cottage-fried potatoes and a totally unseasoned Caesar salad were as disappointing as the rest. Though I have had french-fried onion rings here five times, only once were they not burned. Burning, as a result of quick cooking over very high heat for the sake of speed, occurs often at Pietro's, but no patron we observed seemed to mind at all.

Cheesecake is good but zabaglione is better — when you can get it.

Pirandello
★ ★

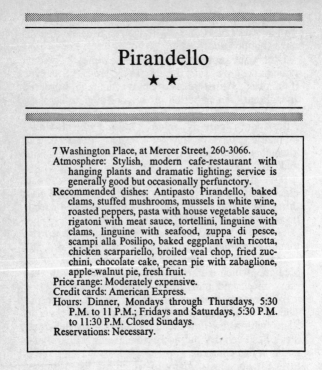

7 Washington Place, at Mercer Street, 260-3066.
Atmosphere: Stylish, modern cafe-restaurant with hanging plants and dramatic lighting; service is generally good but occasionally perfunctory.
Recommended dishes: Antipasto Pirandello, baked clams, stuffed mushrooms, mussels in white wine, roasted peppers, pasta with house vegetable sauce, rigatoni with meat sauce, tortellini, linguine with clams, linguine with seafood, zuppa di pesce, scampi alla Posilipo, baked eggplant with ricotta, chicken scarpariello, broiled veal chop, fried zucchini, chocolate cake, pecan pie with zabaglione, apple-walnut pie, fresh fruit.
Price range: Moderately expensive.
Credit cards: American Express.
Hours: Dinner, Mondays through Thursdays, 5:30 P.M. to 11 P.M.; Fridays and Saturdays, 5:30 P.M. to 11:30 P.M. Closed Sundays.
Reservations: Necessary.

During the last several years, New York has seen the rise of the boutique restaurant, which offers a small, esoteric and stylized representation of a cuisine rather than a full range. For the most part, such restaurants have featured the French nouvelle cuisine, but a few also specialize in North Italian dishes. Pirandello is a perfect example of the Italian boutique restaurant. A dramatic, modern cafe-dining room with its shadowy theatrical lighting, decorative pictures and hanging plants, Pirandello has become popular with Villagers as well as with Off Broadway theatergoers. It certainly has delivered on its earlier promise; when first reviewed, it was given a one-star rating with two stars predicted for the future.

Very little tomato sauce is in evidence here. The whiteness that fashion-conscious diners equate with lightness appears here in butter-cream-cheese sauces on pastas, and in clear white wine and lemon pan juices that result from sautéing meats and poultry. In some cases, dishes are bland, especially in the overly contrived daily specials, but there is more than enough delicious food to make up satisfying dinners.

Appetizers are particularly interesting and well seasoned, including such excellent choices as the crunchy, garlicky baked clams with oregano, mushroom caps baked under a lush mantle of mozzarella cheese, and a gorgeous platter of big, sand-free mussels steamed in a herbaceous white wine sauce. Homemade roasted green peppers, which have a lovely brassy edge to them, can be obtained alone or in an antipasto that includes a cool, delicate rice salad, lusty salami and fresh, moist mozzarella.

Each day Pirandello offers a special pasta or two and a couple of soups. Usually there is some form of short tubular pasta in the house vegetable sauce, a dish that is halfway between minestrone and primavera and altogether delicious. Rigatoni in meat sauce proved exceptionally satisfying. So did the linguine in white clam sauce, the tortellini with cheese and cream and the linguine "tutto mare" — topped with a huge portion of mussels, clams, shrimp and squid, making this as suitable for a main course as for an appetizer. It is the only pasta not available in a half portion. Disappointing pastas were those in which the cream sauce tasted milky — the penne that did not even hint at the sausage said to be in the mix as well as the tagliatelle all'Alfredo. Spicy tortellini in broth should have been cooked a little longer, but their spicy sausage filling imparted a nice edge to steaming, full-bodied broth.

"Tutto mare" is also the label on the Italian fish stew, zuppa di pesce, which is one of the best main courses, along with one Neapolitan offering, the scampi alla Posilipo in a sheer, lightly herbed marinara sauce. A light tomato broth also distinguished a daily special of striped bass in brodetto, garnished with clams, something we had to insist on because the waiter was pushing the spicier Livornese sauce. Southern dishes are so well prepared here that one has to wonder where the chef's heart really lies.

It would be difficult to improve upon the thick, impeccably grilled veal loin chop with its slightly crisp edges and rosy, tender interior. Chicken scarpariello is done properly with chunks of chicken still on the bone, sautéed with garlic in a lemony white wine sauce. Vegetarians should feel no sense of deprivation if the gentle eggplant baked with ricotta cheese filling and a creamy tomato sauce was their main course.

Salads are merely acceptable. A better choice is the cold vegetable of the day with oil and vinegar. Side orders of fried zucchini arrived greaseless and flawless on two out of three visits.

Calorie watchers will find that both bread and desserts are much too good. Chocolate cake with a fluff of whipped cream, a crunchy pecan pie with warm zabaglione, and a walnut-flecked apple tart are all excellent. The assortment of cut fresh fruits tasted as refreshing as it looked. Forget the slightly leaden, overly sweet crème caramel. Service is usually efficient and professional but occasionally is distracted and perfunctory.

Pongsri Thailand Restaurant

★

244 West 48th Street, between Eighth Avenue and
Broadway, 582-3392.

Atmosphere: Trim and sparklingly modern dining
room with tiles, Thai carvings and large bar; service is gracious and helpful despite occasional language difficulties.

Recommended dishes: Egg noodles with roast pork,
roast pork fried rice, crispy rice noodles, fried
Thai noodles with shrimp and peanuts, Thai
stuffed omelet with bean sprouts and coconut,
fried shrimp cakes, shredded papaya salad, sliced
charcoal steak, Chinese sausage salad, shrimp or
squid salad in lime juice, hot and sour shrimp
soup, chicken soup with pickled lemon, frog's legs
Thai style or with garlic and pepper, shrimp with
spicy chili sauce, whole fish with chicken and
tomato, roast duck with bamboo shoots, vegetable
dip, fried banana with bamboo shoots, fried banana with honey, coconut ice cream.

Price range: Moderate.

Credit cards: American Express and Diners Club.

Hours: Seven days, noon to midnight. Open on major
holidays.

Reservations: Necessary for four or more people.

The Theater District is rapidly becoming the city's center for Thai food, and this latest addition can be welcomed not only for its good food and moderate prices
but also for its gracious staff and trimly inviting interi-
or. Its sparklingly modern dining room gets atmospheric touches from colorful tiles, plants, Thai wood
carvings and bright yellow tablecloths kept clean under
glass. There is a large, well-stocked bar (although a request for a glass of dry white wine brought forth
sherry), and from 11 P.M. to 3 A.M. on Friday and
Saturday nights, Thai musicians play Thai and rock
music to a mostly Thai clientele. At that time a long list
of savory and enticing appetizers make up the menu, although main dishes are available on request.

Only a few shortcomings make for some discomfort.
Tables are all rectangular, which for parties of six or
more is less conducive to sharing dishes than a round
shape. In addition, if the restaurant is relatively empty
the air-conditioner is not turned on, and the background music is often too loud. At the gentlest suggestion, however, the air-conditioner is turned up and the
music is turned down, or even off. Clearly, this gentle
and graceful crew is out to please, and the sincerity of
all is at least as refreshing as the spicy and aromatic
food.

An offshoot of the Thailand Restaurant in Chinatown, Pongsri has a kitchen that still needs some fine-
tuning. But there are already more than enough consistently good dishes to assure a delightful meal. Appetizers are wonderful, and a long assortment, plus a soup
and noodle dish, add up to a lovely meal, without hav-

ing to risk some of the second-rate meat and fish main courses.

Bitingly astringent soups often heightened by chili pepper are a Thai specialty: a fiery hot and sour shrimp soup and a soothing, mild lemon-scented chicken soup with winter melon and black mushrooms are perfect examples. Noodle dishes take on many forms. Three worth trying at Pongsri are puffy, crisp mee krob, slightly sweet and pungent and enriched with shrimp; fine fried Thai noodles with shrimp, peanuts and eggs, and gently soft egg noodles with roast pork, which includes fish balls that are rubbery but that can be easily ignored. That same rubberiness, however, spoils the barbecued beef balls.

Beef satays are acceptable, if slightly tough, and their peanut sauce lacks the subtleties it should have. A better choice is warm strips of charcoal-broiled beef sliced into a lemony salad with onions, mint and hot peppers. Similar dressings, based on lemon or lime juice and chili oil, appear on salads of squid, shrimp or Chinese sausage and on delicate shreds of papaya, mellowed with dried shrimp and peanuts. Tender ground shrimp cakes, fried golden brown, are garnished with a cucumber, vinegar, chili oil and peanut sauce, and there is a thick, savory, minced-pork-and-shrimp dip served with such cut raw vegetables as cucumbers, tomato and lettuce.

Another soothing dish is roast pork fried rice threaded with bits of egg, a fine foil for the hotness of chili-spiced shrimp, or piquant Thai-style frog's legs or the same plump and meaty frog's legs glazed with pepper and garlic. Of three whole-fish preparations, the best proved to be sea bass braised with chicken, tomato and mushrooms.

Less satisfactory choices included a slimy, tasteless pork-skin salad; dry chicken, either with cashew nuts or with basil, and beef with green peppers, as well as a few Chinese dishes, including one with less-than-fresh crab in bean sauce and banal lobster Cantonese. If appetizer and noodles or rice leave you hungry, go on to nuggets of roasted duck braised with bamboo shoots or to hot-and-spicy Thai beef coconut curry.

Forks and spoons are the utensils to use, and Thai Singha beer is the most suitable beverage. Unusually good for a Thai restaurant are two desserts — basically Chinese hot honey-glazed bananas with toasted sesame seeds, and coconut ice cream, which is homemade freshly grated coconut and coconut milk frozen to a sherbetlike froth.

Ponte's Steak House

★

39 Desbrosses Street, at the corner of West Street, 226-4621.

Atmosphere: Flashy, upholstered décor that suggests a suburban cocktail lounge or nightclub; noisy when there is live music but otherwise comfortable; excellent service.

Recommended dishes: Clams casino, pasta e fagioli, gnocchi Bolognese, linguine with white clam sauce, rollatine of veal, veal bracciolatini with fettuccine, steak, broiled veal chops, lamb chops, calf's liver scarpariello, chicken and sausage scarpariello, spezzatini of beef or sliced steak pizzaiuola, arugula salad, cheesecake, fresh fruit.

Price range: Moderately expensive.

Credit cards. All major credit cards.

Hours: Mondays through Thursdays, noon to 11 P.M.; Fridays, noon to midnight; Saturdays, 5:30 P.M. to midnight. Closed Sundays.

Reservations: Recommended

Restaurateurs who feel that they must be at the center of things to succeed could learn a lot from Ponte's Steak House, a crowded, lively and colorful restaurant practically in the Hudson River, two blocks south of Canal Street. Drive through this desolate area at night and you will suddenly come upon an oasis of Christmas trees with lights, a parking lot full of Cadillac Sevilles, Mercedes and Continentals and, almost always, a few chauffeured limousines.

This Italian steakhouse is particularly popular with serious eaters from New Jersey and Queens. Its décor suggests a suburban cocktail lounge or nightclub, right from its gussied-up downstairs reception room to its two dining rooms, which are flashy and upholstered with genuine oil paintings and sparkly acoustical ceilings.

As overdone as the setting is, it is interesting to realize how genuinely comfortable the dining rooms are, far more so than many that are more tastefully designed. Tables are large and there is adequate space between them, lighting is excellent, chairs are comfortable and service is professional, polite and efficient. The noise level is bearable on Monday, and would be so on other nights as well except for the strolling musicians who add an intrusive and corny touch.

Ponte's, like Las Vegas, will be enjoyed by those who can give themselves up to the moment and who will be entertained by the unusual and "Guys and Dolls" clientele. If you have a white mink coat, silver sling-back shoes, a red sports jacket, an iridescent suit or large-scale jewelry, this is the place to wear them, and diamond pinky rings for men are practically *de rigueur*.

There are a number of two-star dishes on this menu, most of them Neapolitan specialties. If the cooking were more even, Ponte's could deserve two stars.

Clams casino topped with a little spicy tomato sauce

346

and a crisp sliver of bacon was unusually good, but the clams oreganate were topped with soggy, bland bread crumbs. Prosciutto was only acceptable and neither the hot nor cold antipasto sparkled with quality. Crab meat and lobster cocktails were spongy and washed out, almost as though the shelled meat had been stored directly on ice.

On the other hand, very good first courses included a flavorful pasta e fagioli soup, tinted pink with tomatoes, scented with garlic and thick with ditali pasta and white beans. Slightly chewy gnocchi in a lusty Bolognese meat sauce also were good and the linguine with white clam sauce had just the right accents of toasted garlic cloves.

The only respectable salad was the crisp green arugula. Caesar salad was smothered in a thick dressing and the special house salad incorporated iceberg lettuce, frozen or canned artichoke hearts, California olives and unripe cherry tomatoes.

Steaks and lamb chops, though not quite up to the quality served in the city's top-flight steakhouses, were nonetheless well broiled and acceptable. Tail meat in a broiled three-and-a-half-pound lobster, though not dry, was so hard it could almost not be chewed.

The real winners among main courses included the very original sautéed calf's liver scarpariello style, with garlic, the same scarpariello preparation done with chicken and sausages and both the sliced steak and spezzatini (chunks of beef mantled under a spicy, mushroom-enriched pizzaiuola sauce). Two enjoyable daily specials were the broiled rollatine of veal with a ham filling and the braised bracciolatine of veal with fettuccine in a light tomato sauce.

Boiled beef, a special at some dinners, was well flavored but so overcooked it was almost mashable. Veal piccata was of a fine, snowy quality, but it swam in what could best be described as lemon broth. Veal parmigiana was dry and barely tepid, but a thick loin veal chop retained moistness and tenderness under the broiler and was delicious. Potato croquettes, often served with main courses, were uniformly excellent; roasted potatoes proved a disappointing alternative.

Cheesecake was the best of the otherwise overly sweet and soggy baked desserts. The platter of fresh fruits provided the most appropriately refreshing finish of all.

Unless you drive, Ponte's is best reached by taxi, and be sure to have one called for you before leaving.

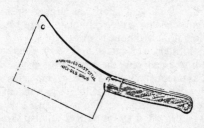

The Post House
Fair

28 East 63rd Street, between Madison and Park Avenues, 935-2888.

Atmosphere: Handsome, spacious dining room with antique touches, good lighting and acoustics; service efficient and polite, but occasionally careless.

Recommended dishes: Lobster cocktail, prime ribs of beef, lemon pepper chicken, veal chop, lobster, scrod, hashed-browned potatoes, cheesecake, hot apple pie or apple Betty, blueberry tart.

Price range: Expensive.

Credit cards: All major credit cards.

Hours: Lunch, Mondays through Fridays, noon to 4 P.M.; dinner, Mondays through Thursdays, 4 P.M. to 11 P.M.; Fridays, 4 P.M. to midnight; Saturdays, 5:30 P.M. to midnight, and Sundays, 5:30 P.M. to 11 P.M.

Reservations: Recommended.

Although the Post House was given two stars in *The New York Times* when the restaurant opened in 1980, that rating no longer seems valid. Based on our half-dozen visits since that first review, the only advantages this steakhouse seems to offer over most others are its handsome setting, a relatively benign noise level and decent service. While these are all important features, they're not quite enough when top prices buy food that is mediocre. On my visits, some chairs extended into aisles or were wedged against service stations, and banquettes have a disconcerting forward pitch; otherwise the modern dining rooms with antique trimmings are comfortable.

The price for prime ribs of beef, lamb chops and steaks is $20.75, strictly à la carte. Of these, the thickly cut, properly rare and tender prime ribs can be recommended. Lamb chops had little flavor, and of several sirloin steaks tasted, only one had that good beefy edge of flavor, and even that one was veined with sinews. Filet mignon was oversoft and bland. Sliced steak on three occasions arrived gray and dry, always smothered with greasy sautéed onions and rimmed with equally greasy fried onion rings — a strange duplication of garnishes. The thick veal chop was properly seared and had a fine, delicate flavor, although there was a high proportion of fat and bone to meat.

Giant lobsters are moist and very good, whether broiled or steamed; only the meat in the claws was overcooked, as it tends to be with such sea monsters.

The best choice on the menu is the pungent lemon-and pepper-burnished broiled chicken. The meat is moist, well protected by the veneer of crisp skin, and at $13.75 it's a relative bargain.

On two occasions, calf's liver was well past freshness and had a bitter, metallic aftertaste, and a veal chop Milanese, though huge and nicely presented, was so heavily breaded that it tasted like a slice of whole-wheat toast. Soft-shell crabs with tough papery skins were no longer really "soft," and tiny scallops, said to be broiled, looked boiled and tasted of paprika. This spice also slightly marred scrod that was described as broiled but that leaked so much water onto the plate that it seemed water-broiled or half-steamed. Still, the inner meat of the fish had the right pearly freshness and firmness; careful draining between platter and plate would have helped. Hashed-brown potatoes proved better than the limp cottage fries and the somewhat stale-tasting baked potato.

Limpness mars salads and all vegetables, which are overcooked. Vegetable appetizers such as ice-cold asparagus and artichokes taste of the refrigerator. Both are topped by a congealed and lumpy mass of vinaigrette dressing.

Crab meat is spongy, and a seafood salad that combines lobster salad, crab meat and shrimp is far too cold. As with the vegetable appetizers, this assortment seems to have been prearranged on plates and stored in the refrigerator so that the flavor faded. Neither a musty tasting gazpacho nor a cream of celery soup that looks more like cream of wheat is a worthwhile first-course possibility. The one recommendable first course is the lobster cocktail — a whole boiled baby lobster with proper flavor and texture.

The best desserts are the high, firm and creamy cheesecake, a hot crisp apple Betty, which is also called deep-dish apple pie, and a blueberry tart that has a better baked crust than the raspberry tart.

The Quilted Giraffe
★ ★

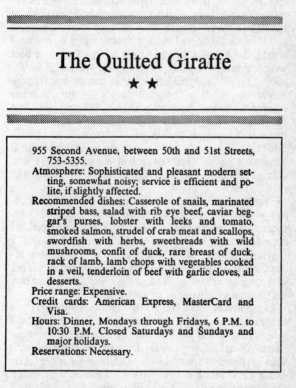

955 Second Avenue, between 50th and 51st Streets, 753-5355.

Atmosphere: Sophisticated and pleasant modern setting, somewhat noisy; service is efficient and polite, if slightly affected.

Recommended dishes: Casserole of snails, marinated striped bass, salad with rib eye beef, caviar beggar's purses, lobster with leeks and tomato, smoked salmon, strudel of crab meat and scallops, swordfish with herbs, sweetbreads with wild mushrooms, confit of duck, rare breast of duck, rack of lamb, lamb chops with vegetables cooked in a veil, tenderloin of beef with garlic cloves, all desserts.

Price range: Expensive.

Credit cards: American Express, MasterCard and Visa.

Hours: Dinner, Mondays through Fridays, 6 P.M. to 10:30 P.M. Closed Saturdays and Sundays and major holidays.

Reservations: Necessary.

A consistent problem with many of the self-taught young cooks who are in a hurry to open their own restaurants without working enough for experienced chefs is that they get little opportunity to develop their palates. With apprenticeship to a master, their own natural talents would be honed against the classics, and gradually they would achieve the best sort of creativity — an individual style rooted in tradition. It is unusual for a self-taught chef who is not drawing from a family or ethnic-food background to achieve a dependably sure hand in an idiom not basically his or her own.

An exception is Barry Wine, originally a lawyer, who turned chef and is now the guiding influence in his kitchen at the Quilted Giraffe. Two recent visits indicate that he has come a long way since he opened his doors at this site, when the restaurant rated one star. Coming to New York City after several years of experience in his restaurant at New Paltz, he already showed talent in certain directions — mostly in preparing duck, calf's liver and desserts. But he was skittish and unpredictable, with a penchant for sweetness in the wrong places.

In general, the food now prepared by Mr. Wine and Mark Chayette, the chef, is delicious and delicately complicated, if esoteric in appeal. The nouvelle cuisine is still the theme in this small, plush and clublike setting. Noisier than it used to be now that tables and chairs have replaced thickly upholstered banquette-booths, The Quilted Giraffe is nonetheless felicitous and well lighted with graceful bouquets and decorative table appointments. Unfortunately, the generally efficient service is still pretentious.

The $45 dinner includes a number of interesting specialties, among them such appetizers as a copper casserole of snails simmered in a creamy wild-mushroom sauce and given crunch with minced pignoli nuts, a cool, lightly marinated striped bass sparked by mustard cream sauce and a salad of rare slices of rib eye beef wrapped around scallions and topped with wild mushrooms. One irresistible conceit that carries a surcharge is a serving of four "beggar's purses" — tiny pouches formed of crepes tied with chives, holding excellent caviar and a dab of crème fraîche. For a supplement, there is a warm appetizer of lobster with tomato in cream, good but not really worth the price, or beautiful smoked salmon, plain or rolled around caviar and crème fraîche — the latter for those who love smoked salmon less.

Excellent main courses were again two duck specialties — a crisply roasted confit on sliced gratinéed potatoes and a rare-roasted breast of duck with winy pickled sour cherries. Equally good was a moist, beautifully sautéed swordfish steak in a beurre blanc sauce brightened with tarragon and parsley. A flaky strudel filled with crab meat and scallops, though excellent, is so rich that it would be better as an appetizer.

Lamb lovers will have a hard time choosing between the rare-roasted rack served with Chinese mustard greens and the chops "in a veil" of caul fat enrobing julienne slivers of vegetables. Braised sweetbreads with wild mushrooms scented with Madeira were more interesting than bland though well-cooked kidneys (when the captain says very pink, he means blood red), and sliced beef tenderloin with butter-soft cloves of garlic could not be improved upon.

Shades of the old Barry Wine are exhibited in an acidic and fishy duck consommé garnished with lobster, in an awful tuna-and-noodle casserole, in which barely heated tuna strips looked like spoiled beef and imparted no flavor to the noodles, and in sweetbreads with braised lettuce in a creamy butter sauce that lacked textural contrast. And his recidivist sweet tooth crops up to inspire a bowl of melon balls with goat cheese in port wine, a sweet and filling appetizer that would be better listed as a dessert. The arrangement was studied, with melon balls and triangles of cheese placed in a geometric pattern that suggested there might be an archeologist in the kitchen reproducing the Stonehenge megaliths in food.

Of the cheeses, only the chèvres were in top condition at two dinners; the others were lifeless. Desserts are superb. A gorgeous madness billed as "the grand dessert," which carries a surcharge, is worth every bit of the price. Included in this heady parade might be four or five of the following: golden summer fruits poached in raspberry eau-de-vie, a burnished mauve sherbet of blueberries and maple syrup topped with fresh berries or a lemony Armagnac sherbet, a miraculous espresso ice cream and hot chocolate sauce fleshed out with a slice of dark, intense flourless chocolate torte, a satiny chocolate mousse, chewy, honeyed pecan squares reminiscent of the Passover candy nougat, and, the least interesting offering, sliced poached peaches with praline ice cream and a somewhat soggy crepe inexplicably wrapped around one of the peach slices. Chocolate-dipped strawberries are passed for those with limitless capacity and a tolerance for that ill-conceived combination.

Those with a penchant for tasting can order "the grand menu," about seven courses for $65 as this book goes to press.

Decent, moderate-priced wines, especially those from California, appear on what is described as a "hi-tech" wine list — neatly typed pages in a metal cover — presenting information clearly and without unnecessary falderal. A 1977 Cabernet Sauvignon was full flavored, satisfying and decently priced. Another good value was a 1970, light, rose-scented Beaune. There is a new dining room upstairs, best suited to private parties, and French moderne washrooms that are knockouts.

Raga

★ ★ ★

57 West 48th Street, between Fifth Avenue and Avenue of the Americas, 757-3450.

Atmosphere: Stunning and romantic Indian décor with comfortable seating and noise level; good service.

Recommended dishes: All first courses except tomato soup, all breads, lobster Malabar, murg tikke makhani, murg Jalfrazie, all tandoori chicken dishes, seekh kebob, gosht do peaza, nargisi kofta, all rice pilafs, eggplant bhurta, stuffed capsicum, masala dal, raita, kulfi, special kheer, gulab jamun, mango and chocolate-cinnamon ice creams.

Price range: Moderately expensive.

Credit cards: All major credit cards.

Hours: Lunch, Mondays through Fridays, noon to 2:45 P.M.; dinner, seven days, September through March, 5:30 P.M. to 11:15 P.M., April through August, 5 P.M. to 10:45 P.M. Dinner only on major holidays.

Reservations: Necessary.

In recent years, Indian food has come to be one of our more fashionable cuisines, served in handsomely decorated, expensive restaurants that are far cries from the murky, tacky holes-in-the-wall we usually had to rely on before that time. Raga was not the first of the stylish and elegant Indian restaurants, but since it opened in January 1977, its tone and cooking have proved to be the most consistent.

Not merely opulent, the interior has great character and originality, with a carved wooden gateway on one wall, tall carved columns that divide the comfortable room into intimate sections, heavy silken fabrics and beautiful antique musical instruments mounted on the walls. At dinner on most evenings, musicians play the sitar, the tabla and the flute, and this is one of the few instances where background music is atmospheric and entertaining without being intrusive. Only the woven striped carpet has worn badly and somewhat destroys the atmosphere of elegance.

Everything else at Raga has improved since the restaurant first opened, and it now is the best of the formal Indian restaurants in the city. Service is prompt and polite and a bit impatient only occasionally at lunch.

There are a number of meat, poultry and seafood specialties broiled in the igloo-shaped stone tandoor or oven. Some of these are served without sauce, pungently seasoned by their bright red, spicy marinades, while in other dishes the tandoor-grilled food is further simmered in complex sauces redolent of ingredients such as onions, ginger, saffron, green herbs and tomato. Seasonings tend to be on the mild side, but to the management's credit, if you ask that food be really hotly spiced, you will be taken at your word.

Most of the appetizers were excellent. Mulligatawny

soup, golden with curry spices and a purée of yellow beans and flecked with bits of chicken, proved to be an exceptional example of that standard soup. Tiny, plump oysters Bombay sautéed with onions and ginger were served in a flared scallop shell, and a ceramic crab ramekin held spicy crab Goa smothered with onions, tomato and spices. Lemon and cucumber added the right accents. Dal papri (a combination of crisp lentil wafers and diced potatoes in a hotly spiced yogurt sauce) and murg ke pakore (bits of chicken dipped in curd batter and fried) came with their own minted yogurt dip.

There is a delicious assortment of hot appetizers large enough for a party of four to share, including nuggets of fried fish, lamb-and-lentil croquettes, and bits of fried chicken and miniature kebobs.

Madras tomato soup, though smooth, soothing and buttery, seemed less inspired than other first courses.

Plain grilled tandoori specialties such as chicken, lamb (ground or in cubes) and the ground chicken reshmi kebobs were invariably excellent at dinner. But at lunch a few times, the boneless chunks of chicken tikke came to the table tepid and dry, as though they had been precooked and reheated to order. Shrimp were invariably overcooked and hard and should probably not be subjected to the tandoor's extreme heat.

Raga excels in its sauces, nowhere more than in lobster Malabar, with chunks of rock lobster smothered in a velvety mantle of onions, tomatoes and ginger. Chicken tikke makhani (bits of tandoori chicken in butter-tomato and herb sauce), and murg Jalfrazie (chicken with spices, peppers and tomatoes), were both expertly prepared and served incendiarily hot when ordered that way.

Ground lamb packed around hard-cooked eggs and braised in golden-brown curry spices (nargisi kofta), and chunks of mild-flavored lamb simmered in a sauce of melted onions topped with whole onion rings lightly simmered in the final sauce (gosht do peaza), both proved exceptional on several tries. So did the spinach-and-spice purée that topped cubes of lamb (gosht palak). Unfortunately, the lamb seemed to have been cooked separately and merely turned through the sauce; as a result, none of the verdant overtones of the spinach permeated the somewhat stringy meat.

Beautiful rice combinations, such as the Kashmiri pilaf, dotted with fruits and nuts, or the mutter pilaf tossed wth green peas or the saffron-gilded rice, all provided savory and substantial bases for the sauces. Vegetable preparations are among the high spots of the Indian kitchen and Raga's are no exception. Try the silken eggplant bhurta that is baked over an open flame, then mashed with sautéed onions or the extraordinary stuffed capsicum — green pepper halves baked with a golden, molten filling of cottage cheese, diced potatoes, peas and spices.

Creamy, bronzed lentil purée (masala dal) and the mint-cooked cucumber and yogurt sauce (raita) were wonderful spooned over rice and topped with chopped, hot, green chilies, raw onions and tomatoes, provided on the relish tray along with mango chutney and the brassy, acidic lemon, lime and lotus-root pickles.

All of the wondrous Indian breads are available on Raga's menu, including the light, crisp puffs of tandoori roti (a pizzalike dough cooked on the sides of the tandoor) and the layered, buttered, whole-wheat partha, plain or filled with potatoes. Onion kulcha, lamb-filled keema nan and the fragile balloon puffs, puris, are all equally irresistible.

Usually, we pass on Indian desserts, but Raga's are delicately light and cool, providing gentle surcease from the exotic spicing of other courses. Kulfi, a cold white and pastel dessert halfway between ice cream and halvah in texture, was aromatic with cardamom and saffron and topped with crushed pistachios and gold threads of sweet rice-paste noodles. Mango or chocolate-cinnamon ice cream were delicious and the very best of the desserts, the special kheer, combined honey, cardamom, fruits, milk and puréed rice in a rich and creamy froth. Gulab jamun — warm, spongy, round pastries in a light honey syrup — were gentle and totally lacking in the cloying sweetness of most Indian pastries. Fresh fruit salad is always on hand, but at times contains unripe melons and an overabundance of apples.

Coffee left something to be desired, but the Darjeeling and spiced teas were lovely. There is full bar service and Indian Eagle brand beer which would be more appreciated if it were served really cold.

Rao's
★ ★ ★

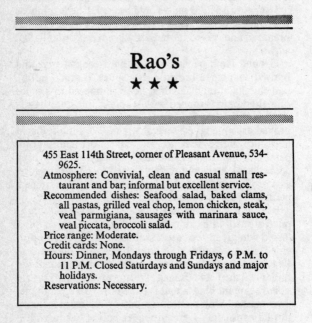

455 East 114th Street, corner of Pleasant Avenue, 534-9625.

Atmosphere: Convivial, clean and casual small restaurant and bar; informal but excellent service.

Recommended dishes: Seafood salad, baked clams, all pastas, grilled veal chop, lemon chicken, steak, veal parmigiana, sausages with marinara sauce, veal piccata, broccoli salad.

Price range: Moderate.

Credit cards: None.

Hours: Dinner, Mondays through Fridays, 6 P.M. to 11 P.M. Closed Saturdays and Sundays and major holidays.

Reservations: Necessary.

A lot has happened to this tiny, unprepossessing corner bar and grill since it first was given three stars in 1977. Set on a corner in the totally devastated neighborhood just behind Benjamin Franklin High School, and with only eight tables to its name, Rao's has become a sort of uptown Elaine's, attracting writers, media and publishing types who go for the offbeat setting and good, lusty Italian food. Included in the scenario of Lieut. David Durk's book "The Pleasant Avenue Connection," dealing with Mafia and drug activities in that neighborhood, Rao's still attracts a local crowd that suggests a movie set based on Durk's book.

In addition to the bar with its year-round Christmas decorations and its thumping juke box, there are some interesting tropical-fish tanks, a handsome old metal ceiling that's golden brown from eighty years of varnishing, and only eight tables. Half of them seat four, while the other half accommodate six to eight, and all are covered with brightly fresh white tablecloths. And against this unpretentious but comfortable backdrop, each evening "from five until ..." as the chef-proprietor, Vincent Rao, puts it, the restaurant serves wonderfully simple, honest and completely delicious Italian food, all prepared strictly alla casalinga — home style.

The service is crisp and efficient. Course by course is the way to order so you can gauge your appetite as the meal progresses and rest as each course is cooked to order. There is no precooking at all here (except for the marinara sauce), which means there are no baked pastas, roasts, stews or rolled, braised meat specialties, although the Raos will prepare such dishes, if ordered a day or two in advance, for groups of six or more.

The best appetizer is the only really expensive dish in the house — seafood salad (also called fish salad), which consists of the tenderest squid and slivered scungilli I've ever tasted, combined with shrimp and lobster meat in a sauce of olive oil and lemon.

Homemade, sweet roasted red peppers, satiny with oil, and baked clams under a mantle of breadcrumbs scented with garlic and oregano are also good choices. There are innumerable shapes of pasta to be had here, generally the imported De Cecco brand, though occasionally a box of Ronzoni slips in. Spaghetti with clam sauce comes topped wtih plenty of scrubbed, fresh clams still in their shells, complemented with garlic, oil and parsley. The marinara is light and faintly perfumed with basil, the nuggets of garlic in the aglio-olio are exactly the right shade of nut brown, and the cream and cheese Alfredo sauce is decent, if not quite a match for the original. In addition, there are homey pastas, such as the short, tubular ditali with peas or beans and tomatoes, and a soup of escarole and white beans that is close to poetic, especially if you flick a little crushed hot red pepper on its surface.

The single most unforgettable main course here is the lemon chicken, for which Vincent Rao would deserve a place in the culinary hall of fame, if such an institution existed. Half-grilled under a red-hot restaurant broiler, the chicken is then turned over and placed in a sizzle pan and topped with lots of lemon juice and olive oil, to form a light, pungent sauce as the top side of the chicken is charred to flaky perfection. A close second is the combination of sautéed chicken, hot sausage, roasted peppers and onions. Crisply breaded veal topped with fresh mozzarella and the light marinara becomes one of the city's best veal parmigianas; the piccata is delicate and lemony; the garlic and fennel sausage is succulent with its tomato-sauce topping, and the grilled steaks are a steal.

So is the marvelous portion of two, thick veal chops so expertly broiled they remain tender and moist. Several salads can be ordered, the best among them being the cold broccoli with oil and lemon. There is usually very fresh fish of the day, always carefully broiled.

There are no desserts at Rao's other than fresh fruit, but it is doubtful that anyone would have room for more. Espresso coffee is hot, dark and strong, and the house gift is a bottle of anisette placed on the table to be poured into the coffee at will.

It is best to go to Rao's by car — parking space is ample and safe. If you go by taxi, the management will call a private car or cab to take you home. Patience is required when making reservations because the place is so small and popular.

Raoul's
Fair

---

180 Prince Street, near Sullivan Street, 966-3518.
Atmosphere: Hectic, noisy, crowded and uncomfortable SoHo bistro; service friendly and efficient or slow and indifferent.
Recommended dishes: Pâté, smoked trout, asparagus vinaigrette, entrecôte, steak au poivre, leg of lamb, banana cake, marquise.
Price range: Moderately expensive.
Credit cards: American Express, MasterCard and Visa.
Hours: Dinner, Sundays through Thursdays, 6:30 P.M. to midnight; Fridays and Saturdays, 6:30 P.M. to 12:30 A.M. Sunday brunch, noon to 3:30 P.M.
Reservations: Recommended.

Raoul's, one of the most popular SoHo haunts, has slipped so much in recent months that I was hard pressed to find a really good dish on the menu. Having maintained a one-star rating since it opened in 1976, this noisy, jammed bistro, with its tin ceiling, poster-filled walls, convivial bar and snug booths, now cannot be rated more than fair.

The problems are food and service. At a recent dinner, red snapper in a saffron cream sauce was so spoiled that it smelled like garbage. When I sent it back, the waiter and then the manager argued about it, saying it was the saffron, not the fish. "The kitchen thinks it's fine," someone in charge said after a ten-minute lapse. Finally, he asked if I would order something else; the replacement, steak au poivre, proved far superior and altogether respectable. When the check came, I discovered a $10 error in my favor. When I told the cashier of the error, he thanked me, but, amazingly enough, he picked up the argument of the spoiled fish, still insisting it had been fine.

Anyone who wants to partake of the casual bonhomie at Raoul's would do well to rely on such appetizers as the decent, if not exceptional, coarse pâté de campagne, smoked trout with bright vegetable salads or asparagus vinaigrette. Snails Polignac are drowned in a muddy mushroom sauce, cream soups taste of raw flour, oysters are too warm, and the sweetbreads in a salad had been held too long in the refrigerator. Beside the steak au poivre, pungent and broiled as ordered, the plain steak pommes frites is a favorite, although the potatoes are unevenly fried and tasteless. Roast leg of lamb, though underseasoned, was rare and tender as ordered. Striped bass was well broiled, but the pasty cucumber sauce obscured its fresh flavor.

Sautéed chicken chasseur and veal with chanterelles tasted like cafeteria food. And mushy calf's liver had a metallic flavor that was not improved by an acidic vinegar sauce.

A dark, moist and spicy banana cake is delicious if you avoid its cloyingly sweet white icing. What is called a marquise is not the usual rectangular, chocolate mousse cake, but rather a layer of génoise sponge cake topped with almonds and filled with custard pastry cream, a pleasant dessert by any name.

Red Tulip
★ ★

439 East 75th Street, between York and First Avenues, 650-0537 or 734-4893.

Atmosphere: Charming Hungarian country setting with folk art; convivial and noisy; slow and inept service.

Recommended dishes: Gulyas, Hungarian sausage, breaded mushrooms, stuffed cabbage, duck, stuffed roast chicken, veal shank, chicken paprikas, grilled trout, veal cutlet with sour cream and palacsinta with poppy seeds or cheese.

Price range: Moderate.

Credit cards: American Express.

Hours: Dinner, Wednesdays through Sundays, 6 P.M. to midnight. Closed Mondays and Tuesdays. Open major holidays.

Reservations: Recommended.

Decorated in what might be termed Hungarian provincial, this lively restaurant provides an enchanting setting with the nostalgic warmth of a far-off Ruritania. The most striking touches come by way of the lavishly carved and painted peasant-style woodwork. Doors are decorated wtih tulip-and-heart motifs to match carved chairs and high-backed booths. Painted antiques hang on walls, and racks close to the dark wood ceiling display floral-patterned pottery, the design of which is repeated on the cornices on other sides of the room. The embroidered red-and-white fabrics used for tablecloths and curtains are said to be antique, and Kazner Kovacs, the owner, notes that he made all of the woodwork himself, a project that took two years.

This is no place for a quiet talk. Go only if you are in a party spirit, for the place is gay, lively, crowded and noisy, the last condition accentuated by musicians (gypsies, what else?) who play violin, bass and the xylophonelike cimbalom (the "c" pronounced as if it were "tz"). It is too bad the music played is not Hungarian. It is a little difficult to get authentic tzigane pathos into "Fascination" or "Bei Mir Bist Du Schoen." That, along with paper napkins, inadequate air-conditioning — which is being adjusted — and slow service are the big flaws.

Although other Hungarian menus in town offer more unusual and innovative dishes, few achieve the consistent level of robustly good cooking that is produced at the Red Tulip. Paprika-burnished gulyas can be had in small portions as a soup or as a main course served from a small copper kettle hanging over what should be a flame. There was no flame and the gulyas could have been hotter, but it was richly scented and flavored with beef, vegetables and the chewy, pinched egg dumplings, scipetke.

The best stuffed cabbage I have ever had in a restaurant was here, too — meaty filling, firm but tender cabbage on a bed of sauerkraut that gave a piquant edge to the tomato-and-sour-cream sauce. This, too, can be ordered as an appetizer or as a main course.

Crisp and savory breaded mushrooms and the grilled Hungarian Debrecen sausage with mustard and horseradish were knockouts among appetizers. Sour cherry soup should have been colder and winier and less aromatic with cinnamon.

Very good main courses included a crackling, greaseless half-duck with caraway-flavored red cabbage, creamy, soothing chicken paprikas with the same pinched dumplings, braised veal steak in a pleasant sour cream sauce, and a wonderfully golden brown, braised veal shank. Pan-fried veal, somewhat like a stew, was undistinguished, and, in fact, is being dropped from the menu. Fortunately, the firm, perfectly grilled trout and the roast chicken with an herb-scented bread and chicken-liver stuffing will remain.

Try to ignore the ubiquitous iceberg lettuce used for salad and, as an unnecessary and costly garnish, ignore the tartar sauce made with mayonnaise, wine and lemon, which tasted disturbingly like Miracle Whip. The best desserts were the folded crepes, palacsinta, filled with poppy seeds or cheese. Other desserts were disappointing, as was the grainy, tasteless chestnut pâté and the chocolate mousse cake Rigo Jancsi topped with unreal-looking whipped cream. Two interesting wines were the dry, gold-colored Tokay Szamorodni and the red Egri Bikaver (Bull's Blood).

Regine's
Poor

502 Park Avenue, between 59th and 60th Streets, 826-0990.

Atmosphere: Dramatic and glittery mirrored supper-club setting with adjoining discothèque; chairs are uncomfortable and many tables are badly placed. Staff is pretentious, rude and inefficient.

Recommended dishes: None.

Price range: Expensive.

Credit cards: All major credit cards.

Hours: Lunch, Mondays through Fridays, noon to 3:30 P.M.; dinner, Mondays through Saturdays, 6 P.M. to midnight. Closed Sundays.

Reservations: Necessary.

In seven years of reviewing, I have never come across service and food that have been so consistently poor as that found at Regine's, the well-known Park Avenue discothèque and restaurant. Regine's would be considered beneath serious criticism were it not such a highly visible restaurant garnering much publicity from its fashionable clientele and from its former connections with the talented French chef Michel Guerard, who used to be the consultant to this New York branch of Regine's Paris original.

I encountered rudeness and overbearing pretentiousness starting with the man who guards the door right through to checkroom employees who are insolent about the mandatory but unposted checkroom charge and to the maître d'hôtel, captains and waiters.

Arriving with a confirmed reservation for four on a crowded Saturday night, we were met by a maître d'hôtel who said with exasperation, "Oh, I don't know where I'm going to seat you. We're inundated with royalty tonight." Then, in a stage whisper to a captain, he continued, "The king will be here at midnight with six bodyguards."

We four commoners were finally seated at an extended table for two, leaving two of us out in an aisle where chairs were kicked every few minutes. It seemed to take forever to place orders for food and wine and even longer to get what we had ordered. When the captain asked how dinner had been and we indicated it had not been very good, he shrugged and said, "Well, you can't fight City Hall."

The menu opens with desserts because, as a message signed by the hostess says, she is especially proud of that course. But twice we were refused soufflés, once as soon as we ordered because the captain said the chef would make none that night, a second time five minutes after our orders were taken when the captain announced that the soufflé oven was broken. Persisting, we got the soufflés at a third dinner, but the oven may still have been out of whack because not one of the four stodgy and flavorless creations had risen.

Spoiled mussels and stale salmon were only two flaws at a lunch that included many. A mountain of soupy fettuccine with cream and ham tasted like a packaged macaroni-and-cheese dinner, and a shrimp dish arrived in a lobster sauce that could have been achieved with canned lobster bisque. When I complained of slow service, an unshaven captain said: "Well, madame, if you knew how to order properly from a captain instead of from waiters, perhaps you would get things promptly."

On slow nights, staff members stand around in deep conversation, ignoring diners, sipping wine, and non-celebrities are often shown to the worst tables, even when not a single table is occupied. At one dinner we tried to order a fish course, asking to share one of the main course seafoods between appetizer and meat. We were told that could only be done if we paid for an extra complete dinner.

In the course of four recent visits, during which all appetizers and desserts and most of the main courses were tried, I did not find a single dish worth recommending. Shrimp in avocado tasted of iodine, vegetables in an aspic terrine were flavorless, scrambled eggs had been overcooked before being topped with caviar, and quenelles were rubbery on two occasions. The raw beef carpaccio was dark around the edges on one visit, indicating staleness, and on another it was still encrusted with splinters of ice. A metallic flavor overpowered both the duck liver pâté and the hot mussel soup, billi-bi. Smoked salmon, though passable, was hardly worth the surcharge on the dinner.

The most depressing dessert was puff pastry with unripe strawberries. The pastry looked like flaked wet Uneeda Biscuits and the minted cream tasted like toothpaste.

Note: The appointment of a new chef has been announced. Let's hope the change will be for the better.

René Pujol

★

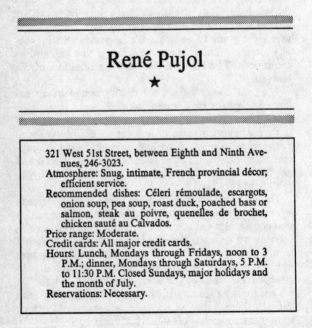

321 West 51st Street, between Eighth and Ninth Avenues, 246-3023.

Atmosphere: Snug, intimate, French provincial décor; efficient service.

Recommended dishes: Céleri rémoulade, escargots, onion soup, pea soup, roast duck, poached bass or salmon, steak au poivre, quenelles de brochet, chicken sauté au Calvados.

Price range: Moderate.

Credit cards: All major credit cards.

Hours: Lunch, Mondays through Fridays, noon to 3 P.M.; dinner, Mondays through Saturdays, 5 P.M. to 11:30 P.M. Closed Sundays, major holidays and the month of July.

Reservations: Necessary.

René Pujol is a pleasant, moderately priced French restaurant convenient to the theater district. If its cooking is less than brilliant, it is at least dependably decent, and the menu offers a range of satisfying, if traditional, choices.

The setting is cozily provincial, although the low ceilings make for noisiness when the place is full, as it usually is during pre-theater hours. The service is courteous and prompt.

Appetizers are unusually good here, beginning with the giveaway pâté, rilettes de Tours, a smooth, unctuously rich spread of pork simmered to spreadability in its own fat. Coarse pâté de campagne is acceptable, if too mildly seasoned. The céleri rémoulade is fresh, crisp and with a brassy mustard tang to its sauce, and plump snails, served not in shells but in fitted dishes, are all they should be. Not so the special clams with almonds, with their pasty cream-sauce topping.

Two soups sampled recently were all well above average. The onion had the right golden-brown onion flavor, the watercress was verdant and peppery, and the Vichyssoise had the perfect consistency of heavy cream and actually tasted of leeks and not of starch, as it all too often does.

Crisp roasted duck with a bitter orange sauce, poached bass or salmon with lobster or hollandaise sauce, and a mellow yet fiery steak au poivre were my favorite main courses. Beef bourguignonne had a sauce that looked as richly dark as hot fudge and which was delicious, but the beef itself was dry and the flavor of the sauce had not penetrated, a similar flaw with the coq au vin. Quenelles de brochet had an excellent fresh fish flavor although they were a bit heavier than they should have been, and a daily special of roast lamb was done to the right tone of pinkness and included the proper subtle hint of garlic. Poulet sauté au Calvados, the tender chicken sautéed and dressed with a cream sauce subtly spiked with apple brandy, was also soothing and satisfying. Pastry was soggy on steamy beef Wellington, a dish the world should have forgotten by now.

Boiled potatoes are properly dry here and vegetables and salads are fair. Desserts, however, are disappointing. Cheeses are invariably dried out and shriveled, and homemade fruit tarts usually have slightly soggy crusts. Crème caramel and napoleon are good choices.

Restaurant Raphaël

★

33 West 54th Street, between Fifth Avenue and Avenue of the Americas, 582-8993.

Atmosphere: Comfortable, small and luxurious chateau setting; excellent service.

Recommended dishes: Fricassee of snails, steamed duck foie gras, lobster velouté, rack of lamb, duck breast with ginger, sautéed salmon, beef with shallots and marrow, goat cheese in olive oil, chocolate mousse, grapefruit sherbet.

Price range: Expensive.

Credit cards: American Express, Diners Club and Carte Blanche.

Hours: Lunch, Mondays through Fridays, noon to 2 P.M.; dinner, Mondays through Fridays, 6 P.M. to 9:30 P.M. Closed Saturdays and Sundays.

Reservations: Necessary.

When the tiny and luxurious Restaurant Raphaël opened four years ago, it was a leading outpost of the prettiest and most engaging examples of nouvelle cuisine. Though the very private and quiet charm of this intimate restaurant has remained intact, recent visits indicate that the food is not quite as good as it once was, nor are the dishes on the new menu as interesting as those on the original. With prices going higher, the kitchen's gradual decline over the past two years makes it necessary to cut the original two-star rating to one.

Raphaël Edery, the owner, and his wife, Mira, still maintain a gracious and restful atmosphere in this chateaulike setting, and the extended dining room now opens onto a leafy pocket-sized garden where drinks can be served before meals.

The consistent flaws in the food are the lack of authoritative flavor and a tendency to oversalt. A few dishes that are still very good include the delicate lobster velouté, a soup rippled with crème fraîche, the gently warm foie gras of duck appetizer, and a subtle fricassee of snails mellowed with truffle-and-morel-perfumed cream. But the once-excellent terrine of vegetables is now mushy and lacks salt, and the decent terrine of duck is ruined by a sweet-sour sauce of pickled strawberries. A pungent blend of crème fraîche and sour cream overpowers the clear, light flavor of raw scallops. And although the tarragon-flavored lobster sauce on green seafood-filled ravioli was delicious, the filling was meager and the pasta undistinguished.

Steamed scallops served with spinach tasted as pallid as they looked, and grilled striped bass tasted of petroleum. Salmon, however, was delicately sautéed and freshly moist. Meat and poultry main courses that still showed some of the original excellence were the rare roasted duck breast, magret de canard, burnished with ginger and the miraculously tender steamed rack of lamb scented with sage. Sliced rare beef with a satiny shallot and marrow sauce, though decent, was less distinguished than the duck or lamb. Greens in a salad had not been dried and so shed their dressing. Crottin de chavignol, an earthy goat cheese, took on luster in its olive-oil marinade.

It would be hard to surpass the grapefruit sherbet for freshness, and those with richer tastes should find solace in the velvety bitter chocolate mousse. Other desserts were disappointing. A 20 percent service charge is automatically added to checks, although the practice is not mentioned on the menu. Payment of that 20 percent, however, is optional and the amount will be altered on request.

Rio de Janeiro/ Boat 57 Seafood House

★ ★

41 West 57th Street, between Fifth Avenue and Ave-
-nue of the Americas, 935-1232.
Atmosphere: Modern, tropical, pleasant and noisy; service is slow but friendly.
Recommended dishes: Clams in garlic sauce, Portuguese sausage, Portuguese clam chowder, broiled salt codfish, mariscadas, lobster à Portuguesa, chicken à bossa velha, filet mignon with fried egg, steak with sliced onions, seafood salads, flan, pasteis de nata (custard tarts), coconut custard.
Price range: Moderate.
Credit cards: American Express, MasterCard and Visa.
Hours: Lunch, Mondays through Saturdays, noon to 5 P.M.; dinner, Mondays through Thursdays, 5 P.M. to 11:30 P.M.; Fridays and Saturdays, 5 P.M. to midnight. Sunday buffet, noon to 10 P.M. Closed major holidays.
Reservations: Generally necessary.

Despite its ridiculously schizophrenic name, Rio de Janeiro/Boat 57 Seafood House provides a most pleasant, all-round Brazilian dining experience. If details of the décor, such as the green-and-white-tropical-leaf-pattern wallpaper in the dining room, are fairly undistinguished, the overall effect, at least, is pleasantly bright and spacious, and noise is kept at a comfortable level. The staff could not be more friendly or sincerely concerned, and one is quite willing to forgo a certain slick professionalism for their obvious good will and desire to please.

If there is any problem with the setup it is that portions are huge, and each course comes with several garnishes, all much too much for the rather small tabletops to accommodate.

For a change, go Brazilian and start your meal with cachaça, the white, potent firewater made of sugar cane, best served with clear, emerald lime juice and ice in the drink known as a caipirinha, after the mountain hillbillies of Brazil.

There are several enticing appetizers at Rio de Janeiro, among them a house giveaway placed on the table when drinks are ordered: fried slices of peppery Portuguese sausage offset by sharp green and oily ripe black olives and with an Italian-style pickled vegetables giardiniere. Those game for still another appetizer would do well to consider fresh clams steamed in a hot chili oil and garlic sauce, or a seafood salad of marinated squid, shrimp and scallops. An avocado stuffed with tiny shrimp was ample and colorfully presented, although the filling lacked distinction.

All of the soups are unusual, and two were excellent — the Portuguese national soup, caldo verde, a thick, steaming combination of puréed potatoes, chopped kale and dicings and slicings of sausage, and a Portuguese clam chowder in a mildly fiery tomato soup. Shrimp soup, also in a tomato base, tasted stale and fishy.

The Brazilian national bean and mixed meat stew, feijoada, is served Wednesdays and Saturdays and is the most extraordinary dish on the menu. Various cuts of pork, sausages, sun-cured salted beef and earthy black beans are simmered to melting tenderness, all spooned over snowy steamed rice and garnished with chopped kale, hot sauce, diced fresh oranges and a sprinkling of manioc flour. The only problem with the feijoada is the staggering size of the portion.

Codfish, fresh or salt-dried, are also standbys in both Brazil and Portugal and are well represented here. Broiled fresh codfish steak is thick, moist and perfectly cooked, while dried cod is simmered under a tomato and onion sauce sparked with hot chili oil and rimmed with homemade mashed potatoes. This same spicy tomato-onion sauce, with the addition of wine and with the onions a bit firm, does wonders for bife acebolada, a delicious steak, and for shrimp Rio de Janeiro. Other well-prepared shrimp dishes include the Nazaré, grilled and fried with chili pepper oil, and cascais crisply fried in egg batter. Tender squid Nazaré (in hot sauce), a special on Tuesday, and lobster, perfectly grilled and served with lemon butter and hearts of palm, or à Portuguesa, in a tomato sauce with mussels, clams, scallops and shrimps, were all beautifully cooked. So was the chicken à bossa velha, fried golden brown in olive oil with cracklings of garlic.

In addition to a bland, textureless bread, there were a few other important flaws at Rio de Janeiro, all with meat dishes.

One of Portugal's best and least likely dishes — loin of pork à Alentejana — clams in the shells steamed with cubed pork, tomatoes and coriander — was ruined by hard, tough cubes of meat, which should have been simmered longer and more slowly to tenderness. Iscas à Lisboeta, at its most authentic, sparkling fresh liver marinated in red wine, then braised, here had the rough texture, dryness and overpowering metallic taste of beef liver that has been frozen.

Churrasco à Gaucho, a marinated broiled steak, was full of flavor but slightly tough, although the rice, manioc farofa and sausage with it were fine. Steak à Portuguesa in red wine tasted all right, but again was tough. But picadinho à Brasilia, a fried-egg-topped, ground-meat cross between chili and hash, was soothing and satisfying.

Side orders of broccoli in garlic sauce would have been better had the broccoli not been overcooked, but leaf spinach, with bits of ham and melted cheese topping, was delicious. Black beans with rice are served with virtually every dish.

Desserts include one of the best homemade flan custards in the city, a refreshing coconut pudding and those delectable tiny custard tart morsels, pasteis de nata, encrusted with cinnamon sugar.

Strawberries à Sintra, in what seemed to be a combination of white wine and a hint of brandy, were also cool, clear and refreshing. Guava desserts, either with cheese or with ice cream, like Rio de Janeiro Scotch sundae custard, were less interesting than their descriptions promised.

The Brazilian beer, Brahma, was at first subtle and bracing when it was icy cold, but its flavor cloyed and became thick on the tongue as the beer warmed. The Portuguese wine, Dão, was a far better choice. Brazilian coffee was properly dark, strong and hot.

Ristorante Toscana
★

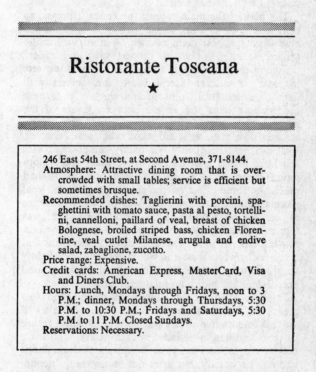

246 East 54th Street, at Second Avenue, 371-8144.
Atmosphere: Attractive dining room that is over-crowded with small tables; service is efficient but sometimes brusque.
Recommended dishes: Taglierini with porcini, spaghettini with tomato sauce, pasta al pesto, tortellini, cannelloni, paillard of veal, breast of chicken Bolognese, broiled striped bass, chicken Florentine, veal cutlet Milanese, arugula and endive salad, zabaglione, zucotto.
Price range: Expensive.
Credit cards: American Express, MasterCard, Visa and Diners Club.
Hours: Lunch, Mondays through Fridays, noon to 3 P.M.; dinner, Mondays through Thursdays, 5:30 P.M. to 10:30 P.M.; Fridays and Saturdays, 5:30 P.M. to 11 P.M. Closed Sundays.
Reservations: Necessary.

It is more disappointing to come across a restaurant that is a near miss than it is to encounter a total failure. A case in point has always been Toscana, an Italian restaurant that would almost certainly be worth two stars if the dining room and kitchen were operated with a little more care and discipline. Everything about this place indicates a certain laxity on the part of management, which is too bad because the dining room is plush and private in feeling and the kitchen, which now produces food that averages out to be decently good, shows just enough flashes of excellence to indicate considerable capability.

The simple, white dining room with its white silk curtains and velvety brown upholstery can be restful and appealing. Tables are unfortunately too small for comfortable eating. And though the staff is less overbearing than it was in years past, there is still a certain distracted note to the service.

As for the food, most pastas were excellent, whether we tried the fettuccine in a creamy sauce topped with shavings of porcini mushrooms, the thin spaghettini with a light tomato sauce or linguine al pesto that was just a bit dry. The less said about the cold version of this dish, the better. Cannelloni with a spinach-and-chicken filling in a cream-pink Bolognese-style sauce, and the tortellini in a buttery cheese and prosciutto sauce were delicious. Pasta primavera, however, is merely buttered thin pasta topped with boiled vegetables.

It's a good idea to choose pasta for a first course, as appetizers are much less appealing. Well-seasoned baked clams had a bread-crumb topping that became overdone and dry, and cold antipasto was a mushy mess of dried salami and prosciutto, with half a shrimp smeared with cocktail sauce.

The plainer the main course, the better it proved to be. Paillard of veal and moist, snowy, broiled striped bass were the best main courses. A fried veal cutlet Milanese needed salt but was properly crisp and tender.

Two of the satisfying, if not brilliant, specialties were the sautéed chicken breast Florentine, served with lightly sautéed fresh spinach, and chicken Bolognese sandwiching ham and cheese between layers of the white breast meat. Spinach accompanied the second chicken dish also, as it did most other main courses. Veal of fine, pale quality was overly complicated with artichoke hearts and mushrooms to make the scaloppine Toscana, and much the same preparation had much the same effect on the chicken Gioconda. Veal piccata, though well seasoned, was pasty. Mignonettes of beef, served in a thick filmy Barolo wine sauce, was topped with cold, uncooked marrow — in other words, raw fat. Heavily sautéed scallops al vino bianco showed no traces of white wine and were overdone and slightly tough. Throughout, top-quality ingredients were used but all deserved more careful preparation.

Fried zucchini could have been crisper and less greasy and once was sandy. But a fresh, icy salad of arugula and endive slivers was perfect, as was a rather hefty zabaglione, well laced with Marsala. Chocolate cake, from Délices La Côte Basque, was dark, moist and rich on one try, but dried out on another. Zucotto, the cream-filled cake that is usually chocolate flavored, here was like a soft cassata, but was delicious.

River Café

★

1 Water Street, Brooklyn, 522-5200.

Atmosphere: Spectacular view of New York skyline from a dining room that might be found on a luxury yacht, with high noise level and inadequate lighting; service polite but disorganized and slow.

Recommended dishes: Sturgeon with quail's eggs, oysters with sea urchins, steamed clams with periwinkles, wild mushrooms in puff pastry, artichokes with goat cheese, poached salmon trout, pheasant with cornbread dressing, rack of lamb, saddle of veal, fillet of beef with thyme sauce, strawberries, chocolate marquise cake.

Price range: Expensive.

Credit cards: American Express, Diners Club and Carte Blanche.

Hours: Lunch, Mondays through Fridays, noon to 2:30 P.M.; dinner, Sundays through Thursdays, 6:30 P.M. to 10:30 P.M.; Fridays and Saturdays, 7 P.M. to 11 P.M.; brunch, Saturdays and Sundays, noon to 3 P.M.

Reservations: Necessary.

A view of New York from atop one of its taller buildings is an experience as breathtaking as it is famous. What is perhaps less widely appreciated, but no less captivating, is a view of the city at water level. Anyone who doubts that should take an evening off and spend it at the River Café, firmly planted on a solidly based barge on the Brooklyn side of the East River and nestled in the shadow of the Brooklyn Bridge at the Fulton Ferry landing. The cafe-restaurant offers an incomparable view of Lower Manhattan and the river, with Coast Guard cutters, Circle Line excursion boats, sailboats, tugs and tankers passing by almost close enough to be touched.

Depending on the direction one is facing, there is a postcard view of the Statue of Liberty or the garlands of lights that outline the East River bridges. The most magical time of all is dusk, when it is still light enough to see details of ships, streets and buildings yet dark enough to give lights a golden, sparkling meaning, and there are two charming outdoor deck verandas for extra-clear viewing.

The interior of the cafe, with its porthole rear windows and riverfront glass wall, is simply and glowingly done up like the dining room of an elegant yacht, with creamy white walls, pale silken lampshades on tables and, here and there, nosegays of flowers spotlighted from above. The bar is dramatically set so that guests face out across the river. Window tables are the prizes, of course, but it is impossible to get confirmed reservations for them. On one visit, several window tables were empty, but we were told ungraciously that they were "for friends of the owner."

Ear-splitting noise and inadequate lighting mar the beauty of the setting, especially at peak hours, when piano music compounds the cacophony. Moreover, the service is a variation on the old army game of "hurry up and wait" — only here the process is reversed to "wait and hurry up." Time lapses between courses can be agonizing, and the management sometimes offers wine as an apology. Once the food arrives, the staff hovers around, snatching plates away and pressing slow eaters to hurry.

The chef is imaginative and talented, but the results of his efforts are disappointingly uneven. He buys such unusual and excellent products as smoked salmon from Bellingham Bay in Washington, briny periwinkles for fish soups and sauces, quails' eggs to garnish sturgeon, pungent goat cheese, which is baked atop braised artichoke bottoms, and tender New Jersey pheasants, which he nests on cornbread dressing.

California miner's lettuce, a wild green with the pleasantly aromatic flavor of lightly mentholated cabbage, and steamed green cattails were interesting and much like woody asparagus.

Some of this food turns out to be delicious, and it is possible to choose a two-star meal. But too many dishes arrive tepid or downright cold, and there are a number of misguided combinations in every course. That silky smoked salmon, for instance, hardly needs a mushy smoked-salmon-mousse filling, and the smoked shrimp turned salty with caviar, were tough when served plain and were musty as the basis of a bisque. Mushrooms were misplaced in a thick, overly peppery tomato-based clam chowder.

Terrine of game proved far too sweet, but both cheese-topped artichoke and wild mushrooms in puff pastry were lovely appetizers. So were steamed clams in buttery broth with periwinkles and poached Belon oysters sparked with sea urchins.

A stew of Eastern fish was a mess, however, bitter in an overconcentrated, soupy green-herb sauce. Claw meat of lobster steamed over seaweed was soft and characterless as custard, and it was chilled by cold herb-butter sauce. But poached salmon trout with lobster sauce was delicious.

A sticky molasses glaze destroyed the flavor of Muscovy duck. Filet of veal saddle could not have been snowier or more tender (or colder). Rack of lamb was far better than lamb in a crust turned soggy by spinach, and filet of beef, glossed with thyme-scented sauce, was among the best choices.

Steamed snow peas were firmer and brighter than a limp "compote" of vegetables. A galette of white and sweet potatoes was stodgy and undistinguished. Pastries are flashed briefly to prompt quick choices, but of those tried, only a velvety bitter-chocolate marquise cake with coffee-cream sauce was worthwhile. Beautiful ripe strawberries are served with two sauces, Grand Marnier cream being more appropriate than bitter chocolate. Italian wines are the only good buys on the illegible list.

The River Café is a difficult spot to get to without a car (parking space is ample) — even if you arrive by taxi, you will hardly find one waiting to take you back. It is possible to take the A train to High Street and walk seven blocks to the restaurant, an interesting stroll through a colorful area in daylight but a somewhat awesome trek after dark.

R. J. Scotty's
Fair

202 Ninth Avenue, between 22nd and 23rd Streets, 741-2148.

Atmosphere: Convivial and casual pub-tavern with copper pans, stained glass panels and plants; bar scene is lively and service is good-natured, if absent-minded.

Recommended dishes: Steamed mussels, fettuccine Alfredo, linguine with clam sauce, spaghetti aglio-olio, linguine Scotty's, sole piccata, chicken oreganata, cappuccino.

Price range: Moderate.

Credit cards: American Express, MasterCard and Visa.

Hours: Lunch, Mondays through Fridays, noon to 5 P.M.; dinner, seven days, 5 P.M. to 1 A.M.; brunch, Saturdays and Sundays, 10 A.M. to 4 P.M. Closed on Christmas Day only.

Reservations: Suggested.

Dark wood, stained glass and old copper pans set the tone at R. J. Scotty's, and the young staff is friendly, if somewhat inept and forgetful. Beef and veal are of poor quality, but pasta and fish dishes are good. The house triumph is the steamed mussels, one of the best buys around. A big bowl of plump, fresh mussels steamed in a garlic and tomato broth makes a wonderfully satisfying main course or a shared appetizer.

Fettuccine Alfredo, linguine with clam sauce and spaghetti aglio-olio — garlic and oil — are also above average. Linguine Scotty's is a rich combination of mussels, squid and other seafood on a mound of pasta so enormous it seems doubtful that one person could finish it; the brothlike sauce is lovely, and the dish easily serves two. Sole piccata had a pungent lemon sauce.

Salads of iceberg lettuce are awful, as are vegetables, soups and cakes. Chicken gets better treatment, especially when sautéed in boneless chunks, oreganata style. Hamburgers and lunch omelets are acceptable, but the chili, under a gummy cheese topping, seemed to be all beans and salt.

Cappuccino, with a snow peak of whipped cream and a generous dusting of cinnamon, was the best dessert.

Ruc

★

312 East 72nd Street, between First and Second Avenues, 650-1611.

Atmosphere: Redecorated dining room is pleasantly bright and informal; large, tiered garden is one of the city's most pleasant. Service is perfunctory and often slow.

Recommended dishes: Ham salad, all soups, roast duck, roast chicken, roast veal shank, boiled beef with dill sauce, Wiener schnitzel, breaded calf's brains, bread dumplings, red cabbage, apricot dumplings, palacinky.

Price range: Moderate.

Credit cards: All major credit cards.

Hours: Dinner, Mondays through Fridays, 5 P.M. to 11 P.M.; Saturdays and Sundays, noon to 11 P.M.

Reservations: Necessary.

As soon as summer approaches, thoughts of New Yorkers inevitably turn to garden restaurants. For twenty years, one of the most beguiling has been the large, informal, somewhat Bohemian setting tucked away behind Ruc, the modestly priced Czechoslovak restaurant.

The tiered garden seems fresher and even more engaging than before, and a glass-enclosed garden has been created between the front dining room and the great outdoors, allowing those who prefer the breezes of an air-conditioner to have a view of the outdoor garden. The dining room itself is brightly attractive, with schmaltzy but decorative folkloric paintings. Service remains perfunctory and uneven. Reservations are taken, but seating is first come, first served, and it would be more straightforward not to take them at all.

The kitchen's level of performance seems to have gone down slightly in recent years, but enough good dishes remain to warrant a one-star rating, especially when one considers the amazingly low prices at Ruc (which is pronounced to rhyme with book).

Oddly enough, the paprika-and-sour-cream-sauced stew dishes, such as goulash and chicken paprikash, are disappointing, even though they are what one would expect to be acceptable at low prices. Instead, it is the crisp, roast half-duck, the fresh and generous portion of roast chicken and the braised veal shank that are preferable. Boiled beef suffers somewhat from being sliced far in advance, but it is saved by a pungent dill cream sauce. The Wiener schnitzel, though hardly made of first-class veal, is satisfying, and so are the breaded, fried calf's brains.

Main courses such as the dreary, overcooked stuffed cabbage, the dry and contorted veal steak à la Ruc and the oversteamed, stringy smoked loin of pork were among the poorer dishes.

Complete dinners begin with soup and the kitchen does a very good job on it, whether the day's choice is beef consommé with spätzle-type dumplings or with peppery liver dumplings, or lentil soup with frankfurters. The cream of giblet and vegetable soup would be better if it were thinner, but even so a dash of salt and pepper make it palatable. Except for a pleasant, creamy ham salad that fills a tomato, à la carte appetizers are not worth their price.

Big, airy bread dumplings are served with most main courses and are much better than the greasy, flat-tasting potatoes. Hot sauerkraut and sweet-and-sour red cabbage can be fine when freshly cooked, as they usually are on weekends, or mushy when reheated on slow weeknights. That is generally true of other dishes. Cucumber salad and pickled beets are livelier than other salads.

Well-made palacinky crepes filled with apricot jam, and apricot dumplings with a creamed-cheese topping, are the best desserts. Skip wine in favor of Pilsner Urquell beer and, for openers, try the fiery prune brandy, slivovitz.

Russian Tea Room
★ ★

150 West 57th Street, between Seventh Avenue and Avenue of the Americas, 265-0947.
Atmosphere: Big, glowing musical-comedy Russian, popular with music and theater personalities; service is sometimes good, often bad.
Recommended dishes: Hot cabbage borscht, herrings, blini, pirojok, red caviar, sirniki, cheese blinchiki, omelets, Caucasian shashlik, Karsky shashlik, chicken Kiev, côtelette de volaille, roast duck, sautéed calf's liver.
Price range: Moderately expensive.
Credit cards: All major credit cards.
Hours: Lunch, seven days, 11:30 A.M. to 4 P.M.; dinner, seven days, 4:30 P.M. to 9:30 P.M.; supper, seven days, 11:30 P.M. to 12:30 A.M. Open on all major holidays.
Reservations: Recommended.

All too often, a decorating job on a supremely comfortable interior means that its particular brand of magic is destroyed as new glitter replaces the mellow patina of age. Fortunately, no such disaster has befallen this festive landmark. Although some obvious changes have been made in recent years, for the most part one is hard pressed to recognize exactly which features account for its new, broad spaciousness and livelier, brighter look.

Three additions are improvements. A carpet has been added over what were bare hard floors, and an acoustical ceiling has been installed to cut the noise level to a more comfortably muffled pitch, although the ceiling is a bit too light in color. The previous deep-pink tone was perhaps preferable, though the new tone is much improved when the lights are dimmed. In addition, the bar has been cut in half to make room for an extra curved banquette in this cafe entrance, and marble, brass and polished mahogany give this area considerable style.

The same pine-green walls, pink cloths, cranberry-glass hurricane lamps, the mixmatch of paintings, the brilliantly polished brass samovars and the glittering Christmas-tree tinsel and ornaments combine to create an atmosphere that is still *uyutno* — about as close as the Russian language comes to that particular homey charm the Germans describe as *gemütlich*.

The same convivial clientele crowds this dining room at all hours of the day — perhaps the most colorful after theater when it is favored by personalities from the theater and music worlds, and most especially, it seems, stand-up comics.

Considering the general air of conviviality and the mellow afterglow of the iced pepper vodka or the amber-colored, aged vodka, starka, it is more difficult than usual to retain objectivity here in evaluating the food. But if one does, the whole is bound to add up to more than the sum of the parts. For although the Russian Tea Room consistently turns out some excellent specialties, it is equally consistent in the mediocrity of other dishes.

Among its triumphs is the hot cabbage borscht, perfumed with dill, thick with vegetables, rosy with tomatoes and beets and enriched with a cloudlet of sour cream. Unfortunately, the soup is not always steamingly hot as it should be.

Herrings here are superb, with the silky, raw red maatjes having the slightest edge over the pickled schmaltz herring in sour cream. Blini, those light, grainy buckwheat crepes served with fresh red caviar and sour cream, are ethereally delicious, although one cannot help wishing that there was enough caviar and cream to fill the seven crepes served. Try as we might, we could not stretch the supply beyond five blini.

Pirojok, the flaky puff-pastry packets of mildly seasoned meat filling, are almost always crisp and savory — only occasionally soggy and leaden. The appetizer of mushrooms à la grecque is fresh and properly piquant.

Fresh red caviar was perfect and honey soft, and only mildly saline three out of four tries. The fourth time it was hard, dry and too salty, as though it had been left out uncovered too long.

Sirniki, delicate cheese pancakes served as a main course at brunch or lunch, were wonderful, lightly sprinkled with sugar and topped with sour cream. The blinchiki, thin rolled crepes, were equally good when filled with cheese, but fruit variations were too cloyingly sweet. Omelets are well made and especially good with caviar fillings and are favorites midday or at late supper.

Whether one tries the Caucasian shashlik of marinated spring lamb broiled on a skewer with onions and tomatoes, or the more elegant karsky shashlik, a filet of lamb with kidneys, one is bound to be more than minimally satisfied. Crisply breaded boneless breast of chicken Kiev, rolled around a potential fountain of butter, and côtelette de volaille, a breast of chicken stuffed with minced chicken then breaded and fried, are among the consistently best offerings. Well-roasted duck with a winy, slightly vinegary cherry sauce and fresh, tender, impeccably sautéed calf's liver are also dependably excellent.

Among the homemade desserts the best are the Russian cream that is halfway between vanilla ice cream and whipped cream, the chocolate glazed boats of almond pastry (lodichka); the turban of sponge cake filled with custard (charlottka) and the delicate baklava with its honey sauce.

If the above dishes made up the entire menu at the Tea Room, this restaurant would easily rate three stars. Unfortunately, the remaining half of the menu ranges from poor to fair. One of the big flaws is sweetness where none belongs — most notably in the eggplant orientale, an appetizer that tastes more like tomato sauce than eggplant. Cold beet borscht, although nicely garnished with crisp cucumber and fresh dill, was so sweet it took the juice of half a lemon to give it even a hint of the tangy, winy quality it should have had. Two soups were awful — a pea soup that was watery both in taste and texture, and a vegetable soup with dumplings that contained (at least in my portion) nothing but carrots.

Roszolnik, a personal favorite that is a creamy soup made with chicken giblets, cucumbers and other vegetables, here was bland and starchy and contained no giblets at all — only wings and necks.

Two Georgian specialties on this menu were total failures — one, a chicken tabaka, is supposed to be pressed flat, highly seasoned with garlic and pepper then fried so parchment crisp that its bones can be eaten. The version here was more like a braised chicken, and the plum sauce served with it lacked the chili pepper, fresh coriander and garlic counterpoints it traditionally has. Chakhobili, another Georgian chicken dish, came as two wing joints, a drumstick and a small piece of breast in a bland, underspiced tomato sauce with onions, again lacking the herbaceous, hearty wallop this dish packs at its most authentic.

Blandness was also the flaw with the otherwise good, fresh chopped chicken livers and the calf's foot aspic, kholodetz.

The buckwheat groats, kasha, served only when requested, turned out to be hard, dry and greasy, and the pojarsky cutlets of ground veal and chicken were ruined by a banal, brown mushroom gravy. Lula kebobs, the ground lamb broiled on skewers, were pink, moist and succulent on one try, but too dense and dry on another. A main course of mushrooms à la Russe au gratin was tasteless, mostly because the insipid American mushrooms lack the flavor to carry this dish. The Russian mushrooms with their earthy, antique savor have the body this simple preparation requires. And the beef stroganoff was minimally acceptable and far from inspired.

Kasha à la Gourieff, usually a pleasantly warm and soothing dessert pudding of semolina, was served red hot with canned peaches on top, an altogether dreadful conclusion to a heavy meal. And surely in a Russian restaurant one has the right to expect pumpernickel with more grain and body than that served here, especially when several examples are readily available in New York.

Service is generally friendly, if informal, and occasionally slapdash. At one lunch I had a waitress who spilled soup and pushed my hands aside so she could serve, and at another I was asked to contribute my salt sticks to a table that had none.

Sahib
★ ★

222 East 86th Street, between Second and Third Avenues, 535-6760.

Atmosphere: Trim, attractive, modern setting; noisy when full; service is slow and lacks professionalism, but waiters are polite.

Recommended dishes: Chicken chat, assorted appetizers, Sahib's special salad, kati kebab, onion kulcha, papad, aloo paratha, kali dal, tandoori chicken and prawns, tandoori prawns masala, seekh kebab, Major Burke Sahib's makhani chicken, chicken tikka masala, lamb shahi, lamb sagwala, mughlai biryani, peas pullao, kheer, Colonel Hooper Sahib's tea, fruit salad, ragmalai, kheer.

Price range: Moderate.

Credit cards: American Express, MasterCard and Visa.

Hours: Lunch, seven days, noon to 3 P.M.; dinner, Mondays through Saturdays, 5:30 P.M. to 11 P.M.; Sundays, 5:30 P.M. to 10:30 P.M. Closed only on Christmas Day and Thanksgiving Day.

Reservations: Recommended.

When waiters ask if guests want their food flavored hot and spicy at Sahib, and you do, be sure to say very, very, very spicy. The owner here says it takes three very's to get it that way. On the other hand, dishes at Sahib also are mild or medium spiced when so ordered. But it is the essential hotness of Indian food, combined with soothing rice pullao, cool, cucumber-flecked yogurt, the gentle brown lentil stew known as kali dal, and mint chutney that really makes for the seductive contrast of flavors and textures that distinguishes this cuisine.

The food at Sahib is certainly well above average and the menu offers a number of enticing possibilities, all in a setting that is trimly modern but stylishly atmospheric. If the noise level were not quite so high it would be even more felicitous.

The star among appetizers is chicken chat, a cold salad of freshly cooked boneless chunks of chicken marinated in a spicy, lemony sauce that would make a delightful main course on a hot summer day. Vegetable fritters such as the triangular samosas and the batter-dipped pakoras are crisp and savory. When ordered on the mixed appetizer tray they are accompanied by tender pieces of tandoori baked chicken and the moist, lightly packed seekh kebabs that are one of the kitchen's real triumphs.

Made of ground lamb packed onto a skewer in a sausage shape, seekh kebabs are generally served too dense and dry at New York restaurants that offer them. But the chef at Sahib obviously knows better, and his kebabs are one of the best choices for a main course or appetizer. Kati kebab is a large rolled chapati pancake filled wtih diced lamb and onions. It is especially good when some mint or taramind chutney is spooned into the filling.

Indian breads are among that country's greatest culinary triumphs. Many at Sahib are disappointing, but a few are excellent, among them the onion filled kulcha, the spicy, grilled lentil flour wafers known as papad, and the aloo paratha, flat layered whole-wheat bread filled with potatoes and peas. Plainer breads such as tandoori roti are a bit leaden and the plain nan lacks the lightness and crispness it should have.

Lovers of fiery seasonings will appreciate Sahib's mixed vegetable salad — special because it is incendiary. After sampling it, a few spoonfuls of the yogurt and cucumber sauce, raita, will be much appreciated. The raita here would be improved if the cucumber in it were crisp rather than limp, but it performs its cooling function, nonetheless.

Vegetarians are in luck in Indian restaurants because there are so many varied nonmeat dishes from which to choose. Kali dal, a saucelike stew of nut-brown lentils, and peas pullao or vegetable biryani, both on a bed of herb-scented rice, are delicious, whether eaten alone or in combination with meat or fish dishes. So is the eggplant with potatoes.

Tandoori baking is a specialty at Shaib, and the chicken is moist and tender whether in halves or in the small boneless pieces known as tikka. Chicken tikka masala — the chicken pieces in a velvety curry sauce — and tandoori prawns, also available plain or in the masala sauce, are excellent. So is Major Burke Sahib's makhani chicken — again tandoori chicken, but this time on the bone and in a light tomato and butter sauce.

Lamb shahi is a dish for those who like mild seasonings, with chunks of lamb, just a little drier than they should be, in a cream sauce accented wtih ginger and almonds. Lamb or chicken sagwala, in a spinach cream sauce, are also mild but subtly flavored. Boti kebabs — chunks of tandoori cooked lamb — were hard, bland and dry, and tandoori fish, an imported pomfret marinated in spiced yogurt and cooked in the tandoor, is much too fishy for my taste.

Indian desserts, usually so chokingly sweet, are better than average at Sahib. Kheer — a soupy rice pudding — is delicately flavored with raisins and honey, and even the rasmalai — pressed cheeselike patties in pistachio-flecked milk sauce — is not too objectionable. Mango ice cream, however, was so frozen when served it was not edible when I tried it.

In addition to the Indian yogurt drink, lassi, Sahib offers full bar service and the Indian beer, Eagle. It is one of the world's weaker and more watery brews, and I found Heineken's far preferable.

Dinner prices are fairly reasonable, especially since appetizers, rice dishes and breads are shared, and buffet lunches are unbelievably inexpensive and copious — $5.95 to $6.95 as I write.

The Saloon
Fair

1920 Broadway, at 64th Street, Lincoln Center, 874-1500.

Atmosphere: Huge, sprawling indoor-outdoor cafe much like a covered street, noisy and convivial; service is amateurish, friendly and often agonizingly slow and badly timed.

Recommended dishes: Spinach and avocado salad, fried mozzarella, fried wontons, ravioli in salsa forte, breast of duckling, marinated lamb steak, roast chicken with shallots, salad of chicken breast and spinach, tournedos of beef with mushroom sauce, English-cut saddle lamb chops, Mississippi Mud cake, shoofly pie, plain cheesecake.

Price range: Moderately expensive.

Credit cards: All major credit cards.

Hours: Seven days, 11:30 A.M. to 2 A.M.

Reservations: Recommended.

Anyone walking into a huge brick cavern of a restaurant that seats about 240 people and finds a menu listing 202 items probably would expect the worst. If the restaurant is The Saloon, the apprehension is well placed because the food and service leave almost everything to be desired. But with its highly visible sidewalk cafe and its location across from Lincoln Center, it is one of the few options in that heavily trafficked area.

Wondering why anyone would do things on such a scale, I called and asked Stewart Rosen, one of the Saloon's four owners. "It's a terrible menu for an owner and a terrible menu for the kitchen, but our chef just loves doing it," Mr. Rosen said. "He's only twenty-seven and is self-taught and he likes to expose people to all kinds of different food." Whether walking or gliding on roller skates in this fun food fair, waiters and waitresses are patient, polite and friendly, but the service is inevitably slow, especially when the restaurant is not crowded. Timing is somewhat better during a rush, oddly enough, although dishes for various members of the same party do not arrive together.

At The Saloon no dish or culinary style is left unturned. Quiche and ravioli, wontons and tacos, omelets and Chinese stir-fried dishes, Tex-Mex chili and nouvelle cuisine salads, hamburgers and sandwiches on croissants, dozens of Continental and Asian creations and who knows what else are here along with squash blossoms, sweetbreads, sushi, every kind of fish and meat and what seems to be a culinary cast of thousands.

The omelets are musty and leaden, made from eggs that do not seem to have been broken fresh — all must have begun as frozen mixes. The quiche gave off such an offensive smell that eating it was out of the question. Croissants for sandwiches were soggy and squashed. Hamburgers were dry and crumbly, cold pastas were pasty, and a mixed grill of sausages and meats arrived burned and arid. The chili might have been acceptable had it not been tepid, but the greasy, heavy cornbread with it did not even hint at the hot jalapeño peppers said to be inside. Cajun soused shrimp and Italian seafood salad had the identical oily metallic dressing, and wherever they appeared, the stale shrimp reeked of iodine.

Surprisingly, it was the simple, heavier meat dishes and a few of the vegetable salads that offered the only passable choices. (Recommended here means passable, in fact.) Both the spinach salad with alfalfa sprouts and avocado, and the julienne breast of chicken with spinach were fine if served with oil and vinegar and not the slimy house dressing. There were also two decent deep-fried appetizers, one of mozzarella cubes, the other of peppery wontons in a fairly light tomato sauce. And for larger appetites, there is edible, though reheated, roast chicken with shallots, a thick leg of lamb steak that had been marinated and sautéed, beef tournedos in a passable brown sauce hinting at wild mushrooms, perhaps in powder form, and English-cut saddle lamb chops topped with pignoli nuts and garnished with steamed snow peas. The chops would have been the best dish of all had they been delivered medium rare instead of well done. Indonesian lemon duck was burned black, but breast of duckling was rare, thinly sliced and pleasantly garnished with papaya. Meat-filled ravioli in a pungent salsa forte proved better than angel-hair pasta with stale and fishy crab meat. Excellent leaf or red-tipped lettuce underlines all salads, although iceberg fleshes out the house green salad. Among desserts, the only acceptable choices were a thick chocolate fudge cake called Mississippi Mud, a frothy, lemony cheesecake and a molasses-rich shoofly pie.

Prices are high, but portions are huge and the management is graceful about dividing dishes, time permitting.

Salta in Bocca
★ ★

179 Madison Avenue, between 33rd and 34th Streets, 684-1757.

Atmosphere: Pleasant if undistinguished dining room that is extremely noisy when full; service is polite, efficient and accommodating.

Recommended dishes: Baked clams, mussels Riviera, roast peppers with mozzarella cheese, minestrone, pasta e fagioli, fettuccine casalinga, spaghetti carbonara, spaghetti al sugo, capelli d'angelo with seafood, linguine with white clam sauce, tortellini gratinati, fettuccine all'Amatriciana, fried squid, red snapper Livornese, scampi fra diavolo, chicken piccata, chicken scarpara, veal Genovese, veal paillard, osso buco, veal cutlet Milanese, veal cutlet Fiorentina, grilled veal chop, fried zucchini, sautéed escarole, zucchini with tomatoes, arugula salad, cheesecake, zabaglione, cheese and fruit platter.

Price range: Expensive.

Credit cards: All major credit cards.

Hours: Lunch, Mondays through Saturdays, noon to 3 P.M.; dinner, Mondays through Thursdays, 4:30 P.M. to 10:30 P.M.; Fridays and Saturdays, 4:30 P.M. to 11 P.M. Closed Sundays and major holidays.

Reservations: Necessary for lunch.

Next to moving its location, the most trying test for a well-established restaurant is a change of chefs. By all indications, Salta in Bocca has weathered just such a change and has exhibited no evidence of disruption in the kitchen's performance, a tribute to the experience and diligence of its owner, Fulvio Tramontina. Since it opened several years ago, this newly decorated, pleasant North Italian restaurant with its rose-glow walls and its abundance of bright mosaics has been mobbed at lunch by business people in the area. The noise and pace at that time of day are frantic and dizzying. But at night, things calm down to an easygoing hum, and on Friday and Saturday nights, when the neighborhood virtually shuts down, Salta in Bocca is an uncrowded and comfortable find, a place worth remembering for a leisurely and elegantly satisfying meal.

Service is both friendly and professional, a combination that comes as something of a relief compared with the many dining rooms where the staffs are often friendly but unpolished. Here captains and waiters actually understand the food they are serving. And if anyone wants a dish that deviates a bit from the menu norm, it is readily provided.

At Salta in Bocca it is quite possible to have a three-star meal, though the overall performance averages out to a two-star rating. A three-star meal would go something like this: Two people could first share an order of either the crusty, garlicky baked clams oreganate or the superb, huge mussels Riviera in a heady garlic, herb and tomato broth. Or they could have a wonderful combination of roasted red peppers baked under a mantle of mozzarella cheese, an appetizer not listed on the menu. The next course might be a shared pasta — say the luxurious green and white fettuccine casalinga to be twirled in a sauce of cream, prosciutto and onions, or the spaghetti carbonara with egg yolks enfolding prosciutto and onions. If seafood is not ordered as a first course, the pasta could be the lacy thin capelli d'angelo in a light shellfish and tomato sauce or the linguine in white clam sauce that has just the right underpinning of sautéed garlic and hot pepper flakes. Paglia e fieno — the "straw and hay" combination of green and white noodles — is nestled in a cream sauce with prosciutto and peas. Tortellini gratinéed under golden cheese and the fettuccine all'Amatriciana with ham, onions and tomatoes are also excellent.

A simple meat dish would be the best choice to follow pasta — the grilled loin veal chop, the paillard of veal or the huge, butterflied veal cutlet Milanese. The butterflied veal chop lightly layered with spinach makes up the veal cutlet Fiorentina, also a first-rate specialty. A cool, fresh arugula salad or the lightly steamed escarole with olive oil and garlic are good company to the veal, as is the crisp fried zucchini.

A beautifully arranged cheese platter combining provolone, grana and asiago cheese with sliced pears, apples and melon, crisp, cold fennel and bunches of grapes in a bowl of ice water will satisfy those who do not feel dessert has to be sweet. For lovers of sweets, the hot zabaglione or homemade cheesecake are in order, far better than the cannoli, the rum cake or the chocolate mousse, which might easily be credited to My-T-Fine.

Salta in Bocca falls down considerably on appetizers. Other than the three mentioned, all are disappointing. The quality of the prosciutto leaves much to be desired, and the cheese, ham and bread combination, spiedino Romano, is sometimes too darkly fried yet uncooked inside. Both the cannelloni and lasagne suffered from a very salty filling that seemed to be sausage meat, and oversalting also flawed the veal scaloppine Bolognese topped with prosciutto and mozzarella cheese.

Judging by local examples, calf's liver Veneziana seems to be the most difficult Italian dish to prepare properly. An overdose of acidic white wine marred the version here, and the thickly cut liver slices were toughened in the sautéing.

Fra diavolo sauce at Salta in Bocca, a lusty blend of tomatoes, garlic, herbs and hot peppers, is superb either on the crunchy, fried squid or on the scampi. Poached bass Triestina style with mussels and clams improves with the addition of tomatoes to its white wine base, so order it that way, and the red snapper Livornese, while very good, would be better with less salt and without the California olives.

Osso buco, at times a daily special, has a rich sauce and is meltingly tender, as is the boneless chicken scarpara sautéed with garlic and shallots, or the breast of chicken piccata, savory with sweet butter and lemon juice. Veal Genovese in a pesto sauce of basil, garlic, pignoli nuts and olive oil is novel and refreshing. There is a good selection of Italian wines, and prices are only moderately high. Those in the mood for a splurge, should try the lusty but mellow Barolo or the less complex but sprightly Barbaresca.

Sammy's Rumanian Jewish Restaurant
★ ★ ★

157 Chrystie Street, near Delancey Street, 673-0330, 673-5526 and 475-9131.

Atmosphere: Casual, convivial and crowded restaurant that suggests a big house party; housekeeping is careless; service is remarkably efficient and good-natured.

Recommended dishes: All appetizers except meatballs and chopped liver; mushroom and barley soup, Rumanian tenderloin steak, rib steak, mush steak, broiled veal chops, broiled chicken, boiled beef flanken, stuffed cabbage, potato pancakes, mashed potatoes, silver-dollar potatoes, kasha varnishkes.

Price range: Moderate.

Credit cards: American Express.

Hours: Saturdays, 3:30 P.M. to 2 A.M.; all other days, 3:30 P.M. to midnight.

Reservations: Necessary on weekends, suggested on weekdays.

The Cadillacs and Rolls-Royces are still double-parked along the otherwise dark and deserted street, the blue-glass seltzer bottles and pitchers of golden chicken fat shimmer on the tables, walls are hung with a rag-bag of memorabilia and the singing of Jewish and Israeli folk songs continues at the same ear-shattering pitch — all instant assurances that Sammy's Rumanian Jewish (but not kosher) restaurant is playing to packed houses. Through it all, the owner, Stan Zimmerman, roams around kibbitzing and often sits down to take sips of leftover drinks. Generally his stopovers are felicitous; occasionally he overstays his welcome.

The best news is that when I returned on a jam-packed Mother's Day after a four-year absence I found the food and service better than ever. Considering the adults and children crowded around tables and the line of waiting customers spilling onto Chrystie Street, it was almost a miracle that the food was fresh and savory and that the young staff remained cool, efficient and graciously good-humored. "Look, I'm bringing all of your appetizers right away," our waitress said, "but you'll have to give me a break on the main courses; they may take a while."

Put that way, the wait was easy to take, especially when time could be passed nibbling on the firm, sour pickles and the jade-green tomatoes, on the crunchy fried onions and grated radish mellowed with chicken fat and on the imcomparable roasted green peppers redolent of garlic. Breads could be better, but everything meant to be spread on them could hardly be improved. As a second visit on a quieter night indicated, Sammy's is now worth three stars instead of the earlier two.

Except for some dry and mealy meatballs and overly wet chopped liver, all appetizers are exceptional. The whipped-eggplant salad with its crunchy green pepper, tomatoes and onion is one of the best versions of that salad I have ever had. Equally good are the broiled chicken livers with baked unborn eggs (the yolks found in fresh-killed spring chickens), the garlic-scented calf's foot jelly that is pitcha and the garlicky grilled beef and veal sausages, Rumanian karnatzlach, that sometimes are a bit dry. The fried kreplach meat dumplings arrive crisp and hot, and the stuffed derma is still the best I know outside of a home kitchen. The filling for this intestine casing is heady with onion, and the slices are broiled after being cut so they are crisp instead of soggy. Brains sprinkled with lemon juice and pepper are refreshing and satiny.

Chicken soup is not as satisfying as the smoky, earthy mushroom and barley combination that can serve as a first course or as a main course ladled over the meltingly tender, boiled beef flanken. Broiling is the strong point of Rumanian kitchens, and it is well executed here on chicken and on that beautifully tender beef-cut known as skirt steak or Rumanian tenderloin, an extraordinary strip of beef that improves with a topping of minced garlic if used in moderation. Other excellent broiled meats are the juicy, fragrant rib steak or the eye of the rib known as mush steak and the huge, moist veal chops. These are better choices than the big, fried, veal rib chops that can be underdone and fatty. Stuffed cabbage in a gently sweet-sour tomato sauce seems much improved.

Like the meatballs, a fricassee of random chicken parts leaves something to be desired, and broiled sweetbreads range from excellent to slightly dry. A choice of vegetables here means crisp and oniony potato pancakes, mashed potatoes with chicken fat and greeven cracklings, kasha varnishkes that combine the nutty buckwheat with pasta bowties and fried silver-dollar potatoes.

When it's time for dessert, a container of milk and a bottle of Fox's u-bet chocolate syrup are placed on the table for do-it-yourself egg creams. And that is about as good as dessert can get because the cakes, cookies and chocolate pudding are skippable. Portions are gigantic, and there is much sharing and packing of doggie bags.

San Marco
★ ★

36 West 52nd Street, between Fifth Avenue and Avenue of the Americas, 246-5340.

Atmosphere: Slightly tacky and dated, dark interior
that needs brightening; noisy when full, but generally comfortable; service is very professional and
good-natured at uncrowded times but can be
brusque and pushy when things are rushed.

Recommended dishes: Shrimp San Marco, baked
clams, peppers and anchovies, spiedino Romano,
mozzarella in vettura, cappelletti in broth, stracciatella, cannelloni, manicotti, gnocchi al pesto,
spaghetti carbonara, striped bass pescatora,
scampi fra diavolo, veal cutlet Milanese, grilled
chicken with sage, arugula salad, zabaglione.

Price range: Expensive.

Credit cards: All major credit cards.

Hours: Lunch, Mondays through Fridays, noon to 3
P.M.; dinner, Mondays through Saturdays, 5:30
P.M. to 10:30 P.M. Closed Sundays and major
holidays; closed Saturdays in summer.

Reservations: Necessary for lunch; recommended for
dinner.

As much as one can appreciate innovation and fashionable presentations of food, all too often those features
are achieved at the sacrifice of standard favorites. It was
encouraging, therefore, to return to San Marco after an
absence of five or six years and find that all of the classic old Italian dishes, popular in the late 50's and 60's,
are reproduced here and are as good as they ever were.
What does need refurbishing, however, is the dining
room, for there is a decided has-been air about it that
belies the kitchen's prowess. Owners Bruno Alessio and
Peppino Zirardi are graduates of the original Romeo
Salta's, and they took the tone and style for their own
restaurant from that once excellent establishment. Having been at the height of contemporary fashion when it
was created, it now seems dated.

That aside, the very professional staff knows how to
dish up what the very professional kitchen turns out.
Only at busy times can that staff be rude and pushy;
generally they are polite and accommodating, if slightly
offhand.

The menu is large and varied, primarily North Italian
in focus but still with a number of the lighter southern
specialties as well. Among the more beguiling appetizers are the gently broiled shrimp with a spicy light
tomato dipping sauce, rosy, fresh roasted peppers
spiked with plump anchovy fillets and two mozzarella
specialties that are extraordinary. The first is spiedino
Romano, alternating slices of bread and cheese deep-
fried but not at all greasy, then dressed with an anchovy, butter and lemon sauce. Mozzarella in vettura
(cheese baked on a slice of toast) is a delicate variation
on the french-toasted sandwich mozzarella in carrozza
and much easier to take as a first course.

Beautifully crafted cappelletti, the delicate pasta dumplings filled with chicken and what seemed to be a touch of sausage meat, were adrift in golden and heady chicken and beef consommé.

These same dumplings can be had baked au gratin. Gnocchi, the cloudlike dumplings of potato dough, are tricky to produce, but the kitchen here turns them out not at all sticky, yet never leaden. They may be had with several sauces, none better than the spring-green pesto, perfumed with basil, cheese and garlic. Another great pasta combination at San Marco is the spinach-and-meat-filled cannelloni paired with creamy cheese-filled manicotti with a meaty Bolognese tomato-cream sauce.

Branzino alla pescatora, a moist, fresh slab of striped bass simmered in a tomato white-wine bouillon, then garnished with mussels and clams, was light and savory, as was half a grilled chicken with sage butter and the sautéed calf's liver and onion specialty, fegato Veneziana.

The arugula salad was glowingly fresh, if overly sharpened with vinegar, and an order of fried zucchini could not have been better.

Among appetizers, only the prosciutto seemed less convincing than it used to be, a result, no doubt, of the disappearance of really good prosciutto from our midst now that manufacturers do not take time to age it properly. The other consistent flaw is a certain disquieting fishiness in dishes such as vermicelli with shellfish and squid Luciana, both of which do not seem truly fresh, especially on Saturday nights. One dish that has improved markedly, oddly enough, is the very simple veal cutlet Milanese. This used to be greasy at San Marco, but on a recent try it arrived as crisp as gold leaf, totally greaseless and with just the right accent of butter setting off the tender meat.

Chicken Casorza, sautéed with tomato, mushrooms, and peppers, had delicate hints of garlic, as did the beefsteak San Marco in the spicy pizzaiuola tomato sauce.

Zabaglione is the best of the desserts, every bit as frothy, rich and delicately Marsala-scented as that hot, whipped specialty is supposed to be.

Sardi's
Fair

234 West 44th Street, between Broadway and Eighth Avenue, 221-8440.

Atmosphere: Convivial Broadway landmark with good acoustics and poor housekeeping; service is careless.

Recommended dishes: Clams or oysters on the half shell, white meat of chicken salad with vinaigrette dressing, crab meat salad, chicken sandwich without mayonnaise, lamb chops, roast beef, spinach salad, pound cake, melon.

Price range: Expensive.

Credit cards: All major credit cards.

Hours: Lunch, Mondays through Saturdays, 11:30 A.M. to 3:30 P.M.; dinner, seven days, 3:30 P.M. to 8 P.M.; supper, Mondays through Thursdays, 8 P.M. to 12:30 A.M.; Fridays and Saturdays, 8 P.M. to 1 A.M., Sundays, 8 P.M. to 11 P.M.; Sunday brunch, 11:30 A.M. to 3 P.M. Open on major holidays.

Reservations: Necessary.

It would be hard to imagine that anyone who grew up in New York loving the city and its traditions would not harbor at least a small, lurking fondness for Sardi's. The restaurant has been a theater district landmark since 1921, and much of the Sardi mystique remains intact. It is virtually a club favored by leading lights of the theater and Broadway buffs of all sorts. It is the most popular gathering place for meals before and after the theater, and the number-one setting for opening-night parties, complete with paparazzi shooting pictures at the door. Those who go to the restaurant to observe celebrities will rarely be disappointed. Those who go for good food that is well served will rarely be satisfied.

For reasons that remain a mystery, food, service and housekeeping at Sardi's leave almost everything to be desired. Service is perfunctory and careless, and waiters never know who gets what.

On the plus side are the excellent acoustics in the downstairs dining room where one can carry on a comfortable conversation even when it is crowded, and the well-made drinks always generously laced with the appropriate alcohol. A Bloody Mary ordered straight up and cold arrives just right, and the Irish coffee is distinguished by the strength of both coffee and whiskey. The newly created downstairs bar is convivial, if jam-packed.

In at least a dozen recent visits, I have tried all appetizers, most of the soups, salads, grilled meats and the house and daily specials, as well as salads and desserts. Except for a few dishes to be recommended, all offerings were seriously flawed because of overcooking or undercooking, ineptly made and heavy sauces or stale ingredients.

Even the few recommendations must be made with caveats. The roast beef is flavorful and fine if it is not cold. The lamb chops are good if they are not dried out. The chicken salad of white meat will probably be satisfying if you skip the sweetish Russian dressing and use vinaigrette. Lump crab meat salad is acceptable if it is not past its prime, which it sometimes is. Order the white meat of chicken sandwich from the modestly priced upstairs luncheon club menu and you will have a perfectly acceptable meal, providing you have it on toast or rye bread and skip the mayonnaise, which is often rancid. Spinach salad is fresh and sparkling and includes crisp nuggets of raw zucchini, but weed out the greasy chunks of ice-cold half-cooked bacon.

The rest is best forgotten, including the two highly touted house specialties — deviled roast beef bones that taste like deep-fried fat, and cannelloni, which is always a pasty mass, filled with stale, nameless meat and smothered by an orange cheese sauce that suggests a Kraft dinner. For dessert, good melon is usually on hand, as well as an above-average pound cake. All other cakes, frozen or liqueured, and the puddings and parfaits are inelegantly commercial.

Say Eng Look
★ ★ ★

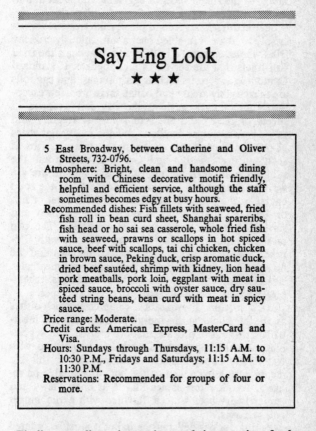

5 East Broadway, between Catherine and Oliver Streets, 732-0796.

Atmosphere: Bright, clean and handsome dining room with Chinese decorative motif; friendly, helpful and efficient service, although the staff sometimes becomes edgy at busy hours.

Recommended dishes: Fish fillets with seaweed, fried fish roll in bean curd sheet, Shanghai spareribs, fish head or ho sai sea casserole, whole fried fish with seaweed, prawns or scallops in hot spiced sauce, beef with scallops, tai chi chicken, chicken in brown sauce, Peking duck, crisp aromatic duck, dried beef sautéed, shrimp with kidney, lion head pork meatballs, pork loin, eggplant with meat in spiced sauce, broccoli with oyster sauce, dry sautéed string beans, bean curd with meat in spicy sauce.

Price range: Moderate.

Credit cards: American Express, MasterCard and Visa.

Hours: Sundays through Thursdays, 11:15 A.M. to 10:30 P.M., Fridays and Saturdays; 11:15 A.M. to 11:30 P.M.

Reservations: Recommended for groups of four or more.

Finding excellent, interesting and inexpensive food served by a pleasant, efficient staff in a festive, sparklingly clean restaurant may sound like a dream of paradise. Yet it is a dream that seems to come true at Say Eng Look in Chinatown.

Now a few doors north of its original location, Say Eng Look is newly done up with flamboyant red walls,

Chinese decorative motifs and a fairly effective acoustical ceiling. It even has generally clean washrooms, a miracle in this part of town. The setting makes this restaurant's existence even more surprising because though many Chinatown restaurants offer bargains in food, they usually do so in rooms that are at best nondescript and more often messy or dirty.

Since Say Eng Look, which features Shanghai cooking, received a two-star rating a few years ago, it has consistently improved and it is now well worth three stars. At busy times, an occasional dish may taste of overheated grease or oversalting, but only such flaws and the lack of attention paid to the "tourist dishes" detracted from recent experiences there.

Service is friendly and accommodating, although it can become hectic at peak times. Almost all waiters speak enough English to explain the unusual dishes. If any of those dishes are marked spicy, they will be exactly that, even if no special plea has been made when ordering. A hefty belt of chili oil brings life to the moist tender chunks of tai chi chicken stir-fried with black mushrooms, to the satiny squares of bean curd with ground pork, to both the prawns and scallops in spiced sauce, to the silken slices of eggplant with meat and to the firm sautéed string beans flecked with pork.

Seaweed lends a verdant, parsleylike freshness when crisply fried and crumbled over a miraculously crunchy fried whole sea bass or in the batter that coats the fried fish fillets that are served as an appetizer. If standard Cantonese appetizers such as shrimp toast and egg rolls are inexcusably greasy and banal, there are a few exceptional alternatives, such as the fish roll wrapped in sheets of bean curd fried to gold-leaf fragility and topped with minced scallions and the meaty flat strips of marinated pork that are Shanghai-style spareribs. If such soups as the hot and sour combination and the subgum bean cake are undistinguished, there are the wonderful casseroles that may be ordered as the soup course or the main course. These combine meat or fish or both with vegetables and noodles, steamed and served in wire-bound stoneware casseroles. The two most exceptional are the fish-head casserole with Chinese cabbage and glassy bean-thread noodles and the ho sai sea casserole, a broth afloat with pork meatballs, steamed fishballs, deep-fried hard-cooked eggs, vegetables, noodles, shrimp and strips of egg-yolk crepes.

Rich, soothing brown sauces complement such dishes as the big, light garlic-and-ginger-scented pork meatballs known as lion heads that are braised with vegetables, and the sugar-glazed pork loin brightened with watercress. Though not listed on the menu, this big meaty pork loin cooked on the bone is available on request. Another top choice that is at once chewy and tender is dry beef sautéed, flavored with garlic, ginger and scallions.

Peking duck is delicious here, but it must be ordered twenty-four hours in advance. The same is true of the more unusual and interesting crisp aromatic duck that is served with steamed buns. Fresh coriander should be served with this duck, but it was missing from a recent order.

No hard liquor or wine is sold here, but you can provide your own. The management accepts reservations for two or three people but at crowded times does not honor them. Count on a firm reservation only for groups of four or more.

Sea Fare of the Aegean
★

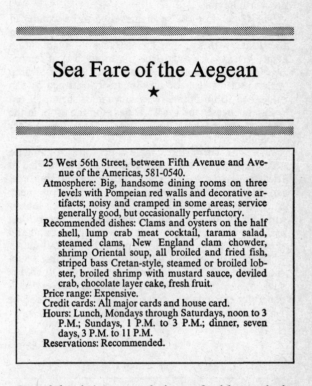

25 West 56th Street, between Fifth Avenue and Avenue of the Americas, 581-0540.
Atmosphere: Big, handsome dining rooms on three levels with Pompeian red walls and decorative artifacts; noisy and cramped in some areas; service generally good, but occasionally perfunctory.
Recommended dishes: Clams and oysters on the half shell, lump crab meat cocktail, tarama salad, steamed clams, New England clam chowder, shrimp Oriental soup, all broiled and fried fish, striped bass Cretan-style, steamed or broiled lobster, broiled shrimp with mustard sauce, deviled crab, chocolate layer cake, fresh fruit.
Price range: Expensive.
Credit cards: All major cards and house card.
Hours: Lunch, Mondays through Saturdays, noon to 3 P.M.; Sundays, 1 P.M. to 3 P.M.; dinner, seven days, 3 P.M. to 11 P.M.
Reservations: Recommended.

One of the city's more enduring seafood houses is the attractive Sea Fare of the Aegean, the offspring of the long-gone Sea Fare that opened 47 years ago in Greenwich Village. Six years ago, the modern Sea Fare merited a three-star rating. But as prices have risen and the competition grown keener, the restaurant's worth declined, and it now merits just one star. Still beautiful with Pompeian red walls and decorative artifacts, Sea Fare was sold by Chris Bastis to three former managers, Gus Gounaris, Nicholas Tsigakos and Joseph Milukas.

As always, the quality of almost all fish and shellfish is topnotch. "Almost" here refers to the second-rate Alaskan king crab cocktail and to one serving of an appetizer of far-from-fresh steamed crab claws. Otherwise, all main ingredients are fresh and both broiling and frying are impeccable, so that the fish retains moisture and flavor. This is no small triumph, but when most of that fish is fairly expensive for a relatively small portion, it is hard to forgive frozen french fries, a salad of wet lettuce that sheds its dressing, cold, tasteless rice and spinach and soggy rolls.

Clams and oysters on the half shell are cold and sparklingly fresh, but the ketchup-based cocktail sauce is the only dressing offered. Similarly, slick Russian dressing masks the otherwise inviting cold poached salmon. Lump crab meat cocktail is also delicious so long as it is not ordered Aegean-style, with olive oil overpowering the fresh sea flavor of the crab meat. Steamed clams with broth and butter, shrimp cocktail and tarama salad — the Greek purée of fish roe — are consistently first rate. Most of the soups are thick and bland; only the New England clam chowder and the shrimp Oriental are worth having.

The Greek-inspired specialties used to be wonderful here, but only a few can now be recommended. Even the dishes with egg and lemon sauce — avgolemono style — are starchy and lack the sunny bite of lemon. Specialties that have stood up are the broiled shrimp with mustard sauce and the Cretan-style striped bass in an herbed fish broth. A sweet sauce mars shrimp baked with feta cheese, and grease settles atop the broth in the steamed striped bass Rodos-style and on the meager bouillabaisse.

Newburg, curry and Creole sauces are of cafeteria quality. Steamed or broiled lobster, sautéed, broiled or fried scallops, soft-shell crabs and, in season, shad roe, are also dependable, as is the spicy deviled crab meat. But that crab meat piled on grilled shrimp or lobster turns the meat soggy. An expensive salad of crab meat and salty lobster is garnished like a drugstore salad and served with commercial mayonnaise and cocktail sauce.

The only dessert that will satisfy those who like a substantial ending is the chocolate layer cake. Otherwise, stick to melon, strawberries or grapefruit. Service is generally efficient and professional, although it can be perfunctory at busy times.

Seeda Thai
★ ★

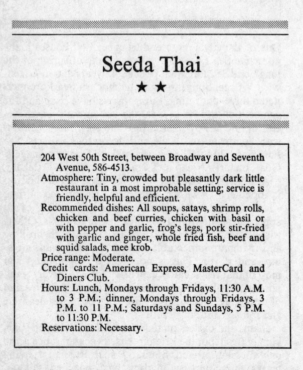

204 West 50th Street, between Broadway and Seventh Avenue, 586-4513.

Atmosphere: Tiny, crowded but pleasantly dark little restaurant in a most improbable setting; service is friendly, helpful and efficient.

Recommended dishes: All soups, satays, shrimp rolls, chicken and beef curries, chicken with basil or with pepper and garlic, frog's legs, pork stir-fried with garlic and ginger, whole fried fish, beef and squid salads, mee krob.

Price range: Moderate.

Credit cards: American Express, MasterCard and Diners Club.

Hours: Lunch, Mondays through Fridays, 11:30 A.M. to 3 P.M.; dinner, Mondays through Fridays, 3 P.M. to 11 P.M.; Saturdays and Sundays, 5 P.M. to 11:30 P.M.

Reservations: Necessary.

Right in the midst of the theater district, this dark, handsome interior with a Thai roof, pierced metal lampshades and huge wall mirror comes as a surprise considering the tackiness of the Broadway block on which it is to be found. The help is unusually handsome and ingratiating. So are the chicken fried rice, the beef or chicken curry, the whole fried fish, the disks of pork stir-fried with garlic and ginger and the best beef or squid salad and crispest shrimp rolls you'll find at any Thai restaurant in town. Sweet and sour pork and egg roll were not up to the other dishes, but mee krob was crunchy. Soups are excellent.

Note: For a complete description of Thai food, see the review of Bangkok Cuisine.

Sheba

★

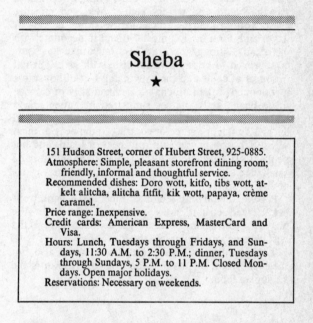

151 Hudson Street, corner of Hubert Street, 925-0885.
Atmosphere: Simple, pleasant storefront dining room; friendly, informal and thoughtful service.
Recommended dishes: Doro wott, kitfo, tibs wott, atkelt alitcha, alitcha fitfit, kik wott, papaya, crème caramel.
Price range: Inexpensive.
Credit cards: American Express, MasterCard and Visa.
Hours: Lunch, Tuesdays through Fridays, and Sundays, 11:30 A.M. to 2:30 P.M.; dinner, Tuesdays through Sundays, 5 P.M. to 11 P.M. Closed Mondays. Open major holidays.
Reservations: Necessary on weekends.

If the polite and gentle personnel at the Sheba Restaurant in TriBeCa have their way, New York can begin to learn a whole new food vocabulary, one that will include words like bereberé, doro wott, kitfo, alitcha and injera. They are all offered on the menu of what so far remains New York's only Ethiopian restaurant. This simple storefront restaurant is clean, modern and bright, decorated with an attractive striped wall fabric, some Ethiopian pictures and a handsome, brass-filigree Coptic Cross. A new branch of the restaurant, called Abyssinia, is expected to open soon in SoHo.

Members of the staff are most helpful in demonstrating how the stews and braised meats are to be eaten, and to do that authentically, forks should be shunned, although they are available. The main eating implement is the thin, flat, moist injera (in-JER-a), a crepelike bread with which food is picked up, dipped in sauce and then eaten. As in Arab countries and India, only the right hand is considered correct for this purpose. Encou Ephrem, an Ethiopian by birth who has lived in this country since 1968, is one of the partners, and she is also the cook. Chicken and beef make up the bulk of the menu selections, with fish offered occasionally as a special. For the most part, dishes resemble stews with spices and sauces close to those of India's Madras region. As prepared at Sheba, the food and sauces seemed overcooked and just a bit greasy, but most of the dishes I tried were satisfying, savory and probably would be considered entertaining by venturesome eaters in search of the exotic.

Some of the dishes are marked wott, which, a waitress told me, means they are hotly seasoned. But what's hot and what's not is apparently a matter of taste, so I was pleased to find that the incendiary Ethiopian spice paste, bereberé, was available on the side, to be added to dishes at will. Doro wott was a rich chicken stew that contained a hard-cooked egg, while tibs wott and alitcha fitfit were basically mild-flavored, pleasant beef stews. The least interesting of these braised beef dishes was the bland and watery kelil merek, and minchet abesh wott (ground beef in sauce) was thin, lacking in flavor and, for a novice, most difficult to negotiate with the bread. Kitfo, ground raw beef much like steak tartare, proved to be my favorite dish, with its bright red freshness of color and the convincing belt of hot spices it contained. Atkelt alitcha — a mixed stew of carrots, string beans and potatoes simmered in butter spiced with cardamom, garlic, ginger and turmeric — provided decorative flavor and color contrast to the heavier meat stews. Kik wott, made with split peas or lentils and hot pepper, is a sauce close to the Indian dahl and may be eaten as a separate course or spooned over the vegetables.

Papaya, melon with lemon or lime, and a light, well-caramelized custard were perfect desserts after the heavily spiced main courses. Beer, available here, is the best beverage to accompany the food.

There are burgers and omelets on the menu also, but the real reason for making the trek to TriBeCa is the Ethiopian food.

Shezan
Fair

8 West 58th Street, between Fifth Avenue and Avenue of the Americas, 371-1414.
Atmosphere: Subtle, sparkling and handsome modern dining room with good acoustics and large, comfortable tables and seating; service is polite and helpful but often slow and distracted.
Recommended dishes: Mulligatawny soup, karahi kebob Khyberi, saag gosht, chicken rice biryani, dal, raita, nan, paratha, carrot halvah, cardamom-flavored ice cream.
Price range: Moderately expensive.
Credit cards: All major credit cards.
Hours: Lunch, Mondays through Fridays, noon to 2:30 P.M; dinner, Mondays through Saturdays, 6 P.M. to 10:45 P.M. Closed Sundays and major holidays.
Reservations: Necessary.

When the owners of Shezan, a successful Indian-Pakistani restaurant in London, decided to open in New York, they undoubtedly tried to avoid all of the clichés of décor and menu associated with Indian restaurants usually found here. And in designing this stunning downstairs restaurant, that is exactly what the architects Charles Gwathmey and Robert Siegel managed to do. It is, plain and simple, a knockout, with a soft shimmery scheme of gold-beige and silver-gray in mirrors and polished aluminum acoustical ceilings, Ultrasuede banquettes and chairs, rose-glow mirrors, gray carpeting on walls, and glass brick partitions that let light through to dispel the feeling of being below street level. The bar is sophisticated and conducive to conversation, and just a few pieces of very good Indian folkcrafts are mounted on the wall abstractly, here and there.

Most magical of all are the double reflection of the mirrored walls and polished ceiling, creating the effect of a hanging reflecting pool, with the watery image above instead of below. The final adornment is the extraordinarily attractive clientele.

The only flaws in the interior design are the somewhat anonymous stairway entrance that made me wonder if I had, in fact, taken a wrong turn somewhere, and a kitchen door that opens into the dining room every other minute, changing both the lighting and heat levels in the room to a distracting degree.

Unfortunately, the service here remains uneven. At best it is friendly and graciously polite. At worst it is downright inefficient, with long waits between courses.

The menu itself is a disappointment. It offers none of the more fascinating Indian breads such as the wafer-crisp chapatti or the ballooning puri, nor does it list any of the sambals, chutneys or relishes that give an Indian meal its sensuous counterpoints of texture and flavor.

Seasonings at Shezan unquestionably are tempered to timid palates, not only because the gorgeously fiery chilies are withheld, but also because all other spicing is effetely restrained. Other shortcomings include a dull appetizer selection with a hearty and excellent mulligatawny soup, a fair consommé (neither soup hot enough) and a ridiculous salad of crab meat in an avocado.

Because of the pleasantly comfortable surroundings and a few really delicious main courses, Shezan originally received a one-star rating. Now, however, there are so few recommendable dishes, that the rating must be reduced to fair. Two dishes that held up well are the karahi kebob Khyberi (chunks of chicken with tomatoes, green peppers and onions brought sizzling to the table) and saag gosht, chunks of lamb gentled in a spinach and coriander sauce. Tandoori chicken and the murgh tikka, quarters of tandoori broiled chicken, were chokingly dry and stale at a recent lunch.

Murgh korma shahi, billed as the king of curries, tasted as though it was at least three days old, and jhinga shahi, prawns broiled in the tandoor, had been overheated to become as appetizing as dry, hard curls of wood. The spiced beef patties, shami kebob, tasted like warm, wet gingerbread, and the sausage-shaped ground meat sheesh kebob had been overbroiled to become tough and dry.

When I asked to have dishes really spicy, there was compliance only with the excellent rice biryani that in-

cluded tender moist chicken. The lentil purée, dal, and
the soothing cool yogurt raita, with currants and raisins,
were good accompaniments, as were the pizzalike
bread, nan, and the buttered, whole-wheat paratha.

Desserts were better than I remembered them. A carrot halvah served hot had a gentle, soothing quality,
and the cardamom-flavored ice cream with chopped
pistachio nuts made a refreshing windup.

Shinbashi
★

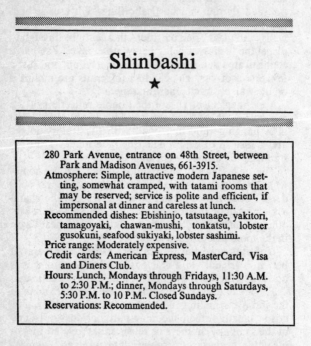

280 Park Avenue, entrance on 48th Street, between
Park and Madison Avenues, 661-3915.
Atmosphere: Simple, attractive modern Japanese setting, somewhat cramped, with tatami rooms that
may be reserved; service is polite and efficient, if
impersonal at dinner and careless at lunch.
Recommended dishes: Ebishinjo, tatsutaage, yakitori,
tamagoyaki, chawan-mushi, tonkatsu, lobster
gusokuni, seafood sukiyaki, lobster sashimi.
Price range: Moderately expensive.
Credit cards: American Express, MasterCard, Visa
and Diners Club.
Hours: Lunch, Mondays through Fridays, 11:30 A.M.
to 2:30 P.M.; dinner, Mondays through Saturdays,
5:30 P.M. to 10 P.M.. Closed Sundays.
Reservations: Recommended.

When it was originally reviewed, Shinbashi merited a
two-star rating. Recent visits, however, show a wide dis-
crepancy between the quality of dishes served at lunch
and those at dinner, making a one-star rating more accurate now.

At midday, this simple, attractive modern restaurant
is jammed with office workers, and the food and service
suggest a coffee shop, Japanese style. Sushi and the
sliced raw fish sashimi are limp and stale, as though
they had been set out on trays long in advance, and
wilted iceberg lettuce salads accompany main courses as
they would on the most banal blue-plate special. There
is even a washed-out blandness to the cold bean curd,
which should be on ice but comes in tepid water. Teriyaki-style broiled meat and fish arrive dry and barely
warm, and shrimp and vegetable tempura often taste of
overused grease. Add slapdash service to that and you
get the unpleasant picture.

At night, there are fewer diners, more Japanese and a
higher-priced menu — and things change completely.
Though teriyaki, tempura, sushi and sashimi are not up
to past standards, other specialties are. Among the best
small dishes at night are chawan-mushi, the steamed
custard with shrimp, fish cake, gingko nuts, lemon rind
and fragments of vegetables, and the tatsutaage, boneless nuggets of fried chicken as moist and silken as
sweetbreads. This same delicacy distinguishes yakitori,
chicken bits grilled on skewers. Ebishinjo, the crisp,

scallion-flavored shrimp croquettes, are also delicious; so is tamagoyaki, the sake-flavored omelet.

Negimayaki, thin beef rolled around scallions and grilled, has a leathery, overwet quality, even at dinner. Shabu shabu, the boiled dinner of meat and vegetables simmered at the table, has no more flavor or zest now than it did in the past. Three main courses that are up to former levels are the crisply fried pork cutlet, tonkatsu, the seafood sukiyaki made with fish, lobster, clams and vegetables, and the lobster gusokuni — fresh, salty lobster simmered in a briny stock with bean thread noodles. Fresh fruits are the best desserts.

Shun Lee Dynasty

★

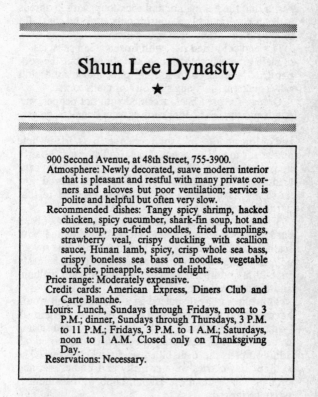

900 Second Avenue, at 48th Street, 755-3900.
Atmosphere: Newly decorated, suave modern interior that is pleasant and restful with many private corners and alcoves but poor ventilation; service is polite and helpful but often very slow.
Recommended dishes: Tangy spicy shrimp, hacked chicken, spicy cucumber, shark-fin soup, hot and sour soup, pan-fried noodles, fried dumplings, strawberry veal, crispy duckling with scallion sauce, Hunan lamb, spicy, crisp whole sea bass, crispy boneless sea bass on noodles, vegetable duck pie, pineapple, sesame delight.
Price range: Moderately expensive.
Credit cards: American Express, Diners Club and Carte Blanche.
Hours: Lunch, Sundays through Fridays, noon to 3 P.M.; dinner, Sundays through Thursdays, 3 P.M. to 11 P.M.; Fridays, 3 P.M. to 1 A.M.; Saturdays, noon to 1 A.M. Closed only on Thanksgiving Day.
Reservations: Necessary.

The chef-owner of this restaurant, as well as of Shun Lee Palace, Shun Lee West and Hunam, T. T. Wang, is said to visit each of his outposts daily to check on ingredients and to oversee the preparation of basic sauces. He is also said to hire personnel, develop basic recipes and cook in each kitchen at intervals.

Unfortunately, such peripatetic culinary efforts leave much to be desired, for Shun Lee Palace far outshines Mr. Wang's other restaurants, and this is the least proficient of them all. Although good, the food is far from inspired, but a recently redone interior makes it a generally comfortable and quiet setting. Even here, however, there are some undesirable tables, and it is too bad that those are the ones given out first to unknown customers even though better tables are unoccupied.

Now a suave and restful, modern mélange of gray glass bricks and white tile, the large dining room is comfortably divided into intimate corners and alcoves, all with decent noise levels, good lighting and just a slight problem with ventilation. The bar, with a few tables, has an inviting clublike atmosphere. Service is polite but often very slow.

There are a few unusually interesting and well-prepared dishes on the menu. Skip such banal Cantonese hot appetizers as spring rolls and shrimp toast, and opt instead for the three appealing and hotly seasoned cold hors d'oeuvres — the tangy, spicy shrimp, the fresh and tender hacked chicken in a chili-oil sauce bedded down on cool, subtly gelatinous bean-paste noodles and the marinated spiced slivers of cucumber. Fried and steamed crescent dumplings were also satisfying.

Both subgum wonton soup and sizzling rice soup were as characterless as in any neighborhood chop suey parlor, but the Peking hot and sour soup, with its shreds of bean curd and black mushrooms, and the shark-fin soup with egg drops were both delicious.

Dry and cold fried rice, with frozen green peas, tasted of stale grease both at lunch and dinner, but the soft, pan-fried noodles with shrimp, pork and a mild chili sauce makes a satisfying side dish or main course.

Orange-flavored beef, accented with hot pepper, was tough and dry. Far better choices were boneless, ginger-scented sea bass in a dark, pungent sauce served on a bed of fine noodles and spicy, crisp sea bass, fried whole and adrift in a Hunan hot sauce. Calf's liver is a fairly unusual dish in a Chinese restaurant, and Hunan sautéed liver, with a garnish of fresh spinach, proved how much we have missed by not being exposed to that particular specialty.

Vegetable duck pie — parchment-crisp layers of bean curd wrapped in a Chinese crepe and flavored with scallions and hoisin sauce — had much the same savory appeal as the equally crisp duckling fried in a meaty cake form and liberally doused with a verdant scallion-and-coriander sauce.

Thin slices of veal sautéed in a hot pepper oil would have been quite ordinary had it not been for the garnish — a circlet of "strawberries" formed of pounded shrimp coated with red-dyed sesame seeds, then deep fried, all adding up to the dish billed as strawberry veal. The shrimp strawberries were crunchy and interesting, and brought life to the meat. Hunan lamb with scallions is not to be missed.

All other dishes tried were decent but totally lacking in distinction. Fillets of sea bass with shrimp roe sauce was overcooked and tasted merely fishy, lacking the subtle, fiery pungency it should have, and squirrel fish was smothered in a dreadful sweet sauce.

Disappointments included General Ching's chicken, served mild when it was ordered fiery, and Lake Tung Ting shrimp with the flavor and aroma of overheated grease, as did an order of beef with snow peas and the slivered filling for mo-shu-ro pork (greasiness, in fact, was a common flaw in other dishes). Vegetables were all badly prepared and much overcooked. Canned mushrooms were common to many dishes.

Fresh pineapple, the coolest and most refreshing of the desserts, seemed the wisest choice, and sesame delight was an interesting offbeat alternative, a sort of fried custard cut in strips and dredged in sesame seeds and pink sugar.

The kitchen is good about omitting monosodium glutamate, cornstarch and sugar upon request.

Shun Lee Palace

★ ★

155 East 55th Street, between Lexington and Third Avenues, 371-8844.

Atmosphere: Interior is being redecorated; service is good.

Recommended dishes: Hacked chicken, velvety shrimp puffs, spicy, crisp, whole sea bass, double-fried pork, Hunan duckling with smoke flavor, lobster Sichuan, pork or shrimp with black bean sauce, vegetable duck pie.

Price range: Expensive.

Credit cards: American Express, Diners Club and Carte Blanche.

Hours: Lunch, Mondays through Fridays, noon to 3 P.M.; dinner, Mondays through Thursdays, 3 P.M. to 11 P.M.; Fridays, 3 P.M. to midnight; Saturdays, noon to midnight; Sundays, noon to 11 P.M. Open major holidays.

Reservations: Necessary.

T. T. Wang, the chef and owner of Shun Lee Palace, is certainly one of the city's most talented Chinese chefs. Several years ago a private banquet I attended at his restaurant showed he was capable of extraordinary feats, as we ate our way through course after course of what was perhaps the most breathtaking and original Chinese meal I have had this side of Singapore.

Even on ordinary, nonbanquet days, the five chefs who staff the kitchen can turn out some of the best Hunan, Sichuan and Cantonese food available uptown, in a setting that is extravagantly if garishly plush, although redecoration is under way as this book goes to press. Those who prefer a quiet background for dining should ask for reservations in the clublike, less decorated front section, a request that is not always granted. But many guests apparently prefer the lighter, brighter big dining room despite the closeness of tables.

The real key to obtaining the best food at Shun Lee Palace lies in establishing rapport with the management. Unknown diners have to take the time and trouble to convince the manager, Michael Tong, or one of his captains that they really know and care about Chinese food or, at the very least, that they are interested in learning. Otherwise, they may be served food that is certainly decent but which in no way approaches the kitchen's full measure of ability — or makes the high prices seem worthwhile.

As do the staffs of so many other Chinese restaurants, the Shun Lee Palace culinary staff puts its best efforts behind what it considers the most interesting dishes. Vegetable duck pie, for example, a layered affair that is really all egg and vegetables fried to resemble duck and served in a crepe with hoisin sauce, was delicious, and could not have been prepared in advance. Nor could the excellent velvet shrimp puffs with water chestnuts and bamboo shoots, a main course shared as an appetizer. Also, cold, tender, hacked white meat of chicken in a sesame paste and chili sauce was equally good on a night when I was not known.

On one of the occasions when I was recognized, I had a hot appetizer, Yank Chow chicken soon, a fiery, stir-fried dish that was very good, and a pleasant "three-delicacy combination platter" of cold appetizers that included a spicy shrimp combination, a cold version of the vegetable duck pie and a somewhat disappointing third accompaniment that tasted like sweet kosher pickles.

On a night when I was unrecognized, the hot and sour soup tasted like chili sauce in hot water. Sampled again when I was known, it was thick with slivers of bean curd, vegetables and chicken and had a mellow sour and pungent sting. Wontons at Shun Lee Palace are unusually good, but the broth in which they are served is nothing short of a disgrace.

In addition, so-called Hunan appetizers turned out to be neighborhood-style egg roll, spare ribs, fried wontons, dim sum and good shrimp balls. And sweet-and-sour duck was the reddish, sticky banality it usually is but does not have to be.

Among the dishes I would list as excellent are a spicy, crisp whole sea bass that is bathed in a rich, Hunan-style hot sauce and accented with slivers of crackling vegetables; Hunan duckling with smoke flavor — tender, moist slices of lean meat with smoky parchment skin — and twice-fried pork, fork-tender and fiery with chili sauce. A combination of slippery white-meat chicken and chicken cooked brown, both with fresh spinach, is a gentle and soothing dish that is recommended for diners who prefer mildly flavored food. Lobster Sichuan with bamboo shoots, hearts of scallions and pungent ginger was also excellent, as were fillets of sea bass in a spicy shrimp roe sauce.

Far less good, however, was dragon and phoenix — a stir-fried combination of diced chicken and lobster in what is billed as a Sichuan sauce — which on the night I was not known tasted only of chili sauce and was served simply spooned onto plates. Ordered again when I was recognized, dragon and phoenix was not only subtly and engagingly herbed and spiced but was also gorgeously presented in a bright-red lobster shell, mantled with meringue at tail and head. Similarly, moo shu filling was very good on the night I was unknown, but only after asking was a guest at my table able to have a torn-to-shreds crepe replaced with a properly intact one.

Hunan lamb with scallions was fair and slightly greasy on two tries, as were Lake Tung Ting shrimp and General Ching's chicken. In the past I have had a lovely, velvety, rich black-bean sauce here, both on shrimp or pork, and very fine steamed bass or flounder.

It was also interesting to note that on the night I was unrecognized I asked to have the spicy food seasoned in the kitchen's normal way, and dishes had barely any hotness at all. The same request, made when I was known, resulted in food that bordered on the blissfully incendiary.

Desserts such as caramelized apples and bananas with sesame seeds were fair, and the standard premeal giveaway of sugar-glazed walnuts was delicious. Fortune cookies were optimistic, as usual.

Wines are suggested, but as pleasant as were the two German vintages I tasted, they seemed lost on the intensely flavored food. Beer still seems the wiser choice.

When asked if the food is cooked the same for all customers and on all days of the week, Mr. Tong said: "Customers from New Jersey and Long Island who come in on Saturday night do not usually like to try new things or highly spiced dishes. So unless we get to know them and can convince them to experiment, we cook it their way."

Shun Lee West
★ ★

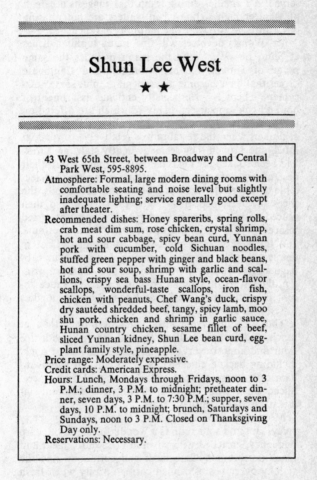

43 West 65th Street, between Broadway and Central Park West, 595-8895.

Atmosphere: Formal, large modern dining rooms with comfortable seating and noise level but slightly inadequate lighting; service generally good except after theater.

Recommended dishes: Honey spareribs, spring rolls, crab meat dim sum, rose chicken, crystal shrimp, hot and sour cabbage, spicy bean curd, Yunnan pork with cucumber, cold Sichuan noodles, stuffed green pepper with ginger and black beans, hot and sour soup, shrimp with garlic and scallions, crispy sea bass Hunan style, ocean-flavor scallops, wonderful-taste scallops, iron fish, chicken with peanuts, Chef Wang's duck, crispy dry sautéed shredded beef, tangy, spicy lamb, moo shu pork, chicken and shrimp in garlic sauce, Hunan country chicken, sesame fillet of beef, sliced Yunnan kidney, Shun Lee bean curd, eggplant family style, pineapple.

Price range: Moderately expensive.

Credit cards: American Express.

Hours: Lunch, Mondays through Fridays, noon to 3 P.M.; dinner, 3 P.M. to midnight; pretheater dinner, seven days, 3 P.M. to 7:30 P.M.; supper, seven days, 10 P.M. to midnight; brunch, Saturdays and Sundays, noon to 3 P.M. Closed on Thanksgiving Day only.

Reservations: Necessary.

"Very good — considering it's near Lincoln Center" has until now been the standard qualification for any halfway decent restaurant in the West Sixties. But at last a "very good" without any qualifications is in order for Shun Lee West, which opened in the summer of 1981 and is turning out more than enough delicious and savory Chinese food to make it worth a journey for its own sake, never mind about tickets to a musical event across the way.

Laid out in the spacious dining rooms formerly occupied by Le Poulailler, Shun Lee West is under the direction of T. T. Wang, the chef, and Michael Tong, who also operate Shun Lee Palace, Shun Lee Dynasty and Hunam. This newest addition already seems to be operating at the level of Shun Lee Palace despite some consistent flaws, most especially late at night when dining room and kitchen staffs operate well below acceptable standards. Redecorated in a somewhat formal modern style, the dining rooms are comfortable with deep banquettes, widely spaced tables and excellent acoustics. But slightly inadequate lighting casts a gloom over the gray-and-maroon color scheme. Somewhat unfelicitous, too, is the entryway past a long and generally unoccupied bar; a more crowded scene there would add a convivial note. The large dining room is used only at night; less busy lunches and weekend dim sum brunches are served in a smaller dining room that suggests a cafe, a pleasant enough setting when waiters are not wearing dirty shirts, as two were one Saturday at lunch.

Mr. Wang's devotees will find many familiar dishes at Shun Lee West, and the menu includes the same range of Hunan, Sichuan, Yunnan and Cantonese dishes that have become his trademark, plus some newcomers. There is an especially enticing assortment of hot and cold appetizers, many of which are offered on the weekend dim sum menu. Most, however, are better at dinner, when the restaurant is relatively crowded; at lunch and brunch they seemed slightly stale, as if they had been cooked the night before and reheated. At their best, chewy, caramelized honey spareribs were as delectable as the petite, crackling Shanghai spring rolls, the slices of green pepper stuffed with shrimp and then sauced with black beans and ginger, the crisply fried minced crystal shrimp, crunchy with water chestnuts, and the delicate crab-meat-filled dumplings. Cool in temperature but fiery in seasoning, hot and sour cabbage added crunchy contrast to the silky Sichuan wonton, the slivers of Yunnan pork in a pungent sauce accented by cucumber icicles and cold Sichuan noodles tossed with a sesame-chili oil sauce.

Those noodles were also better at dinner than at lunch, and so were mellow steamed spareribs with rice flour and almost every dish based on chicken or duck, including hacked chicken, the fried chicken balls with ham called rose chicken and chicken with five spices. Sliced duck with ginger root, which I tried only at lunch, tasted of reheated grease.

Most of the food at Shun Lee West is served properly spicy. Hot and sour soup is a wonderful blend of sharp pungency, enriched with slivered bean curd, meat and black mushrooms. Crab meat and corn soup had the starchy overtones of canned corn — a pity when fresh corn is easily obtainable.

Seafood is well represented on the menu and equally well prepared. Firm shrimp, hotly seasoned and accented with garlic and scallions, and iron fish (braised on an iron pan) subtly sauced with fermented black beans proved fair matches for the magnificent Hunan sea bass, crisply fried and festive with a confettilike topping of minced red and green chilies, ginger and scallions. Ocean-flavor scallops, thinly sliced and stir fried with ginger, vinegar, sugar and soy sauce, were as intriguing as the aptly named wonderful-taste scallops — whole sea scallops lightly glazed and burnished with combined oyster and brown sauces. Hot chili oil cast a rosy haze over the Sichuan lobster, sprightly with ginger. An order of Lake Tung Ting shrimp turned out gray and watery, totally devoid of taste, and General Ching's shrimp are also-rans compared with the other seafood possibilties.

Shrimp combined with chicken in a gentle garlic sauce was one of the better nonspicy dishes. Another was Chef Wang's braised duck (to be ordered six hours in advance), perfumed with garlic and ginger and topped with ginkgo nuts, bamboo shoots and tiny ears of corn — far better, by the way, than the dried-out Sichuan duck. Other excellent mild dishes included moo shu pork, shredded with vegetables to be enfolded in crepes, equally good as appetizer or main course.

Peking duck is well worth ordering in advance, with its parchment-crisp skin, tender crepes and subtle hoisin-based sauce and scallions; a special treat is the leftover duck leg and wing joints, left on the platter for final munching when all of the crepes are gone. Crispy orange beef, tried at lunch, was leathery and afloat in orange grease. It didn't come close to the excellence of the crunches of glazed, shredded dry sautéed beef tossed with slivers of incendiary green chilies that I sampled one night at dinner. Choose the moistly tender Hunan country chicken breast rather than the less interesting cubed tangy spicy chicken, and try slivered tangy lamb with green chilies instead of leg of lamb Hunan style.

Lusty appetites will favor the solidity of sesame filet of beef or the satiny sliced kidney stir fried with bamboo shoots and cucumber. The best vegetables are braised eggplant and bean curd, either minced as an appetizer and topped with crushed peanuts, or sliced and sautéed in a chili-burnished brown sauce.

Pan-fried noodles and fried rice both hinted at overheated or overused grease, and the only dessert worth saving room for is fresh pineapple. A chokingly sweet and dry shower of pink sugar turned otherwise wellfried bananas into a near miss.

It is to be hoped that the menu format will be simplified at Shun Lee West. Right now it is an elaborate triptych listing different prices for some of the same dishes at different times of day — pretheater, dinner and supper. Service is generally good but can be overbearing. There is full bar service, and Chinese beer is on hand.

Siam Inn
★ ★

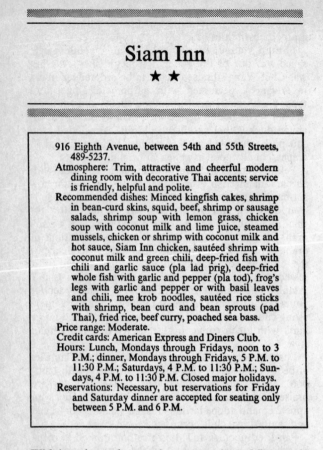

916 Eighth Avenue, between 54th and 55th Streets, 489-5237.

Atmosphere: Trim, attractive and cheerful modern dining room with decorative Thai accents; service is friendly, helpful and polite.

Recommended dishes: Minced kingfish cakes, shrimp in bean-curd skins, squid, beef, shrimp or sausage salads, shrimp soup with lemon grass, chicken soup with coconut milk and lime juice, steamed mussels, chicken or shrimp with coconut milk and hot sauce, Siam Inn chicken, sautéed shrimp with coconut milk and green chili, deep-fried fish with chili and garlic sauce (pla lad prig), deep-fried whole fish with garlic and pepper (pla tod), frog's legs with garlic and pepper or with basil leaves and chili, mee krob noodles, sautéed rice sticks with shrimp, bean curd and bean sprouts (pad Thai), fried rice, beef curry, poached sea bass.

Price range: Moderate.

Credit cards: American Express and Diners Club.

Hours: Lunch, Mondays through Fridays, noon to 3 P.M.; dinner, Mondays through Fridays, 5 P.M. to 11:30 P.M.; Saturdays, 4 P.M. to 11:30 P.M.; Sundays, 4 P.M. to 11:30 P.M. Closed major holidays.

Reservations: Necessary, but reservations for Friday and Saturday dinner are accepted for seating only between 5 P.M. and 6 P.M.

With its spicy and aromatic counterpoints of flavor and the lively textural contrasts it affords, the food of Thailand is certainly one of the world's most entertaining and engaging cuisines. Influenced by India in the use of herbs and spices, and borrowing cooking techniques from the Chinese, the Thais over the centuries have added innovations that resulted in an original and diverting collection of dishes. At the Siam Inn, dozens of beguiling Thai specialties are skillfully prepared and attractively presented by a shyly gracious and efficient staff. If some of the kitchen's efforts are lackluster, most of the dishes offered are skillfully seasoned with onions, coriander, crushed roasted peanuts and fiery chilies, mellowing garlic and cooling cucumber and the highly perfumed juices of lemons and exotic Kaffir limes. Basil, lemon grass and brassy curry spices also give Thai food its character, and the basic stir-fry, steaming and grilling techniques are competently performed.

Add to this low to moderate prices, an attractive, trim modern dining room brightened by Thai accessories and the restaurant's proximity to the theater district, Columbus Circle and even Lincoln Center, and you come up with a winning combination. Generally more crowded during the later lunch and dinner hours, the Siam Inn has a loyal coterie of aficionados who order their way through a long progression of dishes, generally shared Chinese-style. Chopsticks can be provided, but the traditional Thai combination of fork and spoon is more correct and convenient. Air conditioning can be overdone, chilling customers along with food, but it is quickly adjusted upon request.

The one appetizer to avoid is the egg roll, a greasy and banal failure, far outclassed by such choices as the ground shrimp and grated garlic wrapped in bean-curd skin and looking disconcertingly like stuffed derma, the squid salad with its lime juice and chili paste accents, and minced kingfish and shrimp cakes topped with a sparkling cucumber and peanut dressing. Thai soups are heady with aromatic herbs and lemony grasses, and two are done to perfection here — the clear shrimp broth with straw mushrooms, chili and lime juice, and the pleasantly astringent chicken soup with coconut milk and ginger.

Degrees of hotness are indicated on the menu by asterisks, three marking the spiciest dishes. Even so, if you like food really hot, request it that way and you will get it. In addition, fiery condiments are traditional, to be added at the table. The best are the sliced red chilies in vinegar, with a ground variation and crushed peanuts also on hand to stabilize the effects of the chilies.

Certain basic sauces and preparations are common to various ingredients. For example, a glaze of garlic and pepper is equally good on fried shrimp and fried pork, and it reaches its ultimate on tender, meaty frog's legs. Those plump legs are almost as delicious in a hotly flavored combination of basil and chilies, seasonings that can also be had on sautéed boneless chicken, beef, shrimp and pork.

Various curry styles are native to the Thai kitchen, and red curries here are the most incendiary. Good examples are the coconut milk and red chili curry based on chicken, beef or shrimp. Green curries, also with coconut milk, are best here with shrimp and chicken.

Thai salads, suitable as appetizer or main course, are prepared with onions, parsley, lime juice and chili oil, and can be had with shrimp, beef or, most interestingly, with warm, fried sliced Chinese pork sausage.

Whole crisply fried sea bass, with either chili and garlic sauce (pla lad prig) or garlic and pepper (pla tod), are beautifully moist and delicately flavored. So is a menu clip-on special of "red snapper" steamed and served over a brazier. The only problem is that the fish is not red snapper but sea bass. When asked about this, the waiter said: "Yes, all of our red snapper is sea bass. We haven't bothered to change the menu yet." Or even bothered to inform people when they order.

Other clip-on specials, though good, did not seem to approach regular menu offerings in interest. Siam Inn chicken, prettily presented in straw serving dishes, had a richly complicated tamarind and garlic sauce that did not adequately permeate the chicken, and the Bangkok duck with similar seasonings again fell short of the house's best efforts. Not so the almost miraculous mussels, which were plump, fresh as a sea breeze, steamed in a lemony white wine and ginger broth and served in a handsome earthenware casserole.

Sauce for the grilled beef satays was a wonderful blend of peanuts and hot oil, but the meat itself had been sliced a little too thin for broiling.

Creamy fried rice, almost like risotto, was good even with king crab meat, and two noodle dishes were superb

— the traditional mee krob of fine golden crisp-fried noodles tossed with shrimp, pork, tamarind sauce and bean sprouts, and the soft pad Thai, rice noodles with shrimps, egg and dried bean cake.

Desserts are suffocatingly thick and sweet, but for the persistently curious there are pumpkin custard, a coconut cake much like a thick, dry macaroon and a sort of jelled custard. Fresh fruit seemed preferable.

There is full bar service and Thai beer is the most appropriate beverage for the food. Dishes on the lunch menu are remarkably low priced and the full dinner menu is also available at that time, offering more interesting, if more expensive, choices.

Sichuan Pavilion

★

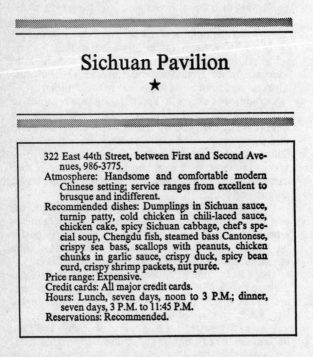

322 East 44th Street, between First and Second Avenues, 986-3775.
Atmosphere: Handsome and comfortable modern Chinese setting; service ranges from excellent to brusque and indifferent.
Recommended dishes: Dumplings in Sichuan sauce, turnip patty, cold chicken in chili-laced sauce, chicken cake, spicy Sichuan cabbage, chef's special soup, Chengdu fish, steamed bass Cantonese, crispy sea bass, scallops with peanuts, chicken chunks in garlic sauce, crispy duck, spicy bean curd, crispy shrimp packets, nut purée.
Price range: Expensive.
Credit cards: All major credit cards.
Hours: Lunch, seven days, noon to 3 P.M.; dinner, seven days, 3 P.M. to 11:45 P.M.
Reservations: Recommended.

It is difficult to say whether the food or the service has deteriorated more since Sichuan Pavilion was awarded three stars. Although at times service can still be efficient and thoughful, unless the party is large and a special plea is made for attention, the staff is brusque and impervious to requests that spicy dishes be really spicy and that only a few dishes be brought at a time.

This is a shame because the menu at this handsome modern restaurant offers some of the most unusual and interesting Chinese specialties in town, and formerly most were well prepared. If one wanted a single test by which to evaluate the management's commitment to the comfort of diners, it would be to arrive at a crowded time with a party of three. Treated properly, a party of three should be given a table for four. But on a busy Saturday night, three diners were crammed at a table for two. Since the earlier review recommending a wide variety of dishes, the staff has discouraged the ordering of many of the more complicated specialties.

There is still evidence of the restaurant's former excellence, especially in such appetizers as the silky little dumplings in a spicy Sichuan sauce, the cool, peppery

Sichuan cabbage, the cold unusual-tasting chicken in a dark chili-laced sauce crunchy with sesame seeds and the crisply fried nuggets known as chicken cake. Turnip patties with ham also remain good. But the greasiness and staleness characteristic of several main courses were also apparent in other appetizers, such as the spring rolls, the spareribs and beef strips served in small steamers and the dried-out smoked fish fillets. Hot and sour soup was neither hot nor sour, and the wonton soup tasted like unseasoned vegetable water. Only the chef's special soup with pork, mushrooms and greens was up to former standards, although it was not served in the individual steamers, as described on the menu.

Whole fish are among the best main courses, whether you choose the crispy sea bass in its dark pork enriched sauce, the gently steamed Cantonese bass with slivers of scallions and ginger or the Chengdu-style bass with minced vegetables in a sauce that is delicious, if not adequately spiced. Crispy shrimp packets — pounded shrimp deep-fried in wrappings of golden, crackling bean curd sheet — and scallions stir-fried with peanuts remain excellent. But shrimp in other dishes reeked of iodine and lobster was tough, pallid and tepid.

The acrid overtones of stale cooking oil flawed pan-fried noodles, fried rice, eggplant in garlic sauce, pork with peanuts and slivered duck. Staleness marred shredded rabbit meat and sliced fried lamb. Better choices were the crispy duck with a salt-glazed, greaseless skin, chicken chunks in garlic sauce and the bean curd slices with ground pork that were properly dosed with chili oil. Perhaps the biggest disappointment on two recent visits was Buddha's duck, formerly a meltingly tender braised duck aromatic with anise and now a fatty, stale and bland misrepresentation.

The walnut purée is the best dessert.

Simon's

★

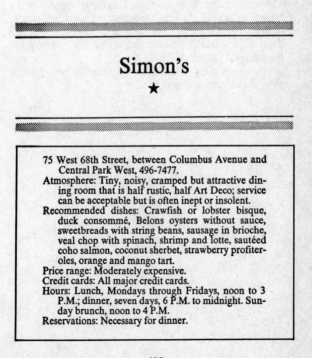

75 West 68th Street, between Columbus Avenue and Central Park West, 496-7477.

Atmosphere: Tiny, noisy, cramped but attractive dining room that is half rustic, half Art Deco; service can be acceptable but is often inept or insolent.

Recommended dishes: Crawfish or lobster bisque, duck consommé, Belons oysters without sauce, sweetbreads with string beans, sausage in brioche, veal chop with spinach, shrimp and lotte, sautéed coho salmon, coconut sherbet, strawberry profiteroles, orange and mango tart.

Price range: Moderately expensive.

Credit cards: All major credit cards.

Hours: Lunch, Mondays through Fridays, noon to 3 P.M.; dinner, seven days, 6 P.M. to midnight. Sunday brunch, noon to 4 P.M.

Reservations: Necessary for dinner.

The missing ingredient at Simon's is experience. Talent in the kitchen seems less of a problem. Here in a tiny boîte done up in rustic wood and Art Deco mirrors, a creditable version of the nouvelle cuisine is served up. Just a short walk from Lincoln Center, Simon's was the setting for a farewell party for Walter Cronkite. From then on, it was on the must list of the au courant.

Although it's a busy restaurant, the noise level is almost bearable when the electric piano is not on. Some of the waiters affect a style that they seem to think is breezy but which is really intrusive and insolent. There is also a tendency to use the kindergartenish "we." Spilling wine on a cloth and menu, the waiter soothed an annoyed patron with, "We're not going to let that spoil our evening, are we?"

Against this backdrop, however, as appetizers one is offered crystal-clear Belons oysters (best without any of the overpowering toppings available), crisp nuggets of sweetbreads bordered with slim French string beans and just about the richest, most superbly spiced crawfish or lobster bisques I have ever had. Duck consommé accompanied by a purée of duck liver on a crouton was another excellent daily special, as was the sausage in a roll of brioche crust. Less appealing were musty artichokes in a cloying sauce, sticky and greasy pasta with basil sauce and, at lunch, a Chinese vegetable salad overpowered with heavy sesame oil.

Red shrimp and tiny medaillons of the snowy, firm fish, lotte, had a satiny beurre blanc sauce and a sublime mousse of roasted red peppers. And there was a golden veal chop filled with Pernod-scented spinach and foie gras nestled beside noodles mellowed by a classic, light truffle sauce. One evening, coho salmon was so skillfully sautéed that its skin took on a crackling crisp glaze of brown butter.

A disappointment among main courses was the surf and turf — lobster beurre blanc and beef tournedos — a dish that suffered from the main ingredients' being served in tandem. Also disappointing were an overly soupy stew of lobster, oysters and vegetables; calf's liver; a ham and cheese omelet, and a candy-sweet sea trout teriyaki at lunch.

For dessert, try strawberry profiteroles or, if available, the orange and mango tart.

Sloppie Louie's

★

92 South Street, between Fulton and John Streets, 952-9657.

Atmosphere: Pleasantly ramshackle but clean fish-market restaurant that is being refurbished; noisy, crowded and convivial; prompt, no-frills service.

Recommended dishes: Clams or oysters on the half shell, fried soft clams, fish chowder, bouillabaisse, all broiled and fried fish.

Price range: Moderate.

Credit cards: None.

Hours: Mondays through Fridays, 11 A.M. to 8 P.M. Closed Saturdays, Sundays and major holidays.

Reservations: Necessary for large groups only.

For almost fifty years, this landmark on South Street near the Fulton Fish Market has been serving simple, moderately priced fish and seafood unmatched for freshness. And in good weather, there is the bonus of being able to sit on the pier of the South Street Seaport Museum or to walk among the enticing alleyways of the financial district and to marvel at the lobbies of some of the more interesting buildings, such as the Cocoa Exchange.

Although an averaging out of the menu results in a one-star rating, there are some dishes of outstanding quality that diners are advised to stick to for a satisfying meal.

The plainer the better is the rule here. Clams and oysters on the half shell are always fresh and opened to order, although they sometimes are less chilled than they should be. Among the soups, fish chowder is a unique masterpiece, a strong, thick, pale-golden soup with chunks of fish and celery. It is somewhat better than the merely decent, tomato-rich Manhattan clam chowder. The small bouillabaisse, an assortment of fish, squid and fragments of shellfish in a rich, oily tomato broth, is delicious when hot enough, but is difficult to eat in the tiny saucer in which it is served. Better to order the rugged, full-portion bouillabaisse as a main course, one of the city's best bargains, which contains generous helpings of firm, fresh assorted fish.

Forget about preparations such as New Orleans shrimp creole and spaghetti with clam sauce and stick to the simplest, freshest broiled and fried fish dishes. The daily specials posted on wall signs are usually the wisest choices. All broiled fish is topped with a coating of fine cornmeal and flour to protect it from the drying ravages of open flame, a precaution that results in moist, tender fish with a light, golden crusty topping. Frying in a crisper breading is also well done, but what is billed as sautéed comes in a sauce that is essentially the bouillabaisse broth — strong, spicy, very good, but a surprise if you are expecting a plain sauté.

Thick codfish steaks, delicate fillets of ocean perch, Kennebec salmon, perfect lemon sole, local bluefish, Boston scrod broiled to just the right degree of doneness without being at all dried out, are among the better choices. So are the wonderful fried soft clams, available as a main course but even better as a shared appetizer.

If any fish is not available fresh, it is not available at Sloppy Louie's. Thus, items on the menu are often not to be had. There are also assorted plates of fried or broiled fish and shellfish to satisfy the indecisive.

But when it comes to trimmings, beware. The salad is simply iceberg lettuce with bottled dressing, so opt for cole slaw if given a choice. All potatoes, whether french fried, baked or boiled, are unworthy of the fish they accompany, as is the starchy over-cooked instant rice. Banana shortcake used to be the one memorable dessert at Sloppy Louie's, a generous helping of sliced ripe bananas and genuine whipped cream on a token slab of pound cake. But on recent tries, the combination was marred somewhat by the use of ultrapasteurized cream for the topping, which added the unpleasant yeasty flavor of boiled milk.

Big tables are shared by several parties, paper napkins are in dispensers and paper mats are placed on plain wood-topped tables. There are a handsome, pressed-tin ceiling and antique mirrors and coat hooks, a nostalgic, old-fashioned touch, albeit one that is unnecessarily ramshackle. Perhaps the current restoration of the building will improve things.

When it comes to service, "sloppy" is no idle adjective. Little care is taken to prevent soup or coffee from spilling over from cup to saucer, side dishes of cole slaw are slapped down in the center of a group to be grabbed for, and bowls of oyster crackers and lemon wedges are shared among strangers who sit at the same table. Waiters range from informally polite and friendly to rude.

The house has no liquor license, so take your own beer or wine.

SoHo Charcuterie
★★

195 Spring Street, corner of Sullivan Street, 226-3545.
Atmosphere: Fresh, romantic and young setting with pleasant lighting but uncomfortable chairs and a high noise level when busy; service is friendly and attentive but often slow.
Recommended dishes: Quiches, omelets, pâté de campagne, curried tuna salad, chicken salad with tarragon mayonnaise, smoked fish platter, charcuterie salads, cream of mushroom soup, sautéed duck livers, mousse of shrimp, scallop and spinach, assortment of hams, angel hair pasta with leeks and shitake mushrooms, soft-shell crabs, salmon stuffed with spinach and watercress, filet of beef tenderloin, rack of baby lamb, brook trout sautéed with almond flour, roast baby chicken, roast pheasant, rhubarb sherbet, lemon mousse, chocolate almond cake, rhubarb and strawberry pie, orange and mango tart, lemon tart.
Price range: Moderately expensive.
Credit cards: American Express and Visa.
Hours: Lunch, Tuesdays through Fridays, noon to 3:30 P.M.; Saturdays, 11:30 A.M. to 4:30 P.M.; dinner, Tuesdays through Fridays, 6 P.M. to 11 P.M.; Saturdays, 6 P.M. to 11:30 P.M.; brunch, Sundays, 11 A.M. to 4:30 P.M. Closed Mondays.
Reservations: Necessary for brunch.

The new philosophy of cooking that might well be considered an emerging American cuisine is exemplified pleasantly and, generally, deliciously here. This young and fresh style of cooking and food presentation borrows freely from Continental kitchens, with much from France, Italy and Germany, along with overtones of things American and Oriental. Sesame oil, shitake mushrooms, authentic French pâtés, delicate pastas sheathed in sheer sauces of cream and leeks, German hams, Eastern curries gentling salads of tuna fish, apples, almonds and currants and a menu printed blessedly and unaffectedly in English are all part of the tone.

At weekend brunches, puffy quiches and omelets are fine alternatives to the exquisite smoked fish platter, and the only fault to be found with the assorted salad platters is that the combinations are too rich. One of the best, however, is the chicken in homemade mayonnaise, sprightly with tarragon and green peppercorns.

Dinners in this bright and fresh setting are romantically lit by floating candles, but the elimination of background music would be an improvement. That way one would be better able to relax and appreciate appetizers such as the sautéed duck liver in a Madeira sauce topped with diced celery root, or the superb froth of shrimp and scallop mousse interwoven with spinach, all in a sauce that blends reduced fish stock, cream and hints of red pepper and sweet paprika. The pâté de campagne made of pork and veal is the house's best, whether plain or fired by green peppercorns. But the assortment of hams with chèvre cheese and apples is a meal in itself, and far too large for an appetizer.

The richness of salmon baked in a fragile turban of phyllo pastry was eased by a filling of spinach and watercress and a sheer beurre blanc sauce. A fist of beef tenderloin, rose-red and fork-tender, picked up flavor from the Westphalian ham and the earthy mushrooms around it. Peppercorns lent bite to a lovely rack of lamb that had only a bit too much rosemary, and brook trout sautéed in a coating of almond flour remained moist and pearly. Boned baby chicken nested on creamed watercress, spinach, dill and chives, and the tender, fresh baby pheasant with red cabbage and ham were also far above average. So were tiny soft-shell crabs in a buttery sauce brightened with salmon caviar.

A puréed cream of mushroom soup was a far more engaging choice than a cloying, curried zucchini soup. Among main courses, the least satisfactory were the fine-quality loin of veal, sticky sweet in an orange sauce, and the overdone sliced duck breast.

Desserts seductive enough to tempt even the most devout sugarphobe included a light and velvety chocolate and almond cake, a rhubarb and strawberry tart and an orange and mango tart. Only the kiwi and strawberry tart and a mint sherbet that suggested frozen toothpaste were disappointing. Rhubarb sherbet with accents of cassis, the black currant liqueur, and a cold lemon mousse were light and lovely. So was a lemon curd pie adrift with cloudlets of whipped cream.

The best buy at the SoHo Charcuterie for those who enjoy a three-course meal is the fixed-price menu with very good choices. The food justifies the price, but the simplicity of the setting and casualness of the service make the check seem high compared to more ambitious and formal uptown alternatives that surely have higher overheads. The wine list is minimally adequate.

Soomthai

★

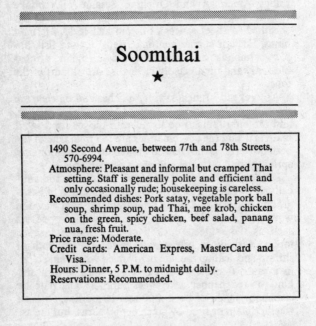

1490 Second Avenue, between 77th and 78th Streets, 570-6994.

Atmosphere: Pleasant and informal but cramped Thai setting. Staff is generally polite and efficient and only occasionally rude; housekeeping is careless.

Recommended dishes: Pork satay, vegetable pork ball soup, shrimp soup, pad Thai, mee krob, chicken on the green, spicy chicken, beef salad, panang nua, fresh fruit.

Price range: Moderate.

Credit cards: American Express, MasterCard and Visa.

Hours: Dinner, 5 P.M. to midnight daily.

Reservations: Recommended.

Although it is still possible to get a very good meal at this atmospheric Thai restaurant, chances of doing so are a little slimmer than they were when it opened in 1979. Unevenness now marks the kitchen's performance, accounting for the one-star rating instead of the original two. Fish and mussels are not always as fresh as they should be and now cannot be recommended. Nevertheless, this is generally a dependable choice for moderately priced Thai food on the Upper East Side.

In general, the food of the country that used to be known as Siam combines the ingredients and many of the cooking methods of China with the curry spices of India and adds a number of Malaysian touches to the mix. The result is steamed, fried and stir-fried dishes brightened with Oriental vegetables and often hotly spiced. A variety of green and red chili peppers is accented by aromatic fresh coriander, scallions and onions, the pungent sweetness of lime and the perfume of lemon grass and basil. Garlic, peanuts, coconut and cucumbers are among the more soothing flavors.

Soomthai offers a limited but tempting array of dishes, starting with such appetizers as grilled pork satays served with peanut sauce and the cucumber salad. Two good soups are the tom yam koong, shrimp in a lemony, chili-spiked broth with mushrooms and parsley, and the mild-flavored but satisfying vegetable and pork ball soup. This is as good a time as any to say that the food here is served hotly spiced even when not so requested, and if you ask for yours extra hotly spiced, be prepared to be taken seriously. Thai hotness can be a bit deceptive. At first taste it may seem mild, but a fiery glow builds up in the throat, so add chili oil judiciously.

There are two intriguing noodle dishes to be had as main courses or side dishes. Pad Thai combines soft noodles with sautéed onions, egg, shrimp, bean curd and the ground peanut and chili oil sauce, while for mee krob the thread-thin rice noodles are fried as crisp and golden as spun glass and then tossed with shrimp, egg and bean sprouts, all seasoned at once mildly sweet and pungent. At times these may hint at overheated grease, but usually they do not.

Chicken on the green, a combination of sliced chicken breast meat on vegetable greens with a nut sauce, and the incendiary spicy chicken, a green curry with basil, chili peppers and fish sauce, are both commendable main sauces. The slightly warm beef salad made with slices of charcoal-broiled beef marinated in a chili and fish sauce, with lemon mint leaves, lemon grass, slivers of red onions and coriander leaves, was delightful even though the meat was just a bit drier than it should have been.

Shrimp can be had in a similar salad or in a mild red curry and onion sauce that, although decent, was not quite up to other choices, especially when the shrimp are stale. Better to try the panang nua, beef sautéed with red curry, coconut milk and green chili.

Pork fried rice is a hardy and soothing foil for the sharply flavored foods. Thai desserts tend to be sweetly sticky and cloying, and Soomthai's are no exceptions. The platter of sliced watermelon and honeydew melon is a better windup for the meal.

There is full bar service, with the light Thai beer, Singha, to be had. Service is considerate and polite as a rule; once in a while it becomes rushed and rude. Tables are a bit too cramped for comfort, especially when the dining room is full. Thai background music is fairly pleasant until the room becomes crowded and noisy.

Portions are large, and, as in Chinese restaurants, it is a good idea to go with several people and share dishes.

Souen

★

210 Avenue of the Americas, between Prince and King Streets, 242-9083.

Atmosphere: Simple, attractive and immaculate cafe-restaurant; service is good natured, helpful and efficient though unpolished.

Recommended dishes: Mushroom and barley soup, brown rice with tahini-oat sauce, tofu, tofu nori roll, agetofu, chef's salad, all broiled fish, sole roll, kara-age, norimaki, cold soba, fried soba, all tempuras, taboulleh, apple crunch.

Price range: Inexpensive.

Credit cards: American Express.

Hours: Sundays through Thursdays, noon to 11 P.M., Fridays and Saturdays, noon to midnight.

Reservations: Necessary for large groups.

Souen specializes in food prepared according to the macrobiotic principles laid down by George Ohsawa as a guide to both spiritual and physical harmony with nature. Macrobiotic cookery features grains, vegetables and noodle and bean curd combinations cooked in the Japanese style. Some fish and occasional frying apparently are permitted for the less orthodox devotees.

Spirituality aside, you don't have to be macrobiotic to enjoy a satisfying and soothing meal at the new Souen (pronounced SOO-en), a far better and more amiable place than its dark, crowded and mediocre original on Upper Broadway. In the Village branch, a bright and simple wood, tile and glass dining room suggests a cross between Scandinavian and Japanese designs. The spotless appointments, the big cafe windows and the friendly and accommodating staff create a felicitous mood, a mood marred only occasionally by a whiff of frying oil from the cleverly enclosed kitchen.

To be sure, there are all the simple steamed and stir-fried vegetable and noodle dishes, plus the millet and brown rice specialties that the strictest followers of George Ohsawa depend on. But if one where not aware of this esoteric bias, Souen would seem to be a terrific find. A hearty, flawlessly fried tempura combination of fish, shrimp and gorgeous vegetables, or an even more diverting kakiage tempura — big lacy swirls of chopped shrimp and vegetables that are crunchy and grease-free — can be had inexpensively. An all-vegetable tempura, also very inexpensive, can be turned into a thoroughly delicious main course by adding some nutlike brown rice with a sesame and oat sauce.

Borrowing a technique from the sushi makers, Souen prepares versions of seaweed nori rolls. For sole roll, the fragrant seaweed is wrapped around sole, filled with vegetables, then deep fried. The tofu nori roll is fishless, but it includes the custardy bean curd, tofu. For nori-maki, the seaweed encloses brown rice and vegetables. This and other main courses are served with a subtly soft mixed vegetable stew, and often with the grated radish, daikon.

Broiled fish, whether teriyaki-style or in a miso bean sauce, is fresh and pleasant, if less engaging than the fried specialties. The blander steamed and stir-fried dishes such as the vegetable soba with buckwheat noodles and the simmered sukiyaki of fish, tofu and vegetables seemed tasteless and boring, although they were sparklingly fresh and certainly a boon to those interested in holding down on fat, salt and calories (and possibly flavor).

A mushroom-and-barley soup, thick as porridge, was almost a meal in itself, and stir-fried soba noodles with vegetables or the cold soba with soy sauce and seaweed proved refreshing. Yakko, the cold tofu with tamari soy sauce, and deep-fried agetofu with ginger sauce were diverting as appetizers or side dishes. Like all other choices here, they can be shared.

Bread was extremely heavy and sourish, and steamed seaweed (hiziki) tasted like iodine, perhaps the very feature that makes it most desirable to aficionados. The chef's salad changes from day to day, and mine was a brilliant rainbow of barely blanched cauliflower, broccoli and raw chicory, watercress, carrots, celery and tomatoes with a marvelous sunny sauce of sesame paste, soy oil and carrots — a copious and genuine bargain. The only recommendable dessert is apple crunch, a baked apple topped with cinnamon-scented nut and granola crumbles. What a pity that dairy products are verboten in the macrobiotic format. Cream would have done wonders for the apple crunch.

The young staff here beams with good will, and all are endlessly patient about explaining the dishes and the way they are eaten.

Sparks Steakhouse
★

210 East 46th Street, between Second and Third Avenues, 687-4855.

Atmosphere: Nondescript but typical pseudo-pub, steakhouse setting; noisy and crowded; service can be good but is generally careless, slow and inattentive.

Recommended dishes: Broiled shrimp scampi style, clams on the half shell, sirloin or filet mignon steaks, baked potato, cheesecake.

Price range: Expensive.

Credit cards: All major credit cards.

Hours: Lunch, Mondays through Fridays, noon to 3 P.M.; dinner, Mondays through Thursdays, 5 P.M. to 11 P.M.; Fridays and Saturdays, 5 P.M. to 11:30 P.M. Closed Sundays.

Reservations: Necessary.

This huge, multiroomed, gaudy and noisy steakhouse has a large and loyal following, which on weeknights consists mostly of men who seem to stop for dinner after meetings. It is decorated in a style I think of as "Kansas City fancy" — lots of dark wood, an overabundance of antique kitsch and enormous displays of wine of which the management has a staggering and excellent selection. It is surprising, then, to discover how lax waiters can be about taking wine orders, and on recent visits I had a hard time getting any. Only once did a very attentive waiter take time out to ask about wine and to make suggestions.

Once known for the low prices charged in its original location on 18th Street, Sparks moved to Steak Row in 1977 and prices soared to equal those of its august neighbors, making it unremarkable.

Steaks, the main business at hand here, are usually very good and only occasionally are not broiled as ordered. Giant lobsters were more expensive than those at comparable places, and though one I had was moist, tender and delicious, two others were tough, rubbery and tasteless. The same unevenness is apparent with shrimp cocktails — sometimes perfect, other times bland because of shrimp that may have been held too long on ice after being peeled. Broiled shrimp scampi style with garlic butter were consistently good as appetizer or main course, but a really disgraceful dish on one occasion was the overcooked, broiled red snapper, past its peak of freshness. Pasty baked clams and leathery prosciutto are also skippable.

Tender beef slices were overpowered by a thick, brown gravy loaded with green peppers and mushrooms. The spinach is soggy and overcooked, and hashed-brown potatoes may either be good or burned. The only dependable choice is the crusty, steaming-hot baked potatoes.

On one occasion, a salad ordered with vinaigrette

dressing arrived with Roquefort instead, and when the correct version was brought, the dressing was bitingly acidic and salty. Walnut pie is good when moist and chewy but is often dry, and one portion of strawberries had been around so long the berries were faded and mushy. Cheesecake is excellent — creamy but with texture and only gently sweet. Because the steaks and a few trimmings are consistently good and are the main reason for this restaurant's being, Sparks is worth a single star.

Suzanne
Fair

313 East 46th Street, between First and Second Avenues, 832-2888.
Atmosphere: Attractive dining room that is generally comfortable, although lighting is inadequate; service is careless and indifferent.
Recommended dishes: Cha gio rice-paper rolls, spicy lemon shrimp soup, beef brochette with sesame seeds, com tay cam casserole.
Price range: Moderately expensive.
Credit cards: All major credit cards.
Hours: Lunch, Mondays through Fridays, 11:30 A.M. to 3 P.M.; dinner, Mondays through Saturdays, 5:30 P.M. to 10:30 P.M. Closed Sundays. Closed on Christmas Day and New Year's Day.
Reservations: Necessary at lunch.

If Vietnamese cuisine were less interesting, and if the Suzanne restaurant were not the most visible uptown source for it in Manhattan, there would be little reason for a review. The restaurant, owned by Huy Ty Pham, a former South Vietnamese representative at the United Nations, and his wife, Suzanne, opened about four years ago as the Griffin, featuring fairly decent Continental food. The brick-and-wood contemporary décor is intact, and in the evenings, there is still a piano player adding to the cocktail-lounge atmosphere. Popular at lunch with United Nations personnel but fairly empty at dinner, the Suzanne restaurant has an unattractive bar scene on some evenings.

Oddly enough, the Continental food formerly served was better than the bland and carelessly prepared Vietnamese dishes now featured. All of the Vietnamese food is certainly edible, but considering the fascinating contrasts of texture and flavor in the food of that Southeast Asian country, the examples at Suzanne are lackluster. Neither the staff nor the management takes much trouble to explain the cuisine, and only occasionally does Suzanne Pham make suggestions.

The only consistently good appetizers among four sampled were cha gio, crisply fried rice-paper rolls filled with crab meat, chicken, noodles and mushrooms. Although less delicate than versions tried in Paris and

Washington, those at Suzanne proved satisfying. Not so the barbecued spareribs, which were stale and dry at both lunch and dinner, nor a watery pork salad. Shrimp grilled on skewers of sugar cane was unavailable on three visits.

Spicy lemon shrimp soup, though made with ice-cold raw tomatoes, did have a good belt of hot and sour seasonings as well as generous portions of shrimp and bean sprouts.

Brochettes of pork and chicken had no flavor and were tough and dry, and so was grilled lemon-grass chicken, but grilled beef brochettes, topped with a crunchy sprinkling of sesame seeds and bedded down on a cushion of soft rice noodles, were delicious. So was a soul-satisfying, steamed earthenware casserole, com tay cam, combining shrimp, chicken, bamboo shoots, mushrooms and scallions. Crispy noodles topped with vegetables and chicken, pork or shrimp brought back memories of neighborhood Chinese restaurant-style chop suey. Shrimp, Saigon style, bore almost no traces of the garlic and ginger seasonings the menu attributed to them.

Two sauces were meant to accent some of the dishes. One was a clear blend of fermented fish sauce and hot chili oil, the other a thicker sweet-and-pungent dip for the brochettes. Sometimes the sauces arrived after the meat had been eaten, other times not at all.

Stick to fresh fruit if you want dessert. Service is slow, especially at lunch.

Sweets
★

2 Fulton Street, corner of South Street, 344-9189.
Atmosphere: Pleasantly antique, Old New York settings; fair service.
Recommended dishes: Clams on the half shell, crab meat cocktail, fried or broiled oysters, clam broth, fried soft-shell crabs, clam or oyster stew, finnan haddie à la Sweets, broiled lobster, broiled bay scallops, broiled fish.
Price range: Moderately expensive.
Credit cards: None.
Hours: Mondays through Fridays, 11:30 A.M. to 8:30 P.M. Closed Saturdays, Sundays and major holidays.
Reservations: Not accepted.

It is hard to imagine that anyone who is interested in New York and its past would not be lured at least occasionally to Sweets, the city's oldest seafood restaurant, opened in 1842 at the edge of the Fulton Fish Market. Unfortunately, it was recently renovated and made characterless, but still another refurbishing is planned that will, perhaps, restore the antique charm. In the best of all possible worlds the experience would be as satisfying gastronomically as it is romantically. I have never found that to be the case, even though optimism draws me back time and time again. Because of its proximity to the wholesale fish market, Sweets does offer fish and seafood that are fresh and of high quality, but the disappointing final results are due to the cooking (or, more exactly, the overcooking) and to the inferior quality of secondary dishes, such as vegetables, sauces, salads and desserts. Nevertheless, those who enjoy walking around the South Street Seaport Museum and the interesting side streets of this beguiling old neighborhood can find enough acceptably prepared dishes on the Sweets menu for a satisfying if not inspiring dinner.

The general rule worth remembering is to order the simpler dishes on the menu. Sauces, such as those used for the creole, au gratin and Newburg dishes, are, plain and simple, awful. But the broiled fish such as the true gray sole, red snapper, swordfish, halibut and bluefish are always far better, if invariably overcooked. The same flaw slightly mars what must be the tiniest and sweetest bay scallops available — worth recommending in spite of the overcooking. It is possible that the kitchen takes fish orders from the broiler before they are overdone, but because broiling is done on heavy metal sizzle platters that hold the heat, the cooking continues as the fish is being carried to the table and even as it is being eaten. Often the fish sticks to the platter and must be scraped off to be eaten. Frying is done very well, whether for the appetizer oysters or for the lusciously fat soft-shell crabs. Broiled lobster, protected by a coating of bread crumbs, is also recommendable, even though small at the price. Smoky finnan haddie à la Sweets (broiled in milk) was lusty, and the salty flavor was mellowed by the milk-and-butter sauce.

The best appetizers sampled were plump and juicy oysters broiled in butter and clams on the half shell, always cold and sparkling. Clam or oyster stews, preferably in cream, were properly briny and satisfying. Clam chowder was consistently disappointing, tasting almost exclusively of canned tomatoes. The hot clam broth is more bracing for someone who considers soup essential.

Cold and unseasoned plain boiled rice or a crisp and well-roasted potato are served with all hot main courses. An order of fried eggplant tasted overwhelmingly of the bread crumbs that coated the slices, but the frying, again, was crisp and greaseless.

If you feel like dessert, stick to the lovely ripe fresh melon. Ice cream and cheese cake are dreadful choices, as are Jell-O with whipped cream and the commercial tortoni and spumoni. The sophistication of the wine list matches that of the dessert selection; better to order one of the good imported beers or ales. There is usually a fast-moving waiting line at Sweets, and it is worth adding a few minutes to that wait to sit in the front dining room. The back room, with the slamming doors of the kitchen and the bathrooms and the brusque help that works there, is most uncomfortable.

Szechuan Cuisine
Poor

30 East Broadway, between Catherine and Division
Streets, 966-2326.
Atmosphere: Messy, dirty, confused dining room;
service is brusque, distracted, careless and rude.
Recommended dishes: All dumplings, cold Sichuan
cabbage, carp with hot bean sauce, prawns with
walnuts.
Price range: Inexpensive.
Credit cards: None.
Hours: Wednesdays through Mondays, 11 A.M. to 10
P.M.; closed Tuesdays. Open on holidays.
Reservations: Suggested on weekdays.

Like so many other restaurants, Szechuan Cuisine has
its walls and windows plastered with reprints of a two-
star rating it received in 1977. It would be nice to be
able to rip such old reviews off those walls and windows
in a case such as this, when service and food have deteriorated to a poor rating. There are still a few good
dishes to be had here at low prices, but considering
more pleasant options in Chinatown, there is no reason
to stand the gaff here.

Even when the place is empty the young staff is surly,
indifferent and so careless they literally slide dishes
across the table at you, all the while looking off in the
opposite direction. The owner (or manager) brings a
check long before one is asked for, and rice is sometimes scorched brown on the bottom. It is changed on
request but hardly with good grace.

Much of the fiery character of the Sichuan dishes has
been eliminated, and even hacked chicken is now sweet
and mawkish. Assorted dumplings and cold Sichuan
cabbage in chili oil served for the early morning weekend breakfast and dim sum for lunch hours are the most
interesting features on the menu, but they too can be
had in more congenial quarters. A whole fried sea bass
reeked of fishiness, indicating it was far from fresh, and
it seemed to have been precooked then reheated. Carp
with hot bean sauce, however, was far better, as were
prawns stir-fried with walnuts. Grease-soaked eggplant,
fibrous string beans and fried boneless chicken, once a
glory of this place, could be equaled at any Kentucky
Fried Chicken outpost.

Other disappointments were the broccoli with garlic
sauce, now hopelessly limp with overcooking, and the
honey bananas and apple fritters tasting of acrid oil.

Table d'Hôte

★

44 East 92nd Street, between Madison and Park Avenues, 348-8125.

Atmosphere: Intimate and romantic, storefront cafe-restaurant with Early American overtones and inadequate ventilation; service is friendly and casual.

Recommended dishes: Chicken liver pâté, house pâté of three meats, asparagus vinaigrette, chicken breast in cream, roast veal, veal scaloppine in caper sauce, lamb chops with herb butter, coffee walnut mousse, poached pear.

Price range: Moderately expensive.

Credit cards: None.

Hours: Dinner, Tuesdays through Saturdays, 6:30 P.M. to 9:30 P.M. Closed Sundays, Mondays and major holidays.

Reservations: Necessary.

Small restaurants with very limited menus, serving near-private dinners to guests by reservation only, seem to be a trend around town, and this is one of the more romantically charming. Lighted only by candles and oil lamps, this small, storefront cafe-restaurant has painted white wainscotted walls and a felicitous mismatch of furniture and china that suggests an Early American setting.

All of the cooking and serving is done by Lauri Gibson, Vivek Bandhu and Stuart Shultz, who love to cook, live in the neighborhood and believed it needed a restaurant where fresh, stylishly prepared dinners could be offered at moderate prices. Whether $30 a person is what most people consider moderate is open to question, but at those prices, these young people serve an interesting and satisfying meal that includes an appetizer or soup, a main course with vegetables, salad, dessert and coffee. They now have a wine license, but you may still bring your own, an additional saving on that score.

The menu changes weekly and each offers a choice of three appetizers, three main courses and three desserts, always with one fish or seafood selection among the main courses.

My most recent dinner at Table d'Hôte began with a creditable and satisfying pâté of three meats studded with walnuts or hazelnuts, and firm, brightly green asparagus in a piquant vinaigrette dressing. Pleasant is the word that comes to mind most often in evaluating main courses here. Cooking is done with a light hand and all ingredients are of top quality; what is lacking to make the food truly exciting is the extra measure of artfulness that seems just beyond the cook's reach. Nevertheless, the level achieved assures a felicitous dining experience.

Veal scaloppine, although not sufficiently pounded and so too thick, was tender and well accented by a lemony caper sauce, and sautéed lamb chops mellowed under a dab of herb butter. Salad of red-tipped lettuce had a light vinaigrette dressing and both whole-wheat and sourdough white breads were delicious. The delicate desserts of a walnut-topped coffee mousse and a pear poached in white wine then soothed with a lightly caramelized butter, wine and sugar sauce flavored with vanilla proved to be refreshing and easy to take.

An earlier dinner at Table d'Hôte began with a pleasant pâté of herbed chicken livers on French bread, which was followed by a light and creamy, green vegetable soup that was a purée of asparagus, celery, mushrooms and, I suspected, leeks. The only flaw was the strings of celery or asparagus that should have been strained out; they were unpleasant distractions in the otherwise silken potage.

Boneless breast of chicken baked in cream was delicate and satisfying, although a bit too strongly flavored with rosemary, apparently a predilection of the kitchen. With it came well-cooked rice and firm, whole fresh green beans, lightly steamed. Mixed green salad had a good, oily dressing. Dessert that night was a baked ricotta pudding in a ramekin, like a slightly dry, mild-flavored cheesecake filling; a topping of strawberries brightened it considerably.

On our next visit the appetizer combined a slice of prosciutto with a topping of céleri rémoulade that would have been perfect if its dressing had been just a little bit oilier and more clinging. Cream of asparagus soup followed (again with unstrained strings), and the main course was a savory veal shoulder roast stuffed with hard-cooked egg, spinach and, alas, too much rosemary. Rice was good, although it did not seem to be risotto as billed, and asparagus was perfectly cooked. The same excellent green salad was served, and dessert consisted of fresh, ripe strawberries with cream.

Prospective guests can find out each day's menu by calling the restaurant during the dinner hours and getting a direct answer, or by calling during the day and leaving their names with the answering machine. One of the proprietors calls back to explain the day's menu and to confirm a reservation.

The seating capacity at Table d'Hôte is twenty-four at peak, but the place is far more comfortable with only eighteen or nineteen guests because space becomes cramped, and the noise level can get high. Better ventilation in the kitchen would prevent cooking odors from becoming overpowering in the dining room, as they do at times.

Taj Mahal

★

1154 First Avenue, between 63rd and 64th Streets, 755-3017.

Atmosphere: Small intimate dining room with draped walls and shadowy lighting; background music is annoying; good and friendly service.

Recommended dishes: Samosas, shami kebob, tandoori chicken, chicken tikka, chicken makhanala, chicken or lamb shag, beef kurma, poori, papadum, paratha, lamb biryani, onion relish, cabbage, raita, baklava.

Price range: Moderate.

Credit cards: All major credit cards.

Hours: Full menu, Mondays through Fridays, noon to midnight; Saturdays and Sundays, 3 P.M. to 1 A.M.

Reservations: Recommended.

This fairly small and vaguely atmospheric restaurant offers some good dishes at modest prices. Walls and ceilings are draped with fabric, and Indian lanterns cast a soporifically inadequate light. That and the constant clatter of Indian music in the background can be wearing to the untutored ear, but the pleasant service and food partially counteract those drawbacks.

Among appetizers, those we found best were the meat-filled fried turnovers (samosas), the chopped-meat patty (shami kebob) served with poori, the balloon-like bread puffs, and the onion relish. Coconut and mulligatawny soups are mawkish and unpleasant.

Lamb biryani made with tender chunks of meat in a spicy rice pillaw, chicken or lamb shag (simmered with spinach and spices) and chicken makhanala sauced with tomatoes, butter, cream and aromatic spices, were all delicious. So were the tandoori-broiled, chicken tikka pieces garnished with onion, and the half tandoori chicken. Beef kurma curry was tender and the sauce had a burnishing of toasted spices. Several other dishes were disappointing. Duck curry was greasy and the cuts of duck seemed to be all bones. Vindaloo curries, a personal favorite because they are usually fiery hot, were bland even though requested extra spicy. Poori puffs, crisp papadum and leafy paratha were excellent breads. The worst dish by far was the most expensive, a whole fish tandoori style that tasted every bit as awful as it smelled. When we asked what kind of fish it was, we were told it was a pompano imported frozen from India — a mistake, as any fresh local fish would have been preferable. Relishes and side dishes were very good, including the cucumber and yogurt raita, the hot lemon pickle, the incendiary onion relish and the soothing steamed cabbage.

Desserts were the typical Indian sweet-and-sticky. Walnut baklava proved the best choice. Such authentic beverages as lassi (yogurt with rosewater, milk and sugar) are on hand, as is complete bar service. The best buys are the complete dinners and lunches.

Takesushi

★ ★

71 Vanderbilt Avenue (230 Park Avenue), at 45th Street, 867-5120.

Atmosphere: Spacious and handsome modern sushi parlor with counter, tables and two private tatami rooms; service is polite, efficient and helpful.

Recommended dishes: All sushi, especially sea urchin, fatty tuna, warm eel, red caviar, octopus, squid, egg pancake, cockle, red snapper, futomaki roll and California roll, sashimi, chirashi, clear soup, bean soup, clam soup.

Price range: Moderately expensive.

Credit cards: All major credit cards.

Hours: Lunch, Mondays through Fridays, noon to 3 P.M.; dinner, Mondays through Fridays, 5 P.M. to 10 P.M.; Saturdays, 1 P.M. to 8 P.M. Closed Memorial Day Monday.

Reservations: Necessary for sushi bar and private tatami rooms; recommended for tables.

Although the Japanese raw fish specialties, sushi and sashimi, are becoming relatively commonplace in New York, they are usually dispensed in settings notably devoid of charm. But the new Takesushi is a handsome exception. The same skillful preparations of sashimi, the sliced raw fish, and sushi, the raw and cooked fish compacted on warm, mild vinegar rice, are turned out here as at the Takezushi on 45th Street and Avenue of the Americas (which spells its name with a "z") and as they were at the former location on East 48th Street.

The setting is bright and festive with the grass-green carpet, blond wood and the rock-garden path leading from the entrance, through the bar and on to the comfortably lit dining room. The scene is complemented by a helpful and efficient staff. There are two private tatami rooms — one for parties of four, the other for groups of eight — as well as small and large tables in the dining room. The real floor show is at the sushi bar, where the edible handicrafts are prepared by sushi masters who roll or press the rice and fish together, with or without bindings of crisp, gold-green dried seaweed. Only the slight sogginess of that seaweed (nori), a certain blandness in the rice and uneven preparation account for a two-star instead of a three-star rating.

The best of the sushi are those not in the standard assortment. Ask for tender, white cooked octopus, delicate red snapper or fluke, the fatty tuna called toro, the briny sea urchin that is uni, and the warm, soy-sauce-glazed eel, anago. At the counter for lunch that eel was simply laid over rice, but at a table for dinner one night, it appeared topped with slivered scallion and bound with seaweed, an extraordinary variation. Choose the big red salmon-roe caviar instead of the tiny, salty red variation. Squid, abalone and clam muscle or cockle add chewy textural contrast and the gently sweet egg pancake, tamago, is the perfect windup. Sushi made with seaweed include the cucumber and tuna rolls,

420

which are best in an unsliced handroll. Futomaki is a wide roll lined with rice and inset with bits of tuna, cucumber and omelet, and the trendy, interesting California roll features layers, from the outside in, of rice around seaweed, around rice, around avocado.

All these fish, as well as smoked salmon, shrimp and yellow-tail, are also available as sashimi. A combination of those fish on a bed of rice make up the satisfying chirashi assortment served in a square lacquer box. Meals can begin here with a soothing clear soup, a smoky bean soup or two clams in their own broth as bracing as a sea breeze. On Saturdays there is a dinner served in three stacked lacquer boxes, with yakimono (broiled fish on rice), nimono (boiled fish) and sashimi.

There is full bar service, but warm sake or tea are the best choices to enhance the cool, subtly flavored fish. Prices are moderate to start, but for those with large appetites they add up rapidly, especially if items are ordered singly.

Takezushi
★ ★

101 West 45th Street, at the Avenue of the Americas, 391-1045.

Atmosphere: Small, modern upstairs dining room with tiny sushi bar; stairway and entrance are shabby but dining room is cheerful; service at tables is a little slow, but friendly and helpful.

Recommended dishes: All sushi and especially futomaki, warm eel (anago), sea urchin, red caviar, octopus and shrimp; all sashimi, especially the mackerel, fatty tuna, salmon and red snapper; chirashi, bean soup, nutta, natto, chawan-mushi, vanilla ice cream with red beans.

Price range: Moderate.

Credit cards: American Express, Diners Club and MasterCard.

Hours: Lunch, Mondays through Fridays, noon to 3 P.M.; dinner, Mondays through Fridays, 5 P.M. to 10 P.M.; Saturdays, 1 P.M. to 8 P.M. Closed Sundays and holidays.

Reservations: Not necessary.

Like all sushi restaurants, this one prepares a full array of sashimi, the sparklingly dewy raw fish slices. The most dedicated aficionados of this informal and entertaining eating discipline are apt to shun house assortments, varied and excellent though they may be, preferring to pick the particular types of sushi and sashimi that interest them.

To do so, they sit at the sushi bar, pointing out this or that as the spirit moves them. At tables it is usually necessary to take the assortments, limiting the favorites one can consume. The prizes among the sashimi choices are fatty tuna, which is far more supple and flavorful than the leaner variety, marinated mackerel edged with a fine silver-blue line of its own skin, bright coral salmon and, when in season, red snapper. Octopus, which is cooked, is also a favorite, and so is raw squid, scored for tenderness.

The two basic categories of sushi are nigiri sushi, based on raw fish or shellfish, skillfully compacted onto vinegared rice, and nori sushi, wrapped in seaweed. Deluxe sushi are made with red caviar and sea urchins, as well as egg cake. Another delectable winner is the warm glazed eel, anago.

Further variations of nori are skillfully prepared here. Futomaki is the ultimate nori sushi, about an inch and a half in diameter, the seaweed wrapped around rice inlaid with tuna, crunches of cucumber and a cube of omelet cake, also a sushi specialty, all subtly sweetened and salted with pickled and preserved vegetables and mushrooms.

Chirashi is a convenient and diverting meal in a shiny rectangular lacquer box, holding a base of rice on which are artful arrangements of raw fish and pickles.

The Takezushi special is a complete meal centered on three stacked lacquer boxes holding yakimono (broiled fish bits on rice), nimono (boiled fish) and a sashimi combination. Clear soup and earthy miso bean soup are served along with a few additional specialties that must be requested — natto (a mix of fermented soy beans, egg yolk and scallions), nutta (diced tuna in a mustardy sauce) and chawan-mushi, here a rather lusty custard, inset with greens and shrimp. Fruit is the best dessert. Vanilla ice cream with sweet red beans proved more of a curiosity than a culinary triumph, but was, in any case, refreshing.

Although the quality of ingredients is generally first-rate, there are occasional lapses in freshness that keep this restaurant from maintaining consistent excellence. Warm sake, Japanese beer and tea are all available.

Tamu

★

340 West Broadway, at the corner of Grand Street, 925-2751.

Atmosphere: Romantic, handsome tropical-island setting with bamboo chairs, basket lampshades, batiks and comfortable seating; service is slow and unprofessional but friendly and good-natured.

Recommended dishes: Beef saté Madura, chicken saté Bali, soto Madura chicken soup, gado-gado salad, acar vegetable salad, opor ayam chicken in spicy coconut cream, ayam Panggang broiled chicken, rendang spiced beef, sambal goreng udang fried shrimp in curry sauce, ikan kuning fillet of sole, ikan bumbu Bali codfish.

Price range: Moderate.

Credit cards: All major credit cards.

Hours: Dinner, 6 P.M. to midnight, daily.

Reservations: Suggested weekdays for parties of four or more; necessary on weekends.

Since the closing many years ago of the colorful little East of Suez, New Yorkers have lacked an atmospheric restaurant in which to have a decent, full-fledged rijstafel. A Dutch word meaning rice table, a rijstafel is based on Indonesian curries, stews and grills, served around rice with pungent condiments. Characteristic flavors include such seasonings as chilies, ginger, coriander and lemon grass, combined in mellow contrast to freshly made peanut butter, soy sauce, coconut cream and palm sugar.

That missing element on the local scene is now pleasantly filled by the brand-new Tamu, a handsome and romantic tropical restaurant arranged on two tiers in a SoHo building at the corner of West Broadway and Grand Street. Basketry lamp shades, colorful batiks, brick walls and bamboo chairs make this an especially palmy and inviting setting. Although service is unprofessional and slow, especially for groups larger than four, the staff is friendly, polite and well-meaning.

The twelve-dish rijstafel is an easy introduction to the esoteric intricacies of the cuisine of the country once known as the Spice Islands. With only a few exceptions, the best dishes are in the rijstafel. It is ample for two people — if it is shared, a service charge is added — and the array includes charcoal-grilled beef and chicken satés and soto ayam — chicken broth heady with lemon grass and enriched with fine noodles, bits of chicken, vegetables and astringent lemon grass. Gado-gado, the Indonesian mixed-vegetable salad, has a velvety peanut sauce that needs only a drop of chili relish to brighten it, and acar, cold pickled mixed vegetables, comes to the table with the proper peppery sting.

The best dishes served with those salads include rendang, a savory beef stew made with coconut cream; ikan bumbu Bali, codfish with turmeric in a garlic-and-ginger-scented red sauce, and udang tumis, shrimp braised with mushrooms, coriander and lemon juice. The only two disappointing dishes were gulai kambing, overcooked stewed lamb that was greasy and tasteless, and care ayam, chicken that seemed to have been reheated once too often.

Other good dishes not included in the rijstafel but available à la carte were ayam panggung, charcoal-broiled chicken, seasoned with a mixture of caraway, pepper, garlic, coriander and bay leaf, and opor ayam, chicken breast in the only really fiery sauce we encountered. Sambal goreng udang, large fried shrimp in a brassy coconut-curry sauce, and ikan kuning, a gently curried fillet of sole, were also savory and satisfying. Daging bakar, strips of charcoal beef, was oversweetened with pineapple. Asinan, a satisfying salad of bean curd and bean sprouts, had an interesting palm-sugar-and-vinegar dressing.

It's too bad the management underestimates the American tolerance for hot spices and underseasons its dishes. It is possible to get a brightly piquant relish-sauce of red chili peppers, garlic and lemon to spoon into dishes yourself, but the effect would be more harmonious and authentic if the seasonings were cooked with the other ingredients.

The only dessert available so far, fried bananas with whipped cream, is minimally acceptable and sometimes greasy. Another dessert, sliced bananas sautéed in butter and sauced with orange and lemon juice, cinnamon and rum and served over ice cream, has so far been unavailable. Plain fresh fruit would be appropriate and welcome. Considering the high quality of Java and Sumatra coffees that grow in Indonesia, it's a pity Tamu serves such a pallid, overboiled brew.

In a setting so handsome, background music is hardly necessary, let alone the Spanish music that the management has chosen, when the liquid, lyrical plunks of a gamelan orchestra would be more in keeping. It is also to be hoped that the delightful staff can serve food a little more quickly and that waiters downstairs will not forget customers upstairs.

Tandoor
★ ★

40 East 49th Street, between Park and Madison Avenues, 752-3334.

Atmosphere: Pleasant and trim dining room with Indian overtones; service is fair to good but sometimes unfriendly.

Recommended dishes: Chicken pakora, chicken chaat, vegetable pakora, alu chaat, mulligatawny soup, nan, Tandoori special nan, papadum, tandoori chicken, sheekh kebob, makhni chicken, chicken tikka masala, chicken muslum, lamb rogan josh, chicken Jalfrezi, lamb or pork vindaloo, kofta masala, vegetable Jalfrezi, dal, raita, vegetable or chicken pullao.

Price range: Moderately expensive.

Credit cards: All major credit cards.

Hours: Lunch, Mondays through Saturdays, noon to 3 P.M.; dinner, seven days, 5:30 P.M. to 11 P.M. Open major holidays.

Reservations: Necessary.

The igloo-shaped clay oven known as the tandoor is most closely identified with Indian cooking. But, in fact, that excellent method of baking meats, poultry, fish and bread is believed to have originated in Afghanistan where it was picked up by the Mogul rulers who took it south to India and north to what is now Soviet Georgia. In all cases, the meat, poultry or fish is first marinated in a roseate spice mixture and is impaled on long skewers that are lowered into the tandoor. Sheets of a pizzalike bread dough, which in India is called nan, are also slapped against the sides of the oven and peeled off when crisply charred and blistered.

As its name implies, the Tandoor restaurant has made a specialty of this lean and savory method of cooking since it opened in 1975. The succulently moist, hotly spiced tandoori chicken remains not only the best dish on the menu, but also one of the best examples of this dish in town. But while a number of other specialties at Tandoor approach their former excellence, there is often a hint of carelessness about some others.

Even the handsome, restful décor with its subtle and stylish Indian overtones is in need of sprucing up, and ventilation is inefficient.

The main problem with the food is that too many dishes are prepared long in advance and are merely heated to order, so they become limp and taste of over-heated cooking oil.

Nevertheless, there are some enticing and appetite-whetting first courses to choose from. Both the alu chaat, a spiced potato salad redolent of coriander, and the chicken chaat with bits of tender breast meat in the same pungent green sauce were excellent, as were the chicken pakora, joints of greaseless deep-fried chicken that profited by a dip into the mint and yogurt chutney.

Mulligatawny soup is a far more robust blend than is usually found elsewhere, a rice-thickened chicken stock with enough body to hold the golden hue and flavor of the spice blend.

Some of the Indian breads, such as the onion kulcha and the chapati, are less distinguished than they might be, but the plain nan and the tandoori special nan with its charred, sweet mincings of nutmeats are perfect foils to the incendiary spicing, which, fortunately, the management does provide when ordered. Although one has to insist firmly to be taken seriously about wanting food hotly spiced, once that point is made the kitchen complies. I have found (as recommended to us elsewhere) that the use of three "very's" before the word "hot," ensures that you will be taken at your word.

The hotness is especially well suited to the tender tandoori chicken that sizzles on a bed of almost raw onions, or in the chicken Jalfrezi mixed with tomatoes, onions and peppers. Chicken tikka — chunks of boneless tandoori chicken — and the ground meat seekh kebobs flavored with onions and herbs are among other beautifully prepared tandoori offerings.

In some dishes, tandoori-baked chicken and meat are tossed in a variety of sauces, hot or mild in flavor, although always warm in temperature. Two of the best of these are the makhni chicken in a mild-flavored tomato and butter sauce and the chicken muslum in a cream and egg sauce. Cubes of lamb or pork vindaloo were tender, lean and mild, and their sauces struck the perfect balance between hotness and acidity, just as vindaloo should. Kofta masala — ground meatballs in a gently spiced brown sauce — were also good.

Flaws are exhibited mainly in combinations such as the assorted hors d'oeuvres that included the vegetable fritters samosa, the crisp pakora vegetable turnovers, bits of tandoori-baked chicken tikka and the ground meat shammi kebob. Served with a parasol topping of flaky, nut-sweet papadum and accompanied by an aromatic green mint and yogurt sauce, these appetizers would have been delectable if freshly fried or baked. Similarly, an order of fried vegetable cutlets were reheated when ordered and when they were sent back, replacements that were merely fried longer and to the burning point were served.

The lamb stew, rogan josh, had just the right fiery spicing, and was delicious. The tandoori shrimp, generally proved second-rate; even when I managed to get them freshly cooked they tasted of iodine, indicating they were past their prime. Fish, braised in a thick, masala spice sauce, also should have been fresher, judging by the scent and flavor.

There is an interesting array of vegetarian dishes at Tandoor, among them the spicy vegetable Jalfrezi, and a fragrant and satisfying vegetable pullao with saffron-gilded rice. Rice, cooked with peas (peas pullao), was tepid and dry.

To offset the fiery sting of the curry spices, try a few spoonfuls of the cooling cucumber and mint yogurt sauce, raita. It is this counterpoint of flavors and textures — the cool and hot, the crisp and the gentle — that make Indian food as appealing and entertaining as it is.

The appeal of desserts here, as in most other Indian restaurants, escapes me entirely. Suffice it to say that those tried from the wagon at Tandoor were a little less cloyingly sweet than most. Would that all Indian restaurants offered a bright assortment of cut fresh fruits, or even one choice of honey-ripe melon.

Tea on two occasions was bitter and overbrewed. Eagle beer from India is available and interesting to try, though light; Beck's will prove more satisfying. There is a limited wine list; although most offerings clash with the intense spicing of this cuisine, the softer Moselles seem more complementary than most.

Tang Tang

★

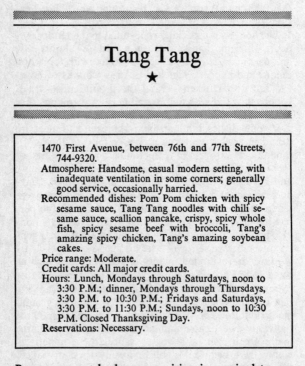

1470 First Avenue, between 76th and 77th Streets, 744-9320.

Atmosphere: Handsome, casual modern setting, with inadequate ventilation in some corners; generally good service, occasionally harried.

Recommended dishes: Pom Pom chicken with spicy sesame sauce, Tang Tang noodles with chili sesame sauce, scallion pancake, crispy, spicy whole fish, spicy sesame beef with broccoli, Tang's amazing spicy chicken, Tang's amazing soybean cakes.

Price range: Moderate.

Credit cards: All major credit cards.

Hours: Lunch, Mondays through Saturdays, noon to 3:30 P.M.; dinner, Mondays through Thursdays, 3:30 P.M. to 10:30 P.M.; Fridays and Saturdays, 3:30 P.M. to 11:30 P.M.; Sundays, noon to 10:30 P.M. Closed Thanksgiving Day.

Reservations: Necessary.

Because so much close supervision is required to run even one restaurant kitchen successfully, it is somewhat startling to learn that Queh-yuen Tang is supervising the cooking not only at her original and very good Hwa Yuan Szechuan Inn on East Broadway in Chinatown, but now also at several other outposts scattered around the city. Even if the word "supervising" is given the loosest interpretation, it is hard to believe that any one person can exercise meaningful control over so large and far-flung a culinary fiefdom.

One of her efforts is the Tang Tang and based on the sampling of some twenty dishes, it appears that Mrs. Tang is spreading her talents much too thin. Although there are several dishes good enough to rely on if one is in this neighborhood, the kitchen's performance is less consistent than that of the superior parent restaurant downtown. The management seems to be caught off guard so frequently that it is unprepared for busy evenings. The result is a sense of emergency that is communicated to diners, spoiling the easy relaxation that the simple and handsome modern wood-structured interior might otherwise impart.

To its credit, Tang Tang does mean what it says when it promises dishes that are hot and spicy; the menu offers to adjust seasonings to taste, but in the absence of such a request, the kitchen opts for hotness. That heady spiciness, fiery as it is, stops short of obliterating the flavors of garlic or ginger, scallions, sesame oil or smoky, fermented black beans. Thus the dishes to rely on are those bathed in sauces with those ingredients. Among appetizers these choices include hot Tang Tang noodles in chili-sesame sauce and pom pom chicken, slim slivers of tender white meat doused with the same sauce. Both are far better than the banally commercial assorted array of spareribs, greasy spring rolls, pasty fried shrimp or the heavy, doughy dumplings or "plus silver treasure chicken." Scallion pancakes, though slightly heavier than they need to be, are crisp and savory.

Main-course dishes that profit from the pungent black-bean sauces are crispy, spicy whole fish (not to be confused with the golden crisp whole fish), Tang's amazing spicy chicken, with large, moist squares of breast meat in a subtle blend of garlic, scallions and hot chili peppers, mellowed by black beans, and Tang's amazing soybean cakes, in a similar, somewhat lighter sauce. Morsels of beef flecked with sesame seeds and tossed with flowerets of broccoli is another dish worth trying.

The smoked duck sampled, though lean and meaty, lacked the overtones of camphorwood and tea with which it was said to be smoked. A spicy, tomato-base Sichuan sauce on lobster was delicious, but the lobster itself was so overcooked that it was almost impossible to dig the meat out of the shell. Lake Tang Tang shrimp and Sichuan lamb were overpowered by chunks of red and green pepper. Mrs. Tang's triple delight was a tasteless tossing of pork, shrimp and chicken, and the flat-tasting, fibrous filling for the moo shu pork spoils that popular dish. Dry sautéed string beans, based on beans as tough as waxed paper, and dreadful, barely fried fried rice were among other disappointments. Strips of Mongolian beef with scallions, though acceptable, were flawed by greasiness, as were many other dishes.

Although service is polite and well-meaning, waiters usually assume customers want dishes portioned out for them. It is a better idea to ask, so that those who enjoy eating Chinese family style have the option to do so.

One word of caution: there are excerpts of favorable reviews posted that one or another of the Tang restaurants have earned, including one from this reviewer for the Hwa Yuan Szechuan Inn. It should be made clear that that was the only Tang restaurant discussed in the review, and what was said does not apply to later additions.

Tastings
★

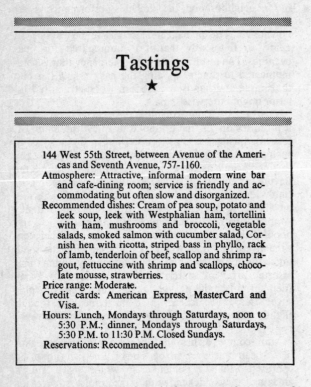

144 West 55th Street, between Avenue of the Americas and Seventh Avenue, 757-1160.

Atmosphere: Attractive, informal modern wine bar and cafe-dining room; service is friendly and accommodating but often slow and disorganized.

Recommended dishes: Cream of pea soup, potato and leek soup, leek with Westphalian ham, tortellini with ham, mushrooms and broccoli, vegetable salads, smoked salmon with cucumber salad, Cornish hen with ricotta, striped bass in phyllo, rack of lamb, tenderloin of beef, scallop and shrimp ragout, fettuccine with shrimp and scallops, chocolate mousse, strawberries.

Price range: Moderate.

Credit cards: American Express, MasterCard and Visa.

Hours: Lunch, Mondays through Saturdays, noon to 5:30 P.M.; dinner, Mondays through Saturdays, 5:30 P.M. to 11:30 P.M. Closed Sundays.

Reservations: Recommended.

Tastings, as in wine tastings, is the name and purpose of a pleasant new cafe-restaurant recently opened directly across from the City Center. It is especially welcome there since it provides a variety of diverting dishes well suited to dining before or after performances.

It is an adjunct of the International Wine Center in the same building, where wine courses and tastings are held. The restaurant has a long wine bar, where food is also served, and a casual, handsome dining room with brick walls, mirrors and green glass lampshades. Twenty wines may be ordered by the half glass as well as by the full glass, thus enabling tastings during a meal. The device that makes it possible to keep so many open bottles of wine in good condition is the Cruvinet, a dispenser that holds reds and whites at correct temperatures and automatically pipes nitrogen into bottles to replace wine that is poured, thereby preventing the remaining wine from being oxidized. Although the prices for glasses and half glasses are steep compared to the cost of wine by the bottle, it is interesting to be able to sample several wines.

The management of the SoHo Charcuterie served as consultants here, setting up the kitchen, finding a staff and devising menu and recipes.

Those efforts are more successful with appetizers than with main courses. There were two excellent soups, one a bright, verdant cream of green pea, the other a satiny hot leek-and-potato combination. Cold leeks wrapped in Westphalian ham was a bright and refreshing first course, as were the assortment of vegetable salads and the delicate pink smoked salmon, marred only by musty American caviar. Ask them to hold the caviar, and perhaps substitute some of the fresh cucumber salad. Tortellini in cream with ham and broccoli were lusty and delicious. Wellfleet oysters should have been colder, and the pâté de campagne was greasy.

Firm, snowy striped bass baked in flakey phyllo dough and lightly doused with a beurre blanc sauce and half of a rock Cornish hen filled with ricotta cheese and spinach were among the best main courses. Close seconds were the rose-pink rack of lamb scented with rosemary and thyme and the rare beef tenderloin, which was only slightly overpowered by the strongly flavored Westphalian ham.

The broiled veal chop was dry and tough, and chicken pie, despite its heady Madeira sauce and crisp phyllo crust, was unsatisfactory because the chicken seemed to be stale. The same condition also detracted from the chicken and broccoli quiche at lunch. Tiny scallops and large shrimp with snow peas and cèpes were good, and so were the same shellfish tossed with green fettuccine and a basil-perfumed pesto cream sauce. Unfortunately, all dishes with shrimp seemed much overpriced for what looked like appetizer portions.

Cheeses on display were woebegone. Those ordered were in better condition but still somewhat past their prime. Bitter chocolate mousse and ripe red strawberries topped with Grand Marnier-spiked whipped cream were the best desserts.

An omelet at lunch was well made, but its Brie filling added too much salt to the combination. Salads and sandwiches at that meal are composed of appetizer and main-dish elements.

One overall problem with the food is its relationship to wine tasting. The rock Cornish hen, for example, would enhance wine more if it were simply roasted or broiled without the creamy cheese. Too many dishes include asparagus, broccoli and spinach, or are garnished with them.

Service is disorganized and slow even when the place is half empty. Busing stations are needed too, since there is much scurrying when a piece of silver is requested. Nevertheless, the tone here is friendly and felicitous, and Tastings is the sort of casual restaurant every good neighborhood deserves.

Tavern on the Green
Fair

In Central Park at 67th Street and Central Park West,
873-3200.
Atmosphere: Glittering fairyland of flowers, crystal
chandeliers, etched glass and incomparable views
of the park; noisy and hectic; service is chaotic.
Recommended dishes: Clams or oysters on the half
shell, hamburger, spinach salad, eggs Benedict or
Florentine, calf's liver, lamb chops, chocolate
cake, pecan pie, banana split.
Price range: Moderately expensive.
Credit cards: All major credit cards.
Hours: Lunch, Mondays through Fridays, 11:30 A.M.
to 3:30 P.M.; dinner, daily, 5 P.M. to midnight;
brunch, Saturdays and Sundays, 10 A.M. to 3:30
P.M.
Reservations: Necessary.

From the day it opened in 1976, this extravagantly
beautiful fairyland of a restaurant in Central Park has
been one of the city's most disappointing experiences. If
it were not for the unique setting and the lavish décor, it
would not be worth considering at all. The series of
bars, dining rooms, private rooms and, in good weather,
a garden cafe, are all joys to behold. Crystal chandeliers, etched glass, wood carvings, gleaming brass and
pastel floral decorations on ceilings, walls and tablecloths are brought to life by a garden of real blooming
plants and floral bouquets. It is exactly the sort of setting one dreams of finding in the park, whether in summer when the landscape is leafy or in winter when snow
is highlighted by the tiny light bulbs shining through
bare branches.

Operated by Warner LeRoy, the Hollywood born
and raised impresario who also runs Maxwell's Plum,
the Tavern has a similar menu and similar flaws, although here the flaws are far greater. Service is chaotic,
a condition that becomes obvious even when you call
for reservations. Speak to two different people and you
will have two different sets of answers about hours and
space available. Reservations are also confused at the
door, and one person may say you will have to wait
thirty minutes, even as another comes to usher you to a
table. Pacing is uneven. At times guests sit and wait almost forever for an order to be taken, only to have
courses arrive on top of each other.

Bloody Marys are short on vodka, and Irish coffee is
pale and watery. Often food meant to be served hot arrives barely tepid, and much of it is ineptly prepared. At
one lunch, thinking buttered spaghetti would be a fool-
proof main course for a young child lunching with me, I
ordered it. It was not possible to guess that the water
would not be drained from the pasta, and so the melted
butter was diluted, forming an unpleasant soup.

The enormous and dazzling original menu has been
much edited and simplified, a move one would have

430

thought to be an improvement. Apparently the easy demands on the kitchen staff have not helped, for the same fair batting average still exists.

To enjoy the leafy, shining splendor of the setting, either go for drinks or to eat only the simplest things on the menu. For appetizers, that means clams or oysters on the half shell but not the mushy gravlax or greasy, overchilled pâtés. Spinach salad is far better than the limp Caesar salad with its waxen cheese. Hamburgers, lamb chops and calf's liver with bacon (not with the greasy onions) have been acceptable. Omelets are leaden, but poached eggs Benedict or Florentine are all right for brunch or lunch. Fettuccine or linguine primavera can be soothing and satisfying if the creamy sauce is not too thick, as it sometimes is, and if the vegetables are not so overcooked that they suggest Campbell's vegetable soup.

If the weather is warm and cold poached salmon is on the menu, it will probably rank among the better choices. And if fresh and not dried out, the grilled snapper with mustard sauce should pass muster. Desserts can make up for a lot here if you have the chocolate cake, the pecan pie or the banana split. Fried bananas are gross and overpowering, and the once-excellent cheesecake can be gummy.

Even though they are not as good as they originally were, breads still carry a separate charge — about one dollar for two people, so if you do not want it, have it removed. It represents a cover charge in disguise.

Tavola Calda da Alfredo

★

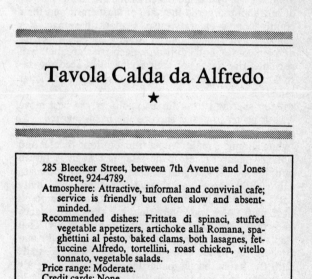

285 Bleecker Street, between 7th Avenue and Jones Street, 924-4789.
Atmosphere: Attractive, informal and convivial cafe; service is friendly but often slow and absentminded.
Recommended dishes: Frittata di spinaci, stuffed vegetable appetizers, artichoke alla Romana, spaghettini al pesto, baked clams, both lasagnes, fettuccine Alfredo, tortellini, roast chicken, vitello tonnato, vegetable salads.
Price range: Moderate.
Credit cards: None.
Hours: Thursdays through Tuesdays, noon to 10:30 P.M. Closed Wednesdays.
Reservations: Not accepted.

In Italy, the term tavola calda — literally, hot table — was originally applied to small, coffeeshop-style eating places that usually had counters and offered simple hot dishes often kept warm on steam tables. But as with other restaurant designations such as trattoria, bistro and cafe, the meaning gradually blurred. In northern

Italy especially, one now finds that a tavola calda is a rather stylish modern cafe-bistro still featuring a wide array of light to heavy dishes served up with relative dispatch.

Tavola Calda da Alfredo in Greenwich Village is an attractive cafe offering a moderately priced assortment of dishes that range from choices as light as stuffed vegetables or cold vegetable salads through a selection of pastas to several substantial meat and poultry dishes featured each day. The setting is simple and bright, though crowded and noisy, and the tone is casual. It is extremely popular with those who wish to enjoy diverting and satisfying food without having to wear anything more formal than blue jeans and T-shirts. It is also entertaining to be able to eat Italian food Chinese style, sharing the generously portioned appetizers, pastas, main courses and salads.

Considering the enticing menu and the wide appeal of the concept and the fact that the owner of the Tavola Calda is Alfredo Viazzi, who also runs his justly famous Trattoria on Hudson Street, one cannot help wishing that the Bleecker Street establishment was more even in quality and service. For though it is certainly possible to put together a very good meal there, the kitchen is all too often careless about overcooking and undercooking and the service can be painfully slow at peak hours.

The huge appetizers are among the best choices. Stuffed zucchini, mushrooms and eggplant are well cooked and their meat fillings are gently herbed. The hot artichoke in its green herb dressing is fragrant and quite superb, and if the baked clams are somewhat shy of oregano and garlic they are at least fresh and their crumb topping emerges crisp. Frittata di spinaci is a pancake-style spinach omelet equally good as appetizer or main course. Supli di risotto, deep-fried croquettes of seasoned rice, tasted of their frying oil. Sliced mozzarella and tomatoes needed better cheese and better tomatoes.

After sharing two or three appetizers, the best move was to go on to pastas such as the basil-flavored spaghettini al pesto or either the lasagne di carnevale (white lasagne noodles with a filling of four cheeses and a meat-tomato sauce) or the lasagne bolognese (green noodles with meat and cheese baked with tomato sauce). Both versions are fine when not burned. A daily pasta of orrechiette with sausages and flecks of broccoli in tomato sauce was interesting, but the tomato sauce had cooked down too much and was a bit heavy. That flaw was even more apparent in the perciatelli all'Amatriciana and in the cannelloni. Carbonara sauce made with the Italian bacon, pancetta, was decent if slightly too milky, and both the tortellini and fettuccine Alfredo have generally proved to be well above average.

Vitello tonnato, cold veal with a creamy tuna fish and caper sauce, was delicious as a main course, and there is also a veal of the day. If you're lucky you will be there when it is veal scaloppine marengo; if you're unlucky you will be faced with stuffed scaloppine that have a soggy limp breading. Roast whole tiny chicken with rosemary and a herbed-bread stuffing was very well prepared, as was half a roast duck with a compote of dried and fresh fruits that flavored a sauce remarkably unsweet.

Forget the ill-conceived layering of broccoli, dried wild mushrooms and washed-out prosciutto as well as the dreadful insalata marinara that combines squid and scallops in a vinegar-sharp sauce that included onions and bay leaves and tasted like pickled herring. Garlic does wonders for the stringbean salad, and the broccoli salad with anchovies is fine if you add olive oil to the meager dressing.

There is usually one baked dessert, and when it is the mocha-mousse cream pie don't miss it. Strawberries are decent but the cream served with them one Sunday evening was very warm and off in flavor — not quite spoiled, but not quite fresh.

Espresso is excellent and there is a moderately priced selection of Italian and California wines as well as San Pellegrino mineral water. Most of the menu items are available for take-out. There is a minimum at dinner, and the amount must be spent on food, not wine.

10th Street Cafe

★

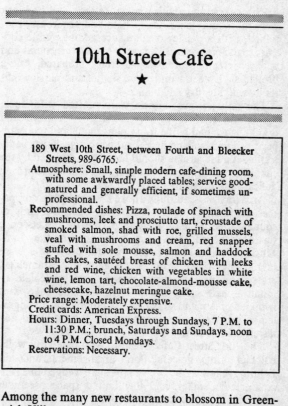

189 West 10th Street, between Fourth and Bleecker Streets, 989-6765.

Atmosphere: Small, simple modern cafe-dining room, with some awkwardly placed tables; service good-natured and generally efficient, if sometimes unprofessional.

Recommended dishes: Pizza, roulade of spinach with mushrooms, leek and prosciutto tart, croustade of smoked salmon, shad with roe, grilled mussels, veal with mushrooms and cream, red snapper stuffed with sole mousse, salmon and haddock fish cakes, sautéed breast of chicken with leeks and red wine, chicken with vegetables in white wine, lemon tart, chocolate-almond-mousse cake, cheesecake, hazelnut meringue cake.

Price range: Moderately expensive.

Credit cards: American Express.

Hours: Dinner, Tuesdays through Sundays, 7 P.M. to 11:30 P.M.; brunch, Saturdays and Sundays, noon to 4 P.M. Closed Mondays.

Reservations: Necessary.

Among the many new restaurants to blossom in Greenwich Village recently, the 10th Street Cafe is one of the more modest and charming. Owned by Martin Wood, who was one of the original partners in the first Woods restaurant on Madison Avenue, this small and intimate cafe reflects a genuine concern for lightness and originality, with the emphasis on fresh and unusual vegetables.

The limited but well-balanced menu is made up of innovative interpretations of Continental dishes. The most successful among the appetizers are a pizza enriched with four cheeses on a puff-pastry crust, mellowed with a light tomato sauce, a roulade of spinach enfolding mushrooms in a delicate tomato cream sauce and a flaky tart filled with minced leeks and prosciutto. Pastry croustades hold excellent smoked salmon topped with sour cream and caviar, and mussels grilled with snail butter nest on leaves of radicchio, the red lettuce. An enticing appetizer featured some evenings is a fillet of shad filled with roe and a sole mousse. A first-course pasta was an uninteresting combination of fettuccine, dill, cream and snow peas.

There is usually a game soup on the menu, and the one I tried, quail with Jerusalem artichokes and parsnips, was a near miss, flawed only by a slight sweetness that resulted from an overabundance of root vegetables with a high sugar content.

Although most main courses were pleasant, few came up to the level of the excellent appetizers. Chicken breast sautéed with Jerusalem artichokes was delicate and satisfying, and so was chicken with leeks and red wine.

Fish cakes made with smoked salmon and haddock were thoroughly delicious — light and generously portioned, with a parsley cream sauce adding gentle contrast to the crisp crust. Veal with black mushrooms and a sheer cream sauce was carefully prepared, but a broiled shell steak with lemon, shallot and parsley butter was slightly dry and bland.

The only serious failures were roasted wild duck, tough and rubbery (a pity because its papaya and orange sauce had a fine fruity pungency), and red snapper filled with sole mousse. The snapper itself was badly spoiled, and its aroma should have been detected by the chef. On another night, however, the same dish proved delicate and diverting.

An array of beautifully cooked vegetables accompanies all main courses. Huge, crisp-crusted rounds of country bread, handsomely displayed in baskets on a rustic sideboard, taste every bit as good as they look. Much the same can be said for such desserts as a lemony cheesecake with an edging of caramelized crushed graham crackers, orange-flavor chocolate-almond-mousse cake, a hazelnut meringue cake with whipped cream and strawberries and brightly astringent lemon tarts. The one disappointment was a bland and tasteless apple tart.

The 10th Street Cafe is restful, with pale-gray walls, colorful prints, graceful floral arrangements and soft lighting. A few of the twelve tables are wedged in at uncomfortable angles, and the limited space precludes really comfortable accommodations for parties of more than four. Service can slow down at times, but the staff is friendly, helpful and polite. There are some good buys on the limited wine list.

The Terrace
★ ★

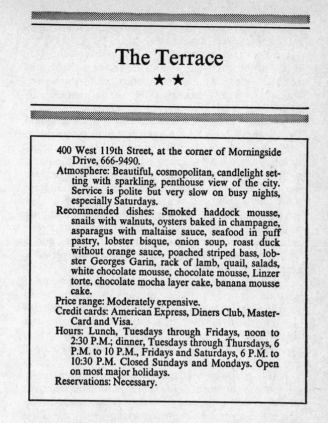

400 West 119th Street, at the corner of Morningside Drive, 666-9490.

Atmosphere: Beautiful, cosmopolitan, candlelight setting with sparkling, penthouse view of the city. Service is polite but very slow on busy nights, especially Saturdays.

Recommended dishes: Smoked haddock mousse, snails with walnuts, oysters baked in champagne, asparagus with maltaise sauce, seafood in puff pastry, lobster bisque, onion soup, roast duck without orange sauce, poached striped bass, lobster Georges Garin, rack of lamb, quail, salads, white chocolate mousse, chocolate mousse, Linzer torte, chocolate mocha layer cake, banana mousse cake.

Price range: Moderately expensive.

Credit cards: American Express, Diners Club, MasterCard and Visa.

Hours: Lunch, Tuesdays through Fridays, noon to 2:30 P.M.; dinner, Tuesdays through Thursdays, 6 P.M. to 10 P.M., Fridays and Saturdays, 6 P.M. to 10:30 P.M. Closed Sundays and Mondays. Open on most major holidays.

Reservations: Necessary.

Anyone who loves to get credit for knowing out-of-the-way restaurants that are beguiling surprises, should add this lovely place to his or her repertory. Set atop Columbia University's Butler Hall, this flower and plant trimmed, candlelit dining room, with its mirrors and sparkling view of the George Washington Bridge and the city skylines, combines very good food with moderately high prices. On most evenings, a lyrical backdrop of live chamber music only occasionally becomes intrusive.

The flaws here are the uneven service that can be agonizingly slow, especially on crowded weekend nights, and the sudden shabbiness of the room when seen by daylight, as it is for lunch. On the plus side, however, is a pretty night-time bar with hamburgers for those who wish to eat lightly or inexpensively, and a generally felicitous atmosphere throughout.

Among appetizers, fluffy smoked mousse of haddock and oysters baked with champagne and cream are excellent, and so are escargots baked with minced walnuts. Serving the snails in three ramekins seems a bit awkward, but the arrangement is manageable and well worth negotiating. An orangy sauce maltaise is a bright alternative to hollandaise on asparagus, also one of the better hors d'oeuvres.

Flaky puff pastry with an array of fresh shellfish and tiny quenelles in a froth of a butter and cream sauce is almost substantial and satisfying enough to be a main course. A lovely, gentle-pink lobster bisque was a marked improvement over an earlier version. Onion soup was strong and bracing, but an order of cream of asparagus soup had an unpleasant metallic edge. An acceptable but bland pâté was the only other disappointment among first courses.

Lobster salad is a wonderful first course at the Terrace, but there is a thirty-minute wait for it that is still not acknowledged either on the menu or by the waiter, which adds greatly to the delay for all first courses. This half-lobster, freshly cooked and trimmed with minced vegetables, was so good it seemed a pity that it should have been the cause for the unexplained discomfort.

Poaching of fish is a difficult and delicate operation, especially in a busy restaurant kitchen, yet striped bass with a mushroom duxelle and slivers of vegetables emerged as sheer perfection, firmly intact yet tenderly moist and without any of the petroleum trace that often contaminates bass. Nut-brown roasted quails, rose pink at the bone, as they should be, carried the subtle sweetness of a sheer sauce accented by green grapes, and it would be hard to find a rack of lamb more perfectly rose pink, as ordered.

Lobster Georges Garin (named for the proprietor of what was one of Paris's best restaurants) was described as being steamed and baked. Whatever that combination entails, it resulted in meat that was pearly and tender yet full of lobster flavor. A beurre blanc sauce sparkled with lemon and herbs and could not have been improved upon.

Puffy, crisp-skinned duck would have been better without the cloying orange sauce that was spooned over it, and though a steak marchand du vin was above average, it was no match for the more inspired choices. Neither were the sweetbreads, escalopes of veal nor a sautéed breast of chicken. Vegetables and salads are carefully prepared at the Terrace, but wild rice seems to give the kitchen trouble. It is undercooked, cold and woody.

The dessert wagon rolling along with triple-tiered temptations is worth stopping. One of the best chocolate mousses in the city is on it, along with a lemony, white-chocolate mousse, a thin crunch of a Linzer torte and lusty strawberry and kiwi tarts. Kept chilled in the kitchen are a cloudlike, mildly sweet banana mousse cake and a slim, stylish chocolate mocha layer cake. Strawberry dacquoise sounds and looks better than it tastes because of an overpowering quantity of creamy filling between the nut and meringue layers.

Texarkana

★

64 West 10th Street, between Fifth Avenue and Avenue of the Americas, 254-5800.

Atmosphere: Casual and stylish dining room with a handsome, lively bar; lighting is inadequate; service is friendly and polite but inept and slow.

Recommended dishes: Charred rare beef, barbecued pork, pickled shrimp, seafood gumbo, orange and onion salad, barbecued chicken, breast of duck, barbecued lamb chops, sirloin steak, salmon with lemon butter, Gulf shrimp Acadian, dirty rice, french fries, wilted spinach, banana fool, rhubarb and strawberry tart, pear or pecan pies.

Price range: Moderately expensive.

Credit cards: American Express.

Hours: Dinner, seven days, 6 P.M. to midnight; supper, Tuesdays through Saturdays, midnight to 3:45 A.M.

Reservations: Necessary.

Much is heard these days about the emergence of a new American cuisine, an innovative combination of our own regional cooking with Continental influences. Anyone who doubts that such a cuisine can enjoy high-fashion status should visit Texarkana in Greenwich Village, in premises formerly occupied by Peter's Backyard. Texarkana, with its adobe peach walls and courtyard atmosphere, is owned by Abe De La Houssaye, who has attracted a casually stylish crowd that gathers at 9 P.M. and later.

What lures this handsome young clientele is not only the attractive, low-key setting but also the enticing adaptations of dishes from the Gulf Coast and Southwestern states. At Texarkana, Mr. De La Houssaye, who is also the chef, displays much the same creativity he exhibits at his first restaurant, La Louisiana. Here he barbecues meat and poultry over mesquite and adds sauces based on jalapeño peppers, sharply burnished homemade ketchup or horseradish with crème fraîche.

Although much of this sounds better than it turns out to be, a number of preparations are successful enough for a satisfying and diverting meal. The kitchen is half a level above the dining room, which slows service and causes food to arrive tepid. But patience can bring rewards by way of such appetizers as the pickled Gulf shrimp marinated in vinegar, lemon juice and olive oil, the charred rare beef, much like a cold London broil, and slivers of spicy barbecued pork to be rolled in lettuce leaves. One refreshing first course was the orange and onion salad with sesame oil, vinegar and black pepper. But crawfish as an appetizer or in bisque and étouffé are dry and tasteless. Oysters were wilted and inadequately chilled. The seafood gumbo with okra was subtle and rich, but other soups were pallid and lacked sufficient seasonings.

Between courses, there are interesting morsels to nibble on — pickled okra and pearl onions, marinated black-eyed peas and cole slaw. The corn muffins, however, are leaden, and the ice-cold butter is impossible to spread; the softer whipped honey butter served with fried chicken would be preferable.

Don't miss the long, crisp and gently starchy french-fried potatoes and the mellow dirty rice, a sort of Cajun risotto "dirtied" with the chopped giblets of chicken and duck. Wilted spinach is more successful than the stodgy fried okra. Any of the side dishes go well with the sautéed salmon in lemon butter (a more generous and successful specialty than the meager portion of swordfish), with the marinated barbecued boned breast of chicken and with the beautifully moist and tender sautéed duck breast enlivened with jalapeño peppers.

Grilled lamb chops with the brassy barbecue sauce were meaty and perfectly cooked, but both the tepid medaillons of beef with peppercorns and the lackluster catfish were disappointing. Fried chicken was decent if less inspired than the barbecued version, and calf's liver brightened by scallions was just slightly less interesting than other meat dishes. Scallions add a verdant touch to sautéed shrimp with lemon and garlic.

The waiters describe many daily specials not on the menu, but the only one for which a price is given is the porterhouse steak for two — and a good thing that it is, because the $45 price tag might send customers into shock. Nothing about the steak justified that price — not the size nor the flavor nor the inept way in which it was carved, with one person given the tail piece and the other the choice center. The barbecued single sirloin at $18 is a much better buy.

In addition to their ineptitude in carving, waiters have trouble opening wine, often breaking corks. They also fail to clear tables promptly and to bring clean napkins when needed. The most memorable desserts were the strawberry and rhubarb tart, the pear pie, the pecan pie and the banana fool, a custard topped with whipped cream. Steamed chocolate pudding was overly dense and hard as a rock.

Overhead fans, a handsome sculptured bar designed by George Nakashima and a big fireplace in which suckling pigs will be barbecued add to the atmosphere. But lighting is inadequate and the menu and the modest wine list are hard to read.

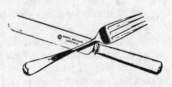

Thailand Restaurant

★ ★

---

106 Bayard Street, between Baxter and Mulberry
Streets, 349-3132.
Atmosphere: Typical Chinatown luncheonette setting
that is crowded, bright and cheerful; service is fast
and strictly no-frills.
Recommended dishes: Beef or chicken curries, beef or
squid salad, fried rice with shrimp, lemon shrimp
soup, cabbage and shrimp soup, whole fried fish,
crabs with garlic bean sauce, chicken with basil.
Price range: Inexpensive.
Credit cards: None.
Hours: Lunch and dinner, seven days, 11:30 A.M. to
11:30 P.M. Open on major holidays.
Reservations: Necessary on weekends or for groups
larger than two.

One of the best and least expensive Thai restaurants in
the city, this one offers nothing in the way of atmosphere or décor and service is merely utilitarian. It is
especially well located for lunch while on jury duty, for
it is possible to have a satisfying meal in very little time.

But if the setting is a bit tacky, the cooking is anything but. Thai soups such as the creamy coconut-based
chicken broth and the shrimp soup astringent with
lemon grass and hot chili oil are bracing, and the cabbage and shrimp combination is sustaining. Beef or
chicken curries, whether marked mild or spicy, are all
spicy, so be warned. Whole fried fish is crisp and
decked out with a hearty sauce heightened by ginger
and garlic, and, when available, hard cracked crabs get
a glossing of a heady garlic-flavored bean sauce.

Fried rice with shrimp rounds out a meal, as do several filling, soothing noodle dishes. Satays were a bit
tough and dry, but the piquant, cool salads crunchy
with onion and fragrant with coriander are delicious;
try those based on beef or squid.

The uptown branch of this restaurant is Pongsri Thailand. See that review.

For more details on Thai food, see the review of
Bangkok Cuisine.

Tibetan Kitchen

★

---

444 Third Avenue, between 30th and 31st Streets, 684-9209.

Atmosphere: Simple, small storefront restaurant with Tibetan decorations; ventilation is poor; service is friendly, helpful and slow.

Recommended dishes: Spicy cabbage and carrot salad, fried meat or vegetable dumplings, beef and onion in bread patty, sautéed noodles and vegetables with or without beef, lamb curry, chicken curry, sliced steak with hot bread, peas with beef and egg, Chinese cabbage with chicken, vegetable patty in bread dough.

Price range: Inexpensive.

Credit cards: None.

Hours: Lunch, Mondays through Fridays, noon to 3 P.M.; dinner, Mondays through Saturdays, 5:30 to 10:30 P.M. Closed Sundays.

Reservations: Not necessary, but will be accepted.

If gastronomic esoterica is the prize, it can certainly be found here at what is said to be the first and only Tibetan restaurant in the country.

The storefront dining room with just seven tables is bright, clean and trim and is decorated with Tibetan scrolls and motifs. Tibetans do the cooking and the one lively and amusing American waitress, who is inordinately proud of the cuisine, offers detailed instructions on the dishes. Her chattiness can wear thin, however, when you are waiting for water, rice or a check, especially annoying lapses when the kitchen slows down.

In general, Tibetan cooking combines the stir-fry techniques and vegetables of China with the curried chicken and lamb reminiscent of India. Sephan, a fiercely hot paste of chili, garlic and coriander, is blended with soy sauce to make a wonderful dip for momo — dumplings filled with meat or vegetables that are good steamed and even better fried. The same sauce sparks dishes such as the shaphali — sautéed beef and onion or vegetables enfolded in steamed bread, and the shapta, sliced steak with vegetables eaten with a flat bread much like the Indian chapati. Other savory meat main courses include the noodles with beef and vegetables (gyathuk ngopa), the sautéed Chinese cabbage with chicken (patsel) and the ground beef tossed with peas and egg drops (tentsel). Most of these dishes are soupy and mild-flavored, relying for interest primarily on onions and the subtle overtones of fresh coriander.

The two anise-scented curries are lively and lusty, though one billed as mutton was really lamb. Steamed rice is the perfect buffer and the chili-spiked salad of shredded cabbage and carrots (tang tsel) provides refreshing contrast. Other dishes were greasy or too limp and liquid.

As in other Asian cuisines, the sharing of dishes results in the most satisfying meals, so go with a few people, although not more than four because that is the most that can be accommodated comfortably. If you want wine or beer, take your own because there is no liquor license. And unless sweet warm rice with yogurt and sugar (deysee) is your idea of a great dessert, finish up with black tea. An alternative beverage is bocha — tea with butter and salt, a special taste that is perhaps acquired if one lives long enough.

Low prices apply at lunch and dinner. The downstairs room for private parties looks positively conspiratorial and is not recommended for those with even the mildest case of claustrophobia.

Toraji
★

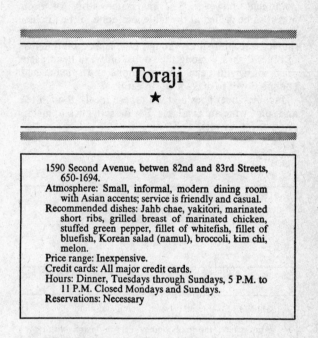

1590 Second Avenue, betwen 82nd and 83rd Streets, 650-1694.

Atmosphere: Small, informal, modern dining room with Asian accents; service is friendly and casual.

Recommended dishes: Jahb chae, yakitori, marinated short ribs, grilled breast of marinated chicken, stuffed green pepper, fillet of whitefish, fillet of bluefish, Korean salad (namul), broccoli, kim chi, melon.

Price range: Inexpensive.

Credit cards: All major credit cards.

Hours: Dinner, Tuesdays through Sundays, 5 P.M. to 11 P.M. Closed Mondays and Sundays.

Reservations: Necessary

Everything about this trim and informal Korean-Japanese restaurant reflects a modest ambition modestly realized. An interesting dinner can be had for $10 or less. Add $3 or $5 to that and you'll have an even more engaging meal, especially if three or four people share dishes from the à la carte menu. Dinner here is satisfying not only because of the quantity of food but also because of the delicate play of contrasting seasonings — winy, fermented soy sauce, hot chili peppers, scallions and garlic, pungent ginger and crackling sesame seeds.

Cold vegetables, more or less pickled in brine, are Korean specialties, represented here in the crisp, hotly flavored cabbage called kim chi and in the assorted namul — barely blanched spinach, bean sprouts and string beans in a sesame oil, garlic and soy dressing. Either of these specialties works as appetizer or side dish, and so do the broccoli sautéed with garlic and the jahb chae, a stir-fried vegetable assortment given heft with sliced beef and slippery bean thread or rice noodles. Along with the vegetables, try the yakitori, tiny nuggets of marinated chicken grilled on bamboo skewers, then have the more substantial kalbi kui — marinated and grilled short ribs with a sweet and pungent glaze. Other interesting main courses include a moist and tender breast of chicken, also marinated and grilled, and a fillet of bluefish in a similar teriyaki-style sauce but baked in an envelope of foil, the sharpness of the marinade doing much to ameliorate the oiliness of this strongly flavored fish.

Slim fillets of whitefish fried in a pale, egg batter proved better than the shrimp similarly prepared, mainly because the shrimp were not fresh and their oil had been overheated. Another mild and soothing dish was the green pepper that was stuffed with ground beef and turkey, fried in a light egg batter and accented by a sweet-sour dipping sauce.

Kogi, a favorite of the Korean kitchen, was a disappointment, however. The marinated strips of beef, meant to be grilled at the table, are done in the kitchen and arrive tough and limp. Stuffed mushrooms and sautéed zucchini slices, though fair, lacked the interest of other dishes. Among the soups, only the bean paste miso shiru with bean curd, scallions and spinach had enough flavor to make it worth eating.

Japanese beer goes best with these meals, though tea and some wine are available. For dessert, stick to melon or other fresh fruits.

Tout Va Bien
★

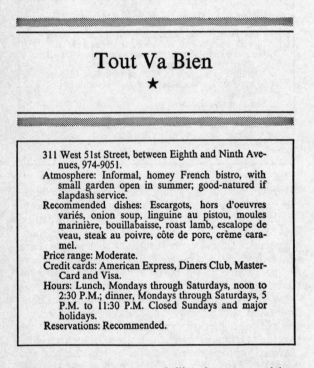

311 West 51st Street, between Eighth and Ninth Avenues, 974-9051.
Atmosphere: Informal, homey French bistro, with small garden open in summer; good-natured if slapdash service.
Recommended dishes: Escargots, hors d'oeuvres variés, onion soup, linguine au pistou, moules marinière, bouillabaisse, roast lamb, escalope de veau, steak au poivre, côte de porc, crème caramel.
Price range: Moderate.
Credit cards: American Express, Diners Club, Master-Card and Visa.
Hours: Lunch, Mondays through Saturdays, noon to 2:30 P.M.; dinner, Mondays through Saturdays, 5 P.M. to 11:30 P.M. Closed Sundays and major holidays.
Reservations: Recommended.

Although it may not sound like the most enticing recommendation, Tout Va Bien should be regarded as a utility French restaurant. This small, informal, family-run bistro, with its veneer paneling, pictures of Broadway-celebrity customers, red-checkered tablecloths and long, friendly bar is so quintessentially French, I never enter without immediately feeling in the mood for a licorice-flavored, cloudy yellow pastis.

The food at Tout Va Bien is best described as workingman French — ruggedly hearty, if lacking in finesse, moderately priced and decently satisfying. Add to that the convenience of having all of this on the edge of the theater district, and you'll understand its utility designation. It is best to avoid selections that rely on complicated, sophisticated sauces. Stick to plain choices and you are more certain to be pleased.

There is a pleasant hors d'oeuvres variés, a pinwheeled array of a good quality sardine, a silky salad of roasted peppers, firm chickpeas or white beans with onion slivers, a piquant beef salad and two different varieties of salami, both unusually savory. The coarse pâté de campagne can be good but sometimes is too soft; and both the escargots and clams baked with the traditional shallot parsley butter are respectably prepared.

A mild, golden onion soup with a thin crust of cheese that is not too cloying is bracing. An order of linguine au pistou, shared among two or three as a first course, is a lovely, creamy blend of basil in a golden cheese sauce that almost seemed to be enriched with egg.

On another occasion, mussels marinière, listed as a main course, were shared by three as an appetizer, and if not the most inspired version of this dish we've ever had, it did consist of sand-free, briny fresh mussels in a well-garlicked wine broth.

One of the best main courses at Tout Va Bien is steak au poivre, based on a really lusty black-pepper sauce. Good quality, properly white escalope of veal sautéed with lemon and butter is a close second to the steak. Veal kidneys Bordelaise, blanketed with mushroom and onion in a thick red-wine sauce is acceptable, as is a daily special of a grilled pork chop only lightly glazed with a much reduced red-wine sauce.

Far less pleasant is the boeuf Bourguignonne, for though the meat is lean and fork tender, the pale, tomato-to-red sauce is thick with flour. Another near-disaster is veal Pojarsky, a daily special of a breaded ground-veal patty drowned to sogginess in an acidy, tomato-thickened sauce. Omelets at lunch tend to be overcooked, but the fillet of sole meunière is carefully, freshly prepared. The Friday bouillabaisse is always creditable, as is roast lamb, when it is on the menu.

The crisp green salad is glossed with a properly mustardy vinaigrette dressing, and the slim, gently crisp french fries are delicious. Not so the ubiquitous, hopelessly overcooked and waterlogged string beans, which appear and reappear at every meal.

There is also a tendency to garnish luncheon dishes drugstore-style, with a wedge of unripe tomato and a limp lettuce leaf.

The only really delicious dessert at Tout Va Bien is crème caramel. Cheese is served too cold, the pastry is leaden and the chocolate mousse pallid.

Since prices are low, it will not be too surprising to learn that quarters are cramped and service is somewhat slapdash. Above all, avoid the tightly pocketed front-window table if there are more than two in your party. Otherwise, at least one member in a larger party will be wedged against a scorching-hot radiator throughout the meal.

There is a small, pretty garden where food is served in summer.

Tovarisch
★

38 West 62nd Street, Broadway at Lincoln Center, 757-0168.

Atmosphere: Small, pleasant dining rooms with Russian overtones; service is generally acceptable but sometimes slow and overbearing.

Recommended dishes: Yogurt cheese, eggplant caviar, calf's foot gelatin, basturma, hot and cold borscht, salmon solyanka, rassolnik, schav, lamb shashlik, chicken tabaka, Siberian pelmeny, roast quail, blinchiki with kasha, fruit compote, délice Anna Pavlova.

Price range: Moderate.

Credit cards: American Express, MasterCard and Visa.

Hours: Lunch, Mondays through Saturdays, 11:30 A.M. to 2:30 P.M.; dinner, Mondays through Saturdays, 5:30 P.M. to 10 P.M.; supper, Mondays through Saturdays, 10 P.M. to 11:30 P.M. Closed Sundays.

Reservations: Necessary.

Because Russian food seems especially appropriate before or after concerts and the ballet, it seems equally appropriate to have it represented near Lincoln Center, as it is at Tovarisch. This snug restaurant is divided into two rooms, and though the front dining room is livelier, both have a warm and festive glow. The warmth is created by a combination of an orange paisley fabric on the wall, mirrors with colorful lacquer frames, pretty flowers and candlelight. Slightly cramped tables and banal background music (much like the "Volga Boatman" as rendered by Mantovani) detract somewhat from the overall experience. So do the slow service, the overbearing staff and food that is not always hot.

Nevertheless, Tovarisch provides a gently pleasant experience, enhanced by some good and interesting food prepared by a chef who is said to have arrived recently from the Soviet Union.

Rich and luxuriously oily zakuska, or appetizers, include a puréed eggplant salad, the tangy yogurt cheese with scallions, kholodets, a garlicky calf's foot aspic, and basturma, the leathery, earthy Georgian, air-cured beef. Maatjes, schmaltz and marinated herrings were decent, though they could have been more tender and succulent. The pashtet, a pâté, was too mushy, fatty and bland. Smoked salmon had a delicate flavor but was too thickly cut. The only caviars available when I ordered were a dry and overly salty salmon roe and a mushy, bitter American sturgeon product. Buttery, grainy blini pancakes should have been thinner, but they were delicious as part of the Blini Imperial, a Lazy Susan of dishes filled with a variety of appetizers.

When I attempted to order this assortment as an appetizer instead of as a main course, the captain objected, saying it would be too much to eat, and for a while it looked as though he would not serve it. But persistence won out, and the assortment, though generous, left room for main courses.

Soups are hearty, especially the hot, red-beet and cabbage borscht and the rassolnik made with chicken giblets, vegetables and pickled cucumbers. Both are accompanied by sour cream and dill. So are the cold beet borscht and the sorrel soup — schav. Smoked salmon, potatoes and onions flavor the unusually soothing solyanka soup. But the meat-and-kasha-filled pastry turnovers — piroshki — were insufficiently heated and greasy as a result.

Two main courses were outstanding: the Siberian pelmeny, which are meat-filled dumplings in a dill-scented chicken broth, and the chicken tabaka, a Georgian specialty of a small, flattened chicken fried under pressure and served with tkemali sauce, a blend of prunes, garlic, chili peppers, onions and coriander. Because American prunes tend to be sweeter than those from the Georgian Republic, a few drops of vinegar would improve flavor contrasts in this sauce. It also accompanies the acceptable lamb shashlik and the oniony ground lamb lyulya kebabs that were a little too firmly packed. Cutlet Kiev was totally uninspired and too darkly fried and a paillard of veal with caviar and a sour cream-mustard sauce proved to be a poor combination. You'll do better with the light blinchiki crepes enfolding kasha with sautéed mushrooms and onions.

Fried herring at lunch was breathtakingly salty even for salty herring. When I ordered the Mongolian fire pot, with its chicken, lamb, beef and vegetables to be cooked in broth at the table, I was told this table procedure had been discontinued because it proved too difficult to handle. On my next visit, however, this service was offered but it did indeed prove awkward and not worth the effort.

Among game dishes on the menu, only roast quail was available. It was tender and delicious both times I ordered it. But vegetables are dull and are generally covered with heavy-handed sauces and the bread should be more interesting. Whole-grain kasha added a nutlike crunch to many courses. Stewed fruit with nuts was among the better dessert choices, along with délice Anna Pavlova, the mocha and hazelnut meringue cake that is a trademark of Délices La Côte Basque, the bakery that provides it. Skip the chocolate cake and the cloyingly sweet combination of cheesecake with walnuts in syrup. The fruit dessert, kissel, was too liquid, and tea with cherry preserves should be brewed.

Trastevere

★ ★ ★

309 East 83rd Street, between First and Second Avenues, 734-6343.

Atmosphere: Tiny, intimate and Bohemian storefront restaurant, noisy and convivial. Service is generally good, but sometimes unevenly paced.

Recommended dishes: Spiedino alla Romana, mussels in brodetto, vegetable antipasto, vegetable salad, vegetable soup, all pastas, chicken alla Romana, chicken alla Elvira, veal all'Anna, rack of veal Trastevere, calamari, sole, zuppa di pesce, all desserts except chestnut mousse.

Price range: Moderately expensive.

Credit cards: American Express. Personal checks are also accepted.

Hours: Dinner, seven days, 5 P.M. to 10:30 P.M. Closed most holidays.

Reservations: Necessary.

Trastevere is not everyone's bowl of pasta. But the consistently full house indicates there are more than enough diners who like the intimate and Bohemian setting, no matter how cramped and noisy, and the lusty, earthy food, no matter how large the portions and how redolent of garlic. Named for the ancient, colorful Trastevere section of Rome, where some of the poorest of its citizens and some of its best trattorie co-exist, this brick-walled slice of a restaurant with its old prints, pot-bellied stove and candlelit tables makes sitting elbow-to-elbow seem convivial — as though at a lively house party. Even the background music of operatic arias and Neapolitan ballads seems acceptable here because it is so much in character.

Discomfort sets in with parties larger than four, however, because only one table adequately seats more. There can also be gusts of icy air when the door is opened and closed, and at times, the kitchen activity backs up and service is unevenly paced.

Certain tables afford a bright view of the tiny kitchen, with hanging iron pots and a good-natured crew that includes the brothers who own the restaurant — Paul Lattanzi, who with his mother, Erminia, oversees the cooking, and Maurizio, who manages the dining room. A third brother, also a chef, has recently arrived from their native Rome to operate their new venture, Trastevere 84, which has just opened.

Several important changes at Trastevere account for the improved rating since it was first reviewed. Previously, too many cloves of half-cooked garlic were left in sauces — booby traps for unsuspecting palates. Also, pasta was cooked a little too al dente, leaving it slightly crisp in the center. Now, garlic is still well-represented, but most of the cloves are removed, and the pasta can be obtained a bit mellower on request. Also, larger bowls now facilitate the handling of seafood dishes.

Generous appetizer portions lend themselves to sharing. The sandless and sparkling fresh mussels steamed in a tomato, garlic and hot pepper sauce are as inspired as the vegetable antipasto, based on a lightly sautéed combination that might include zucchini, peppers, eggplant and broccoli, sometimes dressed only with oil, other times with vinegar and capers. Lightly blanched vegetables in a lusciously oily dressing make up the insalata Trastevere. The spiedino alla Romana, although done as a fried mozzarella and prosciutto sandwich instead of on a spiedo or skewer, is sparked by a lemony caper and anchovy sauce.

Even vegetable soup is exceptional, cooked to order with broccoli, zucchini or peas. Chicken and veal broth make up the base in which the vegetables cook for two minutes, along with a touch of tomato and garlic, all to be finished with a sprinkling of grated Parmesan and black pepper. It's a tossup between the soup and one of the four or five delicious pasta creations. Nowhere will you get better linguine with white clam sauce, though clams out of the shell would be an improvement, and the thick strands of bucatini wound around an Amatriciana sauce of tomatoes, shallots and pancetta is a close second. On some days, gnocchi, green with the basil purée stirred into them, are blanketed by a pizzaiuola sauce made with pancetta bacon. Other regulars include fettuccine Trastevere with fresh peas, mushrooms and cream, and the capellini primavera with vegetables. Although an overabundance of sauce sometimes make those last two a little soupy, they can hardly be faulted for flavor.

Except for lackluster scampi, the seafood dishes are excellent, whether you choose the tender, moist calamari or the mixed fish and shellfish zuppa de pesce. All contain garlic, tomato and a touch of hot red pepper flakes, but some are thinned with fish stock.

Beautifully sautéed sole is rimmed with an herbed tomato salad much like the one that turns the rack of veal Trastevere into a minor miracle. Never in my experience has a veal cutlet Milanese been more imaginatively or successfully presented. Bland and wet veal piccante leaves something to be desired, but veal all'Anna, with mushrooms, Marsala and a brown ragout gravy is delicious. So is the chicken Elvira done with much the same sauce. Chicken Gaetano with mushrooms is more savory than before, but it is still a bit pallid compared to the chicken Romano sautéed with green peppers and rosemary.

Napoleons, cream puffs in chocolate sauce, chocolate mousse and a chocolate ice cream tartufo are up to the level of other dishes. Only the Monte Bianco, the Italian version of the chestnut purée and whipped cream Mont Blanc, was too dry and dense.

The wine list is limited to four whites and four reds. Among the latter, Gattinara proved a better choice than the Riservato Agli Amici, a blend of Nebbiola and Barbaresco grapes.

Trattoria da Alfredo
★ ★

90 Bank Street, at Hudson Street, 929-4400.
Atmosphere: Bright, lively and attractive Mediterranean cafe setting; good service.
Recommended dishes: Artichokes alla Romana, all stuffed vegetables, baked clams oreganate, carpaccio, all pastas, salad of raw spinach with mushrooms and pancetta, chicken with rosemary, arugula salad, Gino's chocolate cake and dacquoise.
Price range: Moderately expensive.
Credit cards: None.
Hours: Lunch, Mondays through Saturdays, except Tuesdays, noon to 2 P.M.; dinner, Mondays through Saturdays, 6 P.M. to 10 P.M.; Sundays, 5 P.M. to 9 P.M. On major holidays, open for dinner only.
Reservations: Necessary.

It has been almost ten years since Alfredo Viazzi, a native of the Ligurian city of Savona and an already experienced New York restaurateur, opened his modest, informal and instantly successful Trattoria da Alfredo in Greenwich Village, and a double trend was born. This was one of the earliest storefront restaurants with a limited but stylish North Italian menu and a variety of foods that allowed a diner to choose a meal that was light, heavy or halfway between.

Captivated by the bright blue-and-white Mediterranean cafe setting and the excellent antipasto, salads and pasta specialties, members of the publishing and fashion worlds took this place over as their own, making reservations inordinately difficult to get, especially on weekends. Fortunately for the management, the early success proved to be enduring.

The mainstay of the menu is its pasta selection, all expertly and enticingly conceived and prepared. All personal favorites are the light and delicate tortellini della nonna in a gossamer cream and cheese sauce that only occasionally is oversalty with chunks of prosciutto; the herbaceous pesto sauce on spaghettini and the thicker perciatelli all'Amatriciana, with tomatoes, onion and pancetta. The spaghettini, prepared with white clam sauce or puttanesca style (tomato sauce with black olives, capers, tuna fish, anchovies), are invariably delicious. At times, the pasta arrives undercooked.

Those with somewhat heartier appetites can precede the pastas with one of the enticing appetizers, several of which also can be combined to make a complete, light meal. Stuffed vegetables are succulent and colorful specialties and include baked mushrooms with minced mushroom stems, prosciutto, cheese and parsley, zucchini filled with ground beef, sausage and cheese, and peppers enclosing a pungent mix of tuna fish, anchovies, pimentos, capers, cheese and a little bread softened in cream to bind and mellow the combination. Baked stuffed clams oreganate are crisp with bread crumbs and fragrant with parsley. All as satisfying as they are hearty are garlic cheese and oregano, carpaccio, the pounded raw beef, with a tangy sauce, and a supple, gently simmered, warm artichoke alla Romana, flavored with olive oil, garlic and parsley.

Also available is an excellent cold antipasto assortment of garlicky Italian salami and properly aged prosciutto and a raw-mushroom salad with a garlic and parsley dressing. Arugula salad, spinach with raw mushrooms and pancetta were fresh and sprightly.

Add to all of this the irresistible desserts, Gino's chocolate cake and hazelnut dacquoise, and you might expect this restaurant to have at least a three-star rating. Unfortunately, a number of main courses that might be considered after the pastas do not live up to the food already described. Each day, one veal scaloppine dish is available, and invariably the veal is insufficiently seared, the sauce pallid. A simple fish preparation can be acceptable, but the meager Livornaise fish soup, cacciucco, often contains fish that is either overcooked or undercooked, as unpleasant a circumstance as having it overcooked. Chicken sautéed with rosemary and black olives was delicious.

An attractive array of cooked vegetables with coarse garlic sausage and green sauce — stronzata di verdure miste e cotechino con salsa verde — was disappointing because the vegetables were so underdone they were virtually raw and unduly filling. Undercooking also marred a side order of asparagus with parmesan cheese, and asparagus with egg and cheese was another vegetable dish that proved uninspired.

Prices are moderate, especially for the pastas, which can be shared, but there is a minimum. No liquor license, so take your own wine.

Tre Scalini
★ ★

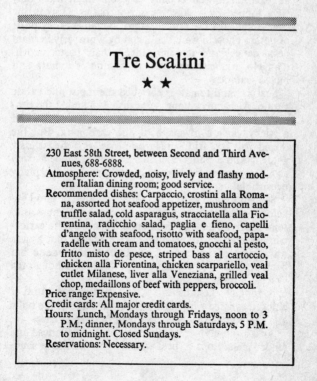

230 East 58th Street, between Second and Third Avenues, 688-6888.

Atmosphere: Crowded, noisy, lively and flashy modern Italian dining room; good service.

Recommended dishes: Carpaccio, crostini alla Romana, assorted hot seafood appetizer, mushroom and truffle salad, cold asparagus, stracciatella alla Fiorentina, radicchio salad, paglia e fieno, capelli d'angelo with seafood, risotto with seafood, paparadelle with cream and tomatoes, gnocchi al pesto, fritto misto de pesce, striped bass al cartoccio, chicken alla Fiorentina, chicken scarpariello, veal cutlet Milanese, liver alla Veneziana, grilled veal chop, medaillons of beef with peppers, broccoli.

Price range: Expensive.

Credit cards: All major credit cards.

Hours: Lunch, Mondays through Fridays, noon to 3 P.M.; dinner, Mondays through Saturdays, 5 P.M. to midnight. Closed Sundays.

Reservations: Necessary.

When Tre Scalini opened, the ambitious menu and the proficiency of the kitchen earned it a three-star rating. But six months later, after a change of chefs and many complaints about service, that rating nose-dived to fair. More recently, with a new chef in command and better manners on the part of the management, Tre Scalini fully deserves two stars — very good, if not yet returned to its early level of excellence.

The kitchen's strong points are the appetizers, pastas and fish dishes, as well as all frying and broiling, a combination that accounts for a considerable part of the menu. Weak spots are in sautéed dishes with overdoses of wine and an overabundance of mushrooms to impart a pseudo-elegance.

The best appetizers now include raw sliced beef, carpaccio, with a sharp and refreshing green sauce, a delicately fried crostini of mozzarella cheese served with both a tomato sauce and a light golden haze of anchovies, and a fine, earthy combination of white truffles and raw mushrooms slivered into a salad accented by chips of celery and Parmesan cheese. Cold asparagus with a festive minced pimento and parsley vinaigrette and the hot assorted seafood appetizer in an herb-scented tomato sauce were also delicious, excepting only the dreadful canned or frozen artichoke heart that appeared as a garnish.

Soup lovers would do well to consider the stracciatella alla Fiorentina, a sunny broth given substance by a fluff of minced spinach, beaten egg and grated cheese.

Some excellent pastas were sampled; all would be equally good in half portions as appetizers or as complete main courses. The green-and-white noodles, paglia e fieno, were about as good as they can get in a gossamer cream-and-cheese sauce flecked with bits of prosciutto and green peas. The wide, short noodles known as paparadelle were equally good one night when they were topped by a sauce of cream, butter, Gorgonzola cheese and just the faint blush of tomatoes. Airy puffs of potato gnocchi were blanketed by a properly verdant pesto sauce, and the thin angel's hair pasta, capelli d'angelo, was elegant under its mantle of tomato and mixed seafood.

Seafood and tomatoes enriched the moist and subtle risotto. Also-rans among pasta dishes included the cannelloni with a filling that was far too pasty and dry and a sticky version of spaghetti alla carbonara. But the mixed fish fry, fritto misto de pesce, was greaselessly golden. And a pungent homemade tartar sauce as well as a hotly spiced fra diavolo tomato sauce were equally irresistible.

Striped bass in cartoccio (a huge balloon of a foil envelope) was baked with tomatoes, clams and mussels to send forth a briny, garlic-scented essence as the cartoccio was opened, and the promise made by that aroma was delivered in flavor. Striped bass in brodetto has been braised to firm but moist perfection, although the sauce itself was too sharply acidy.

Among chicken dishes, stick to the tiny spezzatini of chicken sautéed with garlic and white wine, or the polla alla Fiorentina, tender breasts over fresh spinach.

An absolutely perfect fried veal cutlet Milanese and tender medaillons of beef with a light pizzaiuola sauce brightened by red and green peppers proved to be the best meat dishes, although the calf's liver Veneziana sautéed with onions and the broiled, petal-pink veal chop were almost as good. Tender quails, done a disservice by soggy, leaden diamonds of polenta, were nevertheless worth ordering.

Veal scallopini piccante was unpleasantly steamy and stringy, and the combination of veal, lamb and mushrooms known as abbacchio alla Tre Scalini is the sort of dish that seems wonderful after the first bite but cloys by the third. The bitter Italian broccoli di rape, steamed with olive oil and garlic, is a better vegetable choice than the acceptable but relatively tasteless fried zucchini. The ruby-red leaf lettuce, radicchio, makes a refreshingly tart and bitter salad.

Zabaglione thickened with crushed macaroons is the best dessert. Both the chocolate ganache cake and the gâteau St.-Honoré were uninteresting.

Banquettes and chairs are uncomfortable, and though the noise level in this gaudy, modern Roman setting has been mellowed somewhat, it is still distracting.

Trumpets
★

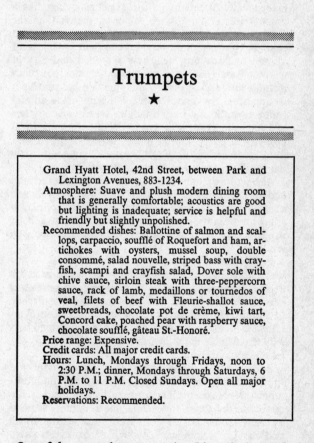

Grand Hyatt Hotel, 42nd Street, between Park and Lexington Avenues, 883-1234.
Atmosphere: Suave and plush modern dining room that is generally comfortable; acoustics are good but lighting is inadequate; service is helpful and friendly but slightly unpolished.
Recommended dishes: Ballottine of salmon and scallops, carpaccio, soufflé of Roquefort and ham, artichokes with oysters, mussel soup, double consommé, salad nouvelle, striped bass with crayfish, scampi and crayfish salad, Dover sole with chive sauce, sirloin steak with three-peppercorn sauce, rack of lamb, medaillons or tournedos of veal, filets of beef with Fleurie-shallot sauce, sweetbreads, chocolate pot de crème, kiwi tart, Concord cake, poached pear with raspberry sauce, chocolate soufflé, gâteau St.-Honoré.
Price range: Expensive.
Credit cards: All major credit cards.
Hours: Lunch, Mondays through Fridays, noon to 2:30 P.M.; dinner, Mondays through Saturdays, 6 P.M. to 11 P.M. Closed Sundays. Open all major holidays.
Reservations: Recommended.

One of the more pleasant surprises I have had recently is Trumpets, the spacious and comfortably appointed restaurant in the Grand Hyatt. After passing through the glitzy and extravagant lobby, Trumpets turns out to be plush, somewhat sedate and thoroughly restful. Long, beveled mirrors reflect the sparkle of candlelight, floral arrangements are graceful and the noise level is benign even when the place is filled or when the pianist plays in the adjoining cocktail lounge. The only flaws in the setting are chairs that are too low and slightly inadequate lighting that makes it difficult to read menus and checks. The staff is friendly and efficient, if somewhat unpolished. An especially hospitable touch comes in the matchbooks stamped with the name in which the reservation was made.

Despite some serious flaws, the kitchen's efforts are already worth a single star and with just a little fine tuning, the restaurant could easily rate two. The menu is ambitious and stylish with nouvelle cuisine overtones. Both the cold table of appetizers and the dessert buffet indicate skilled craftsmen are at work. But in both cases offerings look better than they taste, indicating more experience is needed with seasonings.

When I was recognized, it became impossible to order the duck or pheasant pâtés. On three attempts I was told they were not fresh, yet both were on display and both were being served to other guests. Finally, through a bit of subterfuge, I did manage to try both. Though the duck proved acceptable, the pheasant was indeed stale. Assorted cold fish appetizers, including a potpourri of seafood, were somewhat better than the charcuterie, but they were still inferior to other first courses. One exception was the excellent ballottine of salmon and scallops, delicately seasoned and airy of texture. Raw beef carpaccio gained proper pungency from its mustardy dressing, and a golden hot soufflé of Roquefort cheese and Westphalian ham made an elegant starter. So did fresh artichoke bases under oysters and spinach glossed with cream. Double consommé was properly assertive, and at lunch there is a superb saffron-gilded cream of mussel soup. Among soups, only the bouillon of snails came as a watery failure.

Also at lunch, there is a delicate salad of cool scampi and fresh crayfish over a crunchy mound of julienne strips of raw vegetables. Another salad, breast of pheasant with walnuts and chanterelles, would have been equally good had the creamy mayonnaise dressing been less sweet.

Fish quenelles are frequently the daily special. At one lunch, these dumplings made with salmon had been too densely compacted, but the Nantua seafood sauce was perfect. Another time, the quenelles of white-fleshed fish were light and airy, but the sauce had been oversalted. Dover sole in chive cream sauce and striped bass with crayfish could not be faulted, but salmon with sorrel sauce was dried out.

Both the medaillons of veal with lemon balm and spinach and the thick tournedos of veal atop wild mushrooms were extraordinary, primarily because of the quality of the moist, fork-tender meat. Almost as good were filets of beef in a Fleurie wine sauce accented with shallots. The sirloin steak, though it required a sharp knife, had excellent flavor, compromised somewhat by an overdose of pink peppercorns. Rack of lamb scented with rosemary and fired with Dijon mustard had exceptional flavor, but lamb chops of equally high quality were ruined by a bittingly salty Roquefort glaze. Tarragon and mint lent interesting counterpoints of flavor to sweetbreads, but breast of duck was overdone in a raspberry sauce as thick and sweet as jam.

The salad nouvelle was cool and crisp with its slim green beans and poached julienne vegetables. In general, interesting vegetables accompanied the main courses.

Among the superior desserts were the chocolate soufflé (better than the bland chestnut or Grand Marnier alternatives), the satiny chocolate pot de crème and a poached pear with raspberry purée sauce nestled in chocolate-tipped butter cookies and garnished with kiwi slices on whipped cream. Among the pastries, the best choices were the kiwi tart, the Concord cake with its chocolate meringue and creamy chocolate filling and the gâteau St.-Honoré, unconventional with its chocolate and vanilla whipped cream underlying custard cream.

The wine list has many excellent choices but prices are exorbitant. French imports were marked up 300 to 400 percent and Californias 200 to 250 percent.

Tse Yang

★

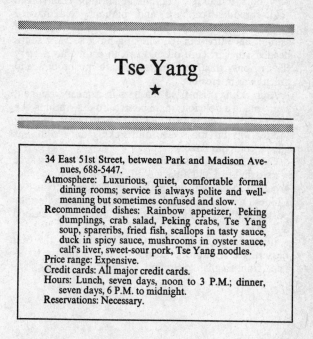

34 East 51st Street, between Park and Madison Avenues, 688-5447.
Atmosphere: Luxurious, quiet, comfortable formal dining rooms; service is always polite and well-meaning but sometimes confused and slow.
Recommended dishes: Rainbow appetizer, Peking dumplings, crab salad, Peking crabs, Tse Yang soup, spareribs, fried fish, scallops in tasty sauce, duck in spicy sauce, mushrooms in oyster sauce, calf's liver, sweet-sour pork, Tse Yang noodles.
Price range: Expensive.
Credit cards: All major credit cards.
Hours: Lunch, seven days, noon to 3 P.M.; dinner, seven days, 6 P.M. to midnight.
Reservations: Necessary.

Although there are excellent Vietnamese restaurants in Paris, Chinese food there ranges from mildly pleasant to poor. So it was hardly exciting to learn that Tse Yang, the expensive new Chinese restaurant that opened recently, is the spin-off of a Paris original. It is certainly the most lavish Chinese restaurant in New York, with intricately worked Chinese motifs hammered into copper wall panels, thick carpeting, large, widely spaced tables with starchy linens, graceful floral arrangements and a black-mirrored ceiling that dramatically reflects candlelit tabletops.

There are also a fishless fish tank, an intimate bar and a few private dining rooms. Because the low noise level makes it possible to hold quiet conversations and because the formal and polite captains and waiters make helpful suggestions, a meal at Tse Yang can be relaxing. Only occasionally is the service slow and forgetful, most especially when things are slow.

It is the comfort of the place and the only moderately expensive lunches that make this restaurant worth a star. For the sky-high dinner prices and the relatively small portions of pleasant but undistinguished food, it would be rated only fair.

One of the biggest flaws in the kitchen is the acrid overtone of stale cooking oil in such dishes as shrimp-filled autumn rolls, pork-filled spring rolls, fried rice, Singapore rice vermicelli, caramelized apples and fried phoenix jade shrimp. Blandness alternates with saltiness, and there is a boring similarity between the brown stir-fried dishes, such as veal with scallions, Tse Yang chicken, a bitingly salty sole in spicy sauce and Tse Yang pork.

Appetizers are appealing, and the best are delicate meat-filled Peking dumplings served in a bamboo steamer, meaty spareribs, a cool crab salad and the rainbow hors d'oeuvres, combining shrimp, chili-spiked cold shredded cabbage and piquant cold hacked chicken with chili pepper and cashews. Chunks of salmon have dried in the smoking process. Most soups needed vinegar, chili oil and salt to counteract watery flavors; only the Tse Yang soup with mushrooms and greens was interesting.

A crackling crisp-fried sea bass in a meaty, pungent sauce made a delicious main course. So did scallops in a sheer spicy sauce and stuffed, fried crab claws. Sichuan lobster was far too sweet, and Peking duck skin was glassy, cold and flavorless.

Calf's liver with scallions and duck in spicy sauce were delightful and a harmonious sweet and sour sauce accented the lemon-flavored pork. A silken mixture of Chinese mushrooms in oyster sauce complemented the pork and the Tse Yang noodles, sautéed with seafood and vegetables.

Beautifully arranged cut fresh fruits make the best dessert. Descriptions of dishes on the menu are translated from English to French, a pretentious touch.

Tucano
★★

333 East 60th Street, between First and Second Avenues, 308-2333.

Atmosphere: Festive tropical setting, amusing and comfortable; restaurant and adjoining disco attract a late and stylish crowd; banquettes are too low, but noise level is bearable; service crisp, polite and professional but sometimes hectic.

Recommended dishes: Smoked salmon, pâté of pigeon, terrine of fish, mosaic of vegetables, salad with frog's legs, string bean salad with foie gras, snails in garlic cream, cream of lettuce soup, cold lobster bisque, cream of mussel soup, quenelles, scallops in pastry, sole frères Troisgros, ragout of lobster, paillard of beef beurre rouge, tournedos Bressane, veal chop with morels, chicken au vinaigre, seafood salad, green salad with walnuts, spinach salad with smoked salmon, cassis cake, lemon cake, chocolate cake, chocolate mousse, apple or orange sherbet.

Price range: Moderately expensive.

Credit cards: All major credit cards.

Hours: Lunch, Mondays through Fridays, noon to 2:30 P.M.; dinner, Mondays through Saturdays, 7 P.M. to 11:30 P.M. Closed Sundays.

Reservations: Recommended for lunch; necessary for dinner.

There is a festive, distinctively Brazilian stylishness about Tucano, the posh and pleasant restaurant that adjoins Club A, the private disco club. Owned by Richard Amaral, who modeled this New York operation after his clubs in Rio de Janeiro and Paris, Tucano is named for the brilliant toucan, the tropical bird, which is celebrated here on painted panels. Illumination comes from big glass lighting fixtures shaped like the bananas, pineapples, oranges and apples that used to be piled on Carmen Miranda's hats.

Polished dark wood, mirrors and striped velvet upholstery add to the handsome effect, marred only by uncomfortably low banquettes. The chairs at square tables are far more comfortable. The dressy swinging international crowd that favors Tucano gathers in the cocktail lounge just before nine and files into the dining room about 9:30.

Because ultra-chic restaurants like this are often painfully pretentious, it comes as a pleasant surprise that Tucano is definitely not, a tribute, perhaps, to Jean Claude Pujol, Mr. Amaral's partner, who keeps a watchful eye on proceedings. The staff seems good natured and thoroughly professional, if somewhat too crisply businesslike, and at crowded times the pace is hectic. Otherwise, Tucano is just plain fun, and the quality of the food, prepared under the direction of Gerard Reuther, the chef, is as surprisingly good as the service.

The menu is nouvelle cuisine to the core and most of the dishes are light, delicate and attractively turned out.

Ingredients are first class, so that whether you have an appetizer as simple as the pale pink, gently smoky salmon or a creation as intricate as a mosaic of vegetables and veal molded in aspic, you will be off to a wonderful start. When pâté of squab is not too cold, it is as good as the rose-pink terrine of salmon and turbot.

Two refreshing appetizer salads are mixed greens tossed with warm, boneless nuggets of frog's legs and slim haricots verts with julienne slivers of foie gras and raw mushrooms. There is also a light, fresh fine pasta verdant with a creamy pistou basil sauce. An artichoke in a piquant vinaigrette sauce was a bit too cold, as was a tiny half-lobster with mayonnaise and vegetable salad.

Such soups as pungent cream of lettuce and sorrel, satiny cold cream of mussel and pearl-pink lobster bisque rival the appetizers as satisfying first courses.

Both the snails in garlic cream and the whole fresh truffles we tried were excellent, but each was slightly marred by the overpowering, soggy pastry wrapped around them. Those flaws are evident in all pastry crusts at Tucano, not only with appetizers but also with such main courses as bland filet of lamb en croûte, fruit tarts and napoleon. The only dish that survives the pastry is sea scallops en croûte, baked in a big seashell that is prettily bedded down on seaweed.

Sauces are strong points, especially on fish and shellfish. For instance, airy pike quenelles are highlighted by a shellfish-enriched sauce Nantua, and a whisky-shellfish sauce brightens a ragout of tender lobster. One of the prettiest and best creations is tresse de sole frères Troisgros, a tribute to the Troisgros brothers, who operate the three-star restaurant in Roanne, France. In this dish, strips of green and pink noodles form a basket weave with firm, fresh strips of snowy sole, all underlined with diced tomatoes sautéed in cream. Overcooking made red snapper and escallops of salmon chokingly dry, but sautéed soft-shell crabs could not be improved upon.

A paillard of beef is properly seared — rare inside, but with a beefy burnish outside — and its beurre rouge of shallots, butter and red wine gives it the right mellow overtones. Thick tournedos with pistachios and truffles didn't quite match the paillard, but they were good nonetheless. So were a veal chop with morels and roseate medaillons of veal with wild mushrooms. Only a small sirloin steak was a disappointment, acrid as it was from too many pink peppercorns. Chicken braised in a mahogany-colored wine vinegar is mellow and tender, but a jam-thick raspberry purée makes roast duck seem like dessert.

Fresh, firm vegetables or well-cooked wild or white rice accompany main courses. With some main courses, the standard garnish is a custard timbale set with bits of vegetables — an attractive presentation that lacks flavor.

Dinner salads such as spinach with smoked salmon and mixed greens with walnuts have a sprightly vinaigrette dressing, and a rich, oily homemade mayonnaise sparks a lunch salad of mixed greens and shellfish. Scrambled eggs topped with red caviar are perfectly prepared, but the portion is much too large. A contrasting element would alleviate the richness of the eggs.

Among desserts, individual soufflés are too tough and eggy, and fruit tarts suffer from poor pastry. Far better choices are green-apple and blood-orange fruit sherbets and Bavarian cream cakes in lemon and cassis flavors. Chocolate cake has just the right combination of lightness and richness, and so does the marvelously velvety chocolate mousse. Petits fours are elaborate, and the best among them are little cream-puff swans and puffs topped by thick, dark fudgelike chocolate.

The adjoining disco is a private club, but those dining at Tucano are admitted. It is a suave setting where the new rage is old-style touch dancing.

24 Fifth Avenue
★ ★

24 Fifth Avenue, at the corner of Ninth Street, 475-0880.
Atmosphere: Graceful, glassed-in cafe, bar and dining room with Art Deco flower motifs and flattering rose-beige color scheme; service slows down between appetizer and main course; staff is friendly but service is erratic.
Recommended dishes: Cold lamb salad, snails, duck liver and veal pâté, Roquefort beignets with apple purée, smoked salmon, gazpacho without cheese, clear fish soup, soft-shell crabs, swordfish, double breast of chicken with two mustards, duck stew, roast lamb, pasta with porcini and pancetta, filet mignon with red wine and port, roast beef sandwich, omelet with curried crab meat, lemon tart, espresso crème caramel, bread pudding.
Prices: Moderately expensive.
Credit cards: All major credit cards.
Hours: Lunch, Mondays through Fridays, 11:45 A.M. to 3:15 P.M.; dinner, Mondays through Saturdays, 5:30 P.M. to 11:15 P.M.; Sundays, 5:30 P.M. to 10:30 P.M.; brunch, Saturdays and Sundays, 11:30 A.M. to 4 P.M.
Reservations: Recommended.

Friends of Leslie Revsin who have missed her light, delicate nouvelle American style of cooking since her Restaurant Leslie closed last year should be delighted to find her holding forth as executive chef at this graceful and romantic new restaurant. There is already a late and stylish singles bar scene on weekends that overflows into the dining room.

Miss Revsin has brought along many of her trademark dishes, such as crisp and airy Roquefort beignets with apple purée and moist, tender grilled breast of chicken glazed with two mustards. These and other dishes are already being turned out with considerable skill at the cafe-restaurant, whose name is also its address. The building used to be the Fifth Avenue Hotel.

The action now centers around the glassed-in cafe, which affords a clear view of street activity while offering protection from the elements, albeit with noisy air-conditioning. In cold weather, the inner dining rooms may seem snugger, with their gleaming brass trim, restful rose-beige walls and stylized Art Deco floral motifs. The staff needs to overcome a certain lack of polish, especially noticeable when wine is being poured, but the waiters are pleasant, good-natured and eager to accommodate. The frequent slowdowns between appetizers and main courses seem to be the fault of the kitchen, even though the restaurant was less than half full on each of my five visits. Early complaints about poor service seem to have subsided.

Miss Revsin has a talent for creating refreshing and beguiling combinations, though her original penchant for using too many nuts and overstrong cheeses perists. So does her relative lack of skill in making desserts, although the sunny, astringent lemon tart, custard bread pudding and crème caramel burnished with espresso that I tried were delicious. Not so the bland chocolate cakes, the thin vanilla ice cream awkwardly presented in a soup plate or the chef's sundae, an uncoordinated combination of sherbet and ice cream, sticky-sweet fruit sauce and slices of unripe melon.

Meat dishes are generally excellent, whether as appetizers or main courses. Cool, rare slices of lamb in an appetizer salad are trimmed with hearts of palm, roasted peppers and flowerets of cauliflower in a grainy mustard sauce. Duck liver and veal are combined in a garlic-scented pâté. Filet mignon in a velvety red-wine-and-port sauce was perfect once, although on a second occasion it was served medium rare instead of rare. The same applied to a mellow, aged sirloin steak. And the fried, breaded mushrooms with the sirloin were perfectly crisp and greaseless at one dinner, though slightly greasy at another. Hot roast beef on a crusty roll, served for lunch and brunch, was thick, rare and well accented by natural juices and mustard horseradish butter, but the huge sandwich had to be eaten with knife and fork. A curried crab meat omelet had a wonderful flavor, if a slightly slick texture.

Braised boneless duck in a stew with olives could not have been better, and the purée of turnips with it provided a gently soft accent. The only disappointing meat dishes were a slightly tough quail and a bland scallop of veal with eggplant.

Roquefort beignets were not too overpowering as a first course because they were small, but Gorgonzola with walnuts made a main course portion of undercooked fettuccine almost inedible. Oysters simmered in red wine looked uninviting and added nothing to an appetizer of pasta in red-wine-and-cream sauce. However, fettuccine with porcini mushrooms and pancetta, the salt-cured Italian bacon, had an irresistibly earthy richness. Crisply sautéed soft-shell crabs and grilled swordfish, mellowed by a herbaceous purée of sweet peppers, proved better fish dishes than the sole meunière. The sole was fresh and decent, but it lacked the crisp patina that distinguishes this preparation. Lovely, lightly cooked vegetables and golden-brown Savoyard potatoes complemented most main courses, green salads were sprightly and refreshing, and both whole wheat and white breads were lusty and satisfying.

The best appetizers, in addition to those mentioned, were smoked salmon and tiny, tender snails mantled with cream, leeks and hazelnuts. Smoked trout was dry and hard, and cold poached scallops were bland. A fragrant clear fish broth had just the right accent of saffron, and a thick, well-chilled gazpacho would be even better without the cheese garnish.

The "21" Club

★

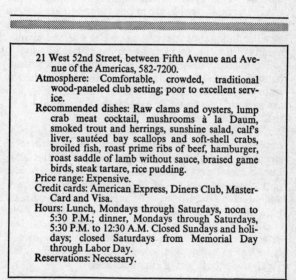

21 West 52nd Street, between Fifth Avenue and Avenue of the Americas, 582-7200.
Atmosphere: Comfortable, crowded, traditional wood-paneled club setting; poor to excellent service.
Recommended dishes: Raw clams and oysters, lump crab meat cocktail, mushrooms à la Daum, smoked trout and herrings, sunshine salad, calf's liver, sautéed bay scallops and soft-shell crabs, broiled fish, roast prime ribs of beef, hamburger, roast saddle of lamb without sauce, braised game birds, steak tartare, rice pudding.
Price range: Expensive.
Credit cards: American Express, Diners Club, MasterCard and Visa.
Hours: Lunch, Mondays through Saturdays, noon to 5:30 P.M.; dinner, Mondays through Saturdays, 5:30 P.M. to 12:30 A.M. Closed Sundays and holidays; closed Saturdays from Memorial Day through Labor Day.
Reservations: Necessary.

It is probably safe to say that no restaurant in New York is more controversial than the "21" Club, that sixty-year-old landmark distinguished by its black iron gate, the painted-jockey hitching posts and the lines of chauffeured limousines double- and triple-parked outside it each afternoon and evening.

To the movers and doers who are its prime regulars, "21" is indeed a club, in spirit if not in fact. To the tourists and celebrity watchers who make up the other half of the clientele, a visit here may prove corny or disappointing or offer an adrenaline-boosting brush with fame. It's just a matter of what turns you on.

But no matter how you feel about it, one thing is certain — the "21" Club is New York's prime crossroads for celebrities in every field, bringing together such diverse talents as Frank Sinatra, Alan King, Otto Preminger and Howard Johnson III, or Dan Rather and almost any candidate running for city or state office in the tristate area. It is hard to imagine how anyone who appreciates the New York scene in all its varied aspects would not be entertained by at least an occasional visit.

The history of "21" is almost as well known as its name. Begun in 1922 by Jack Kriendler and Charles Berns — and still referred to by old-timers as Jack and Charlie's — "21" had three locations before moving to its present resting place in 1930, and taking its name from its address, 21 East 52d Street. During those years, it always was a restaurant, but it gained its greatest notoriety as a speakeasy during Prohibition.

Anyone can go, of course, simply by calling and making a reservation, but not everyone will be accorded the same choice of seating, careful service or warm greeting at the door. The greeting can vary from the effusively welcoming to the officiously impersonal. Prime seating areas are the noisy jampacked downstairs bar, with its red-checkered tablecloths and low ceiling hung with toy models of products made by the companies whose executives frequent the premises, and the "celebrity bay," the first third of the brighter upstairs dining room, where the faces most likely to be recognized are always in view. Seating moves backward to the far end of the upstairs dining room depending on one's degree of anonymity or the amount of money spent with regularity.

Throughout these dining rooms, and the six private banquet rooms as well, dark-wood paneling, touches of leather, sculptures and drawings by Frederick Remington and an assortment of silver trays and trophies add to the clublike atmosphere.

As might be guessed, service varies enormously. It can be impatient and coolly indifferent toward total strangers or almost suffocatingly diligent for the best-known customers. Through the years, I have had ample opportunities to eat at "21," both known and unknown, and so have sampled the full range of service and seating arrangements.

Oddly enough, and most important, there is far less difference in food when one is known or unknown. I have had excellent, bad, good, poor, mediocre and fair meals under both sets of circumstances.

It is hard to believe that anyone would go to "21" deliberately for the food. In fact, it is possible that in the midst all this power playing, the bland anonymity of the food is a distinct advantage. Really great and original fare might prove to be a distraction from all of the wheeling and dealing. It must be stated that certain offerings are always of impeccable quality. If you find yourself hungry and on these premises, stick to the simplest dishes based on the best products. That means you will begin with clear, cold clams or oysters, snowy, lumped crab meat, glistening caviar (if you have brought a trunkload of money) and, usually, smoked Nova Scotia salmon, although on occasion it can be inexcusably dry and flaky.

It also means you will avoid such dishes as the dreadful snails bourguignon that smell and taste of cheese, although they seem to contain none, the nondescript purée of chicken livers billed as pâté and the spongy frozen Dungeness crab.

Mushrooms à la Daum, sliced and sautéed with onions and bits of bacon or ham and served on toast, is one of the only really good cooked appetizers offered. Among soups, the gazpacho or hot or cold beef borscht, clear petite marmite and oxtail all were passable.

Sautéed bay scallops are usually excellent, as are such broiled fish as sole and snapper, although the snapper can be a shade overdone. It is possible to have soft-shell crabs exquisitely sautéed to gold-brown crispness or burned black, apparently depending on your luck.

Steak is about the best one can buy, but it can arrive as dry and as contorted as burned wood. Roast beef is usually roseate as ordered, though the so-called Yorkshire pudding served with it comes as a popover as tough as papier-mâché. Rack of lamb, gently, tenderly, pink, is beautifully done, but avoid the overpungent tarragon sauce that may be offered with it. As a matter of fact, avoid all sauces, including Choron, the tasty white sauce served with game, the underseasoned béarnaise and the horseradish cream served with the lovely, smooth smoked trout.

The "21" Club prepares excellent steak tartare, mixed to subtle piquancy with hard-cooked egg white and yolk as well as raw yolk, capers, mustard, onions, parsley and whatever else you indicate. Game, most often frozen, is surprisingly flavorful, especially when braised. Scandinavian snow grouse, though less rare than it should have been, was excellent, but a roast pheasant was not quite up to the richness and delicacy of a braised pheasant sampled a few months back. Calf's liver is fresh and properly seared and grilled.

The famed "21" hamburger can be delicious — big, puffy and perfectly broiled; if it's not, send it back. Duck is lean, moist and delicate, but the sauce bigarade is much too sweet. There are two chicken hashes. The better is the "21" version of wild rice under a cheese crust. On the other hand, chicken hash and cream were prepared in a chafing dish by a captain who poured what seemed to be one-third of a bottle of sherry into the mix, and then served up this winy soup as though everything were perfectly fine. And chicken hash in a crepe on spinach is a mess.

Escalopine de veau Charleroi was a travesty — thin scallops of veal under a heavy cheese topping — with canned peas. "Petits pois," Sheldon Tannen, a "21" vice president, corrected when this was pointed out to him. But petits pois or not, they were canned peas. Also, what were listed as new peas on the menu were frozen and then cooked to near-paste consistency. All other vegetables were fresh but overcooked without exception. Wild rice was also madly overboiled and totally without salt. A popular luncheon item is sunshine salad. It is much like a finely chopped bacon, tomato and lettuce sandwich complete with minced toast, strange but soothing.

Garnishes belie this restaurant's reputation for sophistication. A typical example accompanied the steak tartare — iceberg lettuce, a slice of overripe tomato and sweet gherkins — and, again, there was iceberg lettuce under an otherwise respectable chicken salad.

The captains showed a reluctance to serve certain dishes even when I was known. I asked for the roast chicken for two but was told it would take at least an hour and a half to prepare. "Nonsense," Mr. Tannen replied when I told him about it. "It would take no more than forty minutes, but he just didn't want to serve it to you." Twice I was put off in an attempt to order soufflés and crêpes soufflé, but on a third attempt I made it. The chocolate soufflé lacked the deep, rich flavor it should have and was dryly cakelike; the crêpe soufflé had almost no filling and was caustic with alcohol.

Other disappointments were desserts such as a zabaglione that was too airy and bland when it should have been satiny and thick and well laced with Marsala or sherry. Fresh berries with real whipped cream was a far better choice, as was rice pudding.

One "21" specialty I favor is the homemade rye melba toast, served only in the evening. And in the outstanding collection of wines from this almost legendary cellar there are some exceptionally good buys.

The Ukrainian Restaurant
Fair

140 Second Avenue, between Eighth and Ninth Streets, 533-6765.

Atmosphere: Simple and somewhat drab dining rooms, generally filled with a convivial crowd; service is often slow and unprofessional but well-meaning.

Recommended dishes: Jellied pigs' feet, pickled herring, borscht, chicken soup with noodles, pierogi filled with meat, cheese or cabbage, bigos, kielbasa with sauerkraut, kasha with beef, veal cutlet, breaded pork chop, cheese blintzes.

Price range: Inexpensive.

Credit cards: None.

Hours: Dinner, Sundays through Thursdays, noon to 11 P.M.; Fridays and Saturdays, noon to midnight.

Reservations: Necessary for large groups.

Were it not for its East Village location and its very low prices, there would probably be no reason to report on the Ukrainian Restaurant. But considering the lack of options in this neighborhood, its proximity to many Off Off Broadway theaters and the fact that it is possible to have a substantial and acceptable main course inexpensively, the Ukrainian certainly is worth noting.

The entrance to the restaurant is through a long and drab hall. Whether you consider the dining rooms dreary or Bohemian will depend on your mood. Regulars include Ukrainian families and young and impecunious residents of the neighborhood, making for a convivial mix. The low-ceilinged front dining room is more pleasant than the banquet-size back room, and the service is more efficient in the front room as well.

While main courses are fairly large, people with ambitious appetites might want to start with one of the better first courses, such as the pickled fillet of herring with onion or the very good mold of jellied pigs' feet, brightened with lemon or a little vinegar. The beet and cabbage borscht is savory when hot. The golden chicken soup that is often available is also very good.

Soup and other courses are often barely tepid, so ask for them hot when you order. Avoid the Ukrainian combination platter that includes overcooked stuffed cabbage with a mealy meat filling. Instead, order the decent version of bigos — the Polish and Ukrainian stew — the acceptable breaded veal cutlet or fried pork chop.

Pungent sauerkraut is available as a vegetable with all main courses, but it is best suited to the garlicky kielbasa. Kasha with chunks of beef in gravy is satisfying. For lunch, brunch or a nonmeat dinner, the boiled dough turnovers, pierogi or varenyky, are served with brown sautéed onions and sour cream. The best are filled with meat, cheese or cabbage; those with potato are pasty.

Crisply fried cheese blintzes work well as a light main course or dessert. Gray, steamy flank steak, floury goulash and stringy boiled beef, in a sauce like library paste, are best ignored. Avoid the soggy, greasy French toast, too. There are a few interesting Russian and Polish vodkas here and eighteen kinds of beer.

Uzie's
★

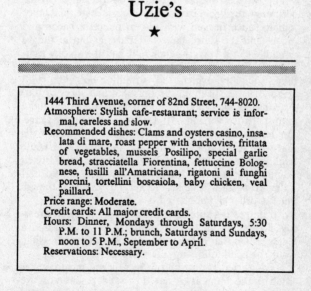

1444 Third Avenue, corner of 82nd Street, 744-8020.
Atmosphere: Stylish cafe-restaurant; service is informal, careless and slow.
Recommended dishes: Clams and oysters casino, insalata di mare, roast pepper with anchovies, frittata of vegetables, mussels Posilipo, special garlic bread, stracciatella Fiorentina, fettuccine Bolognese, fusilli all'Amatriciana, rigatoni ai funghi porcini, tortellini boscaiola, baby chicken, veal paillard.
Price range: Moderate.
Credit cards: All major credit cards.
Hours: Dinner, Mondays through Saturdays, 5:30 P.M. to 11 P.M.; brunch, Saturdays and Sundays, noon to 5 P.M., September to April.
Reservations: Necessary.

The stylish casualness of Uzie's makes it a popular lunch, dinner and late-night eating place. The menu of Italian dishes is enticing, offering anything from a one-dish snack to a complete meal, and the trim, tailored modern setting is aglow with a few Art Deco touches. Uzie's should be a place one is pleased to recommend.

Unfortunately, the management (Giancarlo Uzielli and Robert Shapiro, who also own Hoexter's next door) has a long way to go toward correcting problems in both the dining room and kitchen. Service is chaotic, as it has been since the opening, and there are some painfully long lapses between courses, occurring whether Uzie's is crowded or half empty.

It is too bad that such flaws are not corrected, because one can easily choose an entertaining and satisfying meal from among the many appetizers, and a few very good pastas. There is one appetizer so wildly delicious that it alone is worth a visit to Uzie's. This is the special garlic bread, a whole, slim crusty Italian loaf baked with Gorgonzola cheese and plenty of garlic and olive oil. The toasted bread, contrasted with the meltingly rich sting of the cheese and the heady garlic, would make a meal in itself if accompanied by a green salad and a glass of white wine. As it is, this is a wonderful dish to share while waiting for the rest of the meal.

Other excellent appetizers include the rose-red raw beef carpaccio with a verdant green sauce; fresh, tenderly baked clams and oysters casino; the insalata di mare, consisting mostly of tender squid and shellfish, and plump, large, briny mussels Posilipo, in a frothy tomato broth. Sweet, crimson roasted peppers with anchovies were refreshing, and though what is called a frittata here is not an omelet at all, but rather an individual quiche, the type made with vegetables is equally good as a luncheon main course or as an hors d'oeuvre. The only disappointment among the appetizers tasted was the mozzarella fritta — thick, heavily breaded, sausage-shaped rolls of mozzarella that are deep-fried and so over-cooked that the cheese melted and disappeared altogether, leaving empty breading casings.

The two best pastas proved to be the short, twisted corkscrew fusilli prepared Amatriciana style, in a spicy tomato sauce flecked with bits of pancetta bacon and onion, and the short, large, tubular rigatoni ai funghi porcini — in a velvety sauce that had the smoky richness of the dried wild porcini mushrooms in it. Although slightly overcooked, tortellini boscaiola with cream, cheese, sliced mushrooms and half slices of Italian sausages was good. So was the fettuccine in a light, almost creamy version of the standard Bolognese sauce. Far less satisfactory were the linguine with meat balls that were too soft and pasty, and the green and white paglia e fieno Ronis, dotted with salty, fishy, smoked salmon and sauced with dill-flavored cream. No half orders of pasta will be served here, by the way, though one full order can be shared.

An interesting spinach salad with a hot bacon dressing, acceptable but slightly limp, fried zucchini and a Caesar salad that is fine when not drowned in dressing, would be good follow-ups after pasta.

Having tried almost all of the fish and meat courses listed on the menu as entrees, I can report that most are very badly prepared. The exceptions are the grilled choices such as the rosemary-scented baby chicken and the paillard of veal. Paillard of beef lacked flavor but was fair, and the veal chop, though good, seemed minuscule.

Desserts were not any better than main courses. If you must end with something sweet, have the pear in Chianti or the coupe Uzie, described as crème brûlée but really whipped cream flavored with caramelized sugar, served over fruit. All cakes were poor.

Espresso and cappucino were well made. Italian wines are well selected and represent the fairest-priced category on the list.

Vanessa
★

289 Bleecker Street at Seventh Avenue South, 243-4225.

Atmosphere: Spacious and romantic Art Deco setting that becomes crowded and noisy; air-conditioning is uneven; service is good-natured but often slow and unprofessional.

Recommended dishes: Shrimp and leek salad, shellfish salad, flan Vanessa, snails with herbs, gazpacho, seafood bisque, shrimp in tomato, basil and cream sauce, baby chicken with herb butter, calf's liver, medaillons of beef with leek, mushroom and herb sauce, poached salmon, omelet Basquaise, poached eggs en croûte with Black Forest ham and spinach, smoked-fish platter, warmed filet of chicken breast salad, raspberry tart, walnut tart, chocolate roll, crème brûlée.

Price range: Moderately expensive.

Credit cards: All major credit cards.

Hours: Dinner, seven days, 6 P.M. to midnight. Sunday brunch, noon to 4 P.M. Open major holidays.

Reservations: Necessary.

It would not be hard to believe that there are two entirely different restaurants named Vanessa, both on the same site on Bleecker Street, and both with the same handsome and romantic deep-purple walls and gleaming Art Deco brass lighting fixtures. One Vanessa is quiet, cool and airy, with well-paced service and pleasantly pretty food in the style best described as nouvelle American, and it attracts a mild-mannered young and informal following. The other Vanessa is jam-packed, crashingly noisy, often stifling, with painfully slow and inept service and food so contrived that it is difficult to swallow more than a few bites. In the later hours when the restaurant is most uncomfortable, oddly enough, the crowd is older and more seriously and stylishly dressed.

To experience Vanessa-the-Fair, go for Sunday brunch or before 7:30 any evening, and you will probably have a thoroughly enjoyable, moderately priced meal, especially if you stick to appetizers and desserts.

Like so many restaurants with an expressionist chef who free associates, Vanessa falls down on main courses, primarily because intricate and complicated flavorings and food combinations that can be diverting in appetizer-size portions become cloying in larger amounts.

But it would be hard to imagine anyone disliking a brunch that began with some of his icy, spicy gazpacho or a smoked fish platter that included moist and pearly sable, trout and salmon with a mild horseradish cream

465

sauce. A hefty omelet Basquaise, filled with zucchini, peppers and onion in a light tomato sauce, would be as satisfying a follow-up as the more original poached eggs en croûte, layered between squares of puff pastry with spinach, Black Forest ham and an airy, lemony hollandaise sauce. A salad of strips of warmed chicken breast in a hot and heady vinegar dressing on red leaf lettuce gained textural interest from crisp nutmeats and a sprinkling of pimento and onion.

The most successful course on the dinner menu is unquestionably the first, with such entertaining and savory selections as a light custard flan encasing bits of shellfish; a warm shrimp and leek salad with a vinaigrette dressing; tiny snails blanketed in a finely minced mushroom cream sauce aromatic with herbs, and a soothingly tepid shellfish salad — mine consisted mainly of sea scallops — in a green herb dressing. The only disappointments were pasty chicken livers overspiked with Madeira and a slightly spoiled raw beef carpaccio. A rich coral seafood bisque could have been lighter, but it could hardly have had a more sparkling seafood freshness.

Follow one or two of these appetizers with a dessert such as the lovely crème brûlée with its soft custard and caramelized sugar topping, or a perfect raspberry tart based on a butter-cookie crust, which also distinguishes the walnut tart. There is sometimes a frothy chocolate roll cake with cloudlets of half-whipped cream and always a decent, bright fresh fruit platter. Neither an insipid white chocolate mousse nor an intensely thick chocolate mousse with strawberry sauce matched the pastries, but a luxurious coupe of vanilla ice cream with warm blueberry sauce did.

If you are intent on having a more conventional dinner that includes a bona fide main course, order poached salmon with beurre blanc or hollandaise sauce, shrimp in tomato, basil and cream sauce or the tiny broiled chicken glossed with herb butter. Calf's liver with bacon and pearl onions was also good. So were the medaillons of beef under a sauce that combined slivered leeks and mushrooms. Main courses that proved hard to take included roast rack of lamb overperfumed with fresh mint; dry, cold poached salmon, and striped bass with orange slices and caviar. Veal, either sautéed with lemon or Vanessa-style (drowned in a salty brown sauce), proved as unsatisfactory as a tough beefsteak with three peppercorns and an impossibly rich chicken with écrevisses, which turned out to be shrimp, not crayfish. The sauce for this seemed to be a thickened version of the seafood bisque — far too intense for a portion of this size. Pasta creations were either bland and pasty or stingingly salty.

Wine service is poor, with incorrect vintages delivered by waiters and waitresses who often seem not to have opened a bottle before. This, coupled with a broken air-conditioner and back-to-back chairs constantly being kicked by passers-by, indicates how bad things can get at Vanessa.

Variations

★

358 West 23rd Street, between Eighth and Ninth Avenues, 691-1559.

Atmosphere: Stylish, candlelit supper-club setting with piano music; service is good, if somewhat precious.

Recommended dishes: Tortellini, pâté de campagne, quiche, marinated mussels, oysters baked in cream, fish cakes without sauce, steak au poivre, duck in apricot glaze, beef Bourguignon, ginger pear cake, apple walnut cake with cranberry sauce.

Price range: Moderate.

Credit cards: American Express, MasterCard and Visa.

Hours: Lunch, Tuesdays through Saturdays, 11:30 A.M. to 3:30 P.M.; dinner, Sundays through Thursdays, 5:30 P.M. to 11:30 P.M.; Fridays and Saturdays, 5:30 P.M. to 12:30 A.M.; brunch, Sundays, noon to 5 P.M. Open all major holidays.

Reservations: Recommended.

A departure from the antique settings typical of Chelsea restaurants is this intimate and stylish little supper club, with light and diverting piano music, flowers and candles to brighten tables and service that is well meaning and polite, if a bit precious. The kitchen is competent with first courses such as tortellini in a lush cream and cheese sauce, often a very good pâté de campagne based on chicken, pork, veal and ham, unusually light and fluffy quiches, refreshing marinated mussels (although a few were sandy) and oysters gently baked in cream. Both the seafood bisque and a misbegotten invention of clams, pimento, cream and caraway seed indicate that soup is not the chef's strong point. A sprightly salad of five greens deserves a dressing with more character, although the one served was by no means bad.

Fish cakes here are almost like fish hash — coarse chunks of fish and potato crisply fried — a comforting creation marred by a pasty mustard cream sauce. Fresh lemon juice is a better complement.

Broiled bay scallops turned leathery from too much heat. But steak au poivre was tender and beefy, and its coarsely crushed peppercorns were mellowed by a touch of cream. Other good main courses were duck with an apricot glaze and beef Bourguignon that seemed more like hearty American-style beef stew with barely a hint of wine.

The chocolate mousse should appeal to those who like it smoothly creamy rather than porous or grainy, and the ginger pear cake is soothingly moist and aromatically spiced. Cheesecake was fair; a puddinglike apple walnut cake, served with a hot cranberry sauce, could be a soul-warming meal in itself.

Victor's Cafe 52
Fair

236 West 52nd Street, between Eighth Avenue and
  Broadway, 586-7714.
Atmosphere: Modern cafe-restaurant, large, noisy and
  lively; polite service but very slow at peak hours.
Recommended dishes: Soups, roast suckling pig,
  clams in green sauce, "Durán Victory" Cuban-
  style steak, gypsy pudding, flan, coconut flan.
Price range: Moderate.
Credit cards: All major credit cards.
Hours: Lunch, seven days, noon to 3 P.M.; dinner,
  Sundays through Thursdays, 3 P.M. to midnight;
  Fridays and Saturdays, 3 P.M. to 1 A.M. Open
  major holidays.
Reservations: Recommended.

A branch of Victor's Cafe, which has been operating on
Columbus Avenue for seventeen years, this newer,
modern and more ambitious outpost on 52nd Street in
the theater district sparkles with tiny light bulbs, mirrored panels and potted palms, and a Cuban band plays
at dinner Wednesdays through Sundays. It is noisy, hectic, popular with Cubans, and if the food were improved, it could be an entertaining corner of Havana.

Old Havana hands who valued that pearl of an island
at least in part for its savory, peasant cuisine must find
the dearth of good Cuban food on Manhattan Island
deplorable. This newcomer does not seem destined to
improve matters. After one lunch and three dinners that
took me through a fair sampling of appetizers, soups,
fish, meats and poultry, and both the Spanish and
Cuban specialties, the sad report is that with only a few
exceptions the kitchen never rises above mediocrity and
all too often does worse.

Soup seems to be the kitchen's strong point, whether
you try the spicy, thick and cool gazpacho, crunchy with
chopped cucumbers, green peppers and tomatoes, or the
earthy and smoky black-bean soup, which is a rival for
the world's best as it used to be served in Havana's Flo-
ridita restaurant. Garlic soup, richly oily, is garnished
with a poached egg, and on Sunday night, Galician
white-bean soup takes on thickness and savor from pigs'
knuckles and cooked greens. Lentil soup had just the
right lustiness, but a stale and musty Friday fish soup
had a decidedly reheated taste.

Recooking and reheating sum up the consistent flaws
at Victor's Cafe 52. Almost everything had murky, un-
fresh steam-table overtones. That was true of shrimp,
either creole or asopao style, lobster catalano, and
chicken fried or in fricassee, as well as several beef
dishes listed as Cuban specials. Only the "Durán Victory" Cuban steak (named for the Panamanian boxer)
was a decent cut, well broiled and accented by raw
onion rings. The meat of roast suckling pig proved
tender and mellow on three tries, but its skin was as

tough as the pigskin of football and virtually impossible to cut and chew.

A thick overdose of dreadful canned peas ruined an otherwise aromatic garlic green sauce that blanketed many fish and shellfish dishes. Clams came off best in this sauce, but mussels, again, were gritty and spoiled every dish in which they were included, such as paella and mariscada.

The eggy custard desserts, although extremely sweet, are more worthwhile than main courses. The best of them are gypsy pudding, which is reminiscent of Italian rum cake, and flan, either plain or with coconut.

Vienna Park
★ ★ ★

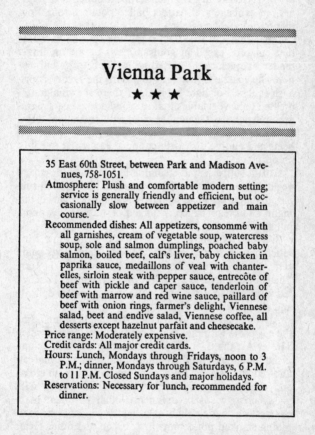

35 East 60th Street, between Park and Madison Avenues, 758-1051.

Atmosphere: Plush and comfortable modern setting; service is generally friendly and efficient, but occasionally slow between appetizer and main course.

Recommended dishes: All appetizers, consommé with all garnishes, cream of vegetable soup, watercress soup, sole and salmon dumplings, poached baby salmon, boiled beef, calf's liver, baby chicken in paprika sauce, medaillons of veal with chanterelles, sirloin steak with pepper sauce, entrecôte of beef with pickle and caper sauce, tenderloin of beef with marrow and red wine sauce, paillard of beef with onion rings, farmer's delight, Viennese salad, beet and endive salad, Viennese coffee, all desserts except hazelnut parfait and cheesecake.

Price range: Moderately expensive.

Credit cards: All major credit cards.

Hours: Lunch, Mondays through Fridays, noon to 3 P.M.; dinner, Mondays through Saturdays, 6 P.M. to 11 P.M. Closed Sundays and major holidays.

Reservations: Necessary for lunch, recommended for dinner.

Vienna Park is an offshoot of the four-star restaurant Vienna '79 on East 79th Street. Walter Krajnc, who manages the newer restaurant, is in partnership with Peter Grunauer, the originator of the '79. Instead of opting for the obvious by creating a folklorically gemütlich setting, the owners here, as uptown, have wisely chosen sophistication, with restful taupe walls and cushy banquettes and a mural that is a blown-up antique map of Vienna. Reddish-brown matted prints of the famed white Lippizaner dancing horses and colorful floral arrangements add to the elegance. Tables are less cramped than in many Upper East side restaurants, but the noise level can become slightly too high at peak hours. There is a stunning long bar at the entrance and an attractive room for private parties of thirty to forty guests.

Anyone stuck with the archetypal image of Austrian-German food is in for a surprise here, for traditional specialties have been given a nouvelle cuisine gloss with light, bright and fresh touches by way of sheer sauces, barely cooked vegetables and leafy garnishes. The airy flavor of dill accents the home-cured salmon, gravlax, served with marinated striped bass and a sweet-hot mustard sauce. Dill also brightens lightly steamed kohlrabi, often served as a vegetable, and the heady, fragrant beef consommé that may be garnished with liver rice (tiny dumplings) or strips of crepes. Sour cream and apple rings enhance satiny matjes herring fillets and a smooth, fiery horseradish cream sauce puts a spin on the marvelously lush and tender thick boiled beef. Garnet red cabbage and perfect boiled potatoes round out that traditional beinfleisch.

Other characteristic flavors include paprika in sauces that enhance excellent goulash stews or the meltingly tender baby chicken braised with slivers of green pepper. The spätzle is just right to absorb the savory paprikash sauces. For light beginnings, there are vinaigrette-dressed cold vegetables that may include leeks, asparagus or artichoke. Cucumber salad with cream and dill is available as a first course or side dish. So is the slivered beets and endive dish with chopped egg and a touch of onion.

Cream soups served steaming hot, such as the mixed vegetable or watercress, are excellent. Other well-prepared appetizers include delicious snails in a garlic, tarragon and cream sauce, arranged on puff pastry, and a pungent head cheese.

Sole and salmon dumplings in a creamy white wine sauce have a clear, fresh flavor. The dumplings could sometimes be a little less dense, but even so they are fine choices either as appetizer or main course. Poached baby salmon in a red and white wine sauce is delicate and altogether satisfying.

All versions of steak are expertly handled, including the entrecôte with pickle and caper sauce, the rostbraten Tiroler Art that is a paillard with crisp onion rings and diced tomatoes, and the tenderloin of beef with marrow and red wine sauce. Tender veal medaillons with cream and chanterelles and perfect calf's liver topped with glassy crisp wisps of onion are other excellent main courses. Farmer's delight is a hearty winter dish, combining smoked pork, bratwurst, bacon and other meats over golden braised sauerkraut.

The one flaw that persists is the frying. It is hard to understand how a chef as adept as this one can do such a lackluster job on Wiener schnitzel. It has never been right here, tasting of overheated oil and covered by a fluffy breading that does not stick to the veal. Natur schnitzel, sautéed without breading, is only a slight improvement. The beer batter for fried shrimp still arrives limp, and on one visit the shrimp reeked of iodine, indicating staleness.

Dieters should be warned: most desserts are totally irresistible. Whipped cream mousses are wonderful whether based on kiwi, sour cherries, lingonberries or strawberries, and the vanilla mousse is positively addictive. Flaky warm strudel and a palatschinken crepe filled with fresh fruits and covered with both a bittersweet fudge sauce and a vanilla sauce are beautiful, as are the cloudlike poached egg whites, schneenockerln, floating on a satiny crème Anglaise. Sacher torte is decently prepared here, but the cheesecake is sometimes too stiff. Hazelnut parfait is acceptable, but no match for the inspired competitors.

Whipped cream is much in evidence with desserts, and if you can stand any more of it, order Viennese coffee. To find good, drinkable Austrian wines, one must choose with care. Reds are skippable, but there are several clear, dry and pleasantly aromatic whites. Except for some confusion at the door when guests enter, and an occasional delay between appetizers and main courses, service is friendly and professional.

Vienna '79

★ ★ ★ ★

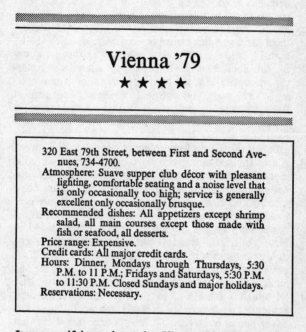

320 East 79th Street, between First and Second Avenues, 734-4700.

Atmosphere: Suave supper club décor with pleasant lighting, comfortable seating and a noise level that is only occasionally too high; service is generally excellent only occasionally brusque.

Recommended dishes: All appetizers except shrimp salad, all main courses except those made with fish or seafood, all desserts.

Price range: Expensive.

Credit cards: All major credit cards.

Hours: Dinner, Mondays through Thursdays, 5:30 P.M. to 11 P.M.; Fridays and Saturdays, 5:30 P.M. to 11:30 P.M. Closed Sundays and major holidays.

Reservations: Necessary.

It was gratifying to learn that Vienna '79, which first received a three-star rating, not only has been able to cope with success but has improved to the point where it well deserves a four-star rating. Full credit for this achievement belongs to Peter Grunauer, the proprietor, a dedicated cook and student of cuisine. Mr. Grunauer's consistent standards and knowledge of the cuisine has bridged the gap between staff changes, and his almost constant presence has kept cooks and waiters working smoothly and professionally.

The cuisine that Mr. Grunauer has devised for his restaurant could be described as nouvelle Viennoise, styles that at first glance might seem mutually exclusive, considering the lightness of the nouvelle cuisine and the heaviness of traditional Austrian fare. But by lightening up on fats and flour and by garnishing dishes with an unusual rainbow of bright steamed and sautéed vegetables, Mr. Grunauer and his chef are devising what is virtually an original cuisine. It is true that many of the themes considered new by the French chefs who are credited with inventing France's nouvelle cuisine are inherent in Austrian-German cooking. Among these, the most obvious are the accents of sweet and sour fruit sauces with meat dishes, the use of cool-flavored green herbs and aromatic spices such as dill, juniper and caraway, and the frothy, brightly refreshing eisbecher — a sundae of sherbet, fruits and ice cream.

In addition to the original repertory of dishes developed for this restaurant, new candidates are constantly on the drawing board and both the owner and chef work on their refinement. Their Wachau-style snails laced with cream and perfumed with garlic, shallots and parsley, all baked in a crusty kaiser roll, are as inspired as the velvety, moist Sacher torte or the Viennese cheesecake. The latter is a fluff of cheese whipped with cream, lemon zest and Grand Marnier spread between layers of a golden sponge cake. Slivers of beef marinated in a vinaigrette dressing and served as a first-course salad with crisp threads of green pepper and onion, and the perfect, tender but meaty liver dumplings adrift in a lusty consommé require as much craftsmanship and flavoring artistry as the Salzburger nockerl, the cloudlets of soufflé baked on a huge silver platter and adrift on a sea of crème Anglaise, or the meltingly rich, warm rahmstrudel, a cream-filled puff of flaky pastry in the same sweet, vanilla-scented sauce.

From appetizers through desserts, the kitchen's performance almost invariably lives up to the menu's promise. Equally elegant first courses are the sweet, pearly smoked trout with horseradish-spiked whipped cream, or the homemade dill-cured salmon, gravlax, with an appropriate mustard sauce. There is usually a smooth and rich vegetable cream soup — a purée of mushroom, perhaps, or a lush broccoli potage. And the onion soup attains a golden richness rarely found in New York. Homemade head cheese of pork, celery, onions and herbs in aspic generally achieves a delicate perfection; occasionally, however, it is too stiffly set and lacks sufficient meat. Breaded mushrooms, the one dish on which I have had two complaints from readers, generally are as crisply breaded and soothing as this homespun appetizer should be, but once in a while they are overdone and tough. At all times their green herb tartar sauce adds a note of verdant freshness.

Frying is beautifully, greaselessly accomplished, whether for the golden Wiener schnitzel based on tender pink veal or for the Wiener backhuhn, the boneless and flattened breast that makes the world's most elegant fried chicken. Lacy onions, deep fried to match the crisp fragility of spun glass, garnish the rose-rare tender beefsteak (zwiebelrostbraten) as well as the fresh calf's liver slices sautéed with apples. Medaillons of veal with mushroom-flecked cream sauce and fork-tender boiled beef (tafelspitz) with chive cream sauce and horseradish-sharpened applesauce have been consistently excellent. And marinated venison, either in a gamy ragout or delicately sautéed, profits from its garnishes of winy red cabbage and half a fresh poached pear jeweled with preserved lingonberries.

Peter Grunauer insists on serving ducks that are raised by a Chinese poultryman in New Jersey who can supply only fifteen a week, so this specialty is not often available. When it is, be prepared for an extraordinarily flavorful and satiny roast, complemented by wild rice and a burnished orange sauce with perfectly balanced tart-sweet counterpoints .

Other inspirations are lean loin sautéed lamb chops that are first marinated in olive oil with caraway seeds, oregano, bay leaves, salt and pepper, and the veal goulash with a bright paprika patina, and curlicued spätzle, the tiny dumplings that absorb the peppery gravy.

Salads, either of icy cucumbers in a sheer sour cream sauce or a combination of cucumber, potato salad and bibb lettuce, add their own sparkle to dinner, and so do the vegetables chosen for each day's main courses — julienne strips of carrots and kohlrabi sautéed in butter, purée of yellow turnips in puff pastry cups, Jerusalem artichokes and potatoes as croquettes or pancakes or in tiny, fluted, deep-fried peaks.

Keep desserts firmly in mind as you work your way through earlier wonders here. In addition to the Salzburger nockerl, the dessert that must be ordered in advance is the kaiserschmarren, the torn, puffy, eggy pancakes tossed with raisins and sugar and topped with fresh fruit compote, such as apples stewed with lemon, cloves and cinnamon. In the fall, the small blue plums, zwetschgen, make an even more vivid and luxurious garnish. My first choice here is the nockerl. The kaiserschmarren are worth trying, too, although sometimes they are too generously studded with raisins. The kitchen can handle only 10 portions of each of these desserts in an evening, so order well in advance.

Palatschinken are superb. The large, magically light crepes are rolled around a smooth chestnut purée and are finished with a bittersweet chocolate sauce laced with kirsch and crowned with whipped cream. Kirsch also sparks the chocolate sauce on the freshly poached poire belle Hélène, with ice cream and whipped cream added to the combination. It is just a little hard to handle in the long-stemmed wineglass, but it's worth the effort. Lemon sherbet whipped with champagne and mantled with cut fresh fruit adds up to eisbecher Johann Strauss, a dessert that by comparison seems dietetically lean.

Extraordinary does not mean perfection, of course, and really no restaurant can maintain that lofty state consistently. Flaws at Vienna '79 include inferior rolls and breads that could easily be improved upon, canned asparagus in the otherwise good shrimp salad appetizer, and fish dishes that are uniformly mediocre.

Austrian vineyards offer lean pickings for wine lovers, but there are a few fine choices I have come to rely on here. The only red in this category is the 1976 Pinot Noir. By far the best white sampled was the Grinzinger-Nussberger Pinot Chardonnay 1979 that provides a soft, flowery background for poultry and salads. The Kremser Pfaffenberger Grüner Veltliner '77 was a little cleaner and thinner in flavor, although still characteristically fruity and pungent.

Describe an interior as glowing with gemütlichkeit and you summon up images of velvet, lace, painted furniture and antique porcelain stoves. At Vienna '79, warmth and snugness are achieved in a suave, gray modern interior that suggests a smart supper club, North European style. Service is generally good but has been known to deteriorate at peak hours.

473

The Village Green
★ ★

531 Hudson street, near Charles Street, 255-1650.

Atmosphere: Beautiful country tavern that is stylish, rustic and contemporary; service is pretentious and management can be sassy when taking reservations or greeting people at the door; dining room staff is efficient and professional.

Recommended dishes: Escargots, frog's legs Provençale, gazpacho, spinach and avocado salad, shrimp rémoulade, stuffed mushrooms, pasta with vegetables, crisp duck, steak au poivre, rack of lamb, sweetbreads, chicken with morels, bananas Foster, chocolate mousse, crème brûlée.

Prices range: Moderately expensive.

Credit cards: American Espress, MasterCard and Visa.

Hours: Dinner, Mondays through Saturdays, 5:30 P.M. to 11 P.M.; Sundays 5 P.M. to 10 P.M.; brunch, winter only, Sundays, noon to 3 P.M.

Reservations: Necessary.

Operating in a wide old brownstone on two levels, the Village Green suggests a charming and glowing English or Colonial inn, with fireplaces trimmed with brass, a two-story window that is virtually a greenhouse, baskets of mauve and straw-colored dried flowers against natural rose brick walls, banquettes covered in a red-and-blue plaid, starchy white cloths, glittering crystal, silver and pewter and graceful floral sprays on every table.

The lighting is especially comfortable — soft, romantic but affording perfect visibility — a feat achieved with warm ceiling reflector bulbs, candles on tables and old carriage-lantern wall brackets. Perhaps the only error in the furnishing was the choice of uncomfortably low chairs facing the banquettes. When all forty seats are occupied, the quarters seem a bit cramped. The kitchen can be extremely slow and the management can be inhospitably sassy and precious. Waiters, however, are efficient.

The well-planned menu is just about as beguiling and inviting as the setting. Limited to just eleven main courses, half a dozen appetizers and desserts and three soups and salads, the combination is so expertly thought out that the diner is faced with a choice best described as delightfully perplexing.

Select the hot champignons farcis and enjoy firm mushroom caps pungent with cheese, onion, minced shrimp and a hint of white wine. Large meaty snails are gentled in garlic cream sauce. The unusually light, puffy quiche in a buttery, flaky crust has a rich and soothing cream dressing that waiters insist is the chef's best-guarded secret. Pâté is decent, if much too cold, and the big firm, fresh shrimp with their tails still on are served with a herbaceous and creamy rémoulade sauce.

A good dark onion soup has just the right amount of thin cheese glaze and is properly scalding. Gazpacho is sparked with crisp vegetables. Avocado and spinach salads are delicious, and the house salad, served with all main courses, consists of fresh, curly greens in a pleasantly sharp mustard vinaigrette dressing.

Broiled or poached fish is usually carefully cooked and fresh. The brown pepper sauce formerly served with the steak au poivre has given way to a creamy version that is only slightly less appropriate. Crackling crisp duck flambéed with Grand Marnier has a tangy caramelized orange edge to its flavor, and morels in cream add richness to sautéed chicken breast.

Tender nuggets of sweetbreads are doused with a white wine sauce enriched with truffles. Fresh peas served with that dish were almost raw and pebble-like — a mistake in texture with the gentle, satiny sweetbreads. Otherwise, main courses were accompanied with firm, al dente vegetables such as slivers of carrots, string beans, snow peas, sugar snap peas and flowerets of broccoli.

In the past, chicken Cordon Bleu, though done originally enough as a sort of croquette-shaped roll, needed the more interesting flavors of prosciutto (rather than boiled ham) and Parmesan to offset the mild Gruyère-type cheese. Veal scaloppine was simmered in a sweet rather than a dry Marsala, making it more like a dessert than an entree, and shrimp with ratatouille were too soft and their vegetable dressing too sparse. It was also a mistake to offer the other mixed vegetables with this dish.

Bananas Foster, the creation of Brennan's restaurant in New Orleans, has always been far better at the Village Green than at its original home. Lengths of bananas are browned in a sauce that seems to combine rum and Grand Marnier, then flambéed and topped with vanilla ice cream. Fresh ripe strawberries in Grand Marnier sauce and a velvety chocolate mousse with a dry and intense chocolate flavor are also excellent, as is the crème brûlée.

Sunday brunch is an especially pleasant meal here if you get by the officious reservation clerk. Duck liver and tongue pâté, quiches of various sorts and savory deep-fried Scotch eggs are among the best choices. Poached eggs Sardou on artichoke bottoms with spinach all topped with hollandaise are acceptable, as is the creamed chipped beef. Bloody Marys are not, however, being much too watery.

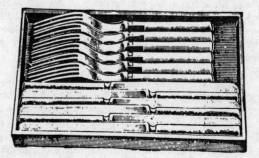

Vivolo
★

140 East 74th Street, between Lexington and Park
Avenues, 628-4671.

Atmosphere: Downstairs dining room is wood paneled, intimate and clublike but terribly noisy and
crowded; upstairs dining room is a little less noisy
and more formal but slightly gloomy; service is
casual, friendly and fast, but often pushy and perfunctory.

Recommended dishes: Seafood salad, eggplant rollantine, agnolotti, fettuccine fileto di pomodoro or
Alfredo, shrimp fra diavolo, veal chop Valdostana
or pizzaiuola, veal scaloppine with cheese, chicken
casalinga, endive and raw mushroom salad, strawberries with cold zabaglione, cheesecake, cannoli.

Price range: Moderate.

Credit cards: All major credit cards.

Hours: Dinner, Mondays through Saturdays, 5:30
P.M. to 11:30 P.M. Closed Sundays. Open on
major holidays.

Reservations: Necessary.

This has become one of the city's more popular and
bustling neighborhood Italian restaurants. The local
regulars constitute a fairly smart and lively group, and
at first glance one almost wishes to become part of the
scene. The downstairs bar and dining room with wood-
paneled walls suggest an intimate, comfortable club.
The staff is young, friendly and engagingly informal,
and the small menu, with moderately priced, enticing
choices, indicates that the approach is more a boutique
than a full department-store menu of Italian specialties.

But as the evening unwinds, one disappointment follows another. The room is mellow and attractive, all
right, but as tables are taken and the mob waiting for
the second seating backs up at the bar, the noise becomes positively dizzying. The nice young waiters call
off so many daily specials that the invitingly simple
basic menu suddenly seems confused and — a surprise
that comes later — all of those specials average about
fifteen percent higher in price than similar dishes on the
regular menu. Only if asked will waiters indicate the
prices of the specials. Service becomes pushy and slam-
bang, and finally, where some restaurants automatically
serve petits fours or chocolates with coffee, Vivolo automatically serves the check — ready or not, here it
comes.

Action in the upstairs dining room is slightly more
restful because the noise level is a pitch more bearable,
but the gloomy lighting and the special house rush act
keep a dinner at Vivolo from being as satisfying as it
might be.

The menu offers a comfortable range of simple Italian dishes, and if none are extraordinarily good, neither
is anything really bad. A decent, pleasant average is
struck, especially considering the fair prices. The bright,
fresh insalata ai frutti di mare is a seafood appetizer

large enough for two that includes tender squid, octopus and firm fresh shrimp, all at room temperature. Rollantine of eggplant, filled with ricotta cheese and topped with a light, fragrant tomato sauce, was equally good. Most of the vegetables in the hot antipasto arrived barely tepid; mozzarella in carrozza was too heavily fried, and baked clams were soggy, but several pasta dishes made excellent first or main courses. Among these were agnolotti — semicircular ravioli — and good, chewy fettuccine al filetto di pomodoro in a sauce of chopped tomatos and chunks of onions melted to tenderness. The same fettuccine took on a soothing quality in a mild Alfredo cream and cheese sauce, but linguine with clams lacked the punch of sufficiently sautéed garlic. Only a banal macaroni-and-cheese type of sauce spoiled the subtlety of the cannelloni; if the sauce had had more character, the dish would have been excellent.

Large veal chops are prepared in several interesting styles, the best of which are those with a tomato, oregano and garlic pizzaiuola sauce and the Valdostana chops, which are stuffed with cheese and prosciutto and then carefully sautéed to a deep golden-brown finish. Scaloppine of veal, either with Marsala or sautéed in a cheese glaze, proved to be above average, and so did chicken casalinga — a sauté finished with white wine and mushrooms. Shrimp fra diavolo with mussels blanketed by a properly spicy hot-pepper-and-tomato sauce was a better main course than the zuppa di pesce, a bland mixed-seafood soup. Chicken scarpariello and a dense, tough grilled beef steak pulled down the kitchen's batting average. A salad of endives and raw mushrooms lent a refreshingly crisp touch to all main courses.

Desserts were pleasant enough, the best two being big ripe strawberries in a froth of cold zabaglione, and spumone, which was served in scoops rather than in the usual frozen slice. A light Italian cheesecake and cannoli filled with delicately whipped ricotta were also above average.

With a shared appetizer, a three-course dinner is a very good value, if one happens to be in this neighborhood and if the management could make life within these walls a little more felicitous.

Wally's

★

---

224 West 49th Street, between Broadway and Eighth
Avenue, 582-0460.

Atmosphere: Gaudy, noisy cocktail lounge setting;
service can be friendly and efficient but is often
rude and careless.

Recommended dishes: Crab meat cocktail, baked
clams oreganate, linguine with white clam sauce,
fettuccine Alfredo, broiled lobster, steaks, lamb
chops, steak à la stone, cottage fries, cheesecake.

Price range: Expensive.

Credit cards: All major credit cards.

Hours: Dinner, Mondays through Saturdays, 4:30
P.M. to 11:30 P.M. Closed Sundays and major
holidays.

Reservations: Recommended, especially before theater.

Just about twelve years ago, the son of one of the owners of the Palm, with two partners, opened Wally's in
the theater district. Two years later, the Palm interests
sold out and moved even farther west to Los Angeles.
But the new owners of Wally's still maintain the same
cooking style although they present a menu, whereas
the original Palm did not. Then too, the Wally's décor
lacks the stylish brio of the East Side outpost, but is instead done up like a gaudy cocktail lounge. The management sometimes has the unfortunate habit of giving
the worst tables away first, and the help remains intran-
sigent about making changes.

Although the cooking at Wally's is not nearly as inspired as that of its illustrious ancestor, it is one of the
better choices in its particular neighborhood. Steaks,
chops, lobsters and Italian dishes make up the menu.
The most noteworthy dishes were some of those Italian
specialties, including the best baked clams oreganate
I've had in a long time, the whole clams hot but tender
and moist under a light, crisp herb and crumb topping.

Just as good was the al dente linguine in a white clam
sauce which had just the right accent of golden garlic
flecks: considering the elemental simplicity of this specialty, it is amazingly difficult to find it properly prepared, but this one was total perfection. Fettuccine Alfredo was a bit dry, but well-flavored with cheese, and
the steaming vegetable-thickened minestrone was
earthy and satisfying. So was the excellent crab meat,
now served with cocktail sauce on the side.

Lamb chops and steaks were delicious. A house salad
of iceberg lettuce and unripe tomatoes was not. Calf's
liver was dry and so strongly flavored that it could not
have been as fresh as it should have been. Veal parmigiana was unusual here and decent, made with fontina
cheese instead of mozzarella and only lightly glazed
with tomato sauce. The veal itself was white, tender and
delicious.

The best, and really excellent, main course was the

monster of a broiled lobster, as fresh, moist and succulent as could be. Even at lofty prices for this four-pound behemoth, which we shared, it seemed a great buy. Waiters, unfortunately, try to discourage ordering it, emphasizing how long it takes to prepare — twenty-five minutes, during which one could have a drink and an appetizer. Steak à la stone, a Palm signature dish of sliced steak over onions and pimento, is a lusty approximation of the original.

Cottage fries were thin, crisp and poetic; hashed browns were mushy and tasteless. There are good, creamy New York-style cheesecake, ripe strawberries topped with whipped cream, and hefty drinks.

West Bank Cafe

★

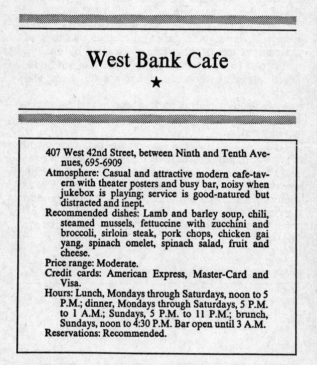

407 West 42nd Street, between Ninth and Tenth Avenues, 695-6909

Atmosphere: Casual and attractive modern cafe-tavern with theater posters and busy bar, noisy when jukebox is playing; service is good-natured but distracted and inept.

Recommended dishes: Lamb and barley soup, chili, steamed mussels, fettuccine with zucchini and broccoli, sirloin steak, pork chops, chicken gai yang, spinach omelet, spinach salad, fruit and cheese.

Price range: Moderate.

Credit cards: American Express, Master-Card and Visa.

Hours: Lunch, Mondays through Saturdays, noon to 5 P.M.; dinner, Mondays through Saturdays, 5 P.M. to 1 A.M.; Sundays, 5 P.M. to 11 P.M.; brunch, Sundays, noon to 4:30 P.M. Bar open until 3 A.M.

Reservations: Recommended.

Two-and-a-half years ago, the West Bank Cafe was by far the best restaurant in the Manhattan Plaza complex and well worth two stars. Although it was somewhat uneven then, its highs were exceptional. Now this lively, attractive, modern pub performs more unevenly than ever, and there are far fewer high points.

The blackboard wall menu combines American, Italian and Oriental dishes, and there is always a good range of light to heavy options, especially convenient before and after performances in the theaters across the street. Sauces are best had on the side or avoided altogether. Broiled meats such as steaks, chicken and the deliciously crisp-crusted, tender pork chops are still satisfying. A generous half-chicken gai yang, well-marinated and then roasted, has a pungent, peppery sting to it, and the meat is moist, but the once fiery sauce served with it has become chokingly sweet and sour.

Sirloin steak is far more satisfying than teriyaki steak, barbecued ribs and chicken, all of which are syrupy sweet. The sauces on them seem better suited to desserts than to main courses. Coarse-cut roasted potatoes and well-cooked vegetables, such as zucchini with tomatoes, enhance main courses.

Fish has never been handled well at the West Bank, but omelets remain excellent, a personal favorite being the verdant spinach omelet. Fettuccine in a creamy cheese sauce flecked with bits of zucchini and broccoli makes a rich and soul-soothing main course or an appetizer when shared, and spinach salad is abundant and sprightly. Steak sandwiches, formerly excellent, now arrive dry, tough and shriveled.

Onion soup is generally fine at the West Bank, good, lusty and golden brown, but it was so salty on a recent try that it seems risky to recommend it. Lamb and barley soup, on the other hand, had just the right mellow flavor and creamy texture.

One of the house classics is mussels steamed in white wine with butter and garlic, altogether delicious as shared appetizer or main course, accented by disks of garlic toast to munch on along with the fragrant broth. Clams are similarly steamed but are too large and tough.

A well-spiced chili is an inexpensive and satisfying lunch or supper dish, and hamburgers are passable, if not inspired.

Desserts have deteriorated. Pecan pie, once good when warm, now arrives ice cold, and so does apple pie and a lackluster chocolate mousse pie. The cold zabaglione on strawberries I tried bore faint traces of onion, as though it had been left uncovered in the refrigerator. Service is absent-minded and altogether slapdash, although good-natured and friendly when you make eye contact.

West Boondock

★

114 Tenth Avenue, corner of 17th Street, 929-9645.
Atmosphere: Pleasantly casual old bar-and-grill setting with stained glass and plants; staff is efficient and helpful.
Recommended dishes: Fried chicken, ham hocks, spareribs, smothered pork chops, chitterlings, yams, collard greens, black-eyed peas and potato salad, sweet potato pie, Irish coffee.
Price range: Moderate.
Credit cards: All major credit cards.
Hours: Lunch, Mondays through Fridays, noon to 3 P.M.; dinner, seven days, 5 P.M. to 12:30 A.M. Closed Christmas Day.
Reservations: Not accepted.

"Boss soul food and fine drinks," the menu promises, and the West Boondock has been delivering on that promise for fifteen years. Old and pleasantly broken down without being self-consciously antique, this tavern-restaurant offers good jazz and fried chicken that's always crackling crisp yet moist.

Meltingly tender ham hocks and meaty spareribs are other above-average examples of soul food, along with the smothered pork chops and chitterlings simmered to a tender but slightly crackling stage. Yams, collard greens, black-eyed peas, cornbread and potato salad are mellow and authentic, as is the sweet potato pie. Vegetables such as string beans are hopelessly over-cooked as is turkey with gravy and stuffing when available.

The Irish coffee packs a wallop and prices are moderate.

Windows on the World
★

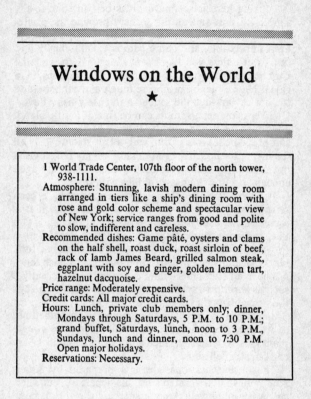

1 World Trade Center, 107th floor of the north tower, 938-1111.
Atmosphere: Stunning, lavish modern dining room arranged in tiers like a ship's dining room with rose and gold color scheme and spectacular view of New York; service ranges from good and polite to slow, indifferent and careless.
Recommended dishes: Game pâté, oysters and clams on the half shell, roast duck, roast sirloin of beef, rack of lamb James Beard, grilled salmon steak, eggplant with soy and ginger, golden lemon tart, hazelnut dacquoise.
Price range: Moderately expensive.
Credit cards: All major credit cards.
Hours: Lunch, private club members only; dinner, Mondays through Saturdays, 5 P.M. to 10 P.M.; grand buffet, Saturdays, lunch, noon to 3 P.M., Sundays, lunch and dinner, noon to 7:30 P.M. Open major holidays.
Reservations: Necessary.

Ever since it opened in 1976, I have been trying to find passable-to-good things to eat at Windows on the World. This is not an easy task, for the kitchen has always overreached itself with elaborate offerings more praiseworthy for their originality than for their execution. That situation has not changed, but neither have the most breathtaking views of New York, and from any side of the bar or dining rooms the cityscape is the world's best. For that reason, the few dishes that have seemed dependable on this frequently changing menu make it worth one star instead of a fair. Service does not help, for even when I am recognized here things become slow and confused. A few times when I have not been recognized, service was polite but even slower and more absentminded.

The large dining room was handsomely designed by Warren Platner, with lush fabrics and details and a color scheme of rose, gold and beige offset by glints of mirror, brass and gold leaf. Its tiered levels and personnel dressed in white uniforms with gold epaulets suggest nothing so much as a ship's dining room. Strips of mirrors above wall banquettes provide a moving frieze of activity to divert the people who sit facing inward, often a boring, out-of-it position since one misses what is going on around the room. The big flaw in the design is the very cold air that is chilling at window tables; a shawl or jacket will be welcomed by the scantily dressed, especially in summer. There is an absurd rule here, by the way, categorically prohibiting blue denim. This really means the management would like people fairly formally dressed (ties and jackets always) but that is a bad way to put it, considering some of the handsome denim clothing now very high styled.

Cooking here is so uneven it is best to stick to the simplest dishes and let the scenery provide the excitement. Clams and oysters on the half shell have always been impeccable, and game pâté is usually meaty and lusty, but unless you like sweet sauce, ask to have the Cumberland dressing on the side. Sea scallops in a caviar beurre blanc sauce were tough and rubbery, and the hot caviar gave the sauce an intensely fishy flavor. Quail eggs on bean sprouts can be fine, if a little bland, and soups tend to lack body. If cervelat of seafood — a sort of quenelles in a casing with a fish velouté — is on the menu, try it; it has been missing on my recent visits but used to be a fine choice. Prosciutto is rarely aged enough and Brie is a dreadful idea with snails.

The three consistently good main courses have been crisp-roasted duck, roast sirloin of prime beef, if it is served hot and cooked to the degree of doneness you like, and a rosy-pink rack of lamb James Beard with a Provençal blend of tomatoes, leeks and pungent little black Nice olives. Grilled salmon with béarnaise sauce has been a better choice than contrived fish alternatives such as shrimp wrapped in leeks that were scorched or the striped bass that tasted of petroleum.

Salads are acceptable although greens are sometimes so wet they shed their dressing. But silky slices of eggplant glossed with soy sauce and spiced with ginger are consistently delicious.

The once sensational desserts prepared by Albert Kumin have deteriorated since his departure, but a few still work quite well. Among such are the very lemony golden lemon tart and the crunchy hazelnut meringue dacquoise with a mocha butter cream that even seems to have improved. Chocolate pastry cake is much less chocolately than it used to be and frozen soufflés are splintered with ice.

I recently looked over the grand buffet served from brunch through dinner on Sundays, and, as so many readers have reported, the selection contains too many cheap fillers of corner-deli-type salads and cold cuts. But herrings, pickled shrimp and some of the hot meat sliced as the day progresses are the best choices. If one chooses carefully, this Saturday lunch and all-day Sunday buffet can offer decent value for the price. Desserts and coffee are served by waiters, but trips to the buffet must be made by customers for other courses. In good weather, when crowds flock to this buffet, choices are the least interesting and service gets pushy in the interest of turnover.

The Hors D'Oeuvrerie is a separate part of this restaurant, featuring substantial international appetizers at very high prices, a served brunch drawn from various ethnic cuisines, afternoon tea, and dancing to the music of a trio from 7:30 P.M. to 1 A.M., Mondays through Saturdays. Music without dancing is played from about 4:30 in the afternoon. There is a cover charge after 7:30 P.M. A series of appetizers can make up a light but costly meal. Offerings include Japanese sashimi, Greek tarama, chicken yakitori, Indonesian satays in peanut sauce, and a dozen or so international specialties. Most are moderately well turned out, if slightly less so than originally.

Sunday brunch from noon to 3 P.M. is à la carte but also offers a fair Mexican breakfast, a dreadful Chinese tea lunch, and a satisfying Scandinavian breakfast that includes herrings and salads, scrambled eggs and steamed potato with dill. On the à la carte menu, James Beard's chicken hash turned out soupy, and eggs Sardou arrived on ice-cold spinach heaped on what tasted like a tinned or jarred artichoke base. Better stick to scrambled eggs with smoked salmon and onion, coconut shrimp or an omelet. The casserole of grits with Jack cheese and bacon is a delicious side dish. The Hors D'Oeuvrerie dining room faces across the Hudson to New Jersey, one of the least impressive views, but the bar and dance floor overlook the Statue of Liberty and the Narrows.

There are other interesting rooms for drinks here, among them the Statue of Liberty lounge, and there are several handsome rooms for private parties of various sizes. Keep the food simple in any of these facilities.

Wings
★ ★

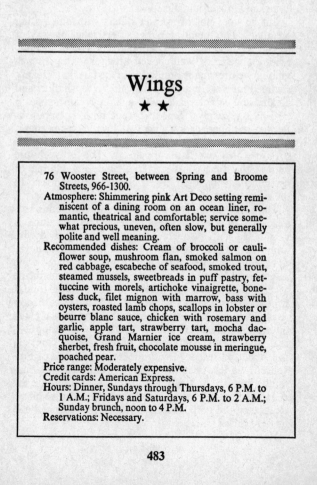

76 Wooster Street, between Spring and Broome Streets, 966-1300.
Atmosphere: Shimmering pink Art Deco setting reminiscent of a dining room on an ocean liner, romantic, theatrical and comfortable; service somewhat precious, uneven, often slow, but generally polite and well meaning.
Recommended dishes: Cream of broccoli or cauliflower soup, mushroom flan, smoked salmon on red cabbage, escabeche of seafood, smoked trout, steamed mussels, sweetbreads in puff pastry, fettuccine with morels, artichoke vinaigrette, boneless duck, filet mignon with marrow, bass with oysters, roasted lamb chops, scallops in lobster or beurre blanc sauce, chicken with rosemary and garlic, apple tart, strawberry tart, mocha dacquoise, Grand Marnier ice cream, strawberry sherbet, fresh fruit, chocolate mousse in meringue, poached pear.
Price range: Moderately expensive.
Credit cards: American Express.
Hours: Dinner, Sundays through Thursdays, 6 P.M. to 1 A.M.; Fridays and Saturdays, 6 P.M. to 2 A.M.; Sunday brunch, noon to 4 P.M.
Reservations: Necessary.

Going to restaurants seven nights a week, I rarely feel called upon to dress up; usually, a simple, unobtrusive outfit suffices. But I discovered that dinner at the recently opened Wings in SoHo is something else again, with a dining room that suggests a dream-world Art Deco ocean liner. The romantic room, with its pink walls, rose-velvet banquettes, serpentine streak of blue neon across the ceiling and fantastic, stylized fabric-flower sculptures, is a stage that inspires appropriate costumes from its cast of diners. At the very least, a marvelous silk shirt seems called for, preferably in pink, rose, white or silver gray, the most flattering colors in this softly diffuse lighting.

Whether drinking at the street-level bar, which creates a balcony, or downstairs in the huge dining room, the cast is especially engaging after 9:30 or 10 each evening, when costumes range from punk to retro to classic, restrained elegance. But best of all, Wings is a beautiful restaurant where very good food seems to be the rule.

The chef turns out original, often improbable-sounding creations, but magically, most of them work. Who would expect, for example, that gently sweet and sour red cabbage with almond slices would set off the smoky and saline flavors of smoked salmon? Yet that combination is one of the best appetizers at Wings, others being fettuccine tossed in a cream, morel and chive sauce, escabeche of marinated cooked seafood, sunny with carrots and scented with coriander and fennel, and hot custard flan burnished with mushrooms and a sauce of cream and mushroom duxelles.

But he does not overpower diners with unrelenting creativity. The menu at Wings offers relief by way of classic dishes, classically prepared. These include, among appetizers, well-cooked artichokes (the French vinaigrette dressing is preferable to the tarragon cream), steamed mussels in a broth of white wine, shallots and cream, and sweetbreads with a light cream sauce in puff-pastry casings. Smoked trout with horseradish-flecked whipped cream and two lovely cream soups, one a satiny cauliflower, the other verdant with broccoli, were also excellent appetizers. The only failure among the first courses I tried was a galantine of chicken that suggested boiled chicken held too long in the refrigerator.

The same mixture of new and traditional lends balance to the main courses. Boneless braised duck is brightened with raspberry vinegar and garnished with kumquats, a main course as satisfying as it is innovative, while the filet mignon with marrow in red-wine sauce might have been cooked verbatim from the recipe in Escoffier. Evidence of seaweed was missing from a firm and meaty sea bass that was said to be steamed in seaweed, but its velouté sauce and briny oysters created interesting flavor contrasts. Roasted lamb chops — really boneless slices of a rack of lamb — are carefully prepared and seasoned with the aromatic herbs of Provence. Fragilely crisp straw potatoes and delicious ratatouille garnish the lamb. Big, briny sea scallops are excellent, either in lobster sauce or in a sheer beurre blanc. Rosemary and garlic added gentle touches to moist and tender braised chicken.

Loin of pork with prunes and spinach was a near miss, primarily because of an overdose of cumin in the sauce. Near misses also included veal in basil cream, which was awkwardly thick and needed a flavor link to the sauce, and paupiettes of sole enfolding salmon mousse, primarily because the sole was almost raw. "A little too nouvelle for you, I guess," a staff member said as he returned the fish for additional cooking. The only total failure was a veal chop in a sauce described as a smoky bordelaise, which seemed, unfortunately, to be exactly that, with its palate-jangling combination of smokiness (achieved with smoked trout heads) and red wine.

Greens in one salad had not been dried sufficiently, and they watered down the somewhat heavy dressing. Bread seems good only when warm, and diners can eat too much of it waiting for the lagging service between courses.

When desserts finally arrive, they prove worth the wait, the only disappointments being an ice-cold slice of cheesecake overpowered by strawberry sauce, a chocolate ganache cake that was dry where it should have been creamy, and both an apricot and pear tart with a base of cloying almond paste. In the dacquoise, hazelnut meringue layers and mocha buttercream had exactly the right textural and flavor contrasts. Crisp, buttery crusts distinguished both apple and strawberry tarts, and a snowy meringue shell held a velvety chocolate mousse, the shell acting as a foil between the chocolate and a fresh strawberry sauce. Poached pear in red wine, fresh fruit, homemade strawberry sherbet and Grand Marnier ice cream provided refreshing finishes. The wine list combines French and California selections, and offers some good choices at fairly high prices.

The staff tends to get flustered at peak hours. Orders are mixed up or forgotten, it becomes hard to get a waiter's attention for water or a check, and off-menu specials are described without price, occasionally without any understanding. One waiter told me twice, at about ten-day intervals, that "this" was his first night. There is also a tendency to overfill wine glasses, emptying a bottle shared by four in a single pouring. The effect of the beautiful, fanciful room is compromised somewhat by the noise level when it is full, a problem worsened by a pianist who also sings after 9 P.M. Chairs and cushy banquettes are comfortable, although some of them face dead corners of the rooms, which would be more interesting if brightened with mirrors.

Wise Maria
Fair

210 Spring Street, at Avenue of the Americas, 925-9257.

Atmosphere: Pretty, delicate but uncomfortable rose and gray setting; service varies from pleasant and efficient to insolent and pretentious.

Recommended dishes: Roasted, marinated peppers, asparagus with butter and grana cheese, grilled pepper chicken, vitello tonnato, calf's liver, arugula salad, ricotta soufflé, chocolate torte.

Price range: Moderately expensive.

Credit cards: American Express, MasterCard and Visa.

Hours: Lunch, Mondays through Fridays, noon to 2:30 P.M.; dinner, Mondays through Saturdays, 6:30 P.M. to midnight; brunch, Saturdays, noon to 3 P.M.; Sundays, noon to 5 P.M.

Reservations: Necessary.

Tempted by the calf's liver on the menu, I asked the waiter how it was prepared. Folding his arms across his chest, he uttered a deep sigh of exasperation. "Why it's done in the classic way, of course — Veneziana," he said, explaining the sautéeing, the onions and the white wine that preparation requires. Never mind that he also needed a shave and wore a soiled apron. Just think of the boring customers he must contend with, all asking the same question that the menu should have answered.

This is more or less the way it went at Wise Maria, in SoHo, characterized as "North Italian dipping into the South" by Philip Idone, co-owner with his wife, Susan, the chef, and Mary Bagley, who manages the dining room. Mrs. Idone used to own and cook at Sabor, a Cuban restaurant in Greenwich Village, and though she didn't have a Cuban background, she did a nice job. The food was not truly Cuban, but it was very good. Now the food is not truly Italian and it is not very good. Cute and pretty applies to the conception of the dishes as much as to the romantically lighted pink-and-gray dining rooms.

Only the front dining room, opposite the bar, is comfortable (though the booths are too cramped for four), and the sound and light are felicitous. But in the back dining room one sits in stiff chairs and always in a traffic pattern.

The food doesn't work any better than the setting, with hardly a dish unaffected by cleverness. Mint replaces basil on a soupy creamed fettuccine with peas and prosciutto to make a cloying, sweetly aromatic sauce that clashes with the cheese sprinkled on it. Although more classic, a small portion of spaghetti al pesto arrived barely tepid and completely pasty.

What is called calzone is a huge appetizer of good, crisp yeasty pastry, disconcertingly filled with strong Gruyère and Montrachet cheese. Pizza is a pie all right, but the raw tomatoes sliced onto the dough turn it to mush in the baking. Better to sauté the tomatoes first to get rid of their water. Littleneck clams touched with herbed butter were hot but not cooked, an unpleasant condition, and sliced tomatoes with smoked mozzarella never caught the perfume of the basil sprinkled on them.

The best appetizers were roasted, marinated peppers with baby eggplants and olives, and firm, bright hot asparagus gilded with butter and sharp grana cheese.

The cook's relentless inventiveness affected the main dishes as well. Gorgonzola cheese blended with butter made grilled veal and lamb chops smell and taste spoiled. Unpleasantly fishy swordfish was overzapped with herbs, and an otherwise tender and succulent steamed lobster was overpowered by a hot vinaigrette dressing heavy with olive oil. A dry, hard, small steak came as a shock at the price, and soft-shell crabs, long past their prime, had been fried without batter so that their shells were unpleasantly brittle.

Pleasant surprises were very good calf's liver, a lovely tiny, juicy chicken grilled under a veneer of crushed peppercorns and tender nuggets of moist chicken sautéed with sliced fresh artichoke hearts. Those dishes, plus a lively arugula salad and superb white, whole-wheat and semolina breads, could make up a delicious if overpriced meal. Finish with the light, chocolate torte adrift in a vanilla-sauce sea or cold ricotta soufflé, much like an airy Italian cheesecake, and you should go away satisfied. Not so if you wind up with the bitter poached pears in a lumpy and cheesy zabaglione sauce or the fig tart with its near-raw dough. Espresso is served in ridiculous thimble-size cups. Based on the three red wines I tried, the selection is better suited to a pizzeria.

Woods (Madison Avenue)
★ ★

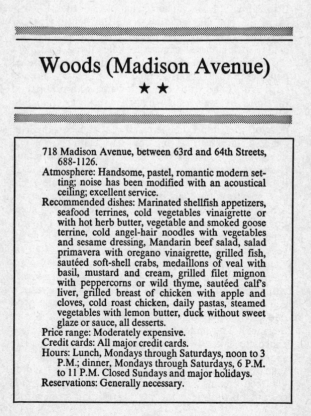

718 Madison Avenue, between 63rd and 64th Streets, 688-1126.

Atmosphere: Handsome, pastel, romantic modern setting; noise has been modified with an acoustical ceiling; excellent service.

Recommended dishes: Marinated shellfish appetizers, seafood terrines, cold vegetables vinaigrette or with hot herb butter, vegetable and smoked goose terrine, cold angel-hair noodles with vegetables and sesame dressing, Mandarin beef salad, salad primavera with oregano vinaigrette, grilled fish, sautéed soft-shell crabs, medaillons of veal with basil, mustard and cream, grilled filet mignon with peppercorns or wild thyme, sautéed calf's liver, grilled breast of chicken with apple and cloves, cold roast chicken, daily pastas, steamed vegetables with lemon butter, duck without sweet glaze or sauce, all desserts.

Price range: Moderately expensive.

Credit cards: All major credit cards.

Hours: Lunch, Mondays through Saturdays, noon to 3 P.M.; dinner, Mondays through Saturdays, 6 P.M. to 11 P.M. Closed Sundays and major holidays.

Reservations: Generally necessary.

Since it opened in 1978, Woods has become headquarters for one of the best representations of the new American cuisine, combining elements of Continental, Oriental and vegetarian cooking concepts to develop a bright, new and fresh food vocabulary. Now with a second branch on West 37th Street, Zeus Goldberg, the president and head overseer, manages to maintain high quality and good service at both. The consistent flaw in the uptown restaurant, which keeps it at a two-star instead of a three-star rating, is a tendency to sweetness in some main courses with the all too frequent appearance of nuts and raisins in dishes where they do not belong, and a few too many sweet vinegar sauces and fruit garnishes. Aside from that, the food is dependably delicious.

From the glowing and felicitous décor to the bright, fresh simplicity of the immaculately well-cooked vegetables, Woods reflects an honest effort, totally without pretensions. By day, the dining room, with its blond-wood chairs, buff-color clothes, café-au-lait walls, attractive photographs and delicate spring bouquets, is cheerful and tailored, and its sunshiny orderliness suggests a Scandinavian interior. At night, with lights dimmed and spots carefully trained on tables with their centerpiece bouquets of yellow, white, red and purple flowers, it becomes intimate and romantic without being the least bit corny.

An acoustical ceiling softens the noise, although not quite enough on busy nights. The young staff is full of good will and manners, and it's easy to see why Woods has become a winner.

The food, which is more or less Continental, is delicately decent, carefully handled and prettily presented. If I deal with the menu somewhat out of order, it is because the real star headliners are the lightly steamed vegetables. The array that wreathes the main courses includes such unusual choices as kale, sliced Jerusalem artichokes, a purée of celery root and potatoes, roasted potatoes in rosy jackets scented with rosemary, almost-crisp carrots and string beans, flowerets of broccoli, and the tiniest Brussels sprouts blanched just long enough to lose their edge of crispness but not so much that they develop the stale cabbage smell that can be repellent. An assortment can be combined as a main course. The house green salad gets an extra touch of springtime freshness from a few snow peas tossed in with the leafy lettuce. Not all of these vegetables are available every day, of course, but there is always a fine assortment.

Several appetizers were equally noteworthy. Exceptional choices are cold angel-hair noodles with Oriental vegetables and a sesame oil dressing, the terrine of vegetables and smoked goose, and a light and silky seviche of marinated raw scallops and crawfish. Also extraordinary were Mandarin beef salad, salad primavera with cheese and vegetables, and asparagus vinaigrette.

To skip around a bit more, the desserts are so good one should save room for them in planning the rest of the meal. The hands-down winner is one of the best chocolate cakes in the city, a roll of dark chocolate sponge, lined with thin sheets of bittersweet chocolate, then rolled around what tastes like espresso-flavored whipped cream. Ripe strawberries nested in a gentle custard fill a butter-cookie tart crust, and strawberries in a chiffon-like Cointreau sauce are also worth their weight in calories. The stingingly ripe Stilton cheese had character; so did the praline cheesecake, pistachio pound cake, lemon cake and a blueberry tart. Skip lemon raspberry mousse and peanut butter chocolate chip cheesecake.

Consistently good main courses include any form of beef prepared with peppercorns, unless it has a sweet accent such as golden raisins; recently it was excellent with wild thyme and red wine sauce. Breast of chicken broiled with apples and cloves is one semi-sweet main course that works, as does the duck breast with a thin glaze of black currant preserves. But impeccable Maryland lump crab meat does not deserve to be compromised by pecans nor does perfectly sautéed calf's liver need pistachios. Ask to have them left off and you will have two perfect dishes.

All forms of lamb — racks or chops — are delicious, as are medaillons of veal in a light sauce of basil, mustard and cream, soft-shell crabs sautéed with Provençal herbs, and a combination of grilled salmon and striped bass with a lemony herb sauce. Lunch specialties, such as pasta, that usually get an Oriental fillip by way of vegetables or oil, and cold roasted chicken are sustaining and diverting. So are most of the stir-fried meats or fish with vegetable combinations when they do not include sweet surprises — ask first. There is usually good decaffeinated coffee, real teas brewed in a Melior pot and a well-thought-out list of moderately priced California, Italian and French wines. Bread is crusty and wheaty.

Woods (37th Street)
★ ★

148 West 37th Street, between Seventh Avenue and Broadway, 564-7340.

Atmosphere: Dramatic modern décor, handsome and stylish, with comfortable lighting and noise level; service generally good but occasionally slow.

Recommended dishes: Marinated shrimp, leek-and-prosciutto tart, duck pâté, spinach soup, mushroom soup, tomato soup, New England clam chowder, leeks Niçoise, grilled shrimp, swordfish, stir-fried chicken, cold chicken breast in spinach-walnut sauce, Korean marinated roast duckling, grilled filet of beef with pink peppercorns, escalope of veal with Calvados and apple, calf's liver, pasta with vegetables, chocolate mocha roulade, royal Viennese walnut torte, cheese and fruit platter, date-pecan ice cream and fresh fruit with fruit sherbets.

Price range: Moderately expensive.

Credit cards: All major credit cards.

Hours: Lunch, Mondays through Fridays, noon to 3 P.M.; dinner, Mondays through Fridays, 5:15 P.M. to 9:30 P.M. Closed Saturdays and Sundays and major holidays.

Reservations: Necessary.

Considering the dearth of good, stylish restaurants close to the garment center, the theater district and Madison Square Garden, a more propitious location could not have been found for the second rendition of Woods. Opened in 1980, this high and boldly handsome modern restaurant has quickly become a lunchtime oasis, and it is rapidly gaining a following for dinner as well. The menu offers the same sort of sparkling fresh, young-spirited and original dishes as the two-and-a-half-year-old Madison Avenue original, but the newcomer is far more comfortable and felicitous. Just a few tables for two are awkwardly placed, and there are still some slowdowns in service at peak hours.

High-fashion photographs pay tribute to the main business at hand in the restaurant's immediate neighborhood, and the huge marble-topped bar attracts a pleasant and convivial crowd. Only a slight brusqueness now and then at the door, and the refusal to seat early arrivals until an entire party is on the premises, detracts from the generally friendly tone.

The style of the food served at Woods can perhaps be best characterized as the new American or new international cuisine, drawing as it does from Continental, American and Oriental kitchens, with a heavy emphasis on the vegetarian look. Fresh and seasonal products are stressed, and culinary boundaries are crossed freely and with style in inventing new dishes.

The appetizer course shows how such invention can work and how it can sometimes fail. Successes include a nearly classic leek-and-prosciutto tart and a duck pâté with chunks of duck meat, which is a far better choice than the lifeless duck terrine with green peppercorns. Leeks Niçoise, again a classic, gets an original and entirely complementary accent with crumbled feta cheese. Whole shrimp marinated with red onions and olive oil take on hints of Southeast Asian cookery, with slices of lime that lend sparkle to both the shrimp and their bed of spinach. A less successful starter was the sliced avocado with scallops in a fresh tomato sauce, which lacked seasonings and therefore interest.

Soups are as delicious as they are refreshing; had they been served hotter, they would have been close to perfection. Even so, those worth trying are a tomato with the subtlest hint of cognac, cream of spinach, an earthy and velvety purée of mushroom with cream and a delicate version of New England clam chowder, with a touch of sherry that adds unexpected elegance.

The steamed vegetable platter, available at both lunch and dinner, is more than enough for two, with such expected choices as carrots, mushrooms, yellow squash, green zucchini, acorn squash, string beans, broccoli and cauliflower. More unusual, but welcome, are purée of yellow turnips, sections of steamed artichoke, snow-pea pods and cuts of unpeeled roasted new potatoes, which are generally excellent, only occasionally tasting of overheated grease.

Kale is the best I have ever eaten — lightly blanched, then glossed with butter so that the usually tough vegetable seems to have melted and absorbed the butter.

Many of these vegetables accompany meat and fish main courses, such as stir-fried chicken in sesame oil and soy sauce, with water chestnuts and bean sprouts;

teriyaki-style swordfish, grilled shrimp with oregano and garlic, beautifully fresh and pink sautéed calf's liver with shallots, and grilled filet of beef in a mustard cream sauce that would be even better if its pink peppercorns were crushed and less liberally sprinkled over the meat. It would seem preferable to vary the combinations of vegetables served with each of these main courses, so that all dishes do not take on a sameness that becomes boring.

At lunch, there is a daily pasta with vegetables: the slim green-and-white noodles, tossed with olive oil, corn oil, broccoli and feta cheese, was entertaining and satisfying. The pasta, ringed with halves of cherry tomatoes, was served with a salad that unfortunately had the very same garnish. Fillet of sole, topped with a beurre blanc sauce flavored with dill and featherings of smoked salmon, took on a saltiness and fishiness from the salmon.

Desserts are simply superb, the only mild exception being a fair mango and strawberry tart. Chocolate mocha roulade, which has become a Woods favorite, is at the new branch, along with other creations, the most inspired of which is a fluffy yet crunchy royal Viennese walnut, chocolate-cream torte. A tart filled with apples, nuts and raisins far outdoes the fruit version, and there are jewel-like homemade fruit sherbets — cranberry-apple, champagne, which gets its golden brilliance from fresh orange and lemon juices, and a cool-as-snow pineapple. Such sherbets arrive amid a rainbow of sparkling, fresh fruits. The lavish fruit and cheese assortment could easily serve as a luncheon or pre-theater main course. Woods has excellent coffees and teas and a decent wine list at fairly moderate prices.

Woo Lae Oak of Seoul
★ ★

77 West 46th Street, between Fifth Avenue and Avenue of the Americas, 869-9958.
Atmosphere: Spacious, attractive modern dining room; service is polite and prompt, but because little English is spoken, the staff is not helpful in explaining dishes.
Recommended dishes: Korean hors d'oeuvres (koo jul pan), egg-rolled fish (saengsun jun), roast marinated beef (bool koki), roast leg of chicken (dak gui), roast tongue (hemmit gui), royal-style tripe casserole (koong joong jungol), casserole cooked in a brazier (shinsullo), assorted plate dinner (jung sik), mixed cold noodles (bibim naeng myun), dumpling soup (mandu kuk), vegetables and vermicelli (jap chae), pickled cabbage (kimchee), pickled radish (kaktoogi), pickled cucumber (oee kimchee), fish casserole (maewoon tang), deep fried fish and vegetables (twikim).
Price range: Moderate.
Credit cards: All major credit cards.
Hours: Seven days, 11:30 A.M. to 11 P.M.
Reservations: Necessary.

Korean food, described in terms of familiar comparisons, is halfway between the cuisines of Japan and Thailand, with a few dishes reminiscent of the Chinese kitchen. The mainstays of the Korean menu are pungently aromatic pickled vegetables such as cabbage (kimchee), radishes (kaktoogi) and cucumbers (oee kimchee), light and satisfying noodle and vegetable combinations that appear in restorative hot and cold soups, bubbling casseroles, and grilled meats that have been marinated in teriyaki-style sauces. Many dishes are cooked at the table, and most are highly seasoned with mustard, chili oil, soy sauce and winy vinegars, usually added as desired.

Barring only its high salt content, Korean food is very much in the modern vein of diet planning because it is low in animal fats and abundant in vegetables and starches that appear in the form of rice and noodles made of wheat flour or bean threads. Of the several Korean restaurants visited in New York, the one I have found to be the most pleasant and authentic is Woo Lae Oak of Seoul, a large, spacious and lively eating place that has branches in Jakarta and Los Angeles, as well as in the South Korean capital.

Woo Lae Oak's waitresses speak very little English and so offer almost no help in explaining dishes and how they should be cooked and eaten. After a brief demonstration, you are strictly on your own. As a result, the best way to discover new and interesting choices is to notice what the regulars are eating, then try and extract the proper names (or numbers) from waitresses.

Seating is around large wooden tables, each of which is supplied with a brazier or burner for broiling meats or simmering sukiyaki-type dishes. Huge vents over each table provide almost adequate ventilation, and the noise level is low enough to allow for comfortable conversation.

When planning for a party of four or more (six is an ideal number), call the manager and order koo jul pan, a huge platter of Korean hors d'oeuvres as colorful and graceful as a flower garden. The arrangement varies but generally includes abalone, squid, octopus, fried and salt-cured fish, exquisitely intricate cold egg dishes and vegetables.

Egg-rolled fish (saengsun jun) are lacy gold rounds of fish dipped in an egg batter then fried, to be shared as an appetizer or eaten as a main course. Among the meats broiled at the table, the marinated beef flavored with scallions (bool koki) is by far the best, although the similarly prepared roast boneless leg of chicken (dak gui) and silken roasted tongue (hemmit gui) also are delicious when dipped into a soy and vinegar sauce and, if you like, further spiked with chili paste. The meat of the broiled marinated ribs (kalbi) proved tough and sinewy and far less pleasant to negotiate. All these meats arrive raw for diners to cook and turn, as needed, with chopsticks.

One of the most extraordinary dishes was maewoon tang, a fish casserole with bean thread noodles, bean curd, vegetables and a fiery dose of chili oil, all arriving so volcanically hot that it seemed to be alive. Koong joong jungol, translated as royal-style casserole, is a mixture of vegetables, tripe, noodles and eggs, simmered in a broth as heady as cider. Shinsullo, a casserole cooked on a brazier with beef, noodles and vegetables topped with hard-cooked eggs, was equally rich and soul warming. All of these soup-casseroles, as well as the cold soups of noodles and vegetables (bibim naeng myun), can be shared, although many Koreans who order them seem to eat them as one-dish meals — no surprise considering how copious the portions are.

Anyone wanting to sample a variety of dishes would do well to order the assorted-plate dinner (jung sik), which includes several of the dishes already described as well as a fragrant bean soup so richly complex it might almost have been fermented. Dumpling soup (mandu kuk) was adrift with meat and vegetables and, again, could be a first course or a hefty meal in itself.

Among the disappointments were the jungol, a casserole much like sukiyaki but made with stringy beef and a cloyingly sweet sauce, and hwe dupbahp — sashimi by another name — lacking the glowing, pearly freshness that assortment of raw fish must have to be worth eating. On the other hand, the Korean version of tempura — twikim — comprising fried shrimp and vegetables was greaseless and crisply delicate.

Essentially peasant food in style and spirit, the Korean dinner usually requires jap chae to be complete. This stir-fried combination of vegetables and vermicelli, which includes several kinds of mushrooms and paper-thin slivers of what seemed to be beef, was so elementally satisfying it might well be considered Korean soul food.

Bean sprouts (unfortunately often wilted and dark) and cold, steamed spinach with sesame oil accompany all main courses and it is worth ordering the previously mentioned pickled vegetables that provide sharp, astringent contrast to the flavors of sesame oil and soy sauce. Fruit and ice cream are the dessert offerings; I always chose melon and found it ripe and freshly cut. Ginseng root is available as tea or as a cocktail somewhat like a sour, but neither beverage affected my psyche or nervous system. Scotch whisky or Japanese beer were more compatible accompaniments.

Xenia
★ ★

871 First Avenue, between 48th and 49th Streets, 838-1191.

Atmosphere: Colorful, informal, folkloric Greek setting with outdoor garden for lunch or dinner, weather permitting; service is slow but friendly.

Recommended dishes: All cold appetizers, hot hors d'oeuvres, spinach pie, moussaka, baby lamb yuvetsi, baked striped bass with tomatoes and onions, fried squid, shish kebab, mixed grill, floghera.

Price range: Inexpensive.

Credit cards: All major credit cards.

Hours: Lunch, Mondays through Fridays, 11:30 A.M. to 3 P.M.; dinner, Mondays through Fridays, 5 P.M. to 11 P.M.; Saturdays and Sundays, noon to 11 P.M. Open on major holidays.

Reservations: Necessary.

In this bright, friendly and colorfully folkloric setting with a small, cheerful garden, pleasant and satisfying Greek food is served at lunch and dinner. Xenia is far busier at midday, attracting a rather late crowd, probably from the United Nations and other nearby office buildings. The food at lunch seems a bit livelier and lighter than at dinner, but at any time, food here is above average compared with many Greek restaurants in town.

The mixed Greek antipasto includes a luxuriously rich and smoky melitzanosalata, a purée of eggplant, whipped to a creamy froth; tzatziki, the sour cream, dill, cucumber and garlic dip; a grape leaf stuffed with herbed rice and sauced with olive and dill, and a small cube of feta cheese. Taramasalata — purée of fish roe whipped with lemon juice, onions and oil — did not have quite the salty tang required, but was acceptable, and the cool, fresh octopus salad was delicious. Any of these appetizers can be had in large single orders or in the assorted mix. All are best accompanied by a glass of the anise-flavored, iced, milky ouzo, the favorite Greek aperitif.

Spanakopita — flaky phyllo dough triangles enclosing a fragrant spinach, onion and cheese filling — were light and enticing, and when served as a main course at lunch, the same pie is made in a large rectangle, from which portions are cut — an even better representation. Hot Greek hors d'oeuvres of liver, sweetbreads and tiny meatballs, braised in a wine and tomato sauce, were lovely, but saganaki, a slice of melted cheese, was tough and leathery.

At dinner one night, egg-lemon soup was thick, pallid and so starchy it was much like porridge, but at lunch on another day, it was pungent with lemon, thinner, and the rice was not overcooked. The salads served with all main courses are poor, composed mostly of iceberg lettuce with a tasteless dressing.

Deep-fried squid were good, if not quite so crisp as they might have been, and shrimp Santorini — baked with a sauce of feta cheese and tomatoes — was done an injustice by the addition of a sherrylike wine, which rendered the whole dish too sweet. Without that touch, the shrimp would have been delicious. Baked striped bass with tomatoes and onions, a daily special at lunch, was well turned out and not at all overcooked, and the same fish broiled looked moist and well prepared, although it was not sampled.

The best meat dishes I tried at Xenia were a light and satisfying moussaka, with a rich and custardy egg-and-cheese topping, and the baby lamb yuvetsi — braised lamb shoulder topped with a Greek pasta, much like giant orzo, which absorbed the meat juices.

Shish kebab was decent, and so was a mixed grill of sweetbreads, liver and a lamb chop, but lamb à la country — sliced roast leg of lamb — was overdone and tasteless. Pastitsio, the Greek version of lasagne, based on layers of tubular macaroni, was very short on the ground meat that the dish should contain. Peas and green beans were badly overcooked, but steamed zucchini was properly done.

Pastries are said to be made on the premises. The baklava was a bit too dense, but the floghera — a roll of phyllo pastry filled with custard and served warm — was excellent. So was the halvah. Greek coffee and wines are on hand, and though the service tends to be slow between appetizers and main course, the staff is friendly and sincere.

Ye Waverly Inn
Fair

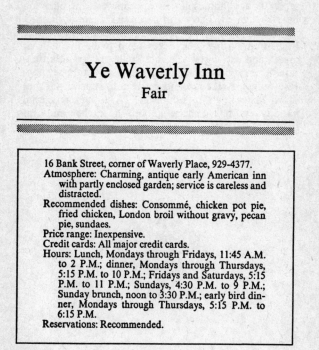

16 Bank Street, corner of Waverly Place, 929-4377.
Atmosphere: Charming, antique early American inn with partly enclosed garden; service is careless and distracted.
Recommended dishes: Consommé, chicken pot pie, fried chicken, London broil without gravy, pecan pie, sundaes.
Price range: Inexpensive.
Credit cards: All major credit cards.
Hours: Lunch, Mondays through Fridays, 11:45 A.M. to 2 P.M.; dinner, Mondays through Thursdays, 5:15 P.M. to 10 P.M.; Fridays and Saturdays, 5:15 P.M. to 11 P.M.; Sundays, 4:30 P.M. to 9 P.M.; Sunday brunch, noon to 3:30 P.M.; early bird dinner, Mondays through Thursdays, 5:15 P.M. to 6:15 P.M.
Reservations: Recommended.

Since 1920, Ye Waverly Inn in Greenwich Village has been valued as a beguiling and dependable source for very good, simple American food at modest prices. Though this 177-year-old tavern with its small, half-covered back garden has retained its charm, the level of cooking and service have declined so markedly that despite its few consistently decent dishes it deserves no more than a fair rating.

Fancy Continental cooking was never a wise choice here, but roast meats, stews, salads and simple homestyle dishes were usually decent, as were the fresh vegetables and home-baked muffins and buns. Now, however, burned, dry meat loaf arrives with huge white clumps of bread in its mixture, roast duck, which is acceptable when fresh, all too often has the acrid aroma and flavor resulting from repeated reheatings, and broiled fish is dry and overcooked. Salads with commercial bottled dressings are disastrous. And though many fresh vegetables, such as yellow squash, acorn squash and collard or turnip greens, are regularly served, they are overcooked and either too sweet or underseasoned.

A dreadful floury brown gravy accompanies many dishes, but it is omitted on request. With that precaution, such choices as London broil and sometimes calf's liver can be acceptable. The most dependable choices for anyone wishing to see this antique landmark and have a modestly priced dinner are the good chicken consommé, a huge quarter of well-fried chicken (again, tell them to hold the gravy) or an individual chicken pot pie with a generous amount of chicken and vegetables in a sauce just a bit too thick, all baked under a crisp, golden brown crust. Barbecued ribs are also decent, although their sauce is on the sweet side.

Hot rolls are textureless and as sweet as cake. Desserts, though homespun in appearance, are also too heavily sugared. The warm pecan pie is one of the better choices, and so are the sundaes. Cobblers are like broken-up syrupy pies, cakes seem to be made from mixes, and cup custard has an unpleasant granular texture. The service is extremely careless. Waitresses confuse orders, spill soup and coffee into saucers and put down dishes in a slapdash fashion. A strong managerial hand is required to shape up both the kitchen and dining-room staffs.

Ying
★ ★

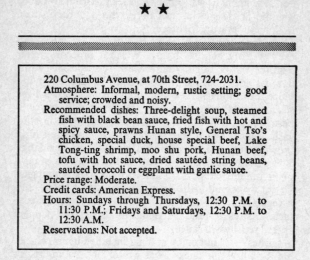

220 Columbus Avenue, at 70th Street, 724-2031.
Atmosphere: Informal, modern, rustic setting; good service; crowded and noisy.
Recommended dishes: Three-delight soup, steamed fish with black bean sauce, fried fish with hot and spicy sauce, prawns Hunan style, General Tso's chicken, special duck, house special beef, Lake Tong-ting shrimp, moo shu pork, Hunan beef, tofu with hot sauce, dried sautéed string beans, sautéed broccoli or eggplant with garlic sauce.
Price range: Moderate.
Credit cards: American Express.
Hours: Sundays through Thursdays, 12:30 P.M. to 11:30 P.M.; Fridays and Saturdays, 12:30 P.M. to 12:30 A.M.
Reservations: Not accepted.

This is one of those Chinese restaurants that does a much better job on its more unusual dishes and gives inexcusably short shrift to commonplace selections, a practice that is as deplorable as it is widespread. Nevertheless, Ying has so many well-prepared dishes that when they are averaged out with the mediocrities, the place still rates two stars and remains one of the best choices in this area.

Skip all appetizers and save room for more inspired dishes. The hot and sour soup, full of vegetables, strips of meat and crunchy tree ears, had a rich and flavorful base, but if you like yours really hot, say so in advance or it will be mild. That rule holds for all dishes here, and the simple addition of hot chili oil is not an altogether effective corrective measure. The best soup on the menu was three-delight, but which of the many ingredients that name refers to is open to question. Scallops, shrimp, chicken, straw mushrooms, tiny ears of corn, carrots and snow peas were all present in the delicious, slightly fishy broth.

I had two excellent fish dishes at Ying, both made with sea bass. The first was the deep-fried whole fish garnished with chopped pork, ginger and vegetables, all in a slightly sweet-sour-hot sauce. More delicate was whole steamed bass in a fragrant, light black-bean sauce.

There were also two beautiful shrimp creations: the Lake Tong-ting version consisted of fresh, firm curls of shrimp, bits of ham, corn and broccoli and snow clouds of egg whites, a mild, soothing and deeply satisfying combination. Prawns Hunan style were fiery with pepper and garnished with tiny, tender straw mushrooms. The same combination of red chili pepper and mushrooms was present in General Tso's chicken, for which the tender boneless chicken was cut into fine nutlike morsels.

The skin of Ying's special duck was fried as crisp as bacon, although its meat was moist and succulent. Shredded vegetables and pork for rolling in crepes (moo shu pork) were well seasoned, and Hunan beef, though not fiery enough, was tender and lean. Richer in flavor was the house special beef done with a darker sauce. Both were served with broccoli.

Unfortunately, and for reasons hard to fathom, the chef at Ying chooses to use Western broccoli rather than the leafier, slightly bitter Chinese species. In addition, he does not actually cook it in the accompanying sauce, but rather serves it on the side, plain boiled (or steamed) and without allowing the flavor of the sauce to permeate it. The one exception was the broccoli with garlic sauce, which was far better, because the satiny brown sauce had imparted its flavor to the vegetable. This same sauce distinguished the finger slivers of eggplant and minced pork. Crumbles of crisp pork and garlic did wonders for the dried, sautéed string beans, and a vegetarian dish of tofu, as gentle and creamy as custard, was really quite marvelous in a sharp but pepper-spiked red-brown sauce.

Dishes I did not enjoy at Ying included lemon chicken, for while the chicken was white, tender and crisply fried, it was ruined by a thick, syrupy lemon sauce suggesting melted marmalade.

Similarly, the lobster Sichuan style, although fresh and generously portioned, was spoiled by the sweetness of its red, cornstarch-thickened sauce. All sparerib dishes were merely adequate, primarily because the meat on the ribs was tough and dry, as though it had been cooked and then left waiting to be combined with sauce for too long. This was true of both the spareribs wtih black-bean sauce and those done Mandarin style.

Sweet-and-hot pickled cabbage, a particular favorite, was missing on all four tries.

Main courses are copious and sharable for three or four. Prices range from inexpensive to moderate. The simple décor is pleasant enough, with raw knotty pine paneling, rough white walls, plants and brown plastic tablecloths. All would look better without the grease-stained, dirty carpet.

Desserts consist of canned fruits and fortune cookies. Mine read: "Speak out as your heart tells you to," and I just did.

Young Bin Kwan

★

10 East 38th Street, between Fifth and Madison Avenues, 683-9031.

Atmosphere: Handsome modern and formal two-story restaurant with convivial bar; service is polite and friendly, but language problems make ordering difficult.

Recommended dishes: Combination appetizers, all meats broiled at the table, kimchee, pickled turnips, spinach and bean sprout salad, pan-fried fillet of flounder (saeng sun jeon), roast whole red snapper in special sauce (domi kui), red snapper or codfish casseroles, cold noodles in broth, hotpot of beef, chicken and vegetables cooked at the table (shin sun lo).

Price range: Moderate.

Credit cards: American Express, MasterCard, Visa and Diners Club.

Hours: Lunch, seven days, noon to 2 P.M.; dinner, seven days, 2 P.M. to 11 P.M.

Reservations: Necessary for lunch.

Young Bin Kwan is a new and elaborate Korean restaurant, with carpeted dining rooms on two floors, modern crystal chandeliers, tablecloths and, at night, an almost continuous slide show of Korean scenes that culminates in a final flash of Leonardo's "Last Supper." At the front there is a big bar where young Koreans gather for drinks and giveaway appetizers and to listen to a stylish Korean chanteuse as she plays the piano and sings French lyrics that she has mastered by rote.

Considering the effort that went into all of this, it is clear that the management has gone out of its way to attract non-Koreans. And on my first visit I felt this effort could be successful. The menu was huge and fascinating, so much so that even though only half of what I ordered was really good, I felt that there were still many fascinating dishes to be tried.

But on subsequent visits there were new menus, listing in English only about half the dishes originally presented, while the other half was listed only in Korean. When I asked about some of the things I remembered and looked forward to, I was told those were not for Americans. Moreover, all of the spicy chili-accented dishes had been eliminated from the English side.

Even with that gastronomic discrimination in force, Young Bin Kwan provides interesting dining experiences. The whole range of meats broiled on gas braziers at the tables is delicious, marinated in a sweet and pungent sauce that adds flavor and tenderness. Bool kogi consists of slender strips of beef cooked this way, and the kal bi kooi, thicker chunks of beef cut from short ribs, are even juicier and more toothsome. Dak gui, or chicken parts, roast beef heart (yom tong gui) and tripe (yang gui) are just a few of the broiled meats worth trying.

Soups were disappointingly bland and watery, but many dishes billed as stews or casseroles turn out to be soup in the Western sense. Among the latter, the hotpot, shin sun lo, cooked at the table, is a bracing combination of beef, chicken and vegetables. Two wonderfully fiery dishes I did manage to get were the red snapper casserole and the codfish casserole, both with hot chili oil sauce and both wonderful. In addition to getting cool and refreshing representations of such Korean pickles as the cabbage kimchee and the barely blanched spinach and bean sprouts (namool), I also managed to cajole the management into giving me some wonderful searingly hot turnip pickles.

Jap chae, a Korean standard of stir-fried vegetables and bean thread noodles, was less interesting here than elsewhere, and the sam hap cho, a combination of abalone, shrimp and beef with vegetables, was a sticky sweet and sour dish that one waitress said was done "American style."

Cold noodles with vegetables in broth were sprightly and refreshing. Saeng sun jeon, thin round fillets of flounder fried in a delicate egg batter, were delicious. So was the domi kui, a whole roasted red snapper dipped in a chili and sesame oil paste.

Prices are moderate by most standards. There are less expensive dishes on the Korean side of the menu.

Yun Luck Rice Shoppe
★ ★

17 Doyers Street, between Mott Street and the Bowery, near Pell Street, 571-1375.
Atmosphere: Noisy, crowded, cheerful luncheonette-dining room; good service.
Recommended dishes: Snails (periwinkles), clams or spareribs in black bean sauce; crab or lobster Cantonese with black beans, Peking chicken, beef with broccoli, steamed flounder, fried sea bass with vegetables and pork, pink pepper shrimp, fried squab.
Price range: Moderate.
Credit cards: None.
Hours: Lunch, Mondays through Fridays, 11:30 A.M. to 3 P.M.; dinner, Mondays through Fridays, 3 P.M. to midnight; Saturdays, 11:30 A.M. to 1 A.M.; Sundays, 11:30 A.M. to midnight. Open major holidays.
Reservations: Necessary for five or more people.

With so much attention being paid nowadays to the Mandarin, Shanghai, Sichuan and Hunan kitchens of China, the food of the southern province of Canton is all too often accorded short shrift. Yet the wide variety of that cuisine, along with its subtly enticing and soul-soothing flavor and textural counterpoints, makes it one of China's most popular and satisfying, even among the Chinese themselves.

Unquestionably, Canton's loss of gourmet status in this country has to do with widespread availability; most of the Chinese who came to this country emigrated from that province. Then, too, most neighborhood Cantonese restaurants feature only banal and Americanized versions of their native fare.

But tucked away in the narrow, winding, helter-skelter streets of Chinatown are a number of small restaurants, most of them suggesting minimal luncheonettes, where delectable and intriguing Cantonese dishes are served to Chinese families, who are usually grouped at round tables. Printed menus in English are offered to the few Westerners who frequent these places, but the Chinese clientele looks for inspiration in the vertical strips of brightly colored paper mounted on the wall, which offer the most authentic of Cantonese specialties in Chinese.

One of the better examples of these Cantonese restaurants is the Yun Luck Rice Shoppe. Yellow oilcloth covers the table, there are touches of red in the typical Chinese restaurant bibelots around the walls, and the sprawling dining room is gay, clattering and convivial. The service is good, and most waiters speak enough English to help explain the menu. If there is one drawback, it is the tendency to bring all the dishes at once, a practice that not only crowds the table, but also causes a number of dishes to grow cold as others are being consumed. I have found the only remedy is to order a few dishes at a time.

It is wise to forget all the Cantonese cliché dishes here. At a restaurant like this, such choices do not measure up to the less common ones. That is inexcusable, of course, because everything on a restaurant's menu should reflect the chef's best efforts.

If a chef considers certain dishes to be beneath his talents, it is understandable and his privilege, but in that case, he should not, out of an instinct for petty opportunism, put them on his menu. Egg rolls, roast pork and wontons are, after all, Chinese inventions, and all can be wonderfully delicious. To serve the most tasteless and commercial variety is reprehensible when a chef knows better — as he surely must here.

Since I first reviewed this restaurant, the kitchen's performance has become somewhat uneven, ranging from excellent to passable. There is a slight tendency to alter dishes served to Westerners, so be sure to ask to have your food served Chinese style.

It is hard to remember ever having had a fish more perfectly cooked than the steamed flounder garnished with soy, scallions and ginger prepared here or, for that matter, the crunchy, deep-fried whole sea bass strewn with vegetables and tender chunks of pork.

Steamed littleneck clams, tiny snails that are really periwinkles, or chunks of lean spareribs may be had, each dish served in a sauce of smoky, salty and winy fermented black beans. The beans are also combined with egg, garlic and crumblings of pork to make the sauce on the fragrant and succulent cut-up fresh crabs or lobsters, Cantonese style.

Pink shrimp, stir-fried to parchment crispness in their split shells, are sparked by black pepper, and slices of steak stir-fried with verdant, leafy, Chinese broccoli in an oyster sauce were tender enough to be nibbled easily when held between chopsticks.

The chewy but delicious scungilli, stir-fried with baby ears of corn, vegetables and mushrooms, was for the more adventurous, and the golden-fried Peking chicken (tell the waiter not to make it crisp and dry, but as the Chinese like it) was cut in strips of tender meat, each gilded with its own paper-thin skin. Although called Peking, this dish is standard at Cantonese restaurants.

Crackling-crisp nuggets of fried squab (complete with head), and tiny chunks of chicken simmered in soy sauce (soy-sauce chicken) were also delicious alternatives.

If you feel that a Chinese meal is incomplete without soup, try the watercress enriched with pork. The so-called kitchen-sink soup — made with third-rate wontons but first-rate slices of meat, chicken, fishcake, shrimp, mushrooms and greens — was certainly decent, but nothing more.

You may take your own beer or wine to Yun Luck, as the house serves no liquor. No desserts are served here either. Non-Orientals have to request chopsticks and porcelain spoons for soup, and if you ask the waiter to remove dishes of mustard and duck sauce, your stock will rise perceptibly.

Zapata
★ ★

330 East 53rd Street, between First and Second Avenues, 223-9408.
Atmosphere: Small, rustic, informal Mexican setting; friendly and efficient service.
Recommended dishes: Guacamole, nachos, seviche, black bean soup, beef tacos, beef or chicken enchiladas, burrito, chilies rellenos with beef, flautas, mole poblano, pollo à la Zapata, carne Tampiqueña, wheat tortillas, natilla.
Price range: Inexpensive.
Credit cards: All major credit cards.
Hours: Lunch, Mondays through Fridays, noon to 3 P.M.; dinner, seven nights, 5 P.M. to 11:30 P.M.
Reservations: Not accepted.

Considering the widespread interest here in new and unusual foods and the wealth of subtle, enticing and varied dishes one finds while traveling through Mexico, it is difficult to understand why no Mexican restaurateur is willing to present a greater range of that savory cuisine in New York. Throughout Mexico one finds delicate and subtle specialties based on fish and shellfish, chicken and pork, a staggering variety of exquisite soups, superb egg dishes and irresistible, chili-spiked pickled vegetables that appear as relishes on many tables.

But in New York, few restaurants go beyond the few standard appetizers, the tortilla-based dishes, tamales, enchiladas and a couple of banal desserts. The problem, perhaps, is that Mexican food is considered cheap, and it would, therefore, be difficult for such a restaurant to charge what would be necessary to prepare more costly ingredients.

Among the Mexican restaurants in New York, Zapata's does a much better job than most. The brick-walled interior with its candlelight, folkloric bric-a-brac and pictures of Zapata, the revolutionary hero, create a pleasant and atmospheric setting. Service in this small, friendly restaurant is suitably informal, accommodating and efficient.

Margaritas are well made here, though perhaps not quite frosty enough for those who like that tequila-and-lime-juice drink straight up rather than with ice. But they go well with the fresh, crisp tostados dipped in a mild, hot sauce or with the savory nachos — tostados spread with refried black beans and glazed with cheese and a sliver of jalapeño pepper. Other good appetizers on the menu include a mild, bright guacamole that improves with the addition of some of the hot sauce and a cool, sprightly seviche of tender, snow-white squid in a sauce not unlike gazpacho.

Unfortunately, that classic soup was served too warm and bland, and chilate, a chicken soup with chili sauce, was equally uninteresting. But the thick, smoky, black bean soup made up for what the other soups lacked.

The whole array of tacos, enchiladas, tamales, tostados, burritos and chilies rellenos are above average and can be had separately or in combination platters. Crisp tacos filled with chicken, soft enchiladas with beef or chicken, and the chili relleno stuffed with beef and baked with cheese were especially well made. So were the big, puffy meat or chicken burritos.

Flautas — rolled, crisp tortillas filled with beef and topped with sour cream and guacamole — were the best of the offerings in this category, and like the others, were garnished with soft, soothing, refried beans and rice that was just a bit too dry.

Fortunately, the Zapata menu does not end with those standard specialties. There is a very good mole poblano, turkey with a dark-as-midnight sauce that blends bitter chocolate, spices, sesame seeds, garlic and chilies. Pollo à la Zapata, chicken in a tomato-and-pepper ranchero sauce, and carne Tampiqueña, steak in a slightly more fiery ranchero sauce, were also satisfying main courses. Cabrito (baby goat) was moist and tender but needed a sauce with more interest than the one in which it was served, and the mole verde — chicken in green sauce — was too bland, although otherwise decent.

Wheat tortillas were better than those of corn, but jalapeño peppers, ordered à la carte, had almost no sting at all. The flan custard should have been smoother, but the natilla, a creamy coconut custard scented with cinnamon, was excellent. Fruited red wine sangria was less cloying than in most places, and Zapata's coffee made with Kahlúa, brandy and whipped cream proved fair.

Mexican beer, Portuguese wine and several mixed-drink specialties also are available.

503

À la Carte

This section of the book is intended as a brief guide to some of the city's less formal eating places that feature one or another ethnic light meals or snacks. They appear in the indexes at the front of the book, preceded by an asterisk.

Country and Western Food (ribs, chili, chicken, barbecue and soul food)

The Lone Star Cafe, 61 Fifth Avenue at 13th Street (242-1664), specializes in live country music, but at lunch, dinner and throughout the evening performances they serve some very good ribs and barbecued brisket flown up from Texas, fried or barbecued chicken and the town's best hotly spiced chili. Barbecue sauce is not up to the quality of the meats. Lone Star beer is the best drink with this food. There is a music charge after 8 or 8:30 at night, but prices are otherwise moderate. Hours: Food served, 11:30 A.M. to 4 P.M. and 6 P.M. to 1 A.M., Mondays through Thursdays, and until 1:30 A.M. on Fridays. Food served 7:30 P.M. to 1:30 A.M., Saturdays. Food served 7:30 P.M. to 1:00 A.M., Sundays. Bar and entertainment until 4 A.M. nightly.

Smokey's, 230 Ninth Avenue at 24th Street (924-8181) and 685 Amsterdam Avenue at 93rd Street (865-2900), has an open-pit barbecue in each dining room and excellent spareribs or baby back ribs with the city's best sauce, be it mild or hot; the latter is incendiary, so be prepared. Fried potato-skin chips are good, too, as is the Rolling Rock beer. Chopped Texas-style beef barbecue is worth trying. Hours: 11 A.M. to 11 P.M., Mondays through Fridays; noon to 11 P.M., Saturdays and Sundays.

Wylie's, 891 First Avenue at 50th Street (751-0700), a stylish East Side pub, also does good baby back ribs with an undistinguished sauce. Beef ribs are gross and tough. Hours: 11:30 A.M. to 1:00 A.M., daily.

Tennessee Mountain, 143 Spring Street at Wooster Street (431-3993), is SoHo's only creditable rib outpost and is a charming setting in which good beef ribs are also served. The sauce is one of the better concoctions *if* it is not burned. Hours: 11:30 A.M. to 11 P.M., Mondays through Thursdays; 11:30 A.M. to midnight, Fridays and Saturdays; 11:30 A.M. to 10:30 P.M., Sundays.

Swiss Chalet, 27 West 72nd Street (873-2004), and **Tony Roma's,** 400 East 57th Street (308-0200), are both branches of international chains that have decent baby back ribs with sauces that are only fair. Tony Roma's is gaudy and garish; Swiss Chalet is more pleasant looking and gets a colorful West Side crowd. Cole slaw is good here. Swiss Chalet hours: Noon to midnight, Sundays through Thursdays; noon to 1 A.M., Fridays and Saturdays. Tony Roma's hours: 11 A.M. to 4 A.M., Mondays through Saturdays; 4 P.M. to 4 A.M., Sundays.

Also see reviews of Cottonwood Cafe, El Coyote, Horn of Plenty, Jack's Nest and West Boondock.

Dairy Restaurants (Kosher/Vegetarian)

Of the dozens of kosher dairy restaurants that used to be in New York, only a few remain and of those, several are beneath serious consideration. Some combine cafeteria and full-service restaurants and all encourage take-out business. Stock-in-trade at these places includes usually very good soups, such as bean, mushroom and barley, cabbage, split pea and potato, and such cold soups as beet borscht and schav (sorrel). Fried fish, whether hot or cold, is generally flavorful, but baked, broiled or boiled fish is almost always overcooked, as are vegetables. Better choices are salad plates with egg, tuna, vegetarian chopped liver and smoked fish as the centerpieces or sandwiches of those same ingredients. Eggs are generally good, especially in the classic preparation — scrambled with onions and smoked salmon or lox. Herring appears in many forms and is very good fried and served with potatoes. Other dependable choices include blintzes (best with cheese) and the dough-filled turnovers, pirogen filled with potato, cabbage, cheese or mushrooms and available boiled or, my preference, fried. There is sour cream in abundance. Matzoh brei (broken matzohs scrambled with eggs) is another standard, as are cinnamon, nut and raisin studded coffeecakes. Because they observe kosher laws, most of these places close Friday night and Saturday for Sabbath and are open Sundays, but it is best to call and check the hours of each. They are listed in order of my preference. Most open for breakfast and serve early dinner.

Gross Dairy Restaurant, 1372 Broadway, between 37th and 38th Streets (921-1969). In the heart of the garment center, this gets a colorful and lively crowd. Salads and French toast are especially good. Hours: 7 A.M. to 9 P.M., Mondays through Thursdays; 7 A.M. to 5 P.M., Fridays; 11 A.M. to 9 P.M., Sundays. Closed Saturdays.

Grand Dairy Restaurant, 341 Grand Street, on the corner of Ludlow Street (673-1904). Crisp apple blintzes are unusual and delicious and egg dishes are especially good, as is rice pudding. Hours: 6 A.M. to 4 P.M., Sundays through Thursdays; 6 A.M. to 3 P.M., Fridays. Closed Saturdays.

Ratner's Dairy Restaurant, 138 Delancey Street, between Norfolk and Suffolk Streets (677-5588). Among other things, baked gefulte fish is unusual and savory.

Soups are very good, as are egg dishes and cakes. Hours: 6 A.M. to midnight, Sundays through Fridays; 6 A.M. to 2 A.M., Saturdays.

B & H Dairy Restaurant, 127 Second Avenue, between St. Marks Place and 7th Street (777-1930). This is really a luncheonette with a counter and just a few tiny tables crammed in. Although the cooking has become careless, there are still good soups and egg dishes as well as lusty pirogen and sandwiches on big rolls. The scene is lively and friendly. Hours: 6 A.M. to 11 P.M., daily.

Gefen's Dairy Restaurant, 297 Seventh Avenue, between 26th and 27th Streets (929-6476). Close to the Institute of Fashion Technology and the garment center, this place has both a counter and a table section. Eggs, pirogen and soups are the safest choices. Cakes and fish are awful. Hours: 7:30 A.M. to 8 P.M., Mondays through Thursdays; 7:30 A.M. to 2:30 P.M., Fridays, 11 A.M. to 5 P.M., Sundays (not during summer). Closed Saturdays.

Famous Dairy Restaurant, 222 West 72nd Street, between Broadway and West End Avenue (595-8487). There is a counter as well as tables, and hot food leaves much to be desired except, of course, for eggs. Soups, salads and sandwiches are the safest choices. Hours: 7:30 A.M. to 11 P.M., Sundays through Thursdays; 7:30 A.M. to 2 P.M., Fridays. Closed Saturdays.

See review, Greener Pastures.

The New York Deli

The deli is a New York Jewish-Eastern European institution, unequaled anywhere else in the country. As reviewed here, they are listed for their delicatessen meats and sandwiches, not for the other kosher-style food they serve. In a few cases where there is an especially good example of a regular dish (soup, meat, etc.), it is noted. All of the following are kosher style and a few are kosher as noted. The pastrami and corned beef were the primary products judged. The delis are listed in order of my preference.

Carnegie Delicatessen and Restaurant, 854 Seventh Avenue near 55th Street (757-2245). Leo Steiner makes his own pastrami and corned beef, both the city's best, and they are piled up handsomely on excellent sandwiches. Tongue is excellent, too, if you ask for center slices. That tongue is also good as tongue and eggs. Pickles are wonderfully garlicky. Chicken soup with matzoh balls, cheese blintzes and boiled short ribs are also delicious. Not kosher. Hours: 6:30 A.M. to 4 A.M., daily.

Bernstein-on-Essex Street, 135 Essex Street between Delancey and East Houston Streets (473-3900). This place observes strict kosher laws and makes very good pastrami, especially the spicy, lean Rumanian pastrami. Corned beef is good. Kosher Chinese food is served here but is skippable. Hours: 8 A.M. to 1 A.M., Sundays through Thursdays; 8 A.M. to 4 P.M., Fridays; 9 P.M. to 3 A.M., Saturdays.

Fine & Schapiro, 138 West 72nd Street, between Broadway and Amsterdam Avenue (877-2874). This kosher delicatessen has improved in the last two years, and pastrami and corned beef are very good, if slightly blander than at the two above. Pot roast is good also. Hours: 11 A.M. to 11:30 P.M., Saturdays through Thursdays, 11 A.M. to 9 P.M., Fridays.

Second Avenue Kosher Delicatessen and Restaurant, 156 Second Avenue at the corner of 10th Street (677-0606). Kosher food is featured with decent delicatessen and very good soups. Corned beef is said to be made on the premises, although pastrami is not. Hours: 6:30 A.M. to 11:30 P.M., daily.

Madison Delicatessen and Restaurant, 1175 Madison Avenue at the corner of 86th Street (369-6670). Food is not kosher and it is expensive but perfectly acceptable. Soups are good, as is some of the cooked food. Hours: 9 A.M. to 10:30 P.M., daily.

Katz's Delicatessen, 205 East Houston Street, at Ludlow Street (254-2246), is the famous Lower East Side deli that is huge, lively and inexpensive. Portions are enormous but quality is below standards, although pastrami is hand-sliced. The real treats are hot dogs with sauerkraut and the local scene. Not kosher. Hours: 8 A.M. to 11:30 P.M., Sundays through Thursdays; 8 A.M. to 1:30 A.M., Saturdays and Sundays.

Marginal delis include Pastrami 'n' Things, The Stage, Wolf's, Orloff's, Sarge's, Gaiety West and Junior's in Brooklyn.

Dim Sum

The tiny dumplings and small dishes of cooked food that make up that tea-lunch known in Chinese as dim sum or yum cha are widely available in New York, especially in Chinatown. The standard serving practice is for waiters and waitresses to circulate around the dining room, each carrying a different type of dim sum. You simply point to what you want among the tiny portions and eat until you have had enough. The check is figured by a count of the saucers left on your table. Tables are usually shared with large groups of strangers and it is best to go with two or three people so you can try a variety of dishes. Dumplings that are steamed or fried may be filled with shrimp, pork, vegetables, lobster or chicken and there are dishes such as the webs of duck and chicken feet, bean curd in sauce, steamed chopped spareribs, chicken livers and so on. Most Chinese families finish up with a platter of noodles stir-fried with seafood and vegetables. Dim sum are mainly breakfast to the Chinese; the downtown places open early. They have become popular weekend brunch items for non-Chinese and so the restaurants are jammed at that time.

Hee Seung Fung (H.S.F.) 46 Bowery (374-1319) and 578 Second Avenue (689-6969). Generally known by its initials, the downtown original continues to offer the most dazzling variety of dim sum and among the best. The uptown branch is more formal and less confusing, but the dim sum are somewhat less lively and sizzling. Try fried shrimp balls in butterfly wings of rice paper. Seafood noodles are among other choices. Hours: 46 Bowery, 7:30 A.M. to 5 P.M., daily; 578 Second, 11:30 A.M. to 3 P.M. Mondays through Fridays, 11:30 A.M. to 5 P.M., Saturdays and Sundays.

Hong Gung, 30 Pell Street (571-0545), also offers a variety of excellent dumplings and small dishes in a lively and friendly atmosphere. Steamed pork or chicken buns are delicious here, as are seafood fried noodles. Hours: 9 A.M. to 3:30 P.M., seven days a week.

Imperial Inn, 23 Pell Street (233-1014). The assortment is smaller here, limited to about ten choices, which are ordered from a menu. All are made to order and are delicious, and this place makes up in quality for what it lacks in diversity. Try steamed or fried dumplings, steamed pork buns, fried turnip cakes and scallion pancakes. Hot and sour soup is one of the city's lustiest. Hours: 11:30 A.M. to 11 P.M., Mondays through Fridays; 11 A.M. to midnight, Saturdays and Sundays.

Cam Fung, 20 Elizabeth Street (964-5256). This is a huge, bright and festive dim sum mecca that is jammed on weekends. Turnip and ham cakes are especially good, as are beef satays, curried squid and the curry-flavored Singapore noodles, mai fon. Hours: 8 A.M. to 4 P.M., seven days a week.

Shun Lee West, 43 West 65th Street, Lincoln Center (595-8895). There is a special menu of dim sum offered from 10 P.M. to midnight, every night, a pleasant supper option after a Lincoln Center performance. There are about 12 dim sum on the menu. They are best when the place is busiest; at off hours, dim sum may have a greasy flavor indicating they have been reheated. Prices are somewhat higher than in Chinatown, but then, so is the overhead. This two-star restaurant also has a full review in the alphabetical listings. Hours: 10 P.M. to midnight, seven days a week; brunch, noon to 4 P.M., Saturdays and Sundays.

Hamburgers

Diane's, 249 Columbus Avenue, near 72nd Street (799-6750). Open 11 A.M. to 2 A.M., daily.

Taste of the Apple, 1000 Second Avenue, near 53rd Street (751-1445). Open 11 A.M. to midnight, Mondays through Saturdays; 1 P.M. to midnight Sundays.

Corner Bistro, 331 West 4th Street, corner Jane Street (242-9502). Open noon to 4 A.M., seven days.

J. G. Melon West, 340 Amsterdam Avenue at 76th Street (874-8291). Open 11:30 A.M. to 1:30 A.M., daily.
J. G. Melon, 1291 Third Avenue at 74th Street (744-0585). Open: 11:30 A.M. to 3 A.M., daily.

Serendipity, 225 East 60th Street, between Second and Third Avenues (838-3531). Open 11:30 A.M. to midnight, weekdays; until 1 A.M. Fridays and 2 A.M. Saturdays.

Elephant & Castle. See review, Elephant & Castle.

Sweet Basil, 88 Seventh Avenue South, near Bleecker Street (242-1785). Open noon to 2 A.M., Sundays through Thursdays; noon to 3 A.M., Fridays and Saturdays.

The Balcony, 2772 Broadway, between 106th and 107th Streets (864-8505). Open noon to midnight, Sundays through Thursdays; noon to 2 A.M., Fridays and Saturdays.

Boodles, 1478 First Avenue, corner 77th Street (628-0900). Open 4 P.M. to 4 A.M., daily.

Charlies', 263 West 45th Street, between Seventh and Eighth Avenues (354-2911). Open noon to 2 A.M., daily.

Joe Allen, 326 West 46th Street, between Eighth and Ninth Avenues (581-6464). Open noon to 2 A.M., daily.

P. J. Clarke's, on Third Avenue at 55th Street and in The Cellar at Macy's, is probably the city's most famous hamburger stop. But the thin, tightly compressed burgers at high prices have not been forgotten in this listing. They are simply not recommended.

Pizza

I know of two places in Manhattan that make what I consider really good, authentic pizzas, baked in stone-floor ovens and with crusts that are blistered and charred around the edges (see below). All three Goldberg's Pizzerias, with their soggy, leaden un-Italian deep-dish pizzas, and the trendy, expensive Rocky Lee's Chu-Cho Bianco, with its tasteless cracker-crust pizzas, are among the city's most overrated culinary specialties.

It is possible that there are other small, old-style pizzerias around, somewhere in the Bronx or Brooklyn, probably, and if you know of one, I'd appreciate hearing about it.

John's Pizzeria, 278 Bleecker Street (242-9529). This Greenwich Village classic serves the best pizza in the city and also offers wonderful calzone — pizza dough wrapped around a ricotta and ham or sausage filling, then baked. Open 11:30 A.M. to 11 P.M., Mondays through Fridays; 11:30 A.M. to 11:30 P.M., Saturdays; noon to 11:30 P.M., Sundays. As this book goes to press, John's is expanding its facilities. There have been some reports lately of careless housekeeping.

Patsy's Pizzeria, 2287 First Avenue, between 117th and 118th Streets (534-9783). This is in East Harlem and is one of the few remnants of the Italian neighborhood that flourished here. The restaurant is neat and tidy, the pizza is wonderful, and so is calzone if it is not too salty. Go there by car or taxi, especially if you go at night. Bus and subway are fine in daylight. Open 11 A.M. to 4 A.M., Tuesdays through Sundays, closed Mondays.

Sushi

See reviews of various Japanese restaurants.

Old New York, or What's Left of It

If food alone is not enough, perhaps history will provide added sustenance. The oldest restaurants in New York include The Old Homestead, Peter Luger, Gage & Tollner and Sweet's. For details on those, see their reviews. Those below have not been fully reviewed or rated:

The oldest restaurant in the city is **Fraunces Tavern,** which is housed in a building of Holland and English brick dating from 1719 that has been the site of the Samuel Fraunces Tavern since 1763. The tavern, at 54 Pearl Street, corner of Broad Street (269-0144), is the establishment in which Washington said farewell to his troops in 1783. The Long Room, where he took his leave, is part of a museum that occupies two floors over the restaurant. The Colonial origins of the building, which was damaged by fire in 1845 and restored in 1907, are best reflected in the corner portion. There is no admission charge to the museum, which is open from 10 A.M. to 4 P.M., Monday through Friday.

Robert Norden, the owner, apparently believes that an international array of fashionable food is called for, but the kitchen is equally inept with sauces, fancy dishes and grilled steaks and chops. Safe choices are fresh and chilled seafood cocktails or cold shellfish platters, pea soup, steamed lobster, broiled fish and roast prime ribs of beef, if they haven't been left under a heat lamp to turn gray. Prices are moderately expensive. Breakfast is served from 8 A.M. to 10 A.M., lunch from noon to 4 P.M. and dinner from 5 P.M. to 9 P.M., Mondays through Fridays. Closed Saturdays and Sundays.

Paddy's Clam House at 215 West 34th Street (244-9123) has been known for seafood since it opened in 1898, and it is close to Madison Square Garden. Although stripped of its antique ornaments, it still reflects traces of its age, especially in the big clam bar-counter and in the simplicity of its dining room furnished with wooden chairs painted a particularly old-time shade of deep apple green.

Prices at Paddy's are low, and the simple dishes are passable. Clams and oysters on the half-shell have always been ice cold and fresh, and broiled fish and lobster are satisfying. Desserts, however, are poor. There is a daily lunch that includes an acceptable chowder and broiled fish with potato and cole slaw and a few desserts, the best of which is grapefruit. The same menu is higher at dinner. Open 11 A.M. to 9:30 P.M., Mondays through Saturdays, and 1 to 9:30 P.M., Sundays.

Dark wood, fancy mirrors, an old tile floor and a magnificent pendulum clock near the bar are reminders of the golden past of **Pete's Tavern,** 129 East 18th Street, at Irving Place (473-7676), a pub that dates to 1864 and which now needs sprucing up. The front booth opposite the bar is where O. Henry is said to have written "The Gift of the Magi," and many photographs, letters and newspaper clippings on the walls are reminders of other writers who were regulars.

The menu offers a mixture of Italian and American dishes, the simplest being the most acceptable. Stay with the hamburgers, baked ziti, spaghetti with garlic and oil, broiled fish or scampi and veal or sausage with peppers, and you will not do too badly. Prices are moderate. Lunch, 11:30 A.M. to 3 P.M., Mondays through Fridays; dinner, 3 P.M. to 12:45 A.M., Mondays through Thursdays; 3 P.M. to 1:45 A.M., Fridays; 4 P.M. to 1:45 A.M., Saturdays, and 4 P.M. to midnight, Sundays. Sunday brunch, 11 A.M. to 4 P.M.

Typical of old-style Germanic bar-and-grill market restaurants, **Suerken's** (962-8053) has been at 27 Park Place, at Church Street, since 1877. Its huge, serpentine bar, fanciful mellow murals, which seem to have been inspired by a Nile theme, its cast-iron Corinthian columns and old etched and stained glass are all in need of repair or restoration. Even so, their inherent beauty still glows.

The German food at Suerken's is stodgy with floury gravies. The best choices are clams or oysters on the half shell, petite marmite soup with chicken, beef and lots of celery, broiled fish, sandwiches, egg dishes, such as a western omelet, and on Thursdays, an excellent chicken pie, filled with white meat and vegetables under a flaky crust. Boiled beef, a Wednesday special, is passable if you have the horseradish sauce on the side, where you can ignore it. Tongue, often available also on Wednesday, is best as a sandwich on rye. Tuesday's corned beef is popular with regulars, although I haven't tried it. A maverick winner is the hefty, fresh-baked apple strudel, which would be a near miracle if it were served warm. Prices are moderate. Lunch and dinner, 11:30 A.M. to 8 P.M., Mondays through Fridays. Closed Saturdays and Sundays.